Over One Thousand Copies Sold!!!

"Jon Sasaki has written a necessary guide for anyone considering [illegible] exam. The business section answers many common questions new brokers face. [illegible] great resource for the new broker"

-Jennifer Henning, LCB, CCS
National Account Manager
SmartBorder

2018 Customs Broker Exam Study Guide & How to Start Your Own CHB Business®

Thru Oct. 2017 Exam Edition

Jon K Sasaki, LCB

ATTACHÉ BOOKS PUBLISHING

Published 2010, 2011, 2012, 2013, 2014, 2015, 2016, 2017, 2018 by CHB Solutions, A division of Attaché Books Publishing, Vancouver, Washington, U.S.A.

CHB Solutions

Manufactured in the United States of America

10 9 8 7 6 5 4 3 2 1

Library of Congress Cataloging-in-Publication Data

Sasaki, Jon K.
2018 Customs Broker Exam Study Guide & How to Start Your Own CHB Business:
Thru Oct. 2017 Exam Edition / Jon K Sasaki, LCB.

Business & Economics, Exports & Imports

ISBN-13: 978-1986651332
ISBN-10: 1986651339

The internet web addresses in this book were confirmed to be valid and correct at the time of the book's publication but may be subject to change.

Disclaimer:

This book is designed to provide expert guidance regarding the subject matter covered. This information is given with the understanding that neither the author nor the publisher is engaged in rendering legal, accounting, or other professional advice. Since the details of your situation are fact dependent, you should also seek the advice of a competent professional.

Contents at a Glance

Book 1

Customs Broker Exam Study Guide

Contents at a Glance

Book 2

How to Start Your Own CHB Business

Book 1 Part 1

Book 1 Introduction

Customs Broker Exam Study Guide

In This Part
Apply "sabermetrics" to the customs broker exam!

"Sabermetrics" -- it is in an analogy of this obscure term that I feel best communicates the spirit of this book.

So, what is "sabermetrics"? It is the empirical (i.e. verifiable) analysis of baseball and baseball statistics. For example, a baseball team utilizing the theory of sabermetrics will measure a baseball player's performance based on the player's slugging percentage and on-base percentage. While in contrast, in the past, baseball teams have dogmatically assumed that a baseball player's worth could be based on traditionally valued statistics such as batting average and stolen bases.

The concept of sabermetrics truly revolutionized the world of major league baseball. They even made a movie on the subject, based on Michael Lewis' book "Moneyball", which centered on one of sabermetrics' major advocates, and whose character portrayed by Brad Pitt. Sabermetrics is now widely recognized as a proven system for locating previously overlooked talent baseball, and occasionally at a deep discount. For nearly half a century it lingered in obscurity. Now, it has been adopted, in at least some shape or form, by all MLB teams.

...why not apply the sabermetrics-like principles to the game of basketball, or to football? Why not apply it to the customs broker exam?

What's the correlation between the sabermetrics phenomenon and the passing of the customs broker exam? Well, why not apply the sabermetrics-like principles to the game of basketball, or to football? Why not apply it to the customs broker exam?

This study guide does its best to dissuade the examinee from studying, in-depth, ALL of the exam reference material, as traditionally may have been the practice for customs broker exams past. Instead, this study guide helps the student target his or her finite study time by isolating the most frequently covered and trending aspects of the exam, working large to small, and based data and observations from previous exams.

Now, visualize yourself and your studies as a laser guided missile amongst a sea of aimless shotguns.

Instead, this study guide helps the student target his or her finite study time by isolating the most frequently covered and trending aspects of the exam, working large to small, and based data and observations from previous exams.

<u>$ Money Saving Tip $</u> The 19 CFR and HTS publications are quite significant investments (approx. $200/ea.). You may save money on these items by buying used or older versions of each. The difference in content from issue to issue and year to year isn't really that significant.

Book 1 Part 2

Getting Started

In This Part
Current web addresses for obtaining essential exam reference material

FOR...

- past customs broker exams and exam keys
- notice of examinations
- application for customs broker license examination (CBP Form 3124E)

GO TO...

US Customs' (CBP) website:

http://www.cbp.gov/document/publications/past-customs-broker-license-examinations-answer-keys

http://www.cbp.gov/trade/broker/exam/announcement

http://www.cbp.gov/document/forms/form-3124-application-customs-broker-license

FOR...

- Code of Federal Regulations (CFR) "online version"

GO TO...

US Government Printing Office (GPO) website:

www.eCFR.gov

FOR...

- Harmonized Tariff Schedule of the United States (HTSUS) "online version"

GO TO...

United States International Trade Commission (ITC) website:

https://hts.usitc.gov/current

FOR...

- "hardcopies" of HTS and CFR Title 19 for sale

GO TO...

Boskage Commerce Publications and/or U.S. Government Bookstore websites:

https://tax.thomsonreuters.com/checkpoint/boskage/trade-publications

http://bookstore.gpo.gov
(and search "Code of Federal Regulations Title 19" and "Harmonized Tariff Schedule of the United States")

Book 1 Part 3

Nature of the Exam

In This Part
Requirements for becoming a licensed customs broker
What types of questions appear on the exam?
Exam reference material breakdown by source and by year
Next exam may be written using what reference materials?

In order to become a customs broker there are a few requirements. Anyone is eligible to apply to become a customs broker as long as they're at least 21 years of age, a US citizen, and not a federal employee. Second, and the aim of this book, is the requirement of passing the customs broker exam—a 4.5 hour open-book test consisting of 80 multiple choice questions and requiring a 75% to pass. As you may already be aware, the exam is administered twice a year, once on the first Wednesday of each April, and once on the first Wednesday of each October. Applications for the exam are to be submitted your nearest service port (or the location where you would like to sit for the exam) within at least about a month prior to the test. A list of customs service ports, sorted by state can be found on Customs' website at http://www.cbp.gov/contact/ports. The exam application and further instructions are found at Customs' website as well (see also previous page). And, ultimately, upon passing the exam, the applicant is to submit their official application to become a customs broker to US Customs.

It is said that the average passing rate for the exam, which, by the way varies remarkably from year-to-year, can be as low as 5 to 10%, though most years it is much higher. Regardless of these statistics, your experience will be entirely unique, based mainly on your preparation and mindset.

... ... I realized a remarkable pattern. A majority of the questions were simply being drawn directly from the 19 CFR (as opposed to the HTSUS, other material, etc.)

Book 1 Part 3: Nature of the Exam

What about my (the author's) experience with the exam? When I made my mind up to start studying for my first attempt at the exam, I began by just reviewing a few of the previous exams. And, in the process I realized a remarkable pattern. A MAJORITY of the questions were simply being drawn directly from the 19 CFR (as opposed to the HTSUS, other material, etc.), AND, many of the same subjects and questions were being repeated from one exam to the next. So, I made note of which 19 CFR Parts, Sections, and Paragraphs were a part of this pattern. I then removed the "unnecessary" parts and pages from my newly purchased 19 CFR, and did my best to focus on the items that would most likely appear on the exam (as I will further outline for you in this book). With this newly conceived strategy of mine, and a commitment to study at least a little each day all the way up to the date of the next exam, the goal was in sight and I felt a surge of confidence. And what was the result? On my first attempt at the exam, I surprised myself by scoring a passing grade!

On the following page is a quick snapshot of each of the major sources of exam reference materials, and the approximate number of occurrences and percentages of each over the last 10 exams.

Exam Reference Material Frequency by Source & Year

of Occurrences per Exam

Exam Date	19 CFR	HTSUS	Form 7501 Inst.	Directives	CATAIR
2017 Oct.	59	19	0	2	0
2017 Apr.	55	15	10	0	0
2016 Oct.	56	22	4	1	1
2016 Apr.	62	11	5	0	2
2015 Oct.	53	20	7	0	0
2015 Apr.	58	18	2	0	1
2014 Oct.	55	21	6	1	0
2014 Apr.	44	28	9	1	0
2013 Oct.	44	34	1	1	0
2013 Apr.	35	34	5	4	2
AVERAGE	**52**	**22**	**5**	**1**	**1**

% of Exam

Exam Date	19 CFR	HTSUS	Form 7501 Inst.	Directives	CATAIR
2016 Oct.	74%	24%	0%	3%	0%
2016 Apr.	69%	19%	13%	0%	0%
2015 Oct.	67%	26%	5%	1%	1%
2015 Apr.	78%	14%	6%	0%	3%
2014 Oct.	66%	25%	9%	0%	0%
2014 Apr.	73%	23%	3%	0%	1%
2013 Oct.	66%	25%	7%	1%	0%
2013 Apr.	54%	34%	11%	1%	0%
2012 Oct.	55%	43%	1%	1%	0%
2012 Apr.	44%	43%	6%	5%	3%
AVERAGE	**65%**	**27%**	**6%**	**1%**	**1%**

It has been announced that the April 2018 examination will be written using the following references:

· Harmonized Tariff Schedule of the United States (2017 Basic Edition)

· Title 19, Code of Federal Regulations (2016, Revised as of April 1, 2016 or 2017, Parts 1 to 199)

· Instructions for Preparation of CBP Form 7501 (July 24, 2012)

· Right to Make Entry Directive 3530-002A

• • • • • • • • •

As the personal finance icon and pragmatist, Dave Ramsey says, "Get gazelle intense!" Act as if you didn't want to take the test more than once.

• • • • • • • • •

Note: See below for CBP's notice in regards to exam reference material.
https://www.cbp.gov/trade/programs-administration/customs-brokers/license-examination-notice-examination

Note Also (per CBP):

Examinees may use any written reference material; however, use of any electronic device during the exam (e.g., laptop, iPad / Nook / Kindle, smart phone, personal digital assistant, etc.) is strictly prohibited.

Cell phones, laptops, pagers, smart watches and other communication devices may not be used inside the examination room.
Any applicant caught cheating will be removed from the exam.

CBP invites the public to submit questions for possible use in future customs broker examinations. See Guidelines for writing questions for the customs broker examination. Please submit your questions to brokermanagement@cbp.dhs.gov. The SUBJECT line must read: Future Exam Questions.

Book 1 Part 4

How to Use This Book

In This Part
Step-by-step instructions for preparing for your studies
How to most effectively study for the exam

This book, by itself, will not guarantee your success on the customs broker exam. It is, however, one of several tools that will best prepare you for the big day. "Preparation" is the key word and preparedness in context of the customs broker exam means studying as efficiently as possible and on a daily basis. As the personal finance icon and pragmatist, Dave Ramsey says, "get gazelle intense!" Act as if you didn't want to take the test more than once. Listed below is a sort of checklist of things we suggest you should do in about the same order before wandering too far into your studies.

√ First, go to the following link to Customs' website.

http://www.cbp.gov/trade/broker/exam/announcement

Here, you will find a list of all the reference materials (HTSUS, 19 CFR, 7501 Instructions etc.) that Customs says it may draw from for the exam. You are not just allowed, but actually encouraged to bring all of these reference materials to the actual exam.

√ Print out all of the reference materials except for the Title 19 Code of Federal Regulations (19 CFR) and the Harmonized Tariff Schedule (HTS). These two items contain too many pages to print on your own. Instead, ask to borrow these items from work or a friend, or purchase from one of the resources listed in the section of this book marked "Getting Started".

Customs Directives (e.g. Right to Make Entry Directive 3530-002A), have only historically appeared on only 1% of the exam.

√ Make yourself familiar with the reference material you have just printed (except for the HTS and 19 CFR, which require more involved study and I will further explain here in a bit). Just be aware and prepared to look something up in these printouts during the actual exam, and I wouldn't recommend starting off trying to memorize too much here. Customs Directives (e.g. Right to Make Entry Directive 3530-002A), have only historically appeared on only 1% of the exam.

√ Next, begin printing out a few of the old exams and exam keys. Take some time to just peruse through these exams and try to get a feeling of what kinds of questions are being asked, and how they are presented, etc. Once you get a little more familiar with everything, you will want to take mock exams utilizing these old exams to improve on your skills and gauge your progress.

√ Once you have a Title 19 CFR available to use, go to the section of this study guide marked "All Sections Appearing on Exams". In this section of the study guide is a table, which lists in order by CFR Part, Section, and Paragraph, all of the 19 CFR-related materials tested over the last 10 exams. With a highlighter, begin highlighting or otherwise notate directly into your 19 CFR, these Parts, Sections, and Paragraphs that most frequently appear on exams as indicated on this table. Not only will this process improve your familiarity with the 19 CFR and these various entries, but it will also make these items more easily stand out when you are searching for answers during your mock exams and during the actual exam.

√ Once you have an HTS at your disposal, you will want to affix sticky tabs for all chapters (on the side) and for all sections (on top) for the purpose of simplified navigation through the HTSUS text. Undoubtedly, the best training method for strengthening your HTS classification skills is to simply go through the Classifications sections of the old exams and try to classify all the different sorts of merchandise described throughout the previous exams. This process will expose you to a wide variety of products and materials. It will also help to get you used to the kinds of HTS-based questions appearing on exams that require you to check chapter notes, section notes, general notes, and consider the general rules of interpretation (GRI) before deciding on the most appropriate classification and answer. This book also includes an "HTS Classification Tips" section, which explains the fundamentals of classification, and dissects a few classification questions derived directly from previous exams.

√ Next, this study guide includes a section called "Most Commonly Tested". This part of the book isolates and quotes the specific "Sections" and "Paragraphs" of the 19 CFR that have most often appeared within exam questions during the last ten customs broker exams. It is, for the sake of prioritizing study time and for ease of navigation, arranged by frequency of appearances in the past ten exams and then numerically by CFR Part, Section, and then by Paragraph. Attempt to memorize as much as you can of this section. The reason for this is that the more you are able to answer exam questions from memory and on the fly, then the more time you will have to focus on the more time-consuming parts, namely HTS classification.

√ Finally, practice taking and re-taking as many mock exams as possible using the free exams and exam keys downloadable from CBP.com. Currently the archive goes back to 2012.

https://www.cbp.gov/document/publications/past-customs-broker-license-examinations-answer-keys

This study guide also includes the most recent exams with commentary and answers. The commentary will provide you with explanations, detailed in proportion to the complexity of each particular exam question. Direct excerpts from the HTSUS, 19 CFR, etc. are also included as supporting points of reference for each answer.

Book 1 Part 5

HTS Classification Tips

Sub-part 1
The HTSUS

In This Sub-part

What is the "HTS"?
The 4 Major Components of the HTSUS
HTSUS Chapters Frequency for last 10 exams
HTSUS General Notes (GN) Frequency for last 10 exams
HTSUS Contents (including Sections Titles & Chapter Titles) at a Glance

The Harmonized Tariff Schedule (HTS) of the United States (HTSUS) is available via both ...

A. hardcopy version:

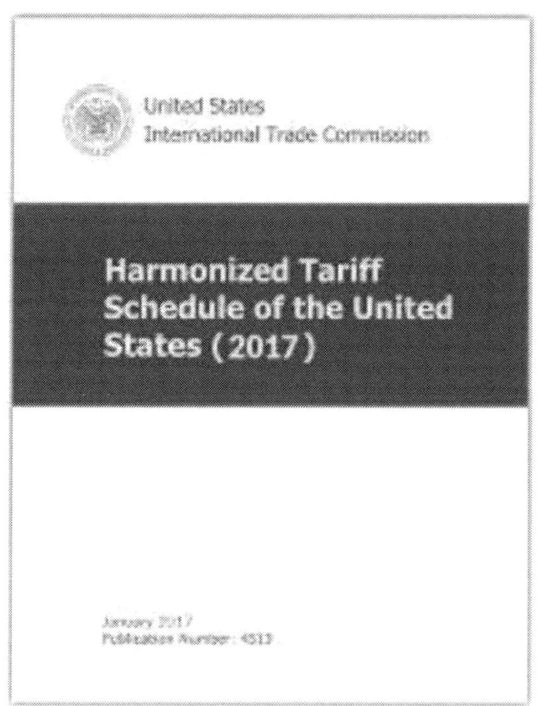

And

B. online version:

https://hts.usitc.gov/current

The HTSUS consists of 4 major components ...

1) The General Rules of Interpretation (GRI), which are U.S. Customs' instructions for HTS classification (see excerpt below):

GENERAL RULES OF INTERPRETATION

Classification of goods in the tariff schedule shall be governed by the following principles:

1. The table of contents, alphabetical index, and titles of sections, chapters and sub-chapters are provided for ease of reference only; for legal purposes, classification shall be determined according to the terms of the headings and any relative section or chapter notes and, provided such headings or notes do not otherwise require, according to the following provisions:

2. (a) Any reference in a heading to an article shall be taken to include a reference to that article incomplete or unfinished, provided that, as entered, the incomplete or unfinished article has the essential character of the complete or finished article. It shall also include a reference to that article complete or finished (or falling to be classified as complete or finished by virtue of this rule), entered unassembled or disassembled.

   (b) Any reference in a heading to a material or substance shall be taken to include a reference to mixtures or combinations of that material or substance with other materials or substances. Any reference to goods of a given material or substance shall be taken to include a reference to goods consisting wholly or partly of such material or substance. The classification of goods consisting of more than one material or substance shall be according to the principles of rule 3.

3. When, by application of rule 2(b) or for any other reason, goods are, prima facie, classifiable under two or more headings, classification shall be effected as follows:

   (a) The heading which provides the most specific description shall be preferred to headings providing a more general description. However, when two or more headings each refer to part only of the materials or substances contained in mixed or composite goods or to part only of the items in a set put up for retail sale, those headings are to be regarded as equally specific in relation to those goods, even if one of them gives a more complete or precise description of the goods.

   (b) Mixtures, composite goods consisting of different materials or made up of different components, and goods put up in sets for retail sale, which cannot be classified by reference to 3(a), shall be classified as if they consisted of the material or component which gives them their essential character, insofar as this criterion is applicable.

   (c) When goods cannot be classified by reference to 3(a) or 3(b), they shall be classified under the heading which occurs last in numerical order among those which equally merit consideration.

4. Goods which cannot be classified in accordance with the above rules shall be classified under the heading appropriate to the goods to which they are most akin.

5. In addition to the foregoing provisions, the following rules shall apply in respect of the goods referred to therein:

   (a) Camera cases, musical instrument cases, gun cases, drawing instrument cases, necklace cases and similar containers,specially shaped or fitted to contain a specific article or set of articles, suitable for long-term use and entered with the articles for which they are intended, shall be classified with such articles when of a kind normally sold therewith. This rule does not,however, apply to containers which give the whole its essential character;

   (b) Subject to the provisions of rule 5(a) above, packing materials and packing containers entered with the goods therein shall be classified with the goods if they are of a kind normally used for packing such goods. However, this provision is not binding when such packing materials or packing containers are clearly suitable for repetitive use.

6. For legal purposes, the classification of goods in the subheadings of a heading shall be determined according to the terms of those subheadings and any related subheading notes and, mutatis mutandis, to the above rules, on the understanding that only subheadings at the same level are comparable. For the purposes of this rule, the relative section, chapter and subchapter notes also apply, unless the context otherwise requires.

2) The General Notes (GN), which include important interpretive notes for using the HTSUS, such as defining what is the "Customs Territory of the United States", outlining the rules of NAFTA and other Free Trade Agreements (FTA), etc. (Excerpt of HTSUS General Notes 1, 2, and partial of 3 below):

General Notes

1 Tariff Treatment of Imported Goods and of Vessel Equipments, Parts and Repairs. All goods provided for in this schedule and imported into the customs territory of the United States from outside thereof, and all vessel equipments, parts, materials and repairs covered by the provisions of subchapter XVIII to chapter 98 of this schedule, are subject to duty or exempt therefrom as prescribed in general notes 3 through 29, inclusive.

2 Customs Territory of the United States. The term "customs territory of the United States", as used in the tariff schedule, includes only the States, the District of Columbia and Puerto Rico.

3 Rates of Duty. The rates of duty in the "Rates of Duty" columns designated 1 ("General" and "Special") and 2 of the tariff schedule apply to goods imported into the customs territory of the United States as hereinafter provided in this note:

(a) Rate of Duty Column 1.

… …

3) Section Notes (HTSUS Section I Notes below):

Harmonized Tariff Schedule of the United States (2016)
Annotated for Statistical Reporting Purposes

SECTION I

LIVE ANIMALS; ANIMAL PRODUCTS

I-1

Notes

1. Any reference in this section to a particular genus or species of an animal, except where the context otherwise requires, includes a reference to the young of that genus or species.

2. Except where the context otherwise requires, throughout the tariff schedule any reference to "dried" products also covers products which have been dehydrated, evaporated or freeze-dried.

& Chapter Notes. (HTSUS Chapter 1 Notes below):

Harmonized Tariff Schedule of the United States (2016)
Annotated for Statistical Reporting Purposes

CHAPTER 1

LIVE ANIMALS

I
1-1

Note

1. This chapter covers all live animals except:

   (a) Fish and crustaceans, molluscs and other aquatic invertebrates, of heading 0301, 0306, 0307 or 0308;

   (b) Cultures of microorganisms and other products of heading 3002; and

   (c) Animals of heading 9508.

Additional U.S. Notes

1. The expression "purebred breeding animals" covers only animals certified to the U.S. Customs Service by the Department of Agriculture as being purebred of a recognized breed and duly registered in a book of record recognized by the Secretary of Agriculture for that breed, imported specially for breeding purposes, whether intended to be used by the importer himself or for sale for such purposes. 1/

2. Certain special provisions applying to live animals are in chapter 98.

4) Classifications and their corresponding descriptions, reportable unit of measure, duty rate, and special program indicator (SPI) availability for anything and everything under the sun. (Excerpt from HTSUS Chapter 1 below):

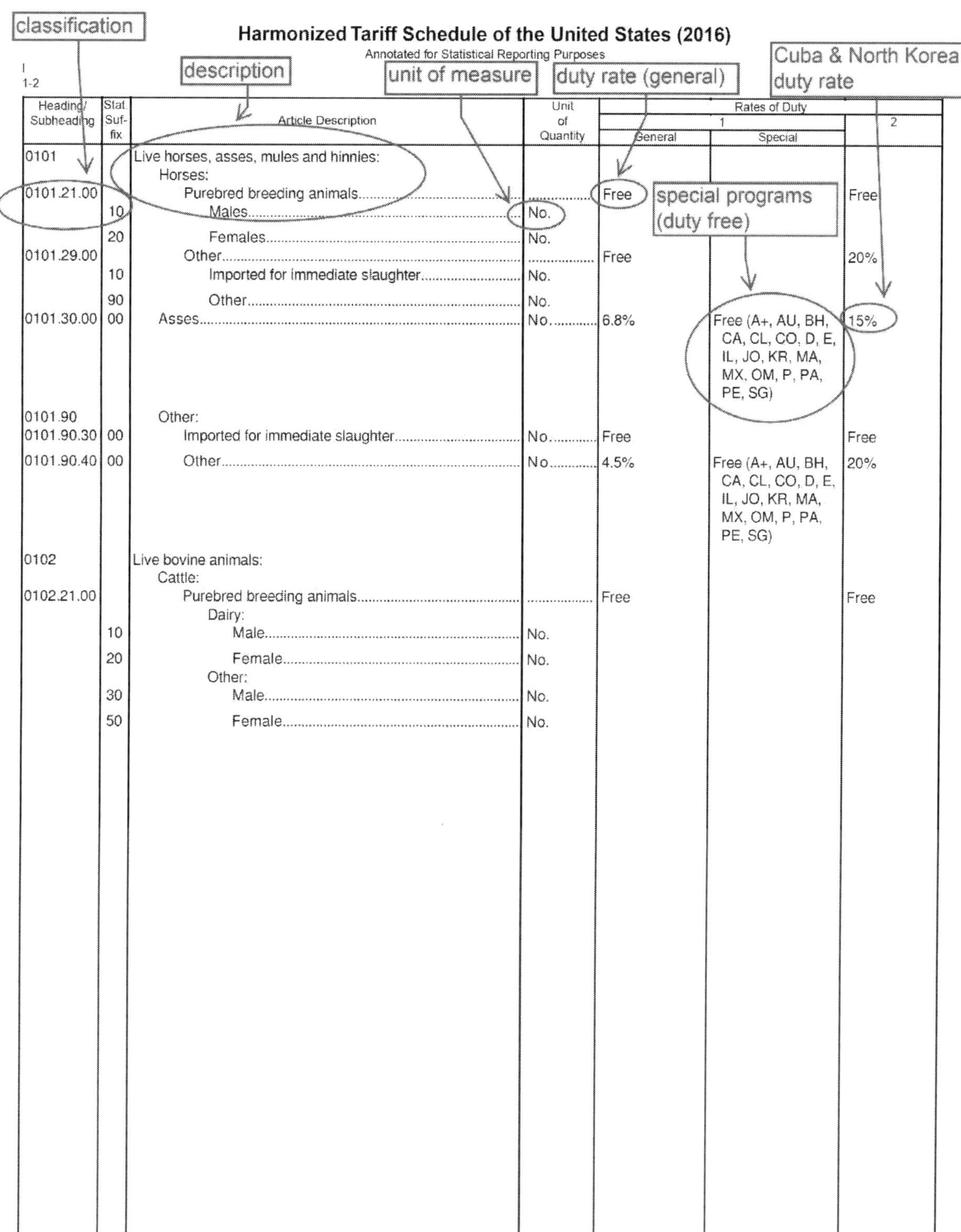

Harmonized Tariff Schedule of the United States (2016)

Annotated for Statistical Reporting Purposes

I
1-2

Heading/ Subheading	Stat. Suf- fix	Article Description	Unit of Quantity	Rates of Duty 1 General	Rates of Duty 1 Special	2
0101		Live horses, asses, mules and hinnies:				
		Horses:				
0101.21.00		Purebred breeding animals		Free		Free
	10	Males	No.			
	20	Females	No.			
0101.29.00		Other		Free		20%
	10	Imported for immediate slaughter	No.			
	90	Other	No.			
0101.30.00	00	Asses	No.	6.8%	Free (A+, AU, BH, CA, CL, CO, D, E, IL, JO, KR, MA, MX, OM, P, PA, PE, SG)	15%
0101.90		Other:				
0101.90.30	00	Imported for immediate slaughter	No.	Free		Free
0101.90.40	00	Other	No	4.5%	Free (A+, AU, BH, CA, CL, CO, D, E, IL, JO, KR, MA, MX, OM, P, PA, PE, SG)	20%
0102		Live bovine animals:				
		Cattle:				
0102.21.00		Purebred breeding animals		Free		Free
		Dairy:				
	10	Male	No.			
	20	Female	No.			
		Other:				
	30	Male	No.			
	50	Female	No.			

HTSUS Chapters Frequency for last 10 exams (thru. October 2017 exam):

HTS Chapter	Occurrences
General Notes	55
1	1
2	2
3	1
4	2
5	1
7	3
8	5
9	1
11	1
12	2
13	1
16	4
17	3
18	1
19	2
20	13
21	5
22	3
25	1
26	2
27	1
28	1
29	6
30	2
31	3
33	3
34	2
38	5
39	7
40	3
42	10
44	4
46	3
48	4
50	1
51	2
52	2
53	1
54	2

HTS Chapter	Occurrences
55	1
58	3
59	2
60	1
61	18
62	14
63	8
64	2
66	1
67	1
68	2
69	8
70	4
71	6
72	4
73	10
74	2
76	1
79	1
82	6
83	2
84	20
85	8
86	1
87	1
88	4
90	5
91	1
92	1
94	3
95	7
96	1
97	4
98	19
99	2
Chemical App.	1
ANNEX A	1
ANNEX B	2
ANNEX C	7

HTSUS General Notes (GN) Frequency over last 10 exams (thru. Oct. 2017 exam):

Exam		General Note Number (Name)	Paragraph
2013 October	GN	2 (Customs Territory of the U.S.)	
2015 October	GN	3 (Rates of Duty)	(a)
2016 April	GN	3 (Rates of Duty)	(c)
2015 April	GN	3 (Rates of Duty)	(c)
2015 April	GN	3 (Rates of Duty)	(c)
2014 October	GN	3 (Rates of Duty)	(c)
2013 October	GN	3 (Rates of Duty)	(c)
2017 October	GN	3 (Rates of Duty)	(e)
2017 April	GN	3 (Rates of Duty)	(e)
2014 April	GN	3 (Rates of Duty)	
2014 October	GN	4 (Generalized System of Preferences)	(a)
2014 April	GN	4 (Generalized System of Preferences)	(b)
2016 October	GN	4 (Generalized System of Preferences)	(c)
2014 October	GN	4 (Generalized System of Preferences)	(c)
2014 April	GN	4 (Generalized System of Preferences)	(d)
2013 October	GN	4 (Generalized System of Preferences)	(d)
2016 April	GN	4 (Generalized System of Preferences)	
2015 October	GN	4 (Generalized System of Preferences)	
2014 October	GN	4 (Generalized System of Preferences)	
2014 April	GN	4 (Generalized System of Preferences)	
2013 October	GN	8 (Israel FTA)	(b)
2014 April	GN	11 (Andean Trade Preference Act)	(a)
2013 April	GN	12 (NAFTA)	(a)
2013 April	GN	12 (NAFTA)	(b)
2013 April	GN	12 (NAFTA)	(c)
2017 October	GN	12 (NAFTA)	(i)
2016 October	GN	12 (NAFTA)	(n)
2016 October	GN	12 (NAFTA)	(q)
2015 October	GN	12 (NAFTA)	(t)
2013 October	GN	12 (NAFTA)	(t)
2013 April	GN	12 (NAFTA)	
2017 April	GN	13 (Pharmaceutical Products)	
2014 October	GN	13 (Pharmaceutical Products)	
2014 October	GN	14 (Intermediate Chemicals for Dyes)	
2015 October	GN	15 (Exclusions)	
TABLE CONTINUED BELOW			

HTSUS General Notes (GN) Frequency over last 10 exams (thru. Oct. 2017 exam):

Exam		General Note Number (Name)	Paragraph
2016 October	GN	16 (African Growth and Opportunity Act)	(a)
2014 October	GN	16 (African Growth and Opportunity Act)	
2017 October	GN	25 (Singapore FTA)	(b)
2014 April	GN	25 (Singapore FTA)	(m)
2017 October	GN	26 (Chile FTA)	(c)
2015 October	GN	27 (Morocco FTA)	
2017 October	GN	28 (Australia FTA)	(c)
2015 April	GN	28 (Australia FTA)	(k)
2014 April	GN	28 (Australia FTA)	(k)
2014 October	GN	29 (Dominican Republic FTA)	(a)
2013 October	GN	29 (Dominican Republic FTA)	(a)
2017 October	GN	29 (Dominican Republic FTA)	(c)
2014 October	GN	29 (Dominican Republic FTA)	(d)
2014 October	GN	29 (Dominican Republic FTA)	
2014 April	GN	33 (Korea FTA)	(c)
2013 October	GN	33 (Korea FTA)	(c)
2014 April	GN	33 (Korea FTA)	(o)
2017 October	GN	34 (Colombia Trade Promotion Agreement)	(c)
2014 October	GN	34 (Colombia Trade Promotion Agreement)	(o)

HTSUS Contents at a Glance:

(please note: Section titles and Chapter titles are for reference purposes only—use the General Rules of Interpretation to classify).

HTSUS Contents at a Glance:

Section III: Animal or Vegetable Fats and Oils and Their Cleavage Products; Prepared Edible Fats; Animal or Vegetable Waxes

Chapter 15 Animal or vegetable fats and oils and their cleavage products prepared edible fats; animal or vegetable waxes

Section IV: Prepared Foodstuffs; Beverages, Spirits, and Vinegar; Tobacco and Manufactured Tobacco Substitutes

Chapter 16 Preparations of meat, of fish or of crustaceans, mollusks or other aquatic invertebrates

Chapter 17 Sugars and sugar confectionery

Chapter 18 Cocoa and cocoa preparations

Chapter 19 Preparations of cereals, flour, starch or milk; bakers' wares

Chapter 20 Preparations of vegetables, fruit, nuts or other parts of plants

Chapter 21 Miscellaneous edible preparations

Chapter 22 Beverages, spirits and vinegar

Chapter 23 Residues and waste from the food industries; prepared animal feed

Chapter 24 Tobacco and manufactured tobacco substitutes

Section V:Mineral Products

Chapter 25 Salt; sulfur; earths and stone; plastering materials, lime and cement

Chapter 26 Ores, slag and ash

Chapter 27 Mineral fuels, mineral oils and products of their distillation; bituminous substances; mineral waxes

Section VI: Products of Chemical or Allied Industries

Chapter 28 Inorganic chemicals; organic or inorganic c compounds of precious metals, of rare-earth metals, of radioactive elements or of isotopes

Chapter 29 Organic chemicals

Chapter 30 Pharmaceutical products

Chapter 31 Fertilizers

Chapter 32 Tanning or dyeing extracts; dyes, pigments, paints, varnishes, putty and mastics

Chapter 33 Essential oils and resinoids; perfumery, cosmetic or toilet preparations

Chapter 34 Soap, organic surface-active agents, washing preparations, lubricating preparations, artificial waxes, prepared waxes, polishing or scouring preparations, candles and similar articles, modeling pastes, "dental waxes" and dental preparations with a basis of plaster

Chapter 35 Albuminoidal substances; modified starches; glues; enzymes

Chapter 36 Explosives; pyrotechnic products; matches; pyrophoric alloys; certain combustible preparations

Chapter 37 Photographic or cinematographic goods

Chapter 38 Miscellaneous chemical products

HTSUS Contents at a Glance:

HTSUS Contents at a Glance:

Section XI: Textile and Textile Articles

Chapter 50 Silk
Chapter 51 Wool, fine or coarse animal hair; horsehair yarn and woven fabric
Chapter 52 Cotton
Chapter 53 Other vegetable textile fibers; paper yarn and woven fabric of paper yarn
Chapter 54 Man-made filaments
Chapter 55 Man-made staple fibers
Chapter 56 Wadding, felt and nonwovens; special yarns, twine, cordage, ropes and cables and articles thereof
Chapter 57 Carpets and other textile floor coverings
Chapter 58 Special woven fabrics; tufted textile fabrics; lace, tapestries; trimmings; embroidery
Chapter 59 Impregnated, coated, covered or laminated textile fabrics; textile articles of a kind suitable for industrial use
Chapter 60 Knitted or crocheted fabrics
Chapter 61 Articles of apparel and clothing accessories, knitted or crocheted
Chapter 62 Articles of apparel and clothing accessories, not knitted or crocheted
Chapter 63 Other made up textile articles; sets; worn clothing and worn textile articles; rags

Section XII: Footwear, Headgear, Umbrellas, Sun Umbrellas, Walking Sticks, Seatsticks, Whips, Riding-Crops and Parts Thereof; Prepared Feathers and Articles Made Therewith; Artificial Flowers; Articles of Human

Chapter 64 Footwear, gaiters and the like; parts of such articles
Chapter 65 Headgear and parts thereof
Chapter 66 Umbrellas, sun umbrellas, walking sticks, seatsticks, whips, riding-crops and parts thereof
Chapter 67 Prepared feathers and down and articles made of feathers or of down; artificial flowers; articles of human hair

Section XIII: Articles of Stone, Plaster, Cement, Asbestos, Mica or Similar Materials; Ceramic Products; Glass and Glassware

Chapter 68 Articles of stone, plaster, cement, asbestos, mica or similar materials
Chapter 69 Ceramic products
Chapter 70 Glass and glassware

Section XIV: Natural or Cultured Pearls, Precious or Semiprecious Stones, Precious Metals, Metals Clad With Precious Metal, and Articles Thereof; Imitation Jewelry; Coin

Chapter 71 Natural or cultured pearls, precious or semi-precious stones, precious metals, metals clad with precious metal and articles thereof; imitation jewelry; coin

HTSUS Contents at a Glance:

Section XV: Base Metals and Articles of Base Metal

Chapter 72 Iron and steel
Chapter 73 Articles of iron or steel
Chapter 74 Copper and articles thereof
Chapter 75 Nickel and articles thereof
Chapter 76 Aluminum and articles thereof
Chapter 77 (Reserved for possible future use)
Chapter 78 Lead and articles thereof
Chapter 79 Zinc and articles thereof
Chapter 80 Tin and articles thereof
Chapter 81 Other base metals; cermets; articles thereof
Chapter 82 Tools, implements, cutlery, spoons and forks, of base metal; parts thereof of base metal
Chapter 83 Miscellaneous articles of base metal

Section XVI: Machinery and Mechanical Appliances; Electrical Equipment; Parts Thereof; Sound Recorders and Reproducers, Television Image and Sound Recorders and Reproducers, and Parts and Accessories of Such Articles

Chapter 84 Nuclear reactors, boilers, machinery and mechanical appliances; parts thereof
Chapter 85 Electrical machinery and equipment and parts thereof; sound recorders and reproducers, television image and sound recorders and reproducers, and parts and accessories of such articles

Section XVII: Vehicles, Aircraft, Vessels and Associated Transport Equipment

Chapter 86 Railway or tramway locomotives, rolling-stock and parts thereof; railway or tramway track fixtures and fittings and parts thereof; mechanical (including electro-mechanical) traffic signaling equipment of all kinds
Chapter 87 Vehicles other than railway or tramway rolling stock, and parts and accessories thereof
Chapter 88 Aircraft, spacecraft, and parts thereof
Chapter 89 Ships, boats and floating structures

Section XVIII: Optical, Photographic, Cinematographic, Measuring, Checking, Precision, Medical or Surgical Instruments and Apparatus; Clocks and Watches; Musical Instruments; Parts and Accessories Thereof

Chapter 90 Optical, photographic, cinematographic, measuring, checking, precision, medical or surgical instruments and apparatus; parts and accessories thereof
Chapter 91 Clocks and watches and parts thereof
Chapter 92 Musical instruments; parts and accessories of such articles

HTSUS Contents at a Glance:

(This Page Intentionally Left Blank)

Book 1 Part 5

HTS Classification Tips

Sub-part 2
The HTS Number

In This Sub-part
What is an "HTS Number"?
HTSUS Number Structure & Breakdown
Basic Classification Procedure
Basic Exam Classification Strategy

An HTS number ("HTS" is the abbreviation for "Harmonized Tariff Schedule") is a 10-digit number (in the case of the United States) and it determines the admissibility of and duty rate for goods imported into the United States. There are over 17,000 HTS numbers within the Harmonized Tariff Schedule of the United States (also known as HTSUS). Let's break it down here!

Here's a breakdown (of the components of) of the HTS classification number:

(Example: HTSUS classification for a male purebred horse)

LIVE ANIMALS	Live horses, asses, mules and hinnies:	Horses: Purebred breeding animals	Males
01	01.	21.00	10
Chapter			
Heading			
Subheading			Statistical

Here's what the classification looks like in the HTSUS:

Heading/ Subheading	Stat. Suf-fix	Article Description	Unit of Quantity	General
0101		Live horses, asses, mules and hinnies:		
		Horses:		
0101.21.00		Purebred breeding animals........	....	Free
	10	Males........	No.	
	20	Females........	No.	

Chapter

The first two digits of the HTS number represent the "Chapter" number. There are 99 chapters (which are further logically sub-divided into 22 sections). Think of these chapters and sections as the A to Z alphabetic lookup system of a city's phone book. For example, if you don't know the spelling of a person's last name you're looking for, the alphabetic lookup will assist, though it is for reference purposes only.

Heading

The first four digits of the HTS number represent the "Heading". The chapter number combined with the subsequent two digits make up what Customs refers to as the classification "Heading". You may think of the "Heading" in the HTSUS as last names (a.k.a. surnames) in a phone book. Meaning, if you're looking for a person in the phone book, first you locate for the person's last name, not the first name first.

Subheading & Statistical

Practically speaking, after the chapter and heading, it is only important to note that the last six digits of the HTS further break down the classifications into increasingly more specific descriptions. This is the person's first and middle name in the above-mentioned phone book analogy.

Here's another example of HTSUS number breakdown:

(Example: HTSUS classification for cross-country skis)

TOYS, GAMES AND SPORTS EQUIPMENT; PARTS AND ACCESSORIES THEREOF	Articles and equipment for general physical exercise, gymnastics, athletics, other sports (including table-tennis) or outdoor games, not specified or included elsewhere in this chapter; swimming pools and wading pools; parts and accessories thereof:	Snow-skis and other snow-ski equipment; parts and accessories thereof:	Cross-country skis	(N/A for this item)
95	06.	11.20		00
Chapter				
Heading				
Subheading				Statistical

Chapter
Using the HTS number for cross-country skis, for example, Chapter 95 is the chapter for "Toys, Games, and Sports Equipment".

Heading
For example, heading 9506 provides for "equipment for … … outdoor games … …"

Subheading & Statistical
The complete classification number for "cross-country skis" is 9506.11.2000.

✓ **Note:** HTSUS article descriptions are separated by either a "," (comma) or by a ";" (semi-colon). The commas are used to continue a description. The semi-colons are used to start a new description

Basic Classification Procedure:

- The structure of the HTS is hierarchical in nature. Start at the appropriate heading (first 4 digits).
- Then work from left-to-right, choosing among the descriptions available at the same indentations.
- Repeat until you arrive at your 10-digit classification.

(The example below shows how we arrive at the HTS classification for cross-country skis.)

Heading/ Subheading	Stat. Suf-fix	Article Description	Unit of Quantity	Rates of Duty 1 General	Special
9505		Festive, carnival or other entertainment articles, including magic tricks and practical joke articles; parts and accessories thereof:			
9505.10		Articles for Christmas festivities and parts and accessories thereof:			
		Christmas ornaments:			
9505.10.10	00	Of glass	X	Free	
		Other:			
9505.10.15	00	Of wood	X	Free	
9505.10.25	00	Other	X	Free	
9505.10.30	00	Nativity scenes and figures thereof	X	Free	
		Other:			
9505.10.40		Of plastics		Free	
	10	Artificial Christmas trees	No.		
	20	Other	X		
9505.10.50		Other		Free	
	10	Artificial Christmas trees	No.		
	20	Other	X		
9505.90		Other:			
9505.90.20	00	Magic tricks and practical joke articles; parts and accessories thereof	X	Free	
9505.90.40	00	Confetti, paper spirals or streamers, party favors and noisemakers; parts and accessories thereof	X	Free	
9505.90.60	00	Other	X	Free	
9506		Articles and equipment for general physical exercise, gymnastics, athletics, other sports (including table-tennis) or outdoor games, not specified or included elsewhere in this chapter; swimming pools and wading pools; parts and accessories thereof:			
		Snow-skis and other snow-ski equipment; parts and accessories thereof:			
9506.11		Skis and parts and accessories thereof, except ski poles:			
9506.11.20	00	Cross-country skis	prs.	Free	
9506.11.40		Other skis		2.6%	Free (A, AU, BH, CA, CL, CO, E, IL, JO, KR, MA, MX, OM, P, PA, PE, SG)

For HTS classification, there's just one more thing to consider, the General Rules of Interpretation (discussed in detail later in this part of the study guide), but essentially that's it. Depending on the item, the process of selecting the correct HTSUS can be either a trek up Mount Everest or a leisurely trip down the bunny hill.

Basic Exam Classification Strategy:

Which chapters do I study?

The exam may produce HTS classification-based questions pulled anywhere from Chapter 1 thru Chapter 99 of the HTS. One could say that for the last ten exams, Customs has pretty evenly spread out the use of the various chapters throughout. However, there are definitely some outliers. Several chapters have, historically speaking, never appeared, and yet others are almost sure to appear on each exam. For example, chapters 61 and 62 (knitted & not knitted apparel, respectively) have, combined, appeared nearly 30 times over the last 10 exams, whereas chapter 65 ("headgear"), also for example, hasn't appeared even once.

Do the classifications last?

The HTS classification portion of the exam can easily end up taking up the lion's share of the examinee's time. Therefore, my first recommendation for those taking the exam, and especially for those whose strong point isn't in classification, is to budget sufficient time for, and tackle the classification part of the test last. It is imperative to have a plan before you enter the test room. Then implement that plan accordingly.

What are your options?

When you take on the classification portion of the exam try this. After you read through the question and have made mental notes on what you guess to be the key points, quickly scan over the five multiple choice answers and take stock of which chapters of the HTS are give to you as an options. You may ask yourself the following types of questions. Which chapters are overrepresented? Are there any seemingly dead giveaways or tells? Which classifications can be disregarded right of the back? Should I skip the question for now and revisit it later?

Several chapters have, historically speaking, never appeared, and yet others are almost sure to appear on each exam.

Book 1 Part 5

HTS Classification Tips

Sub-part 3
The General Rules of Interpretation (GRI)
"HUM SELMA"

In This Sub-part
An easy way to remember the GRI's
Breakdown of each GRI
GRI snapshot from the HTSUS

The complete procedural how-to for correctly classifying imported products and materials is included in the GRI's (General Rules of Interpretation). Basically, there are six GRI's. As is true with any other disciplines, as a person gains more experience in HTS classification, these "rules" eventually almost become second nature, and the act of classification becomes a mostly automatic endeavor.

Let's Get to Know the GRI's

To remember the GRI's, try remembering the following acronym "**HUM SELMA**"

H Headings and any relative Section & Chapter Notes determine the HTS number. **GRI 1**

U Unfinished items are classified as if finished (if unfinished has essential character of finished). **GRI 2(a)**

M Mixtures may be implied (unless prohibited in headings or notes). Go to GRI 3. **GRI 2(b)**

S Specific HTS heading/description preferred (over less descriptive), for prima facie items. **GRI 3(a)**

E Essential character of item determines HTS number (if item cannot be classified by 3(a)), for prima facie items. **GRI 3(b)**

L Last in order HTS# shall be used (if item cannot be classified by 3(a) or by 3(b)), for prima facie items. **GRI 3(c)**

M Most akin item's HTS# is to be used (if not classifiable by the preceding rules). **GRI 4**

A Article-specific cases & packaging are classified with item (unless they are "the item"). **GRI 5(a) & (b)**

BREAKDOWN OF EACH GRI:

GRI 1: Headings and any relative Section & Chapter Notes determine the HTS number.

Most items are classifiable based on GRI 1. The titles of sections & chapters, the HTSUS alphabetical index, etc. are for reference purposes ONLY. To classify, use the Heading Article Description and Section & Chapter Notes. An example of the application of this rule would be the classification of chocolate-covered peanuts. Although Chapter 20 is named "PREPARATIONS OF VEGETABLES, FRUIT, NUTS OR OTHER PARTS OF PLANTS", Chapter 20 Note 2 states that heading 2008 does not apply to "chocolate confectionery (heading 1806)". Instead, the chocolate-covered peanuts would be classified in Chapter 18 (cocoa and cocoa preparations).

Directly quoting GRI 1 from the HTSUS General Rules of Interpretation...

1. The table of contents, alphabetical index, and titles of sections, chapters and sub-chapters are provided for ease of reference only; for legal purposes, classification shall be determined according to the terms of the headings and any relative section or chapter notes and, provided such headings or notes do not otherwise require, according to the following provisions:

BREAKDOWN OF EACH GRI:

GRI 2(a): Unfinished items are classified as if finished (if unfinished item has essential character of finished).

Any reference in an HTS Heading Article Description to an article shall apply to the same article even if the said article is incomplete or unfinished. An example of this would be a pair of basketball shoes imported without its laces. Though not completely functional or ready for use in their imported state, the item is still essentially basketball shoes, even without laces.

Quoting GRI 2(a) directly from the HTSUS General Rules of Interpretation...

2. (a) Any reference in a heading to an article shall be taken to include a reference to that article incomplete or unfinished, provided that, as entered, the incomplete or unfinished article has the essential character of the complete or finished article. It shall also include a reference to that article complete or finished (or falling to be classified as complete or finished by virtue of this rule), entered unassembled or disassembled.

GRI 2(b): Mixtures may be implied (unless otherwise prohibited in the headings or notes). Go to GRI 3.

This rule is, in a way, the flipside of GRI 2(a). GRI 2(b) says that an item may be classified under a specific classification even if the item is combined with other substances. In other words, mixtures may be implied (unless otherwise prohibited in the section notes, chapter notes, or headings). An example of this could be a chrome-plated steel wire garment hanger (clothes hanger). "Garment hangers" are specifically provided for in the HTSUS and classified under 7326.20.0020 following the sub-heading of "Articles of iron or steel wire". Since no Section Note, no Chapter Note, and no Classification Heading advise otherwise, the inconsequential presence of the "chrome plating" in this instance does not affect the classification of the item as a "steel" wire garment hanger. Just to be sure, we proceed to GRI 3.

Quoting GRI 2(b) directly from the HTSUS General Rules of Interpretation...

2. (b) Any reference in a heading to a material or substance shall be taken to include a reference to mixtures or combinations of that material or substance with other materials or substances. Any reference to goods of a given material or substance shall be taken to include a reference to goods consisting wholly or partly of such material or substance. The classification of goods consisting of more than one material or substance shall be according to the principles of rule 3.

BREAKDOWN OF EACH GRI:

GRI 3(a): Specific HTS heading/description preferred (over less descriptive), for prima facie items.

This rule says that, for prima facie items, the HTS heading that most specifically describes the product should be used. "Prima Facie" (often pronounced "preemuh face-she"), in the context of customs, simply means an item is potentially classifiable under more than one classification in the HTS.
For example, which of the two following classifications more specifically describes a keyboard for a desktop computer?

A) 8471.60.2000 Automatic data processing machines and units thereof...>>Input or output units...>>Other>>**Keyboards**

Or

B) 8537.10.9070 Boards, panels, consoles...equipped with two or more apparatus of heading 8535 or 8536, for electric control...>>For a voltage not exceeding 1,000V>>Other>>Other>>Other

"A" is a more specific description than "B". The word "keyboards" is explicitly part of the description (note: Customs' word for "computer" is "Automatic Data Processing Machines"). "B" is a commonly used classification for control units in general.

 Quoting GRI 3(a) directly from the HTSUS General Rules of Interpretation...

3. When, by application of rule 2(b) or for any other reason, goods are, prima facie, classifiable under two or more headings, classification shall be effected as follows:

(a) The heading which provides the most specific description shall be preferred to headings providing a more general description. However, when two or more headings each refer to part only of the materials or substances contained in mixed or composite goods or to part only of the items in a set put up for retail sale, those headings are to be regarded as equally specific in relation to those goods, even if one of them gives a more complete or precise description of the goods.

BREAKDOWN OF EACH GRI:

GRI 3(b): Essential character of item determines HTS# (if unclassifiable by 3(a)), for prima facie items.

If GRI 3(a) does not work, this rule says that products consisting of multiple materials or components, or sets shall be classified under the material which gives the product its essential character. For example, a nice leather baseball glove for an adult, which has been packaged with a gratuitous baseball and small bottle of glove oil, would still just be classified as a baseball glove (4203.21.4000), as this main component of the set clearly gives the set its essential character.

Quoting GRI 3(b) directly from the HTSUS General Rules of Interpretation...

3. When, by application of rule 2(b) or for any other reason, goods are, prima facie, classifiable under two or more headings, classification shall be effected as follows:

(b) Mixtures, composite goods consisting of different materials or made up of different components, and goods put up in sets for retail sale, which cannot be classified by reference to 3(a), shall be classified as if they consisted of the material or component which gives them their essential character, insofar as this criterion is applicable.

GRI 3(c): Last in order HTS# shall be used (if unclassifiable by 3(a) or by 3(b)), for prima facie items.

If neither GRI 3(a) nor GRI 3(b) works, this rule says that the largest (numerically speaking) classification prevails. For example, if an item is classifiable in both chapter 84 AND chapter 85, then choose the classification in chapter 85, as this classification numerically occurs later in the HTSUS than does the chapter 84 item.

Quoting GRI 3(c) directly from the HTSUS General Rules of Interpretation...

3. When, by application of rule 2(b) or for any other reason, goods are, prima facie, classifiable under two or more headings, classification shall be effected as follows:

(c) When goods cannot be classified by reference to 3(a) or 3(b), they shall be classified under the heading which occurs last in numerical order among those which equally merit consideration.

BREAKDOWN OF EACH GRI:

GRI 4: Most akin item's HTS# is to be used (if not classifiable by the preceding rules).

This rule concedes that goods still unclassifiable per the previously mentioned rules (GRI 1 thru. GRI 3) shall be classified under the heading for goods that are most similar in character. For example, a "computer monitor magnifier" (accessory attached to front of monitor to magnify items on screen) is classifiable as 9013.80.2000. This classification's description is "Hand magnifiers, magnifying glasses, loupes, thread counters and similar apparatus", which certainly could be considered most akin to the computer monitor magnifier.

 Quoting GRI 4 directly from the HTSUS General Rules of Interpretation...

4. Goods which cannot be classified in accordance with the above rules shall be classified under the heading appropriate to the goods to which they are most akin.

BREAKDOWN OF EACH GRI:

GRI 5(a) & (b): Article-specific cases & packaging are classified with item (unless *they are* "the item").

These rules deal with (a) cases and (b) packaging, and are fairly self-explanatory.

Example of 5(a): A (real) gold-plated case for reading glasses would not be classified with the relatively insignificant reading glasses for which it contains. The valuable case, itself, would be given its own classification. On the other hand, a basic plastic protective case for and imported with reading glasses would not be separately classified—it would be classified with the glasses.

Example of 5(b): A shipment of bulk-packaged styrofoam packaging peanuts, and nothing else, for a packaging supplies importer, would be classified and entered as styrofoam packaging peanuts. On the other hand, styrofoam peanuts used as protective packaging for delicate electronic goods would not be classified separately—it would be classified with the electronics.

 Quoting GRI 5(a) & (b) directly from the HTSUS General Rules of Interpretation...

5. In addition to the foregoing provisions, the following rules shall apply in respect of the goods referred to therein:

(a) Camera cases, musical instrument cases, gun cases, drawing instrument cases, necklace cases and similar containers, specially shaped or fitted to contain a specific article or set of articles, suitable for long-term use and entered with the articles for which they are intended, shall be classified with such articles when of a kind normally sold therewith. This rule does not, however, apply to containers which give the whole its essential character;

(b) Subject to the provisions of rule 5(a) above, packing materials and packing containers entered with the goods therein shall be classified with the goods if they are of a kind normally used for packing such goods. However, this provision is not binding when such packing materials or packing containers are clearly suitable for repetitive use.

BREAKDOWN OF EACH GRI:

GRI 6: Apply the GRI's to the headings, then the sub-headings, then ...

This means the logic and application of the GRI's are to be applied and repeated from one level (e.g. heading) to the next lower level (e.g. sub-heading), and so on. In our humble opinion, this rule is self-evident, and so we have thus omitted this GRI from the acronym H.U.M. S.E.L.M.A. to keep things as simple as possible.

 Quoting GRI 6 directly from the HTSUS General Rules of Interpretation...

6. For legal purposes, the classification of goods in the subheadings of a heading shall be determined according to the terms of those subheadings and any related subheading notes and, mutatis mutandis, to the above rules, on the understanding that only subheadings at the same level are comparable. For the purposes of this rule, the relative section, chapter and subchapter notes also apply, unless the context otherwise requires.

BREAKDOWN OF EACH GRI:

Additional U.S. Rules of Interpretation:

Also worth noting, but omitted from the acronym are the "Additional U.S. Rules of Interpretation". Notably, Additional Rule 1(c), which says that (in general) "parts and accessories" may be classified as "parts", UNLESS the part in question happens to be specifically provided for in the HTSUS. A good example of this is the question of where to classify a "glass fuse" manufactured for an automobile. Many might just classify as "a part" for an automobile in Chapter 87. However, since a "glass fuse" is specifically provided for in Chapter 85 with other electronics, the fuse if classifiable accordingly in Chapter 85. This rule, however, is just in general. Wherever applicable, Section Notes and Chapter Notes, include instructions for classifying parts for those Sections and Chapters.

Quoting Additional U.S. Rules of Interpretation from the HTSUS General Rules of Interpretation...

ADDITIONAL U.S. RULES OF INTERPRETATION

1. In the absence of special language or context which otherwise requires--

(a) a tariff classification controlled by use (other than actual use) is to be determined in accordance with the use in the United States at, or immediately prior to, the date of importation, of goods of that class or kind to which the imported goods belong, and the controlling use is the principal use;

(b) a tariff classification controlled by the actual use to which the imported goods are put in the United States is satisfied only if such use is intended at the time of importation, the goods are so used and proof thereof is furnished within 3 years after the date the goods are entered;

(c) a provision for parts of an article covers products solely or principally used as a part of such articles but a provision for "parts" or "parts and accessories" shall not prevail over a specific provision for such part or accessory; and

(d) the principles of section XI regarding mixtures of two or more textile materials shall apply to the classification of goods in any provision in which a textile material is named.

GRI snapshot from the HTSUS:

In their entirety, the General Rules of Interpretation as presented on pages 1 & 2 of the HTSUS:

GENERAL RULES OF INTERPRETATION

Classification of goods in the tariff schedule shall be governed by the following principles:

1. The table of contents, alphabetical index, and titles of sections, chapters and sub-chapters are provided for ease of reference only; for legal purposes, classification shall be determined according to the terms of the headings and any relative section or chapter notes and, provided such headings or notes do not otherwise require, according to the following provisions:

2. (a) Any reference in a heading to an article shall be taken to include a reference to that article incomplete or unfinished, provided that, as entered, the incomplete or unfinished article has the essential character of the complete or finished article. It shall also include a reference to that article complete or finished (or falling to be classified as complete or finished by virtue of this rule), entered unassembled or disassembled.

   (b) Any reference in a heading to a material or substance shall be taken to include a reference to mixtures or combinations of that material or substance with other materials or substances. Any reference to goods of a given material or substance shall be taken to include a reference to goods consisting wholly or partly of such material or substance. The classification of goods consisting of more than one material or substance shall be according to the principles of rule 3.

3. When, by application of rule 2(b) or for any other reason, goods are, prima facie, classifiable under two or more headings, classification shall be effected as follows:

   (a) The heading which provides the most specific description shall be preferred to headings providing a more general description. However, when two or more headings each refer to part only of the materials or substances contained in mixed or composite goods or to part only of the items in a set put up for retail sale, those headings are to be regarded as equally specific in relation to those goods, even if one of them gives a more complete or precise description of the goods.

   (b) Mixtures, composite goods consisting of different materials or made up of different components, and goods put up in sets for retail sale, which cannot be classified by reference to 3(a), shall be classified as if they consisted of the material or component which gives them their essential character, insofar as this criterion is applicable.

   (c) When goods cannot be classified by reference to 3(a) or 3(b), they shall be classified under the heading which occurs last in numerical order among those which equally merit consideration.

4. Goods which cannot be classified in accordance with the above rules shall be classified under the heading appropriate to the goods to which they are most akin.

5. In addition to the foregoing provisions, the following rules shall apply in respect of the goods referred to therein:

   (a) Camera cases, musical instrument cases, gun cases, drawing instrument cases, necklace cases and similar containers,specially shaped or fitted to contain a specific article or set of articles, suitable for long-term use and entered with the articles for which they are intended, shall be classified with such articles when of a kind normally sold therewith. This rule does not,however, apply to containers which give the whole its essential character;

   (b) Subject to the provisions of rule 5(a) above, packing materials and packing containers entered with the goods therein shall be classified with the goods if they are of a kind normally used for packing such goods. However, this provision is not binding when such packing materials or packing containers are clearly suitable for repetitive use.

6. For legal purposes, the classification of goods in the subheadings of a heading shall be determined according to the terms of those subheadings and any related subheading notes and, mutatis mutandis, to the above rules, on the understanding that only subheadings at the same level are comparable. For the purposes of this rule, the relative section, chapter and subchapter notes also apply, unless the context otherwise requires.

GRI snapshot from the HTSUS:

ADDITIONAL U.S. RULES OF INTERPRETATION

1. In the absence of special language or context which otherwise requires--

   (a) a tariff classification controlled by use (other than actual use) is to be determined in accordance with the use in the United States at, or immediately prior to, the date of importation, of goods of that class or kind to which the imported goods belong, and the controlling use is the principal use;

   (b) a tariff classification controlled by the actual use to which the imported goods are put in the United States is satisfied only if such use is intended at the time of importation, the goods are so used and proof thereof is furnished within 3 years after the date the goods are entered;

   (c) a provision for parts of an article covers products solely or principally used as a part of such articles but a provision for "parts" or "parts and accessories" shall not prevail over a specific provision for such part or accessory; and

   (d) the principles of section XI regarding mixtures of two or more textile materials shall apply to the classification of goods in any provision in which a textile material is named.

Book 1 Part 5

HTS Classification Tips

Subpart 4
GRI's Explained in Exam Examples

In This Sub-part
Each GRI applied to solve actual previous exam questions
Further GRI 1 through GRI 6 analysis

This subpart puts to use the General Rules of Interpretation by solving actual past exam problems.

Please note that classification descriptions notated to the right of exam question HTSUS number have been added by the author of this book for ease of reference. These classification descriptions are not annotated or provided on the actual exams. Also, some HTSUS numbers and excerpts may not be up-to-date, and some HTSUS numbers have been slightly updated or modified for the sake of these exercises.

Exam Example of GRI 1

"Headings and any relative Section & Chapter Notes determine the HTS#."

(Exam Question) What is the correct classification for fresh sweet corn?

A) 0709.99.4500 Other vegetables, fresh or chilled>>Other>>Other>>Sweet corn

B) 0710.40.0000 Vegetables (uncooked or cooked by steaming or boiling in water), frozen>>Sweet corn

C) 0712.90.8550 Dried vegetables, whole, cut, sliced, broken or in powder, but not further prepared>>Other vegetables; mixtures of vegetables>>Other>>Sweet corn seeds of a kind used for sowing

D) 1005.10.0010 Corn (maize)>>Seed>>Yellow corn

E) 1005.90.4060 Corn (maize)>>Other>>Other>>Other

Here's a perfect exam example to demonstrate the application of GRI 1. The item in question is fresh sweet corn.

First off, as per GRI 1, Chapter titles have no bearing on classification and are for reference purposes only. So, as just a side note, Chapter 7's title is "EDIBLE VEGETABLES AND CERTAIN ROOTS AND TUBERS" and Chapter 10's title is "CEREALS".

GRI 1 dictates that we must classify based on Chapter Notes, Section Notes, and Headings.

Note that Chapter 10, Note 2 says:

CHAPTER 10

CEREALS

II
10-1

Notes

1. (a) The products specified in the headings of this chapter are to be classified in those headings only if grains are present, whether or not in the ear or on the stalk.

   (b) This chapter does not cover grains which have been hulled or otherwise worked. However, rice, husked, milled, polished, glazed, parboiled or broken remains classified in heading 1006.

2. Heading 1005 does not cover sweet corn (chapter 7).

The item in question is fresh sweet corn. Per the note, we may eliminate Heading 1005 multiple choice options "D" and "E".

The heading for multiple choice "B" is for "frozen" vegetables, so we eliminate this one. The heading for multiple choice "C" is for "dried" vegetables, so we may eliminate this one as well.

"A" is the classification for fresh sweet corn, and is the correct answer.

✓ **Just a side note:** "Maize" is a type of corn grown by Native Americans.

Heading/ Subheading	Stat. Suf-fix	Article Description	Unit of Quantity	Rates of Duty 1 General	Rates of Duty 1 Special	Rates of Duty 2
0709 (con.)		Other vegetables, fresh or chilled: (con.)				
		Other:				
0709.91.00	00	Globe artichokes	kg	11.3%	Free (A, AU, BH, CA, CL, CO, E, IL, JO, KR, MA, MX, OM, P, PA, PE, SG)	50%
0709.92.00	00	Olives	kg	8.8¢/kg	Free (A+, AU, BH, CA, CL, CO, D, E, IL, JO, KR, MA, MX, OM, P, PA, PE, SG)	11¢/kg
0709.93		Pumpkins, squash and gourds (*Curcubita* spp.):				
0709.93.10	00	Pumpkins	kg	11.3%	Free (A, AU, BH, CA, CL, CO, E, IL, JO, KR, MA, MX, OM, P, PA, PE, SG)	50%
0709.93.20	00	Squash	kg	1.5¢/kg	Free (A, AU, BH, CA, CL, CO, E, IL, JO, KR, MA, MX, OM, P, PA, PE, SG)	4.4¢/kg
0709.93.30	00	Gourds (*Curcubita* spp.)	kg	20%	Free (A+, BH, CA, CL, CO, D, E, IL, JO, KR, MA, MX, OM, P, PA, PE, SG) 6.5% (AU)	50%
0709.99		Other:				
0709.99.05	00	Jicamas, and breadfruit	kg	11.3%	Free (A, AU, BH, CA, CL, CO, E, IL, JO, KR, MA, MX, OM, P, PA, PE, SG)	50%
0709.99.10	00	Chayote (*Sechium edule*)	kg	5.6%	Free (A, AU, BH, CA, CL, CO, E, IL, JO, KR, MA, MX, OM, P, PA, PE, SG)	50%
0709.99.14	00	Okra	kg	20%	Free (A, AU, BH, CA, CL, CO, E, IL, JO, KR, MA, MX, OM, P, PA, PE, SG)	50%
0709.99.30	00	Fiddlehead greens	kg	8%	Free (A+, AU, BH, CA, CL, CO, D, E, IL, JO, KR, MA, MX, OM, P, PA, PE, SG)	20%
0709.99.45	00	Sweet corn	kg	21.3%	Free (AU, BH, CA, CL, CO, D, E, IL, JO, KR, MA, MX, P, PA, PE, SG) 4.2% (OM)	50%
0709.99.90	00	Other	kg	20%	Free (A+, BH, CA, CL, CO, D, E, IL, JO, KR, MA, MX, OM, P, PA, PE, SG) 6.5% (AU)	50%

(Another) Exam Example of GRI 1 (classifying "parts" of machines)

(Exam Question) What is the CLASSIFICATION for a submersible pump o-ring? The o-ring is made of vulcanized rubber and for use within a saltwater submersible pump.

A. 4016.93.1010	Other articles of vulcanized rubber other than hard rubber>>Other>>Gaskets, washers, and other seals>>Of a kind used in the automotive goods of chapter 87>>O-rings
B. 4016.93.5010	Other articles of vulcanized rubber other than hard rubber>>Other>>Gaskets, washers, and other seals>>Other>>O-rings
C. 4016.93.5050	Other articles of vulcanized rubber other than hard rubber>>Other>>Gaskets, washers, and other seals>>Other>>Other
D. 8413.70.2004	Pumps for liquids, whether or not fitted with a measuring device; liquid elevators; part thereof>>Other centrifugal pumps>>Other>>Submersible pumps
E. 8413.91.9080	Pumps for liquids, whether or not fitted with a measuring device; liquid elevators; part thereof>>Parts>>Of pumps>>Other>>Other

Note that for classifying "parts of" machinery or electronics; refer to the rules for doing so in the Section Notes and/or Chapter Notes (i.e. classify via GRI 1). **The following note is quite relevant as both Chapters 84 & 85 quite often appear on the exams.**

As per Section XVI (Chapters 84 & 85), Note 2:

2. Subject to note 1 to this section, note 1 to chapter 84 and to note 1 to chapter 85, ***parts of machines*** *(not being parts of the articles of heading 8484, 8544, 8545, 8546 or 8547)* ***are to be classified according to the following rules:***

(a) Parts which are goods included in any of the headings of chapter 84 or 85 *(other than headings 8409, 8431, 8448, 8466, 8473, 8487, 8503, 8522, 8529, 8538 and 8548)* ***are in all cases to be classified in their respective headings***

... ...

The above note means that, except for the headings listed in the parentheses of both paragraphs (e.g. 8484, 8409, etc.), if the part is described in another chapter or heading in the HTS, then classify using that ("respective") heading, and do not classify as a "part of" the machine, electronic device, etc.

The item in question is a simple rubber O-ring for use with a submersible pump. Per the above-mentioned Section Note, if O-rings are provided for in another Chapter/Heading, then we'll use that classification, instead of classifying the O-ring as a part of a pump.

The HTSUS does indeed describe "O-rings", in multiple choices "A" and "B". So, we'll disregard the parts of pump classification "E". "A", however, is for O-rings for use in automobiles, and may be disregarded. "B" is the correct answer.

✓ **Just a side note:** An "O-ring" is simply a circular gasket (for creating a water-tight seal, for example) with a round cross-section.

Heading/ Subheading	Stat. Suf- fix	Article Description	Unit of Quantity	Rates of Duty 1 General	Rates of Duty 1 Special	Rates of Duty 2
4016		Other articles of vulcanized rubber other than hard rubber:				
4016.10.00	00	Of cellular rubber	X	Free		25%
		Other:				
4016.91.00	00	Floor coverings and mats	X	2.7% 1/	Free (A,AU,BH,B, CA,CL,CO,E,IL, JO,KR,MA, MX,OM,P, PA,PE,SG)	40%
4016.92.00	00	Erasers	X	4.2% 2/	Free (A,AU,BH, CA,CL,CO,E,IL, JO,KR,MA, MX,OM,P, PA,PE,SG)	35%
4016.93		Gaskets, washers and other seals:				
4016.93.10		Of a kind used in the automotive goods of chapter 87		2.5%	Free (A,AU,BH,B, CA,CL,CO,E,IL, JO,KR,MA, MX,OM,P, PA,PE,SG)	25%
	10	O-Rings	kg			
	20	Oil seals	No. kg			
	50	Other	kg			
4016.93.50		Other		2.5%	Free (A,AU,BH,C, CA,CL,CO,E,IL, JO,KR,MA, MX,OM,P, PA,PE,SG)	25%
	10	O-Rings	kg			
	20	Oil seals	No. kg			
	50	Other	kg			
4016.94.00	00	Boat or dock fenders, whether or not inflatable	X	4.2%	Free (A,AU,BH, CA,CL,CO,E,IL, JO,KR,MA, MX,OM,P, PA,PE,SG)	80%
4016.95.00	00	Other inflatable articles	X	4.2%	Free (A,AU,BH, CA,CL,CO,E,IL, JO,KR,MA, MX,OM,P, PA,PE,SG)	25%

Exam Example of GRI 2(a)

"Unfinished items are classified as if finished (if unfinished has essential character of finished)."

(Exam Question)

A shipment arrives at the port of Champlain, New York, destined for your client, Ice Jewels, located in Burlington, Vermont. The exporter is located in Ottawa, Canada. The merchandise is invoiced as unfinished jewelry boxes. Examination of the load reveals 1,000 boxes (without lids) that are lined with red velvet fabric, 2,000 small steel hinges (2 per box), 1,000 carved wooden lids. You contact your client, who states that he ordered jewelry boxes from the Ottawa company, but had them shipped down unassembled, because of a rush order he received. The correct classification for this merchandise is:

A) Wooden box bottoms-4420.90.80, carved lids-4421.90.94, hinges-8302.10.90.

B) Wooden box bottoms-4420.90.65, carved lids-4421.90.98, hinges-8302.10.90

C) Wooden bottoms and lids-4421.90.98, hinges-8302.10.90

D) 4420.90.65 Wood marquetry and inlaid wood; caskets and cases for jewelry or cutlery and similar articles, of wood; statuettes and other ornaments, of wood; wooden articles of furniture not falling within chapter 94>>Other>>Jewelry boxes, silverware chests, cigar and cigarette boxes, microscope cases, tool or utensil cases and similar boxes, cases and chests, all the foregoing of wood>>Other>>Lined with textile fabrics

E) 4202.39.20 Trunks, suitcases, vanity cases, attache cases, briefcases, school satchels, spectacle cases, binocular cases, camera cases, musical instrument cases, gun cases, holsters and similar containers; ... ...>>Articles of a kind normally carried in the pocket or in the handbag>>Other>>Of material (other than leather, composition leather, sheeting of plastics, textile materials, vulcanized fiber or paperboard) wholly or mainly covered with paper>>Of wood

Here's an easy one! Should the shipment be classified as jewelry boxes, or should each separate component of the boxes be classified separately? Remember that as per GRI 2(a):

"Any reference in a heading to an article shall be taken to include a reference to that article incomplete or unfinished, provided that, as entered, the incomplete or unfinished article has the essential character of the complete or finished article. It shall also include a reference to that article complete or finished (or failing to be classified as complete or finished by virtue of this rule) entered unassembled or disassembled".

In other words, if an unfinished, unassembled, or incomplete item still manages to maintain the essential character (in name and in general) of the item as if it were finished, then the unfinished item should be classified just as the finished item would. So, in terms of the jewelry box in question, although the box is unassembled, it is still considered, for all intents and purposes, to be a jewelry box. Therefore, by application of GRI 2(a), and noting that "jewelry boxes" are provided for in the classification description, we may deduce that the correct answer is "D".

✓ **Note:** The HTS numbers used in this exam question are shortened to 8 digits (instead of the complete 10 digits). The customs broker exam classification questions are occasionally abbreviated this way, possibly in an attempt to simplify things.

Heading/ Subheading	Stat. Suf-fix	Article Description	Unit of Quantity	Rates of Duty 1 General	Special	2
4419.00		Tableware and kitchenware, of wood:				
4419.00.40	00	Forks and spoons	X	5.3%	Free (A, AU, BH, CA, CL, CO, E, IL, JO, KR, MA, MX, OM, P, PA, PE, SG)	33 1/3%
4419.00.80	00	Other	X	3.2%	Free (A, AU, BH, CA, CL, CO, E, IL, JO, KR, MA, MX, OM, P, PA, PE, SG)	33 1/3%
4420		Wood marquetry and inlaid wood; caskets and cases for jewelry or cutlery and similar articles, of wood; statuettes and other ornaments, of wood; wooden articles of furniture not falling within chapter 94:				
4420.10.00	00	Statuettes and other ornaments, of wood	X	3.2%	Free (A, AU, BH, CA, CL, CO, E, IL, JO, KR, MA, MX, OM, P, PA, PE, SG)	33 1/3%
4420.90		Other:				
		Jewelry boxes, silverware chests, cigar and cigarette boxes, microscope cases, tool or utensil cases and similar boxes, cases and chests, all the foregoing of wood:				
4420.90.20	00	Cigar and cigarette boxes	No.	Free		60%
		Other:				
4420.90.45	00	Not lined with textile fabrics	No.	4.3%	Free (A, AU, BH, CA, CL, CO, E, IL, JO, KR, MA, MX, OM, P, PA, PE, SG)	33 1/3%
4420.90.65	00	Lined with textile fabrics	kg No.	Free		11¢/kg + 20%
4420.90.80	00	Other	X	3.2%	Free (A, AU, BH, CA, CL, CO, E, IL, JO, KR, MA, MX, OM, P, PA, PE, SG)	33 1/3%

Exam Example of GRI 2(b)

"Mixtures may be implied (unless otherwise prohibited in the headings or notes). Go to GRI 3."

(Exam Question)

What is the CLASSIFICATION for dried and prepared seaweed from Korea? The edible food is made from raw kelp-type seaweed that is filtered for impurities, pressed, formed into square sheets, dried, and finally roasted and seasoned with sesame oil, salt, MSG, and soy sauce.

A. 1212.21.0000	Locust beans, seaweeds and other algae … of a kind used primarily for human consumption, not elsewhere specified or included>>Seaweeds and other algae>>Fit for human consumption
B. 1212.29.0000	Locust beans, seaweeds and other algae … of a kind used primarily for human consumption, not elsewhere specified or included>>Seaweeds and other algae>>Other
C. 2008.99.6100	Fruit, nuts and other edible parts of plants, otherwise prepared or preserved, whether or not containing added sugar or other sweetening matter or spirit, not elsewhere specified or included>>Other>>Other>>Soybeans
D. 2008.99.9090	Fruit, nuts and other edible parts of plants, otherwise prepared or preserved, whether or not containing added sugar or other sweetening matter or spirit, not elsewhere specified or included>>Other>>Other>>Other>>Other>>Other
E. 2103.10.0000	Sauces and preparations therefore: mixed condiments and mixed seasonings; mustard flour and meal and prepared mustard>>Soy sauce

Simply stated, GRI 2(b) says that an item may be classifiable under a single heading/classification even if the item is combined with other substances.

In other words, mixtures may be implied (unless otherwise prohibited in the section notes, chapter notes, and headings). For the sake of demonstrating this rule, we'll go ahead and disclose that multiple choice "D" is the correct classification for "prepared" edible seaweed.

The dried seaweed snack in question contains, in addition to seaweed, a multitude of other substances (i.e. sesame oil, salt, MSG, and soy sauce). So, can it still be classified as seaweed? Yes, and that is the main point of this exam problem. As per GRI 2(b), these additional ingredients are inconsequential to the nature of the item. This should be further confirmed by going to GRI 3, though for the purpose of explaining the GRI 2(b), we can digress at this point.

✓ **Note:** The other multiple choices may be addressed as per the following. Multiple choices "C" and "E" are the classifications for prepared soybeans and soy sauce, respectively. Both "A" and "B" are located within the heading 1212, which does include items such as seaweed, though ONLY IF the item to be classified is "not elsewhere specified or included" in the HTSUS. However, the item in question IS INDEED (though somewhat vaguely) described under heading 2008, which includes "prepared" plant food items. Prepared "Seaweed" is not specifically provided for in heading 2008, so it is thus classified, as customs brokers commonly say, "other, other". Once again, "D" is the correct answer.

Heading/ Subheading	Stat. Suf- fix	Article Description	Unit of Quantity	Rates of Duty 1 General	Rates of Duty 1 Special	Rates of Duty 2
2008 (con.)		Fruit, nuts and other edible parts of plants, otherwise prepared or preserved, whether or not containing added sugar or other sweetening matter or spirit, not elsewhere specified or included (con.):				
		Other, including mixtures other than those of sub-heading 2008.19 (con.):				
2008.99 (con.)		Other (con.):				
2008.99.40	00	Mangoes	kg	1.5¢/kg	Free (A,AU,BH,CA, CL,CO,E,IL,JO, KR,MA,MX,OM,P, PA,PE,SG)	33¢/kg
		Papayas:				
2008.99.45	00	Pulp	kg	14%	Free (A,AU,BH,CA, CL,CO,E,IL,JO, MA,MX,OM,P,PA, PE,SG) 5.6% (KR)	35%
2008.99.50	00	Other	kg	1.8%	Free (A,AU,BH,CA, CL,CO,E,IL,JO, KR,MA,MX,OM,P, PA,PE,SG)	35%
2008.99.60	00	Plums (including prune plums and sloes)	kg	11.2%	Free (A+,AU,BH, CA,CL,CO,D,E, IL,JO,KR,MX, OM,P,PA,PE,SG) 1.1% (MA)	35%
2008.99.61	00	Soybeans	kg	3.8%	Free (A,AU,BH,CA, CL,CO,E,IL,JO, KR,MA,MX,OM,P, PA,PE,SG)	35%
2008.99.63	00	Sweet ginger	kg	4.4%	Free (A,AU,BH,CA, CL,CO,E,IL,JO, KR,MA,MX,OM,P, PA,PE,SG)	35%
2008.99.65	00	Cassava (manioc)	kg	7.9%	Free (A,AU,BH,CA, CL,CO,E,IL,JO, MA,MX,OM,P,PA, PE,SG) 3.1% (KR)	35%
		Chinese water chestnuts:				
2008.99.70	00	Frozen	kg	11.2%	Free (A+,AU,BH, CA,CL,CO,D,E, IL,JO,MX,OM,P, PA,PE,SG) 1.1% (MA) 6.4% (KR)	35%
2008.99.71		Other		Free		35%
	10	Sliced	kg			
	20	Whole	kg			
		Other:				
2008.99.80	00	Pulp	kg	9.6%	Free (A*,AU,BH, CA,CL,CO,E,IL, JO,KR,MA,MX, OM,P,PA,PE,SG)	35%
2008.99.90		Other		6%	Free (A,AU,BH,CA, CL,CO,E,IL,JO, KR,MA,MX,OM,P, PA,PE,SG)	35%
	10	Bean cake, bean stick, miso and similar products	kg			
	90	Other	kg			

Exam Example of GRI 3(a)

"Specific HTS heading/description preferred (over less descriptive), for prima facie items."

(Exam Question) What is the classification for a diffusing apparatus used for the commercial extraction of sugar juice?

A. 8419.40.0040 Machinery, plant or laboratory equipment, whether or not electrically heated ... ..., for the treatment of materials by a process involving a change of temperature such as heating, cooking, roasting, distilling, rectifying, sterilizing, pasteurizing, steaming, drying, evaporating, vaporizing, condensing or cooling, other than machinery or plant of a kind used for domestic purposes; instantaneous or storage water heaters, nonelectric; parts thereof>>Distilling or rectifying plant>>For food and beverages

B. 8421.22.0000 Centrifuges, including centrifugal dryers; filtering or purifying machinery and apparatus, for liquids or gases; parts thereof>>Filtering or purifying machinery and apparatus for liquids>>For filtering or purifying beverages other than water

C. 8435.10.0000 Presses, crushers and similar machinery, used in the manufacture of wine, cider, fruit juices or similar beverages; parts thereof>>Machinery

D. 8438.30.0000 Machinery, not specified or included elsewhere in this chapter, for the industrial preparation or manufacture of food or drink, other than machinery for the extraction or preparation of animal or fixed vegetable fats or oils; parts thereof>>Machinery for sugar manufacture

E. 8509.40.0030 Electromechanical domestic appliances, with self-contained electric motor, other than vacuum cleaners of heading 8508; parts thereof>>Food grinders, processors and mixes; fruit or vegetable juice extractors>>Juice extractors

The item in question is a commercial sugar juice extractor. To begin with, by application of GRI 1, let's disregard multiple choices "A" and "E", as both headings 8419 and 8509 state in their article descriptions that the machines classified therein are for "domestic" purposes/appliances (i.e. not commercial).

Now, since the item in question is a prima facie item (i.e. classifiable under more than one heading), we first try to apply GRI 3(a), which says to select the most specific description. "D", which is the classification for machinery for "sugar manufacture" is relatively the most descriptive. "B" and "C", which are the classifications for machines for filtering juices, and for juice presses, respectively, are relatively less descriptive, AND each just potentially refers to part of the process of sugar manufacturing. Furthermore, Chapter 84, Note 2 (see below) makes reference that heading 8438 is for "sugar juice extraction". The correct answer is "D".

Heading 8419 does not, however, cover:

... ...

(c) ***Diffusing apparatus for sugar juice extraction (heading 8438);***

✓ **Just a Side Note:** The sugar (cane) manufacturing process (among others steps) washing, crushing, extracting, filtering, evaporating, centrifuging, and drying.

Heading/ Subheading	Stat. Suf- fix	Article Description	Unit of Quantity	Rates of Duty 1 General	Rates of Duty 1 Special	Rates of Duty 2
8438		Machinery, not specified or included elsewhere in this chapter, for the industrial preparation or manufacture of food or drink, other than machinery for the extraction or preparation of animal or fixed vegetable fats or oils; parts thereof:				
8438.10.00		Bakery machinery and machinery for the manufacture of macaroni, spaghetti or similar products		Free		35%
	10	Bakery machinery	No.			
	90	Other	No.			
8438.20.00	00	Machinery for the manufacture of confectionery, cocoa or chocolate	No.	Free		35%
8438.30.00	00	Machinery for sugar manufacture	No.	Free		Free
8438.40.00	00	Brewery machinery	No.	2.3%	Free (A, AU, BH, CA, CL, CO, E, IL, JO, KR, MA, MX, OM, P, PA, PE, SG)	35%
8438.50.00		Machinery for the preparation of meat or poultry		2.8%	Free (A, AU, BH, CA, CL, CO, E, IL, JO, KR, MA, MX, OM, P, PA, PE, SG)	35%
	10	Meat- and poultry-packing plant machinery	No.			
	90	Other	No.			
8438.60.00	00	Machinery for the preparation of fruits, nuts or vegetables	No.	Free		35%
8438.80.00	00	Other machinery	No.	Free		40%
8438.90		Parts:				
8438.90.10	00	Of machinery for sugar manufacture	X	Free		Free
8438.90.90		Other		2.8%	Free (A, AU, BH, CA, CL, CO, E, IL, JO, KR, MA, MX, OM, P, PA, PE, SG)	35%
	15	Of bakery machinery and machinery for the manufacture of macaroni, spaghetti or similar products	X			
	30	Of machinery for the manufacture of confectionery, cocoa or chocolate	X			
	60	Of machinery for the preparation of meat or poultry	X			
	90	Other	X			

Exam Example of GRI 3(b)

Essential character of item determines HTS# (if unclassifiable by 3(a)), for prima facie items.

(Question) What is the CLASSIFICATION for a woven cotton baseball cap with detachable sunglasses attached under the bill of the cap?

A. 6505.90.2590 Hats and other headgear, knitted or crocheted, or made up from lace, felt or other textile fabric, in the piece (but not in strips), whether or not lined or trimmed; ... ... >>Other>>Of cotton, flax or both>>Not knitted>>Other>>Other

B. 9004.10.0000 Spectacles, goggles and the like, corrective, protective or other>>Sunglasses

C. 6505.90.0800 Hats and other headgear, knitted or crocheted, or made up from lace, felt or other textile fabric, in the piece (but not in strips), whether or not lined or trimmed; ... ... >>Other>>Felt hats and other felt headgear ... ... >>Other

D. 9004.90.0000 Spectacles, goggles and the like, corrective, protective or other>>Other

E. 9003.19.0000 Frames and mountings for spectacles, goggles or the like, and parts thereof>>Frames and mountings>>Of other materials

Here's a great example of a prima facie item (i.e. an item classifiable under more than one heading). The item is a cotton woven (i.e. not knitted) baseball cap with detachable sunglasses. First off, we're unable to classify via GRI 3(a), which says to choose the most descriptive heading, as all the headings presented here only refer to parts (i.e. either cap or sunglasses) of the item. So, next we have to try to classify by using GRI 3(b).

Accordingly, as per GRI 3(b), we try to classify based on the "essential character" of the item. It would be reasonable to say that the baseball cap ("A") gives the item its essential character, and that the detachable sunglasses ("B") do not give the item its essential character. Therefore, the correct answer and classification is "A".

Heading/ Subheading	Stat. Suf-fix	Article Description	Unit of Quantity	Rates of Duty 1 General	Rates of Duty 1 Special	Rates of Duty 2
6505		Hats and other headgear, knitted or crocheted, or made up from lace, felt or other textile fabric, in the piece (but not in strips), whether or not lined or trimmed; hair-nets of any material, whether or not lined or trimmed:				
6505.10.00	00	Hair-nets	kg	9.4%	Free (A,AU,BH,CA, CL,E,IL,J,JO, MX, SG) 7.3% (MA) 7.5% (P)	90%
6505.90		Other:				
		Felt hats and other felt headgear, made from the hat bodies, hoods or plateaux of heading 6501, whether or not lined or trimmed:				
6505.90.04		Of fur felt		Free		$16/doz. + 25%
	10	For men or boys	doz. kg			
	50	Other	doz. kg			
6505.90.08	00	Other	No. kg	13.5¢/kg + 6.3% + 1.9¢/article	Free (AU,BH,CA, IL,JO,MX, P,SG) 10.5¢/kg + 4.8% + 1.4¢/article (MA)	88.2¢/kg + 55% + 12.5¢/ article
		Other:				
		Of cotton, flax or both:				
6505.90.15		Knitted		7.9%	Free (AU,BH,CA, CL,E*,IL,JO, MX,P,SG) 6.2% (MA)	45%
		Of cotton:				
	15	For babies (239)	doz. kg			
		Other:				
	25	Visors, and other headgear which provides no covering for the crown of the head (359)	doz. kg			
	40	Other (359)	doz. kg			
	60	Other (859)	doz. kg			
		Not knitted:				
6505.90.20		Certified hand-loomed and folklore products; and headwear of cotton		7.5%	Free (AU,BH,CA, E*,IL,J*,JO, MX,P,SG) 5.9% (MA)	37.5%
	30	For babies (239)	doz. kg			
	60	Other (359)	doz. kg			
6505.90.25		Other		7.5%	Free (AU,BH,CA, CL,E*,IL,JO, MX,P,SG) 5.9% (MA)	37.5%
	45	Visors, and other headgear of cotton which provides no covering for the crown of the head (359)	doz. kg			
	90	Other (859)	doz. kg			

Exam Example of GRI 3(c)

"Last in order HTS# shall be used (if item cannot be classified by 3(a) or by 3(b)), for prima facie items."

(Question)

Which of the following HTS headings should be used in classifying the following hairdressing set?

Towel classified in HTS heading 6302
Shampoo classified in HTS heading 3305
Hair gel classified in HTS heading 3305
Brush classified in HTS heading 9603
Comb classified in HTS heading 9615
Hair dryer classified in HTS heading 8516
Leather case to hold the above items classified in HTS heading 4202

A. 6302
B. 3305
C. 9615
D. 8516
E. 4202

The format of this particular previous exam question provides an easy-to-understand example of applying GRI 3(c).

First, note that the item, a hairdressing set, is prima facie (i.e. classifiable under more than one heading) as it contains 7 different components. No single classification specifically provides for a "hairdressing set" so we cannot classify by GRI 3(a). Further, no single classification clearly imparts the essential character of the set, so we cannot classify by GRI 3(b). Therefore, we classify based on last option GRI 3(c), which says to classify the prima facie item by selecting the heading/classification that occurs numerically last. 9615 is highest number here, so we conclude that the correct answer is "C".

Heading/ Subheading	Stat. Suf-fix	Article Description	Unit of Quantity	Rates of Duty 1 General	Rates of Duty 1 Special	2
9615		Combs, hair-slides and the like; hairpins, curling pins, curling grips, hair-curlers and the like, other than those of heading 8516, and parts thereof:				
		Combs, hair-slides and the like:				
9615.11		Of hard rubber or plastics:				
		Combs:				
9615.11.10	00	Valued not over $4.50 per gross	gross	14.4¢/gross + 2%	Free (A, AU, BH, CA, CL, CO, E, IL, JO, KR, MA, MX, OM, P, PA, PE, SG)	$1.44/gross + 25%
		Valued over $4.50 per gross:				
9615.11.20	00	Of hard rubber	gross	5.2%	Free (A, AU, BH, CA, CL, CO, E, IL, JO, KR, MA, MX, OM, P, PA, PE, SG)	36%
9615.11.30	00	Other	gross	28.8¢/gross + 4.6%	Free (A, AU, BH, CA, CL, CO, E, IL, JO, KR, MA, MX, OM, P, PA, PE, SG)	$2.88/gross + 35%
		Other:				
9615.11.40	00	Not set with imitation pearls or imitation gemstones	X	5.3%	Free (A, AU, BH, CA, CL, CO, E, IL, JO, KR, MA, MX, OM, P, PA, PE, SG)	80%
9615.11.50	00	Other	X	Free		110%
9615.19		Other:				
		Combs:				
9615.19.20	00	Valued not over $4.50 per gross	gross	9.7¢/gross + 1.3%	Free (A, AU, BH, CA, CL, CO, E, IL, JO, KR, MA, MX, OM, P, PA, PE, SG)	$1.44/gross + 25%
9615.19.40	00	Valued over $4.50 per gross	gross	28.8¢/gross + 4.6%	Free (A, AU, BH, CA, CL, CO, E, IL, JO, KR, MA, MX, OM, P, PA, PE, SG)	$2.88/gross + 35%
9615.19.60	00	Other	X	11%	Free (A, AU, BH, CA, CL, CO, E, IL, JO, MA, MX, OM, P, PA, PE, SG) 5.5% (KR)	110%

(ANOTHER) Exam Example of GRI 3(c)

"Last in order HTS# shall be used (if item cannot be classified by 3(a) or by 3(b)) for prima facie items."

(Question)

What is the CLASSIFICATION for a high-end youth fishing combo set composed of 1 fishing rod, 1 fishing reel, and 1 snelled fish hook? All three articles are packaged together, though they are not attached within the clear plastic packaging, and are all made in Japan. The fishing set is intended for freshwater use and is marketed as a "set" by the manufacturer. The value of the rod is $50 USD. The value of the reel is $50 USD. The value of the hook is $1 USD.

A. 9507.10.0040 Fishing rods, fish hooks and other line fishing tackle; …; parts and accessories thereof>>Fishing rods and parts and accessories thereof>>Fishing rods

B. 9507.10.0080 Fishing rods, fish hooks and other line fishing tackle; …; parts and accessories thereof>>Fishing rods and parts and accessories thereof>>Parts and accessories

C. 9507.20.4000 Fishing rods, fish hooks and other line fishing tackle; …; parts and accessories thereof>>Fish hooks, whether or not snelled>>Snelled hooks

D. 9507.30.6000 Fishing rods, fish hooks and other line fishing tackle; …; parts and accessories thereof>>Fishing reels and parts and accessories thereof>>Fishing reels>>Valued over $8.45 each

E. 9507.90.8000 Fishing rods, fish hooks and other line fishing tackle; …; parts and accessories thereof>>Other>>Other, including parts and accessories>>Other, including parts and accessories

The item in question is "Prima Facie" (i.e. classifiable under two or more different headings). There are three distinct items (rod, reel, & hook) within the fishing combo set, and they are represented by multiple choices "A", "D", and "C", respectively.

Each item is specifically provided for within the HTSUS, though all refer to only part of the item. Thus, the set cannot be classified under GRI 3(a). Next, GRI 3(b) says to classify based on the component that gives the set its essential character. The fishing hook definitely does not do this, so we may disregard "C". However, in the case of the fishing rod compared to the fishing reel, neither value nor functionality of either definitively imparts the essential character of the set over the other.

Subsequently we proceed to GRI 3(c), which says to classify based on the classification that (numerically) occurs last. Accordingly, 9507.30.6000 (the reel) occurs in order after 9507.10.0040 (the rod). "D", the reel classification, is the correct answer.

Heading/ Subheading	Stat Suf-fix	Article Description	Unit of Quantity	Rates of Duty 1 General	Rates of Duty 1 Special	Rates of Duty 2
9507		Fishing rods, fish hooks and other line fishing tackle; fish landing nets, butterfly nets and similar nets; decoy "birds" (other than those of heading 9208 or 9705) and similar hunting or shooting equipment; parts and accessories thereof:				
9507.10.00		Fishing rods and parts and accessories thereof.		6%	Free (A+,AU,BH, CA,CL,CO,D,E,IL, JO,KR,MA,MX, OM,P,PA,PE,SG)	55%
	40	Fishing rods.	No.			
	80	Parts and accessories.	X			
9507.20		Fish hooks, whether or not snelled:				
9507.20.40	00	Snelled hooks.	X.	4%	Free (A,AU,BH,CA, CL,CO,E,IL,JO, KR,MA,MX,OM, P,PA,PE,SG)	55%
9507.20.80	00	Other.	X.	4.8%	Free (A,AU,BH,CA, CL,CO,E,IL,JO, KR,MA,MX,OM, P,PA,PE,SG)	45%
9507.30		Fishing reels and parts and accessories thereof:				
		Fishing reels:				
9507.30.20	00	Valued not over $2.70 each.	No.	9.2%	Free (A+,AU,BH, CA,CL,CO,D,E,IL, JO,KR,MA,MX, OM,P,PA,PE,SG)	55%
9507.30.40	00	Valued over $2.70 but not over $8.45 each.	No.	24¢ each	Free (A+,AU,BH, CA,CL,CO,D,E,IL, JO,KR,MA,MX, OM,P,PA,PE,SG)	55%
9507.30.60	00	Valued over $8.45 each.	No.	3.9%	Free (A,AU,BH,CA, CL,CO,E,IL,JO, KR,MA,MX,OM, P,PA,PE,SG)	55%
9507.30.80	00	Parts and accessories.	X.	5.4%	Free (A,AU,BH,CA, CL,CO,E,IL,JO, KR,MA,MX,OM, P,PA,PE,SG)	55%
9507.90		Other:				
9507.90.20	00	Fishing line put up and packaged for retail sale.	X.	3.7%	Free (A,AU,BH,CA, CL,CO,E,IL,JO, KR,MA,MX,OM, P,PA,PE,SG)	65%
9507.90.40	00	Fishing casts or leaders.	doz.	5.6%	Free (A,AU,BH,CA, CL,CO,E,,IL, JO,KR,MA,MX, OM,P,PA,PE,SG)	55%
9507.90.60	00	Fish landing nets, butterfly nets and similar nets.	No.	5%	Free (A,AU,BH,CA, CL,CO,E,IL,JO, KR,MA,MX,OM, P,PA,PE,SG)	40%
		Other, including parts and accessories:				
9507.90.70	00	Artificial baits and flies	doz.	9%	Free (A+,AU,BH, CA,CL,CO,D,E,IL, JO,KR,MA,MX, OM,P,PA,PE,SG)	55%
9507.90.80	00	Other, including parts and accessories.	X.	9%	Free (A,AU,BH,CA, CL,CO,E,IL,JO, KR,MA,MX,OM, P,PA,PE,SG)	55%
9508		Merry-go-rounds, boat-swings, shooting galleries and other fairground amusements; traveling circuses and traveling menageries; traveling theaters; parts and accessories thereof:				
9508.10.00	00	Traveling circuses and traveling menageries; parts and accessories.	X.	Free		35%
9508.90.00	00	Other	X.	Free		35%

Exam Example of GRI 4

"Most akin item's HTS# is to be used (if not classifiable by the preceding rules)."

(Question)

What is the CLASSIFICATION for a "dummy launcher"? The dummy launcher is a stationary device that uses a .22 caliber blank to launch a bird dummy (not included with item) in the air from the ground for the purpose of training hunting dogs.

A. 9303.90.4000 Other firearms and similar devices which operate by the firing of an explosive charge (for example, sporting shot- guns and rifles, muzzle-loading firearms, Very pistols and other devices designed to project only signal flares, pistols and revolvers for firing blank ammunition, captive-bolt humane killers, line-throwing guns)>>Other>>Pistols and revolvers designed to fire only blank cartridges or blank ammunition

B. 9303.90.8000 Other firearms and similar devices which operate by the firing of an explosive charge (for example, sporting shot- guns and rifles, muzzle-loading firearms, Very pistols and other devices designed to project only signal flares, pistols and revolvers for firing blank ammunition, captive-bolt humane killers, line-throwing guns)>>Other>>Other

C. 9304.00.4000 Other arms (for example, spring, air or gas guns and pistols, truncheons), excluding those of heading 9307>>Pistols, rifles and other guns which eject missiles by release of compressed air or gas, or by the release of a spring mechanism or rubber held under tension>>Other

D. 9503.00.0090 Tricycles, scooters, pedal cars and similar wheeled toys; dolls' carriages; dolls, other toys; reduced-scale ("scale") models and similar recreational models, working or not; puzzles of all kinds; parts and accessories thereof>>Other

E. 9506.99.6080 Articles and equipment for general physical exercise, gymnastics, athletics, other sports (including table-tennis) or outdoor games, not specified or included elsewhere in this chapter, swimming pools and wading pools; parts and accessories thereof>>Other>>Other>>Other>>Other

The item in question, a dummy launcher, does not appear to be specifically provided for or otherwise described in any of the classification options, nor do the Section or Chapter Notes instruct how they are to be classified (no GRI 1).

Furthermore, the dummy launcher does not appear to be a prima facie (i.e. classifiable under more than one heading) item (no GRI 2(b) & no GRI 3).

Therefore, and as a last resort, we use the classification of the item that is most akin to the item to be classified by applying GRI 4. One could make a reasonable case that "line-throwing guns" are most akin to our dummy launcher. Line-throwing guns are described under multiple choice "B".

Just a Side Note: A "line-throwing gun", as the name suggests, launches a lifeline to a boat or person in distress.

Heading/ Subheading	Stat. Suf-fix	Article Description	Unit of Quantity	Rates of Duty 1 General	Rates of Duty 1 Special	2
9303		Other firearms and similar devices which operate by the firing of an explosive charge (for example, sporting shot- guns and rifles, muzzle-loading firearms, Very pistols and other devices designed to project only signal flares, pistols and revolvers for firing blank ammunition, captive-bolt humane killers, line-throwing guns):				
9303.10.00	00	Muzzle-loading firearms	No.	Free		Free
9303.20.00		Other sporting, hunting or target-shooting shotguns, including combination shotgun-rifles		2.6%	Free (A, AU, BH, CA, CL, CO, E, IL, JO, KR, MA, MX, OM, P, PA, PE, SG)	65%
		Shotguns:				
	20	Autoloading	No.			
	30	Pump action	No.			
	40	Over and under	No.			
	65	Other	No.			
	80	Combination shotgun-rifles	No.			
9303.30		Other sporting, hunting or target-shooting rifles:				
9303.30.40		Valued over $25 but not over $50 each		3.8% on the value of the rifle + 10% on the value of the telescopic sight, if any	Free (A, AU, BH, CA, CL, CO, E, IL, JO, KR, MA, MX, OM, P, PA, PE, SG)	65%
	10	Telescopic sights imported with rifles	No. 1/			
		Rifles:				
	20	Centerfire	No. 1/			
	30	Rimfire	No. 1/			
9303.30.80		Other		3.1% on the value of the rifle + 13% on the value of the telescopic sight, if any	Free (A, AU, BH, CA, CL, CO, E, IL, JO, KR, MA, MX, OM, P, PA, PE, SG)	65%
	05	Telescopic sights imported with rifles	No. 1/			
		Rifles:				
		Centerfire:				
	10	Autoloading	No. 1/			
		Bolt action:				
	12	Single shot	No. 1/			
	17	Other	No. 1/			
	25	Other	No. 1/			
	30	Rimfire	No. 1/			
9303.90		Other:				
9303.90.40	00	Pistols and revolvers designed to fire only blank cartridges or blank ammunition	No.	4.2%	Free (A, AU, BH, CA, CL, CO, E, IL, JO, KR, MA, MX, OM, P, PA, PE, SG)	105%
9303.90.80	00	Other	No.	Free		27.5%

Exam Example of GRI 5 (a)

"Article-specific cases are classified with item (unless they are 'the item')"

(Question)

What is (are) the classification(s) of a clarinet and its fitted case, with an outer surface of plastic sheeting, imported together from China?

A. 9205.90.4020	Wind musical instruments (for example, keyboard pipe organs, accordions, clarinets, trumpets, bagpipes), other than fairground organs and mechanical street organs>>Other>>Woodwind instruments>>Other>>Clarinets
AND 9209.99.4040	Parts (for example, mechanisms for music boxes) and accessories (for example, cards, discs and rolls for mechanical instruments) of musical instruments; metronomes, tuning forks and pitch pipes of all kinds>>Other>>Other>>Other>>For other woodwind and brass wind musical instruments>>For woodwind musical instruments
B. 9205.90.4020	Wind musical instruments (for example, keyboard pipe organs, accordions, clarinets, trumpets, bagpipes), other than fairground organs and mechanical street organs>>Other>>Woodwind instruments>>Other>>Clarinets
AND 9209.99.4080	Parts (for example, mechanisms for music boxes) and accessories (for example, cards, discs and rolls for mechanical instruments) of musical instruments; metronomes, tuning forks and pitch pipes of all kinds>>Other>>Other>>Other>>For other woodwind and brass wind musical instruments>>Other
C. 9205.90.4020 ONLY	
D. 9205.90.4020	Wind musical instruments (for example, keyboard pipe organs, accordions, clarinets, trumpets, bagpipes), other than fairground organs and mechanical street organs>>Other>>Woodwind instruments>>Other>>Clarinets
AND 4202.92.5000	Trunks, suitcases, vanity cases, attaché cases, …, musical instrument cases, …, and similar containers, of leather or of composition leather, of sheeting of plastics, of textile materials, of vulcanized fiber or of paperboard, or wholly or mainly covered with such materials or with paper>>Other>>With outer surface of sheeting of plastic or textile materials>>Musical instrument cases
E. 4202.92.5000 ONLY	

GRI 5(a) states that cases (including musical instrument cases) fitted to contain a specific article shall be classified with such articles, except when such cases give the whole its essential character.

The correct classification for the "clarinet" is 9205.90.4020. The "clarinet case" will definitely NOT BE CLASSIFED SEPARATELY since it is only of any use as a protective container for the clarinet. . "C" is the correct answer.

Heading/ Subheading	Stat. Suf-fix	Article Description	Unit of Quantity	Rates of Duty 1 General	Special	2
9205		Wind musical instruments (for example, keyboard pipe organs, accordions, clarinets, trumpets, bagpipes), other than fairground organs and mechanical street organs:				
9205.10.00		Brass-wind instruments		2.9%	Free (A,AU,BH,CA, CL,CO,E,IL,JO, KR,MA,MX,OM, P,PA,PE,SG)	40%
	40	Valued not over $10 each	No.			
	80	Valued over $10 each	No.			
9205.90		Other:				
		Keyboard pipe organs; harmoniums and similar keyboard instruments with free metal reeds:				
9205.90.12	00	Keyboard pipe organs	No.	Free		35%
9205.90.14	00	Other	No.	2.7%	Free (A,AU,BH,CA, CL,CO,E,IL,JO, KR,MA,MX,OM,P, PA,PE,SG)	40%
		Accordions and similar instruments; mouth organs:				
		Accordions and similar instruments:				
9205.90.15	00	Piano accordions	No.	Free		40%
9205.90.18	00	Other	No.	2.6%	Free (A,AU,BH,CA, CL,CO,E,IL,JO, KR,MA,MX,OM, P,PA,PE,SG)	40%
9205.90.19	00	Mouth organs	doz.	Free		40%
		Woodwind instruments:				
9205.90.20	00	Bagpipes	No.	Free		40%
9205.90.40		Other		4.9%	Free (A,AU,BH,CA, CL,CO,E,IL,JO, KR,MA,MX,OM, P,PA,PE,SG)	40%
	20	Clarinets	No.			
	40	Saxophones	No.			
	60	Flutes and piccolos (except bamboo)	No.			
	80	Other	No.			
9205.90.60	00	Other	No.	Free		40%
9206.00		Percussion musical instruments (for example, drums, xylophones, cymbals, castanets, maracas):				
9206.00.20	00	Drums	No.	4.8%	Free (A,AU,BH,CA, CL,CO,E,IL,JO, KR,MA,MX,OM, P,PA,PE,SG)	40%
9206.00.40	00	Cymbals	No.	Free		40%
9206.00.60	00	Sets of tuned bells known as chimes, peals or carillons	No.	Free		50%
9206.00.80	00	Other	No.	5.3%	Free (A,AU,BH,CA, CL,CO,E,IL,JO, KR,MA,MX,OM, P,PA,PE,SG)	40%

Exam Example of GRI 5 (b)

"Packaging is classified with item (unless it is 'the item')"

(Question)

An importer in the U.S. receives 500 single action economy stopwatches shipped by air from Munich, Germany. The stopwatches are individually packaged in plastic blister packaging for retail sale. Which statement regarding the plastic blister packaging is TRUE?

- **A.** The packaging is classified with the stopwatches
- **B.** The packaging is classified separately as articles of plastic
- **C.** The packaging costs are deducted from the entered value
- **D.** The importer's name must be on the packaging
- **E.** The manufacturer's name must be on the packaging

Paraphrasing GRI 5(b), packaging used as packaging is to be classified with the goods packaged therein. "A" is the correct answer.

Just a Side Note: Occasionally, the Classification Section of the exam will include a GRI-focused narrative-type question such as this one. These are by far easier and much less time consuming than the traditional Classification Section questions with HTS number lookups.

(This Page Intentionally Left Blank)

Book 1 Part 6

Free Trade Agreements
(FTA's)

In This Part
What kinds of FTA questions & topics appear on the exam?
Table of Special Programs Quick Reference & Guide
Table of Countries and Their Eligible Special Programs
Rules to determine special program eligibility (in general)

The "Free Trade Agreements" portion of the exam is one of the more time-consuming sections of the exam. Free Trade Agreements are unique in that they are explained in length in both the HTSUS (General Notes) AND in the 19 CFR (Part 10). **Bookmark the three quick reference tables on the next three pages as they include important and time-saving information such as each special program's symbol, HTSUS General Note number, starting page number in the HTSUS, MPF & HMF exemption status, corresponding 19 CFR Parts, Tariff Change Rules starting page number in the HTSUS, all countries eligible for which special programs, and each special program countries list.**

What are the Free Trade Agreements and Preferential Trade Programs?

Free Trade Agreements and Preferential Trade Programs are "special programs" in place for the purpose of allowing qualifying products the benefit of duty free (or at least reduced duty) entry into the United States.

What kinds of FTA questions & topics appear on the exam?

- Is this (described) shipment eligible for GSP (or other special program)?
- Is the special program-eligible shipment exempt from the Merchandise Processing Fee?
- Is the percentage of value from beneficiary inputs sufficient to make the item eligible for the special program?
- The certificate of origin must be kept on file / maintained for five years.
- Which of the following countries designated as beneficiaries (a.k.a. signatories or parties to the agreement) of the (named) special program?
- Distinguish between the special program-eligible inputs and ineligible inputs.
- What is the Special Program Indicator (SPI) symbol for the (named) FTA?
- Does the (described) HTSUS tariff number change make the transformed item eligible for the special program?

Just a Side Note: FTA tool at http://export.gov/fta/ftatarifftool/TariffSearch.aspx

SPECIAL PROGRAMS QUICK REFERENCE & GUIDE (Version: 2016 HTSA Basic Edition)

	SPECIAL PROGRAM	ABBREV.	SPI	GN	PG#	PARTIES	Imported	%	MPF	HMF	SEE ALSO	TCR PG#
1	**African Growth and Opportunity Act**	AGOA	D	16	194	38	Directly	35 ≤			19 CFR 10.211-217	n/a
2	**Australia FTA**	UAFTA	AU	28	407	1		10 >	EXEMPT	EXEMPT	19 CFR 10.721-741	417
3	**Automotive Products**	APTA	B	5	16	1		n/a			19 CFR 10.84	n/a
4	**Bahrain FTA**	UBFTA	BH	30	568	1	Directly	35 ≤	EXEMPT	EXEMPT	19 CFR 10.801-10.827	573
5	**Caribbean Basin Economic Recovery Act**	CBERA	E, E*	7	17	18	Directly	35 ≤	EXEMPT	EXEMPT	19 CFR 10.191-199	n/a
6	**Caribbean Basin Trade Partnership Act**	CBTPA	R	17	196	8	Directly	7 >			19 CFR 10.221-237	n/a
7	**Chile FTA**	UCFTA	CL	26	301	1		10 >	EXEMPT	EXEMPT	19 CFR 10.401-10.490	309
8	**Civil Aircraft Agreement on Trade**	n/a	C	6	17	all**		n/a	EXEMPT		19 CFR 10.183	n/a
9	**Colombia TPA**	COTPA	CO	34	750	1		10 >	EXEMPT	EXEMPT	19 CFR 10.3001-3034	762
10	**Dominican Republic-Central America**	DR-CAFTA	P, P+	29	480	6		10 >	EXEMPT	EXEMPT	19 CFR 10.581-625	493
11	**Generalized System of Preferences**	GSP	A, A*, A+	4	10	122		35 ≤	EXEMPT*	EXEMPT*	19 CFR 10.171-178	15
12	**Intermediate Chemicals for Dyes (Uruguay round)**	n/a	L	n/a	897	all**		n/a	EXEMPT		n/a	n/a
13	**Israel FTA ACT**	ILFTA	IL	8	20	3	Directly	35 ≤	EXEMPT	EXEMPT	n/a	n/a
14	**Jordan FTA ACT**	JOFTA	JO	18	198	1	Directly	35 ≥			19 CFR 10.701-712	n/a
15	**Korea FTA**	UKFTA	KR	33	679	1		10 >	EXEMPT	EXEMPT	19 CFR 10.1001-1034	689
16	**Morocco FTA**	UMFTA	MA	27	386	1	Directly	35 ≤			19 CFR 10.761-787	391
17	**North American Free Trade Agreement**	NAFTA	CA, MX	12	22	2		7 >	EXEMPT	EXEMPT	19 CFR 181	32
18	**Oman FTA**	UOFTA	OM	31	587	1	Directly	35 ≤	EXEMPT	EXEMPT	19 CFR 10.861-890	592
19	**Panama TPA**	PATPA	PA	35	823	1		10 >	EXEMPT	EXEMPT	19 CFR 10.2001-2034	836
20	**Peru TPA**	PTPA	PE	32	605	1		10 >	EXEMPT	EXEMPT	19 CFR 10.901-934	618
21	**Pharmaceutical Products (Agreement on Trade in)**	ATP	K	13	193	all**		n/a	EXEMPT		HTSUS Pharma. Appendix	n/a
22	**Singapore FTA**	SFTA	SG	25	201	1		10 >	EXEMPT	EXEMPT	19 CFR 10.501-570	220

LEGEND:
GN = HTSUS General Note
PG# = general note for the special program starts on this page number in version of the HTSUS
PARTIES = number of beneficiary countries (not including the U.S.)
IMPORTED: must be imported directly from a beneficiary country to the U.S. to qualify for the special program
% = allowable percentage of originating or non-originating inputs that qualifies or disqualifies the product for the special program
MPF = Merchandise Processing Fee
HMF = Harbor Maintenance Fee
TCR PG# = Tariff Change Requirements starts on this page (also known as product specific rules)

* exemption applies to GSP "least-developed beneficiary countries" (i.e. SPI symbol "A+")
** generally applies to all countries with normal trade relations (NTR) with the U.S. (i.e. other than "Column 2 Countries" Cuba or North Korea)
≤ originating inputs value must be greater than or equal to this percentage
> non-originating inputs value must be less than this percentage

COUNTRIES AND ELIGIBLE SPECIAL PROGRAMS QUICK REFERENCE & GUIDE

Country	*Special Program*	Country	*Special Program*	Country	*Special Program*
Anguilla	*GSP*	Falkland Islands	*GSP*	Oman	*UOFTA*
Antigua and Barbuda	*CBERA*	Fiji	*GSP*	Pakistan	*GSP*
Armenia	*GSP*	Gabon	*GSP, AGOA*	Panama	*PATPA*
Aruba	*CBERA*	Gambia, The	*GSP*	Papua New Guinea	*GSP*
Australia	*UAFTA*	Georgia	*GSP*	Paraguay	*GSP*
Azerbaijan	*GSP*	Ghana	*GSP, AGOA*	Peru	*PTPA*
Bahamas	*CBERA*	Grenada	*GSP, CBERA*	Philippines	*GSP*
Bahrain	*UBFTA*	Guatemala	*DR-CAFTA*	Pitcairn Islands	*GSP*
Barbados	*CBERA, CBTPA*	Guinea	*GSP*	Republic of Yemen	*GSP*
Belize	*GSP, CBERA, CBTPA*	Guinea-Bissau	*GSP, AGOA*	Rwanda	*GSP, AGOA*
Benin	*GSP, AGOA*	Guyana	*GSP, CBERA, CBTPA*	Saint Helena	*GSP*
Bhutan	*GSP*	Haiti	*GSP, CBERA, CBTPA*	Saint Lucia	*GSP, CBERA, CBTPA*
Bolivia	*GSP*	Heard and McDonald Islands	*GSP*	Saint Vincent/ Grenadines	*GSP, CBERA*
Bosnia and Herzegovina	*GSP*	Honduras	*DR-CAFTA*	Samoa	*GSP*
Botswana	*GSP, AGOA*	India	*GSP*	Sao Tomé and Principe	*GSP, AGOA*
Brazil	*GSP*	Indonesia	*GSP*	Senegal	*GSP, AGOA*
British Indian Ocean Territory	*GSP*	Iraq	*GSP*	Serbia	*GSP*
Burkina Faso	*GSP, AGOA*	Jamaica	*GSP, CBERA, CBTPA*	Seychelles	*GSP, AGOA*
Burundi	*GSP*	Jordan	*GSP, JOFTA*	Sierra Leone	*GSP, AGOA*
Cambodia	*GSP*	Kazakhstan	*GSP*	Singapore	*SFTA*
Cameroon	*GSP, AGOA*	Kenya	*GSP, AGOA*	Solomon Islands	*GSP*
Canada	*NAFTA, APTA*	Kiribati	*GSP*	Somalia	*GSP*
Cape Verde	*GSP, AGOA*	Korea	*UKFTA*	South Africa	*GSP, AGOA*
Central African Republic	*GSP*	Kosovo	*GSP*	South Sudan	*GSP*
Chad	*GSP, AGOA*	Kyrgyzstan	*GSP*	Sri Lanka	*GSP*
Chile	*UCFTA*	Lebanon	*GSP*	St. Kitts and Nevis	*CBERA*
Christmas Island (Australia)	*GSP*	Lesotho	*GSP, AGOA*	Suriname	*GSP*
Cocos (Keeling) Islands	*GSP*	Liberia	*GSP, AGOA*	Swaziland	*GSP*
Colombia	*COTPA*	Macedonia	*GSP*	Tanzania	*GSP, AGOA*
Comoros	*GSP, AGOA*	Madagascar	*GSP, AGOA*	Thailand	*GSP*
Congo (Brazzaville)	*GSP, AGOA*	Malawi	*GSP, AGOA*	Timor-Leste	*GSP*
Congo (Kinshasa)	*GSP, AGOA*	Maldives	*GSP*	Togo	*GSP, AGOA*
Cook Islands	*GSP*	Mali	*GSP, AGOA*	Tokelau	*GSP*
Costa Rica	*DR-CAFTA*	Mauritania	*GSP, AGOA*	Tonga	*GSP*
Côte d'Ivoire	*GSP, AGOA*	Mauritius	*GSP, AGOA*	Trinidad and Tobago	*CBERA, CBTPA*
Curacao	*CBERA, CBTPA*	Mexico	*NAFTA*	Tunisia	*GSP*
Djibouti	*GSP, AGOA*	Moldova	*GSP*	Turkey	*GSP*
Dominica	*GSP, CBERA*	Mongolia	*GSP*	Tuvalu	*GSP*
Dominican Republic	*DR-CAFTA*	Montenegro	*GSP*	Uganda	*GSP, AGOA*
Ecuador	*GSP*	Montserrat	*GSP, CBERA*	Ukraine	*GSP*
Egypt	*GSP*	Morocco	*UMFTA*	Uruguay	*GSP*
El Salvador	*DR-CAFTA*	Mozambique	*GSP, AGOA*	Uzbekistan	*GSP*
Eritrea	*GSP*	Namibia	*GSP, AGOA*	Vanuatu	*GSP*
Ethiopia	*GSP, AGOA*	Nepal	*GSP*	Venezuela	*GSP*
Anguilla	*GSP*	Netherlands Antilles	*CBERA*	Virgin Islands, British	*GSP, CBERA*
Antigua and Barbuda	*CBERA*	Nicaragua	*DR-CAFTA*	Wallis and Futuna	*GSP*
Armenia	*GSP*	Niger	*GSP, AGOA*	West Bank and Gaza Strip	*GSP, ILFTA*
Aruba	*CBERA*	Nigeria	*GSP, AGOA*	Western Sahara	*GSP*
Australia	*UAFTA*	Niue	*GSP*	Zambia	*GSP, AGOA*
Azerbaijan	*GSP*	Norfolk Island	*GSP*	Zimbabwe	*GSP*

Beneficiary Countries Sorted by Special Program (excludes single-country programs)

GSP			AGOA	CBERA	CBTPA	DR-CAFTA	NAFTA	APTA
Afghanistan+	Grenada	Pitcairn Islands	Angola	Antigua and Barbuda	Barbados	Costa Rica	Canada	Canada
Albania	Guinea+	Republic of Yemen+	Benin	Aruba	Belize	Dominican Rep.	Mexico	
Algeria	Guinea-Bissau+	Rwanda+	Botswana	Bahamas	Costa Rica*	El Salvador		
Angola+	Guyana	Saint Helena	Burkina Faso	Barbados	Curacao	Guatemala		
Anguilla	Haiti+	Saint Lucia	Cameroon	Belize	Dominican Republic*	Honduras		
Armenia	Heard Island/McDonald Is.	Saint Vincent/Grenadines	Cape Verde	Costa Rica*	El Salvador*	Nicaragua		
Azerbaijan	India	Samoa+	Central African Rep.*	Curacao	Guatemala*			
Belize	Indonesia	Sao Tomé and Principe+	Chad	Dominica	Guyana			
Benin+	Iraq	Senegal+	Comoros	Dominican Republic*	Haiti			
Bhutan+	Jamaica	Serbia	Congo (Brazzaville)	El Salvador*	Honduras*			
Bolivia	Jordan	Seychelles	Congo (Kinshasa)	Grenada	Jamaica			
Bosnia and Hercegovina	Kazakhstan	Sierra Leone+	Côte d'Ivoire	Guatemala*	Nicaragua*			
Botswana	Kenya	Solomon Islands+	Djibouti	Guyana	Panama*			
Brazil	Kiribati+	Somalia+	Eritrea*	Haiti	Saint Lucia			
British Indian Ocean Territory	Kosovo	South Africa	Ethiopia	Honduras*	Trinidad and Tobago			
Burkina Faso+	Kyrgyzstan	South Sudan+	Gabon	Jamaica				
Burundi	Lebanon	Sri Lanka	Ghana	Montserrat				
Cambodia+	Lesotho+	Suriname	Guinea-Bissau	Netherlands Antilles				
Cameroon	Liberia+	Swaziland	Kenya	Nicaragua*				
Cape Verde	Macedonia	Tanzania+	Lesotho	Panama*				
Central African Republic+	Madagascar+	Thailand	Liberia	Saint Lucia				
Chad+	Malawi+	Timor-Leste+	Madagascar	Saint Vincent/Grenadines				
Christmas Island (Australia)	Maldives	Togo+	Malawi	St. Kitts and Nevis				
Cocos (Keeling) Islands	Mali+	Tokelau	Mali	Trinidad and Tobago				
Comoros+	Mauritania+	Tonga	Mauritania	Virgin Islands, British				
Congo (Brazzaville)	Mauritius	Tunisia	Mauritius					
Congo (Kinshasa)+	Moldova	Turkey	Mozambique					
Cook Islands	Mongolia	Tuvalu+	Namibia					
Côte d'Ivoire	Montenegro	Uganda+	Niger					
Djibouti+	Montserrat	Ukraine	Nigeria					
Dominica	Mozambique+	Uruguay	Rwanda					
Ecuador	Namibia	Uzbekistan	Sao Tomé and Principe					
Egypt	Nepal+	Vanuatu+	Senegal					
Eritrea	Niger+	Venezuela	Seychelles					
Ethiopia+	Nigeria	Virgin Islands, British	Sierra Leone					
Falkland Islands (Is. Malvinas)	Niue	Wallis and Futuna	South Africa					
Fiji	Norfolk Island	West Bank and Gaza Strip	Tanzania					
Gabon	Pakistan	Western Sahara	Togo					
Gambia, The+	Papua New Guinea	Zambia+	Uganda					
Georgia	Paraguay	Zimbabwe	Zambia					
Ghana	Philippines							

*** former beneficiary countries**
+ GSP least-developed beneficiary

Rules to determine special program eligibility (in general*):

1) The product must have the special program indicator (SPI) symbol included in the "Special" subcolumn of the HTSUS column 1, AND

(Example of DR-CAFTA SPI symbol "P" available for food processors as per HTSUS Chapter 85)

Heading/ Subheading	Stat. Suf-fix	Article Description	Unit of Quantity	Rates of Duty 1 General	Rates of Duty 1 Special	Rates of Duty 2
8509		Electromechanical domestic appliances, with self- contained electric motor, other than vacuum cleaners of heading 8508; parts thereof:				
8509.40.00		Food grinders, processors and mixers; fruit or vegetable juice extractors........................	....	4.2% 1/	Free (A, AU, BH, CA, CL, CO, E, IL, JO, MA, MX, OM, P, PA, PE, SG) 2.1% (KR)	40%

2) The country of origin(s) of the product is listed as a designated beneficiary country, AND

(Snapshot of DR-CAFTA beneficiary countries list per HTSUS GN 29)

DR-CAFTA

(iii) except as provided in individual notes or tariff provisions, the terms "party to the Agreement" and "parties to the Agreement" refer to the following countries: Costa Rica, Dominican Republic, El Salvador, Guatemala, Honduras, Nicaragua or the United States.

3) The product officially qualifies as an "originating good" of the beneficiary country(s), meaning ANY of the following:

a) the product wholly originates from the beneficiary country(s) OR

(Partial excerpt from HTSUS GN 29 definition of a good "wholly obtained or produced")

(i) For purposes of subdivision (b)(i) of this note, the expression "good wholly obtained or produced" means any of the following goods:

(A) plants and plant products harvested or gathered in the territory of one or more of the parties to the Agreement;

(B) live animals born and raised in the territory of one or more of the parties to the Agreement;

b) each non-originating material undergoes a specific change in HTS number OR

(Example of an eligible HTSUS DR-CAFTA Tariff Change Requirement [TCR] range that includes a change to the food processor subheading 8509.40 from any other article subheading)

(n) Change in tariff classification rules.

(A) A change to subheadings 8509.10 through 8509.80 from any other heading;

c) the values attributed to the subject country(s), is within the allowable %

(Excerpt from the HTSUS DR-CAFTA de minimis [i.e. maximum % of non-originating inputs allowed] explanation)

(e) De minimis amounts of nonoriginating materials.

(i) Except as provided in subdivisions (d)(i), (e)(ii) and (m) below, a good that does not undergo a change in tariff classification pursuant to subdivision (n) of this note is an originating good if--

(A) the value of all nonoriginating materials that--

(1) are used in the production of the good, and

(2) do not undergo the applicable change in tariff classification set out in subdivision (n) of this note,

does not exceed 10 percent of the adjusted value of the good;

Note: The above rules for determining special program eligibility are broad in scope. To verify eligibility, refer also to the appropriate HTSUS General Note.

So, for example, the following three shipments would qualify for duty-free treatment under the DR-CAFTA free trade agreement.

Example a) An electronic food grinder is assembled in Costa Rica from materials wholly produced in The Dominican Republic. The food grinder is wholly obtained from and produced by parties to the agreement, and is thus eligible for duty free treatment under the DR-CAFTA.

Example b) An electronic food processor is assembled in El Salvador from electronic components, wholly produced in either Guatemala or China. When assembled into a food processor, the electronic components sourced from China all undergo an HTSUS tariff number change to subheading 8509.40. The food processor's non-originating material underwent a qualifying change in HTS number, and is thus eligible for duty-free treatment under the DR-CAFTA.

Example c) An electronic fruit juice extractor wholly originates in Honduras, except for the unit's specially designed printed circuit board assembly, which is produced in Mexico. The printed circuit board's HTSUS tariff number heading is 8509 (i.e. no tariff change occurs), yet represents only 9 % of the juice extractor's total value. The juice extractor's non-originating material does not exceed 10% of the finished good, and is thus eligible for duty-free treatment under the DR-CAFTA.

Book 1 Part 7

Most Commonly Tested

TITLE 19 CFR & Other

In This Part
Overview of the most commonly tested 19 CFR sections and paragraphs
Overview of the most commonly tested Directives & 7501 Instructions parts
Organized by frequency of occurrence **for maximum study prioritization!!!**

Mainly, this section singles out parts, sections, and paragraphs of the 19 CFR that have most often appeared as questions over the last ten exams. It is arranged by frequency of appearances from the past ten exams, and then numerically by CFR Part, Section, and then by Paragraph. Attempt to memorize as much as you can of the major points of this part of the study guide. The more you are able to answer exam questions "on the fly" (i.e. without having to refer to your 19 CFR, HTS, directives, etc.), then the more time you will have to focus on the more time-consuming parts of the exam, especially HTS classification questions.

Most Commonly Tested
CBP FORM 7501 INSTRUCTIONS

BLOCK 2
ENTRY TYPE

Number of times appearing in last 10 exams: 15
Last appeared in exam: April 2017

The gist of it...

The instructions for this block of CBP Form 7501 lists all the possible entry types and type codes. It also lists all of the different kinds of ABI indicators and what they stand for.

Excerpt from CBP FORM 7501 INSTRUCTIONS...

BLOCK 2) ENTRY TYPE

Record the appropriate entry type code by selecting the two-digit code for the type of entry summary being filed. The first digit of the code identifies the general category of the entry (i.e., consumption = 0, informal = 1, warehouse = 2). The second digit further defines the specific processing type within the entry category. The following codes shall be used:

Consumption Entries

Free and Dutiable	*01*
Quota/Visa	*02*
Antidumping/Countervailing Duty (AD/CVD)	*03*
Appraisement	*04*
Vessel Repair	*05*
Foreign Trade Zone Consumption	*06*
Quota/Visa and AD/CVD combinations	*07*
Duty Deferral	*08*

Informal Entries

Free and Dutiable	*11*
Quota Other than textiles	*12*

Warehouse Entries

Trade Fair	*24*
Permanent Exhibition	*25*
Foreign Trade Zone Admission	*26*
Warehouse Withdrawal For Consumption	*31*

Quota/Visa 32

AD/CVD 34

Quota/Visa and AD/CVD combinations 38

Government Entries

Defense Contract Management Command 51

Any U.S. Federal Government agency 52

Note: When the importer of record of emergency war materials is not a government agency, entry type codes 01, 02, 03, etc., as appropriate, are to be used.

Transportation Entries

Immediate Transportation 61

Transportation and Exportation 62

Immediate Exportation 63

Automated Broker Interface (ABI) processing requires an ABI status indicator. This indicator must be recorded in the entry type code block. It is to be shown for those entry summaries with ABI status only, and must be shown in one of the following formats:

ABI/S = ABI statement paid by check or cash

ABI/A = ABI statement paid via Automated Clearinghouse (ACH)

ABI/P = ABI statement paid on a periodic monthly basis

ABI/N = ABI summary not paid on a statement

Note: Either a slash (/) or hyphen (-) may be used to separate ABI from the indicator

(i.e., ABI/S or ABI-S).

A "LIVE" entry is when the entry summary documentation is filed at the time of entry with estimated duties. Warehouse withdrawals are always considered "LIVE" entries. When a "LIVE" entry/entry summary is presented, an additional indicator is required to be shown in the following formats:

ABI/A/L = ABI statement paid via ACH for a "live" entry/entry summary

ABI/N/L = ABI "live" entry/entry summary not paid on a statement

"LIVE" or "L" = non-ABI "live" entry/entry summary

Most Commonly Tested
TITLE 19 CFR

Part 152.103(a)
CLASSIFICATION AND APPRAISEMENT OF MERCHANDISE>>Valuation of Merchandise>>Transaction value>>Price actually paid or payable

Number of times appearing in last 10 exams: 12
Last appeared in exam: October 2017

The gist of it...

This paragraph explains that the price actually paid or payable is to be used when determining an import's transaction value, which may be derived by means of additions to or deductions from the invoice value (e.g. deducting freight charges from invoice value, etc.). Several helpful examples are provided as a reference.

Excerpt from 19 CFR...

(a) Price actually paid or payable—(1) General. In determining transaction value, the price actually paid or payable will be considered without regard to its method of derivation. It may be the result of discounts, increases, or negotiations, or may be arrived at by the application of a formula, such as the price in effect on the date of export in the London Commodity Market. The word "payable" refers to a situation in which the price has been agreed upon, but actual payment has not been made at the time of importation. Payment may be made by letters of credit or negotiable instruments and may be made directly or indirectly.

Example 1. In a transaction with foreign Company X, a U.S. firm pays Company X $10,000 for a shipment of meat products, packed ready for shipment to the United States. No selling commission, assist, royalty, or license fee is involved. Company X is not related to the U.S. purchaser and imposes no condition or limitation on the buyer.

The customs value of the imported meat products is $10,000—the transaction value of the imported merchandise.

Example 2. A foreign shipper sold merchandise at $100 per unit to a U.S. importer. Subsequently, the foreign shipper increased its price to $110 per unit. The merchandise was exported after the effective date of the price increase. The invoice price of $100 was the price originally agreed upon and the price the U.S. importer actually paid for the merchandise.

How should the merchandise be appraised?

Actual transaction value of $100 per unit based on the price actually paid or payable.

Example 3. A foreign shipper sells to U.S. wholesalers at one price and to U.S. retailers at a higher price. The shipment undergoing appraisement is a shipment to a U.S. retailer. There are continuing shipments of identical and similar merchandise to U.S. wholesalers.

How should the merchandise be appraised?

Actual transaction value based on the price actually paid or payable by the retailer.

Example 4. Company X in the United States pay $2,000 to Y Toy Factory abroad for a shipment of toys. The $2,000 consists of $1,850 for the toys and $150 for ocean freight and insurance. Y Toy Factory would have *charged Company X $2,200 for the toys; however, because Y owed Company X $350, Y charged only $1,850 for the toys. What is the transaction value?*

The transaction value of the imported merchandise is $2,200, that is, the sum of the $1,850 plus the $350 indirect payment. Because the transaction value excludes C.I.F. charges, the $150 ocean freight and insurance charge is excluded.

Example 5. A seller offers merchandise at $100, less a 2% discount for cash. A buyer remits $98 cash, taking advantage of the cash discount.

The transaction value is $98, the price actually paid or payable.

(2) Indirect payment. An indirect payment would include the settlement by the buyer, in whole or in part, of a debt owed by the seller, or where the buyer receives a price reduction on a current importation as a means of settling a debt owed him by the seller. Activities such as advertising, undertaken by the buyer on his own account, other than those for which an adjustment is provided in §152.103(b), will not be considered an indirect payment to the seller though they may benefit the seller. The costs of those activities will not be added to the price actually paid or payable in determining the customs value of the imported merchandise.

(3) Assembled merchandise. The price actually paid or payable may represent an amount for the assembly of imported merchandise in which the seller has no interest other than as the assembler. The price actually paid or payable in that case will be calculated by the addition of the value of the components and required adjustments to form the basis for the transaction value.

Example 1. The importer previously has supplied an unrelated foreign assembler with fabricated components ready for assembly having a value or cost at the assembler's plant of $1.00 per unit. The importer pays the assembler 50¢ per unit for the assembly. The transaction value for the assembled unit is $1.50.

Example 2. Same facts as Example 1 above except the U.S. importer furnishes to the foreign assembler a tooling assist consisting of a tool acquired by the importer at $1,000. The transportation expenses to the foreign assembler's plant for the tooling assist equal $100. The transaction value for the assembled unit would be $1.50 per unit plus a pro rata share of the tooling assist valued at $1,100.

(4) Rebate. Any rebate of, or other decrease in, the price actually paid or payable made or otherwise effected between the buyer and seller after the date of importation of the merchandise will be disregarded in determining the transaction value under §152.103(b).

(5) Foreign inland freight and other inland charges incident to the international shipment of merchandise—(i) Ex-factory sales. If the price actually paid or payable by the buyer to the seller for the imported merchandise does not include a charge for foreign inland freight and other charges for services incident to the international shipment of merchandise (an ex-factory price), those charges will not be added to the price.

… …

Most Commonly Tested

TITLE 19 CFR

Part 24.23(c)
CUSTOMS FINANCIAL AND ACCOUNTING PROCEDURE>>Fees for processing merchandise>>Exemptions and limitations

Number of times appearing in last 10 exams: 10
Last appeared in exam: October 2017

The gist of it...

This paragraph lists the transactions that are exempt from the Merchandise Processing Fee (MPF), such as most all of the HTSUS Chapter 98 items (e.g. U.S. Goods Returned), multiple Free Trade Agreements, etc.

Excerpt from 19 CFR...

(c) Exemptions and limitations. (1) The ad valorem fee, surcharge, and specific fees provided for under paragraphs (b)(1) and (b)(2) of this section will not apply to:

(i) Except as provided in paragraph (c)(2) of this section, articles provided for in chapter 98, Harmonized Tariff Schedule of the United States (HTSUS; 19 U.S.C. 1202);

(ii) Products of insular possessions of the U.S. (General Note 3(a)(iv), HTSUS);

(iii) Products of beneficiary countries under the Caribbean Basin Economic Recovery Act (General Note 7, HTSUS);

(iv) Products of least-developed beneficiary developing countries (General Note 4(b)(i), HTSUS); and

(v) Merchandise described in General Note 19, HTSUS, merchandise released under 19 U.S.C. 1321, and merchandise imported by mail.

(2) In the case of any article provided for in subheading 9802.00.60 or 9802.00.80, HTSUS:

(i) The surcharge and specific fees provided for under paragraphs (b)(1)(ii) and (b)(2) of this section will remain applicable; and

(ii) The ad valorem fee provided for under paragraph (b)(1)(i) of this section will be assessed only on that portion of the cost or value of the article upon which duty is assessed under subheadings 9802.00.60 and 9802.00.80.

... ...

Most Commonly Tested

TITLE 19 CFR

Part 111.30(d)
CUSTOMS BROKERS>>Duties and Responsibilities of Customs Brokers>>Notification of change of business address, organization name, or location of business records; status report; termination of brokerage business>>Status Report

Number of times appearing in last 10 exams: 9
Last appeared in exam: April 2017

The gist of it...

This paragraph provides instructions on the customs broker triennial status report. The next status reports are due Feb. 2021 & Feb. 2024.

Excerpt from 19 CFR...

(d) Status report—(1) General. Each broker must file a written status report with Customs on February 1, 1985, and on February 1 of each third year after that date. The report must be accompanied by the fee prescribed in §111.96(d) and must be addressed to the director of the port through which the license was delivered to the licensee (see §111.15). A report received during the month of February will be considered filed timely. No form or particular format is required.

(2) Individual. Each individual broker must state in the report required under paragraph (d)(1) of this section whether he is actively engaged in transacting business as a broker. If he is so actively engaged, he must also:

(i) State the name under which, and the address at which, his business is conducted if he is a sole proprietor;

(ii) State the name and address of his employer if he is employed by another broker, unless his employer is a partnership, association or corporation broker for which he is a qualifying member or officer for purposes of §111.11(b) or (c)(2); and

(iii) State whether or not he still meets the applicable requirements of §111.11 and §111.19 and has not engaged in any conduct that could constitute grounds for suspension or revocation under §111.53.

(3) Partnership, association or corporation. Each corporation, partnership or association broker must state in the report required under paragraph (d)(1) of this section the name under which its business as a broker is being transacted, its business address, the name and address of each licensed member of the partnership or licensed officer of the association or corporation who qualifies it for a license under §111.11(b) or (c)(2), and whether it is actively engaged in transacting business as a broker, and the report must be signed by a licensed member or officer.

(4) Failure to file timely. If a broker fails to file the report required under paragraph (d)(1) of this section by March 1 of the reporting year, the broker's license is suspended by operation of law on that date. By March 31 of the reporting year, the port director will transmit written notice of the suspension to the broker by certified mail, return receipt requested, at the address reflected in Customs records. If the broker files the required report and pays the required fee within 60 calendar days of the date of the notice of suspension, the license will be reinstated. If the broker does not file the required report within that 60-day period, the broker's license is revoked by operation of law without prejudice to the filing of an application for a new license. Notice of the revocation will be published in the Customs Bulletin.

Most Commonly Tested
TITLE 19 CFR

Part 111.23(b)
CUSTOMS BROKERS>>Duties and Responsibilities of Customs Brokers>>Retention of records>>Period of retention

Number of times appearing in last 10 exams: 8
Last appeared in exam: October 2017

The gist of it...

This paragraph simply describes the length of time (generally 5 years) required, for customs brokers' record keeping.

Excerpt from 19 CFR...

(b) Period of retention. The records described in this section, other than powers of attorney, must be retained for at least 5 years after the date of entry. Powers of attorney must be retained until revoked, and revoked powers of attorney and letters of revocation must be retained for 5 years after the date of revocation or for 5 years after the date the client ceases to be an "active client" as defined in §111.29(b)(2)(ii), whichever period is later. When merchandise is withdrawn from a bonded warehouse, records relating to the withdrawal must be retained for 5 years from the date of withdrawal of the last merchandise withdrawn under the entry.

Most Commonly Tested

TITLE 19 CFR

Part 152.103(d)
CLASSIFICATION AND APPRAISEMENT OF MERCHANDISE>>Valuation of Merchandise>>Transaction Value>>Assist

Number of times appearing in last 10 exams: 8
Last appeared in exam: October 2017

The gist of it...

This paragraph explains methods for and examples of assessing the value for assists. Particularly, the exam often makes reference to the fact that design work done in the U.S. (as opposed to foreign design work) does not count as an assist.

Excerpt from 19 CFR...

(d) Assist. If the value of an assist is to be added to the price actually paid or payable, or to be used as a component of computed value, the port director shall determine the value of the assist and apportion that value to the price of the imported merchandise in the following manner:

(1) If the assist consist of materials, components, parts, or similar items incorporated in the imported merchandise, or items consumed in the production of the imported merchandise, acquired by the buyer from an unrelated seller, the value of the assist is the cost of its acquisition. If the assist were produced by the buyer or a person related to the buyer, its value would be the cost of its production. In either case, the value of the assist would include transportation costs to the place of production.

(2) If the assist consists of tools, dies, molds, or similar items used in the production of the imported merchandise, acquired by the buyer from an unrelated seller, the value of the assist is the cost of its acquisition. If the assist were produced by the buyer or a person related to the buyer, its value would be cost of its production. If the assist has been used previously by the buyer, regardless of whether it had been acquired or produced by him, the original cost of acquisition or production would be adjusted downward to reflect its use before its value could be determined. ... ...

Example 1. A U.S. importer supplied detailed designs to the foreign producer. These designs were necessary to manufacture the merchandise. The U.S. importer bought the designs from an engineering company in the U.S. for submission to his foreign supplier.

Should the appraised value of the merchandise include the value of the assist?

No, design work undertaken in the U.S. may not be added to the price actually paid or payable.

Example 2. A U.S. importer supplied molds free of charge to the foreign shipper. The molds were necessary to manufacture merchandise for the U.S. importer. The U.S. importer had some of the molds manufactured by a U.S. company and others manufactured in a third country.

Should the appraised value of the merchandise include the value of the molds?

Yes. It is an addition required to be made to transaction value.

Most Commonly Tested

Directive 3530-002A Right to Make Entry

Section 5
RIGHT TO MAKE ENTRY>>PROCEDURES

Number of times appearing in last 10 exams: 7
Last appeared in exam: October 2017

The gist of it...

Most notably, this section states that only the importer or a customs broker may be the importer of record, the party with a right to make customs entry.

Excerpt from Directive 3530-002A...

5.1.1 RIGHT TO MAKE ENTRY

5.1.2 Section 484 provides that only the "importer of record" has the right to make entry. "Importer of Record" is defined as the owner or purchaser of the goods, or when designated by the owner, purchaser, or consignee, a licensed Customs broker.

5.1.3 A nominal consignee may designate a Customs broker to make entry on his behalf but may not make entry on his own behalf. If a Customs broker makes entry for a nominal consignee, the broker must appear as importer of record.

5.1.4 The purpose of the amendment to Section 484 was to prevent nominal consignees, other than licensed Customs brokers, from filing entries and thereby engaging in the transaction of Customs business without a license.

... ...

Most Commonly Tested

TITLE 19 CFR

Part 111.2(a)
CUSTOMS BROKERS>>General Provisions>>License and district permit required>>License

Number of times appearing in last 10 exams: 6
Last appeared in exam: October 2016

The gist of it...

This section explicitly describes which "customs-related activities" do (and do not) necessitate the possession of a customs broker license.

Excerpt from 19 CFR...

(a) License—(1) General. Except as otherwise provided in paragraph (a)(2) of this section, a person must obtain the license provided for in this part in order to transact customs business as a broker.

(2) Transactions for which license is not required—(i) For one's own account. An importer or exporter transacting customs business solely on his own account and in no sense on behalf of another is not required to be licensed, nor are his authorized regular employees or officers who act only for him in the transaction of such business.

(ii) As employee of broker—(A) General. An employee of a broker, acting solely for his employer, is not required to be licensed where:

(1) Authorized to sign documents. The broker has authorized the employee to sign documents pertaining to customs business on his behalf, and has executed a power of attorney for that purpose. The broker is not required to file the power of attorney with the port director, but must provide proof of its existence to Customs upon request; or

(2) Authorized to transact other business. The broker has filed with the port director a statement identifying the employee as authorized to transact customs business on his behalf. However, no statement will be necessary when the broker is transacting customs business under an exception to the district permit rule.

(B) Broker supervision; withdrawal of authority. Where an employee has been given authority under paragraph (a)(2)(ii) of this section, the broker must exercise sufficient supervision of the employee to ensure proper conduct on the part of the employee in the transaction of customs business, and the broker will be held strictly responsible for the acts or omissions of the employee within the scope of his employment and for any other acts or omissions of the employee which, through the exercise of reasonable care and diligence, the broker should have foreseen. The broker must promptly notify the port director if authority granted to an employee under paragraph (a)(2)(ii) of this section is withdrawn. The withdrawal of authority will be effective upon receipt by the port director.

... ...

Most Commonly Tested
TITLE 19 CFR

Part 111.28(b)
CUSTOMS BROKERS>>Duties and Responsibilities of Customs Brokers>>Responsible supervision>>Employee information

Number of times appearing in last 10 exams: 6
Last appeared in exam: October 2017

The gist of it...

This paragraph outlines the customs broker's reporting requirements for reporting current, new, and terminated employee information to the affected port director(s).

Excerpt from 19 CFR...

(b) Employee information—(1) Current employees—(i) General. Each broker must submit, in writing, to the director of each port at which the broker intends to transact customs business, a list of the names of persons currently employed by the broker at that port. The list of employees must be submitted upon issuance of a permit for an additional district under §111.19, or upon the opening of an office at a port within a district for which the broker already has a permit, and before the broker begins to transact customs business as a broker at the port. For each employee, the broker also must provide the social security number, date and place of birth, current home address, last prior home address, and, if the employee has been employed by the broker for less than 3 years, the name and address of each former employer and dates of employment for the 3-year period preceding current employment with the broker. After the initial submission, an updated list, setting forth the name, social security number, date and place of birth, and current home address of each current employee, must be submitted with the status report required by §111.30(d).

(ii) New employees. In the case of a new employee, the broker must submit to the port director the written information required under paragraph (b)(1)(i) of this section within 10 calendar days after the new employee has been employed by the broker for 30 consecutive days.

(2) Terminated employees. Within 30 calendar days after the termination of employment of any person employed longer than 30 consecutive days, the broker must submit the name of the terminated employee, in writing, to the director of the port at which the person was employed.

(3) Broker's responsibility. Notwithstanding a broker's responsibility for providing the information required in paragraph (b)(1) of this section, in the absence of culpability by the broker, Customs will not hold him responsible for the accuracy of any information that is provided to the broker by the employee.

Most Commonly Tested

TITLE 19 CFR

Part 111.29(a)
CUSTOMS BROKERS>>Duties and Responsibilities of Customs Brokers>>Diligence in correspondence and paying monies>>Due diligence by broker

Number of times appearing in last 10 exams: 6
Last appeared in exam: October 2017

The gist of it...

This paragraph states the responsibilities of customs broker in making payments to Customs on behalf of their customers. Payments from clients must be made to Customs by the due date, or within 5 working days of receipt if received late from client.

Excerpt from 19 CFR...

(a) Due diligence by broker. Each broker must exercise due diligence in making financial settlements, in answering correspondence, and in preparing or assisting in the preparation and filing of records relating to any customs business matter handled by him as a broker. Payment of duty, tax, or other debt or obligation owing to the Government for which the broker is responsible, or for which the broker has received payment from a client, must be made to the Government on or before the date that payment is due. Payments received by a broker from a client after the due date must be transmitted to the Government within 5 working days from receipt by the broker. Each broker must provide a written statement to a client accounting for funds received for the client from the Government, or received from a client where no payment to the Government has been made, or received from a client in excess of the Governmental or other charges properly payable as part of the client's customs business, within 60 calendar days of receipt. No written statement is required if there is actual payment of the funds by a broker.

Most Commonly Tested

TITLE 19 CFR

Part 111.29(b)
CUSTOMS BROKERS>>Duties and Responsibilities of Customs Brokers>>Diligence in correspondence and paying monies>>Notice to client of method of payment

Number of times appearing in last 10 exams: 6
Last appeared in exam: October 2017

The gist of it...

This paragraph 1) spells out the "notice to client of method of payment" notification that customs brokers must provide their clients and 2) dictates that the notification must be with the POA as well as sent annually to active clients.

Excerpt from 19 CFR...

(b) Notice to client of method of payment. (1) All brokers must provide their clients with the following written notification:

If you are the importer of record, payment to the broker will not relieve you of liability for customs charges (duties, taxes, or other debts owed CBP) in the event the charges are not paid by the broker. Therefore, if you pay by check, customs charges may be paid with a separate check payable to the "U.S. Customs and Border Protection" which will be delivered to CBP by the broker.

(2) The written notification set forth in paragraph (b)(1) of this section must be provided by brokers as follows:

(i) On, or attached to, any power of attorney provided by the broker to a client for execution on or after September 27, 1982; and

(ii) To each active client no later than February 28, 1983, and at least once at any time within each 12-month period after that date. An active client means a client from whom a broker has obtained a power of attorney and for whom the broker has transacted customs business on at least two occasions within the 12-month period preceding notification.

Most Commonly Tested

TITLE 19 CFR

Part 111.45(a) & (b)
CUSTOMS BROKERS>>Duties and Responsibilities of Customs Brokers>>Revocation by operation of law

Number of times appearing in last 10 exams: 6
Last appeared in exam: April 2016

The gist of it...

Although there is an exception request available for the district permit rule, here, the regulations explain that a customs brokerage operation must maintain at least one license holder to avoid revocation of the business' customs license and permit(s).

Excerpt from 19 CFR...

(a) License. If a broker that is a partnership, association, or corporation fails to have, during any continuous period of 120 days, at least one member of the partnership or at least one officer of the association or corporation who holds a valid individual broker's license, that failure will, in addition to any other sanction that may be imposed under this part, result in the revocation by operation of law of the license and any permits issued to the partnership, association, or corporation. The Assistant Commissioner or his designee will notify the broker in writing of an impending revocation by operation of law under this section 30 calendar days before the revocation is due to occur.

(b) Permit. If a broker who has been granted a permit for an additional district fails, for any continuous period of 180 days, to employ within that district (or region, as defined in §111.1, if an exception has been granted pursuant to §111.19(d)) at least one person who holds a valid individual broker's license, that failure will, in addition to any other sanction that may be imposed under this part, result in the revocation of the permit by operation of law.

(c) Notification. If the license or an additional permit of a partnership, association, or corporation is revoked by operation of law under paragraph (a) or (b) of this section, the Assistant Commissioner or his designee will notify the organization of the revocation. If an additional permit of an individual broker is revoked by operation of law under paragraph (b) of this section, the Assistant Commissioner or his designee will notify the broker. Notice of any revocation under this section will be published in the Customs Bulletin.

(d) Applicability of other sanctions. Notwithstanding the operation of paragraph (a) or (b) of this section, each broker still has a continuing obligation to exercise responsible supervision and control over the conduct of its brokerage business and to otherwise comply with the provisions of this part. Any failure on the part of a broker to meet that continuing obligation during the 120 or 180-day period referred to in paragraph (a) or (b) of this section, or during any shorter period of time, may result in the initiation of suspension or revocation proceedings or the assessment of a monetary penalty under subpart D or subpart E of this part.

Most Commonly Tested
TITLE 19 CFR

Part 141.34
ENTRY OF MERCHANDISE>>Powers of Attorney>> Duration of power of attorney

Number of times appearing in last 10 exams: 6
Last appeared in exam: October 2017

The gist of it…

Power of attorneys from partnerships are unique from POA's received from other legal entities in that the partnership POA is valid for a maximum of 2 years, at which time a new POA must be issued.

Excerpt from 19 CFR…

141.34 Duration of power of attorney.

Powers of attorney issued by a partnership shall be limited to a period not to exceed 2 years from the date of execution. All other powers of attorney may be granted for an unlimited period.

Most Commonly Tested

TITLE 19 CFR

Part 152.103(b)
CLASSIFICATION AND APPRAISEMENT OF MERCHANDISE>>Valuation of Merchandise>>Transaction value>>Additions to price actually paid or payable

Number of times appearing in last 10 exams: 6
Last appeared in exam: April 2016

The gist of it...

This paragraph states that packing costs, selling commissions, assists, royalties, and proceeds to seller are to be added to the transaction value, to arrive at the entered value. You just have to remember the acronym "C.R.A.P.P." (Commissions, Royalties, Assists, Packaging, Proceeds).

Excerpt from 19 CFR...

(b) Additions to price actually paid or payable. (1) The transaction value of imported merchandise is the price actually paid or payable for the merchandise when sold for exportation to the United States, plus amounts equal to:

(i) The packing costs incurred by the buyer with respect to the imported merchandise;

(ii) Any selling commission incurred by the buyer with respect to the imported merchandise;

(iii) The value, apportioned as appropriate, of any assist;

(iv) Any royalty or license fee related to the imported merchandise that the buyer is required to pay, directly or indirectly, as a condition of the sale of the imported merchandise for exportation to the United States; and

(v) The proceeds of any subsequent resale, disposal, or use of the imported merchandise that accrue, directly or indirectly, to the seller.

(2) The price actually paid or payable for imported merchandise will be increased by the amounts attributable to the items (and no others) described in paragraphs (b)(1) (i) through (v) of this section to the extent that each amount is not otherwise included within the price actually paid or payable, and is based on sufficient information. If sufficient information is not available, for any reason, with respect to any amount referred to in this section, the transaction value will be treated as one that cannot be determined.

... ...

Most Commonly Tested

TITLE 19 CFR

Part 162.74(b)
INSPECTION, SEARCH, AND SEIZURE>>Special Procedures for Certain Violations>>Prior disclosure>> Disclosure of the circumstances of a violation

Number of times appearing in last 10 exams: 6
Last appeared in exam: October 2017

The gist of it...

This paragraph lists the four specific elements (i.e. circumstances) to be provided to CBP when submitting a prior disclosure.

Excerpt from 19 CFR...

(b) Disclosure of the circumstances of a violation. The term "discloses the circumstances of a violation" means the act of providing to Customs a statement orally or in writing that:

(1) Identifies the class or kind of merchandise involved in the violation;

(2) Identifies the importation or drawback claim included in the disclosure by entry number, drawback claim number, or by indicating each concerned Customs port of entry and the approximate dates of entry or dates of drawback claims;

(3) Specifies the material false statements, omissions or acts including an explanation as to how and when they occurred; and

(4) Sets forth, to the best of the disclosing party's knowledge, the true and accurate information or data that should have been provided in the entry or drawback claim documents, and states that the disclosing party will provide any information or data unknown at the time of disclosure within 30 days of the initial disclosure date. Extensions of the 30-day period may be requested by the disclosing party from the concerned Fines, Penalties, and Forfeitures Officer to enable the party to obtain the information or data.

Most Commonly Tested

TITLE 19 CFR

Part 163.6(b)
RECORDKEEPING>> Production and examination of entry and other records and witnesses; penalties>> Failure to produce entry records

Number of times appearing in last 10 exams: 6
Last appeared in exam: April 2017

The gist of it...

In this paragraph Customs outlines a penalty schedule for failing to produce entry records, describes penalty exceptions and mitigation, etc.

Excerpt from 19 CFR...

(b) Failure to produce entry records—(1) Monetary penalties applicable. The following penalties may be imposed if a person fails to comply with a lawful demand for the production of an entry record and is not excused from a penalty pursuant to paragraph (b)(3) of this section:

(i) If the failure to comply is a result of the willful failure of the person to maintain, store, or retrieve the demanded record, such person shall be subject to a penalty, for each release of merchandise, not to exceed $100,000, or an amount equal to 75 percent of the appraised value of the merchandise, whichever amount is less; or

(ii) If the failure to comply is a result of negligence of the person in maintaining, storing, or retrieving the demanded record, such person shall be subject to a penalty, for each release of merchandise, not to exceed $10,000, or an amount equal to 40 percent of the appraised value of the merchandise, whichever amount is less.

(2) Additional actions—(i) General. In addition to any penalty imposed under paragraph (b)(1) of this section, and except as otherwise provided in paragraph (b)(2)(ii) of this section, if the demanded entry record relates to the eligibility of merchandise for a column 1 special rate of duty in the Harmonized Tariff Schedule of the United States (HTSUS), the entry of such merchandise:

(A) If unliquidated, shall be liquidated at the applicable HTSUS column 1 general rate of duty; or

(B) If liquidated within the 2-year period preceding the date of the demand, shall be reliquidated, notwithstanding the time limitation in 19 U.S.C. 1514 or 1520, at the applicable HTSUS column 1 general rate of duty.

(ii) Exception. Any liquidation or reliquidation under paragraph (b)(2)(i)(A) or (b)(2)(i)(B) of this section shall be at the applicable HTSUS column 2 rate of duty if Customs demonstrates that the merchandise should be dutiable at such rate.

... ...

Most Commonly Tested

TITLE 19 CFR

Part 133.21(b)
TRADEMARKS, TRADE NAMES, AND COPYRIGHTS>>Importations Bearing Recorded Marks or Trade Names>> Articles suspected of bearing counterfeit marks>> Detention, notice, and disclosure of information

Number of times appearing in last 10 exams: 5
Last appeared in exam: October 2017

The gist of it...

This paragraph lays out the Customs procedure for responding to suspected trademark violations, including notice to the importer and what details at what stage may be disclosed to the owner of the trademark.

Excerpt from 19 CFR...

(b) Detention, notice, and disclosure of information—(1) Detention period. CBP may detain any article of domestic or foreign manufacture imported into the United States that bears a mark suspected by CBP of being a counterfeit version of a mark that is registered with the U.S. Patent and Trademark Office and is recorded with CBP pursuant to subpart A of this part. The detention will be for a period of up to 30 days from the date on which the merchandise is presented for examination. In accordance with 19 U.S.C. 1499(c), if, after the detention period, the article is not released, the article will be deemed excluded for the purposes of 19 U.S.C. 1514(a)(4).

(2) Notice of detention to importer and disclosure to owner of the mark—(i) Notice and seven business day response period. Within five business days from the date of a decision to detain suspect merchandise, CBP will notify the importer in writing of the detention as set forth in §151.16(c) of this chapter and 19 U.S.C. 1499. CBP will also inform the importer that for purposes of assisting CBP in determining whether the detained merchandise bears counterfeit marks:

(A) CBP may have previously disclosed to the owner of the mark, prior to issuance of the notice of detention, limited importation information concerning the detained merchandise, as described in paragraph (b)(4) of this section, and, in any event, such information will be released to the owner of the mark, if available, no later than the date of issuance of the notice of detention; and

(B) CBP may disclose to the owner of the mark information that appears on the detained merchandise and/or its retail packaging, including unredacted photographs, images, or samples, as described in paragraph (b)(3) of this section, unless the importer presents information within seven business days of the notification establishing that the detained merchandise does not bear a counterfeit mark.

(ii) Failure of importer to respond or insufficient response to notice. Where the importer does not provide information within the seven business day response period, or the information provided is insufficient for CBP to determine that the merchandise does not bear a counterfeit mark, CBP may proceed with the disclosure of information described in paragraph (b)(3) of this section to the owner of the mark and will so notify the importer.

... ...

Most Commonly Tested

TITLE 19 CFR

Part 134.2
COUNTRY OF ORIGIN MARKINGS>>General Provisions>>Additional duties

Number of times appearing in last 10 exams: 5
Last appeared in exam: October 2016

The gist of it...

Imports missing proper country of origin markings may either be 1) destroyed, 2) exported, or 3) entered and assessed an additional 10% in duties.

Excerpt from 19 CFR...

134.2 Additional duties.

Articles not marked as required by this part shall be subject to additional duties of 10 percent of the final appraised value unless exported or destroyed under Customs supervision prior to liquidation of the entry, as provided in 19 U.S.C. 1304(f). The 10 percent additional duty is assessable for failure either to mark the article (or container) to indicate the English name of the country of origin of the article or to include words or symbols required to prevent deception or mistake.

Most Commonly Tested

TITLE 19 CFR

Part 152.102(a)
CLASSIFICATION AND APPRAISEMENT OF MERCHANDISE>>Valuation of Merchandise>>Definitions>>Assist

Number of times appearing in last 10 exams: 5
Last appeared in exam: October 2016

The gist of it...

Here, an "assist" is defined as an item provided free-of-charge or at a discount from the importer to the foreign manufacturer and used in or to make the imported product. Design work undertaken in the U.S., however, is not considered to be an "assist".

Excerpt from 19 CFR...

152.102 Definitions.

As used in this subpart, the following terms will have the meanings indicated:

(a) Assist. (1) "Assist" means any of the following if supplied directly or indirectly, and free of charge or at reduced cost, by the buyer of imported merchandise for use in connection with the production or the sale for export to the United States of the merchandise:

(i) Materials, components, parts, and similar items incorporated in the imported merchandise.

(ii) Tools, dies, molds, and similar items used in the production of the imported merchandise.

(iii) Merchandise consumed in the production of the imported merchandise.

(iv) Engineering, development, artwork, design work, and plans and sketches that are undertaken elsewhere than in the United States and are necessary for the production of the imported merchandise.

(2) No service or work to which paragraph (a)(1)(iv) of this section applies will be treated as an assist if the service or work:

(i) Is performed by an individual domiciled within the United States;

(ii) Is performed by that individual while acting as an employee or agent of the buyer of the imported merchandise; and

(iii) Is incidental to other engineering, development, artwork, design work, or plans or sketches that are undertaken within the United States.

(3) The following apply in determining the value of assists described in paragraph (a)(1)(iv) of this section:
... ...

Most Commonly Tested

TITLE 19 CFR

Part 152.102(f)
CLASSIFICATION AND APPRAISEMENT OF MERCHANDISE>>Valuation of Merchandise>>Definitions>>Price Actually paid or payable

Number of times appearing in last 10 exams: 5
Last appeared in exam: April 2017

The gist of it...

This paragraph defines the customs phrase "price actually paid or payable", otherwise known as the "transaction value". Remember that international freight and insurance charges are excluded from the transaction value.

Excerpt from 19 CFR...

(f) Price actually paid or payable. "Price actually paid or payable" means the total payment (whether direct or indirect, and exclusive of any charges, costs, or expenses incurred for transportation, insurance, and related services incident to the international shipment of the merchandise from the country of exportation to the place of importation in the United States) made, or to be made, for imported merchandise by the buyer to, or for the benefit of, the seller.

Most Commonly Tested

TITLE 19 CFR

Part 171 APPENDIX B
FINES, PENALTIES, AND FORFEITURES>> Guidelines for the Imposition and Mitigation of Penalties for Violations of 19 U.S.C. 1592

Number of times appearing in last 10 exams: 5
Last appeared in exam: April 2016

The gist of it...

Here Customs incorporates Title 19 of the United States Code (U.S.C), Part 1592 into the customs regulations as an appendix to Title 19 CFR Part 171. This appendix is essentially a rulebook for customs officers to refer to when imposing and mitigating penalties.

Excerpt from 19 CFR...

Appendix B to Part 171 – Customs Regulations, Guidelines for the Imposition and Mitigation of Penalties for Violations of 19 U.S.C. 1592

A monetary penalty incurred under section 592 of the Tariff Act of 1930, as amended (19 U.S.C. 1592; hereinafter referred to as section 592) may be remitted or mitigated under section 618 of the Tariff Act of 1930, as amended (19 U.S.C. 1618), if it is determined that there are mitigating circumstances to justify remission or mitigation. The guidelines below will be used by the Customs Service in arriving at a just and reasonable assessment and disposition of liabilities arising under section 592 within the stated limitations. It is intended that these guidelines shall be applied by Customs officers in pre-penalty proceedings and in determining the monetary penalty assessed in any penalty notice. The assessed penalty or penalty amount set forth in Customs administrative disposition determined in accordance with these guidelines does not limit the penalty amount which the Government may seek in bringing a civil enforcement action pursuant to section 592(e). It should be understood that any mitigated penalty is conditioned upon payment of any actual loss of duty as well as a release by the party that indicates that the mitigation decision constitutes full accord and satisfaction. Further, mitigation decisions are not rulings within the meaning of part 177 of the Customs Regulations (19 CFR part 177). Lastly, these guidelines may supplement, and are not intended to preclude application of, any other special guidelines promulgated by Customs.

... ...

Most Commonly Tested

TITLE 19 CFR

Part 191.3(b)
DRAWBACK>>General Provisions>>Duties and fees subject or not subject to drawback>>Duties and fees not subject to drawback

Number of times appearing in last 10 exams: 5
Last appeared in exam: October 2015

The gist of it...

This paragraph states that (in general) fees and duties paid for HMF, MPF, and ADD/CVD will NOT be refunded with drawback.

Excerpt from 19 CFR...

(b) Duties and fees not subject to drawback include:

(1) Harbor maintenance fee (see §24.24 of this chapter);

(2) Merchandise processing fees (see §24.23 of this chapter), except where unused merchandise drawback pursuant to 19 U.S.C. 1313(j) or drawback for substitution of finished petroleum derivatives pursuant to 19 U.S.C. 1313(p)(2)(A)(iii) or (iv) is claimed; and

(3) Antidumping and countervailing duties on merchandise entered, or withdrawn from warehouse, for consumption on or after August 23, 1988.

Most Commonly Tested

TITLE 19 CFR

Part 351.402(f)
ANTIDUMPING AND COUNTERVAILING DUTIES>>Calculation of export price and constructed export price; reimbursement of antidumping and countervailing duties

Number of times appearing in last 10 exams: 5
Last appeared in exam: April 2016

The gist of it...

Most notably, this paragraph states that the importer must have an antidumping/countervailing duty non-reimbursement certificate on file for all applicable entries.

Excerpt from 19 CFR...

... ...

(2) Certificate. The importer must file prior to liquidation a certificate in the following form with the appropriate District Director of Customs:

I hereby certify that I (have) (have not) entered into any agreement or understanding for the payment or for the refunding to me, by the manufacturer, producer, seller, or exporter, of all or any part of the antidumping duties or countervailing duties assessed upon the following importations of (commodity) from (country): (List entry numbers) which have been purchased on or after (date of publication of antidumping notice suspending liquidation in the Federal Register) or purchased before (same date) but exported on or after (date of final determination of sales at less than fair value).

(3) Presumption. The Secretary may presume from an importer's failure to file the certificate required in paragraph (f)(2) of this section that the exporter or producer paid or reimbursed the antidumping duties or countervailing duties.

Most Commonly Tested

TITLE 19 CFR

Part 24.23(b)
CUSTOMS FINANCIAL AND ACCOUNTING PROCEDURE>>Fees for processing merchandise>>Fees

Number of times appearing in last 10 exams: 4
Last appeared in exam: October 2017

The gist of it...

This paragraph outlines the calculation of merchandise processing fees for both formal and informal entries.

Excerpt from 19 CFR...

(b) Fees—(1) Formal entry or release—(i) Ad valorem fee—(A) General. Except as provided in paragraph (c) of this section, merchandise that is formally entered or released is subject to the payment to CBP of an ad valorem fee of 0.3464 percent. The 0.3464 ad valorem fee is due and payable to CBP by the importer of record of the merchandise at the time of presentation of the entry summary and is based on the value of the merchandise as determined under 19 U.S.C. 1401a. In the case of an express consignment carrier facility or centralized hub facility, each shipment covered by an individual air waybill or bill of lading that is formally entered and valued at $2,500 or less is subject to a $1.00 per individual air waybill or bill of lading fee, as adjusted in accordance with the terms of §24.22(k) of this part, and, if applicable, to the 0.3464 percent ad valorem fee in accordance with paragraph (b)(4) of this section.

(B) Maximum and minimum fees. Subject to the provisions of paragraphs (b)(1)(ii) and (d) of this section relating to the surcharge and to aggregation of the ad valorem fee respectively, the ad valorem fee charged under paragraph (b)(1)(i)(A) of this section must not exceed $485, as adjusted in accordance with the terms of §24.22(k) of this part, and must not be less than $25, as adjusted in accordance with the terms of §24.22(k) of this part.

... ...

Most Commonly Tested

TITLE 19 CFR

Part 111.1
CUSTOMS BROKERS>>General Provisions>>Definitions

Number of times appearing in last 10 exams: 4
Last appeared in exam: April 2017

The gist of it…

This list of definitions includes the meanings of terms such as "customs business" and "responsible supervision and control" as defined by CBP, which are often incorporated into the exam

Excerpt from 19 CFR…

When used in this part, the following terms have the meanings indicated:

Assistant Commissioner. "Assistant Commissioner" means the Assistant Commissioner, Office of International Trade, U.S. Customs and Border Protection, Washington, DC.

Broker. "Broker" means a customs broker.

Corporate compliance activity. "Corporate compliance activity" means activity performed by a business entity to ensure that documents for a related business entity or entities are prepared and filed with CBP using "reasonable care", but such activity does not extend to the actual preparation or filing of the documents or their electronic equivalents. For purposes of this definition, a "business entity" is an entity that is registered or otherwise on record with an appropriate governmental authority for business licensing, taxation, or other legal purposes, and the term "related business entity or entities" encompasses a business … …

Customs broker. "Customs broker" means a person who is licensed under this part to transact customs business on behalf of others.

Customs business. "Customs business" means those activities involving transactions with CBP concerning the entry and admissibility of merchandise, its classification and valuation, the payment of duties, taxes, or other charges assessed or collected by CBP on merchandise by reason of its importation, and the refund, rebate, or drawback of those duties, taxes, or other charges. "Customs business" also includes the preparation, and activities relating to the preparation, of documents in any format and the electronic transmission of documents and parts of documents intended to be filed with CBP in furtherance of any other customs business activity, whether or not signed or filed by the preparer. However, "customs business" does

… …

Responsible supervision and control. "Responsible supervision and control" means that degree of supervision and control necessary to ensure the proper transaction of the customs business of a broker, including actions necessary to ensure that an employee of a broker provides substantially the same quality of service in handling customs transactions that the broker is required to provide. While the determination of what is … …

Most Commonly Tested
TITLE 19 CFR

Part 132.5
QUOTAS>>General Provisions>>Merchandise imported in excess of quota quantities

Number of times appearing in last 10 exams: 4
Last appeared in exam: April 2016

The gist of it...

This section covers the two different types of quota merchandise—1) Absolute Quota Merchandise & 2) Tariff-Rate Quota Merchandise. It also lists options for disposal of items imported in excess of quota limits. Just remember that absolute quotas are different than tariff-rate quotas in that absolute quotas are "absolute" (i.e. fixed, and "absolutely" cannot be entered in excess of the quote; even at a higher duty rate).

Excerpt from 19 CFR...

(a) Absolute quota merchandise. Absolute quota merchandise imported in excess of the quantity admissible under the applicable quota must be disposed of in accordance with paragraph (c) of this section.

(b) Tariff-rate quota merchandise. Merchandise imported in excess of the quantity admissible at the reduced quota rate under a tariff-rate quota is permitted entry at the higher duty rate. However, it may be disposed of in accordance with paragraph (c) of this section.

(c) Disposition of excess merchandise. Merchandise imported in excess of either an absolute or a tariff-rate quota may be held for the opening of the next quota period by placing it in a foreign-trade zone or by entering it for warehouse, or it may be exported or destroyed under Customs supervision.

Most Commonly Tested

TITLE 19 CFR

Part 134.32
COUNTRY OF ORIGIN MARKING>>Exceptions to Marking Requirements>> General exceptions to marking requirements

Number of times appearing in last 10 exams: 4
Last appeared in exam: October 2016

The gist of it…

This section of the regulations lists, in general, the types of products that are (reasonably) excepted from the country of origin marking requirements. It would be impossible, for example to mark crude oil product.

Excerpt from 19 CFR…

134.32 General exceptions to marking requirements.

The articles described or meeting the specified conditions set forth below are excepted from marking requirements (see subpart C of this part for marking of the containers):

(a) Articles that are incapable of being marked;

(b) Articles that cannot be marked prior to shipment to the United States without injury;

(c) Articles that cannot be marked prior to shipment to the United States except at an expense economically prohibitive of its importation;

(d) Articles for which the marking of the containers will reasonably indicate the origin of the articles;

(e) Articles which are crude substances;

(f) Articles imported for use by the importer and not intended for sale in their imported or any other form;

(g) Articles to be processed in the United States by the importer or for his account otherwise than for the purpose of concealing the origin of such articles and in such manner that any mark contemplated by this part would necessarily be obliterated, destroyed, or permanently concealed;

(h) Articles for which the ultimate purchaser must necessarily know, or in the case of a good of a NAFTA country, must reasonably know, the country of origin by reason of the circumstances of their importation or by reason of the character of the articles even though they are not marked to indicate their origin;

(i) Articles which were produced more than 20 years prior to their importation into the United States;

(j) Articles entered or withdrawn from warehouse for immediate exportation or for transportation and exportation;

… …

Most Commonly Tested

TITLE 19 CFR

Part 134.33
COUNTRY OF ORIGIN MARKING>>Exceptions to Marking Requirements>>J-List exceptions

Number of times appearing in last 10 exams: 4
Last appeared in exam: April 2017

The gist of it...

Customs provides quite a detailed and thorough list of items that, for practical reasons, are excepted from meeting the country of origin marking requirements—the J-List Exceptions.

Excerpt from 19 CFR...

§134.33 J-List exceptions.

Articles of a class or kind listed below are excepted from the requirements of country of origin marking in accordance with the provisions of section 304(a)(3)(J), Tariff Act of 1930, as amended (19 U.S.C. 1304(a)(3)(J)). However, in the case of any article described in this list which is imported in a container, the outermost container in which the article ordinarily reaches the ultimate purchaser is required to be marked to indicate the origin of its contents in accordance with the requirements of subpart C of this part. All articles are listed in Treasury Decisions 49690, 49835, and 49896. A reference different from the foregoing indicates an amendment.

Articles	***References***
Art, works of.	
Articles classified under subheadings 9810.00.15, 9810.00.25, 9810.00.40 and 9810.00.45, Harmonized Tariff Schedule of the United States	*T.D. 66-153.*
Articles entered in good faith as antiques and rejected as unauthentic.	
Bagging, waste.	
Bags, jute.	
Bands, steel.	
Beads, unstrung.	
Bearings, ball, 5/8-inch or less in diameter.	
Blanks, metal, to be plated.	
Bodies, harvest hat.	
Bolts, nuts, and washers.	

... ...

Most Commonly Tested

TITLE 19 CFR

Part 159.32
LIQUIDATION OF DUTIES>>Conversion of Foreign Currency>>Date of exportation

Number of times appearing in last 10 exams: 4
Last appeared in exam: April 2017

The gist of it...

Customs states that that the currency conversion rate to be used to convert commercial invoice values stated in foreign currency amounts is to be based on the date of exportation. The related section 152.1 defines "date of exportation".

Excerpt from 19 CFR...

159.32 Date of exportation.

The date of exportation for currency conversion shall be fixed in accordance with §152.1(c) of this chapter.

152.1 Definitions.

The following are general definitions for the purposes of part 152:

(a)-(b) [Reserved]

(c) Date of exportation. "Date of exportation," or the "time of exportation" referred to in section 402, Tariff Act of 1930, as amended (19 U.S.C. 1401a), means the actual date the merchandise finally leaves the country of exportation for the United States. If no positive evidence is at hand as to the actual date of exportation, the port director shall ascertain or estimate the date of exportation by all reasonable ways and means in his power, and in so doing may consider dates on bills of lading, invoices, and other information available to him.

Most Commonly Tested

TITLE 19 CFR

Part 163.5(b)
RECORDKEEPING>>Methods for storage of records>> Alternative method of storage

Number of times appearing in last 10 exams: 4
Last appeared in exam: April 2016

The gist of it...

This paragraph explains that alternative (to physical paper copies) methods for recordkeeping are available, though advance notification must be sent to the "CBP Regulatory Audit office in Charlotte, NC".

Excerpt from 19 CFR...

(b) Alternative method of storage—(1) General. Any of the persons listed in §163.2 may maintain any records, other than records required to be maintained as original records under laws and regulations administered by other Federal government agencies, in an alternative format, provided that the person gives advance written notification of such alternative storage method to the Regulatory Audit, U.S. Customs and Border Protection, 2001 Cross Beam Dr., Charlotte, North Carolina 28217, and provided further that the Director of Regulatory Audit, Charlotte office does not instruct the person in writing as provided herein that certain described records may not be maintained in an alternative format. The written notice to the Director of Regulatory Audit, Charlotte office must be provided at least 30 calendar days before implementation of the alternative storage method, must identify the type of alternative storage method to be used, and must state that the alternative storage method complies with the standards set forth in paragraph (b)(2) of this section. If an alternative storage method covers records that pertain to goods under CBP seizure or detention or that relate to a matter that is currently the subject of an inquiry or investigation or administrative or court proceeding, the appropriate CBP office may instruct the person in writing that those records must be maintained as original records and therefore may not be converted to an alternative format until specific written authorization is received from that CBP office. A written instruction to a person under this paragraph may be issued during the 30-day advance notice period prescribed in this section or at any time thereafter, must describe the records in question with reasonable specificity but need not identify the underlying basis for the instruction, and shall not preclude application of the planned alternative storage method to other records not described therein.

(2) Standards for alternative storage methods. Methods commonly used in standard business practice for storage of records include, but are not limited to, machine readable data, CD ROM, and microfiche. Methods that are in compliance with generally accepted business standards will generally satisfy CBP requirements, provided that the method used allows for retrieval of records requested within a reasonable time after the request and provided that adequate provisions exist to prevent alteration, destruction, or deterioration of the records. The following standards must be applied by recordkeepers when using alternative storage methods ... ...

Most Commonly Tested

TITLE 19 CFR

Part 171 APPENDIX C (V)
FINES, PENALTIES, AND FORFEITURES>>Customs Regulations Guidelines for the Imposition and Mitigation of Penalties for Violations of 19 U.S.C. 1641>>Violation of Any Law Enforced by the Customs Service or the Rules or Regulations Issued Under Any Such Provision

Number of times appearing in last 10 exams: 4
Last appeared in exam: October 2016

The gist of it...

Here Customs incorporates Title 19 of the United States Code (U.S.C), Part 1592 into the customs regulations as an appendix to Title 19 CFR Part 171. This appendix is basically a rulebook for customs officers to refer to when imposing and mitigating penalties.

Excerpt from 19 CFR...

V. Section 1641(d)(1)(C) – Violation of Any Law Enforced by the Customs Service or the Rules or Regulations Issued Under Any Such Provision

A. Penalties under this section may be imposed in addition to any penalty provided for under the law enforced by Customs. Exception: Penalties imposed against a broker under 19 U.S.C. 1592 at a culpability level of less than fraud or under 19 U.S.C. 1595a(b) shall not be imposed in addition to a broker's penalty.

B. Additional penalties under this section shall also be imposed against any broker where the other statute violated only moves against property, or the violator has demonstrated a continuing course of illegal conduct or evidence exists which indicates repeated violations of other statutes or regulations.

C. Conducting Customs business without a permit penalties should be assessed under this section.

1. The penalty notice should also cite 19 CFR 111.19 as the regulation violated. A party operating without a permit is required to apply for one under the above-noted regulation.

2. Assessment amount – $1,000 per transaction conducted without a permit.

3. Mitigation.

a. Negligence, mitigate to $250-$500 per transaction depending on the presence of mitigating factors (lack of knowledge of permit requirement).

b. Intentional, grant no relief.

c. No mitigation if permit revoked by operation of law.

4. Generally, a separate penalty should not be assessed for each non-permitted transaction if numerous transactions occurred contemporaneously. For example, if a broker files 30 entries the day after a permit expires, the 30 filings should be treated as one violation, not 30 separate violations.

... ...

Most Commonly Tested
CBP FORM 7501 INSTRUCTIONS

APPENDIX 2
RULES FOR CONSTRUCTING THE MANUFACTURER IDENTIFICATION CODE

Number of times appearing in last 10 exams: 4
Last appeared in exam: October 2015

The gist of it...

Here the Form 7501 instructions spell out the rules (and additional special rule for Canada) for making the Manufacturer Identification (MID) Code from elements of the manufacturer's name and address.

Excerpt from CBP FORM 7501 INSTRUCTIONS...

Appendix 2

RULES FOR CONSTRUCTING THE MANUFACTURER IDENTIFICATION CODE

These instructions provide for the construction of an identifying code for a manufacturer or shipper from its name and address. The code can be up to 15 characters in length, with no inserted spaces.

To begin, for the first 2 characters, use the ISO code for the actual country of origin of the goods. The exception to this rule is Canada. "CA" is NOT a valid country for the manufacturer code; instead, show as one of the appropriate province codes listed below:

ALBERTA	*XA*
BRITISH COLUMBIA	*XC*
MANITOBA	*XM*
NEW BRUNSWICK	*XB*
NEWFOUNDLAND (LABRADOR)	*XW*
NORTHWEST TERRITORIES	*XT*
NOVA SCOTIA	*XN*
NUNAVUT	*XV*
ONTARIO	*XO*
PRINCE EDWARD ISLAND	*XP*
QUEBEC	*XQ*
SASKATCHEWAN	*XS*
YUKON TERRITORY	*XY*

Next, use the first three characters from the first two "words" of the name. If there is only one "word" in the name, then use only the first three characters from the first name. For example, Amalgamated Plastics Corp. would be "AMAPLA;" Bergstrom would be "BER."

If there are two or more initials together, treat them as a single word. For example, A.B.C. Company or A B C Company would yield "ABCCOM." O.A.S.I.S. Corp. would yield "OASCOR." Dr. S.A. Smith yields "DRSA," Shavings B L Inc. yields "SHABL."

In the manufacturer name, ignore the English words a, an, and, of, and the. For example, "The Embassy of Spain" would yield "EMBSPA."

Portions of a name separated by a hyphen are to be treated as a single word. For example, "Rawles-Aden Corp." or "Rawles – Aden Corp." would both yield "RAWCOR."

Some names will include numbers. For examples, "20th Century Fox" would yield "20TCEN" and "Concept 2000" yields "CON200."

Most Commonly Tested
CBP FORM 7501 INSTRUCTIONS

OTHER FEE SUMMARY FOR BLOCK 39

Number of times appearing in last 10 exams: 4
Last appeared in exam: October 2016

The gist of it...

The "Other Fee Summary for Block 39" is the Form 7501 block in which the code for each fee applicable to the entry is listed along with the charge for each. The total for this block is entered in "Block 39", which is a separate block than the "Other Fee Summary for Block 39" block.

Excerpt from CBP FORM 7501 INSTRUCTIONS...

OTHER FEE SUMMARY FOR BLOCK 39

For entries subject to payment of AD/CVD and/or any of the various fees, each applicable fee must be indicated in this area, and the individual amount of each fee must be shown on the corresponding line. AD/CVD amounts are to be included in the summary only when they are actually deposited. Bonded amounts should not be included. The Block 39 Summary must be on the first page if the entry summary consists of more than one page.

The applicable collection code must be indicated on the same line as the fee or other charge or exaction. Report the fees in the format below:

AD	*012*
CVD	*013*
Tea Fee	*038*
Misc. Interest	*044*
Beef Fee	*053*
Pork Fee	*054*
Honey Fee	*055*
Cotton Fee	*056*
Pecan Fee	*057*
Sugar Fee	*079*
Potato Fee	*090*
Mushroom Fee	*103*
Watermelon	*104*
Blueberry Fee	*106*
Avocado	*107*
Mango	*108*
Informal Entry MPF	*311*
Dutiable Mail Fee	*496*
Merchandise Processing Fee (MPF)	*499*
Manual Surcharge	*500*
Harbor Maintenance Fee (HMF)	*501*

There is no de minimis collection for the MPF. There is an established minimum and maximum due on each formal entry, release or withdrawal from warehouse for consumption. Report the actual MPF due unless the perspective amount due is less than the established minimum (record the minimum), or exceeds the established maximum (record the maximum).

There is a de minimis on the HMF if it is the only payment due on the entry summary. If such is the case, HMF of $3 or less will not be collected. The grand total user fee in this block should be reported as the total fee amount of all line items, but the amount in block 39 should be reported as $0.

Goods originating under a Free Trade Agreement (FTA) may be exempt from MPF. To obtain this exemption, the importer must indicate the appropriate SPI for each HTS number in Column 27.

Most Commonly Tested
CBP FORM 7501 INSTRUCTIONS

COLUMN 27) LINE NUMBER

Number of times appearing in last 10 exams: 4
Last appeared in exam: October 2015

The gist of it...

Column 27 is for the Entry Summary line item number, Special Program Indicator (e.g. "CA" for NAFTA), and country of origin (if multiple country of origins for the entry).

Excerpt from CBP FORM 7501 INSTRUCTIONS...

COLUMN 27) LINE NUMBER

Record the appropriate line number, in sequence, beginning with the number 001.

A "line number" refers to a commodity from one country, covered by a line which includes a net quantity, entered value, HTS number, charges, rate of duty and tax. However, some line numbers may actually include more than one HTS number and value. For example, many items in Chapter 98 of the HTS require a dual HTS number. Articles assembled abroad with U.S. components require the HTS number 9802.00.80 along with the appropriate reporting number of the provision in Chapters 1 through 97.

Also, many items in Chapter 91 of the HTS require as many as four HTS numbers. Watches classifiable under subheading 9101.11.40, for example, require that the appropriate reporting number and duty rate be shown separately for the movement, case, strap, band or bracelet, and battery. A separate line item is also required for each commodity that is the subject of a Customs binding ruling. Proper format is listed under the instructions for HTS number.

Where a reporting number is preceded by an alpha character designating a special program (i.e., NAFTA = "CA" or "MX"; GSP = "A"), that indicator is to be placed in column 27, directly below the line number. The special program indicator (SPI) should be right justified on the same line and immediately preceding the HTS number to which it applies. If more than one HTS number is required for a line item, place the SPI on the same line as the HTS number upon which the rate of duty is based. If more than one SPI is used, the primary indicator that establishes the rate of duty is shown first, followed by a period and the secondary SPI immediately following.

If "MULTI" was recorded in block(s) 10, 14, 15, and/or 19, the appropriate codes or dates are to be shown in column 27 below the SPI. See specific instructions for those items with multiple elements.

Book 1 Part 8

All Sections Appearing on Exams

TITLE 19 CFR

This section of the study guide lists nearly all instances of Title 19 of the United States Code of Federal Regulations (19 CFR) appearing throughout the last 10 exams.

The contents of all Titles of the Code of Federal Regulations (CFR) are logically organized in hierarchical order. Essentially, the United States regulations publications are broken down first by 1) "Title", then 2) "Part", then 3) "Section", then 4) "Paragraph", and then in some cases additionally by 5) "Subparagraph". So, for example, 19 CFR 134.1(b) (the paragraph of the regulations where Customs defines the term "country of origin") is located within Title 19, Part 134, Section 1, Paragraph (b). You can remember this structure of the regulations by remembering the initials "P.S.P.S" (part, section, paragraph, and sub-paragraph).

Accordingly, the following "All 19 CFR Sections Appearing on Exams Table" is arranged in ascending order by "Part", then by "Section", then by "Paragraph" level, and then further sorted by exam date with the most recent exam instances appearing first for each repeating set of section and paragraph occurrences. Within the table, if reference to a specific "Paragraph" has been left blank, then either there may not be a "Paragraph" breakdown for that particular "Section", or the answer for that particular exam question may refer to multiple "Paragraphs" within that Section. As you can see from the table, we start from "Part" 4, because "Part" 0 (Transferred or Delegated Authority) has not appeared in any of the last 10 exams. It is a safe bet to assume that although you can be aware that this part exists, there is no reason to memorize anything contained therein.

The best way to make use of the "All 19 CFR Sections Appearing on Exams Table" is as follows. First, feel free to remove from your 19 CFR binder the "Parts" that do not appear on the "Parts List" (located on the following page). You can move these extra pages to a different folder or binder that can be label "just in case" if, by chance, these obscure Parts show up in the next exam. By doing so, you reduce the number of pages you must shuffle through to find what you're looking for. This is helpful during both study time and exam time.

Next, go through the remaining part of your newly condensed 19 CFR, and with a highlighter marker, highlight onto your CFR, as many "Sections", and "Paragraphs" as possible that appear in the All 19 CFR Sections Appearing on Exams Table. This is a great way to get to know the regulations better, and it will also allow these frequently tested items to jump out at you when you're speedily scanning through the pages during exam time.

$ Money Saving Tip $
Let your employer know that you're interested in taking the exam. Ask if they can help cover some of the expenses. Or, they may do so on the condition that you pass in order to get reimbursed.

19 CFR "Parts List"

Of the 70 Parts that comprise Title 19 CFR, only the following 41 Parts (and even then, some appear only once or twice) have appeared on the last 10 customs broker exams...

Part 4:	VESSELS IN FOREIGN AND DOMESTIC TRADES
Part 7:	CUSTOMS RELATIONS WITH INSULAR POSSESSIONS AND GUANTANAMO BAY
Part 10:	ARTICLES CONDITIONALLY FREE, SUBJECT TO A REDUCED RATE, ETC.
Part 11:	PACKING AND STAMPING; MARKING
Part 12:	SPECIAL CLASSES OF MERCHANDISE
Part 18:	TRANSPORTATION IN BOND AND MERCHANDISE IN TRANSIT
Part 19:	CUSTOMS WAREHOUSES, CONTAINER STATIONS AND CONTROL OF MERCHANDISE
Part 24:	CUSTOMS FINANCIAL AND ACCOUNTING PROCEDURE
Part 101:	GENERAL PROVISIONS
Part 102:	RULES OF ORIGIN
Part 103:	AVAILABILITY OF INFORMATION
Part 111:	CUSTOMS BROKERS
Part 113:	CUSTOMS BONDS
Part 114:	CARNETS
Part 122:	AIR COMMERCE REGULATIONS
Part 123:	CBP RELATIONS WITH CANADA AND MEXICO
Part 132:	QUOTAS
Part 133:	TRADEMARKS, TRADE NAMES, AND COPYRIGHTS
Part 134:	COUNTRY OF ORIGIN MARKING
Part 141:	ENTRY OF MERCHANDISE
Part 142:	ENTRY PROCESS
Part 143:	SPECIAL ENTRY PROCEDURES
Part 144:	WAREHOUSE AND REWAREHOUSE ENTRIES AND WITHDRAWALS
Part 146:	FOREIGN TRADE ZONES
Part 148:	PERSONAL DECLARATIONS AND EXEMPTIONS
Part 151:	EXAMINATION, SAMPLING, AND TESTING OF MERCHANDISE
Part 152:	CLASSIFICATION AND APPRAISEMENT OF MERCHANDISE
Part 159:	LIQUIDATION OF DUTIES
Part 161:	GENERAL ENFORCEMENT PROVISIONS
Part 162:	INSPECTIONS, SEARCH, AND SEIZURE
Part 163:	RECORDKEEPING
Part 165:	INVESTIGATION OF CLAIMS OF EVASION OF ANTIDUMPING/COUNTERVAILING DUTIES
Part 171:	FINES, PENALTIES, AND FORFEITURES
Part 172:	CLAIMS FOR LIQUIDATED DAMAGES; PENALTIES SECURED BY BONDS
Part 173:	ADMINISTRATIVE REVIEW IN GENERAL
Part 174:	PROTESTS
Part 176:	PROCEEDINGS IN THE COURT OF INTERNATIONAL TRADE
Part 177:	ADMINISTRATIVE RULINGS
Part 181:	NORTH AMERICAN FREE TRADE AGREEMENT (NAFTA)
Part 191:	DRAWBACK
Part 351:	ANTIDUMPING AND COUNTERVAILING DUTIES

All 19 CFR Sections Appearing on Exams Table

EXAM DATE	"PART"	"SECTION"	"PARAGRAPH"
Part 4: VESSELS IN FOREIGN AND DOMESTIC TRADES			
2017 October	4	7	(b)
2017 April	4	7	(b)
2015 April	4	37	(a)
Part 7: CUSTOMS RELATIONS WITH INSULAR POSSESSIONS AND GUANTANAMO BAY			
2013 April	7	2	(c)
Part 10: ARTICLES CONDITIONALLY FREE, SUBJECT TO A REDUCED RATE, ETC.			
2016 October	10	1	(h)
2016 October	10	16	(a)
2013 October	10	16	(b)
2013 October	10	16	(c)
2017 October	10	31	(f)
2016 October	10	31	(f)
2015 October	10	31	(h)
2016 April	10	37	
2013 October	10	37	
2016 April	10	39	(e)
2016 April	10	39	(f)
2015 April	10	39	(f)
2013 April	10	100	
2016 October	10	101	(d)
2016 October	10	151	
2017 October	10	175	(c)
2014 October	10	175	(c)
2013 October	10	175	(d)
2014 April	10	176	(a)
2016 April	10	178	
2015 April	10	440	
2015 October	10	761	
2015 April	10	910	
2014 October	10	910	
2015 October	10	1005	(a)
2015 April	10	1010	
2017 April	10	1026	
2015 April	10	3010	
Part 11: PACKING AND STAMPING; MARKING			
2015 October	11	12	(b)
Part 12: SPECIAL CLASSES OF MERCHANDISE			
2014 April	12	3	(b)
2016 October	12	10	
2016 October	12	26	(a)
2017 October	12	39	(b)

All 19 CFR Sections Appearing on Exams Table

EXAM DATE	"PART"	"SECTION"	"PARAGRAPH"
2016 April	12	39	(b)
2015 October	12	39	(b)
2017 April	12	42	(a)
2016 October	12	42	(b)
2016 October	12	42	
2016 October	12	43	(a)
2013 October	12	73	(d)
2016 October	12	73	(e)
2017 October	12	98	(c)
2017 October	12	99	(a)
2013 April	12	115	
2013 April	12	121	(a)
2017 October	12	150	(a)
2013 October	12	150	(a)
Part 18: TRANSPORTATION IN BOND AND MERCHANDISE IN TRANSIT			
2014 October	18	8	
2016 October	18	10	
2017 October	18	25	(a)
2014 April	18	25	(a)
2014 April	18	25	(b)
Part 19: CUSTOMS WAREHOUSES, CONTAINER STATIONS AND CONTROL OF MERCHANDISE THEREIN			
2017 October	19	1	(a)
2017 October	19	1	(a)
2017 April	19	1	(a)
2014 April	19	4	(b)
2017 April	19	6	(d)
2017 October	19	11	(d)
2014 October	19	11	(d)
2017 October	19	12	(d)
2014 October	19	12	(d)
2013 October	19	12	(d)
2013 April	19	44	(a)
2015 April	19	48	(a)
Part 24: CUSTOMS FINANCIAL AND ACCOUNTING PROCEDURE			
2016 April	24	3	(e)
2015 April	24	3	(e)
2016 October	24	3a	(c)
2015 October	24	5	(c)
2013 April	24	5	(e)
2013 April	24	5	
2017 October	24	23	(b)
2016 October	24	23	(b)
2015 October	24	23	(b)
2015 October	24	23	(b)
2017 October	24	23	(c)
2017 April	24	23	(c)
2017 April	24	23	(c)
2016 October	24	23	(c)
2016 April	24	23	(c)

All 19 CFR Sections Appearing on Exams Table

EXAM DATE	"PART"	"SECTION"	"PARAGRAPH"
2014 October	24	23	(c)
2014 October	24	23	(c)
2014 October	24	23	(c)
2014 April	24	23	(c)
2013 October	24	23	(c)
2016 April	24	23	(d)
2014 October	24	24	(c)
Part 101: GENERAL PROVISIONS			
2017 April	101	1	
2014 April	101	1	
2016 October	101	2	(a)
2017 April	101	3	(b)
Part 102: RULES OF ORIGIN			
2017 October	102	0	
2016 October	102	13	(c)
2013 April	102	20	(g)
2016 April	102	21	(b)
Part 103: AVAILABILITY OF INFORMATION			
2013 October	103	31	(d)
Part 111: CUSTOMS BROKERS			
2017 April	111	1	
2016 April	111	1	
2014 October	111	1	
2014 April	111	1	
2016 October	111	2	(a)
2015 October	111	2	(a)
2015 April	111	2	(a)
2015 April	111	2	(a)
2014 October	111	2	(a)
2014 October	111	2	(a)
2014 October	111	2	(b)
2013 April	111	2	(b)
2013 April	111	2	(b)
2013 April	111	2	
2014 April	111	11	(a)
2017 October	111	11	
2017 April	111	19	(b)
2017 April	111	19	(c)
2014 October	111	19	(d)
2017 October	111	19	(f)
2013 October	111	21	(a)
2017 October	111	23	(b)
2016 October	111	23	(b)
2016 October	111	23	(b)
2015 October	111	23	(b)
2015 April	111	23	(b)
2014 October	111	23	(b)
2013 October	111	23	(b)
2013 October	111	23	(b)

All 19 CFR Sections Appearing on Exams Table

EXAM DATE	"PART"	"SECTION"	"PARAGRAPH"
2017 October	111	28	(b)
2016 October	111	28	(b)
2014 October	111	28	(b)
2014 October	111	28	(b)
2014 April	111	28	(b)
2014 April	111	28	(b)
2014 April	111	28	(c)
2017 October	111	29	(a)
2016 October	111	29	(a)
2014 October	111	29	(a)
2013 October	111	29	(a)
2013 October	111	29	(a)
2013 April	111	29	(a)
2017 October	111	29	(b)
2017 October	111	29	(b)
2017 April	111	29	(b)
2016 October	111	29	(b)
2014 October	111	29	(b)
2013 October	111	29	(b)
2013 October	111	30	(a)
2016 October	111	30	(c)
2016 October	111	30	(c)
2017 April	111	30	(d)
2016 April	111	30	(d)
2014 October	111	30	(d)
2014 October	111	30	(d)
2014 April	111	30	(d)
2014 April	111	30	(d)
2013 October	111	30	(d)
2013 April	111	30	(d)
2013 April	111	30	(d)
2015 April	111	31	(c)
2013 April	111	31	(c)
2016 April	111	36	(a)
2013 April	111	36	(c)
2013 April	111	37	
2013 April	111	39	(b)
2014 April	111	42	(a)
2016 April	111	45	(a)
2016 April	111	45	(a)
2015 April	111	45	(a)
2016 April	111	45	(b)
2015 October	111	45	(b)
2015 April	111	45	(b)
2013 April	111	45	(b)
2013 October	111	53	(e)
2013 April	111	53	(e)
2016 October	111	56	
2014 April	111	79	

All 19 CFR Sections Appearing on Exams Table

EXAM DATE	"PART"	"SECTION"	"PARAGRAPH"
2013 April	111	81	
2015 April	111	91	(b)
2013 October	111	91	(b)
2015 April	111	92	(b)
2014 April	111	96	(c)
2013 October	111	96	(d)
Part 113: CUSTOMS BONDS			
2015 April	113	1	
2014 April	113	1	
2014 October	113	11	
2017 October	113	13	(a)
2014 October	113	13	(a)
2017 April	113	13	(b)
2017 April	113	13	(c)
2016 October	113	13	(d)
2014 April	113	23	(b)
2017 October	113	26	(a)
2014 October	113	26	(a)
2017 April	113	37	(g)
2017 April	113	38	(b)
2014 April	113	40	(a)
2017 April	113	52	
2016 April	113	62	(j)
2014 October	113	62	
2016 April	113	63	(c)
2016 October	113	66	(b)
2016 April	113	66	(b)
2014 April	113	66	
Part 114: CARNETS			
2016 October	114	1	(c)
2017 October	114	23	(a)
2015 April	114	23	(a)
2017 April	114	31	(a)
Part 122: AIR COMMERCE REGULATIONS			
2014 October	122	50	(a)
Part 123: CBP RELATIONS WITH CANADA AND MEXICO			
2017 October	123	10	(b)
2014 October	123	10	(b)
Part 132: QUOTAS			
2015 April	132	3	
2014 April	132	3	
2015 April	132	5	(c)
2016 April	132	5	
2015 October	132	5	
2013 April	132	5	
2016 April	132	13	(a)
2015 April	132	17	(c)
2016 October	132	22	
2016 October	132	24	

All 19 CFR Sections Appearing on Exams Table

EXAM DATE	"PART"	"SECTION"	"PARAGRAPH"
Part 133: TRADEMARKS, TRADE NAMES, AND COPYRIGHTS			
2013 April	133	1	
2015 April	133	2	(e)
2017 April	133	3	(b)
2016 April	133	3	(b)
2017 April	133	6	(b)
2016 October	133	12	
2016 October	133	21	(a)
2015 April	133	21	(a)
2017 October	133	21	(b)
2017 October	133	21	(b)
2016 April	133	21	(b)
2015 October	133	21	(b)
2015 April	133	21	(b)
2017 October	133	21	(e)
2016 October	133	21	(g)
2016 April	133	21	(g)
2015 October	133	21	(g)
2014 April	133	21	
2013 April	133	21	
2015 April	133	23	(a)
2015 April	133	23	(a)
2013 October	133	23	(a)
2015 October	133	23	(b)
2017 October	133	23	(c)
2013 October	133	25	(a)
2015 April	133	25	(b)
2017 April	133	27	(b)
2013 October	133	34	(b)
2016 April	133	51	(b)
2016 April	133	52	(c)
2016 April	133	53	
Part 134: COUNTRY OF ORIGIN MARKING			
2015 October	134	1	(b)
2013 April	134	1	(b)
2016 October	134	2	
2016 October	134	2	
2016 April	134	2	
2014 April	134	2	
2014 April	134	2	
2017 October	134	11	
2017 April	134	12	
2017 October	134	26	(a)
2016 October	134	32	
2016 April	134	32	
2015 October	134	32	
2015 April	134	32	
2017 April	134	33	
2015 October	134	33	

All 19 CFR Sections Appearing on Exams Table

EXAM DATE	"PART"	"SECTION"	"PARAGRAPH"
2015 April	134	33	
2015 April	134	33	
2015 April	134	41	(a)
2014 October	134	43	(a)
2017 April	134	46	
2017 October	134	51	(a)
2014 October	134	51	(a)
2013 October	134	51	(a)
2017 October	134	54	(a)
2016 October	134	54	(a)
Part 141: ENTRY OF MERCHANDISE			
2016 April	141	2	
2014 October	141	2	
2017 April	141	4	(c)
2016 October	141	4	(c)
2014 October	141	4	(c)
2017 October	141	4	
2017 April	141	5	
2015 October	141	18	
2017 April	141	20	(a)
2015 October	141	20	(a)
2014 October	141	20	(a)
2017 October	141	31	(a)
2016 October	141	31	(a)
2017 October	141	32	
2016 October	141	32	
2016 April	141	32	
2017 October	141	34	
2017 April	141	34	
2016 October	141	34	
2016 April	141	34	
2015 April	141	34	
2014 April	141	34	
2017 October	141	35	
2015 October	141	35	
2017 April	141	36	
2013 October	141	37	
2016 April	141	39	(a)
2015 April	141	39	(a)
2014 April	141	39	(a)
2017 October	141	46	
2016 October	141	46	
2016 October	141	46	
2016 April	141	57	(b)
2017 October	141	57	(i)
2014 April	141	61	(b)
2015 October	141	68	(c)
2015 April	141	69	(b)
2014 April	141	69	(b)

All 19 CFR Sections Appearing on Exams Table

EXAM DATE	"PART"	"SECTION"	"PARAGRAPH"
2017 April	141	86	(a)
2013 October	141	86	(a)
2017 April	141	86	(j)
2017 April	141	89	(a)
2017 April	141	89	(a)
2014 April	141	89	
2013 April	141	92	(a)
2013 April	141	113	(b)
2013 October	141	113	(c)
Part 142: ENTRY PROCESS			
2016 April	142	4	(a)
2015 April	142	12	(b)
2017 April	142	15	
2015 October	142	15	
Part 143: SPECIAL ENTRY PROCEDURES			
2016 April	143	2	
2016 October	143	8	
2017 April	143	21	(k)
2015 October	143	28	
Part 144: WAREHOUSE AND REWAREHOUSE ENTRIES AND WITHDRAWALS			
2015 April	144	1	(a)
2015 April	144	41	(a)
Part 146: FOREIGN TRADE ZONES			
2013 October	146	22	(a)
2015 October	146	25	(a)
2015 April	146	25	(a)
2014 April	146	25	(a)
2015 October	146	32	(a)
2014 October	146	32	(a)
2014 April	146	35	(b)
2017 April	146	39	(a)
2015 October	146	39	(a)
2015 April	146	44	(c)
2017 April	146	52	(a)
2016 April	146	52	(a)
2014 April	146	53	(b)
2016 October	146	53	(d)
2016 April	146	62	(b)
2016 April	146	63	(c)
2015 April	146	63	(c)
2016 October	146	64	(d)
2015 April	146	66	(a)
2016 October	146	71	(c)
Part 148 PERSONAL DECLARATIONS AND EXEMPTIONS			
2017 April	148	55	
Part 151: EXAMINATION, SAMPLING, AND TESTING OF MERCHANDISE			
2013 October	151	16	(c)
2015 October	151	16	(f)
2017 October	151	42	(a)

All 19 CFR Sections Appearing on Exams Table

EXAM DATE	"PART"	"SECTION"	"PARAGRAPH"
Part 152: CLASSIFICATION AND APPRAISEMENT OF MERCHANDISE			
2017 April	152	1	(c)
2014 October	152	1	(c)
2017 October	152	2	
2015 April	152	2	
2013 April	152	13	
2015 April	152	23	
2014 October	152	101	(d)
2014 April	152	101	(d)
2016 October	152	102	(a)
2016 October	152	102	(a)
2016 April	152	102	(a)
2014 October	152	102	(a)
2014 April	152	102	(a)
2017 April	152	102	(c)
2016 October	152	102	(c)
2014 April	152	102	(d)
2017 April	152	102	(f)
2015 April	152	102	(f)
2014 October	152	102	(f)
2014 October	152	102	(f)
2014 October	152	102	(f)
2016 April	152	102	(g)
2016 April	152	102	(g)
2014 October	152	102	(g)
2014 April	152	102	(i)
2017 October	152	103	(a)
2016 April	152	103	(a)
2015 October	152	103	(a)
2015 April	152	103	(a)
2015 April	152	103	(a)
2015 April	152	103	(a)
2014 October	152	103	(a)
2014 April	152	103	(a)
2013 October	152	103	(a)
2013 October	152	103	(a)
2013 October	152	103	(a)
2013 April	152	103	(a)
2016 April	152	103	(b)
2016 April	152	103	(b)
2015 October	152	103	(b)
2014 October	152	103	(b)
2014 April	152	103	(b)
2013 October	152	103	(b)
2017 October	152	103	(d)
2017 April	152	103	(d)
2016 October	152	103	(d)
2015 October	152	103	(d)
2014 October	152	103	(d)

All 19 CFR Sections Appearing on Exams Table

EXAM DATE	"PART"	"SECTION"	"PARAGRAPH"
2014 April	152	103	(d)
2013 October	152	103	(d)
2013 October	152	103	(d)
2013 October	152	103	(e)
2015 October	152	103	(i)
2014 October	152	103	(j)
2013 October	152	103	(j)
2013 October	152	103	(k)
2015 April	152	104	(d)
2014 April	152	105	(d)
2013 October	152	106	(a)
2013 October	152	106	(b)
2014 April	152	107	(b)
2017 October	152	108	(c)
2016 October	152	108	(c)
2017 April	152	108	(g)
2017 October	152	108	
Part 159: LIQUIDATION OF DUTIES			
2013 October	159	1	
2014 April	159	9	(c)
2017 October	159	11	(a)
2014 October	159	11	(a)
2015 October	159	12	(a)
2015 October	159	12	(a)
2013 April	159	12	(a)
2015 October	159	12	(e)
2013 April	159	12	(e)
2015 October	159	12	(f)
2017 April	159	32	
2015 October	159	32	
2014 October	159	32	
2013 October	159	32	
2015 October	159	51	
2016 April	159	61	(c)
Part 161: GENERAL ENFORCEMENT PROVISIONS			
2017 October	161	5	
Part 162: INSPECTIONS, SEARCH, AND SEIZURE			
2015 October	162	0	
2016 October	162	23	
2013 October	162	73	(b)
2017 April	162	74	(a)
2014 October	162	74	(a)
2017 October	162	74	(b)
2017 April	162	74	(b)
2016 October	162	74	(b)
2016 April	162	74	(b)
2015 October	162	74	(b)
2014 October	162	74	(b)
2016 April	162	74	(c)

All 19 CFR Sections Appearing on Exams Table

EXAM DATE	"PART"	"SECTION"	"PARAGRAPH"
2014 October	162	74	(c)
2015 April	162	74	(h)
2013 April	162	74	
2016 April	162	77	(b)
Part 163: RECORDKEEPING			
2017 October	163	2	(e)
2014 October	163	4	(a)
2017 October	163	4	(b)
2016 October	163	4	(b)
2016 October	163	4	(b)
2016 April	163	5	(b)
2015 April	163	5	(b)
2014 October	163	5	(b)
2013 October	163	5	(b)
2017 April	163	6	(b)
2017 April	163	6	(b)
2016 April	163	6	(b)
2015 October	163	6	(b)
2015 April	163	6	(b)
2013 October	163	6	(b)
Part 165: INVESTIGATION OF CLAIMS OF EVASION OF ANTIDUMPING AND COUNTERVAILING DUTIES			
2017 October	165	1	
2017 October	165	14	(b)
Part 171: FINES, PENALTIES, AND FORFEITURES			
2015 October	171	2	(b)
2015 April	171	2	(b)
2015 April	171	2	(c)
2015 April	171	22	
2013 April	171	23	
2017 October	171	32	
2015 October	171	62	(a)
2016 April	171	APPENDIX B	C
2013 October	171	APPENDIX B	E
2013 October	171	APPENDIX B	F
2016 October	171	APPENDIX B	
2015 April	171	APPENDIX B	
2015 October	171	APPENDIX C	V.
2016 October	171	APPENDIX C	
2016 October	171	APPENDIX C	
2015 April	171	APPENDIX C	
Part 172: CLAIMS FOR LIQUIDATED DAMAGES; PENALTIES SECURED BY BONDS			
2012 April	172	1	
2015 October	172	2	(a)
2016 April	172	3	(b)
2012 April	172	11	
2015 October	172	31	
2013 October	172	41	

All 19 CFR Sections Appearing on Exams Table

EXAM DATE	"PART"	"SECTION"	"PARAGRAPH"
Part 173: ADMINISTRATIVE REVIEW IN GENERAL			
2016 October	173	2	
2016 April	173	5	
Part 174: PROTESTS			
2014 October	174	12	(a)
2013 October	174	12	(b)
2016 October	174	12	(e)
2015 April	174	12	(e)
2017 October	174	13	(a)
2017 April	174	13	(a)
2014 October	174	13	(a)
2014 April	174	22	(d)
2016 April	174	31	
2015 October	174	31	
2017 April	174	32	
Part 176: PROCEEDINGS IN THE COURT OF INTERNATIONAL TRADE			
2017 April	176	11	
Part 177: ADMINISTRATIVE RULINGS			
2016 April	177	23	
Part 181: NORTH AMERICAN FREE TRADE AGREEMENT (NAFTA)			
2016 October	181	11	(b)
2017 April	181	11	(d)
2015 October	181	21	(a)
2014 April	181	21	(b)
2013 April	181	21	
2016 April	181	22	(a)
2017 April	181	22	(b)
2014 October	181	22	(b)
2014 October	181	22	(b)
2016 October	181	31	
2016 April	181	31	
2014 October	181	31	
2015 April	181	32	(a)
Part 191: DRAWBACK			
2014 April	191	2	(g)
2014 April	191	2	(i)
2016 October	191	2	(o)
2015 October	191	3	(b)
2015 April	191	3	(b)
2015 April	191	3	(b)
2014 April	191	3	(b)
2014 April	191	3	(b)
2016 April	191	6	(a)
2017 October	191	11	(a)
2016 October	191	11	(a)
2016 April	191	14	(c)
2013 October	191	15	
2015 October	191	21	
2015 April	191	21	

All 19 CFR Sections Appearing on Exams Table

EXAM DATE	"PART"	"SECTION"	"PARAGRAPH"
2015 October	191	22	
2015 April	191	22	
2014 April	191	28	
2015 October	191	31	
2015 April	191	31	
2017 October	191	33	(a)
2017 April	191	35	(a)
2014 October	191	35	(a)
2015 April	191	41	
2016 April	191	42	(c)
2015 October	191	51	(a)
2015 October	191	51	(b)
2015 April	191	51	(b)
2014 October	191	51	(e)
2014 April	191	51	(e)
2016 April	191	52	(a)
2017 October	191	52	(c)
2017 October	191	71	(a)
2017 April	191	112	(b)
2016 October	191	166	(b)
2015 October	191	171	
2015 April	191	171	
2016 April	191	192	(b)
Part 351: ANTIDUMPING AND COUNTERVAILING DUTIES			
2015 April	351	107	(a)
2015 October	351	107	(b)
2013 April	351	206	(a)
2016 April	351	402	(f)
2015 October	351	402	(f)
2015 April	351	402	(f)
2015 April	351	402	(f)
2014 October	351	402	(f)

Phew…

Book 1 Part 9

Exam with Broker Commentary

October 2017 Customs Broker License Examination

This section of the study guide analyzes an actual customs broker exam. It presents the actual question and its multiple choices. For HTSUS classification questions, the author of this book has included abbreviated HTSUS Article Descriptions notated directly to the right of each multiple choice classification for the student's convenience and ease of reference purposes. As necessary, and in proportion to the complexity of each particular exam question, an analysis of the question and path to the correct answer has been provided. Direct excerpts from the HTSUS, 19 CFR, etc. are also included as supporting points of reference for each answer, as necessary. This exam (without commentary, etc.) and its answer key, as well as other previous customs exams can be downloaded directly from Customs' website at...

http://www.cbp.gov/document/publications/past-customs-broker-license-examinations-answer-keys

Exam Refs: **Harmonized Tariff Schedule of the United States**
Title 19, Code of Federal Regulations
Instructions for Preparation of CBP Form 7501
Right to Make Entry Directive, 3530-002A

Exam Breakdown by Subject:

Category I – Antidumping/Countervailing Duties	**Questions 1 - 3**
Category II – Bonds	**Questions 4 - 6**
Category III – Broker Compliance	**Questions 7 - 14**
Category IV – Classification	**Questions 15 - 29**
Category V – Drawback	**Questions 30 - 33**
Category VI – Entry	**Questions 34 - 43**
Category VII – Fines and Penalties	**Questions 44 - 48**
Category VIII – Free Trade Agreements	**Questions 49 - 53**
Category IX – Foreign Trade Zones/Warehouses	**Questions 54 - 58**
Category X – Intellectual Property Rights	**Questions 59 - 63**
Category XI – Marking	**Questions 64 - 67**
Category XII – Power of Attorney	**Questions 68 - 70**
Category XIII – Practical Exercise	**Questions 71 – 75**
Category XIV – Value	**Questions 76 – 80**

Category I – Antidumping/Countervailing Duties

1. Which of the following would NOT be referred to as an "interested party" in proceedings relating to allegations by the public for an investigation regarding the evasion of antidumping and countervailing duty AD/(CVD) orders and procedures by which CBP investigates such claims consistent with the Trade Facilitation and Trade Enforcement Act of 2015 ("TFTEA")?

A. Foreign manufacturer of covered merchandise
B. Manufacturer or producer of a domestic like product in the United States
C. Trade association a majority of the members of which produce a domestic like product in the United States
D. Certified union that is representative of an industry engaged in the wholesale of a domestic like product in the United States
E. Coalition that is representative of processors of non-agricultural products

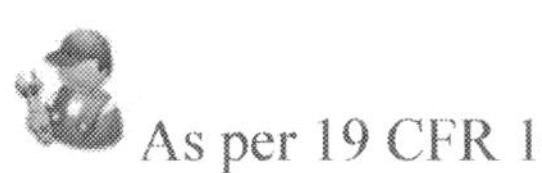
As per 19 CFR 165.1:

§165.1 Definitions.

As used in this part, the following terms will have the meanings indicated unless either the context in which they are used requires a different meaning or a different definition is prescribed for a particular section of this part:

… …

Interested party. **The term "interested party" in this part refers only to the following**:

(1) **A foreign manufacturer**, producer, or exporter, or any importer (not limited to importers of record and including the party against whom the allegation is brought), **of covered merchandise** or a trade or business association a majority of the members of which are producers, exporters, or importers of such merchandise;

(2) **A manufacturer, producer, or wholesaler in the United States of a domestic like product**;

(3) **A certified union or recognized union or group of workers that is representative of an industry engaged in the manufacture, production, or wholesale in the United States of a domestic like product**;

(4) **A trade or business association a majority of the members of which manufacture, produce, or wholesale a domestic like product in the United States**;

(5) An association a majority of the members of which is composed of interested parties described in paragraphs (2), (3), and (4) of this definition with respect to a domestic like product; or,

(6) If the covered merchandise is a processed agricultural product, as defined in 19 U.S.C. 1677(4)(E), a coalition or trade association that is representative of any of the following: processors; processors and producers; or processors and growers.

Although credit was given to all examinees for this question, we can reasonably infer that the correct answer is "E".

✔ **JUST A SIDE NOTE:** In regards to the above-mentioned TFTEA, Customs' website explains…

Title IV, Section 421 of the Trade Facilitation and Trade Enforcement Act of 2015, commonly referred to as EAPA, establishes a formal process for CBP to investigate allegations of evasion of AD/CVD orders. Specifically, it provides for a transparent administrative proceeding where parties can both participate in and learn the outcome of the investigation. It also provides an option for both administrative and judicial appeals of the investigation.

2. All of the following information must be included in Federal agency requests for investigations in proceedings relating to allegations by the public for an investigation regarding the evasion of antidumping and countervailing duty (AD/CVD) orders and the procedures by which CBP investigates such claims consistent with the Trade Facilitation and Trade Enforcement Act of 2015 ("TFTEA"), EXCEPT:

A. **Name of importer against whom the allegation is brought**
B. **Description of the covered merchandise**
C. **Applicable AD/CVD orders**
D. **Harmonized Tariff Numbers**
E. **Identification of a point of contact at the agency**

As per 19 CFR 165.14(b):

§165.14 Other Federal agency requests for investigations.

(a) *Requests for investigations.* Any other Federal agency, including the Department of Commerce or the United States International Trade Commission, may request an investigation under this part. CBP will initiate an investigation if the Federal agency has provided information that reasonably suggests that an importer has entered covered merchandise into the customs territory of the United States through evasion, unless the agency submits a request to withdraw to the designated email address specified by CBP.

(b) *Contents of requests.* The following information must be included in the request for an investigation:

(1) Name of importer against whom the allegation is brought;

(2) Description of the covered merchandise;

(3) Applicable AD/CVD orders;

(4) Information that reasonably suggests that an importer has entered covered merchandise into the customs territory of the United States through evasion;

(5) Identification of a point of contact at the agency; and

(6) Notification of any knowledge of or reason to suspect that the covered merchandise poses any health or safety risk to U.S. consumers.

HTS numbers are not a required part of the request for AD/CVD investigation. The correct answer is "D". Credit was given to all test takers for the question.

✓ **JUST A SIDE NOTE:** CBP accepts questions, comments, and allegations of evasion of AD/CVD orders via email at:

eapallegations@cbp.dhs.gov

3. Big Mouth Bearing Company imported eight ball bearings with integral shafts from Germany, which are classified under subheading 8482.10.10, Harmonized Tariff Schedule of the United States, at a 2.4% ad valorem duty rate and subject to antidumping duties. The ball bearings are shipped by air and formally entered at John F. Kennedy International Airport. The total value of the shipment is $7,134.00. The applicable antidumping duty case deposit rate is 69.88%. What is the total amount of fees and estimated duties that should be reported on CBP Form 7501?

A. $171.22
B. $5,181.17
C. $5,181.46
D. $5,009.95
E. $4,985.24

 As per 19 CFR 24.23(b):

(b) *Fees*—(1) *Formal entry or release*—(i) *Ad valorem fee*—(A) *General.* Except as provided in paragraph (c) of this section, merchandise that is formally entered or released is subject to the payment to CBP of an *ad valorem* fee of 0.3464 percent. The 0.3464 *ad valorem* fee is due and payable to CBP by the importer of record of the merchandise at the time of presentation of the entry summary and is based on the value of the merchandise as determined under 19 U.S.C. 1401a. In the case of an express consignment carrier facility or centralized hub facility, each shipment covered by an individual air waybill or bill of lading that is formally entered and valued at $2,500 or less is subject to a $1.00 per individual air waybill or bill of lading fee, as adjusted in accordance with the terms of §24.22(k) of this part, and, if applicable, to the 0.3464 percent *ad valorem* fee in accordance with paragraph (b)(4) of this section.

(B) *Maximum and minimum fees.* Subject to the provisions of paragraphs (b)(1)(ii) and (d) of this section relating to the surcharge and to aggregation of the ad valorem fee respectively, **the ad valorem fee charged under paragraph** (b)(1)(i)(A) of this section must not exceed $485, as adjusted in accordance with the terms of §24.22(k) of this part, and **must not be less than $25**, as adjusted in accordance with the terms of §24.22(k) of this part.

... ...

 The correct answer is "C".

$171.22 (duty rate 0.024 x value $7,134.00)
+$4,985.24 (antidumping duty rate 0.6988 x value $7,134.00)
+$25.00 (MPF rate 0.003464 x value $7,134.00 = $24.71 [use minimum $25.00])
=$5,181.46

✓ **JUST A SIDE NOTE:** "Ad valorem" is Latin with a literal meaning of "according to value". For Customs, it means to multiply the applicable rate against the value of the merchandise.

4. A continuous bond, and any associated application required by 19 CFR 113.11, or rider, may be filed up to ________ days prior to the effective date requested for the continuous bond or rider.

A. 30
B. 45
C. 60
D. 120
E. 365

 As per 19 CFR 113.26(a):

§113.26 Effective dates of bonds and riders.

(a) *General.* **A continuous bond, and any associated application required by §113.11, or rider, may be filed up to 60 days prior** to the effective date requested for the continuous bond or rider.

A continuous bond may be filed up to 60 days prior to the effective date of the Customs bond (application). The correct answer is "C".

✓ **JUST A SIDE NOTE:** According to CBP's General Guidelines for Completing the CBP Form 301 (Customs Bond):

All continuous bonds are to be filed with the Revenue Division Bond Team in Indianapolis, IN. Note: … … The Bond Team will accept bond submissions via email or fax. It is preferred that the submissions are transmitted via email … …

5. What is the minimum amount of any CBP bond?

A. Not less than $100, except when the law or regulation expressly provides that a lesser amount may be taken

B. Not less than $100, without exception

C. Not less than $1000, without exception

D. The CBP bond must be equal to the value of the merchandise.

E. A minimum of 50 percent of duties, taxes and fees

 As per 19 CFR 113.13(a):

§113.13 Amount of bond.

(a) *Minimum amount of bond.* **The amount of any CBP bond must not be less than $100, except when the law or regulation expressly provides that a lesser amount may be taken.** Fractional parts of a dollar will be disregarded in computing the amount of a bond. The bond always will be stated as the next highest dollar.

 The correct answer is "A".

✓ **JUST A SIDE NOTE:** As per 19 CFR 113.11, **a Customs bond application must contain:**

(i) The general character of the merchandise to be entered; and

(ii) The total amount of ordinary customs duties (including any taxes required by law to be treated as duties), plus the estimated amount of any other tax or taxes on the merchandise to be collected by CBP, accruing on all merchandise imported by the principal during the calendar year preceding the date of the application. The total amount of duties and taxes will be that which would have been required to be deposited had the merchandise been entered for consumption even though some or all of the merchandise may have been entered under bond. If the value or nature of the merchandise to be imported will change in any material respect during the next year the change must be identified. If no imports were made during the calendar year prior to the application, a statement of the duties and taxes it is estimated will accrue on all importations during the current year shall be submitted.

6. When a resident of France temporarily imports articles under subheading 9813.00.50, HTSUS, and formal entry is made, the importer of record shall be required to file a bond in what amount?

A. 110 percent of estimated duties and fees
B. 110 percent of estimated duties
C. 3 times the entered value
D. 200 percent of estimated duties and fees, if payable
E. An amount equal to the entered value plus duties, taxes and fees

 As per 19 CFR 10.31(f):

§10.31 Entry; bond.

… …

(f) With the exceptions stated herein, a bond shall be given on CBP Form 301, containing the bond conditions set forth in §113.62 of this chapter, in an amount equal to double the duties, including fees, which it is estimated would accrue (or such larger amount as the Center director shall state in writing or by the electronic equivalent to the entrant is necessary to protect the revenue) had all the articles covered by the entry been entered under an ordinary consumption entry. In the case of samples solely for use in taking orders entered under subheading 9813.00.20, HTSUS, motion-picture advertising films entered under subheading 9813.00.25, HTSUS, and professional equipment, tools of trade and repair components for such equipment or tools entered under subheading **9813.00.50, HTSUS, the bond required to be given shall be in an amount equal to 110 percent of the estimated duties**, including fees, determined at the time of entry. If appropriate a carnet, under the provisions of part 114 of this chapter, may be filed in lieu of a bond on CBP Form 301 (containing the bond conditions set forth in §113.62 of this chapter). Cash deposits in the amount of the bond may be accepted in lieu of sureties. When the articles are entered under subheading 9813.00.05, 9813.00.20, or 9813.00.50, HTSUS without formal entry, as provided for in §§10.36 and 10.36a, or the amount of the bond taken under any subheading of Chapter 98, Subchapter XIII, HTSUS, is less than $25, the bond shall be without surety or cash deposit, and the bond shall be modified to so indicate. In addition, notwithstanding any other provision of this paragraph, in the case of professional equipment necessary for carrying out the business activity, trade or profession of a business person, equipment for the press or for sound or television broadcasting, cinematographic equipment, articles imported for sports purposes and articles intended for display or demonstration, if brought into the United States by a resident of Canada, Mexico, Singapore, Chile, Morocco, Australia, El Salvador, Guatemala, Honduras, Nicaragua, the Dominican Republic, Costa Rica, Bahrain, Oman, Peru, the Republic of Korea, Colombia, or Panama and entered under Chapter 98, Subchapter XIII, HTSUS, no bond or other security will be required if the entered article is a good originating, within the meaning of General Notes 12, 25, 26, 27, 28, 29, 30, 31, 32, 33, 34, and 35, HTSUS, in the country of which the importer is a resident.

 The correct answer is "A".

✓ **NOTE:** The above-mentioned HTSUS 9813.00.50 provides for…

Professional equipment, tools of trade, repair components for equipment or tools admitted under this heading and camping equipment; all the foregoing imported by or for nonresidents sojourning temporarily in the United States and for the use of such nonresidents

7. After a new employee has been employed by the broker for 30 consecutive days, the Broker has 10 calendar days to provide CBP with all of the following information, EXCEPT:

A. Social Security number
B. Passport number
C. Previous employment if employed by the broker for less than 3 years
D. Current and prior home address
E. Place and date of birth

As per 19 CFR 111.28(b):

§111.28 Responsible supervision.

… …

(b) *Employee information*—(1) *Current employees*—(i) *General.* Each broker must submit, in writing, to the director of each port at which the broker intends to transact customs business, a list of the names of persons currently employed by the broker at that port. The list of employees must be submitted upon issuance of a permit for an additional district under §111.19, or upon the opening of an office at a port within a district for which the broker already has a permit, and before the broker begins to transact customs business as a broker at the port. **For each employee, the broker also must provide the social security number, date and place of birth, current home address, last prior home address, and, if the employee has been employed by the broker for less than 3 years, the name and address of each former employer and dates of employment for the 3-year period preceding current employment with the broker.** After the initial submission, an updated list, setting forth the name, social security number, date and place of birth, and current home address of each current employee, must be submitted with the status report required by §111.30(d).

(ii) *New employees.* **In the case of a new employee, the broker must submit to the port director the written information required under paragraph (b)(1)(i) of this section** within 10 calendar days after the new employee has been employed by the broker for 30 consecutive days.

… …

For a new employee, after 30 days of employment, the customs broker must provide the port director the same information required for current employees. The employee's passport number is not provided. The correct answer is "B".

✓ **JUST A SIDE NOTE:** The regulations define "Responsible supervision and control" as the "degree of supervision and control necessary to ensure the proper transaction of the customs business of a broker, including actions necessary to ensure that an employee of a broker provides substantially the same quality of service in handling customs transactions that the broker is required to provide."

8. Which of the following individuals will be granted an exception to the requirements of maintaining records?

A. **An agent of a consignee who imports goods under a Temporary Importation Bond (Type 23 entry)**

B. **A traveler who made a baggage or oral declaration of non-commercial merchandise upon arrival**

C. **An importer who files a drawback claim for previously imported merchandise**

D. **An exporter who has exported goods to Canada or Mexico for which a certificate of origin was completed and signed pursuant to NAFTA agreement**

E. **A customs broker making entry on behalf of an importer**

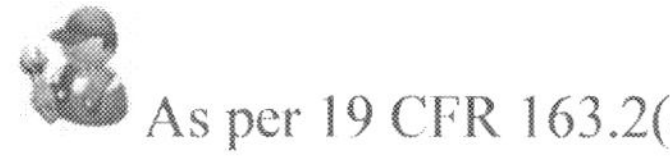

As per 19 CFR 163.2(e):

§163.2 Persons required to maintain records.

… …

(e) *Recordkeeping not required for certain travelers.* After having physically cleared the Customs facility, **a traveler who made a baggage or oral declaration upon arrival in the United States will not be required to maintain supporting records regarding non-commercial merchandise** acquired abroad which falls within the traveler's personal exemptions or which is covered by a flat rate of duty.

Common sense and Customs say the correct answer is "B".

✓ **JUST A SIDE NOTE:** As per CBP's website, CBP either restricts or prohibits travelers from bringing into the United States meat, milk, eggs, poultry, and products made with these items.

9. Who can apply for a National Permit?

A. An attorney

B. An importer

C. A freight forwarder

D. A customs licensed broker

E. A foreign Importer

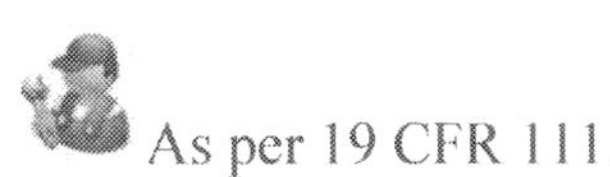

As per 19 CFR 111.19(f):

§111.19 Permits.

… …

(f) ***National permit.*** **A broker who has a district permit issued under paragraph (a) or paragraph (e) of this section may apply for a national permit** for the purpose of transacting customs business in any circumstance described in §111.2(b)(2)(i). An application for a national permit under this paragraph must be in the form of a letter addressed to the Office of International Trade, U.S. Customs and Border Protection, Washington, DC 20229, and must:

(1) Identify the applicant's broker license number and date of issuance;

(2) Set forth the address and telephone number of the office designated by the applicant as the office of record for purposes of administration of the provisions of this part regarding all activities of the applicant conducted under the national permit. That office will be noted in the national permit when issued;

(3) Set forth the name, broker license number, office address, and telephone number of the individual broker who will exercise responsible supervision and control over the activities of the applicant conducted under the national permit; and

(4) Attach a receipt or other evidence showing that the fees specified in §111.96(b) and (c) have been paid in accordance with paragraph (c) of this section.

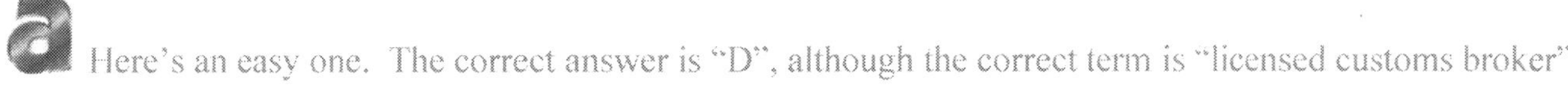

Here's an easy one. The correct answer is "D", although the correct term is "licensed customs broker".

✓ **JUST A SIDE NOTE:** The above 19 CFR 111.19(f)(4) mentions proof of payment of "fees specified in 111.96(b) and (c)" which are the $100 district permit fee and $138 annual broker permit user fee, for a total of $238.

10. How often should brokers advise their active clients of their rights to pay duties, taxes, and fees directly to CBP, in writing?

A. At least once upon first importation
B. Annually
C. At least once within each 12-month period
D. Every five years
E. Upon each update of Power of Attorney

 As per 19 CFR 111.29(b):

§111.29 Diligence in correspondence and paying monies.

… …

(b) *Notice to client of method of payment.* **(1) All brokers must provide their clients with the following written notification:**

If you are the importer of record, payment to the broker will not relieve you of liability for customs charges (duties, taxes, or other debts owed CBP) in the event the charges are not paid by the broker. Therefore, if you pay by check, customs charges may be paid with a separate check payable to the "U.S. Customs and Border Protection" which will be delivered to CBP by the broker.

(2) The written notification set forth in paragraph (b)(1) of this section must be provided by brokers as follows:

(i) On, or attached to, any power of attorney provided by the broker to a client for execution on or after September 27, 1982; and

(ii) To each active client no later than February 28, 1983, and **at least once at any time within each 12-month period** after that date. An active client means a client from whom a broker has obtained a power of attorney and for whom the broker has transacted customs business on at least two occasions within the 12-month period preceding notification.

a Although it might seem that multiple choice "B" would be sufficient, the words "at least once" distinguishes "C" from "B". The correct answer is "C".

✓ **JUST A SIDE NOTE:** A customs broker can take care of the above-mentioned requirement (ii) by always including the liability for duties and taxes notification on their invoices to their clients.

11. What chapter of the Federal Regulations (CFR) sites the basic requirements for a Customs Broker License?

A. **19 CFR 111.11**
B. **19 CFR 111.18**
C. **19 CFR 111.15**
D. **19 USC 1641**
E. **19 USC 1592**

As per 19 CFR 111.11:

§111.11 Basic requirements for a license.

(a) *Individual.* In order to obtain a broker's license, an individual must:

(1) Be a citizen of the United States on the date of submission of the application referred to in §111.12(a) and not an officer or employee of the United States Government;

(2) Attain the age of 21 prior to the date of submission of the application referred to in §111.12(a);

(3) Be of good moral character; and

(4) Have established, by attaining a passing (75 percent or higher) grade on an examination taken within the 3-year period before submission of the application referred to in §111.12(a), that he has sufficient knowledge of customs and related laws, regulations and procedures, bookkeeping, accounting, and all other appropriate matters to render valuable service to importers and exporters.

(b) *Partnership.* In order to qualify for a broker's license, a partnership must have at least one member of the partnership who is a broker.

(c) *Association or corporation.* In order to qualify for a broker's license, an association or corporation must:

(1) Be empowered under its articles of association or articles of incorporation to transact customs business as a broker; and

(2) Have at least one officer who is a broker.

The correct answer is "A". Technically, the regulations covering the "basic requirements for a license" are under Title 19 of the Code of Federal Regulations (CFR), Volume 1, Chapter I, Part 111, Section 11.

✓ **JUST A SIDE NOTE:** Here's a snapshot of the basic structure of the 19 CFR.

Title	Volume	Chapter	Browse Parts	Regulatory Entity
Title 19 Customs Duties	1	I	0-140	U.S. CUSTOMS AND BORDER PROTECTION, DEPARTMENT OF HOMELAND SECURITY; DEPARTMENT OF THE TREASURY
	2		141-199	
	3	II	200-299	UNITED STATES INTERNATIONAL TRADE COMMISSION
		III	300-399	INTERNATIONAL TRADE ADMINISTRATION, DEPARTMENT OF COMMERCE
		IV	400-599	U.S. IMMIGRATION AND CUSTOMS ENFORCEMENT, DEPARTMENT OF HOMELAND SECURITY [RESERVED]

12. An importer sends a check, payable to a licensed broker, for payment of duties and fees applicable to an entry after the due date of the duties and fees. When is the broker required to submit payment for the duties and fees owed to CBP?

A. The same day the payment is received from the importer
B. Within five calendar days from receipt of the payment by the broker
C. Within ten calendar days from receipt of the payment by the broker
D. Within five working days from receipt of the payment by the broker
E. The estimated duties shall be immediately deposited with CBP.

 As per 19 CFR 111.29(a):

§111.29 Diligence in correspondence and paying monies.

(a) *Due diligence by broker.* Each broker must exercise due diligence in making financial settlements, in answering correspondence, and in preparing or assisting in the preparation and filing of records relating to any customs business matter handled by him as a broker. Payment of duty, tax, or other debt or obligation owing to the Government for which the broker is responsible, or for which the broker has received payment from a client, must be made to the Government on or before the date that payment is due. **Payments received by a broker from a client after the due date must be transmitted to the Government within 5 working days** from receipt by the broker. Each broker must provide a written statement to a client accounting for funds received for the client from the Government, or received from a client where no payment to the Government has been made, or received from a client in excess of the Governmental or other charges properly payable as part of the client's customs business, within 60 calendar days of receipt. No written statement is required if there is actual payment of the funds by a broker.

 The correct answer is "D".

JUST A SIDE NOTE: Customs may use CBP Form 6084 (bill form) for issuing a bill to an importer. It includes the details of the charge(s) as well as a remittance copy/slip at the bottom of the form for the payer to include with their payment to be mailed to the listed CBP address.

13. A separate entry for any portion of a split shipment is required for which of the following:

A. **A pre-filed entry notifying Customs that a single entry will be filed for shipments released incrementally**

B. **The portion of the shipment that arrived ten calendar days after the first portion**

C. **The portion of the shipment that arrived at a different port and was transported in-bond to the port of destination where entry was made for the other portions of the shipment**

D. **The portion of the shipment which results in the application of different duty rates for merchandise classifiable under the same subheading of the Harmonized Tariff Schedule of the United States (HTSUS)**

E. **The portion arriving after the importer of record filed and was granted a special permit for immediate delivery when the first portion arrived**

 As per 19 CFR 141.57(i):

§141.57 Single entry for split shipments.

… …

(i) ***Separate entry required***—(1) *Untimely arrival.* **The importer of record must enter separately those portions of a split shipment that do not arrive at the port of entry within 10 calendar days of the portion that arrived there first** (see paragraph (b)(3) of this section).

(2) *Different rates of duty for identically classified merchandise.* **An importer of record will be required to file a separate entry for any portion of a split shipment if necessary to preclude the application of different rates of duty on a split shipment entry for merchandise that is classifiable under the same subheading of the Harmonized Tariff Schedule of the United States (HTSUS).**

The exam key states that the correct answer is "D". However, "B" should also be considered a correct answer.

✔ **JUST A SIDE NOTE:** 19 CFR 141.57(b) spells out, in detail, three conditions necessary for a shipment to be treated as a "split shipment".

(b) *Split shipment defined.* A "split shipment", for purposes of this section, means a shipment:

(1) Which may be accommodated on a single conveyance, and which is delivered to and accepted by a carrier in the exporting country under one bill of lading or waybill, and is thus intended by the importer of record to arrive in the United States as a single shipment;

(2) Which is thereafter divided by the carrier, acting on its own, into different portions which are transported and consigned to the same party in the United States; and

(3) Of which the first portion and all succeeding portions arrive at the same port of entry in the United States, as listed in the original bill of lading or waybill; and all the succeeding portions arrive at the port of entry within 10 calendar days of the date of the first portion. If any portion of the shipment arrives at a different port, such portion must be transported in-bond to the port of destination where entry of the shipment is made.

14. Certain documents required for the entry of merchandise must be maintained by brokers for 5 years and produced to CBP upon reasonable demand. The following documents are subject to this requirement, EXCEPT:

A. Evidence of the right to make entry
B. Invoices
C. Packing Lists
D. Bond information
E. Export certificates for beef or sugar-containing products subject to tariff-rate quota

 As per 19 CFR 163.4(b):

§163.4 Record retention period.

(a) *General.* Except as otherwise provided in paragraph (b) of this section, any record required to be made, kept, and rendered for examination and inspection by Customs under §163.2 or any other provision of this chapter shall be kept for 5 years from the date of entry, if the record relates to an entry, or 5 years from the date of the activity which required creation of the record.

(b) *Exceptions.* (1) Any record relating to a drawback claim shall be kept until the third anniversary of the date of payment of the claim.

(2) Packing lists shall be retained for a period of 60 calendar days from the end of the release or conditional release period, whichever is later, or, if a demand for return to Customs custody has been issued, for a period of 60 calendar days either from the date the goods are redelivered or from the date specified in the demand as the latest redelivery date if redelivery has not taken place.

(3) A consignee who is not the owner or purchaser and who appoints a customs broker shall keep a record pertaining to merchandise covered by an informal entry for 2 years from the date of the informal entry.

(4) Records pertaining to articles that are admitted free of duty and tax pursuant to 19 U.S.C. 1321(a)(2) and §§10.151 through 10.153 of this chapter, and carriers' records pertaining to manifested cargo that is exempt from entry under the provisions of this chapter, shall be kept for 2 years from the date of the entry or other activity which required creation of the record.

(5) If another provision of this chapter sets forth a retention period for a specific type of record that differs from the period that would apply under this section, that other provision controls.

 A packing list, or its equivalent, is not required to be kept for five years. The correct answer is "C".

✓ **JUST A SIDE NOTE:** There are many different names for "Packing Lists", including:

- Packing Slip
- Shipping List
- Transport Note
- Customer Receipt

(This Page Intentionally Left Blank)

15. What is the CLASSIFICATION of check valves that regulate the flow of hydraulic fluid? The check valves are made of iron and are used in the oil well industry.

A. 8431.43.4000 Parts suitable for use solely or principally with the machinery of headings 8425 to 8430>>Of machinery of heading 8426, 8429 or 8430>>Parts for boring or sinking machinery of subheading 8430.41 or 8430.49>>Of offshore oil and natural gas drilling and production platforms

B. 8481.20.0040 Taps, cocks, valves and similar appliances, for pipes, boiler shells, tanks, vats or the like, including pressure-reducing valves and thermostatically controlled valves; parts thereof>>Valves for oleo hydraulic or pneumatic transmissions>>Hydraulic valves>>Flow control type

C. 8481.30.2010 Taps, cocks, valves and similar appliances, for pipes, boiler shells, tanks, vats or the like, including pressure-reducing valves and thermostatically controlled valves; parts thereof>>Check (nonreturn) valves>>Of iron or steel>>Of iron

D. 8481.30.9000 Taps, cocks, valves and similar appliances, for pipes, boiler shells, tanks, vats or the like, including pressure-reducing valves and thermostatically controlled valves; parts thereof>>Check (nonreturn) valves>>Other

E. 8431.43.8060 Parts suitable for use solely or principally with the machinery of headings 8425 to 8430>>Of machinery of heading 8426, 8429 or 8430>>Parts for boring or sinking machinery of subheading 8430.41 or 8430.49>>Other>>Of oil and gas field machinery>>Other

 As per HTSUS Chapter 84, Subheading Note 3:

Subheading Notes

1. For the purposes of subheading 8465.20, the term "machining centers" applies only to machine tools for working wood, cork, bone, hard rubber, hard plastics or similar hard materials, which can carry out different types of machining operations by automatic tool change from a magazine or the like in conformity with a machining program.

2. For the purposes of subheading 8471.49, the term "systems" means automatic data processing machines whose units satisfy the conditions laid down in note 5(C) to chapter 84 and which comprise at least a central processing unit, one input unit (for example, a keyboard or a scanner), and one output unit (for example, a visual display unit or a printer).

3. For the purposes of subheading 8481.20, **the expression "valves for oleo hydraulic or pneumatic transmissions" means valves which are used specifically in the transmission of "fluid power" in a hydraulic or pneumatic system, where the energy source is supplied in the form of pressurized fluids (liquid or gas). These valves may be of any type (for example, pressure-reducing type, check type). Subheading 8481.20 takes precedence over all other subheadings of heading 8481.**

As per GRI 1, goods are first and foremost to be classified according to the applicable Section and Chapter Notes, and according to the classifications' Headings. As per the above-mentioned Chapter 84 Subheading Note 3, if the classification Subheading 8481.20 applies, which it does here (for a hydraulic valve), then it shall be used instead of any other possibly applicable valve type (check valve, etc.) classified under Heading 8481. HTSUS 8481.20.0040 provides for "flow control type" (i.e. "that regulate the flow") hydraulic valves. The correct answer is "B".

✓ **NOTE:** Multiple choices "A" and "E" make reference to Headings 8425 to 8430, which among other items, include jacks (for lifting), cranes, forklifts, elevators, bull-dozers, snowplows, etc., etc.

Heading/ Subheading	Stat. Suf- fix	Article Description	Unit of Quantity	Rates of Duty 1 General	Rates of Duty 1 Special	Rates of Duty 2
8481		Taps, cocks, valves and similar appliances, for pipes, boiler shells, tanks, vats or the like, including pressure-reducing valves and thermostatically controlled valves; parts thereof:				
8481.10.00		Pressure-reducing valves		2%	Free (A, AU, B, BH, CA, CL, CO, D, E, IL, JO, KR, MA, MX, OM, P, PA, PE, SG)	35%
	20	Hydraulic fluid power type	No. kg			
		Pneumatic fluid power type:				
	40	Filter-regulators and filter-regulator-lubricators	No. kg			
	60	Other	No. kg			
	90	Other	No. kg			
8481.20.00		Valves for oleohydraulic or pneumatic transmissions		2%	Free (A, AU, B, BH, CA, CL, CO, D, E, IL, JO, KR, MA, MX, OM, P, PA, PE, SG)	35%
		Hydraulic valves:				
		Directional control				
	10	Manual type	No. kg			
	20	Solenoid type	No. kg			
	30	Other	No. kg			
	40	Flow control type	No. kg			
	50	Other	No. kg			
		Other:				
		Directional control:				
	60	Solenoid type	No. kg			
	70	Other	No. kg			
	80	Other	No. kg			

16. Roma Sports Company intends to import backpacks into the United States. The backpacks are constructed with a cotton textile base. The textile is coated on one side with polyvinyl chloride (PVC) plastic sheeting. The coating makes up the outermost surface of the backpack. The PVC is embossed to simulate leather. What is the CLASSIFICATION of the backpacks?

A. 4202.92.1500 Trunks, suitcases, vanity cases, … …, knapsacks and backpacks, handbags, shopping bags, wallets, purses, map cases, cigarette cases, tobacco pouches, tool bags, sports bags, bottle cases, jewelry boxes, powder cases, cutlery cases and similar containers, of leather or of composition leather, of sheeting of plastics, of textile materials, of vulcanized fiber or of paperboard, or wholly or mainly covered with such materials or with paper>>Other>>With outer surface of sheeting of plastics or of textile materials>>Travel, sports and similar bags>>With outer surface of textile materials>>Of vegetable fibers and not of pile or tufted construction>>Of cotton

B. 4202.92.3305 Trunks, suitcases, vanity cases, … …, knapsacks and backpacks, handbags, shopping bags, wallets, purses, map cases, cigarette cases, tobacco pouches, tool bags, sports bags, bottle cases, jewelry boxes, powder cases, cutlery cases and similar containers, of leather or of composition leather, of sheeting of plastics, of textile materials, of vulcanized fiber or of paperboard, or wholly or mainly covered with such materials or with paper>>Other>>With outer surface of sheeting of plastics or of textile materials>>Travel, sports and similar bags>>With outer surface of textile materials>> Of paper yarn or of cotton; containing 85 percent or more by weight of silk or silk waste>>Of paper yarn

C. 4202.91.9030 Trunks, suitcases, vanity cases, … …, knapsacks and backpacks, handbags, shopping bags, wallets, purses, map cases, cigarette cases, tobacco pouches, tool bags, sports bags, bottle cases, jewelry boxes, powder cases, cutlery cases and similar containers, of leather or of composition leather, of sheeting of plastics, of textile materials, of vulcanized fiber or of paperboard, or wholly or mainly covered with such materials or with paper>>Other>> With outer surface of leather or of composition leather>>Other>>Travel, sports and similar bag

D. 4202.92.4500 Trunks, suitcases, vanity cases, … …, knapsacks and backpacks, handbags, shopping bags, wallets, purses, map cases, cigarette cases, tobacco pouches, tool bags, sports bags, bottle cases, jewelry boxes, powder cases, cutlery cases and similar containers, of leather or of composition leather, of sheeting of plastics, of textile materials, of vulcanized fiber or of paperboard, or wholly or mainly covered with such materials or with paper>>Other>>With outer surface of sheeting of plastics or of textile materials>>Travel, sports and similar bags>>Other

E. 4202.22.1500 Trunks, suitcases, vanity cases, … …, knapsacks and backpacks, handbags, shopping bags, wallets, purses, map cases, cigarette cases, tobacco pouches, tool bags, sports bags, bottle cases, jewelry boxes, powder cases, cutlery cases and similar containers, of leather or of composition leather, of sheeting of plastics, of textile materials, of vulcanized fiber or of paperboard, or wholly or mainly covered with such materials or with paper>> Handbags, whether or not with shoulder strap, including those without handle>>With outer surface of sheeting of plastics or of textile materials>> With outer surface of sheeting of plastics

 As per HTSUS Chapter 42 Additional U.S. Notes 1 & 2:

Additional U.S. Notes

1. For the purposes of heading 4202, the expression **"travel, sports and similar bags" means** goods, other than those falling in subheadings 4202.11 through 4202.39, of a kind designed for carrying clothing and other personal effects during travel, **including backpacks** and shopping bags of this heading, but does not include binocular cases, camera cases, musical instrument cases, bottle cases and similar containers.

2. For purposes of classifying articles under subheadings 4202.12, 4202.22, 4202.32, and 4202.92, **articles of textile fabric** impregnated, **coated**, covered or laminated **with plastics** (whether compact or cellular) **shall be regarded as having an outer surface of textile material or of sheeting of plastics, depending upon whether and the extent to which the textile constituent or the plastic constituent makes up the exterior surface of the article.**

a All of the multiple choices here contain the Heading 4202, which may have one of the longest HTSUS Article Descriptions in the HTSUS. The plastic, not the cotton textile, makes up the exterior surface of the backpack, so as per the above Additional U.S. Note 2, we may disregard multiple choice "A". Similarly, we may disregard "B", which is for "of paper yarn". The outer surface of the item in question is made of artificial leather, not leather, so we may disregard "C". As per Additional U.S. Note 1, "travel, sports and similar bags" includes backpacks, so we choose "D" as the right answer, not "E", which is for handbags.

Heading/ Subheading	Stat. Suf-fix	Article Description	Unit of Quantity	Rates of Duty 1 General	Rates of Duty 1 Special	2
4202 (con.)		Trunks, suitcases, vanity cases, attache cases, briefcases, school satchels, spectacle cases, binocular cases, camera cases, musical instrument cases, gun cases, holsters and similar containers; traveling bags, insulated food or beverage bags, toiletry bags, knapsacks and backpacks, handbags, shopping bags, wallets, purses, map cases, cigarette cases, tobacco pouches, tool bags, sports bags, bottle cases, jewelry boxes, powder cases, cutlery cases and similar containers, of leather or of composition leather, of sheeting of plastics, of textile materials, of vulcanized fiber or of paperboard, or wholly or mainly covered with such materials or with paper: (con.)				
		Other: (con.)				
4202.92 (con.)		With outer surface of sheeting of plastics or of textile materials: (con.)				
		Travel, sports and similar bags: (con.)				
		With outer surface of textile materials: (con.)				
4202.92.39	00	Other (870) 1/	No. kg	17.6%	Free (A, AU, BH, CA, CL, CO, D, IL, JO, KR, MA, MX, NP, OM, P, PA, PE, SG) 16.6% (E)	65%
4202.92.45	00	Other 2/	No. kg	20%	Free (A, AU, BH, CA, CL, CO, D, IL, JO, KR, MA, MX, NP, OM, P, PA, PE, R, SG) 17.5% (E)	45%
4202.92.50	00	Musical instrument cases	No.	4.2%	Free (A, AU, BH, CA, CL, CO, D, E, IL, JO, KR, MA, MX, OM, P, PA, PE, SG)	50%

17. What is the CLASSIFICATION of a stainless steel bolt imported together with a corresponding stainless steel nut? The bolt has a round head and a threaded shank that measures 5.6 mm in diameter and 27 mm in length. It is used exclusively in central heating radiators.

A. 7318.15.2051	Screws, bolts, nuts, coach screws, screw hooks, rivets, cotters, cotter pins, washers (including spring washers) and similar articles, of iron or steel>>Threaded articles>>Other screws and bolts, whether or not with their nuts or washers>>Bolts and bolts and their nuts or washers entered or exported in the same shipment>>Having shanks or threads with a diameter of 6 mm or more>>Other>>With round heads>>Of stainless steel
B. 7318.29.0000	Screws, bolts, nuts, coach screws, screw hooks, rivets, cotters, cotter pins, washers (including spring washers) and similar articles, of iron or steel>>Non-threaded articles>>Other
C. 7318.15.2010	Screws, bolts, nuts, coach screws, screw hooks, rivets, cotters, cotter pins, washers (including spring washers) and similar articles, of iron or steel>>Threaded articles>>Other screws and bolts, whether or not with their nuts or washers>>Bolts and bolts and their nuts or washers entered or exported in the same shipment>> Having shanks or threads with a diameter of less than 6 mm
D. 7318.16.0060	Screws, bolts, nuts, coach screws, screw hooks, rivets, cotters, cotter pins, washers (including spring washers) and similar articles, of iron or steel>>Threaded articles>>Nuts>>Other>>Of stainless steel
E. 7318.19.0000	Screws, bolts, nuts, coach screws, screw hooks, rivets, cotters, cotter pins, washers (including spring washers) and similar articles, of iron or steel>>Threaded articles>>Other

As per HTSUS Chapter 73 (see following page):

We may eliminate "A" since the item in question has shanks of less than 6 mm in diameter. Next, we may eliminate "B" as the bolt in question is threaded. "C" is a correct description of the item in question, which logically excludes the alternate of "Other" "than this" in "E". Further, in regards to "C" & "D", since the item is prima facie (i.e. classifiable under multiple classifications) we jump to GRI 3. GRI 3(a) does not apply as "C" and "D" each refer to part only of the bolt ("C") & nut ("D") set/composite good. So, on to GRI 3(b), which says to classify based on the component that gives the set its essential character, the bolt (not the nut). The correct answer is "C".

✓ **JUST A SIDE NOTE:** The "shank" of a bolt is the narrow length of the bolt, either threaded and/or non-threaded, and does not include the head.

Heading/ Subheading	Stat. Suf-fix	Article Description	Unit of Quantity	Rates of Duty 1 General	Rates of Duty 1 Special	Rates of Duty 2
7318 (con.)		Screws, bolts, nuts, coach screws, screw hooks, rivets, cotters, cotter pins, washers (including spring washers) and similar articles, of iron or steel: (con.)				
		Threaded articles: (con.)				
7318.15		Other screws and bolts, whether or not with their nuts or washers:				
7318.15.20		Bolts and bolts and their nuts or washers entered or exported in the same shipment		Free		3.5%
	10	Having shanks or threads with a diameter of less than 6 mm	kg			
		Having shanks or threads with a diameter of 6 mm or more:				
	20	Track bolts	kg			
	30	Structural bolts	kg			
		Bent bolts:				
	41	Right-angle anchor bolts	kg			
	46	Other	kg			
		Other:				
		With round heads:				
	51	Of stainless steel	kg			
	55	Other	kg			
		With hexagonal heads:				
	61	Of stainless steel	kg			
	65	Other	kg			
		Other:				
	91	Of stainless steel	kg			
	95	Other	kg			
7318.15.40	00	Machine screws 9.5 mm or more in length and 3.2 mm or more in diameter (not including cap screws)	kg	Free		2.2¢/kg
7318.15.50		Studs		Free		45%
	30	Of stainless steel	kg			
		Other:				
		Continuously threaded rod:				
	51	Of alloy steel	kg			
	56	Other	kg			
	90	Other	kg			

18. What is required for men's 100% polyester (synthetic) trousers to be classified as water resistant?

A. The trousers must be completely water proof with no penetration of water when tested for water resistance under AATCC Test Method 35.

B. The trousers must have critically sealed seams, be visibly coated with plastic, and when sprayed with water using a head pressure of 600 millimeters, not have more than 1.0 gram of water penetrate after two minutes when tested in accordance with AATCC Test Method 35.

C. Men's trousers cannot be classified as water resistant.

D. The trousers must have a water resistance such that, under a head pressure of 600 millimeters, not more than 1.0 gram of water penetrates after two minutes when tested in accordance with AATCC Test Method 35 and the water resistance must be as a result of an application of rubber or plastics on the outer shell, lining, or inner lining.

E. The trousers must have a water resistance such that, under a head pressure of 600 millimeters, not more than 1.0 gram of water penetrates after two minutes when tested in accordance with AATCC Test Method 35.

 As per HTSUS Chapter 62 Additional U.S. Note 2:

2. For the purposes of subheadings 6201.92.17, 6201.92.35, 6201.93.47, 6201.93.60, 6202.92.05, 6202.92.30, 6202.93.07, 6202.93.48, 6203.41.01, 6203.41.25, 6203.43.03, 6203.43.11, 6203.43.55, 6203.43.75, 6204.61.05, 6204.61.60, 6204.63.02, 6204.63.09, 6204.63.55, 6204.63.75 and 6211.20.15, the term **"water resistant" means that garments classifiable in those subheadings must have a water resistance** (see current version of ASTM D7017) such that, **under a head pressure of 600 millimeters, not more than 1.0 gram of water penetrates after two minutes when tested in accordance with the current version of AATCC Test Method 35. This water resistance must be the result of a rubber or plastics application to the outer shell, lining or inner lining.**

 The correct answer and definition of "water resistant" is in "D".

✓ **NOTE:** "ASTM", as referenced in the above Additional U.S. Note, stands for American Society for Testing and Materials. ASTM is a global products and services standards organization, is headquartered in Pennsylvania, and has a membership of over 30,000 entities.

(This Page Intentionally Left Blank)

19. What is the CLASSIFICATION of a machine that produces glass fibers? This machine is a highly specialized piece of equipment that operates at elevated temperatures to produce glass fibers using molten glass. Due to the size of the complete machine, it cannot be shipped on a single conveyance. It will enter the United States disassembled and in multiple shipments within 6 days to the Port of Newark. After the components are imported, they will be delivered directly to the customer and will be assembled then.

A. 8475.29.0000	Machines for assembling electric or electronic lamps, tubes or flashbulbs, in glass envelopes; machines for manufacturing or hot working glass or glassware; parts thereof>>Machines for manufacturing or hot working glass or glassware>>Other
B. 8444.00.0090	Machines for extruding, drawing, texturing or cutting man-made textile materials>>Other
C. 8479.89.9499	Machines and mechanical appliances having individual functions, not specified or included elsewhere in this chapter; parts thereof>>Other machines and mechanical appliances>>Other>>Other>>Other
D. 8464.90.0110	Machine tools for working stone, ceramics, concrete, asbestos-cement or like mineral materials or for cold working glass>>Other>>Other
E. 8475.90.9000	Machines for assembling electric or electronic lamps, tubes or flashbulbs, in glass envelopes; machines for manufacturing or hot working glass or glassware; parts thereof>>Parts>>Other

 As per HTSUS GRI 2(a):

2. (a) Any reference in a heading to an article shall be taken to include a reference to that article incomplete or unfinished, provided that, as entered, the incomplete or unfinished article has the essential character of the complete or finished article. It shall also include a reference to that article complete or finished (or falling to be classified as complete or finished by virtue of this rule), entered unassembled or disassembled.

As per GRI 2(a), items maintaining their essential character, even if unassembled, should be classified under the applicable classification as if they were assembled. The specialty glass fiber machine in question does not simply turn into a bunch of generic nuts and bolts when in unassembled form for shipment. It maintains its essential character as a disassembled glass fiber machine. The correct answer is "A" (as opposed to "E").

✓ **JUST A SIDE NOTE:** "cold working" glass (as opposed to "hot working") involves grinding, sandblasting, and other mechanical means for shaping glass without the addition of heat.

Heading/ Subheading	Stat. Suf- fix	Article Description	Unit of Quantity	Rates of Duty 1 General	Special	2
8474		Machinery for sorting, screening, separating, washing, crushing, grinding, mixing or kneading earth, stone, ores or other mineral substances, in solid (including powder or paste) form; machinery for agglomerating, shaping or molding solid mineral fuels, ceramic paste, unhardened cements, plastering materials or other mineral products in powder or paste form; machines for forming foundry molds of sand; parts thereof:				
8474.10.00		Sorting, screening, separating or washing machines		Free		35%
	10	Portable	No.			
	90	Stationary	No.			
8474.20.00		Crushing or grinding machines		Free		35%
	10	Portable	No.			
		Stationary:				
	50	Crushing	No.			
	70	Other	No.			
		Mixing or kneading machines:				
8474.31.00	00	Concrete or mortar mixers	No.	Free		35%
8474.32.00	00	Machines for mixing mineral substances with bitumen	No.	Free		35%
8474.39.00	00	Other	No.	Free		35%
8474.80.00		Other machinery		Free		35%
		For agglomerating, shaping or molding solid mineral fuels, ceramic paste, unhardened cements, plastering materials or other mineral products in powder or paste form:				
	10	Designed for use with ceramic paste, unhardened cements and plastering materials	No.			
	15	Other	No.			
	20	Machines for forming foundry molds of sand	No.			
	80	Other	No.			
8474.90.00		Parts		Free		35%
	10	Of sorting, screening, separating or washing machines	X			
	20	Of crushing or grinding machines	X			
	50	Of mixing or kneading machines	X			
	90	Other	X			
8475		Machines for assembling electric or electronic lamps, tubes or flashbulbs, in glass envelopes; machines for manufacturing or hot working glass or glassware; parts thereof:				
8475.10.00	00	Machines for assembling electric or electronic lamps, tubes or flashbulbs, in glass envelopes	No.	Free		35%
		Machines for manufacturing or hot working glass or glassware:				
8475.21.00	00	Machines for making optical fibers and preforms thereof	No.	Free		35%
8475.29.00	00	Other	No.	Free		35%
8475.90		Parts:				
8475.90.10	00	Of machines for assembling electric or electronic lamps, tubes or flashbulbs, in glass envelopes	X	Free		35%
8475.90.90	00	Other	X	Free		35%

20. What is the CLASSIFICATION of an unfolded, uncoated, rectangular sheet of gift-type tissue paper containing 30 percent of fibers obtained by a chemi-mechanical process, weighing 27 g/m^2, measuring 50cm by 80cm, that is colored throughout the mass, and that has been printed with a flower design?

A. 4804.39.4041 Uncoated kraft paper and paperboard, in rolls or sheets, other than that of heading 4802 or 4803>>Other kraft paper and paperboard weighing 150 g/m^2 or less>>Other>>Wrapping paper>>Other>>Tissue paper having a basis weight not exceeding 29 g/m^2, in sheets

B. 4811.90.9010 Paper, paperboard, cellulose wadding and webs of cellulose fibers, coated, impregnated, covered, surface-colored, surface-decorated or printed, in rolls or rectangular (including square) sheets, of any size, other than goods of the kind described in heading 4803, 4809 or 4810>>Other paper, paperboard, cellulose wadding and webs of cellulose fibers>>Other>>Tissue papers having a basis weight not exceeding 29 g/m^2, in sheets

C. 4803.00.4000 Toilet or facial tissue stock, towel or napkin stock and similar paper of a kind used for household or sanitary purposes, cellulose wadding and webs of cellulose fibers, whether or not creped, crinkled, embossed, perforated, surface-colored, surface decorated or printed, in rolls or sheets>>Other

D. 4811.90.6010 Paper, paperboard, cellulose wadding and webs of cellulose fibers, coated, impregnated, covered, surface-colored, surface-decorated or printed, in rolls or rectangular (including square) sheets, of any size, other than goods of the kind described in heading 4803, 4809 or 4810>>Other paper, paperboard, cellulose wadding and webs of cellulose fibers>>In strips or rolls of a width exceeding 15 cm or in rectangular (including square) sheets with one side exceeding 36 cm and the other side exceeding 15 cm in the unfolded state>>Other>>Other>>Other>>Weighing over 15 g/m^2 but not over 30 g/m^2

E. 4802.69.3000 Uncoated paper and paperboard, of a kind used for writing, printing or other graphic purposes, and non perforated punch-cards and punch tape paper, in rolls or rectangular (including square) sheets, of any size, other than paper of heading 4801 or 4803; hand-made paper and paperboard>>Other paper and paperboard, of which more than 10 percent by weight of the total fiber content consists of fibers obtained by a mechanical or chemi-mechanical process>>Other>>Other

As per Chapter 48 Note 6:

6. In this chapter "kraft paper and paperboard" means paper and paperboard of which not less than 80 percent by weight of the total fiber content consists of fibers obtained by the chemical sulfate or soda processes.

We may eliminate "A" as the Chapter 48 Note 6 definition of "kraft paper" shows that the item in question does not contain a high enough % of fibers obtained by a chemi-mechanical process to qualify as kraft paper. We may eliminate multiple choice "B" as its description is "Other" than multiple choice "D", which is a correct description of the item in question exceeding 36 cm x 15 cm. We may eliminate "C" as the gift-type tissue paper in question is not toilet paper, facial tissue, cellulose wadding, etc. As previously mentioned, "D" is a correct description of the item and we may choose it if there is no other classification with a correct description to choose from (i.e. prima facie). We may disregard "E" as the item in question is not for writing, printing, punch card/tape, and not hand-made. So, through the process of elimination, we may infer that "D" is the correct answer.

✓ **NOTE:** Chapter 48 Note 5 confirms that the gift-type tissue paper commodity in question is not of a kind used for writing, etc. as described in multiple choice "E".

5. For the purposes of heading 4802, **the expressions "paper and paperboard, of a kind used for writing, printing or other graphic purposes" and "nonperforated punch-cards and punch tape paper" mean paper** and paperboard made mainly from bleached pulp or from pulp **obtained by a mechanical or chemi-mechanical process and satisfying any of the following criteria:**

For paper or paperboard weighing not more than 150 g/m$_2$:

(a) Containing 10 percent or more of fibers obtained by a mechanical or chemi-mechanical process, and

1. weighing not more than 80 g/m$_2$, or

2. colored throughout the mass; or

Heading/ Subheading	Stat. Suf- fix	Article Description	Unit of Quantity	Rates of Duty 1 General	Special	2
4811 (con.)		Paper, paperboard, cellulose wadding and webs of cellulose fibers, coated, impregnated, covered, surface-colored, surface-decorated or printed, in rolls or rectangular (including square) sheets, of any size, other than goods of the kind described in heading 4803, 4809 or 4810: (con.)				
4811.90		Other paper, paperboard, cellulose wadding and webs of cellulose fibers:				
		In strips or rolls of a width exceeding 15 cm or in rectangular (including square) sheets with one side exceeding 36 cm and the other side exceeding 15 cm in the unfolded state:				
4811.90.10	00	Handmade paper	kg	Free		27%
		Other:				
4811.90.20	00	Wholly or partly covered with flock, gelatin, metal or metal solutions	kg	Free		22.5%
		Other:				
4811.90.30	00	Impregnated with latex	kg	Free		25%
		Other:				
4811.90.40		Weighing not over 15 g/m²		Free		30%
	10	Tissue papers, in sheets	kg			
	90	Other	kg			
4811.90.60		Weighing over 15 g/m² but not over 30 g/m²		Free		20%
	10	Tissue papers having a basis weight not exceeding 29 g/m², in sheets	kg			
	90	Other	kg			
4811.90.80		Weighing over 30 g/m²		Free		18.5%
	20	Gift Wrap (other than tissue)	kg			
	30	Direct thermal coated paper	kg			
	50	Other	kg			
4811.90.90		Other		Free		35%
	10	Tissue papers having a basis weight not exceeding 29 g/m², in sheets	kg			
	30	Direct thermal coated paper	kg			
	35	Paper in sheets, lined or ruled, having a width of 152.4 to 360 mm inclusive and a length of 225.25 to 360 mm inclusive	kg			
	80	Other	kg			
4812.00.00	00	Filter blocks, slabs and plates, of paper pulp	kg	Free		20%
4813		Cigarette paper, whether or not cut to size or in the form of booklets or tubes:				
4813.10.00	00	In the form of booklets or tubes	kg	Free 1/		60% 1/
4813.20.00	00	In rolls of a width not exceeding 5 cm	kg	Free		60%
4813.90.00	00	Other	kg	Free		60%

21. What is the CLASSIFICATION of an unadorned basket constructed of woven 6 mm wide plastic strips? The basket measures 10" square by 4" deep and includes an arched handle.

A. 4202.29.1000 Trunks, suitcases, vanity cases, attache cases, briefcases, school satchels, spectacle cases, binocular cases, camera cases, musical instrument cases, gun cases, holsters and similar containers; traveling bags, insulated food or beverage bags, toiletry bags, knapsacks and backpacks, handbags, shopping bags, wallets, purses, map cases, cigarette cases, tobacco pouches, tool bags, sports bags, bottle cases, jewelry boxes, powder cases, cutlery cases and similar containers, of leather or of composition leather, of sheeting of plastics, of textile materials, of vulcanized fiber or of paperboard, or wholly or mainly covered with such materials or with paper>>Handbags, whether or not with shoulder strap, including those without handle>>Other>>Of materials (other than leather, composition leather, sheeting of plastics, textile materials, vulcanized fiber or paperboard) wholly or mainly covered with paper>>Of plastics

B. 3926.90.1000 Other articles of plastics and articles of other materials of headings 3901 to 3914>>Other>>Buckets and pails

C. 4602.90.0000 Basketwork, wickerwork and other articles, made directly to shape from plaiting materials or made up from articles of heading 4601; articles of loofah>>Other

D. 3923.90.0080 Articles for the conveyance or packing of goods, of plastics; stoppers, lids, caps and other closures, of plastics>>Other>>Other

E. 4602.11.0900 Basketwork, wickerwork and other articles, made directly to shape from plaiting materials or made up from articles of heading 4601; articles of loofah>>Of vegetable materials>>Of bamboo>>Other baskets and bags, whether or not lined>>Other

 As per HTSUS Chapter 42 Note 3, Chapter 39 Note 2, & Chapter 46 Note 1:

(Chapter 42)
3. (A) In addition to the provisions of note 2, above, heading **4202 does not cover**:
(a) Bags made of sheeting of plastics, whether or not printed, with handles, not designed for prolonged use (heading 3923);
(b) Articles of plaiting materials (heading 4602).

(Chapter 39)
2. This chapter does not cover:
... ...
(n) **Plaits**, wickerwork **or other articles of chapter 46;**

(Chapter 46)
1. In this chapter the expression "plaiting materials" means materials in a state or form suitable for plaiting, interlacing or similar processes; it includes straw, osier or willow, bamboos, rattans, rushes, reeds, strips of wood, strips of other vegetable material (for example, strips of bark, narrow leaves and raffia or other strips obtained from broad leaves), unspun natural textile fibers, monofilament **and strip and the like of plastics** and strips of paper, but not strips of leather or composition leather or of felt or nonwovens, human hair, horsehair, textile rovings or yarns, or monofilament and strip and the like of chapter 54.

a As per the Chapter 46 Note on what qualifies as plaited basketwork, it appears that the item in question will be classified under 4602, which is either multiple choice "C" or "E". As per the above-mentioned Chapter 42 and Chapter 39 Notes that list what these chapters do not cover, we may disregard "A", "B", and "D". The plastic basket is not made of vegetable materials, so we may disregard "E". We are left with "C", which is NOT and INCORRECT description of the item in question, and is the correct answer.

✓ **NOTE:** "Woven" is the "interlaced" fibers or strips in one direction with others at a right angle to them.

Heading/ Subheading	Stat. Suf-fix	Article Description	Unit of Quantity	Rates of Duty 1 General	Rates of Duty 1 Special	Rates of Duty 2
4602 (con.)		Basketwork, wickerwork and other articles, made directly to shape from plaiting materials or made up from articles of heading 4601; articles of loofah: (con.)				
		Of vegetable materials: (con.)				
4602.19 (con.)		Other: (con.)				
		Other:				
		Of willow or wood:				
4602.19.35	00	Wickerwork	No.	Free		45%
4602.19.45	00	Other	No.	6.6%	Free (A, AU, BH, CA, CL, CO, D, E, IL, JO, KR, MA, MX, OM, P, PA, PE, SG)	45%
		Other:				
4602.19.60	00	Wickerwork	X	Free		25%
4602.19.80	00	Other	X	2.3%	Free (A, AU, BH, CA, CL, CO, D, E, IL, JO, KR, MA, MX, OM, P, PA, PE, SG)	25%
4602.90.00	00	Other	X	3.5%	Free (A, AU, BH, CA, CL, CO, D, E, IL, JO, KR, MA, MX, OM, P, PA, PE, SG)	80%

22. What is the CLASSIFICATION of a machine that forms pre-scored paperboard into boxes which are used for packing pharmaceuticals? The machine consists of a conveyer-type feeding section, folding and gluing sections, and a controller.

A. 8441.30.0000 Other machinery for making up paper pulp, paper or paperboard, including cutting machines of all kinds, and parts thereof>>Machines for making cartons, boxes, cases, tubes, drums or similar containers, other than by molding

B. 8479.89.9499 Machines and mechanical appliances having individual functions, not specified or included elsewhere in this chapter; parts thereof>>Other machines and mechanical appliances>>Other>>Other>>Other

C. 8422.30.9191 Dishwashing machines; machinery for cleaning or drying bottles or other containers; machinery for filling, closing, sealing or labeling bottles, cans, boxes, bags or other containers; machinery for capsuling bottles, jars, tubes and similar containers; other packing or wrapping machinery (including heat-shrink wrapping machinery); machinery for aerating beverages; parts thereof>>Machinery for filling, closing, sealing or labeling bottles, cans, boxes, bags or other containers; machinery for capsuling bottles, jars, tubes and similar containers; machinery for aerating beverages>>Other>>Other>>Machinery for filling, closing, sealing, capsuling or labeling boxes, bags or similar containers>>Other

D. 8439.20.0010 Machinery for making pulp of fibrous cellulosic material or for making or finishing paper or paperboard (other than the machinery of heading 8419); parts thereof>>Machinery for making paper or paperboard>>New

E. 8441.80.0000 Other machinery for making up paper pulp, paper or paperboard, including cutting machines of all kinds, and parts thereof>>Other machinery

 As per HTSUS Section XVI (Chapters 84 & 85) Note 4 & Chapter 84 Note 7:

(Section XVI Note)

4. **Where a machine** (including a combination of machines) **consists of individual components** (whether separate or interconnected by piping, by transmission devices, by electric cables or by other devices) **intended to contribute together to a clearly defined function covered by one of the headings in chapter 84 or chapter 85, then the whole falls to be classified in the heading appropriate to that function.**

(Chapter 84 Note)

7. **A machine which is used for more than one purpose is, for the purposes of classification, to be treated as if its principal purpose were its sole purpose.**

Subject to note 2 to this chapter and note 3 to section XVI, a machine the principal purpose of which is not described in any heading or for which no one purpose is the principal purpose is, unless the context otherwise requires, to be classified in heading 8479. Heading 8479 also covers machines for making rope or cable (for example, stranding, twisting or cabling machines) from metal wire, textile yarn or any other material or from a combination of such materials.

The item in question is a machine that forms (i.e. puts together or makes up) boxes from paperboard. "A" is not an incorrect description of the item, so this may be the answer. See also the above applicable Section and Chapter Notes. "B", which is for machines that are not otherwise classifiable in Chapter 84, may be disregarded as the item in question is at least already classifiable under "A". We may disregard "C" as the item in question isn't specifically for "filling, closing, sealing, capsuling or labeling boxes". Furthermore, we may disregard "D" and "E" as the item in question is not for making paper or paperboard, and not for cutting. Rather, the item in question takes already pre-scored paperboard and forms it into boxes. We are thus only left with the correct answer is "A".

✓ **JUST A SIDE NOTE:** A "pre-scored" paper item is something that has been partially cut, notched, or pressed to make for easier folding or tearing of the paper.

Heading/ Subheading	Stat. Suf-fix	Article Description	Unit of Quantity	Rates of Duty 1 General	Special	2
8439		Machinery for making pulp of fibrous cellulosic material or for making or finishing paper or paperboard (other than the machinery of heading 8419); parts thereof:				
8439.10.00		Machinery for making pulp of fibrous cellulosic material		Free		35%
	10	New	No.			
	90	Used or rebuilt	No.			
8439.20.00		Machinery for making paper or paperboard		Free		35%
	10	New	No.			
	90	Used or rebuilt	No.			
8439.30.00	00	Machinery for finishing paper or paperboard	No.	Free		35%
		Parts:				
8439.91		Of machinery for making pulp of fibrous cellulosic materials:				
8439.91.10	00	Bed plates, roll bars and other stock-treating parts	X	Free		20%
8439.91.90	00	Other	X	Free		35%
8439.99		Other:				
8439.99.10	00	Of machinery for making paper or paperboard	X	Free		35%
8439.99.50	00	Of machinery for finishing paper or paperboard	X	Free		35%
8440		Bookbinding machinery, including book-sewing machines, and parts thereof:				
8440.10.00	00	Machinery	No.	Free		25%
8440.90.00	00	Parts	X	Free		25%
8441		Other machinery for making up paper pulp, paper or paperboard, including cutting machines of all kinds, and parts thereof:				
8441.10.00	00	Cutting machines	No.	Free		35%
8441.20.00	00	Machines for making bags, sacks or envelopes	No.	Free		35%
8441.30.00	00	Machines for making cartons, boxes, cases, tubes, drums or similar containers, other than by molding	No.	Free		35%
8441.40.00	00	Machines for molding articles in paper pulp, paper or paperboard	No.	Free		35%
8441.80.00	00	Other machinery	No.	Free		35%
8441.90.00	00	Parts	X	Free		35%
8442		Machinery, apparatus and equipment (other than the machines of headings 8456 to 8465), for preparing or making plates, cylinders or other printing components; plates, cylinders and other printing components; plates, cylinders and lithographic stones, prepared for printing purposes (for example, planed, grained or polished); parts thereof:				
8442.30.01		Machinery, apparatus and equipment		Free		Free
	10	Phototypesetting and composing machines	No.			
	50	Other machinery, apparatus and equipment	No.			
8442.40.00	00	Parts of the foregoing machinery, apparatus or equipment	X	Free		Free
8442.50		Plates, cylinders and other printing components; plates, cylinders and lithographic stones, prepared for printing purposes (for example, planed, grained or polished):				
8442.50.10	00	Plates	No.	Free		25%
8442.50.90	00	Other	No.	Free		60%

23. What is the correct CLASSIFICATION for this Light-emitting diode (LED) lamp (bulb)? The lamp or light bulb is described as a shape CA lamp (bulb) that will be used in a chandelier or a ceiling light fixture. It consists of an aluminum screw-in base and has a decorative bent-tip transparent plastic housing (envelope).

A. 9405.10.4010 Lamps and lighting fittings including searchlights and spotlights and parts thereof, not elsewhere specified or included; illuminated signs, illuminated nameplates and the like, having a permanently fixed light source, and parts thereof not elsewhere specified or included>>Chandeliers and other electric ceiling or wall lighting fittings, excluding those of a kind used for lighting public open spaces or thoroughfares>>Of base metal>>Of brass>>Household

B. 8539.50.0010 Electrical filament or discharge lamps, including sealed beam lamp units and ultraviolet or infrared lamps; arc lamps; light-emitting diode (LED) lamps; parts thereof>>Light-emitting diode (LED) lamps>>Of a type specified in statistical note 8(a) to this chapter

C. 8543.70.7100 Electrical machines and apparatus, having individual functions, not specified or included elsewhere in this chapter; parts>>Other machines and apparatus>>Electric luminescent lamps

D. 8539.31.0060 Electrical filament or discharge lamps, including sealed beam lamp units and ultraviolet or infrared lamps; arc lamps; light-emitting diode (LED) lamps; parts thereof>>Discharge lamps, other than ultraviolet lamps>>Fluorescent, hot cathode>>Other>>With a single screw-in base

E. 8539.50.0020 Electrical filament or discharge lamps, including sealed beam lamp units and ultraviolet or infrared lamps; arc lamps; light-emitting diode (LED) lamps; parts thereof>>Light-emitting diode (LED) lamps>>Of a type specified in statistical note 8(b) to this chapter

 As per HTSUS Chapter 94 Note 1(f) & Chapter 85 Statistical Note 8(b):

(Chapter 94 Note 1(f))

Notes

1. **This chapter does not cover**:

… …

(f) **Lamps or lighting fittings of chapter 85**;

(Chapter 85 Statistical Note 8(b))

8. For statistical reporting purposes under subheading 8539.50.00, the types of light-emitting (LED) lamps are defined by American National Standards Institute for Electric Lamps as follows:
(a) ANSI shapes A, BT, P, PS or T described under 8539.50.0010;
(b) ANSI shapes B, BA, C, CA, DC, F, G or ST described under 8539.50.0020;
(c) ANSI shapes R, BR or PAR described under 8539.50.0030; or
(d) ANSI shapes MR11, MR16 or MRX16 described under 8539.50.0040.

a We may eliminate multiple choice "A" as per the above-mentioned Chapter 94 note states that Chapter 94 does not cover lamps (LED, etc.) classifiable in Chapter 85. "B" may be disregarded but "E" is a nominee for correct answer as per the above Chapter 85 Statistical Note. "C" may be disregarded as the item in question is not an electric luminescent lamp. "D" may be disregarded as the item in question is not a fluorescent lamp. Through the process of elimination, we may deduce that the correct answer is "E".

✓ **INTERESTINGLY ENOUGH:** According to thesimpledollar.com, the average life of a traditional incandescent light bulb is just 1,200 hours. Compact Fluorescent Lights (CFL) average 8,000 hours. LED's on the other hand average 25,000 hours.

Heading/ Subheading	Stat. Suf-fix	Article Description	Unit of Quantity	Rates of Duty 1 General	Rates of Duty 1 Special	Rates of Duty 2
8539 (con.)		Electrical filament or discharge lamps, including sealed beam lamp units and ultraviolet or infrared lamps; arc lamps; light-emitting diode (LED) lamps; parts thereof: (con.)				
		Ultraviolet or infrared lamps; arc lamps:				
8539.41.00	00	Arc lamps	No.	2.6%	Free (A, AU, BH, CA, CL, CO, D, E, IL, JO, KR, MA, MX, OM, P, PA, PE, SG)	35%
8539.49.00		Other		2.4%	Free (A, AU, BH, CA, CL, CO, D, E, IL, JO, KR, MA, MX, OM, P, PA, PE, SG)	35%
	40	Ultraviolet lamps	No.			
	80	Other	No.			
8539.50.00		Light-emitting diode (LED) lamps		2%	Free (A, AU, BH, CA, CL, CO, D, E, IL, JO, KR, MA, MX, OM, P, PA, PE, SG)	20%
	10	Of a type specified in statistical note 8(a) to this chapter	No.			
	20	Of a type specified in statistical note 8(b) to this chapter	No.			
	30	Of a type specified in statistical note 8(c) to this chapter	No.			
	40	Of a type specified in statistical note 8(d) to this chapter	No.			
	50	Straight linear tube	No.			
	90	Other	No.			
8539.90.00	00	Parts	X	2.6%	Free (A, AU, BH, CA, CL, CO, D, E, IL, JO, KR, MA, MX, OM, P, PA, PE, SG)	35%

24. What is the CLASSIFICATION of an automatic baseball pitching machine that releases five time-delayed balls in succession? The pitching machine is constructed of bright colored plastic and operates using four D batteries, which power the launcher and audible sound that signals when the next ball is coming. The product also includes a hollow yellow plastic bat and five white hollow plastic balls. Additionally, beginners can convert the product into a miniature T-ball set. It is recommended for children aged 3 years and older.

A. 9504.90.9080 Video game consoles and machines, articles for arcade, table or parlor games, including pinball machines, bagatelle, billiards and special tables for casino games; automatic bowling alley equipment; parts and accessories thereof>>Other>>Other>>Other>>Other

B. 9506.69.2040 Articles and equipment for general physical exercise, gymnastics, athletics, other sports (including table-tennis) or outdoor games, not specified or included elsewhere in this chapter; swimming pools and wading pools; parts and accessories thereof>>Balls, other than golf balls and table-tennis balls>>Other>>Baseballs and softballs>>Baseballs

C. 9503.00.0073 Tricycles, scooters, pedal cars and similar wheeled toys; dolls' carriages; dolls, other toys; reduced-scale ("scale") models and similar recreational models, working or not; puzzles of all kinds; parts and accessories thereof>>"Children's products" as defined in 15 U.S.C. § 2052>>Other>>Labeled or determined by importer as intended for use by persons>>3 to 12 years of age

D. 9503.00.0071 Tricycles, scooters, pedal cars and similar wheeled toys; dolls' carriages; dolls, other toys; reduced-scale ("scale") model and similar recreational models, working or not; puzzles of all kinds; parts and accessories thereof>>"Children's products" as defined in 15 U.S.C. § 2052>>Other>>Labeled or determined by importer as intended for use by persons>> Under 3 years of age

E. 9506.99.1500 Articles and equipment for general physical exercise, gymnastics, athletics, other sports (including table-tennis) or outdoor games, not specified or included elsewhere in this chapter; swimming pools and wading pools; parts and accessories thereof>>Other>>Other>>Baseball articles and equipment, except balls, and parts and accessories thereof

As per HTSUS Chapter 95 Statistical Note 1:

Statistical note

1. **In heading 9503, classification is based on the youngest age for which the product is intended**. For example, an item labeled "For ages 2–5" would be appropriately classified in the "Under 3 years of age" category. Parts and accessories, if not specifically labeled for a specific age, should be classified under the age designation that would be applicable to the finished retail product of which it is a component or in which it is incorporated.

This question I found to be a little tricky. Let's start from the top. We may eliminate "A" as this does not, in any way, describe the item in question. We may disregard "B" as it is for "baseballs", yet the "baseball" pitching machine includes only "hollow plastic balls". "C" is a correct description of the product (other toys for 3 to 12-year olds), but the mutually exclusive "D" is not. "E" also appears to be a correct description, however it should only be applied when the article or equipment to be classified is not otherwise "specified or included elsewhere in this chapter (95)". The article is provided for in the correct answer is "C".

✓ **NOTE:** As made reference to in multiple choice "C", 15 U.S.C. § 2052 defines the term "children's product" as "a consumer product designed or intended primarily for children 12 years of age or younger". The examinee is not expected to know this, but would probably otherwise correctly assume this or something similar.

Heading/ Subheading	Stat. Suf-fix	Article Description	Unit of Quantity	Rates of Duty 1 General	Special	2
9503.00.00		Tricycles, scooters, pedal cars and similar wheeled toys; dolls' carriages; dolls, other toys; reduced-scale ("scale") models and similar recreational models, working or not; puzzles of all kinds; parts and accessories thereof		Free		70%
		"Children's products" as defined in 15 U.S.C. § 2052:				
		Inflatable toy balls, balloons and punchballs, of rubber:				
		Labeled or determined by importer as intended for use by persons:				
	11	Under 3 years of age	No.			
	13	3 to 12 years of age	No.			
		Other:				
		Labeled or determined by importer as intended for use by persons:				
	71	Under 3 years of age	X			
	73	3 to 12 years of age	X			
	90	Other	X			

25. What is the CLASSIFICATION of a dinnerware plate that is made of earthenware, measures 27.9 cm in maximum diameter, is valued at 70 cents per plate, and is offered for sale in the same pattern as a soup bowl? No other articles are offered for sale in that same pattern and the soup bowl is not imported in the same shipment as the plate.

A. 6911.10.3710 Tableware, kitchenware, other household articles and toilet articles, of porcelain or china>>Tableware and kitchenware>>Other>>Other>>Available in specified sets>>In any pattern for which the aggregate value of … …

B. 6911.10.5200 Tableware, kitchenware, other household articles and toilet articles, of porcelain or china>>Tableware and kitchenware>>Other>>Other>>Other>> Cups valued over $8 but not over $29 per dozen; saucers valued over … …

C. 6912.00.3510 Ceramic tableware, kitchenware, other household articles and toilet articles, other than of porcelain or china>>Tableware and kitchenware>>Other>>Other>>Available in specified sets>>In any pattern for which the aggregate value of the articles listed in additional U.S. note 6(b) of this chapter is not over $38>>Plates not over 27.9 cm in maximum dimension; teacups and saucers; mugs; soups, fruits and cereals, the foregoing not over 22.9 cm in maximum dimension

D. 6912.00.4500 Ceramic tableware, kitchenware, other household articles and toilet articles, other than of porcelain or china>>Tableware and kitchenware>>Other>>Other>>Other>> Cups valued over $5.25 per dozen; saucers valued over $3 per dozen; soups, oatmeals and cereals valued over $6 per dozen; plates not over 22.9 cm in maximum diameter and valued over $6 per dozen; plates over 22.9 but not over 27.9 cm in maximum diameter and valued over $8.50 per dozen; platters or chop dishes valued over $35 per dozen; sugars valued over $21 per dozen; creamers valued over $15 per dozen; and beverage servers valued over $42 per dozen

E. 6912.00.4810 Ceramic tableware, kitchenware, other household articles and toilet articles, other than of porcelain or china>>Tableware and kitchenware>>Other>>Other>>Other>>Other>>Suitable for food or drink contact.

As per HTSUS Chapter 69 Additional U.S. Note 5(c) & 6:

(c) The term "earthenware" embraces ceramic ware, whether or not glazed or decorated, having a fired body which contains clay as an essential ingredient, and will absorb more than 3 percent of its weight of water.

6. For the purposes of headings 6911 and 6912:

(a) **The term "available in specified sets"** embraces plates, cups, saucers and other articles principally used for preparing, serving or storing food or beverages, or food or beverage ingredients, which are sold or offered for sale in the same pattern, but **no article is classifiable as being "available in specified sets" unless it is of a pattern in which at least the articles listed below in (b) of this note are sold or offered for sale.**

… …

12 plates of the size nearest to 26.7 cm in maximum dimension, sold or offered for sale,
12 plates of the size nearest to 15.3 cm in maximum dimension, sold or offered for sale,
12 tea cups and their saucers, sold or offered for sale,
12 soups of the size nearest to 17.8 cm in maximum dimension, sold or offered for sale,
… …
1 sugar of largest capacity, sold or offered for sale,
1 creamer of largest capacity, sold or offered for sale.

The item in question is made of earthenware, which as per the above-mentioned Chapter Note 5(c), includes ceramic ware. Accordingly, we may disregard "A" and "B" as they are classifications for porcelain or china. "C" is a classification for applicable items "available in specified sets". We may disregard "C" as the plate in question shares the same pattern with only a soup bowl. These two items, and by themselves, however, do not constitute being "available in specified sets" (the 27.9 cm plate is too large, no tea cups of same pattern, etc., etc.). We may disregard "D" as the plate in question is valued only at $8.40 per dozen ($ 0.70 x 12 = $8.40) as opposed to "D", which is a classification for applicable plates not over 27.9 cm BUT valued over $8.50 per dozen. "E" is "Other" than "D", and if we were to presume that the "dinnerware" plate was suitable for food contact, we could infer that the correct answer is "E".

Heading/ Subheading	Stat. Suf-fix	Article Description	Unit of Quantity	Rates of Duty 1 General	Rates of Duty 1 Special	2
6912.00 (con.)		Ceramic tableware, kitchenware, other household articles and toilet articles, other than of porcelain or china: (con.)				
		Tableware and kitchenware: (con.)				
		Other: (con.)				
		Other: (con.)				
		Other:				
6912.00.41	00	Steins with permanently attached pewter lids; candy boxes, decanters, punch bowls, pretzel dishes, tidbit dishes, tiered servers, bonbon dishes, egg cups, spoons and spoon rests, oil and vinegar sets, tumblers and salt and pepper shaker sets..............	doz. pcs...........	3.9%	Free (A, AU, BH, CA, CL, CO, D, E, IL, JO, KR, MA, MX, OM, P, PA, PE, SG)	55%
6912.00.44	00	Mugs and other steins............................	doz. pcs...........	10%	Free (A*, AU, BH, CA, CL, CO, D, E, IL, JO, KR, MA, MX, OM, P, PA, PE, SG)	55%
6912.00.45	00	Cups valued over $5.25 per dozen; saucers valued over $3 per dozen; soups, oatmeals and cereals valued over $6 per dozen; plates not over 22.9 cm in maximum diameter and valued over $6 per dozen; plates over 22.9 but not over 27.9 cm in maximum diameter and valued over $8.50 per dozen; platters or chop dishes valued over $35 per dozen; sugars valued over $21 per dozen; creamers valued over $15 per dozen; and beverage servers valued over $42 per dozen..........	doz. pcs...........	4.5%	Free (A+, AU, BH, CA, CL, CO, D, E, IL, JO, KR, MA, MX, OM, P, PA, PE, SG)	55%
6912.00.46	00	Serviette rings..	doz. pcs...........	9.8%	Free (A, AU, BH, CA, CL, CO, D, E, IL, JO, KR, MA, MX, OM, P, PA, PE, SG)	55%
6912.00.48		Other..	....	9.8% 1/	Free (A, AU, BH, CA, CL, CO, D, E, IL, JO, KR, MA, MX, OM, P, PA, PE, SG)	55%
	10	Suitable for food or drink contact......	doz. pcs			
	90	Other...	doz. pcs			
6912.00.50	00	Other..	X...............	6%	Free (A, AU, BH, CA, CL, CO, D, E, IL, JO, KR, MA, MX, OM, P, PA, PE, SG)	50.5%

26. What is the CLASSIFICATION of a women's jacket constructed from 80% polyester, 15% cotton, and 5% spandex knitted fabric coated with plastic, which is visible to the naked eye on the inner surface of the shell fabric, and lined with 100% woven polyester fabric?

A. 6102.30.2010 Women's or girls' overcoats, carcoats, capes, cloaks, anoraks (including ski-jackets), windbreakers and similar articles, knitted or crocheted, other than those of heading 6104>>Of man-made fibers>>Other>>Other>>Women's

B. 6113.00.9030 Garments, made up of knitted or crocheted fabrics of heading 5903, 5906 or 5907>>Other>>Coats and jackets>>Other>>Women's or girls'

C. 6113.00.9020 Garments, made up of knitted or crocheted fabrics of heading 5903, 5906 or 5907>>Other>>Coats and jackets>>Of cotton>>Women's or girls'

D. 6102.20.0010 Women's or girls' overcoats, carcoats, capes, cloaks, anoraks (including ski-jackets), windbreakers and similar articles, knitted or crocheted, other than those of heading 6104>>Of cotton>>Women's

E. 6202.93.5511 Women's or girls' overcoats, carcoats, capes, cloaks, anoraks (including ski-jackets), windbreakers and similar articles (including padded, sleeveless jackets), other than those of heading 6204>>Anoraks (including ski-jackets), windbreakers and similar articles (including padded, sleeveless jackets)>>Of man-made fibers>>Other>>Other>>Other>>Other>>Other>>Women's

 As per HTSUS Chapter 59 Note 2 & Chapter 61 Note 8:

(Chapter 59 Note 2)

2. Heading 5903 applies to:

(a) Textile fabrics, impregnated, coated, covered or laminated with plastics, whatever the weight per square meter and whatever the nature of the plastic material (compact or cellular), **other than:**

(1) Fabrics in which the impregnation, coating or covering cannot be seen with the naked eye (usually chapters 50 to 55, 58 or 60); for the purpose of this provision, no account should be taken of any resulting change of color;

(Chapter 61 Note 8)

8. Garments which are, prima facie, classifiable both in heading 6113 and in other headings of this chapter, excluding heading 6111, **are to be classified in heading 6113.**

Articles of clothing made of textiles of heading 5903 applies to the item in question as the item in question is coated with plastic that CAN be seen by the naked eye (as opposed the heading 5903 exclusion of coatings that CANNOT be seen with the naked eye). Next, according to Chapter 61 Note 8, items that are prima facie (i.e. classifiable under more than one classification) and classifiable under 6113 are to be classified in heading 6113. The item is definitely a prima facie item as it appears it could potentially be classified under "A", "B", "D", and "E". So, if we are to classify under heading 6113, we have either "B" or "C" as our options. We may disregard "C" as the item in question does not predominate by weight in cotton. The correct answer then is "B".

✓ **NOTE:** For your reference, above-referenced headings applicable to the question are as follows:

5902	Tire cord fabric of high tenacity yarn of nylon or other polyamides, polyesters or viscose rayon
5903	Textile fabrics impregnated, coated, covered or laminated with plastics, other than those of heading 5902
5906	Rubberized textile fabrics, other than those of heading 5902
5907	Textile fabrics otherwise impregnated, coated or covered; painted canvas being theatrical scenery, studio back-cloths or the like
6104	Women's or girls' suits, ensembles, suit-type jackets, blazers, dresses, skirts, divided skirts, trousers, bib and brace overalls, breeches and shorts (other than swimwear), knitted or crocheted
6111	Babies' garments and clothing accessories, knitted or crocheted

Heading/ Subheading	Stat. Suf- fix	Article Description	Unit of Quantity	Rates of Duty 1 General	Rates of Duty 1 Special	2
6113.00 (con.)		Garments, made up of knitted or crocheted fabrics of heading 5903, 5906 or 5907: (con.)				
6113.00.90		Other		7.1%	Free (AU, BH, CA, CL, CO, E*, IL, JO, KR, MA, MX, OM, P, PA, PE, SG)	65%
		Coats and jackets:				
		Of cotton:				
	15	Men's or boys' (334)	doz. kg			
	20	Women's or girls' (335)	doz. kg			
		Other:				
	25	Men's or boys' (634)	doz. kg			
	30	Women's or girls' (635)	doz. kg			
		Trousers, breeches and shorts:				
		Of cotton:				
	38	Men's or boys' (347)	doz. kg			
	42	Women's or girls (348)	doz. kg			
		Other:				
	44	Men's or boys' (647)	doz. kg			
	52	Women's or girls' (648)	doz. kg			
		Overalls and coveralls:				
		Of cotton:				
	55	Men's or boys' (359)	doz. kg			
	60	Women's or girls' (359)	doz. kg			
		Other:				
	65	Men's or boys' (659)	doz. kg			
	70	Women's or girls' (659)	doz. kg			
		Other:				
		Of cotton:				
	74	Men's or boys' (359)	doz. kg			
	82	Women's or girls' (359)	doz. kg			
		Other:				
	84	Men's or boys' (659)	doz. kg			
	86	Women's or girls' (659)	doz. kg			

27. What is the CLASSIFICATION of agglomerated slate facing tiles which measure approximately 15.25 centimeters long by 15.25 centimeters wide by 1.25 cm thick?

A. 2514.00.0000 Slate, whether or not roughly trimmed or merely cut, by sawing or otherwise, into blocks or slabs of a rectangular (including square) shape

B. 6802.10.0000 Worked monumental or building stone (except slate) and articles thereof, other than goods of heading 6801; mosaic cubes and the like, of natural stone (including slate), whether or not on a backing; artificially colored granules, chippings and powder, of natural stone (including slate)>> Tiles, cubes and similar articles, whether or not rectangular (including square), the largest surface area of which is capable of being enclosed in a square the side of which is less than 7 cm; artificially colored granules, chippings and powder

C. 6802.99.0060 Worked monumental or building stone (except slate) and articles thereof, other than goods of heading 6801; mosaic cubes and the like, of natural stone (including slate), whether or not on a backing; artificially colored granules, chippings and powder, of natural stone (including slate)>>Other>>Other stone>>Other

D. 6803.00.5000 Worked slate and articles of slate or of agglomerated slate>>Other

E. 6810.19.1400 Articles of cement, of concrete or of artificial stone, whether or not reinforced>>Tiles, flagstones, bricks and similar articles>>Other>>Floor and wall tiles>>Other

As per HTSUS Chapter 25 Note 2(e):

(Chapter 25 Note 2(e))
2. This chapter does not cover:
… …
(e) Setts, curbstones or flagstones (heading 6801); mosaic cubes and the like (heading 6802); roofing, facing or damp course **slates (heading 6803)**;

We may disregard "A" as per the above Chapter 25 Note, chapter 25 does not cover slate. We may disregard multiple choices "B" and "C" as the forms of articles of heading 6802 do not correctly describe the item in question. "D" is a correct description of the item. We may disregard "E" as the item in question is neither of cement nor of artificial stone. Through the process of elimination, we find that the correct answer is "D".

✓ **JUST A SIDE NOTE:** Wikipedia defines "slate" as "a fine-grained, foliated, homogeneous metamorphic rock derived from an original shale-type sedimentary rock composed of clay or volcanic ash through low-grade regional metamorphism. It is the finest grained foliated metamorphic rock". Wikipedia defines "agglomerate" as "a coarse accumulation of large blocks of volcanic material that contains at least 75% (volcanic) bombs." A volcanic bomb is a lump of lava thrown out by a volcano, and can be larger than 20 feet in diameter.

Heading/ Subheading	Stat. Suf-fix	Article Description	Unit of Quantity	Rates of Duty 1 General	Rates of Duty 1 Special	Rates of Duty 2
6802 (con.)		Worked monumental or building stone (except slate) and articles thereof, other than goods of heading 6801; mosaic cubes and the like, of natural stone (including slate), whether or not on a backing; artificially colored granules, chippings and powder, of natural stone (including slate): (con.)				
		Other: (con.)				
6802.99.00		Other stone		6.5%	Free (A, AU, BH, CA, CL, CO, D, E, IL, JO, KR, MA, MX, OM, P, PA, PE, SG)	40%
	30	Monuments, bases and markers	t			
	60	Other	t			
6803.00		Worked slate and articles of slate or of agglomerated slate:				
6803.00.10	00	Roofing slate	m^2	3.3%	Free (A, AU, BH, CA, CL, CO, D, E, IL, JO, KR, MA, MX, OM, P, PA, PE, SG)	25%
6803.00.50	00	Other	X	Free		25%
6804		Millstones, grindstones, grinding wheels and the like, without frameworks, for grinding, sharpening, polishing, trueing or cutting, hand sharpening or polishing stones, and parts thereof, of natural stone, of agglomerated natural or artificial abrasives, or of ceramics, with or without parts of other materials:				
6804.10.00	00	Millstones and grindstones for milling, grinding or pulping	No.	Free		Free
		Other millstones, grindstones, grinding wheels and the like:				
6804.21.00		Of agglomerated synthetic or natural diamond		Free		30%
	10	Segments for circular sawblades, consisting of diamond agglomerated with metal	No.			
	80	Other	No.			
6804.22		Of other agglomerated abrasives or of ceramics:				
6804.22.10	00	Bonded with synthetic resins	kg	5¢/kg + 2%	Free (A, AU, BH, CA, CL, CO, D, E, IL, JO, KR, MA, MX, OM, P, PA, PE, SG)	$1.10/kg + 40%
		Other:				
6804.22.40	00	Abrasive wheels	X	Free		20%
6804.22.60	00	Other	X	Free		30%
6804.23.00	00	Of natural stone	No.	Free		Free
6804.30.00	00	Hand sharpening or polishing stones	No.	Free		Free
6805		Natural or artificial abrasive powder or grain, on a base of textile material, of paper, of paperboard or of other materials, whether or not cut to shape or sewn or otherwise made up:				
6805.10.00	00	On a base of woven textile fabric only	kg	Free		20%
6805.20.00	00	On a base of paper or paperboard only	kg	Free		20%
6805.30		On a base of other materials:				
6805.30.10	00	Articles wholly or partly coated with abrasives, in the form of sheets, strips, disks, belts, sleeves or similar forms	kg	Free		20%
6805.30.50	00	Other	kg	Free		20%

28. What is the CLASSIFICATION of women's trousers constructed from 60% polyester and 40% nylon woven fabric? The pull-on trousers feature a functional drawstring threaded throughout the waistband, on-seam front pockets, and long hemmed leg openings with zipper closures at the ankles.

A. 6204.69.4510 Women's or girls' suits, ensembles, suit-type jackets, blazers, dresses, skirts, divided skirts, trousers, bib and brace overalls, breeches and shorts (other than swimwear)>>Trousers, bib and brace overalls, breeches and shorts>>Of other textile materials>>Other>>Of silk or silk waste>>Trousers, breeches and shorts

B. 6204.63.9030 Women's or girls' suits, ensembles, suit-type jackets, blazers, dresses, skirts, divided skirts, trousers, bib and brace overalls, breeches and shorts (other than swimwear)>>Trousers, bib and brace overalls, breeches and shorts>>Of synthetic fibers>>Other>>Other>>Other>>Other>>Other>>Trousers and breeches>>Girls'>>Other

C. 6204.63.9010 Women's or girls' suits, ensembles, suit-type jackets, blazers, dresses, skirts, divided skirts, trousers, bib and brace overalls, breeches and shorts (other than swimwear)>>Trousers, bib and brace overalls, breeches and shorts>>Of synthetic fibers>>Other>>Other>>Other>>Other>>Other>>Trousers and breeches>>Women's

D. 6204.69.2810 Women's or girls' suits, ensembles, suit-type jackets, blazers, dresses, skirts, divided skirts, trousers, bib and brace overalls, breeches and shorts (other than swimwear)>>Trousers, bib and brace overalls, breeches and shorts>>Of other textile materials>>Other>>Of artificial fibers>>Trousers, breeches and shorts>>Other>>Trousers and breeches>>Women's

E. 6204.69.8010 Women's or girls' suits, ensembles, suit-type jackets, blazers, dresses, skirts, divided skirts, trousers, bib and brace overalls, breeches and shorts (other than swimwear)>>Trousers, bib and brace overalls, breeches and shorts>>Of other textile materials>>Other>>Other>>Trousers, breeches and shorts>>Subject to cotton restraints

 As per the HTSUS Chapter 54 (MAN-MADE FILAMENTS) Note 1:

Notes

1. Throughout the tariff schedule, the term "man-made fibers" means staple fibers and filaments of organic polymers produced by manufacturing processes, either:

(a) By polymerization of organic monomers to produce polymers such as polyamides, polyesters, polyolefins or polyurethanes, or by chemical modification of polymers produced by this process (for example, poly(vinyl alcohol) prepared by the hydrolysis of poly(vinyl acetate)); or

(b) By dissolution or chemical treatment of natural organic polymers (for example, cellulose) to produce polymers such as cuprammonium rayon (cupro) or viscose rayon, or by chemical modification of natural organic polymers (for example, cellulose, casein and other proteins, or alginic acid), to produce polymers such as cellulose acetate or alginates.

The terms "synthetic" and "artificial", used in relation to fibers, mean: **synthetic: fibers as defined at (a)**; artificial: fibers as defined at (b). Strip and the like of heading 5404 or 5405 are not considered to be man-made fibers.

The terms "man-made", "synthetic" and "artificial" shall have the same meanings when used in relation to "textile materials".

a Let's start from the top. We may disregard "A" as the item in question is not of silk. We may disregard "B" as this classification is for girls' (as opposed to women's). "C" is a correct description of the polyester/nylon (i.e. synthetic; see also above Note) trousers for women. We may disregard "D" and "E" as these classifications are for "other (than synthetic, etc.) textiles. The correct answer is "C".

✓ **NOTE:** The difference between "synthetic" fibers and "artificial" fibers is that "artificial" fibers are made from naturally-occurring substances, such as plant cellulose. Both, however, are "man-made" fibers. Nylon and polyester are examples of synthetic fibers. Rayon is an example of an artificial fiber.

Heading/ Subheading	Stat. Suf-fix	Article Description	Unit of Quantity	Rates of Duty 1 General	Special	2
6204 (con.)		Women's or girls' suits, ensembles, suit-type jackets, blazers, dresses, skirts, divided skirts, trousers, bib and brace overalls, breeches and shorts (other than swimwear): (con.)				
		Trousers, bib and brace overalls, breeches and shorts: (con.)				
6204.63 (con.)		Of synthetic fibers: (con.)				
		Other: (con.)				
		Other: (con.)				
		Other:				
6204.63.70		Containing 36 percent or more by weight of wool or fine animal hair		13.6%	Free (AU, BH, CA, CL, IL, JO, KR, MA, MX, OM, P, PA, PE, SG)	58.5%
	10	Women's (448)	doz. kg			
	20	Girls' (448)	doz. kg			
		Other:				
6204.63.75		Water resistant trousers or breeches (648)		7.1%	Free (AU, BH, CA, CL, CO, IL, JO, KR, MA, MX, OM, P, PA, PE, SG)	65%
	10	Ski/snowboard pants (648)	doz. kg			
	90	Other (648)	doz. kg			
6204.63.90		Other		28.6%	Free (AU, BH, CA, CL, CO, IL, JO, KR, MA, MX, OM, P, PA, PE, SG)	90%
		Trousers and breeches:				
	10	Women's (648)	doz. kg			
		Girls':				
	25	Imported as parts of playsuits (237)	doz. kg			
	30	Other (648)	doz. kg			
		Shorts:				
	32	Women's (648)	doz. kg			
		Girls':				
	35	Imported as parts of playsuits (237)	doz. kg			
	40	Other (648)	doz. kg			

29. What is the CLASSIFICATION of a hot-rolled, stainless steel sheet imported in coils? The stainless steel sheet measures 750 mm in width and 4 mm in thickness. It is not coated, painted, clad, annealed or pickled.

A. 7219.23.0060 Flat-rolled products of stainless steel, of a width of 600 mm or More>>Not further worked than hot-rolled, not in coils>>Of a thickness of 3 mm or more but less than 4.75 mm>>Other

B. 7220.12.1000 Flat-rolled products of stainless steel, of a width of less than 600 mm>>Not further worked than hot-rolled>>Of a thickness of less than 4.75 mm>>Of a width of 300 mm or more

C. 7225.30.7000 Flat-rolled products of other alloy steel, of a width of 600 mm or more>>Other, not further worked than hot-rolled, in coils>>Of a thickness of less than 4.75 mm>>Other

D. 7219.13.0002 Flat-rolled products of stainless steel, of a width of 600 mm or More>>Not further worked than hot-rolled, in coils>>Of a thickness of 3 mm or more but less than 4.75 mm>>Not annealed or not pickled

E. 7219.32.0060 Flat-rolled products of stainless steel, of a width of 600 mm or more>>Not further worked than cold-rolled>>Of a thickness of 3 mm or more but less than 4.75 mm>>Not in coils>>Other

As per HTSUS Chapter 72 (see following page):

We may disregard "A" as the item in question is "in coils" (as opposed to not in coils). We may disregard "B" as the item in question is 750 mm in width (as opposed to less than 600 mm). We may disregard "C" as the item in question is "stainless steel" (as opposed to alloy steel). "D" is a correct description of the item. "E" may be disregarded as the item in question is "hot rolled" (as opposed to cold-rolled). The correct answer here is "D".

✓ **JUST A SIDE NOTE:** According to Wikipedia "hot rolling" is a metalworking process that occurs above the recrystallization temperature of the material. "Cold rolling" occurs with the metal below its recrystallization temperature (usually at room temperature), which increases the strength via strain hardening up to 20%. It (cold rolling) also improves the surface finish and holds tighter tolerances. "Rolling" refers to the passing of the steel through cylindrical rolls to flatten the steel to the desired thickness. It is similar to the concept of rolling dough.

Heading/ Subheading	Stat. Suf- fix	Article Description	Unit of Quantity	Rates of Duty 1 General	Rates of Duty 1 Special	Rates of Duty 2
7219 (con.)		Flat-rolled products of stainless steel, of a width of 600 mm or more: (con.)				
		Not further worked than hot-rolled, in coils: (con.)				
7219.13.00		Of a thickness of 3 mm or more but less than 4.75 mm		Free		29%
	02	Not annealed or not pickled	kg			
		Other:				
	31	Of a width of 1370 mm or more	kg			
		Other:				
		Containing more than 0.5 percent but less than 24 percent by weight of nickel:				
	51	Containing more than 1.5 percent but less than 5 percent by weight of molybdenum	kg			
	71	Other	kg			
	81	Other	kg			
7219.14.00		Of a thickness of less than 3 mm		Free		29%
	30	Of a width of 1370 mm or more	kg			
		Other:				
	65	Of high-nickel alloy steel	kg			
	90	Other	kg			

Category V – Drawback

30. A Notice of Intent to Export, Destroy, or Return Merchandise for Purposes of Drawback on CBP Form 7553 for merchandise that is going to be destroyed, shall be filed by the claimant with the CBP port where the destruction is to take place at least _______ working day(s) prior to the date of intended destruction.

A. 1
B. 2
C. 7
D. 10
E. 14

 As per 19 CFR 191.71(a):

§191.71 Drawback on articles destroyed under Customs supervision.

(a) *Procedure.* **At least 7 working days before the intended date of destruction of merchandise or articles upon which drawback is intended to be claimed, a Notice of Intent to Export, Destroy, or Return Merchandise for Purposes of Drawback on Customs Form 7553 shall be filed by the claimant with the Customs port** where the destruction is to take place, giving notification of the date and specific location where the destruction is to occur. Within 4 working days after receipt of the Customs Form 7553, Customs shall advise the filer in writing of its determination to witness or not to witness the destruction. If the filer of the notice is not so notified within 4 working days, the merchandise may be destroyed without delay and will be deemed to have been destroyed under Customs supervision. Unless Customs determines to witness the destruction, the destruction of the articles following timely notification on Customs Form 7553 shall be deemed to have occurred under Customs supervision. If Customs attends the destruction, it must certify the Notice of Intent to Export, Destroy, or Return Merchandise for Purposes of Drawback.

 The correct answer is "C".

✔ **JUST A SIDE NOTE:** Companies may file a duty drawback claim with CBP if a previously imported item is to be destroyed or exported. Along with the CBP Form 7553 "heads up", if a company is to export the item, they must provide Customs with a copy of the international bill of lading as part of their drawback claim.

31. Under the provisions for Direct Identification Unused Merchandise Drawback, which party is eligible to claim drawback or issue a waiver of this right to another entity?

A. The manufacturer of the goods

B. The foreign purchaser of the unused imported goods

C. The exporter (or destroyer) of the unused imported goods

D. The party who paid the duties submitted on the associated consumption entry

E. The buyer as identified on the commercial invoice used to make entry

 As per 19 CFR 191.33(a):

§191.33 Person entitled to claim drawback.

(a) ***Direct identification***. (1) Under 19 U.S.C. 1313(j)(1), the exporter (or destroyer) shall be entitled to claim drawback.

(2) **The exporter or destroyer may waive the right to claim drawback and assign such right to the importer or any intermediate party.** A drawback claimant under 19 U.S.C. 1313(j)(1) other than the exporter or destroyer shall secure and retain a certification signed by the exporter or destroyer that such party waived the right to claim drawback, and did not and will not authorize any other party to claim the exportation or destruction for drawback (see §191.82 of this part). The certification provided for under this section may be a blanket certification for a stated period. The claimant shall file such certification at the time of, or prior to, the filing of the claim(s) covered by the certification.

 The correct answer is "C".

✔ **JUST A SIDE NOTE:** Information on ACE (Automated Commercial Environment) drawback procedures, frequently asked questions (such as "What are the elements of a complete (ACE) drawback claim?"), etc. can be found at the following CBP page.

https://www.cbp.gov/trade/automated/news/drawback

32. When can a claimant amend an unliquidated drawback claim?

A. Claims may be amended at any time provided the claim is unliquidated.

B. Within 90 days of the date the claim was received by CBP

C. Within 180 days of the date the claim was received by CBP

D. Within 3 years after the date of exportation or destruction of the claimed merchandise

E. Within 5 years after the date of exportation or destruction of the claimed merchandise

 As per 19 CFR 191.52(c):

§191.52 Rejecting, perfecting or amending claims.

... ...

(c) *Amending the claim; supplemental filing.* **Amendments to claims for which the drawback entries have not been liquidated must be made within three (3) years after the date of exportation or destruction** of the articles which are the subject of the original drawback claim. Liquidated drawback entries may not be amended; however, they may be protested as provided for in §191.84 of this part and part 174 of this chapter.

 The correct answer is "D".

✓ **JUST A SIDE NOTE:** At the time of the writing of this section of the study guide, importers and customs brokers have the option of filing duty drawbacks either via paper submission or electronically via ACE through Feb 23, 2019. After this date, it is scheduled that only duty drawback claims filed electronically via ACE will be accepted (i.e. paper submissions will no longer be accepted). This is subject to change, of course.

33. To comply with manufacturing drawback (direct identification and substitution), the use of domestic merchandise taken in exchange for imported merchandise of the same kind and quality shall be treated as use of the imported merchandise if no certificate of delivery is issued covering the transfer of the imported merchandise. This provision is known as a/an:

A. Interchange

B. Fungibility

C. Trade good

D. Exchange merchandise.

E. Tradeoff

 As per 19 CFR 191.11(a):

§191.11 Tradeoff.

(a) *Exchanged merchandise.* To comply with §§191.21 and 191.22 of this part, **the use of domestic merchandise taken in exchange for imported merchandise of the same kind and quality** (as defined in §191.2(x)(1) of this part for purposes of 19 U.S.C. 1313(b)) **shall be treated as use of the imported merchandise if no certificate of delivery is issued covering the transfer of the imported merchandise. This provision shall be known as tradeoff** and is authorized by §313(k) of the Act, as amended (19 U.S.C. 1313(k)).

 The correct answer is "E".

✔ **JUST A SIDE NOTE:** "Tradeoff" may be applied when domestic merchandise is manufactured with imported merchandise that is subject to drawback."

Category VI – Entry

34. An entry of merchandise is made on January 23, 2017. If the entry is not liquidated within____________, it will be deemed liquidated by operation of law at the rate of duty, value, quantity, and amount of duties asserted by the importer of record.

A. 90 days

B. 4 years

C. 15 months

D. 1 year

E. 180 days

As per 19 CFR 159.11:

§159.11 Entries liquidated by operation of law.

(a) *Time limit generally.* Except as provided in §159.12, **an entry not liquidated within one year from the date of entry of the merchandise**, or the date of final withdrawal of all merchandise covered by a warehouse entry, **will be deemed liquidated by operation of law at the rate of duty, value, quantity, and amount of duties asserted by the importer of record.** Notice of liquidation will be given electronically as provided in §§159.9 and 159.10(c)(3) of this part. CBP will endeavor to provide a courtesy notice of liquidation in accordance with §159.9(d).

The correct answer is "D".

✓ **JUST A SIDE NOTE:** CBP has a page where recently liquidation notices can be viewed, searchable by entry number, importer of record number, etc.

https://bulletin-notice.cbp.dhs.gov/LBNotice

35. The A.T.A. carnet is an international Customs document issued in conformity of the Customs Convention on the A.T.A. carnet for the Temporary Admission of Goods. An A.T.A. carnet may be used to temporarily import certain goods, duty-free. How long are A.T.A carnets valid?

A. One year from date of importation
B. One year from date of issue
C. Two years from date of importation
D. Two years from date of issue
E. Three years from date of issue

 As per 19 CFR 114.23(a):

§114.23 Maximum period.

(a) *A.T.A. carnet.* No A.T.A. carnet with a period of validity exceeding 1 year from date of issue shall be accepted. This period of validity cannot be extended.

(b) *TIR carnet.* A TIR carnet may be accepted without limitation as to time provided it is initially "taken on charge by a customs administration (United States or foreign) within the period of validity shown on its front cover."

(c) *TECRO/AIT carnet.* A TECRO/AIT carnet shall not be issued with a period of validity exceeding one year from the date of issue. This period of validity cannot be extended and must be shown on the front cover of the carnet.

 The correct answer is "B".

✔ **JUST A SIDE NOTE:** The A.T.A. carnet is the most popular type of carnet in the United States, and is an acronym of French and English (Admission Temporaire/Temporary Admission).

36. Which of the following U.S. Government Agencies administer the regulations regarding economic and trade sanctions?

A. Justice Department's Office of International Affairs
B. Commerce Department's Office of Economics and Statistics Administration
C. Treasury Department's Office of Foreign Assets Control
D. State Department's U.S. Foreign Service
E. None of the above

 As per 19 CFR 12.150(a):

§12.150 Merchandise prohibited by economic sanctions; detention; seizure or other disposition; blocked property.

(a) *Generally.* Merchandise from certain countries designated by the President as constituting a threat to the national security, foreign policy, or economy of the United States shall be detained until the question of its release, seizure, or other disposition has been determined under law and regulations issued by the Treasury Department's Office of Foreign Assets Control (OFAC) (31 CFR Chapter V).

(b) *Seizure.* When an unlicensed importation of merchandise subject to OFAC's regulations is determined to be prohibited, no entry for any purpose shall be permitted and, unless the immediate reexportation or other disposition of such merchandise under Customs supervision has previously been authorized by OFAC, the merchandise shall be seized.

(c) *Licenses.* OFAC's regulations may authorize OFAC to issue licenses on a case-by-case basis authorizing the importation of otherwise prohibited merchandise under certain conditions. If such a license is issued subsequent to the attempted entry and seizure of the merchandise, importation shall be conditioned upon the importer:

(1) Agreeing in writing to hold the Government harmless, and

(2) Paying any storage and other Customs fees, costs, or expenses, as well as any mitigated forfeiture amount or monetary penalty imposed or assessed by Customs or OFAC, or both.

(d) *Blocked property.* Merchandise which constitutes property in which the government or any national of certain designated countries has an interest may be blocked (frozen) pursuant to OFAC's regulations and may not be transferred, sold, or otherwise disposed of without an OFAC license.

(e) *Additional information.* For further information concerning importing merchandise prohibited under economic sanctions programs currently in effect, the Office of Foreign Assets Control of the Department of the Treasury should be contacted. The address of that office is 1500 Pennsylvania Ave., NW., Annex 2nd Floor, Washington, DC 20220.

 The correct answer is "C".

✓ **NOTE:** The Office of Foreign Assets Control (OFAC) was founded in 1950 as the Division of Foreign Assets Control. OFAC regularly updates a list of Specially Designated Nationals, which lists over 15,000 entities from over 150 countries, with which U.S. persons are strictly prohibited from doing business with.

37. Which of the following parties does NOT have the right to make entry?

A. **A licensed customs broker designated by a selling agent, to enter merchandise for the agent's client**

B. **A firm importing merchandise on consignment**

C. **A freight forwarder who is identified as the purchaser of an entry of equipment for their new warehouse**

D. **A licensed customs broker who presents a carnet on behalf of an owner of the merchandise**

E. **A freight forwarder who presents a carnet, without a financial interest in the merchandise, on behalf of its client**

 As per Customs Directive 3530-002A, 5.12.1:

5.12 ADMISSION TEMPORAIRE-TEMPORARY ADMISSION CARNETS (A.T.A. CARNET) AND TAIPEI ECONOMIC AND CULTURAL REPRESENTATIVE OFFICE IN THE UNITED STATES AND THE AMERICAN INSTITUTE IN TAIWAN CARNET (TECRO/AIT CARNET)

5.12.1 The requirements applicable to the filing of TIB entries by the importer of record, i.e., the owner, purchaser, or licensed Customs broker, shall be applied to the filing of A.T.A. and TECRO/AIT Carnets. **Such carnets presented by freight forwarders or others without an interest in the merchandise shall not be accepted unless they are a licensed Customs broker.**

 The correct answer is "E".

✔ **NOTE:** The above-mentioned directive does not apply to freight forwarders that are also customs brokerage operations.

38. Which of the following is an example of bulk cargo?

A. 250 40-foot containers of household goods

B. 500 tons of grain stowed loose in the hold of a cargo vessel

C. 1000 cases of wine, each holding 24 bottles

D. 2500 barrels of olive oil

E. 5000 sacks of coffee beans

 As per 19 CFR § 4.7(b):

§4.7 Inward foreign manifest; production on demand; contents and form; advance filing of cargo declaration.

… …

(b)(1) With the exception of any Cargo Declaration that has been filed in advance as prescribed in paragraph (b)(2) of this section, the original and one copy of the manifest must be ready for production on demand. The master shall deliver the original and one copy of the manifest to the CBP officer who shall first demand it. If the vessel is to proceed from the port of arrival to other United States ports with residue foreign cargo or passengers, an additional copy of the manifest shall be available for certification as a traveling manifest (see §4.85). The port director may require an additional copy or additional copies of the manifest, but a reasonable time shall be allowed for the preparation of any copy which may be required in addition to the original and one copy.

… …

(4) Carriers of bulk cargo as specified in paragraph (b)(4)(i) of this section and carriers of break bulk cargo to the extent provided in paragraph (b)(4)(ii) of this section are exempt, with respect only to the bulk or break bulk cargo being transported, from the requirement set forth in paragraph (b)(2) of this section that an electronic cargo declaration be received by CBP 24 hours before such cargo is laden aboard the vessel at the foreign port. With respect to exempted carriers of bulk or break bulk cargo operating voyages to the United States, CBP must receive the electronic cargo declaration covering the bulk or break bulk cargo they are transporting 24 hours prior to the vessel's arrival in the United States (see §4.30(n)). However, for any containerized or non-qualifying break bulk cargo these exempted carriers will be transporting, CBP must receive the electronic cargo declaration 24 hours in advance of loading.

(i) Bulk cargo is defined for purposes of this section as homogeneous cargo that is stowed loose in the hold and is not enclosed in any container such as a box, bale, bag, cask, or the like. Such cargo is also described as bulk freight. Specifically, bulk cargo is composed of either:

(A) Free flowing articles such as oil, grain, coal, ore, and the like, which can be pumped or run through a chute or handled by dumping; or

(B) Articles that require mechanical handling such as bricks, pig iron, lumber, steel beams, and the like.

… …

 The correct answer is "B".

✓ **JUST A SIDE NOTE:** Bulk cargo is classified as either liquid (e.g. petroleum) or dry (e.g. coal). In terms of containerized cargo, however, a "dry" container means one that is non-refrigerated (i.e. a non-refer container).

39. Which of the following is NOT a method of control for the unlading and measurement of petroleum and petroleum products imported in bulk by vessel, truck, railroad car, pipeline, or other carrier?

A. Manufacturer affidavit

B. Shore tank gauging

C. Weighing for trucks and railroad cars

D. Customs-approved metering

E. Sampling installations provided by the importer

 As per 19 CFR 151.42(a):

§151.42 Controls on unlading and gauging.

(a) *Methods of control.* (1) Each port director shall establish **controls and checks on the unlading and measurement of petroleum and petroleum products imported in bulk by vessel, truck, railroad car, pipeline, or other carrier. One of the following methods of control shall be employed:**

(i) Customs-approved metering and sampling installations provided by the importer;

(ii) Shore tank gauging; or

(iii) Weighing for trucks and railroad cars.

(2) Vessel ullages shall be taken in every case unless the port director determines that it is impracticable to do so for safety or technological reasons. Ullages may be taken for trucks and railroad cars if weighing or shore tank gauging is not available as a method of control. Vessel ullages will not be used to determine the quantity unladen unless none of the other methods provided for in this paragraph is available or adequate.

(3) The metering and sampling installations described in paragraph (a)(1)(i) of this section are approved by Customs on a case-by-case basis. Importers seeking approval shall send a complete description of the installation to the port director who, with the concurrence of the Director, Laboratory & Scientific Services, or his designee, shall give approval or shall state, in writing, the reasons for disapproval. Approved installations are subject to periodic verification by Customs. Importers desiring to modify a Customs-approved installation shall obtain Customs approval beforehand.

 The correct answer is "A".

✓ **NOTE:** "Tank gauging" is the use of scanners and sensors to measure storage tank volume.

40. Importations of switchblade knives is permissible by 15 U.S.C 1244 if:

A. The importation is pursuant to a contract with a branch of the State Militia.

B. The importation is destined for a specific member or employee in a branch of the Armed Forces of the United States specifically for personal pleasure off-duty use.

C. The importation of the switchblade knives have a blade not exceeding 6 inches in length.

D. The entry will contain, among other documents, a declaration in duplicate stating that the switchblade knife has a blade not exceeding 3 inches in length and is possessed by and is being transported on the person of an individual who has only one arm.

E. The entry will contain, among other documents, a declaration in duplicate stating that the switchblade knife has a blade not exceeding 6 inches in length.

As per 19 CFR 12.98(c) and § 12.99(a):

§12.98 Importations permitted by statutory exceptions.

The importation of switchblade knives is permitted by 15 U.S.C. 1244, when:

(a) Imported pursuant to contract with a branch of the Armed Forces of the United States;

(b) Imported by a branch of the Armed Forces of the United States or any member or employee thereof acting in the performance of his duty; or

(c) A switchblade knife, other than a ballistic knife, having a blade not exceeding 3 inches in length is in the possession of and is being transported on the person of an individual who has only one arm.

§12.99 Procedures for permitted entry.

(a) *Declaration required.* The entry of switchblade knives, the importation of which is permitted under §12.98 shall be accompanied by a declaration, or its electronic equivalent, in duplicate, of the importer or consignee stating the facts of the import transaction as follows:

(1) *Importation pursuant to Armed Forces contract.* (i) The names of the contracting Armed Forces branch and its supplier;

(ii) The specific contract relied upon identified by its date, number, or other contract designation; and

(iii) A description of the kind or type of knife imported, the quantity entered, and the aggregate entered value of the importation.

(2) *Importation by a branch, member, or employee of the Armed Forces.* (i) The name of the Armed Forces branch by or for the account of which entry is made or the branch of the importing member or employee acting in performance of duty; and

(ii) The description, quantity, and aggregate entered value of the importation.

(3) *Importation by a one-armed person.* A statement that the knife has a blade not exceeding 3 inches in length and is possessed by and transported on the declarant's person solely for his necessary personal convenience, accommodation, and use as a one-armed individual.

Many of the multiple-choice options are just slightly, yet nonetheless, discrepant. The correct answer is "D".

41. Are corpses subject to the provisions of the Harmonized Tariff Schedule of the United States (HTSUS) and therefore required to be entered?

A. **Yes, corpses are goods subject to the provisions of the HTSUS and are entered under subheading 7326.90.8677 as steel or iron burial caskets with a duty rate of 2.9 percent.**

B. **No, corpses are not goods subject to the provisions of the HTSUS, but are required to be entered.**

C. **No, corpses are not goods subject to the provisions of the HTSUS and are not required to be entered.**

D. **Yes, corpses are goods subject to the provisions of the HTSUS, but are not required to be entered.**

E. **Yes, corpses are goods subject to the provisions of the HTSUS and are entered under subheading 4421.91.9730 as wooden burial caskets with a duty rate of 3.3 percent.**

 As per 19 CFR 141.4 & HTSUS General Note 3(e):

§141.4 Entry required.

(a) ***General.*** **All merchandise imported into the United States is required to be entered, unless specifically excepted.**

(b) ***Exceptions.*** **The following are the exceptions to the general rule:**

(1) The exemptions listed in General Note 3(e) to the Harmonized Tariff Schedule of the United States (HTSUS).

… …

(HTSUS General Note 3(e))

(e) Exemptions. For the purposes of general note 1--

(i) corpses, together with their coffins and accompanying flowers,
(ii) telecommunications transmissions,
(iii) records, diagrams and other data with regard to any business, engineering or exploration operation whether on paper, cards, photographs, blueprints, tapes or other media,
(iv) articles returned from space within the purview of section 484a of the Tariff Act of 1930,
(v) articles exported from the United States which are returned within 45 days after such exportation from the United States as undeliverable and which have not left the custody of the carrier or foreign customs service,
… …

are not goods subject to the provisions of the tariff schedule. No exportation referred to in subdivision (e) may be treated as satisfying any requirement for exportation in order to receive a benefit from, or meet an obligation to, the United States as a result of such exportation. … …

a As per HTSUS General Note 3(e), corpses are not subject to the HTSUS. Thus, as per 19 CFR 141.4, corpses are not required to be customs entered. The correct answer is "C".

✓ **JUST A SIDE NOTE:** The above-mentioned General Note 1 says:

(HTSUS General Note 1)
1 Tariff Treatment of Imported Goods and of Vessel Equipments, Parts and Repairs. All goods provided for in this schedule and imported into the customs territory of the United States from outside thereof, and all vessel equipments, parts, materials and repairs covered by the provisions of subchapter XVIII to chapter 98 of this schedule, are subject to duty or exempt therefrom as prescribed in general notes 3 through 29, inclusive.

42. A carrier has custody of in-bond merchandise coming from Mexico or Canada, for which entry has not been made. Within how many calendar days is the carrier required to notify Customs of merchandise for which entry has not been made?

A. 5
B. 10
C. 20
D. 30
E. 45

 As per 19 CFR 123.10(b):

(b) Any merchandise or baggage that is taken into custody from an arriving carrier by any party under a Customs-authorized permit to transfer or in-bond entry may remain in the custody of that party for 15 calendar days after receipt under such permit to transfer or 15 calendar days after arrival at the port of destination. **No later than 20 calendar days after receipt under the permit to transfer** or 20 calendar days after arrival under bond at the port of destination, **the party shall notify Customs of any such merchandise or baggage for which entry has not been made.** Such notification shall be provided in writing or by any appropriate Customs-authorized electronic data interchange system. If the party fails to notify Customs of the unentered merchandise or baggage in the allotted time, he may be liable for the payment of liquidated damages under the terms and conditions of his custodial bond (see §113.63(c)(4) of this chapter).

 The correct answer is "C".

✓ **JUST A SIDE NOTE:** Goods not customs entered within 15 days after arrival at their port of entry become General Order (GO) status merchandise.

43. ABC Corp entered Japanese-manufactured construction equipment into the U.S. in March 2011. At the time, all applicable duties, taxes and fees were paid. In 2014, ABC Corp won a contract to construct a U.S. military facility overseas. ABC Corp sent the equipment overseas in January 2015. It is now being returned to the U.S. Which of the following is TRUE?

A. The equipment is not eligible for duty-free entry under Chapter 98 because is it not of U.S. origin.

B. The equipment is not eligible for duty-free entry under Chapter 98 because it was not exported within 3 years of importation.

C. The equipment is not eligible for duty-free entry because it is not returning temporarily for repair, alteration or processing.

D. The equipment is eligible for duty-free entry because it is being returned to the U.S. within 3 years of exportation.

E. The equipment is eligible for duty-free entry because A-Z Corp is a U.S. Government contractor.

As per HTSUS 9801.00.10:

Heading/ Subheading	Stat. Suf-fix	Article Description
9801.00.10 (con.)		Products of the United States when returned after having been exported, or any other products when returned within 3 years after having been exported, without having been advanced in value or improved in condition by any process of manufacture or other means while abroad (con.)

The exam answer key says the "D" is the correct answer, however we disagree. The exam question states that the item is "Japanese-manufactured", and thus the item cannot be called a "product of the United States", for which there is a provision under HTSUS 9801.00.10 for U.S.-made items returned within 3 years after having been exported. The equipment is not otherwise eligible for duty-free treatment under Chapter 98. The correct answer is "A".

✓ **JUST A SIDE NOTE:** Another helpful provision in Chapter 98 is HTSUS 9801.00.2000, which provides for duty free entry for items previously imported, then exported under lease or similar use agreement, and then reimported to the U.S. The complete HTSUS article description for this is:

9801.00.2000
Articles, previously imported, with respect to which the duty was paid upon such previous importation or which were previously free of duty pursuant to the Caribbean Basin Economic Recovery Act or Title V of the Trade Act of 1974, if (1) reimported, without having been advanced in value or improved in condition by any process of manufacture or other means while abroad, after having been exported under lease or similar use agreements, and (2) reimported by or for the account of the person who imported it into, and exported it from, the United States

Category VII – Fines and Penalties

44. Which section of the CFR determines when a petition for relief for liquidated damages and penalties should be filed with CBP, Fines, Penalties and Forfeitures Office?

A. 19 C.F.R. § 152.13

B. 19 C.F.R. § 172.3

C. 19 C.F.R. § 143.21

D. 19 C.F.R. § 152.2

E. 19 C.F.R. § 181.12

 As per 19 CFR 172.3(b):

172.3 Filing a petition.

(a) *Where filed.* A petition for relief must be filed by the bond principal with the Fines, Penalties, and Forfeitures office whose address is given in the notice.

(b) *When filed.* Petitions for relief must be filed within 60 days from the date of mailing to the bond principal the notice of claim for liquidated damages or penalty secured by a bond.

 The correct answer is "B".

✓ **JUST A SIDE NOTE:** When CBP notifies an importer of the assessment of liquidated damages or penalty, the importer may request cancellation or mitigation of the original assessment.

45. Which of the following information is required in every protest?

A. The name and address of the attorney

B. The number and date of the entry

C. A declaration as to whether or not the entry is subject to anti-dumping

D. CBP Form 301

E. A status report fee

 As per 19 CFR 174.13(a):

§174.13 Contents of protest.

(a) *Contents, in general.* **A protest shall contain the following information:**

(1) The name and address of the protestant, *i.e.*, the importer of record or consignee, and the name and address of his agent or attorney if signed by one of these;

(2) The importer number of the protestant. If the protestant is represented by an agent having power of attorney, the importer number of the agent shall also be shown;

(3) The number and date of the entry;

(4) The date of liquidation of the entry, or the date of a decision not involving a liquidation or reliquidation;

(5) A specific description of the merchandise affected by the decision as to which protest is made;

(6) The nature of, and justification for the objection set forth distinctly and specifically with respect to each category, payment, claim, decision, or refusal;

(7) The date of receipt and protest number of any protest previously filed that is the subject of a pending application for further review pursuant to subpart C of this part and that is alleged to involve the same merchandise and the same issues, if the protesting party requests disposition in accordance with the action taken on such previously filed protest;

(8) If another party has not filed a timely protest, the surety's protest shall certify that the protest is not being filed collusively to extend another authorized person's time to protest; and

(9) A declaration, to the best of the protestant's knowledge, as to whether the entry is the subject of drawback, or whether the entry has been referenced on a certificate of delivery or certificate of manufacture and delivery so as to enable a party to make such entry the subject of drawback (see §§181.50(b) and 191.81(b) of this chapter).

 The correct answer is "B".

✓ **JUST A SIDE NOTE:** As outlined in 19 CFR 174.13(b), a single protest may be filed for multiple entries.

46. According to ____________________, CBP issues a notice for liquidated damages when there is a failure to meet the condition of any bond posted with CBP or for a penalty violation which is secured by a CBP bond.

A. 19 CFR § 19.39

B. 19 CFR § 142.26

C. 19 CFR § 24.1

D. 19 CFR § 163.2

E. 19 CFR § 172.1

 As per 19 CFR 172.1(a):

172.1 Notice of liquidated damages or penalty incurred and right to petition for relief.

(a) *Notice of liquidated damages or penalty incurred.* **When there is a failure to meet the conditions of any bond posted with Customs or when a violation occurs which results in assessment of a penalty which is secured by a Customs bond, the principal will be notified in writing of any liability for liquidated damages** or penalty incurred and a demand will be made for payment. The sureties on such bond will also be notified in writing of any such liability at the same time.

 The correct answer is "E".

✓ **JUST A SIDE NOTE:** Liquidated damages are monetary claims made by CBP. CBP has made available a very helpful Informed Compliance Publication guide related to the subject of liquidated damages, and can currently be found here:

https://www.cbp.gov/sites/default/files/documents/icp052_3.pdf

47. In accordance with 19 C.F.R. 162.74 (prior disclosure), a complete "disclosure of the circumstances of a violation" includes which of the following sets of factual elements?

A. **1) The complete Harmonized Tariff Schedule (HTS) classification for all involved merchandise,**
2) the specific entry/drawback claims by number (including identification of the licensed broker who filed the paperwork, where applicable), and
3) the true and accurate information that should have been provided.

B. **1) The class or kind of merchandise,**
2) the specific import/drawback claims by number (or by the CBP ports of entry and approximate dates of entry/drawback),
3) the material false statements/omissions along with an explanation of how the errors occurred, and
4) the true and accurate information that should have been provided.

C. **1) A complete explanation of the underlying cause(s) of the violation,**
2) a summary of the involved merchandise,
3) the approximate dates the violation occurred,
4) calculation of any applicable loss of revenue to the government, and
5) tender of any unpaid amount.

D. **1) The class or kind of merchandise,**
2) a complete list of the CBP ports of entry along with approximate dates of entry/drawback,
3) a statement of the material error, and
4) the corrective actions that have been or will be implemented for future transactions.

E. **1) The complete Harmonized Tariff Schedule (HTS) classification for all involved merchandise,**
2) the specific import/drawback claims by number (including identification of the licensed broker who filed the paperwork, where applicable),
3) a summary of the error and underlying causes, and
4) documentation to verify that all licensed broker(s) for the affected imports/drawback have been advised of the circumstances.

 As per 19 CFR 162.74(b):

§162.74 Prior disclosure.

… …

(b) *Disclosure of the circumstances of a violation.* The term "discloses the circumstances of a violation" means the act of providing to Customs a statement orally or in writing that:

(1) Identifies the **class or kind of merchandise involved** in the violation;

(2) Identifies the importation or drawback claim included in the disclosure by **entry number, drawback claim number, or by indicating each concerned Customs port of entry and the approximate dates of entry or dates** of drawback claims;

(3) Specifies the **material false statements, omissions or acts including an explanation as to how and when they occurred**; and

(4) Sets forth, to the best of the disclosing party's knowledge, **the true and accurate information or data that should have been provided** in the entry or drawback claim documents, and states that the disclosing party will provide any information or data unknown at the time of disclosure within 30 days of the initial disclosure date. … …

The correct answer is "B".

48. Which statement is NOT correct regarding an offer in compromise submitted pursuant to 19 U.S.C. 1617?

A. The amount of the offer must be deposited with CBP in accordance with the provisions of 19 CFR 161.5.

B. An offer in compromise will be considered accepted only when the offeror is notified in writing.

C. An offer in compromise submitted pursuant to 19 U.S.C. 1617 must expressly state that it is being submitted in accordance with the provisions of that section.

D. The offer shall be limited to the criminal and civil liability of the proponent in the matter which is the subject of the Government's claim.

E. As a condition to accepting an offer in compromise, the offeror may be required to enter into any collateral agreement or to post any security which is deemed necessary for the protection of the interest of the United States.

 As per 19 CFR 161.5 & 171.32:

§161.5 Compromise of Government claims.

(a) *Offer.* An offer made pursuant to section 617, Tariff Act of 1930, as amended (19 U.S.C. 1617), in compromise of a Government claim arising under the Customs laws and the terms upon which it is made shall be stated in writing addressed to the Commissioner of Customs. **The offer shall be limited to the civil liability of the proponent in the matter which is the subject of the Government's claim**.

(b) *Deposit of specific sum tendered.* No offer in which a specific sum of money is tendered in compromise of a Government claim under the Customs laws will be considered by the Commissioner of Customs until due notice is received that such sum has been properly deposited in the name of the person submitting the offer with the Treasurer of the United States or a Federal Reserve bank. A proponent at a distance from a Federal Reserve bank may perfect his offer by tendering a bank draft for the amount of the offer payable to the Secretary of the Treasury for collection and deposit. If the offer is rejected, the money will be returned to the proponent.

§171.32 Acceptance of offers in compromise.

An offer in compromise will be considered accepted only when the offeror is so notified in writing. As a condition to accepting an offer in compromise, the offeror may be required to enter into any collateral agreement or to post any security which is deemed necessary for the protection of the interest of the United States.

a An Offer in Compromise (OIC) by the importer will only be considered by CBP for civil penalties. The correct answer is "D".

✓ **JUST A SIDE NOTE:** An Offer in Compromise is completed when both parties to the issue agree upon the payment settlement. The term "Offer in Compromise" is most commonly used in the context of IRS settlements.

49. The following trade preference programs provide the merchandise processing fee (MPF) exemption, upon importation into the United States, to products of a beneficiary country even without a claim for preferential treatment. Choose the best answer applicable.

A. Chile Free Trade Agreement

B. Caribbean Basin Economic Recovery Act

C. The Israel Free Trade Area Agreement

D. Both "B" and "C"

E. None of the above, as the goods have to "originate" under the program and trade preference must be claimed

As per 19 CFR 24.23(c):

(c) *Exemptions and limitations.* (1) The ad valorem fee, surcharge, and specific fees provided for under paragraphs (b)(1) and (b)(2) of this section will not apply to:

… …

(iii) **Products of beneficiary countries under the Caribbean Basin Economic Recovery Act** (General Note 7, HTSUS);

… …

(5) The ad valorem fee, surcharge, and specific fees provided for under paragraphs (b)(1) and (b)(2) of this section **will not apply to products of Israel** that are entered, or withdrawn from warehouse for consumption, on or after September 16, 1998 (the effective date of a determination published in the FEDERAL REGISTER on September 1, 1998, under section 112 of the Customs and Trade Act of 1990).

… …

(7) The ad valorem fee, surcharge, and specific fees provided under paragraphs (b)(1) and (b)(2)(i) of this section will not apply to **goods that qualify as originating goods under** §202 of **the United States-Chile Free Trade Agreement** Implementation Act (see also General Note 26, HTSUS) that are entered, or withdrawn from warehouse for consumption, on or after January 1, 2004.

The above-mentioned regulations state that even without explicitly requesting trade agreement qualification, goods made in Israel or made in a country named in the Caribbean Basin Economic Recovery Act will benefit from exemption from the MPF payment requirement. The correct answer is "D".

✓ **JUST A SIDE NOTE:** Caribbean Basin Economic Recovery Act (CBERA) countries consist of:

Antigua and Barbuda	Aruba	Bahamas	Barbados	Belize	Curacao
Dominica	Grenada	Guyana	Haiti	Jamaica	Montserrat
Netherlands Antilles	St. Kitts and Nevis	Saint Lucia	Trinidad & Tobago	Virgin Islands, GB	Saint Vincent and the Grenadines

50. In our free trade agreements, the following list of materials is an example of:

- **Fuel and energy**
- **Tools, dies and molds**
- **Spare parts and materials used in the maintenance of equipment or buildings**
- **Lubricants, greases and compounding materials**
- **Gloves, footwear, safety equipment and supplies**
- **Testing or inspection equipment, catalysts, etc.**

A. Indirect materials
B. Accessories, spare parts or tools
C. Intermediate material
D. De minimis materials
E. Assists

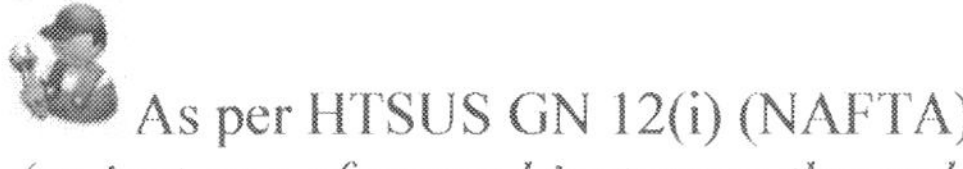

As per HTSUS GN 12(i) (NAFTA):
(as just one of several instances throughout the HTSUS)

(i) Indirect materials. An indirect material shall be considered to be an originating material without regard to where it is produced. The term **"indirect material" means** a good used in the production, testing or inspection of a good but not physically incorporated into the good, or a good used in the maintenance of buildings or the operation of equipment associated with the production of a good, including the following: **fuel and energy**; **tools, dies and molds**; **spare parts and materials used in the maintenance of equipment and buildings**; **lubricants, greases, compounding materials** and other materials used in production or used to operate other equipment and buildings; **gloves, glasses, footwear, clothing, safety equipment and supplies**; equipment, **devices and supplies used for testing or inspecting the goods; catalysts** and solvents; and any other goods that are not incorporated into the good but whose use in the production of the good can reasonably be demonstrated to be a part of that production.

"Indirect Materials" are used in the manufacturing process of the product, but are not part of the manufactured product, itself. The correct answer is "A".

✓ **JUST A SIDE NOTE:** As opposed to "Indirect Materials", what are "Intermediate Materials" as referenced in multiple choice "C"? CBP defines them on its website:

An intermediate material is a self-produced material, designated by the producer, that meets the rules of origin of Article 401 and that is incorporated into the final good. Article 415 defines a self-produced material as a material produced by the same party that produced the final goods and which is used in the production of those final goods.

51. Which free trade agreements take the NAFTA Marking Rules?

A. NAFTA and no others

B. NAFTA and CAFTA-DR

C. NAFTA, Bahrain FTA and Morocco FTA

D. NAFTA, AUFTA, COTPA and KORUS

E. None of the above

 As per 19 CFR 102.0:

§102.0 Scope.

With the exception of §§102.21 through 102.25, **this part sets forth rules for determining the country of origin of imported goods for the purposes specified in paragraph 1 of Annex 311 of the North American Free Trade Agreement ("NAFTA"). These specific purposes are: country of origin marking**; determining the rate of duty and staging category applicable to originating textile and apparel products as set out in Section 2 (Tariff Elimination) of Annex 300-B (Textile and Apparel Goods); and determining the rate of duty and staging category applicable to an originating good as set out in Annex 302.2 (Tariff Elimination). **The rules set forth in §§102.1 through 102.21 of this part will also apply for purposes of determining whether an imported good is a new or different article of commerce under §10.769 of the United States-Morocco Free Trade Agreement regulations and §10.809 of the United States-Bahrain Free Trade Agreement regulations.** The rules for determining the country of origin of textile and apparel products set forth in §102.21 apply for the foregoing purposes and for the other purposes stated in that section. Section 102.22 sets forth rules for determining whether textile and apparel products are considered products of Israel for purposes of the customs laws and the administration of quantitative limitations. Sections 102.23 through 102.25 set forth certain procedural requirements relating to the importation of textile and apparel products.

a This should be considered a challenging question. Neither the question, nor the regulations are straightforward on the subject. However, a case could be made that the correct answer is "C".

✓ **JUST A SIDE NOTE:** NAFTA was implemented in 1994, the Morocco FTA in 2006, and the Bahrain FTA also in 2006.

52. Under what free trade agreement can certain third-country goods originate, and thus be eligible for preferential tariff treatment upon importation into the United States (U.S.) merely for having been entered into the commerce of an FTA Party and then been subsequently imported into the U.S.?

A. The Australia Free Trade Agreement
B. The Morocco Free Trade Agreement
C. The North American Free Trade Agreement
D. The Singapore Free Trade Agreement
E. None of the above

 As per HTSUS General Note 25(b) & (m):

25. <u>United States-Singapore Free Trade Agreement</u>.

(a) Originating goods under the terms of the United States-Singapore Free Trade Agreement (SFTA) are subject to duty as provided herein. For the purposes of this note, goods of Singapore, as defined in subdivisions (b) through (o) of this note, that are imported into the customs territory of the United States and entered under a provision for which a rate of duty appears in the "Special" subcolumn of column 1 followed by the symbol "SG" in parentheses are eligible for the tariff treatment and quantitative limitations set forth in the "Special" subcolumn, in accordance with sections 201 and 202 of the United States-Singapore Free Trade Agreement Implementation Act (Pub.L.108-78; 117 Stat. 948).

(b) For the purposes of this note, subject to the provisions of subdivisions (c), (d), (n) and (o) thereof, goods imported into the customs territory of the United States are eligible for treatment as originating goods of a SFTA country under the terms of this note only if they–

(i) were wholly obtained or produced entirely in the territory of Singapore or of the United States, or both;

(ii) are goods that, in their condition as imported, are enumerated in subdivision (m) of this note and imported from the territory of Singapore; or

… …

<u>(m) Goods that shall be considered originating goods.</u> For the purposes of subdivision (b)(ii) of this note, goods that, in their condition as imported, are classifiable in the tariff provisions enumerated in the first column and are described opposite such provisions, when such goods are imported into the customs territory of the United States from the territory of Singapore, shall be considered originating goods for the purposes of this note:

	Heading/Subheading	Articles Subject to this Note
(1)	3818	Chemical elements doped for use in electronics, in the form of disks, wafers or similar forms; chemical compounds doped for use in electronics
(2)	7017.10.30, 7020.00.30	Quartz reactor tubes and holders designed for insertion into diffusion and oxidation furnaces for production of semiconductor wafers
(3)	8443.31.00, 8443.32.10, 8443.39.00, 8471.49.00, 9017.10.40, 9017.20.70, 9017.90.01	Plotters, whether input or output units of the automatic data processing machines of heading 8471 or drawing or drafting machines of heading 9017
(4)	8443.31.00, 8443.32.50	Facsimile machines
(5)	8443.31.00, 8443.32.10, 8443.99, 8471.60, 8528.41.00, 8528.51.00, 8528.61.00	Input or output units (including printers), whether or not containing storage units in the same housing; parts of printers

… …

Generally speaking, even if a product is not "made in Singapore", if it is imported into the U.S. from Singapore and classified under a Heading or Subheading listed in GN 25(m), it will qualify for preferential duty treatment under the Singapore FTA. For example, a fax machine (Subheading 8443.31.00) made in Malaysia, imported into Singapore (i.e. not just in transit), and exported to the United States can qualify for the Singapore FTA. The correct answer is "D".

53. Which of the following free trade agreements have a remanufacturing provision enabling certain non-originating third-country goods to be disassembled, cleaned, inspected and processed to bring into sound working condition as "recovered goods" and that such "recovered goods" are then considered originating materials when processed into a "remanufactured good".

A. AUFTA, CAFTA-DR, CLFTA & COTPA

B. Israel FTA, Jordan FTA & NAFTA

C. BHFTA, Jordan FTA & OMFTA

D. All of the above

E. None of the above

As per HTSUS General Note 26(c) (Chile FTA), GN 28(c) (Australia FTA), GN 29(c) (Dominican Republic-Central America FTA), GN 34(c) (Colombia FTA):

(using GN 26/Chile FTA as the example)

… …the expression **"wholly obtained or produced" means–**
… … **recovered goods derived in the territory of (Chile/participating country)** or of the United States, or both, from used goods; or

For the purposes of subdivision (i)(J), the term **"recovered goods" means materials in the form of individual parts that are the result of:**

(1) the complete disassembly of used goods into individual parts; and

(2) the cleaning, inspecting, testing or other processing of those parts as necessary for improvement to sound working condition by one or more of the following processes: welding, flame spraying, surface machining, knurling, plating, sleeving, and rewinding; the foregoing in order for such parts to be assembled with other parts, including other recovered parts, in **the production of a remanufactured good** as defined in subdivision (ii)(B).

Here's another challenging one. The AUFTA, DR-CAFTA, CLFTA & COTPA are not the only Free Trade Agreements with remanufacturing provisions. The Singapore FTA, for example, also has this provision. However, as the multiple-choice options are presented for the question here, "A" is the only combination of FTA's for with the remanufacturing provision applies to all in the selection. The correct answer is "A".

✓ **JUST A SIDE NOTE:** The Following Free Trade Agreements contain qualifying provisions for remanufactured goods:

Singapore FTA
Chile FTA
Morocco FTA
Australia FTA
DR-CAFTA
Bahrain FTA
Oman FTA
Peru FTA
Korea FTA
Colombia FTA
Panama FTA

Category IX – Foreign Trade Zones/Warehouses

54. CBP Form _________ must be presented to CBP timely to request a manipulation of freight to remove a prohibited item. Subsequently, in order to get the prohibited item exported, CBP Form___________ must be presented to CBP.

A. 3461 and 7512

B. 3499 and 7501

C. 3499 and 7512

D. 3499 and 1302

E. 4455 and 7512

As per 19 CFR 19.11(d) & 18.25(a):

§19.11 Manipulation in bonded warehouses and elsewhere.

(d) The application to manipulate, which shall be filed on Customs Form 3499 with the port director having jurisdiction of the warehouse or other designated place of manipulation, shall describe the contemplated manipulation in sufficient detail to enable the port director to determine whether the imported merchandise is to be cleaned, sorted, repacked, or otherwise changed in condition, but not manufactured, within the meaning of section 562, Tariff Act of 1930, as amended. If the port director is satisfied that the merchandise is to be so manipulated, he may issue a permit on Customs Form 3499, making any necessary modification in such form. The port director may approve a blanket application to manipulate on Customs Form 3499, for a period of up to one year, for a continuous or a repetitive manipulation. The warehouse proprietor must maintain a running record of manipulations performed under a blanket application, indicating the quantities before and after each manipulation. The record must show what took place at each manipulation describing marks and numbers of packages, location within the facility, quantities, and description of goods before and after manipulation. The port director is authorized to revoke a blanket approval to manipulate and require the proprietor to file individual applications if necessary to protect the revenue, administer any law or regulation, or both. Manipulation resulting in a change in condition of the merchandise, which will make it subject to a lower rate of duty or free of duty upon withdrawal for consumption, is not precluded by the provisions of such section 562.

18.25 Direct exportation.

(a) *Merchandise*—(1) *General*. Except for exportations by mail as provided for in subpart F of part 145 of this chapter (see also §158.45 of this chapter), **an in-bond application must be transmitted as provided under §18.1, for the following merchandise when it is to be directly exported** without transportation to another port:

(i) Merchandise in CBP custody for which no entry has been made or completed;

(ii) Merchandise covered by an unliquidated consumption entry; or

(iii) Merchandise that has been entered in good faith but is found to be prohibited under any law of the United States.

Although not explicitly spelled out in 19 CFR 18.25, an "in-bond application" implies the CBP Form 7512. The correct answer is "C".

✓ **JUST A SIDE NOTE:** A page on CBP's website provides examples of prohibited items, such as:

dangerous toys, cars that don't protect their occupants in a crash, bush meat (the meat of African wild animals), or illegal substances like absinthe (strong alcohol) and Rohypnol (strong tranquilizer).

55. A Foreign Trade Zone Operator shall prepare a reconciliation report within ______ days after the end of the zone/sub zone year unless the port director authorizes an extension for reasonable cause.

A. 30
B. 60
C. 90
D. 120
E. 180

 As per 19 CFR 146.25(a):

146.25 Annual reconciliation.

(a) *Report.* **The operator shall prepare a reconciliation report within 90 days after the end of the zone/subzone year** unless the port director authorizes an extension for reasonable cause. The operator shall retain that annual reconciliation report for a spot check or audit by Customs, and need not furnish it to Customs unless requested. There is no form specified for the preparation of the report.

(b) *Information required.* The report must contain a description of merchandise for each zone lot or unique identifer, zone status, quantity on hand at the beginning of the year, cumulative receipts and transfers (by unit), quantity on hand at the end of the year, and cumulative positive and negative adjustments (by unit) made during the year.

(c) *Certification.* The operator shall submit to the port director within 10 working days after the annual reconciliation report, a letter signed by the operator certifying that the annual reconciliation has been prepared, is available for Customs review, and is accurate. The certification letter must contain the name and street address of the operator, where the required records are available for Customs review; and the name, title, and telephone number of the person having custody of the records. Reporting of shortages and overages based on the annual reconciliation will be made in accordance with §146.53. These reports must accompany the certification letter.

 The correct answer is "C".

✓ **JUST A SIDE NOTE:** A Foreign Trade Zone vs. Subzone. Most U.S. auto manufacturing plants are FTZ subzones. CBP describes subzones on their website per below:

Subzones are normally private plant sites authorized by the Board and sponsored by a grantee for operations that usually cannot be accommodated within an existing general-purpose zone.

56. A Class 11 warehouse is a(n):

A. Duty Free warehouse

B. Public bonded warehouse

C. General Order warehouse

D. Bonded yard

E. Importers' private bonded warehouse

As per 19 CFR 19.1(a):

19.1 Classes of customs warehouses.

(a) *Classifications.* Customs warehouses shall be designated according to the following classifications:

(1) *Class 1.* Premises that may be owned or leased by the Government, when the exigencies of the service as determined by the port director so require, and used for the storage of merchandise undergoing examination … …

(2) *Class 2.* Importers' private bonded warehouses used exclusively for the storage of merchandise belonging or consigned to the proprietor thereof. A warehouse of class 4 or 5 may be bonded exclusively for the storage of … …

(3) *Class 3.* Public bonded warehouses used exclusively for the storage of imported merchandise.

(4) *Class 4.* Bonded yards or sheds for the storage of heavy and bulky imported merchandise; stables, feeding pens, corrals, or other similar buildings or limited enclosures for the storage of imported animals; and tanks for the … …

(5) *Class 5.* Bonded bins or parts of buildings or of elevators to be used for the storage of grain. The bonded portions shall be effectively separated from the rest of the building.

(6) *Class 6.* Warehouses for the manufacture in bond, solely for exportation, of articles made in whole or in part of imported materials or of materials subject to internal-revenue tax; and for the manufacture for home consumption … …

(7) *Class 7.* Warehouses bonded for smelting and refining imported metal-bearing materials for exportation or domestic consumption.

(8) *Class 8.* Bonded warehouses established for the purpose of cleaning, sorting, repacking, or otherwise changing in condition, but not manufacturing, imported merchandise, under Customs supervision and at the expense of the proprietor.

(9) *Class 9.* Bonded warehouse, known as "duty-free stores", used for selling, for use outside the Customs territory, conditionally duty-free merchandise owned or sold by the proprietor and delivered from the Class 9 warehouse … …

(10) [Reserved]

(11) *Class 11.* Bonded warehouses, known as "general order warehouses," established for the storage and disposition exclusively of general order merchandise as described in §127.1 of this chapter.

A Class 11 warehouse is a "General Order Warehouse" (also known as a G.O. Warehouse). The correct answer is "C".

✓ **INTERESTINGLY ENOUGH:** The world's first duty-free store (Class 9 Warehouse in the U.S.) was Shannon Airport, Ireland in 1947.

57. Which statement is TRUE?

A. **The importer must be notified in writing within 5 business days of the date of discovery.**

B. **The importer must pay duties on the affected merchandise within 20 days of the date of discovery.**

C. **The port director must be notified in writing within 20 business days of the date of discovery.**

D. **The proprietor must file a warehouse entry for the affected merchandise within 5 business days of the date of discovery.**

E. **The port director must be notified immediately upon discovery, and must receive written confirmation of the discovery within 5 days of the date the port director received initial notice.**

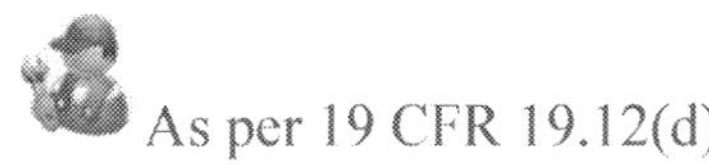
As per 19 CFR 19.12(d):

19.12 Inventory control and recordkeeping system.

… …

(d) *Accountability for merchandise in a warehouse*—(1) *Identification of merchandise.* The customs entry number or unique identifier, as applicable under §19.4(b)(8), will be used to identify and trace merchandise.

… …

(3) *Theft, shortage, overage or damage*—(i) *General.* Except as otherwise provided in paragraph (d)(3)(ii) of this section, **any theft or suspected theft or overage or any extraordinary shortage or damage** (equal to one percent or more of the value of the merchandise in an entry or covered by a unique identifier; or if the missing merchandise is subject to duties and taxes in excess of $100) **must be immediately brought to the attention of the port director, and confirmed in writing within five business days after the shortage, overage, or damage has been brought to the attention of the port director.** An entry for warehouse must be filed for all overages by the person with the right to make entry within five business days of the date of discovery. The responsible party must pay the applicable duties, taxes and interest on thefts and shortages reported to CBP within 20 calendar days following the end of the calendar month in which the shortage is discovered. The port director may allow the consolidation of duties and taxes applicable to multiple shortages into one payment; however, the amount applicable to each warehouse entry is to be listed on the submission and must specify the applicable duty, tax and interest. These same requirements apply when cumulative thefts, shortages or overages under a specific entry or unique identifier total one percent or more of the value of the merchandise or if the duties and taxes owed exceed $100. Upon identification, the proprietor must record all shortages and overages in its inventory control and recordkeeping system, whether or not they are required to be reported to the port director at the time. The proprietor must also record all shortages and overages as required in the CBP Form 300 or annual reconciliation report under paragraphs (g) or (h) of this section, as appropriate. Duties and taxes applicable to any non-extraordinary shortage or damage and not required to be paid earlier must be reported and submitted to the port director no later than the date the certification of preparation of CBP Form 300 is due or at the time the certification of preparation of the annual reconciliation report is due, as prescribed in paragraphs (g) or (h) of this section.

(ii) *Class 9 warehouses.* With respect to Class 9 warehouses, any theft or suspected theft or overage or any extraordinary shortage or damage (equal to one percent or more of the merchandise in an entry or covered by a unique … …

The correct answer is "E".

✓ **JUST A SIDE NOTE:** "Discovery" is a commonly used legal term, meaning "the compulsory disclosure, by a party to an action, of relevant documents referred to by the other party".

58. An article is produced in a beneficiary developing country and shipped to the United States through a free trade zone in a beneficiary developing country. Which of the operations below may be performed in the free trade zone if a claim for duty exemption under the Generalized System of Preferences is to be made upon entry into the United States?

A. Sewing, weaving, and knitting

B. Removal of burs by grinding

C. Sorting, grading, or testing

D. Assembly of parts totaling less than 35% of value of the article entering the zone

E. Annealing or heat treating of metals

 As per 19 CFR 10.175(c):

10.175 Imported directly defined.

Eligible articles shall be imported directly from a beneficiary developing country to qualify for treatment under the Generalized System of Preferences. For purposes of §§10.171 through 10.178 the words "imported directly" mean:

(a) Direct shipment from the beneficiary country to the United States without passing through the territory of any other country; or

(b) If the shipment is from a beneficiary developing country to the U.S. through the territory of any other country, the merchandise in the shipment does not enter into the commerce of any other country while en route to the U.S., and the invoice, bills of lading, and other shipping documents show the U.S. as the final destination; or

(c) If shipped from the beneficiary developing country to the United States through a free trade zone in a beneficiary developing country, the merchandise shall not enter into the commerce of the country maintaining the free trade zone, and

(1) The eligible articles must not undergo any operation other than:

(i) Sorting, grading, or testing,

(ii) Packing, unpacking, changes of packing, decanting or repacking into other containers,

(iii) Affixing marks, labels, or other like distinguishing signs on articles or their packing, if incidental to operations allowed under this section, or

(iv) Operations necessary to ensure the preservation of merchandise in its condition as introduced into the free trade zone.

 The correct answer is "C".

✓ **JUST A SIDE NOTE:** "Grading" refers to assessment of product quality (e.g. steel grade).

59. Which importation data element is CBP NOT permitted to disclose to the owner of a mark during the examination of articles suspected of bearing counterfeit marks?

A. The date of importation
B. The port of entry
C. A description of the merchandise
D. The quantity of the merchandise
E. The importer of the merchandise

 As per 19 CFR 133.21(b):

133.21 Articles suspected of bearing counterfeit marks.

... ...

(b) *Detention, notice, and disclosure of information*—(1) *Detention period.* CBP may detain any article of domestic or foreign manufacture imported into the United States that bears a mark suspected by CBP of being a counterfeit version
... ...

(4) *Disclosure to owner of the mark of limited importation information.* From the time merchandise is presented for examination, CBP may disclose to the owner of the mark limited importation information in order to obtain assistance in determining whether an imported article bears a counterfeit mark. Where CBP does not disclose this information to the owner of the mark prior to issuance of the notice of detention, it will do so concurrently with the issuance of the notice of detention, unless the information is unavailable, in which case CBP will release the information as soon as possible after issuance of the notice of detention. **The limited importation information CBP will disclose to the owner of the mark consists of:**

(i) The date of importation;

(ii) The port of entry;

(iii) The description of the merchandise, for merchandise not yet detained, from the paper or electronic equivalent of the entry (as defined in §142.3(a)(1) or (b) of this chapter), the CBP Form 7512, cargo manifest, advance electronic information or other entry document as appropriate, or, for detained merchandise, from the notice of detention;

(iv) The quantity, for merchandise not yet detained, as declared on the paper or electronic equivalent of the entry (as defined in §142.3(a)(1) or (b) of this chapter), the CBP Form 7512, cargo manifest, advance electronic information, or other entry document as appropriate, or, for detained merchandise, from the notice of detention; and

(v) The country of origin of the merchandise.

a When a suspected counterfeit product is to be "examined", CBP is not permitted to disclose information about the importer to the trademark owner. The correct answer is "E".

✓ **JUST A SIDE NOTE:** As per 19 CFR 133.22(a), A "copying or simulating" trademark or trade name is one which may so resemble a recorded mark or name as to be likely to cause the public to associate the copying or simulating mark or name with the recorded mark or name. See below example.

60. When merchandise is seized, CBP will disclose to the owner of the mark the following comprehensive importation information, if available, within 30 business days from the date of the notice of the seizure, EXCEPT:

A. The date of importation

B. The port of entry

C. The description of the merchandise from the notice of seizure

D. The quantity as set forth in the notice of seizure

E. The value of the merchandise

As per 19 CFR 133.21(e)

(e) *Seizure and disclosure to owner of the mark of comprehensive importation information.* Upon a determination by CBP, made any time after the merchandise has been presented for examination, that an article of domestic or foreign manufacture imported into the United States bears a counterfeit mark, CBP will seize such merchandise and, in the absence of the written consent of the owner of the mark, forfeit the seized merchandise in accordance with the customs laws. When merchandise is seized under this section, **CBP will disclose to the owner of the mark the following comprehensive importation information, if available, within 30 business days from the date of the notice of the seizure:**

(1) The date of importation;

(2) The port of entry;

(3) The description of the merchandise from the notice of seizure;

(4) The quantity as set forth in the notice of seizure;

(5) The country of origin of the merchandise;

(6) The name and address of the manufacturer;

(7) The name and address of the exporter; and

(8) The name and address of the importer.

When a confirmed counterfeit product is "seized", the above-mentioned paragraph (e) outlines what can be disclosed by CBP to the owner of the trademark. The correct answer is "E".

✓ **JUST A SIDE NOTE:** Counterfeit products not only create financial loss for rightful trademark owners, they (counterfeit products) also defraud customers.

61. In regard to "prohibited or restricted importations" relative to "articles involved in unfair competition," after the U.S. International Trade Commission issues an exclusion order pursuant to 19 U.S.C. § 1337, an importer of record has the following option(s) with respect to the entry of merchandise subject to that exclusion order:

A. The importer may enter merchandise subject to an exclusion order if the importer's basic importation bond contains a provision authorizing such action.

B. The importer may enter merchandise subject to an exclusion order for thirty days after the exclusion order issues, at which point the Commission's exclusion order becomes final and entry is no longer permitted.

C. Until the time the Commission's exclusion order becomes final, the importer may enter merchandise subject to the exclusion order by filing a single entry bond with CBP in an amount determined by the U.S International Trade Commission to be sufficient to protect the complainant from any injury.

D. Until the time the Commission's exclusion order becomes final, the importer may enter merchandise subject to the exclusion order by filing a single entry bond with CBP in an amount set by the port director to ensure compliance with the customs and related laws.

E. None of the above because an exclusion order is effective on the date it is issued and merchandise subject to that exclusion order cannot be entered lawfully after this point.

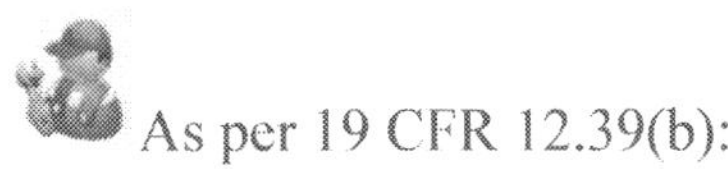

As per 19 CFR 12.39(b):

12.39 Imported articles involving unfair methods of competition or practices.

… …

(b) *Exclusion from entry; entry under bond; notice of exclusion order.* (1) If the Commission finds a violation of section 337, or reason to believe that a violation exists, it may direct the Secretary of the Treasury to exclude from entry into the United States the articles concerned which are imported by the person violating or suspected of violating section 337. The Commission's exclusion order remains in effect until the Commission determines, and notifies the Secretary of the Treasury, that the conditions which led to the exclusion no longer exist, or until the determination of the Commission on which the order is based is disapproved by the President.

(2) During the period the Commission's exclusion order remains in effect, excluded articles may be entered under a single entry bond in an amount determined by the International Trade Commission to be sufficient to protect the complainant from any injury. On or after the date that the Commission's determination of a violation of section 337 becomes final, as set forth in paragraph (a) of this section, articles covered by the determination will be refused entry. If a violation of section 337 is found, the bond may be forfeited to the complainant under terms and conditions prescribed by the Commission. To enter merchandise that is the subject of a Commission exclusion order, importers must:

… …

The correct answer is "C".

✓ **JUST A SIDE NOTE:** An "exclusion order" is a government order denying entry into the country.

62. What statement is FALSE?

A. **An application to record a trademark must include the places of manufacture of goods bearing the recorded trademark.**

B. **The fee to accompany an application of trademark is $190.00 for each class**

C. **The recordation of a trademark shall remain in force for 20 years**

D. **A counterfeit mark may be detained for a period up to 60 days from the date on which the merchandise is presented.**

E. **Protection for a recorded trade name shall remain in force as long as the trade name is used. The recordation shall be canceled upon request of the recordant or upon evidence of disuse.**

 As per 19 CFR 133.21(b):

133.21 Articles suspected of bearing counterfeit marks.

(a) *Counterfeit mark defined.* A "counterfeit mark" is a spurious mark that is identical with, or substantially indistinguishable from, a mark registered on the Principal Register of the U.S. Patent and Trademark Office.

(b) *Detention, notice, and disclosure of information*—(1) *Detention period.* **CBP may detain any article of domestic or foreign manufacture imported into the United States that bears a mark suspected by CBP of being a counterfeit** version of a mark that is registered with the U.S. Patent and Trademark Office and is recorded with CBP pursuant to subpart A of this part. **The detention will be for a period of up to 30 days from the date on which the merchandise is presented for examination.** In accordance with 19 U.S.C. 1499(c), if, after the detention period, the article is not released, the article will be deemed excluded for the purposes of 19 U.S.C. 1514(a)(4).

… …

 The counterfeit mark detention period is 30 (not 60) days. The correct answer is "D".

✓ **JUST A SIDE NOTE:** In certain counterfeit trademark cases, at CBP's discretion, offending importers may be allowed to enter their shipment if all offending trademarks are removed or obliterated prior to customs release.

63. Goods determined to be "restricted gray market":

A. Are subject to immediate seizure

B. Are considered to be counterfeit

C. Are subject to detention

D. Will be excluded from entry but not seized

E. All of the above

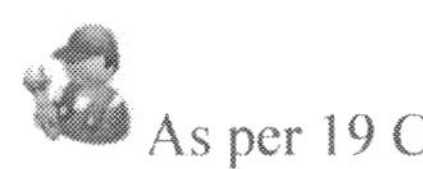As per 19 CFR 133.23(c):

133.23 Restrictions on importation of gray market articles.

… …

(c) *Denial of entry.* **All restricted gray market goods imported into the United States shall be denied entry and subject to detention** as provided in §133.25, except as provided in paragraph (b) of this section.

 The correct answer is "C".

✓ **JUST A SIDE NOTE:** "Gray market goods" are not counterfeit. Rather, they are legitimately produced goods not authorized by the trademark owner for sale in the country they are being illegally imported into.

Category XI – Marking

64. CBP Form ___________ from the port director shall notify the importer of articles or containers that are found upon examination not to be legally marked.

A. 4647

B. 301

C. 7512

D. 434

E. 7501

As per 19 CFR 134.51(a):

134.51 Procedure when importation found not legally marked.

(a) *Notice to mark or redeliver.* **When articles or containers are found upon examination not to be legally marked, the Center director shall notify the importer on Customs Form 4647**, or its electronic equivalent, to arrange with the Center director's office to properly mark the article or containers, or to return all released articles to Customs custody for marking, exportation, or destruction.

The correct answer is "A".

✓ **JUST A SIDE NOTE:** The ACE (Automated Commercial Environment) portal allows ACE users to review and respond to CBP Form 4647 (Notice to Mark/Notice to Re-Deliver).

65. When an Importer submits a Repacking Statement (Certificate of Marking by Importer-Repacked Articles Subject to Marking) to CBP, they are certifying that the imported article ___________________:

A. **Will be sold or transferred to a subsequent purchaser.**

B. **Does not have to be marked with the country of origin.**

C. **Was repacked not to conceal or obscure the country of origin marking, or the container, unless excepted, was marked legibly and indelibly in a conspicuous place.**

D. **Will remain in the Importer's possession.**

E. **Will obscure origin and conceal the country of origin.**

As per 19 134.26(a):

134.26 Imported articles repacked or manipulated.

(a) *Certification requirements.* If an article subject to these requirements is intended to be repacked in retail containers (e.g., blister packs) after its release from Customs custody, or if the Center director has reason to believe such article will be repacked after its release, **the importer shall certify to the Center director that: (1) If the importer does the repacking, he shall not obscure or conceal the country of origin marking** appearing on the article, or else the new container shall be marked to indicate the country of origin of the article in accordance with the requirements of this part; or (2) if the article is intended to be sold or transferred to a subsequent purchaser or repacker, the importer shall notify such purchaser or transferee, in writing, at the time of sale or transfer, that any repacking of the article must conform to these requirements. The importer, or his authorized agent, shall sign the following statement.

CERTIFICATE OF MARKING BY IMPORTER—REPACKED ARTICLES SUBJECT TO MARKING

(Port of entry)

I, ____ of ____, certify that if the article(s) covered by this entry (entry no.(s) __ dated __), is (are) repacked in retail container(s) e.g., blister packs), while still in my possession, the new container(s) will not conceal or obscure the country of origin marking appearing on the article(s), or else the new container(s), unless excepted, shall be marked in a conspicuous place as legibly, indelibly, and permanently as the nature of the container(s) will permit, in such manner as to indicate the country of origin of the article(s) to the ultimate purchaser(s) in accordance with the requirements of 19 U.S.C. 1304 and 19 CFR part 134. I further certify that if the article(s) is (are) intended to be sold or transferred by me to a subsequent purchaser or repacker, I will notify such purchaser or transferee, in writing, at the time of sale or transfer, of the marking requirements.

Date
Importer

The certification statement may appear as a typed or stamped statement on an appropriate entry document or commercial invoice, or on a preprinted attachment to such entry or invoice; or it may be submitted in blanket form to cover all importations of a particular product for a given period (e.g., calendar year). If the blanket procedure is used, a certification must be filed with CBP, either at the port of entry or electronically.

The correct answer is "C".

✓ **JUST A SIDE NOTE:** As per 19 CFR 134.26(d), if the articles subject to repacking requirements are sold, the seller is obligated to provide a "Notice to Subsequent Purchaser or Repacker" to the buyer.

66. Every article of foreign origin imported into the US shall be marked according to the following conditions, EXCEPT:

A. The article must be marked in a conspicuous place.

B. The marking must be as legible, indelible, and permanent as the nature of the article will permit.

C. The marking must indicate the English name of the country of origin of the article at the time of importation.

D. The marking must indicate the year it was produced.

E. The marking should be on each article or its container.

As per 19 CFR 134.11:

134.11 Country of origin marking required.

Unless excepted by law, section 304, Tariff Act of 1930, as amended (19 U.S.C. 1304), requires that **every article of foreign origin (or its container)** imported into the United States **shall be marked in a conspicuous place as legibly, indelibly, and permanently as the nature of the article (or container) will permit**, in such manner as to indicate to an ultimate purchaser in the United States **the English name of the country of origin of the article, at the time of importation into the Customs territory of the United States.** Containers of articles excepted from marking shall be marked with the name of the country of origin of the article unless the container is also excepted from marking.

 correct answer is "D".

✓ **JUST A SIDE NOTE:** Marked "indelibly" means "in a way that cannot be removed or forgotten".

67. A-Z Corp imported a shipment of tote bags from China. These bags will be sold in A-Z Corp's stores throughout the U.S. The entry was covered by a continuous bond for basic importation and entry. CBP discovered that half of the shipment was not properly marked with the country of origin and released it conditionally. What will happen if after Customs Form 4647 is issued, A-Z Corp fails to properly mark or to return to CBP custody for marking, exportation, or destruction?

A. A-Z Corp will be charged additional duties in the amount of 10% of the entire shipment.

B. A-Z Corp will be assessed liquidated damages equal to the lesser of the entered value of the improperly marked merchandise or the amount of the bond.

C. A-Z Corp will be assessed liquidated damages in the amount of three times the value of the merchandise or the amount of the bond, whichever is less.

D. A-Z Corp will be required to re-export or destroy the improperly marked merchandise.

E. A-Z Corp will be considered to be the "ultimate purchaser" of the merchandise.

 As per 19 CFR 134.54(a):

134.54 Articles released from Customs custody.

(a) *Demand for liquidated damages.* If within 30 days from the date of the notice of redelivery, or such additional period as the Center director may allow for good cause shown, the importer does not properly mark or redeliver all merchandise previously released to him, **the port director shall demand payment of liquidated damages incurred under the bond in an amount equal to the entered value of the articles not properly marked or redelivered.**

 The correct answer is "B".

✓ **JUST A SIDE NOTE:** In regards to relief from payment in full of liquidated damages, 19 CFR 134.54(c) says:

Any relief from the payment of the full liquidated damages incurred will be contingent upon the deposit of the marking duty required by 19 U.S.C. 1304(f), and the satisfaction of the Fines, Penalties, and Forfeitures Officer that the importer was not guilty of bad faith in permitting the illegally marked articles to be distributed, has been diligent in attempting to secure compliance with the marking requirements, and has attempted by all reasonable means to effect redelivery of the merchandise.

68. Which of the following principal types of power of attorney are limited to a period not to exceed 2 years from the date of execution?

A. Corporation
B. Partnership
C. Individual
D. Corporation and Partnership
E. Partnership and Individual

 As per 19 CFR 141.34:

141.34 Duration of power of attorney.

Powers of attorney issued by a partnership shall be limited to a period not to exceed 2 years from the date of execution. All other powers of attorney may be granted for an unlimited period.

 The correct answer is "B".

✓ **INTERESTINGLY ENOUGH:** Depending on the jurisdiction, some Power of Attorneys (POA) must be notarized. The POA for US Customs' purposes, however, need not be notarized.

69. When may a power of attorney be revoked?

A. **Prior to last transaction**

B. **Within 30 days from execution**

C. **Upon written approval by the Port Director**

D. **At any time by written notice given to and received by the Port Director**

E. **It may not be revoked**

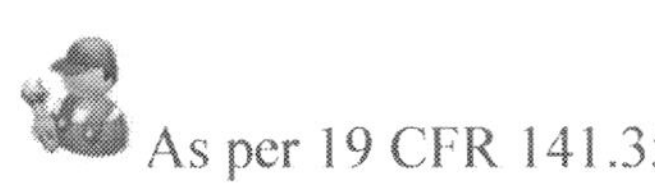

As per 19 CFR 141.35:

141.35 Revocation of power of attorney.

Any power of attorney shall be subject to revocation at any time by written notice given to and received by CBP, either at the port of entry or electronically.

An importer may communicate to their customs broker their wish to revoke a POA at any time. Per the regulations, the POA is officially revoked when advised so by the importer to CBP in writing (e.g. via a letter or email). The correct answer is "D".

✓ **JUST A SIDE NOTE:** CBP recommends that customs brokers and freight forwarders validate the POA's they receive from their customers. This means verifying that the importer or exporter is who they say they are, and that they are not on any of the U.S. government's sanctions lists.

70. CBP Form __________ may be used for giving power of attorney to transact Customs business.

A. 3461

B. 3495

C. 5291

D. 7501

E. 4811

As per 19 CFR 141.32:

141.32 Form for power of attorney.

Customs Form 5291 may be used for giving power of attorney to transact Customs business. If a Customs power of attorney is not on a Customs Form 5291, it shall be either a general power of attorney with unlimited authority or a limited power of attorney as explicit in its terms and executed in the same manner as a Customs Form 5291. The following is an example of an acceptable general power of attorney with unlimited authority:

KNOW ALL MEN BY THESE PRESENTS, THAT

____

(Name of principal)

____________________ ,

(State legal designation, such as corporation, individual, etc.) residing at _______________ and doing business under the laws of the State of ______, hereby appoints

(Name, legal designation, and address)

as a true and lawful agent and attorney of the principal named above with full power and authority to do and perform every lawful act and thing the said agent and attorney may deem requisite and necessary to be done for and on behalf of the said principal without limitation of any kind as fully as said principal could do if present and acting, and hereby ratify and confirm all that said agent and attorney shall lawfully do or cause to be done by virtue of these presents until and including ______, (date) or until notice of revocation in writing is duly given before that date.

Date __________, 19__;.

(Principal's signature)

Although it is not required to be used to give POA, CBP Form 5291 may be used. The correct answer is "C".

✓ **JUST A SIDE NOTE:** One definition of "attorney" is "a person appointed to act for another in business or legal matters". It is derived from the Old French word "atorner" which means "to assign".

Category XIII – Practical Exercise

Using the information provided below, please answer Questions 71 through 75

Below are two Powers of Attorney (POA). The first was received by James Brown, General Manager, South Coast Freight Forwarder & Logistics, Inc. (a freight forwarder), from Hillcrest Merchants Corp., on December 31, 2014 (POA1). The second was issued by South Coast Freight Forwarder & Logistics, Inc., to Barbara Sun, a customs broker doing business as Sunshine Brokers, on January 2, 2015 (POA 2). The importing history between the customs broker on behalf of the importer of record demonstrates that entries were made on February 1, 2015; March 1, 2015 and May 22, 2015.

POA 1: South Coast Freight Forwarder & Logistics, Inc. from Hillcrest Merchants Corp.

CUSTOMS POWER OF ATTORNEY

I hereby authorize South Coast Freight Forwarders & Logistics, Inc. to act as Hillcrest Merchants Corp. agent and customs broker and to file entry/entry summary for all commercial shipments from January 1, 2015 onwards.
Hillcrest Merchants Corp. authorizes other duly licensed customs brokers to act as Grantor's agent.

(Capacity): BUYER Date: DECEMBER 31, 2014 (Signature) ______________ (Signed) ___________

POA 2: South Coast Freight Forwarder & Logistics, Inc. to Barbara Sun dba: Sunshine Brokers

CUSTOMS POWER OF ATTORNEY

KNOW ALL MEN BY THESE PRESENTS: That **HILLCREST MERCHANTS CORP** doing business as a corporation under the laws of the State of **North Carolina** residing or having a place of business at **6231 Waterville Road, Raleigh, North Carolina** hereby constitutes and appoints **Barbara Sun dba SUNSHINE BROKERS**, which may act through any of its licensed officers or employees duly authorized to sign documents by power of attorney as a true and lawful agent and attorney of the grantor named above for and in the name, place, and stead of said grantor from this date and in **ALL Customs Ports** and in no other name, to make, endorse, sign, declare, or swear to any entry, withdrawal, declaration, certificate, bill of lading, carnet, or other document required by law or regulation in connection with the importation, transportation, or exportation of any merchandise shipped or consigned by or to said grantor; to perform any act or condition which may be required by law or regulation in connection with such merchandise; to receive any merchandise deliverable to said grantor.

To receive, endorse and collect checks issued for Customs duty refunds in grantor's name drawn on the Treasurer of the United States.

This power of attorney is to remain in full force and effect until revocation in writing is duly given to and received by grantee (if the donor of this power of attorney is a partnership, the said power shall in no case have any force or effect in the United States after the expiration 2 years from the dates of its execution);

IN WITNESS WHEREOF: the said **HILLCREST MERCHANTS CORP.** has caused these presents to be sealed and signed:

(Signature) __________ (Signed) ________ (Print Name) ____JAMES BROWN ________

(Capacity) _ATTORNEY IN FACT______________ Date: ______JANUARY 2, 2015___________

Witness: (if required) _____________ (Signature) __________________________

If you are the importer of record, payment to the broker will not relieve you of liability for customs charges (duties, taxes, or other debts owed CBP) in the event the charges are not paid by the broker. Therefore, if you pay by check, customs charges may be paid with a separate check payable to U.S. Customs and Border Protection which shall be delivered to CBP by the broker. Importers who wish to utilize this procedure must contact our office in advance to arrange timely receipt of duty checks.

71. Which person or entity may act as the intended importer of record?

A. Hillcrest Merchants Corp.
B. South Coast Logistics, Inc.
C. The nominal consignee
D. Sunshine Brokers
E. James Brown A.I.F.

 As per Customs Directive 3530-002A, Section 5.3:

5.3 OWNER OR PURCHASER DEFINED

5.3.1 The terms "owner" and "purchaser" include any party with a financial interest in a transaction, including, but not limited to, the actual owner of the goods, the actual purchaser of the goods, a buying or selling agent, a person or firm who imports on consignment, a person or firm who imports under loan or lease, a person or firm who imports for exhibition at a trade fair, a person or firm who imports goods for repair or alteration or further fabrication, etc. **Any such owner or purchaser may make entry on his own behalf or may designate a licensed Customs broker to make entry on his behalf and may be shown as the importer of record** on the CF 7501. The terms "owner" or "purchaser" would not include a "nominal consignee" who effectively possesses no other right, title, or interest in the goods except as he possessed under a bill of lading, air waybill, or other shipping document.

5.3.2 Examples of nominal consignees not authorized to file Customs entries are express consignment operators (ECO), freight consolidators who handle consolidated shipments as described in 5.10 below, and Customs brokers who are not permitted to transact business in Customs ports where a shipment is being entered.

Hillcrest Merchants Corp. is the owner/purchaser of the goods, and accordingly will be the importer of record. The correct answer is "A".

✓ **JUST A SIDE NOTE:** Customs Directive 3530-002A, Section 5.1 describes which parties may act as importer of record per below.

5.1.1 RIGHT TO MAKE ENTRY

5.1.2 Section 484 provides that only the "importer of record" has the right to make entry. "Importer of Record" is defined as the owner or purchaser of the goods, or when designated by the owner, purchaser, or consignee, a licensed Customs broker.

5.1.3 A nominal consignee may designate a Customs broker to make entry on his behalf but may not make entry on his own behalf. If a Customs broker makes entry for a nominal consignee, the broker must appear as importer of record.

5.1.4 The purpose of the amendment to Section 484 was to prevent nominal consignees, other than licensed Customs brokers, from filing entries and thereby engaging in the transaction of Customs business without a license.

72. Based on the information provided for POA 1, which statement is TRUE?

A. POA 1 allows the forwarder to create an agency relationship (i.e., assign the POA to a broker).

B. POA 1 allows the South Coast Logistics, Inc. to classify and value the imported merchandise, and report the outcome to U.S. Customs and Border Protection.

C. The Vice President of an incorporated business entity must sign the POA 1.

D. POA 1 is invalid since it does not allow for the service of process.

E. POA 1 must be on CBP Form 5291 "Power of Attorney".

 As per 19 CFR 141.31(a):

141.31 General requirements and definitions.

(a) *Limited or general power of attorney.* **A power of attorney may be executed for the transaction by an agent or attorney of a specified part or all the Customs business of the principal.**

(b) [Reserved]

(c) *Minor agents.* A power of attorney to a minor shall not be accepted.

(d) *Definitions of resident and nonresident.* For the purposes of this subpart, "resident" means an individual who resides within, or a partnership one or more of whose partners reside within, the Customs territory of the United States or the Virgin Islands of the United States, or a corporation incorporated in any jurisdiction within the Customs territory of the United States or in the Virgin Islands of the United States. A "nonresident" means an individual, partnership, or corporation not meeting the definition of "resident."

a The importer, Hillcrest Merchants Corp., authorizes the freight forwarder, South Coast Freight Forwarder & Logistics, Inc., to make customs entries on Hillcrest's behalf via POA 1. POA 1 also authorizes South Coast to authorize other customs brokers to do the same on Hillcrest's behalf. The correct answer is "A".

✓ **JUST A SIDE NOTE:** Both POA's may be considered "general power of attorneys", as both basically give unlimited authority to conduct customs business on the principal's behalf, void of any port, date, or other explicit restrictions.

73. Based on the information provided for POA 2, which statement is FALSE?

A. POA 2 identifies a resident principal.

B. POA 2 omits the "notice to client of method of payment".

C. Failure of the broker to retain a valid POA may result in a monetary penalty in an amount not to exceed an aggregate of $30,000.00 for one or more violations.

D. POA 2 may be granted for an unlimited period of time.

E. POA 2 authorizes the broker to sign documents in Puerto Rico.

 As per 19 CFR 111.29(b):

111.29 Diligence in correspondence and paying monies.

(a) *Due diligence by broker.* Each broker must exercise due diligence in making financial settlements, in answering correspondence, and in preparing or assisting in the preparation and filing of records relating to any customs business matter handled by him as a broker. Payment of duty, tax, or other debt or obligation owing to the Government for which the broker is responsible, or for which the broker has received payment from a client, must be made to the Government on or before the date that payment is due. Payments received by a broker from a client after the due date must be transmitted to the Government within 5 working days from receipt by the broker. Each broker must provide a written statement to a client accounting for funds received for the client from the Government, or received from a client where no payment to the Government has been made, or received from a client in excess of the Governmental or other charges properly payable as part of the client's customs business, within 60 calendar days of receipt. No written statement is required if there is actual payment of the funds by a broker.

(b) *Notice to client of method of payment.* (1) **All brokers must provide their clients with the following written notification:**

If you are the importer of record, payment to the broker will not relieve you of liability for customs charges (duties, taxes, or other debts owed CBP) in the event the charges are not paid by the broker. Therefore, if you pay by check, customs charges may be paid with a separate check payable to the "U.S. Customs and Border Protection" which will be delivered to CBP by the broker.

(2) The written notification set forth in paragraph (b)(1) of this section must be provided by brokers as follows:

(i) On, or attached to, any power of attorney provided by the broker to a client for execution on or after September 27, 1982; and

(ii) To each active client no later than February 28, 1983, and at least once at any time within each 12-month period after that date. An active client means a client from whom a broker has obtained a power of attorney and for whom the broker has transacted customs business on at least two occasions within the 12-month period preceding notification.

a POA 2 duly gives "notice to client of method of payment". The false statement, and thus the correct answer is "B".

✓ **JUST A SIDE NOTE:** POA 1 does not provide the "notice to client of method of payment" statement and thus the customs broker must otherwise provide the notice to the importer (e.g. include with the customs broker's billing invoice to the importer).

74. Upon review of both POAs, which statement is FALSE?

A. The customs broker may prepare and present the entry summary to CBP.

B. South Coast Freight Forwarder & Logistics, Inc. may authorize the customs broker to forward a completed CBP Form 3461.

C. The customs broker shall exercise responsible supervision and control when transacting customs business.

D. The POA may be completed and signed after the merchandise has been released from CBP custody.

E. Hillcrest Merchants Corp. is a resident corporate principal.

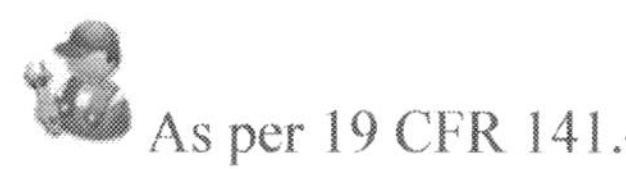

As per 19 CFR 141.46:

141.46 Power of attorney retained by customhouse broker.

Before transacting Customs business in the name of his principal, a customhouse broker is required to obtain a valid power of attorney to do so. He is not required to file the power of attorney with CBP. Customhouse brokers shall retain powers of attorney with their books and papers, and make them available to representatives of the Department of the Treasury as provided in subpart C of part 111 of this chapter.

A Power of Attorney must be valid (i.e. legally binding) prior to a customs broker acting on behalf of the client. The correct answer is "D".

✓ **JUST A SIDE NOTE:** In signing a legal document, such as a POA, blue ink is preferable to black ink as it is more easily identified as an actual signature (as opposed to a copy). Some countries require their customs-related documents be signed with blue ink, though this is not the case in the U.S.

75. The Customs broker shall retain POA 2 for a period of 5 years starting on __________.

A. December 31, 2014

B. January 2, 2015

C. February 1, 2015

D. March 1, 2015

E. May 22, 2015

 As per 19 CFR 111.23(b):

111.23 Retention of records.

(a) *Place of retention.* A licensed customs broker may retain records relating to its customs transactions at any location within the customs territory of the United States in accordance with the provisions of this part and part 163 of this chapter. Upon request by CBP to examine records, the designated recordkeeping contact identified in the broker's applicable permit application, in accordance with §111.19(b)(6) of this chapter, must make all records available to CBP within 30 calendar days, or such longer time as specified by CBP, at the broker district that covers the CBP port to which the records relate.

(b) *Period of retention.* The records described in this section, other than powers of attorney, must be retained for at least 5 years after the date of entry. **Powers of attorney must be retained until revoked, and revoked powers of attorney and letters of revocation must be retained for 5 years after the date of revocation or for 5 years after the date the client ceases to be an "active client"** as defined in §111.29(b)(2)(ii), whichever period is later. When merchandise is withdrawn from a bonded warehouse, records relating to the withdrawal must be retained for 5 years from the date of withdrawal of the last merchandise withdrawn under the entry.

POA 2 must be retained for five years from the last customs transaction date involving the two parties (Hillcrest & Barbara Sun), which was the entry on May 22, 2015. The correct answer is "E".

✓ **JUST A SIDE NOTE:** 19 CFR 111.29(b) defines "active client" as "a client from whom a broker has obtained a power of attorney and for whom the broker has transacted customs business on at least two occasions within the 12-month period preceding notification".

Category XIV – Value

76. If the port director believes that the entered rate or value of any merchandise is too low, or if he finds that the quantity imported exceeds the entered quantity, and the estimated aggregate of the increase in duties on that entry exceeds $15, he shall promptly notify the importer on Customs Form 29, or its electronic equivalent, specifying the nature of the difference on the notice. Liquidation shall be made promptly and shall not be withheld for a period of more than ___________________ days from the date of mailing such notice unless in the judgment of the port director there are compelling reasons that would warrant such action.

A. 5
B. 10
C. 15
D. 20
E. 30

 As per 19 CFR 152.2:

152.2 Notification to importer of increased duties.

If the Center director believes that the entered rate or value of any merchandise is too low, or if he finds that the quantity imported exceeds the entered quantity, and the estimated aggregate of the increase in duties on that entry exceeds $15, he shall promptly notify the importer on Customs Form 29, or its electronic equivalent specifying the nature of the difference on the notice. **Liquidation shall be made promptly and shall not be withheld for a period of more than 20 days** from the date of mailing of such notice unless in the judgment of the Center director there are compelling reasons that would warrant such action.

 The correct answer is "D".

✓ **JUST A SIDE NOTE:** The above-mentioned Notice of Action by CBP via CBP Form 29 is protestable via CBP Form 19 (Protest).

77. A used mold was provided free of charge to a Korean manufacturer by the U.S. importer. The used mold cost the importer $85,000 prior to sending it to Korea. Because of its poor condition, the importer had it repaired for $2,500 before shipping the mold to Korea. The importer paid freight cost of $1,000 and the Korean manufacturer paid $500 import duty for the mold. What is the total value of the assist?

A. $85,000
B. $86,000
C. $87,500
D. $88,500
E. $89,000

 As per 19 CFR 152.103(d):

(d) *Assist.* If the value of an assist is to be added to the price actually paid or payable, or to be used as a component of computed value, the Center director shall determine the value of the assist and apportion that value to the price of the imported merchandise in the following manner:

... ...

(2) If the assist consists of tools, dies, molds, or similar items used in the production of the imported merchandise, acquired by the buyer from an unrelated seller,the value of the assist is the cost of its acquisition. If the assist were produced by the buyer or a person related to the buyer, its value would be cost of its production. If the assist has been used previously by the buyer, regardless of whether it had been acquired or produced by him, the original cost of acquisition or production would be adjusted downward to reflect its use before its value could be determined. If the assist were leased by the buyer from an unrelated seller, the value of the assist would be the cost of the lease. In either case, **the value of the assist would include transportation costs to the place of production. Repairs or modifications to an assist may increase its value.**

 The correct answer is "D".

$85,000 (cost of mold assist)
\+ 2,500 (repairs on assist)
\+ 1,000 (transport cost)
=$88,500 (total value of the assist)

✓ **JUST A SIDE NOTE:** 19 CFR 152.103(e) explains the three ways importers may apportion (i.e. prorate) assists values to their entries:

(e) *Apportionment.* (1) The apportionment of the value of assists to imported merchandise will be made in a reasonable manner appropriate to the circumstances and in accordance with generally accepted accounting principles. The method of apportionment actually accepted by Customs will depend upon the documentation submitted by the importer. If the entire anticipated production using the assist is for exportation to the United States, the total value may be apportioned over (i) the first shipment, if the importer wishes to pay duty on the entire value at once, (ii) the number of units produced up to the time of the first shipment, or (iii) the entire anticipated production. In addition to these three methods, the importer may request some other method of apportionment in accordance with generally accepted accounting principles. If the anticipated production is only partially for exportation to the United States, or if the assist is used in several countries, the method of apportionment will depend upon the documentation submitted by the importer.

(2) *Interpretative note.* An importer provides the producer with a mold to be used in the production of the imported merchandise and contracts to buy 10,000 units. By the time of arrival of the first shipment of 1,000 units, the producer has already produced 4,000 units. The importer may request Customs to apportion the value of the mold over 1,000, 4,000, 10,000 units, or any other figure which is in accordance with generally accepted accounting principles.

78. ABC Inc. purchases 10,000 glass vases from Overseas Trading Company. The wholesale price charged by Overseas Trading Company is $3.00 per vase with the following volume discounts:

1 – 1,000 vases	**full price**
1,001 – 5,000 vases	**5% discount**
5,001 – 15,000 vases	**10% discount**
15,001 – 25,000 vases	**15% discount**

ABC Inc. receives the shipment and finds that 100 of the vases are broken. They contact Overseas Trading Company, who agrees not to charge ABC Inc. for the broken vases. What is the transaction value for the vases?

A. $30,000
B. $29,700
C. $27,000
D. $26,730
E. $26,700

 As per 19 CFR 152.103(a):

152.103 Transaction value.

(a) *Price actually paid or payable*—(1) *General.* **In determining transaction value, the price actually paid or payable will be considered without regard to its method of derivation. It may be the result of discounts, increases, or negotiations, or may be arrived at by the application of a formula**, such as the price in effect on the date of export in the London Commodity Market. The word "payable" refers to a situation in which the price has been agreed upon, but actual payment has not been made at the time of importation. Payment may be made by letters of credit or negotiable instruments and may be made directly or indirectly.

 The correct answer is "C".

$30,000 (10,000 vases x $3.00 ea. price)
<u>- $300</u> (300 broken vases x $3.00 ea. credit)
=$27,000 (transaction value/price actually payable)

✓ **JUST A SIDE NOTE:** A credit for broken or defective merchandise may be deducted from the transaction value. However, a rebate after the date of import for other miscellaneous purposes may not be deducted.

79. Merchandise imported into the United States may be appraised according to:

A. The selling price in the United States of merchandise produced in the United States

B. The price of the merchandise in the domestic market of the country of importation

C. The price of merchandise for export to a country other than the United States

D. Minimum values for appraisement

E. Arbitrary or fictitious values

 As per 19 CFR 152.108:

152.108 Unacceptable bases of appraisement.

For the purposes of this subpart, **imported merchandise may not be appraised on the basis of:**

(a) The selling price in the United States of merchandise produced in the United States;

(b) A system that provides for the appraisement of imported merchandise at the higher of two alternative values;

(c) The price of merchandise in the domestic market of the country of exportation;

(d) A cost of production, other than a value determined under §152.106 for merchandise that is identical merchandise, or similar merchandise, to the merchandise being appraised;

(e) The price of merchandise for export to a country other than the United States;

(f) Minimum values for appraisement;

(g) Arbitrary or fictitious values.

 Through the process of elimination, we may infer that the correct answer here is "B".

✓ **JUST A SIDE NOTE:** The following methods of import value appraisal are to be used, in order, until the appropriate method can be applied. As per 19 CFR 152.101(b):

(b) *Methods.* Imported merchandise will be appraised on the basis, and in the order, of the following:

(1) The transaction value provided for in §152.103;

(2) The transaction value of identical merchandise provided for in §152.104, if the transaction value cannot be determined, or can be determined but cannot be used because of the limitations provided for in §152.103(j);

(3) The transaction value of similar merchandise provided for in §152.104, if the transaction value of identical merchandise cannot be determined;

(4) The deductive value provided for in §152.105, if the transaction value of similar merchandise cannot be determined;

(5) The computed value provided for in §152.106, if the deductive value cannot be determined; or

(6) The value provided for in §152.107, if the computed value cannot be determined.

80. Which statement is TRUE?

A. Interest on overdue bills will be assessed on the delinquent principal amount by 60- day periods. No interest charge will be assessed for the 60-day period in which the payment is actually received at the "Send Payment To" location designated on the bill.

B. Imported merchandise may not be appraised on the basis of the price of merchandise in the domestic market of the country of exportation.

C. For the purpose of the entry of theatrical scenery, properties and apparel under subheading 9817.00.98, Harmonized Tariff Schedule of the United States, animals imported for use or exhibition in theaters or menageries may not be classified as theatrical properties.

D. A person transacting business in connection with entry or clearance of vessels or other regulation of vessels under the navigation laws is required to be licensed as a broker.

E. For purposes of administering quotas, "official office hours" shall mean 8:30 a.m. to 4:30 a.m. in all time zones.

As per 19 CFR 152.108(c):

152.108 Unacceptable bases of appraisement.

For the purposes of this subpart, **imported merchandise may not be appraised on the basis of:**

(a) The selling price in the United States of merchandise produced in the United States;

(b) A system that provides for the appraisement of imported merchandise at the higher of two alternative values;

(c) The price of merchandise in the domestic market of the country of exportation;

(d) A cost of production, other than a value determined under §152.106 for merchandise that is identical merchandise, or similar merchandise, to the merchandise being appraised;

(e) The price of merchandise for export to a country other than the United States;

(f) Minimum values for appraisement;

(g) Arbitrary or fictitious values.

The correct answer is "B".

✓ **JUST A SIDE NOTE:** CBP has a very helpful and in-depth (approx. 580 pages) resource on the subject of appraisement / valuation, titled "U.S. Customs and Border Protection Valuation Encyclopedia", an Informed Compliance Publication, last updated in 2016, and currently at the following url:

https://www.cbp.gov/sites/default/files/assets/documents/2016-Jul/Valuation%20Encyclopedia%20Dec%202015%20final.pdf

Book 1 Part 10

Exam with Broker Commentary

April 2017 Customs Broker License Examination

This section of the study guide analyzes an actual customs broker exam. It presents the actual question and its multiple choices. For HTSUS classification questions, the author of this book has included abbreviated HTSUS Article Descriptions notated directly to the right of each multiple-choice classification for the student's convenience and ease of reference purposes. The indentation and spacing of some questions have been modified for ease of use. As necessary, and in proportion to the complexity of each particular exam question, an analysis of the question and path to the correct answer has been provided. Direct excerpts from the HTSUS, 19 CFR, etc. are also included as supporting points of reference for each answer, as necessary. This exam (without commentary, etc.) and its answer key, as well as other previous customs exams can be downloaded directly from Customs' website at…

http://www.cbp.gov/document/publications/past-customs-broker-license-examinations-answer-keys

Exam Refs:

Harmonized Tariff Schedule of the United States
Title 19, Code of Federal Regulations
Instructions for Preparation of CBP Form 7501
Right to Make Entry Directive, 3530-002A

Exam Breakdown by Subject:

Category I	**Antidumping/Countervailing Duties**	**Questions 1 - 3**
Category II	**Bonds**	**Questions 4 - 8**
Category III	**Broker Compliance**	**Questions 9 - 14**
Category IV	**Classification**	**Questions 15 - 26**
Category V	**Drawback**	**Questions 27 - 30**
Category VI	**Entry**	**Questions 31 - 41**
Category VII	**Fines and Penalties**	**Questions 42 - 47**
Category VIII	**Free Trade Agreements**	**Questions 48 - 53**
Category IX	**Foreign Trade Zones**	**Questions 54 - 57**
Category X	**Intellectual Property Rights**	**Questions 58 - 61**
Category XI	**Marking**	**Questions 62 - 64**
Category XII	**Power of Attorney**	**Questions 65 - 67**
Category XIII	**Practical Exercise**	**Questions 68 - 75**
Category XIV	**Value**	**Questions 76 – 80**

Category I: Antidumping/Countervailing Duties

1. What is the correct entry type code for a warehouse withdrawal for antidumping/countervailing duties (AD/CVD)?

A. 03
B. 21
C. 34
D. 32
E. 31

 As per FORM 7501 INSTRUCTIONS, Block 2:

Consumption Entries	
Free and Dutiable	01
Quota/Visa	02
Antidumping/Countervailing Duty (AD/CVD)	03
Appraisement	04
Vessel Repair	05
Foreign Trade Zone Consumption	06
Quota/Visa and AD/CVD combinations	07
Duty Deferral	08
Informal Entries	
Free and Dutiable	11
Quota Other than textiles	12
Warehouse Entries	
Warehouse	21
Re-Warehouse	22
Temporary Importation Bond	23
Trade Fair	24
Permanent Exhibition	25
Foreign Trade Zone Admission	26
Warehouse Withdrawal	
For Consumption	31
Quota/Visa	32
AD/CVD	**34**
Quota/Visa and AD/CVD combinations	38

… …

 The answer is "C".

✓ **JUST A SIDE NOTE:** CBP defines a "customs bonded warehouse" as "a building or other secured area in which imported dutiable merchandise may be stored, manipulated, or undergo manufacturing operations without payment of duty for up to 5 years from the date of importation."

2. In which column on the CBP Form 7501 would you report the AD/CVD CASE Number?

A. Column 27
B. Column 28
C. Column 29
D. Column 32
E. Column 34

 As per FORM 7501 INSTRUCTIONS, Column 29:

COLUMN 29)

… …

B. AD/CVD CASE NUMBER

Directly below the HTS number, indicate the appropriate AD/CVD case number(s), as assigned by the Department of Commerce, International Trade Administration. The following format shall be used:

A000-000-000 -or- A-000-000-000 (AD)
C000-000-000 -or- C-000-000-000 (CV)

Case numbers with a suffix of 000 (ex. A-000-000-000) should only be used when the manufacturer and/or exporter falls under the "All Other" or country wide provisions of the AD/CVD case.

… …

 The correct answer is "C".

✓ **JUST A SIDE NOTE:** As per the same Form 7501 Instructions for Column 29:

The application of case numbers should follow this hierarchy under the following circumstances:

1. *The exporter has its own rate, use the case assigned to the exporter;*

2. *The exporter does not have its own case, use the case assigned to the manufacturer/producer; OR the case assigned to the exporter/manufacturer combination; or*

3. *Neither the exporter nor the manufacturer/producer nor the exporter/manufacturer combination has its own case, use the "all others" case with a suffix of 000.*

3. Top Dawg imported seven ball bearings with integral shafts from Germany, which are classified under subheading 8482.10.10, Harmonized Tariff Schedule of the United States, at a 2.4% ad valorem duty rate and subject to antidumping duties. The ball bearings are shipped by air and formally entered at John F. Kennedy International Airport. The total value of the shipment is $9,875.00. The applicable antidumping duty case deposit rate is 68.89%. What are the total amount of fees and estimated duties that should be reported on the CBP Form 7501?

A. $237.00
B. $7,039.89
C. $7,074.10
D. $6,837.10
E. $6,802.89

 As per FORM 7501 INSTRUCTIONS, Column 29:

... ...

D. OTHER FEES

Directly below the pertinent line information, on the same line as the applicable rate in column 33, identify any other fee, charge or exaction that applies. Examples include the beef fee, honey fee, pork fee, cotton fee, harbor maintenance fee (HMF), sugar fee, and merchandise processing fee (MPF). All fees, with the exception of the HMF, are to be reported at the line item level. The HMF may be shown either at the line item level or once at the bottom of column 29 on the first page of the summary.

$9,875.00	$9,875.00	$9,875.00 (Value)	
x .024 (Duty)	x .6889 (AD)	x .003464 (MPF)	
$237.00	+$6,802.89	+$34.21	= $7,074.10

This is an easy one to miss since the Merchandise Processing Fee (MPF) is not explicitly referenced in the question. Note, however, that the question asks "What are the TOTAL amount of FEES AND estimated duties". The Harbor Maintenance Fee (HMF) does not apply as the shipment is via air (i.e. not ocean). The correct answer is "C".

✓ **JUST A SIDE NOTE:** MPF Increase

Per CSMS (Cargo Systems Messaging Service)17-000734, effective January 1, 2018, the MPF minimum for formal entries (class code 499) will increase from $25 to $25.67 and the maximum will increase from $485 to $497.99. The ad valorem rate of 0.3464% will NOT change

4. CBP will periodically review each bond on file to determine whether the bond is adequate to protect the revenue and ensure compliance with applicable law and regulations. If CBP determines that a bond is inadequate, the principal and surety will be promptly notified in writing. The principal will have how many days from the date of notification to remedy the deficiency?

A. 10 days
B. 15 days
C. 20 days
D. 25 days
E. 30 days

 As per 19 CFR 113.13(c):

(c) *Periodic review of bond sufficiency*. CBP will periodically review each bond on file to determine whether the bond is adequate to protect the revenue and ensure compliance with applicable law and regulations. If CBP determines that a bond is inadequate, the principal and surety will be promptly notified in writing. **The principal will have 15 days from the date of notification to remedy the deficiency.** Notwithstanding the foregoing, where CBP determines that a bond is insufficient to adequately protect the revenue and ensure compliance with applicable law and regulations, CBP may provide written notice to the principal and surety that, upon receipt thereof, additional security in the form of cash deposit or single transaction bond may be required for any and all of the principal's transactions until the deficiency is remedied.

 The correct answer is "B".

✔ **JUST A SIDE NOTE:** Just as there are mandatory minimum amounts for auto liability insurance that help to ensure that drivers will adequately compensate affected parties for damages caused, a customs bond in a sufficient amount is deemed necessary to guarantee importer payment of duty and tax obligations to Customs.

5. Entry summary documentation was not filed timely for a shipment of $100,000.00 entered with Single Transaction Bond (STB) in the amount of $110,000.00. Liquidated damages will be assessed at:

A. The entire amount of the STB ($110,000)
B. $100,000 plus duties and fees
C. $100,000 plus duties
D. 10% of the value of the merchandise
E. Duties and Fees

 As per 19 CFR 142.15:

If the entry summary documentation is not filed timely, the port director shall make an immediate demand for liquidated damages in the entire amount of the bond in the case of a single entry bond. When the transaction has been charged against a continuous bond, the demand shall be for the amount that would have been demanded if the merchandise had been released under a single entry bond. Any application to cancel liquidated damages incurred shall be made in accordance with part 172 of this chapter.

 The correct answer is “A”.

JUST A SIDE NOTE: As per CBP’s website…

A single entry bond is generally in an amount not less than the total entered value, plus any duties, taxes and fees.

6. In determining whether the amount of a bond is sufficient, CBP will consider all of the below EXCEPT:

A. The value and nature of the merchandise involved in the transaction(s) to be secured.
B. The degree and type of supervision that CBP will exercise over the transaction(s)
C. The volume of import transactions conducted annually.
D. The prior record of the principal in timely payment of duties, taxes, and charges with respect to the transaction(s) involving such payments
E. The prior record of the principal honoring bond commitments, including the payment of liquidated damages.

 As per 19 CFR 113.13(b):

(b) ***Guidelines for determining amount of bond.*** **In determining whether the amount of a bond is sufficient, CBP will consider:**

(1) The prior record of the principal in timely payment of duties, taxes, and charges with respect to the transaction(s) involving such payments;

(2) The prior record of the principal in complying with CBP demands for redelivery, the obligation to hold unexamined merchandise intact, and other requirements relating to enforcement and administration of customs and other laws and CBP regulations;

(3) The value and nature of the merchandise involved in the transaction(s) to be secured;

(4) The degree and type of supervision that CBP will exercise over the transaction(s);

(5) The prior record of the principal in honoring bond commitments, including the payment of liquidated damages; and

(6) Any additional information contained in any application for a bond.

While continuous bond amounts are calculated based on an annual amount of duties and fees with a minimum bond amount of $50,000, the number (i.e. volume) of import transactions is not a factor. The correct answer is "C".

✓ **NOTE:** The current CBP bond formula and worksheet can be found at the following:

https://www.cbp.gov/document/forms/current-bond-formulas

7. If any CBP Bond, except one given only for the production of free-entry or reduced-duty documents, has not been satisfied upon the expiration of _______________ has accrued under the bond, the matter will be reported to the Department of Justice for prosecution unless measures have been taken to file an application for relief or protest to satisfactorily settle this matter.

A. 30 days after liability
B. 60 days after liability
C. 90 days after liability
D. 120 days after liability
E. 180 days after liability

 As per 19 CFR 113.52:

§113.52 Failure to satisfy the bond.

If any CBP bond, except one given only for the production of free-entry or reduced-duty documents (see §113.43(c) of this chapter) **has not been satisfied upon the expiration of 180 days after liability has accrued under the bond**, **the matter will be reported to the Department of Justice for prosecution unless measures have been taken to file an application for relief or protest in accordance with the provisions of this chapter or to satisfactorily settle this matter.**

 The correct answer is "E".

✓ **JUST A SIDE NOTE:** Basic Customs bond conditions include the payment of duties and fees, redelivery to Customs of conditionally released merchandise, etc.

8. Which statement is TRUE concerning Customs Bonds?

A. The surety, as well as the port director, remains liable on a terminated bond for obligations incurred prior to termination.
B. Continuous bond applications must be submitted to the Commissioner of Customs.
C. The principal may list on the bond trade names and the names of unincorporated divisions of the corporate principal which have a separate and distinct legal status who are authorized to use the bond in their own name.
D. A continuous bond is effective on the effective date identified on CBP Form 368.
E. A surety on a CBP bond which is in default may be accepted as surety on other CBP bonds only to the extent that the surety assets are unencumbered by the default.

As per 19 CFR 113.38(b):

(b) *Acceptance as surety when in default as surety on another CBP bond.* **A surety on a CBP bond which is in default may be accepted as surety on other CBP bonds only to the extent that the surety assets are unencumbered by the default.**

The correct statement and answer is "E".

✓ **JUST A SIDE NOTE:** Conversely, an importer (as opposed to a surety company) in default on a Customs bond with surety company A cannot be accepted by surety company B on a separate Customs bond.

9. The triennial process consists of a status report and fee payment that must be submitted by all licensed brokers. The regulations governing this process may be found:

A. 19 CFR § 10.31(3)(ii)
B. 19 CFR § 142.12 (b)
C. 19 CFR § 114.3
D. 19 CFR § 111.30 (d)
E. 19 CFR § 163.4 (a)

 As per 19 CFR 111.30(d):

(d) ***Status report***—(1) General. Each broker must file a written status report with Customs on February 1, 1985, and on February 1 of each third year after that date. The report must be accompanied by the fee prescribed in §111.96(d) and must be addressed to the director of the port through which the license was delivered to the licensee (see §111.15). A report received during the month of February will be considered filed timely. No form or particular format is required.

(2) Individual. Each individual broker must state in the report required under paragraph (d)(1) of this section whether he is actively engaged in transacting business as a broker. If he is so actively engaged, he must also:

(i) State the name under which, and the address at which, his business is conducted if he is a sole proprietor;

(ii) State the name and address of his employer if he is employed by another broker, unless his employer is a partnership, association or corporation broker for which he is a qualifying member or officer for purposes of §111.11(b) or (c)(2); and

(iii) State whether or not he still meets the applicable requirements of §§111.11 and 111.19 and has not engaged in any conduct that could constitute grounds for suspension or revocation under §111.53.
… …

 In general, any item related to custom broker compliance will be found in part 111. The correct answer is "D".

✓ **JUST A SIDE NOTE:** The symbol "§" means "section". So, "§ 111.30", for example, means section 30 of part 111.

10. When must Form 3347, Declaration of Owner, be filed?

A. Within 90 days from the time of entry
B. At the time of entry
C. Any time before final liquidation
D. Within 180 days from the time of entry
E. When entry summary is filed

As per 19 CFR 141.20(a):

(a) *Filing*—(1) Declaration of owner. A consignee in whose name an entry summary for consumption, warehouse, or temporary importation under bond is filed, or in whose name a rewarehouse entry or a manufacturing warehouse entry is made, and who desires, under the provisions of section 485(d), Tariff Act of 1930, as amended (19 U.S.C. 1485(d)), to be relieved from statutory liability for the payment of increased and additional duties shall declare at the time of the filing of the entry summary or entry documentation, as provided in §141.19(a), that he is not the actual owner of the merchandise, furnish the name and address of the owner, and file with CBP, either at the port of entry or electronically **within 90 days from the time of entry (see §141.68) a declaration of the actual owner of the merchandise acknowledging that the actual owner will pay all additional and increased duties. The declaration of owner shall be filed on Customs Form 3347.**

This is somewhat of a trick question. The Declaration of Owner form "can" be submitted at the time of entry (i.e. multiple-choice "B"), however, it "must" be filed within 90 days of this date. The correct answer is "A".

✓ **JUST A SIDE NOTE:** Below is a partial snapshot of what the above-mentioned CBP Form 3347 looks like.

DEPARTMENT OF HOMELAND SECURITY
U.S. Customs and Border Protection

OMB No. 1651-0093
Exp. 12-31-2019

DECLARATION OF OWNER
FOR MERCHANDISE OBTAINED (OTHERWISE THAN) IN PURSUANCE OF A PURCHASE OR AGREEMENT TO PURCHASE
19 CFR 24.11(a)(1), 141.20

This declaration must be presented at the port of entry within 90 days after the date of entry in order to comply with Section 485(d), of the Tariff Act of 1930. **LINE OUT EACH PHRASE SHOWN IN ITALICS NOT APPLICABLE TO THIS DECLARATION.**

1. NAME OF OWNER		2. ADDRESS OF OWNER (STREET, CITY, STATE, ZIP CODE)		3. SUPERSEDING BOND SURETY CODE
4. PORT OF ENTRY	5. PORT CODE	6. IMPORTER NUMBER OF AUTHORIZED AGENT (SHOW HYPHENS)		7. VESSEL/CARRIER ARRIVED FROM
8. IMPORTER NUMBER OF OWNER (SHOW HYPHENS)		9. ENTRY NUMBER	10. DATE OF ENTRY	11. DATE OF ARRIVAL

11. What factor is NOT considered by Customs when measuring if a brokerage is exercising proper supervision and control?

A. Circumstances which indicate that the licensed broker has a real interest in the operations of the business
B. Issuance of written instructions and guidelines to employees of the broker
C. Volume and type of business
D. Location of where records are stored and size of office
E. Extent the local permit qualifying broker is involved in the operation

 As per 19 CFR 111.1 (Definitions):

… …

Responsible supervision and control. "Responsible supervision and control" means that degree of supervision and control necessary to ensure the proper transaction of the customs business of a broker, including actions necessary to ensure that an employee of a broker provides substantially the same quality of service in handling customs transactions that the broker is required to provide. While the determination of what is necessary to perform and maintain responsible supervision and control will vary depending upon the circumstances in each instance, **factors which CBP will consider include, but are not limited to: The training required of employees of the broker; the issuance of written instructions and guidelines to employees of the broker; the volume and type of business of the broker; the reject rate for the various customs transactions; the maintenance of current editions of CBP Regulations, the Harmonized Tariff Schedule of the United States, and CBP issuances; the availability of an individually licensed broker for necessary consultation with employees of the broker; the frequency of supervisory visits of an individually licensed broker to another office of the broker that does not have a resident individually licensed broker; the frequency of audits and reviews by an individually licensed broker of the customs transactions handled by employees of the broker; the extent to which the individually licensed broker who qualifies the district permit is involved in the operation of the brokerage; and any circumstance which indicates that an individually licensed broker has a real interest in the operations of a broker.**

… …

The customs broker may retain records anywhere in the United States, and regardless of office size, provided that the records are readily accessiblé (within 30 days of request for documents). The correct answer is "D".

✓ **JUST A SIDE NOTE:** Customs brokers must keep their clients' customs entry records strictly confidential, and therefore when the time comes to dispose of (e.g. after 5 years from date of entry, unnecessary copies produced, etc.) documents must be shredded.

12. Under which scenario below would a broker be exempt from notifying importers annually of their right to pay CBP directly under 19 CFR 111.29?

A. The importer has contracted for payment through a freight forwarder, and the broker's invoice to the freight forwarder provides notice of the right to pay CBP directly.
B. The broker has not transacted Customs business on behalf of the importer for the preceding six months.
C. The broker has provided clear written instructions to the freight forwarder to provide a copy of the 19 C.F.R. 111.29(b)(1) statement to the importer directly.
D. All of the Above.
E. None of the Above.

As per 19 CFR 111.29(b):

(b) *Notice to client of method of payment.* (1) **All brokers must provide their clients with the following written notification:**

If you are the importer of record, payment to the broker will not relieve you of liability for customs charges (duties, taxes, or other debts owed CBP) in the event the charges are not paid by the broker. Therefore, if you pay by check, customs charges may be paid with a separate check payable to the "U.S. Customs and Border Protection" which will be delivered to CBP by the broker.

(2) The written notification set forth in paragraph (b)(1) of this section must be provided by brokers as follows:

(i) On, or attached to, any power of attorney provided by the broker to a client for execution on or after September 27, 1982; and

(ii) **To each active client no later than February 28, 1983, and at least once at any time within each 12-month period after that date. An active client means a client from whom a broker has obtained a power of attorney and for whom the broker has transacted customs business on at least two occasions within the 12-month period preceding notification.**

The customs broker must provide the duties liability statement to all of their importers, with the only excepting for "non-active clients". The correct answer is "E".

13. For each release of merchandise, what is the maximum penalty that may be assessed against an importer who is negligent in producing entry records at the request of an Import Specialist?

A. An amount not to exceed 40% of the appraised value of the merchandise
B. An amount not to exceed 75% of the appraised value of the merchandise
C. $10,000
D. $100,000
E. $75,000

 As per 19 CFR 163.6(b):

(b) ***Failure to produce entry records***—(1) Monetary penalties applicable. The following penalties may be imposed if a person fails to comply with a lawful demand for the production of an entry record and is not excused from a penalty pursuant to paragraph (b)(3) of this section:

(i) If the failure to comply is a result of the willful failure of the person to maintain, store, or retrieve the demanded record, such person shall be subject to a penalty, for each release of merchandise, not to exceed $100,000, or an amount equal to 75 percent of the appraised value of the merchandise, whichever amount is less; or

(ii) **If the failure to comply is a result of negligence of the person in maintaining, storing, or retrieving the demanded record, such person shall be subject to a penalty, for each release of merchandise, not to exceed $10,000**, or an amount equal to 40 percent of the appraised value of the merchandise, whichever amount is less.
... ...

Although "A" may not appear to be incorrect, the "maximum" penalty amount is $10,000. The technically correct answer is "C".

✔ **JUST A SIDE NOTE:** Generally speaking, entry records must be maintained for 5 years, however, drawback claim records and packing lists must only be kept for three years and 60 days respectively.

14. John Henry received a license through the port of Duluth, MN (3604). John Henry also has a local permit for the port of Duluth, MN (3604). John Henry is now looking to move his business to the port of Minneapolis, MN (3501). Which of the following is the correct course of action for John Henry to take?

A. John Henry should notify the port of Minneapolis, MN of the new address.
B. John Henry should send a letter cancelling the permit to Minneapolis, MN.
C. John Henry should request to be permitted in Duluth, MN.
D. John Henry should apply for a National permit and pay in Duluth, MN.
E. John Henry should send a triennial report and fee to Minneapolis, MN.

As per 19 CFR 111.19 (b) & (c):

(b) ***Submission of application for*** *initial or* ***additional district permit****.* A broker who intends to conduct customs business at a port within another district for which he does not have a permit, or a broker who was not concurrently granted a permit with the broker's license under paragraph (a) of this section, and except as otherwise provided in paragraph (f) of this section, **must submit an application for a permit in a letter to the director of the port at which he intends to conduct customs business**. Each application for a permit must set forth or attach the following:

... ...

(c) *Fees.* Each application for a district permit under paragraph (b) of this section must be accompanied by the fees specified in §§111.96(b) and (c). **In the case of an application for a national permit** under paragraph (f) of this section, the fee specified in §111.96(b) and the fee specified in §111.96(c) **must be paid at the port through which the applicant's license was delivered** (see §111.15) prior to submission of the application. The fee specified in §111.96(c) also must be paid in connection with the issuance of an initial district permit concurrently with the issuance of a license under paragraph (a) of this section.

Although one possible course of action for John Henry to take would be to apply for an additional district permit at the port of Minneapolis, this is not included in the list of multiple choice options. Alternatively, John Henry can apply for a national permit through Duluth, which is provided for in the correct answer "D".

✓ **JUST A SIDE NOTE:** "35" is the district code prefix for "Minneapolis, Minnesota". "36" is the code prefix for separate district "Duluth, Minnesota". See below snapshot from the HTSUS Statistical Annex C:

35. MINNEAPOLIS, MINNESOTA
01. Minneapolis-St Paul, MN
02. Sioux Falls, SD
10. Duluth, MN-Superior, WI
11. Ashland, WI
12. Omaha, NE
13. Des Moines, IA
81. Rochester User Fee Airport,Rochester, MN

36. DULUTH, MINNESOTA
04. International Falls, MN
13. Grand Portage, MN

(This Page Intentionally Left Blank)

15. The duty free provision for returned American Goods is found in ____________________.

A. 9813.00.35
B. 9812.00.20
C. 9801.00.10
D. 9808.00.30
E. 9806.00.50

 As per HTSUS Chapter 98 (see following page):

 The correct answer is "C".

✓ **NOTE:** This 9801.00.10 is not an uncommonly used classification for claiming duty-free entry on U.S.-made goods being returned to the United States. The last two digits of the classification depend on the nature (e.g. Chapter 1 thru. 97 chapter or heading) of the item.

Heading/ Subheading	Stat. Suf-fix	Article Description	Unit of Quantity	Rates of Duty 1 General	Rates of Duty 1 Special	2
9801.00.10		Products of the United States when returned after having been exported, or any other products when returned within 3 years after having been exported, without having been advanced in value or improved in condition by any process of manufacture or other means while abroad		Free		
	10	Articles previously exported with intent to reimport after temporary use abroad	X			
	12	Articles returned temporarily for repair, alteration, processing or the like, the foregoing to be reexported	X			
		Other:				
	15	Meat and poultry products provided for in chapter 2 or 16	kg			
	26	Peanuts provided for in heading 1202	kg			
	27	Articles provided for in chapter 28	X			
	28	Articles provided for in chapter 30	X			
	29	Articles provided for in chapter 37	X			
	30	Articles provided for in chapter 71	X			
	31	Articles provided for in chapter 82	X			
		Articles provided for in chapter 84:				
	35	Articles provided for in headings 8407.10, 8409.10, 8411 or 8412.10	X			
	37	Articles provided for in headings 8419.31, 8424.41, 8424.49, 8424.82, 8424.90, 8429.11, 8429.19, 8431.42, 8432, 8433, 8434 or 8436	X			
	43	Articles provided for in headings 8470, 8471, 8472 or 8473	X			
	45	Other	X			
		Articles provided for in chapter 85:				
	49	Articles provided for in headings 8501, 8502 or 8503	X			
	51	Articles provided for in heading 8504	X			
	53	Articles provided for in headings 8517, 8519, 8525, 8527 or 8529	X			
	55	Other	X			
	59	Articles provided for in chapter 86	X			
		Articles provided for in chapter 87:				
	63	Articles provided for in heading 8701	No.			
	64	Articles provided for in heading 8702	No.			
	65	Articles provided for in heading 8703	No.			
	66	Articles provided for in heading 8704	No.			
	67	Articles provided for in headings 8706, 8707 or 8708	X			
	69	Articles provided for in headings 8705 or 8709	X			
	74	Other	No.			
		Articles provided for in chapter 88:				
	75	Articles provided for in headings 8801 or 8802	X			
	77	Articles provided for in headings 8803 or 8804	X			
	79	Article provided for in heading 8805	X			

16. What is the CLASSIFICATION of a men's woven shirt, made of 65 % rayon and 35 % polyester fiber? The garment features a full front zippered opening, a pocket on the left chest panel, a pointed collar, long sleeves with buttoned cuffs, and a straight hemmed bottom with two side vents.

A. 6205.20.2066	Men's or boys' shirts>>Of cotton>>Other>>Other>>Other>>Other
B. 6205.30.1510	Men's or boys' shirts>>Of man-made fibers>>Other>>Containing 36 percent or more by weight of wool or fine animal hair>>Men's
C. 6205.90.4040	Men's or boys' shirts>>Of other textile materials>>Other>>Other
D. 6205.20.2051	Men's or boys' shirts>>Of cotton>>Other>>Other>>Other>>With two or more colors in the warp and/or the filling>>Other>>Men's
E. 6205.30.2070	Men's or boys' shirts>>Of man-made fibers>>Other>>Other>>Other>>Other>>Men's

 As per HTSUS, SECTION XI (TEXTILES AND TEXTILE ARTICLES) Note 2(A):

2. (A) Goods classifiable in chapters 50 to 55 or in heading 5809 or 5902 and of **a mixture of two or more textile materials are to be classified as if consisting wholly of that one textile material which predominates by weight over each other single textile material.**

When no one textile material predominates by weight, the goods are to be classified as if consisting wholly of that one textile material which is covered by the heading which occurs last in numerical order among those which equally merit consideration.

a Let's disregard some of the "fluffy" overkill in the question's commodity description and just note that the item in question is a men's woven shirt of 100% man-made fiber (65% rayon + 35% polyester). Accordingly, we can narrow down our choices to just "B" and "E". The shirt does not contain wool or any animal hair, so we may eliminate "B". Therefore, by the process of elimination here, we know that the correct answer is "E".

✓ **NOTE:** The difference between "synthetic" fibers and "artificial" fibers is that "artificial" fibers are made from naturally-occurring substances, such as plant cellulose. Both, however, are "man-made" fibers. Nylon, for example, is a synthetic fiber. HTSUS Chapter 54 (Man-made filaments/textiles) Note 1 defines "man-made fibers" as:

Notes

1. **Throughout the tariff schedule, the term "man-made fibers" means staple fibers and filaments of organic polymers produced by manufacturing processes**, either:

(a) By polymerization of organic monomers to produce polymers such as polyamides, polyesters, polyolefins or polyurethanes, or by chemical modification of polymers produced by this process (for example, poly(vinyl alcohol) prepared by the hydrolysis of poly(vinyl acetate)); or

(b) By dissolution or chemical treatment of natural organic polymers (for example, cellulose) to produce polymers such as cuprammonium rayon (cupro) or viscose rayon, or by chemical modification of natural organic polymers (for example, cellulose, casein and other proteins, or alginic acid), to produce polymers such as cellulose acetate or alginates.

... ...

The terms "<u>man-made</u>", "<u>synthetic</u>" and "<u>artificial</u>" shall have the same meanings when used in relation to "<u>textile materials</u>".

Heading/ Subheading	Stat. Suf- fix	Article Description	Unit of Quantity	Rates of Duty 1 General	1 Special	2
6205 (con.)		Men's or boys' shirts: (con.)				
6205.30		Of man-made fibers:				
6205.30.10	00	Certified hand-loomed and folklore products (640)	doz. kg	12.2%	Free (AU, BH, CA, CL, CO, E, IL, JO, KR, MA, MX, OM, P, PA, PE, SG)	76%
		Other:				
6205.30.15		Containing 36 percent or more by weight of wool or fine animal hair		49.6¢/kg + 19.7%	Free (AU, BH, CA, CL, CO, IL, JO, KR, MA, MX, OM, P, PA, PE, SG)	52.9¢/kg + 45%
	10	Men's (440)	doz. kg			
	20	Boys' (440)	doz. kg			
6205.30.20		Other		29.1¢/kg + 25.9%	Free (AU, BH, CA, CL, CO, IL, JO, KR, MA, MX, OM, P, PA, PE, SG)	30.9¢/kg + 76%
		Dress:				
		With two or more colors in the warp and/or the filling:				
	10	Men's (640)	doz. kg			
	20	Boys' (640)	doz. kg			
		Other:				
	30	Men's (640)	doz. kg			
	40	Boys' (640)	doz. kg			
		Other:				
		With two or more colors in the warp and/or the filling:				
	50	Men's (640)	doz. kg			
		Boys':				
	55	Imported as parts of play- suits (237)	doz. kg			
	60	Other (640)	doz. kg			
		Other:				
	70	Men's (640)	doz. kg			
		Boys':				
	75	Imported as parts of play- suits (237)	doz. kg			
	80	Other (640)	doz. kg			

17. What is the CLASSIFICATION of a necklace with a heart pendant made of zinc metal 50 or fewer years old? The value of the item is $600.00.

A. 7111.00.0000	Base metals, silver or gold, clad with platinum, not further worked than semimanufactured
B. 7113.20.5000	Articles of jewelry and parts thereof, of precious metal or of metal clad with precious metal>>Of base metal clad with precious metal>>Other>>Other
C. 7901.11.0000	Unwrought zinc>>Zinc, not alloyed>>Containing by weight 99.9 percent or more of zinc
D. 7117.90.9000	Imitation jewelry>>Other>>Other>>Valued over 20 cents per dozen pieces or parts>>Other>>Other
E. 9706.00.0060	Antiques of an age exceeding one hundred years>>Other

 As per HTSUS, Chapter 71, Note 11 and Chapter 71 Additional U.S. Note 1(a):

11. **For the purposes of heading 7117, the expression "imitation jewelry" means articles of jewelry** within the meaning of paragraph (a) of note 9 above (but not including buttons or other articles of heading 9606, or dress combs, hair slides or the like, or hairpins, of heading 9615), **not incorporating natural or cultured pearls, precious or semiprecious stones (natural, synthetic or reconstructed) nor (except as plating or as minor constituents) precious metal or metal clad with precious metal.**

(a) **The term "unwrought" refers to metals, whether or not refined**, in the form of ingots, blocks, lumps, billets, cakes, slabs, pigs, cathodes, anodes, briquettes, cubes, sticks, grains, sponge, pellets, shot and similar manufactured primary forms, but does not cover rolled, forged, drawn or extruded products, tubular products or cast or sintered forms which have been machined or processed otherwise than by simple trimming, scalping or descaling.

Neither "A" nor "B" are correct as the item in question, a necklace, is not clad with a precious metal (i.e. platinum, gold, or silver). "C" is not correct as the item is not unwrought. "D" correctly describes the item. "E" is not correct as the necklace is 50 or fewer years old. Accordingly, the correct answer is "D".

✔ **JUST A SIDE NOTE:** As per HTSUS Section XV (Base Metals and Articles of Base Metal), Note 3, "base metals" is defined as:

3. Throughout the schedule, the expression **"base metals" means: iron and steel, copper, nickel, aluminum, lead, zinc, tin, tungsten (wolfram), molybdenum, tantalum, magnesium, cobalt, bismuth, cadmium, titanium, zirconium, antimony, manganese, beryllium, chromium, germanium, vanadium, gallium, hafnium, indium, niobium (columbium), rhenium and thallium.**

Heading/ Subheading	Stat. Suf- fix	Article Description	Unit of Quantity	Rates of Duty 1 General	Special	2
7117 (con.)		Imitation jewelry: (con.)				
7117.90		Other:				
7117.90.10	00	Necklaces, valued not over 30 cents per dozen, composed wholly of plastic shapes mounted on fiber string	doz	Free		Free
		Religious articles of a purely devotional character designed to be worn on apparel or carried on or about or attached to the person:				
7117.90.20	00	Rosaries and chaplets	X	3.3%	Free (A, AU, BH, CA, CL, CO, D, E, IL, JO, KR, MA, MX, OM, P, PA, PE, SG)	50%
7117.90.30	00	Other	X	3.9%	Free (A, AU, BH, CA, CL, CO, D, E, IL, JO, KR, MA, MX, OM, P, PA, PE, SG)	45%
		Other:				
		Valued not over 20 cents per dozen pieces or parts:				
7117.90.45	00	Toy jewelry (except parts)	X	Free		45%
7117.90.55	00	Other	X	7.2%	Free (A, AU, BH, CA, CL, CO, D, E, IL, JO, KR, MA, MX, OM, P, PA, PE, SG)	45%
		Valued over 20 cents per dozen pieces or parts:				
7117.90.60	00	Toy jewelry (except parts) valued not over 8 cents per piece	X	Free		110%
		Other:				
7117.90.75	00	Of plastics	X	Free		110%
7117.90.90	00	Other	X	11%	Free (A, AU, BH, CA, CL, CO, D, E, IL, JO, KR, MA, MX, OM, P, PA, PE, SG)	110%
7118		Coin:				
7118.10.00	00	Coin (other than gold coin), not being legal tender	X	Free		Free
7118.90.00		Other		Free		Free
		Gold:				
	11	Canadian maple leaf	g Au g			
	19	Other	g Au g			
	20	Platinum	g Pt g			
	55	Other	X			

18. What is the CLASSIFICATION for an adult size, unisex, pullover constructed from 100% bamboo knit fabric? The Fiber Trade Name is Rayon.

A. 6110.30.3059 Sweaters, pullovers, sweatshirts, waistcoats (vests) and similar articles, knitted or crocheted>>Of man-made fibers>>Other>>Other>>Other>>Other>>Other>>Women's or girls'>>Other

B. 6110.90.9066 Sweaters, pullovers, sweatshirts, waistcoats (vests) and similar articles, knitted or crocheted>>Of other textile materials>>Other>>Sweaters for women or girls>>Other>>Women's or girls'

C. 6110.30.3053 Sweaters, pullovers, sweatshirts, waistcoats (vests) and similar articles, knitted or crocheted>>Of man-made fibers>>Other>>Other>>Other>>Other>>Other>>Other>>Men's or boys'>>Other

D. 6110.90.1060 Sweaters, pullovers, sweatshirts, waistcoats (vests) and similar articles, knitted or crocheted>>Of other textile materials>>Containing 70 percent or more by weight of silk or silk waste>>Other>>Women's or girls'

E. 6110.90.9054 Sweaters, pullovers, sweatshirts, waistcoats (vests) and similar articles, knitted or crocheted>>Of other textile materials>>Other>>Vests, other than sweater vests>>Subject to man-made fiber restraints>>Women's or girls'

 As per HTSUS GRI 3(c):

3. **When**, by application of rule 2(b) or for any other reason, **goods are, prima facie, classifiable under two or more headings, classification shall be effected as follows:**

(a) The heading which provides the most specific description shall be preferred to headings providing a more general description. However, when two or more headings each refer to part only of the materials or substances contained in mixed or composite goods or to part only of the items in a set put up for retail sale, those headings are to be regarded as equally specific in relation to those goods, even if one of them gives a more complete or precise description of the goods.

(b) Mixtures, composite goods consisting of different materials or made up of different components, and goods put up in sets for retail sale, which cannot be classified by reference to 3(a), shall be classified as if they consisted of the material or component which gives them their essential character, insofar as this criterion is applicable.

(c) When goods cannot be classified by reference to 3(a) or 3(b), they shall be classified under the heading which occurs last in numerical order among those which equally merit consideration.

a The pullover is made of Rayon, which is a synthetic (i.e. man-made) fiber, and so we may disregard all multiple-choice options except "A" and "C". The pullover is "unisex", and so by application of GRI 3(c), we must select "A" over "C" since this classification occurs later in order. The correct answer is "A".

✓ **NOTE:** "Prima facie" is Latin and may literally be translated as "at first face/appearance". Customs defines "prima facie" as classifiable under two or more HTS headings. In other legal terms "prima facie" means that something is sufficient to prove as true, until disproved.

Heading/ Subheading	Stat. Suf-fix	Article Description	Unit of Quantity	Rates of Duty 1 General	Rates of Duty 1 Special	2
6110 (con.)		Sweaters, pullovers, sweatshirts, waistcoats (vests) and similar articles, knitted or crocheted: (con.)				
6110.30 (con.)		Of man-made fibers: (con.)				
		Other: (con.)				
		Other: (con.)				
6110.30.30		Other		32%	Free (AU, BH, CA, CL, CO, IL, JO, KR, MA, MX, OM, P, PA, PE, SG)	90%
	05	Boys' and girls' garments imported as parts of playsuits (237)	doz. kg			
		Other:				
		Sweaters:				
	10	Men's (645)	doz. kg			
	15	Boys' (645)	doz. kg			
	20	Women's (646)	doz. kg			
	25	Girls' (646)	doz. kg			
		Vests, other than sweater vests:				
	30	Men's or boys' (659)	doz. kg			
	35	Women's or girls' (659)	doz. kg			
		Sweatshirts:				
	41	Men's (638)	doz. kg			
	44	Boys' (638)	doz. kg			
	45	Women's or girls' (639)	doz. kg			
		Other:				
		Men's or boys':				
	51	Knit to shape articles described in statistical note 6 to this chapter (638)	doz. kg			
	53	Other (638)	doz. kg			
		Women's or girls':				
	57	Knit to shape articles described in statistical note 6 to this chapter (639)	doz. kg			
	59	Other (639)	doz. kg			

19. What is the CLASSIFICATION of a woman's knitted Irish sweater with a fiber content of 50% merino wool and 50% man-made rayon?

A. 6110.30.1520/17%	Sweaters, pullovers, sweatshirts, waistcoats (vests) and similar articles, knitted or crocheted>>Of man-made fibers>>Other>>Containing 23 percent or more by weight of wool or fine animal hair>>Sweaters>>Women's or girls
B. 6110.20.2020/16.5%	Sweaters, pullovers, sweatshirts, waistcoats (vests) and similar articles, knitted or crocheted>>Of cotton>>Other>>Other>>Sweaters>>Women's
C. 6110.30.1020/6%	Sweaters, pullovers, sweatshirts, waistcoats (vests) and similar articles, knitted or crocheted>>Of man-made fibers>>Containing 25 percent or more by weight of leather>>Sweaters>>Women's or girls'
D. 6110.19.0030/16%	Sweaters, pullovers, sweatshirts, waistcoats (vests) and similar articles, knitted or crocheted>>Of wool or fine animal hair>>Other>>Sweaters>>Women's
E. 6105.20.1000/13.6%	Men's or boys' shirts, knitted or crocheted>>Of man-made fibers>>Containing 23 percent or more by weight of wool or fine animal hair

 As per HTSUS, SECTION XI (TEXTILES AND TEXTILE ARTICLES) Note 2(A):

2. (A) Goods classifiable in chapters 50 to 55 or in heading 5809 or 5902 and of a mixture of two or more textile materials are to be classified as if consisting wholly of that one textile material which predominates by weight over each other single textile material.

When no one textile material predominates by weight, the goods are to be classified as if consisting wholly of that one textile material which is covered by the heading which occurs last in numerical order among those which equally merit consideration.

 "B" may be eliminated as the sweater contains no cotton. "C" may be eliminated as the sweater contains no leather. "E" may be eliminated as the sweater is not men's or boys'. The sweater is 50% wool and 50% man-made rayon, so at this point both "A" and "D" (respectively) equally merit consideration. As per the above-mentioned Section Note, and/or by the application of GRI 3(c), instead of HTS numerically earlier "D" subheading of 6110.19 we are to classify under the later "A" subheading of 6110.30. The correct answer is "A".

✓ **JUST A SIDE NOTE 1:** As referenced in the above-mentioned Section XI Note, HTSUS Chapters 50 to 55 include the following:

Chapter 50	*Silk*
Chapter 51	*Wool, fine or coarse animal hair; horsehair yarn and woven fabric*
Chapter 52	*Cotton*
Chapter 53	*Other vegetable textile fibers; paper yarn and woven fabric of paper yarn*
Chapter 54	*Man-made filaments*
Chapter 55	*Man-made staple fibers*

✓ **JUST A SIDE NOTE 2:** Wikipedia differentiates "staple fibers" vs. "filaments" as follows:

Staple refers to fibre of discrete length and may be of any composition. A continuous fibre such as natural silk or synthetic is known as filament rather than staple fibre.

The opposite term is filament fibre, which is fibre that comes in continuous to near continuous lengths for use. Silk, taken from the cocoon of a silkworm, is a filament. Synthetic fibres can also be manufactured as filament. If the filament is then cut into discrete lengths, it becomes staple fibre.

Heading/ Subheading	Stat. Suf-fix	Article Description	Unit of Quantity	Rates of Duty 1 General	Rates of Duty 1 Special	2
6110 (con.)		Sweaters, pullovers, sweatshirts, waistcoats (vests) and similar articles, knitted or crocheted: (con.)				
6110.30		Of man-made fibers:				
6110.30.10		Containing 25 percent or more by weight of leather		6%	Free (AU, BH, CA, CL, CO, IL, JO, KR, MA, MX, OM, P, PA, PE, SG)	35%
		Sweaters:				
	10	Men's or boys' (645)	doz. kg			
	20	Women's or girls' (646)	doz. kg			
		Vests, other than sweater vests:				
	30	Men's or boys' (659)	doz. kg			
	40	Women's or girls' (659)	doz. kg			
		Other:				
	50	Men's or boys' (638)	doz. kg			
	60	Women's or girls' (639)	doz. kg			
		Other:				
6110.30.15		Containing 23 percent or more by weight of wool or fine animal hair		17%	Free (AU, BH, CA, CL, CO, IL, JO, KR, MA, MX, OM, P, PA, PE, SG)	54.5%
		Sweaters:				
	10	Men's or boys' (445)	doz. kg			
	20	Women's or girls' (446)	doz. kg			
		Vests, other than sweater vests:				
	30	Men's or boys' (459)	doz. kg			
	40	Women's or girls' (459)	doz. kg			
		Other:				
	50	Men's or boys' (438)	doz. kg			
	60	Women's or girls' (438)	doz. kg			

20. What is the CLASSIFICATION of tomato juice concentrate with 49% of soluble tomato solids and 51% water that is produced by washing, crushing, screening, centrifuging and concentrating the tomatoes prior to the juice concentrate being aseptically packed into airtight bottles?

A. 2009.50.0010	Fruit juices (including grape must) and vegetable juices, not fortified with vitamins or minerals, unfermented and not containing added spirit, whether or not containing added sugar or other sweetening matter>>Tomato juice>>In airtight containers
B. 2009.50.0090	Fruit juices (including grape must) and vegetable juices, not fortified with vitamins or minerals, unfermented and not containing added spirit, whether or not containing added sugar or other sweetening matter>>Tomato juice>>Other
C. 2009.89.8031	Fruit juices (including grape must) and vegetable juices, not fortified with vitamins or minerals, unfermented and not containing added spirit, whether or not containing added sugar or other sweetening matter>>Juice of any other single fruit or vegetable>>Other>>Vegetable juice>>In airtight containers
D. 2202.90.3600	Waters, including mineral waters and aerated waters, containing added sugar or other sweetening matter or flavored, and other nonalcoholic beverages, not including fruit or vegetable juices of heading 2009>>Other>>Fruit or vegetable juices, fortified with vitamins or minerals>>Other>>Juice of any single fruit or vegetable
E. 2002.90.8050	Tomatoes prepared or preserved otherwise than by vinegar or acetic acid>>Other>>Other>>Other

 As per Chapter 20, Note 4:

4. **Tomato juice the dry weight content of which is 7 percent or more is to be classified in heading 2002.**

a At first glance it appears that "A" might be the correct answer. However, as per GRI 1, items are to be classified according to 1) the terms of the headings AND 2) the Section and Chapter Notes. Per the above-mentioned Chapter 20 Note, tomato juice of 7% or more dry weight is to be classified under heading 2002. The item in question is composed of 49% solids (i.e. dry weight). Accordingly, we can infer that the correct answer is "E".

✓ **INTERESTINGLY ENOUGH:** As per Wikipedia, "In Canada and Mexico, tomato juice is commonly mixed with beer; the concoction is known in Canada as Calgary Red-Eye, and in Mexico as Cerveza preparada."

Heading/ Subheading	Stat. Suf- fix	Article Description	Unit of Quantity	Rates of Duty 1 General	Special	2
2002		Tomatoes prepared or preserved otherwise than by vinegar or acetic acid:				
2002.10.00		Tomatoes, whole or in pieces		12.5%	Free (A+, BH, CA, CL, CO, D, E, IL, JO, KR, MX, OM, P, PA, PE, SG) See 9912.20.05-9912.20.20 (MA) See 9913.95.21-9913.95.30 (AU)	50%
	20	In containers holding less than 1.4 kg	kg			
	80	Other	kg			
2002.90		Other:				
2002.90.40	00	In powder	kg	11.6%	Free (A, BH, CA, CL, CO, D, E, IL, JO, KR, MA, MX, OM, P, PA, PE, SG) 2.5% (AU)	50%
2002.90.80		Other		11.6%	Free (A+, BH, CA, CL, CO, D, E, IL, JO, KR, MX, OM, P, PA, PE, SG) See 9912.20.05, 9912.20.21-9912.20.45 (MA) See 9913.95.31-9913.95.55 (AU)	50%
		Paste:				
	10	In containers holding less than 1.4 kg	kg			
	20	Other	kg			
		Puree:				
	30	In containers holding less than 1.4 kg	kg			
	40	Other	kg			
	50	Other	kg			

21. What is the CLASSIFICATION of frozen, uncooked, shrimp-stuffed ravioli packaged with a white wine sauce made in Italy which contains 51% by weight of shrimp?

A. 1605.29.0500 Crustaceans, molluscs and other aquatic invertebrates, prepared or preserved>>Shrimps and prawns>>Other>>Products containing fish meat; prepared meals

B. 1605.29.1010 Crustaceans, molluscs and other aquatic invertebrates, prepared or preserved>>Shrimps and prawns>>Other>>Other>> Frozen, imported in accordance with Statistical Note 1 to this chapter.

C. 1605.29.1040 Crustaceans, molluscs and other aquatic invertebrates, prepared or preserved>>Shrimps and prawns>>Other>>Other>> Other, imported in accordance with Statistical Note 1 to this chapter

D. 1902.19.4000 Pasta, whether or not cooked or stuffed (with meat or other substances) or otherwise prepared, such as spaghetti, macaroni, noodles, lasagna, gnocchi, ravioli, cannelloni; couscous, whether or not prepared>>Uncooked pasta, not stuffed or otherwise prepared>>Other>>Other, including pasta packaged with sauce preparations

E. 1902.20.0040 Pasta, whether or not cooked or stuffed (with meat or other substances) or otherwise prepared, such as spaghetti, macaroni, noodles, lasagna, gnocchi, ravioli, cannelloni; couscous, whether or not prepared>> Stuffed pasta, whether or not cooked or otherwise prepared>>Other>>Frozen

 As per HTSUS Chapter 16, Note 2 & Chapter 19, Note 1:

(Chapter 16)
2. **Food preparations fall in this chapter provided that they contain more than 20 percent by weight of** sausage, meat, meat offal, blood, fish or crustaceans, **molluscs** or other aquatic invertebrates, or any combination thereof. In cases where the preparation contains two or more of the products mentioned above, it is classified in the heading of chapter 16 corresponding to the component or components which predominate by weight. These provisions do not apply to the stuffed products of heading 1902 or to the preparations of heading 2103 or 2104.

(Chapter 19)
1. **This chapter does not cover**:
(a) **Except in the case of stuffed products of heading 1902**, food preparations containing more than 20 percent by weight of sausage, meat, meat offal, blood, fish or crustaceans, molluscs or other aquatic invertebrates, or any combination thereof (chapter 16);

a The item in question is prima facie (i.e. classifiable under two or more headings) as both "B" and "E" correctly describe the product. So, on to GRI 3(a). However, GRI 3(a) cannot be applied as both "B" and "E" refer only to a part of the shrimp/pasta composite good. So, on to GRI 3(b). One might argue that since the ravioli is 51% by weight of shrimp, then the shrimp gives the meal its essential character. I would argue that the meal is ravioli with shrimp rather than shrimp with ravioli. Inconclusive? So, on to GRI 3(c). The HTS number for "E" occurs later in order than "B", so we may conclude that the correct answer is "E".

✓ **NOTE:** The above-mentioned Chapter 16 and Chapter 19 notes leave the door open to, but do not preclude us from classifying in either Chapters.

Heading/ Subheading	Stat. Suf- fix	Article Description	Unit of Quantity	Rates of Duty 1 General	Rates of Duty 1 Special	Rates of Duty 2
1902		Pasta, whether or not cooked or stuffed (with meat or other substances) or otherwise prepared, such as spaghetti, macaroni, noodles, lasagna, gnocchi, ravioli, cannelloni; couscous, whether or not prepared:				
		Uncooked pasta, not stuffed or otherwise prepared:				
1902.11		Containing eggs:				
1902.11.20		Exclusively pasta		Free		6.6¢/kg
		Product of a European Union (EU) country:				
	10	Subject to the Inward Processing Regime (IPR)	kg			
	20	Subject to the EU reduced export refund in accordance with the US-EU Pasta agreement	kg			
	30	Other	kg			
	90	Product of a country other than an EU country	kg			
1902.11.40	00	Other, including pasta packaged with sauce preparations	kg	6.4%	Free (A, AU, BH, CA, CL, CO, D, E, IL, JO, KR, MA, MX, OM, P, PA, PE, SG)	20%
1902.19		Other:				
1902.19.20		Exclusively pasta		Free		4.4¢/kg
		Product of a European Union (EU) Country:				
	10	Subject to the Inward Processing Regime (IPR)	kg			
	20	Subject to the EU reduced export refund in accordance with the US-EU Pasta agreement	kg			
	30	Other	kg			
	90	Product of a country other than an EU country	kg			
1902.19.40	00	Other, including pasta packaged with sauce preparations	kg	6.4%	Free (A, AU, BH, CA, CL, CO, D, E, IL, JO, KR, MA, MX, OM, P, PA, PE, SG)	20%
1902.20.00		Stuffed pasta, whether or not cooked or otherwise prepared		6.4%	Free (A, AU, BH, CA, CL, CO, D, E, IL, JO, KR, MA, MX, OM, P, PA, PE, SG)	20%
	20	Canned	kg			
		Other:				
	40	Frozen	kg			
	60	Other	kg			
1902.30.00		Other pasta		6.4%	Free (A, AU, BH, CA, CL, CO, D, E, IL, JO, KR, MA, MX, OM, P, PA, PE, SG)	20%
	20	Canned	kg			
		Other:				
	40	Frozen	kg			
	60	Other	kg			

22. What is the CLASSIFICATION of a woven, embroidered, single layer bedspread made of 50% rayon fibers and 50% silk fibers?

A. 6304.11.2000 Other furnishing articles, excluding those of heading 9404>>Bedspreads>>Knitted or crocheted>>Of man-made fibers

B. 6304.11.3000 Other furnishing articles, excluding those of heading 9404>>Bedspreads>>Knitted or crocheted>>Other

C. 6304.19.1500 Other furnishing articles, excluding those of heading 9404>>Bedspreads>>Other>>Of man-made fibers>>Containing any embroidery, lace, braid, edging, trimming, piping or applique work

D. 6304.19.3060 Other furnishing articles, excluding those of heading 9404>>Bedspreads>>Other>>Other>>Other>>Other

E. 9404.90.8536 Mattress supports; articles of bedding and similar furnishing (for example, mattresses, quilts, eiderdowns, cushions, pouffes and pillows) fitted with springs or stuffed or internally fitted with any material or of cellular rubber or plastics, whether or not covered>>Other>>Other>>Other>>Quilts, eiderdowns, comforters and similar articles>>With outer shell of other textile materials>>Other

 As per HTSUS SECTION XI, SUBHEADING NOTE 2 (A):

(A) Goods classifiable in chapters 50 to 55 or in heading 5809 or 5902 and of a mixture of two or more textile materials are to be classified as if consisting wholly of that one textile material which predominates by weight over each other single textile material.

When no one textile material predominates by weight, the goods are to be classified as if consisting wholly of that one textile material which is covered by the heading which occurs last in numerical order among those which equally merit consideration.

The item in question, a bedspread, is woven (as opposed to knitted or crocheted), so this eliminates "A" and "B". The item is single layer (as opposed to stuffed or internally fitted), so that eliminates "E". The item is 50% rayon and 50% silk, so it is classifiable under both "C" and "D" respectively. As per GRI 1, we classify per any relevant Section and/or Chapter Notes, which in this case says to use the classification that occurs last. The correct answer is "D".

✓ **JUST A SIDE NOTE:** Heading 9404 provides for "eiderdowns", which is kind of comforter, traditionally stuffed with duck down feathers. "Eider" are a type of duck.

Heading/ Subheading	Stat. Suf-fix	Article Description	Unit of Quantity	Rates of Duty 1 General	Special	2
6304 (con.)		Other furnishing articles, excluding those of heading 9404: (con.)				
		Bedspreads: (con.)				
6304.19		Other:				
		Of cotton:				
6304.19.05	00	Containing any embroidery, lace, braid, edging, trimming, piping or applique work (362)	No. kg	12%	Free (AU, BH, CA, CL, CO, IL, JO, KR, MA, MX, OM, P, PA, PE, SG)	90%
6304.19.10	00	Other (362)	No. kg	4.4%	Free (AU, BH, CA, CL, CO, IL, JO, KR, MA, MX, OM, P, PA, PE, SG)	25%
		Of man-made fibers:				
6304.19.15	00	Containing any embroidery, lace, braid, edging, trimming, piping or applique work (666)	No. kg	14.9%	Free (AU, BH, CA, CL, CO, IL, JO, KR, MA, MX, OM, P, PA, PE, SG)	90%
6304.19.20	00	Other (666)	No. kg	6.5%	Free (AU, BH, CA, CL, CO, IL, JO, KR, MA, MX, OM, P, PA, PE, SG)	77.5%
6304.19.30		Other		6.3%	Free (AU, BH, CA, CL, CO, E*, IL, JO, KR, MA, MX, OM, P, PA, PE, SG)	90%
	30	Containing 85 percent or more by weight of silk or silk waste	No. kg			
		Other:				
	40	Of wool or fine animal hair (469)	No. kg			
	60	Other (899)	No. kg			

23. Which of the following is required when importing iron or steel classifiable under Chapter 72 or headings 7301 to 7307 HTSUS?

A. Country of Origin certificate.
B. Mill certificate containing percentage by weight of carbon or any metallic elements contained in the imported products.
C. Single entry bond
D. Reimbursement statement
E. ASTM standard specifications for steel

As per 19 CFR 141.89(a):

§141.89 Additional information for certain classes of merchandise.

(a) Invoices for the following classes of merchandise, classifiable under the Harmonized Tariff Schedule of the United States (HTSUS), shall set forth the additional information specified: [75-42, 75-239, 78-53, 83-251, 84-149.]
… …
***Iron or steel* classifiable in Chapter 72 or headings 7301 to 7307, HTSUS** (T.D. 53092, 55977)—**Statement of the percentages by weight or carbon and any metallic elements contained in the articles, in the form of a mill analysis or mill test certificate**.
… …

This question is a little tricky in that it is more of an "Entry/19 CFR" question rather than a "Classification" question. The correct answer is "B".

✓ **JUST A SIDE NOTE:** A "mill certificate" can also referred to as a "mill test report", "mill test certificate", or "inspection certificate", etc.

(This Page Intentionally Left Blank)

24. What is the CLASSIFICATION for dried potato flakes composed of dried potato flakes, sodium acid pyrophosphate (a preservative), sodium bisulfite (a preservative), monoglycerides (an anti-sticking agent), citric acid (an antioxidant), and butylated hydroxyanisole?

A. 0701.90.5065	Potatoes, fresh or chilled>>Other>>Other>>Other>>Other
B. 0712.90.3000	Dried vegetables, whole, cut, sliced, broken or in powder, but not further prepared>>Other vegetables; mixtures of vegetables>>Potatoes whether or not cut or sliced but not further prepared
C. 1105.20.0000	Flour, meal, powder, flakes, granules and pellets of potatoes>>Flakes, granules and pellets
D. 1108.13.0010	Starches; inulin>>Starches>>Potato starch>>For human consumption
E. 2005.20.0070	Other vegetables prepared or preserved otherwise than by vinegar or acetic acid, not frozen, other than products of heading 2006>>Potatoes>>Other

 As per HTSUS Chapter 7 Note 3(c) and Chapter 11 Note 1(d):

3. **Heading 0712 covers all dried vegetables of the kinds** falling in headings 0701 to 0711, **other than**:
(a) Dried leguminous vegetables, shelled (heading 0713);
(b) Sweet corn in the forms specified in headings 1102 to 1104;
(c) Flour, meal, powder, **flakes**, granules and pellets **of potatoes** (heading 1105);

1. **This chapter (11) does not cover:**
(a) Roasted malt put up as coffee substitutes (heading 0901 or 2101);
(b) Prepared flours, groats, meals or starches of heading 1901;
(c) Corn flakes or other products of heading 1904;
(d) **Vegetables, prepared or preserved, of heading 2001, 2004 or 2005**;

a The dried potato flakes are neither fresh nor chilled, so we may disregard "A". The above-mentioned Chapter 7 Note precludes "B" from being considered. The above-mentioned Chapter 11 Note precludes "C" and "D" from consideration. "E" accurately describes the "preserved" potato product. The correct answer is "E".

✓ **JUST A SIDE NOTE 1:** "Butylated hydroxyanisole", as referenced in the question, is an antioxidant.

✓ **JUST A SIDE NOTE 2:** The actual exam copy uses the classification 0701.90.5040 for multiple choice "A". This classification, however, does not exist in any recent versions of the HTSUS. This appears to be a typo. 0701.90.5065 was instead used here for the purposes of this exercise.

Heading/ Subheading	Stat. Suf-fix	Article Description	Unit of Quantity	Rates of Duty 1 General	Rates of Duty 1 Special	Rates of Duty 2
2005		Other vegetables prepared or preserved otherwise than by vinegar or acetic acid, not frozen, other than products of heading 2006:				
2005.10.00	00	Homogenized vegetables	kg	11.2%	Free (A, AU, BH, CA, CL, CO, D, E, IL, JO, KR, MA, MX, OM, P, PA, PE, SG)	35%
2005.20.00		Potatoes		6.4%	Free (A, AU, BH, CA, CL, CO, D, E, IL, JO, KR, MA, MX, OM, P, PA, PE, SG)	35%
	20	Potato chips	kg			
	40	Potato granules	kg			
	70	Other	kg			
2005.40.00	00	Peas (*Pisum sativum*)	kg	Free		4.4¢/kg on entire contents of container
		Beans (*Vigna spp., Phaseolus spp.*):				
2005.51		Beans, shelled:				
2005.51.20		Black-eye cowpeas		1.5¢/kg on entire contents of container	Free (A+, AU, BH, CA, CL, CO, D, E, IL, JO, KR, MA, MX, OM, P, PA, PE, SG)	6.6¢/kg on entire contents of container
	20	Canned dried	kg			
	40	Other	kg			
2005.51.40		Other		2.1¢/kg on entire contents of container	Free (A, AU, BH, CA, CL, CO, D, E, IL, JO, KR, MA, MX, OM, P, PA, PE, SG)	6.6¢/kg on entire contents of container
	20	Canned dried	kg			
	40	Other	kg			
2005.59.00	00	Other	kg	1.5¢/kg on entire contents of container	Free (A, AU, BH, CA, CL, CO, D, E, IL, JO, KR, MA, MX, OM, P, PA, PE, SG)	6.6¢/kg on entire contents of container
2005.60.00	00	Asparagus	kg	14.9%	Free (A+, BH, CA, CL, CO, D, E, IL, JO, KR, MX, OM, P, PA, PE, SG) See 9912.95.01-9912.95.05 (MA) See 9913.95.56-9913.95.60 (AU)	35%

25. What is the CLASSIFICATION of used rescue blankets, not over 3 meters in length, constructed from 50 % polyester and 50 % wool knit fabric that show signs of appreciable wear, but have been cleaned and are individually packaged?

A. 6301.20.0010 I. OTHER MADE UP TEXTILE ARTICLES>>Blankets and traveling rugs>>Blankets (other than electric blankets) and traveling rugs, of wool or fine animal hair>>Not over 3 meters in length

B. 6309.00.0010 III. WORN CLOTHING AND WORN TEXTILE ARTICLES; RAGS>>Worn clothing and other worn articles>>Worn clothing

C. 6301.40.0020 I. OTHER MADE UP TEXTILE ARTICLES>>Blankets and traveling rugs>> Blankets (other than electric blankets) and traveling rugs, of synthetic fibers>>Other

D. 6301.40.0010 I. OTHER MADE UP TEXTILE ARTICLES>>Blankets and traveling rugs>> Blankets (other than electric blankets) and traveling rugs, of synthetic fibers>>Woven

E. 6309.00.0020 III. WORN CLOTHING AND WORN TEXTILE ARTICLES; RAGS>>Worn clothing and other worn articles>>Other

 As per HTSUS Chapter 63 Note 3 and SECTION XI, SUBHEADING NOTE 2 (A):

(Chapter 63 Note)
3. **Heading 6309 applies only to the following goods**:

(a) Articles of textile materials:
(i) Clothing and clothing accessories, and parts thereof;
(ii) Blankets and traveling rugs;
(iii) Bed linen, table linen, toilet linen and kitchen linen;
(iv) Furnishings, other than carpets of headings 5701 to 5705 and tapestries of heading 5805.

(b) Footwear and headgear of any material other than asbestos.

In order to be classified in this heading, the articles mentioned above must comply with both of the following requirements:
(i) They must show signs of appreciable wear; **and**
(ii) **They must be entered in bulk or in bales, sacks or similar packings**.

(SECTION XI Note)
2. (A) Goods classifiable in chapters 50 to 55 or in heading 5809 or 5902 and of a mixture of two or more textile materials are to be classified as if consisting wholly of that one textile material which predominates by weight over each other single textile material.

When no one textile material predominates by weight, the goods are to be classified as if consisting wholly of that one textile material which is covered by the heading which occurs last in numerical order among those which equally merit consideration.

a The item in question is a "rescue blanket". I had to look this up to learn that a rescue blanket is a very light blanket with a highly reflective exterior, and which can be used in an emergency. It turns out that ignorance of this fact has little bearing on the solution to the problem. Just know that it is a "blanket" with certain qualities as described in the question.

The blankets are individually packaged (as opposed to being in bulk packaging), so according to the above-mentioned Chapter 63 Note, we eliminate both "B" and "E" (heading 6309). The blanket is knit (as opposed to woven), so we may disregard "D". At this point the item is classifiable under both "A" (wool) and "C" (synthetic). As per the Section XI Note, we now choose the classification that numerically occurs last. The correct answer is "C".

✓ **JUST A SIDE NOTE:** Even though the correct path to the answer here is by using the Section XI Note, if GRI 3(c) was instead used, we would still arrive at the same correct answer.

Heading/ Subheading	Stat. Suf-fix	Article Description	Unit of Quantity	Rates of Duty 1 General	Rates of Duty 1 Special	Rates of Duty 2
		I. OTHER MADE UP TEXTILE ARTICLES				
6301		Blankets and traveling rugs:				
6301.10.00	00	Electric blankets (666)	No. kg	11.4%	Free (AU, BH, CA, CL, CO, E*, IL, JO, KR, MA, MX, OM, P, PA, PE, SG)	77.5%
6301.20.00		Blankets (other than electric blankets) and traveling rugs, of wool or fine animal hair		Free		$1.10/kg + 60%
	10	Not over 3 meters in length (464)	No. kg			
	20	Over 3 meters in length (410)	m^2 kg			
6301.30.00		Blankets (other than electric blankets) and traveling rugs, of cotton		8.4%	Free (AU, BH, CA, CL, CO, IL, JO, KR, MA, MX, OM, P, PA, PE, SG)	30%
	10	Woven (369)	No. kg			
	20	Other (369)	No. kg			
6301.40.00		Blankets (other than electric blankets) and traveling rugs, of synthetic fibers		8.5%	Free (AU, BH, CA, CL, CO, IL, JO, KR, MA, MX, OM, P, PA, PE, SG)	77.5%
	10	Woven (666)	No. kg			
	20	Other (666)	No. kg			
6301.90.00		Other blankets and traveling rugs		7.2%	Free (AU, BH, CA, CL, CO, E*, IL, JO, KR, MA, MX, NP, OM, P, PA, PE, SG)	90%
	10	Of artificial fibers (666)	No. kg			
		Other:				
	20	Containing 85 percent or more by weight of silk or silk waste	No. kg			
	30	Other (899)	No. kg			

26. The article is a small battery-operated plastic LED flashlight with a bottom split ring onto which is attached two metal key rings, both connected by a cylindrical plastic attachment: by pressing down on the lamp's midsection, a beam of light is activated. What is the CLASSIFICATION for the LED Light keychain?

A. 3924.90.5610 Tableware, kitchenware, other household articles and hygienic or toilet articles, of plastics>>Other>>Other>>Gates for confining children or pets

B. 8513.10.2000 Portable electric lamps designed to function by their own source of energy (for example, dry batteries, storage batteries, magnetos), other than lighting equipment of heading 8512; parts thereof>>Lamps>>Flashlights

C. 7326.20.0071 Other articles of iron or steel>>Articles of iron or steel wire>>Other

D. 8513.90.4000 Portable electric lamps designed to function by their own source of energy (for example, dry batteries, storage batteries, magnetos), other than lighting equipment of heading 8512; parts thereof>>Lamps>>Parts>>Other

E. 9013.80.9000 Liquid crystal devices not constituting articles provided for more specifically in other headings; lasers, other than laser diodes; other optical appliances and instruments, not specified or included elsewhere in this chapter; parts and accessories thereof>> Other devices, appliances and instruments>>Other

 As per HTSUS GRI 3(b):

3. When, by application of rule 2(b) or for any other reason, goods are, prima facie, classifiable under two or more headings, classification shall be effected as follows:

(a) The heading which provides the most specific description shall be preferred to headings providing a more general description. However, when two or more headings each refer to part only of the materials or substances contained in mixed or composite goods or to part only of the items in a set put up for retail sale, those headings are to be regarded as equally specific in relation to those goods, even if one of them gives a more complete or precise description of the goods.

(b) Mixtures, composite goods consisting of different materials or made up of different components, and goods put up in sets for retail sale, **which cannot be classified by reference to 3(a), shall be classified as if they consisted of the material or component which gives them their essential character**, insofar as this criterion is applicable.

(c) When goods cannot be classified by reference to 3(a) or 3(b), they shall be classified under the heading which occurs last in numerical order among those which equally merit consideration.

First off, the item obviously is not a gate for confining children or pets, so we'll eliminate "A". Next, we'll eliminate "D" as the item in question is not a part for lamps. At this point we're left with and the item is potentially classifiable under "B" as a flashlight, "C" as a key ring, or "E" as a light-emitting diode (LED) optical instrument. Since the item is prima facie (i.e. classifiable under more than one heading), as per the General Rules of Interpretation we first try classifying under GRI 3(a). However, GRI 3(a) cannot be applied here as each of the potential classifications only refer to respective parts of the whole product. So, we must move on to GRI 3(b), which says to classify based on what gives the product its essential character, which in this case is the flashlight component. The correct answer is "B".

✓ **JUST A SIDE NOTE:** A light-emitting diode (LED) is a semiconductor device through which electricity passes to produce light.

Heading/ Subheading	Stat. Suf-fix	Article Description	Unit of Quantity	Rates of Duty 1 General	Special	2
8513		Portable electric lamps designed to function by their own source of energy (for example, dry batteries, storage batteries, magnetos), other than lighting equipment of heading 8512; parts thereof:				
8513.10		Lamps:				
8513.10.20	00	Flashlights	No.	12.5%	Free (A, AU, BH, CA, CL, CO, D, E, IL, JO, MA, MX, OM, P, PA, PE, SG) 3.7% (KR)	35%
8513.10.40	00	Other	No.	3.5%	Free (A, AU, BH, CA, CL, CO, D, E, IL, JO, KR, MA, MX, OM, P, PA, PE, SG)	40%
8513.90		Parts:				
8513.90.20	00	Of flashlights	X	12.5%	Free (A, AU, BH, CA, CL, CO, D, E, IL, JO, KR, MA, MX, OM, P, PA, PE, SG)	35%
8513.90.40	00	Other	X	3.5%	Free (A, AU, BH, CA, CL, CO, D, E, IL, JO, KR, MA, MX, OM, P, PA, PE, SG)	40%

27. Company A is the importer of record for widgets in the United States. Company A sold 100 widgets on 1/1/2012 to Company B in United States. Company B sold the widgets to a foreign company and filed drawback for the widgets under unused direct identification 19 USC 1313(j)(1) on 5/1/2012. Which of the following document shows the transfer of the merchandise from Company A to Company B?

A. A waiver of drawback right
B. A certificate of delivery and manufacture
C. A certificate of delivery
D. A notice of intent to export
E. An application of waiver of prior notice of intent to export

 As per 19 CFR 191.34(a):

§191.34 Certificate of delivery required.

(a) *Direct identification; purpose; when required.* **If the exported or destroyed merchandise claimed for drawback under 19 U.S.C. 1313(j)(1) was not imported by the exporter or destroyer, a properly executed certificate of delivery must be prepared by the importer and each intermediate party.** Each such transfer of the merchandise must be documented by its own certificate of delivery.

(1) *Completion.* The certificate of delivery shall be completed as provided in §191.10 of this part. Each party must also certify on the certificate of delivery that the party did not use the transferred merchandise (see §191.31(c) of this part).

(2) *Retention; submission to Customs.* The certificate of delivery shall be retained by the party to whom the merchandise or article covered by the certificate was delivered. Customs may request the certificate from the claimant for the drawback claim based upon the certificate (see §§191.51, 191.52). If the certificate is requested by Customs, but is not provided by the claimant, the part of the drawback claim dependent on that certificate will be denied.

 The correct answer is "C".

✓ **JUST A SIDE NOTE:** On the following page is a snapshot of the two-page Customs Form 7552 (DELIVERY CERTIFICATE FOR PURPOSES OF DRAWBACK).

OMB 1651-0075 Exp. 04/30/2018

DEPARTMENT OF HOMELAND SECURITY
U.S. Customs and Border Protection

DELIVERY CERTIFICATE FOR PURPOSES OF DRAWBACK
19 CFR 191

PAPERWORK REDUCTION ACT NOTICE: This request is in accordance with the Paperwork Reduction Act. We ask for the information in order to carry out U.S. Department of Homeland Security laws and regulations, to determine the eligibility for refund of taxes on domestic alcohol (if applicable), and to determine the proper amount of drawback. Your response is required to obtain or retain a benefit. The estimated average burden associated with this collection of information is 33 minutes per respondent depending on individual circumstances. Comments concerning the accuracy of this burden estimate and suggestions for reducing this burden should be directed to U.S. Customs and Border Protection, Asset Management, Washington, DC 20229, and to the Office of Management and Budget, Paperwork Reduction Project (1651-0075) Washington, DC 20503.

☐ Certificate of Delivery

☐ Certificate of Manufacture and Delivery

1. CM&D No.	2. Port Code	3. DBK Ruling No.

4. Type Code	5. ID No. of Transferor

6. **FROM TRANSFEROR:** Company Name and Complete Address	7. **TO TRANSFEREE:** Company Name and Complete Address	**RECEIVED DATE**

IMPORTED DUTY PAID, DESIGNATED MERCHANDISE OR DRAWBACK PRODUCT

8. Use	9. Import Entry or CM&D Number	10. Port Code	11. Import Date (MM/DD/YYYY)	12. CD	13. (If using 1313(b)) A. Date(s) Received	13. B. Date(s) Used	14. Date Delivered	15. HTSUS No.	16. Description of Merchandise (Include Part/Style/Serial Numbers)	17. Quantity & Unit of Measure	18. Entered Value Per Unit	19. 100% Duty

21. Contact Name and Address	PREPARER	20. **Total**
	Phone Number ______ Ext. ______ FAX Number ______	

CBP Form 7552 (07/08)

22. Quantity & Description of Merchandise Used	23. Date(s) of Manufacture (MM/DD/YYYY)	24. Description of Articles Manufactured or Produced (Include Part/Style/Serial Numbers)	25. Quantity & Unit of Measure	26. Date Delivered

27. Duty Available on Manufacture Articles (Total of Duties in Block 20)	28. Drawback Available Per Unit of Measure on Manufactured Article	29. Factory Location

30. Exhibits to be attached for the following:
☐ Relative Value ☐ Petroleum ☐ Domestic Tax Paid Alcohol ☐ Piece Goods ☐ Waste Calculation ☐ Recycled ☐ Harbor Maintenance Fee ☐ Merchandise Processing Fee ☐ Other Taxes/Fees

31. STATUS - Import Entries listed on this form are subject to (If CD, identify on this form; if CM&D, identify on coding sheet):
☐ Reconciliation ☐ 19 USC 1514, Protest ☐ 19 USC 1520 (c)(1) ☐ 19 USC 1520 (d)

DECLARATIONS

☐ The merchandise transferred on this CD is the imported merchandise.

☐ The merchandise transferred on this CD is pursuant to 19 U.S.C. 1313(j)(2) and will not be designated for any other Drawback purposes.

☐ The article(s) described above were manufactured or produced and delivered as stated herein in accordance with the Drawback ruling on file with CBP and in compliance with applicable laws and regulations.

☐ This Certificate of Delivery is a subsequent transfer and the merchandise is the same as received.

The undersigned acknowledges statutory requirements that all records supporting the information on this document are to be retained by the issuing party for a period of three years from the date of payment of the related drawback entry.

Assignment of Rights is transferred when this form is prepared as a CD or CM&D.

I declare that according to the best of my knowledge and belief, all of the statements in this document are correct and I am fully aware of the sanctions provided in18 U.S.C.1001 and 18 U.S.C. 550 and 19 U.S.C. 1593a.

☐ Member of Firm with Power of Attorney ☐ Officer of Corporation ☐ Broker with Power of Attorney

Printed Name and Title	Signature and Date

CBP Form 7552 (07/08)

28. Which of the following is required when filing drawback for items laden on vessels/aircrafts as supplies?

A. CBP Form 6043
B. CBP Form 7512
C. CBP Form 7514
D. CBP Form 7552
E. CBP Form 7553

 As per the 19 CFR 191.112(b) (Subpart K—Supplies for Certain Vessels and Aircraft):

§191.112 Procedure.

(a) *General.* The provisions of this subpart shall override other conflicting provisions of this part.

(b) *Customs forms.* The drawback claimant shall file with the drawback office the drawback entry on Customs Form 7551 annotated for 19 U.S.C. 1309, **and attach thereto a notice of lading on Customs Form 7514**, in quadruplicate, unless the export summary procedure, provided for in §191.73, is used. If the export summary procedure is used, the requirements in §191.73 shall be complied with, as applicable, and the requirements in paragraphs (d)(1) and (f)(1) of this section shall also be complied with.

A drawback entry is submitted via Customs form 7551, however in the case of a vessel/aircraft drawback, Customs form 7514 must accompany the 7551. The correct answer is "C".

✔ **JUST A SIDE NOTE:** Two common forms of drawback include "Rejected Merchandise Drawback" and "Unused Merchandise Drawback". On the following page is a snapshot of the Customs Form 7551 (DRAWBACK ENTRY).

DEPARTMENT OF HOMELAND SECURITY
U.S. Customs and Border Protection

DRAWBACK ENTRY
19 CFR 191

Paperwork Reduction Act Statement: An agency may not conduct or sponsor an information collection and a person is not required to respond to this information unless it displays a current valid OMB control number and an expiration date. The control number for this collection is 1651-0075. The estimated average time to complete this application is 35 minutes. If you have any comments regarding the burden estimate you can write to U.S. Customs and Border Protection, Office of Regulations and Rulings, 799 9th Street, NW., Washington DC 20229.

Section I - Claim Header Approved OMB No. 1651-0075 Exp. 04/30/2018

1. Drawback Entry Number	2. Entry Type Code	3. Port Code	4. Surety Code	5. Bond Type

6. Claimant ID Number	7. Broker ID Number (CBP 4811)	8. DBK Ruling Number	9. Duty Claimed

10. Puerto Rico Claimed	11. HMF Claimed	12. MPF Claimed	13. Other Taxes/Fees Claimed	14. Total Drawback Claimed	15. Total I.R. Tax Claimed

16. Method of Filing ☐ ABI ☐ Manual	17. NAFTA DBK ☐ Yes ☐ No	18. Privilege Authorized ☐ Accelerated Payment ☐ WPN	19. Drawback Statutory Provision

20. Name and Address of Claimant	21. Contact Name, Address, E-mail, Phone & Fax Numbers of Preparer

Section II - Imported Duty Paid, Designated Merchandise or Drawback Product

22. Import Entry Or CM&D Numbers (List Once in Chronological Order)	23. Port Code	24. Import Date	25. CD	26. (If using 1313(b)) A. Date(s) Received	B. Date(s) Used	27. HTSUS No.	28. Description of Merchandise (Include Part/Style/Serial Numbers)	29. Quantity & Unit of Measure	30. Entered Value Per Unit	31. Duty Rate	32. 99% Duty
										33. Total	

34. STATUS - The Import entries as listed on this form are subject to:
(Must be identified on claim or coding sheet)

☐ Reconciliation ☐ 19 USC 1514, Protest

☐ 19 USC 1520 (c)(1) ☐ 19 USC 1520 (d)

DATE RECEIVED

CBP USE ONLY

Class Code	Accelerated	Liquidated	Bill/Refund
364 Duty			
365 Excise Tax			
369 Puerto Rico			
398 HMF			
399 MPF			
___ Other Tax or Fee			
Total Drawback Claimed			

INTERNAL CONTROL REVIEW Date ____ DS Number ____ ☐ IC OK

Reason ☐ 21 ☐ 23 ☐ 24 ☐ 25 ☐ 26 Specialist Code

CBP Form 7551 (01/11)

Section III - Manufactured Articles

35. Quantity & Description of Merchandise Used	36. Date(s) of Manufacture or Production	37. Description of Articles Manufactured or Produced	38. Quantity and Unit of Measure	39. Factory Location

Section IV - Information on Exported or Destroyed Merchandise

PERIOD COVERED ____ **TO** ____

40. Exhibits to be attached for the following:

☐ Relative Value ☐ Petroleum ☐ Domestic Tax Paid Alcohol ☐ Piece Goods ☐ Waste Calculation ☐ Recycled ☐ Harbor Maintenance Fee ☐ Merchandise Processing Fee ☐ Other Taxes/Fees

41. Date (MM/DD/YYYY)	42. Action Code	43. Unique Identifier No.	44. Name of Exporter/Destroyer	45. Description of Articles (Include Part/Style/Serial Numbers)	46. Quantity and Unit of Measure	47. Export Destination	48. HTSUS No.

Section V - Declarations

☐ Same condition to NAFTA countries - The undersigned herein certifies that the merchandise herein described is in the same condition as when it was imported under above import entry(ies) and further certifies that this merchandise was not subjected to any process of manufacturer or other operation except the following allowable operations:

☐ The undersigned hereby certifies that the merchandise herein described is unused in the United States and further certifies that this merchandise was not subjected to any process of manufacture or other operation except the following allowable operations:

☐ The undersigned hereby certifies that the merchandise herein described is commercially interchangeable with the designated imported merchandise and further certifies that the substituted merchandise is unused in the United States and that the substituted merchandise was in our possession prior to exportation or destruction.

☐ Merchandise does not conform to sample or specifications. ☐ Merchandise was defective at time of importation. ☐ Merchandise was shipped without consent of the consignee.

☐ The undersigned hereby certifies that the merchandise herein described is the same kind and quality as defined in 19 U.S.C. 1313(p)(3)(B), with the designated imported merchandise or the article manufactured or produced under 1313(a) or (b), as appropriate.

☐ The article(s) described above were manufactured or produced and disposed of as stated herein in accordance with the drawback ruling on file with CBP and in compliance with applicable laws and regulations.

The undersigned acknowledges statutory requirements that all records supporting the information on this document are to be retained by the issuing party for a period of three years from the date of payment of the drawback claim. The undersigned is fully aware of the sanctions provided in 18 U.S.C. 1001 and 18 U.S.C. 550 and 19 U.S.C. 1593a.

I declare that according to the best of my knowledge and belief, all of the statements in this document are correct and that the exported article is not to be relanded in the United States or any of its possessions without paying duty.

☐ Member of Firm with Power of Attorney ☐ Officer of Corporation ☐ Broker with Power of Attorney

Printed Name and Title	Signature and Date

CBP Form 7551 (01/11)

29. Which Service Port contains a Drawback unit/office?

A. Boston, MA
B. Detroit, MI
C. Houston, TX
D. Honolulu, HI
E. Miami, FL

 As per 19 CFR 101.3(b)(1):

(b) *List of Ports of Entry and Service Ports.* The following is a list of Customs Ports of Entry and Service Ports. Many of the ports listed were created by the President's message of March 3, 1913, concerning a reorganization of the Customs Service pursuant to the Act of August 24, 1912 (37 Stat. 434; 19 U.S.C. 1). Subsequent orders of the President or of the Secretary of the Treasury which affected these ports, or which created (or subsequently affected) additional ports, are cited following the name of the ports.

(1) *Customs ports of entry.* A list of Customs ports of entry by State and the limits of each port are set forth below:

… …

Boston	Including territory and waters adjacent thereto described in T.D. 56493.

… …

Detroit	Including territory described in E.O. 9073, Feb. 25, 1942 (7 FR 1588), and T.D. 53738.

… …

+ Houston-Galveston	Consolidated port includes territory lying within corporate limits of both Houston and Galveston, and remaining territory in Harris and Galveston Counties, T.D.s 81-160 and 82-15.

… …

Honolulu	Including territory described in T.D. 90-59.

… …

Miami	Including territory described in T.D. 53514.

+ Indicates Drawback unit/office.

 The correct answer here is "C".

✓ **JUST A SIDE NOTE:** The above-referenced list of U.S. Customs ports of entry are, in their totality in the 19 CFR 101.3, arranged by state in alphabetical order.

30. A Notice of Intent to export merchandise which may be the subject of an unused merchandise drawback claim, must be filed at the port of intended exportation on CBP Form 7553 at least _______ working day(s) prior to the date of intended exportation.

A. 1
B. 2
C. 15
D. 30
E. 45

 As per 19 CFR 191.35(a):

§191.35 Notice of intent to export; examination of merchandise.

(a) *Notice.* A notice of intent to export merchandise which may be the subject of an unused merchandise drawback claim (19 U.S.C. 1313(j)) must be provided to the Customs Service to give Customs the opportunity to examine the merchandise. **The claimant, or the exporter, must file** at the port of intended examination a Notice of Intent to Export, Destroy, or Return Merchandise for Purposes of Drawback on **Customs Form 7553 at least 2 working days prior** to the date of intended exportation unless Customs approves another filing period or the claimant has been granted a waiver of prior notice (see §191.91 of this part).

 The correct answer is "B".

✓ **JUST A SIDE NOTE:** An importer may file an "unused merchandise drawback claim" and recover any paid duties, taxes, and fees (including Merchandise Processing Fee [MPF]).

Category VI: Entry

31. Which of the following is an example of bulk cargo?

A. 250 40-foot containers of household goods
B. 500 tons of grain stowed loose in the hold of a cargo vessel
C. 1000 cases of wine, each holding 24 bottles
D. 2500 barrels of olive oil
E. 5000 sacks of coffee beans

 As per 19 CFR 4.7(b):

... ...

(4) Carriers of bulk cargo as specified in paragraph (b)(4)(i) of this section and carriers of break bulk cargo to the extent provided in paragraph (b)(4)(ii) of this section are exempt, with respect only to the bulk or break bulk cargo being transported, from the requirement set forth in paragraph (b)(2) of this section that an electronic cargo declaration be received by CBP 24 hours before such cargo is laden aboard the vessel at the foreign port. With respect to exempted carriers of bulk or break bulk cargo operating voyages to the United States, CBP must receive the electronic cargo declaration covering the bulk or break bulk cargo they are transporting 24 hours prior to the vessel's arrival in the United States (see §4.30(n)). However, for any containerized or non-qualifying break bulk cargo these exempted carriers will be transporting, CBP must receive the electronic cargo declaration 24 hours in advance of loading.

(i) **Bulk cargo is defined for purposes of this section as homogeneous cargo that is stowed loose in the hold and is not enclosed in any container such as a box, bale, bag, cask, or the like.** Such cargo is also described as bulk freight. Specifically, bulk cargo is composed of either:

(A) Free flowing articles such as oil, grain, coal, ore, and the like, which can be pumped or run through a chute or handled by dumping; or

(B) Articles that require mechanical handling such as bricks, pig iron, lumber, steel beams, and the like.

... ...

"Bulk Cargo" must be both 1) stowed loose in cargo hold AND 2) not in any way packaged. "B" meets both of these conditions and is thus correct.

✓ **JUST A SIDE NOTE:** Depending on the cargo vessel type, a vessel's hold can hold either bulk, packaged, and/or containerized cargo.

32. What additional information must be provided on invoices for plastic sheets classified in heading 3920, HTSUS?

A. Statement as to whether the plastic is cellular or non-cellular; the thickness in micrometers; indication of whether or not flexible and whether combined with textile or other material.

B. Statement as to whether the plastic is cellular or non-cellular; stretch factor, in machine direction and in cross direction; indication of whether or not flexible and whether combined with textile or other material.

C. Statement as to whether combined with textile or other material; statement whether the rubber is cellular or non-cellular, unvulcanized or vulcanized, and if vulcanized, whether hard rubber or other than hard rubber.

D. Statement as to whether the plastic is cellular or non-cellular; specification of the type of plastic; indication of whether or not flexible and whether combined with textile or other material.

E. Statement as to whether the plastic is cellular or non-cellular; chemical abstracts service number of the active ingredient; indication of whether or not flexible and whether combined with textile or other material.

 As per 19 CFR 141.89(a) (Additional information for certain classes of merchandise):

(a) Invoices for the following classes of merchandise, classifiable under the Harmonized Tariff Schedule of the United States (HTSUS), shall set forth the additional information specified: [75-42, 75-239, 78-53, 83-251, 84-149.]

… …

Plastic plates, sheets, film, foil and strip **of headings 3920** and 3921—(1) **Statement as to whether the plastic is cellular or noncellular; (2) Specification of the type of plastic; (3) Indication of whether or not flexible and whether combined with textile or other material.**

… …

 The correct answer is "D".

✓ **JUST A SIDE NOTE:** Similarly, as per the same 141.89(a), there are additional information requirements for commercial invoices for printed matter classified in specific HTSUS headings per below.

Printed matter classificable in Chapter 49—Printed matter entered in the following headings shall have, on or with the invoices covering such matter, the following information: (1) *Heading 4901*—(a) Whether the books are: dictionaries, encyclopedias, textbooks, bound newspapers or journals or periodicals, directories, bibles or other prayer books, technical, scientific or professional books, art or pictorial books, or "other" books; (b) if "other" books, whether hardbound or paperbound; (c) if "other" books, paperbound, other than "rack size": number of pages (excluding covers). (2) *Heading 4902*—(a) Whether the journal or periodical appears at least four times a week. If the journal or periodical appears other than at least four times a week, whether it is a newspaper supplement printed by a gravure process, is it a newspaper, business or professional journal or periodical, or other than these; (3) *Heading 4904*—Whether the printed or manuscript music is sheet music, not bound (except by stapling or folding); (4) *Heading 4905*—(a) Whether globes or not; (b) if not globes, whether in book form or not; (c) in any case, whether or not in relief; (5) *Heading 4908*—Whether or not vitrifiable; (6) *Heading 4904*—Whether post cards, greeting cards, or other; (7) *Heading 4910*—(a) … …

33. Which piece of information is NOT a requirement on a commercial invoice?

A. All rebates, drawbacks, and bounties, separately itemized, allowed upon the exportation of the merchandise.

B. The port of entry to which the merchandise is destined.

C. The kind of currency, whether gold, silver or paper.

D. An itemized list by name and amount of packing, cases, containers, and inland freight to the port of exportation, if included in the invoice price, and so identified.

E. The name of a responsible employee of the exporter, who has knowledge, or who can readily obtain knowledge, of the transaction.

 As per 19 CFR 141.86 (a) & (j):

§141.86 Contents of invoices and general requirements.

(a) ***General information required on the invoice***. Each invoice of imported merchandise, must set forth the following information:

(1) **The port of entry to which the merchandise is destined**;

… …

(7) **The kind of currency, whether gold, silver, or paper**;

… …

(9) **All rebates, drawbacks, and bounties, separately itemized, allowed upon the exportation of the merchandise**;

(10) The country of origin of the merchandise; and,

(11) All goods or services furnished for the production of the merchandise (e.g., assists such as dies, molds, tools, engineering work) not included in the invoice price. However, goods or services furnished in the United States are excluded. Annual reports for goods and services, when approved by the Center director, will be accepted as proof that the goods or services were provided.

… …

(j) *Name of responsible individual*. Each invoice of imported merchandise must identify by **name a responsible employee of the exporter**, who has knowledge, or who can readily obtain knowledge, of the transaction.

The regulations do not state that an invoice must have an itemized list by name and amount of packing, etc., and inland freight to the port of exportation. The correct answer is "D".

✓ **JUST A SIDE NOTE:** Some of the above-mentioned invoice requirements are rarely actually included on a commercial invoice. In practice, pieces of information on a commercial invoice that are most helpful in facilitating customs release include: Pieces, Importer, Terms [INCO], Country of origin, Actual manufacturer, Related?, HTSUS, Currency, Description of merchandise.

34. A person claiming an exemption from entry for undeliverable articles under General Note 3(e), HTSUS, must submit a certification. The certification must contain all the following conditions EXCEPT:

A. The merchandise was intended to be exported to a foreign country.

B. The merchandise was not sent abroad to receive benefit from, or fulfill obligations to, the United States as a result of exportation.

C. The merchandise was refused as defective by the foreign consignee.

D. The merchandise is being returned to the United States because it was undeliverable to the foreign consignee.

E. The merchandise is being returned within 45 days of departure from the United States.

As per 19 CFR 141.4(c):

(c) ***Undeliverable articles.*** **The exemption from entry for undeliverable articles under General Note 3(e), HTSUS, is subject to the following conditions**:

(1) The person claiming the exemption must submit a certification (documentary or electronic) that:

(i) **The merchandise was intended to be exported to a foreign country**;

(ii) **The merchandise is being returned within 45 days of departure from the United States;**

(iii) The merchandise did not leave the custody of the carrier or foreign customs;

(iv) **The merchandise is being returned to the United States because it was undeliverable to the foreign consignee;** and

(v) **The merchandise was not sent abroad to receive benefit from, or fulfill obligations to, the United States as a result of exportation.**

(2) Upon request by CBP, the person claiming the exemption shall provide evidence required to support the claim for exemption.

a The exam question makes reference to GN 3(e), which is a list of exemptions in the HTSUS for the purposes of GN 1. GN 1 basically says that all imports are subject to duty. That a shipment was refused by the foreign consignee does not exempt an undeliverable shipment from duties under GN 3(e). The correct answer is "C".

✓ **JUST A SIDE NOTE:** HTSUS General Note (GN) 1 is, in its entirety, is as follows:

General Notes

1 Tariff Treatment of Imported Goods and of Vessel Equipments, Parts and Repairs. All goods provided for in this schedule and imported into the customs territory of the United States from outside thereof, and all vessel equipments, parts, materials and repairs covered by the provisions of subchapter XVIII to chapter 98 of this schedule, are subject to duty or exempt therefrom as prescribed in general notes 3 through 29, inclusive.

35. Which of the following classes of merchandise are NOT exempt from the requirement of entry?

A. Telecommunications transmissions.

B. Vessels classified in headings 8903 and 8907 and subheadings 8905.90.10 and 8906.00.10 or in Chapter 98, HTSUS, such as under subheadings 9804.00.35 or 9813.00.35

C. Corpses, together with their coffins and accompanying flowers.

D. Railway locomotives classified in heading 8601 or 8602, HTSUS, and freight cars classified in heading 8606, HTSUS, on which no duty is owed.

E. Records, diagrams and other data with regard to any business, engineering or exploration operation whether on paper, cards, photographs, blueprints, tapes or other media

As per HTSUS General Note (GN) 3(e) & Chapter 98 Subchapter III (SUBSTANTIAL CONTAINERS OR HOLDERS):

(HTSUS General Note (GN) 3(e))

(e) **Exemptions**. For the purposes of general note 1--

(i) **corpses, together with their coffins and accompanying flowers,**
(ii) **telecommunications transmissions,**
(iii) **records, diagrams and other data with regard to any business, engineering or exploration operation whether on paper, cards, photographs, blueprints, tapes or other media,**
(iv) articles returned from space within the purview of section 484a of the Tariff Act of 1930,
(v) articles exported from the United States which are returned within 45 days after such exportation from the United States as undeliverable and which have not left the custody of the carrier or foreign customs service,
(vi) any aircraft part or equipment that was removed from a United States-registered aircraft while being used abroad in international traffic because of accident, breakdown, or emergency, that was returned to the United States within 45 days after removal, and that did not leave the custody of the carrier or foreign customs service while abroad, and
(vii) residue of bulk cargo contained in instruments of international traffic previously exported from the United States,

(Chapter 98 Subchapter III)

4. **Instruments of international traffic, such as** containers, lift vans, rail cars and **locomotives**, truck cabs and trailers, etc. **are exempt from formal entry procedures** but are required to be accounted for when imported and exported into and out of the United States, respectively, through the manifesting procedures required for all international carriers by the United States Customs Service. Fees associated with the importation of such instruments of international traffic shall be reported and paid on a periodic basis as required by regulations issued by the Secretary of the Treasury and in accordance with 1956 Customs Convention on Containers (20 UST 30; TIAS 6634).

A vessel entry is required on yachts (heading 8903), etc. The correct answer is "B".

✓ **JUST A SIDE NOTE:** A formal "vessel entry" is required for foreign yachts, cargo ships, etc. entering the United States via CBP Form 1300.

36. A warehouse entry is entry type _______.

A. 11
B. 21
C. 23
D. 61
E. 05

 As per FORM 7501 INSTRUCTIONS, Block 2:

Consumption Entries	
Free and Dutiable	01
Quota/Visa	02
Antidumping/Countervailing Duty (AD/CVD)	03
Appraisement	04
Vessel Repair	05
Foreign Trade Zone Consumption	06
Quota/Visa and AD/CVD combinations	07
Duty Deferral	08
Informal Entries	
Free and Dutiable	11
Quota Other than textiles	12
Warehouse Entries	
Warehouse	**21**
Re-Warehouse	22
Temporary Importation Bond	23
Trade Fair	24
Permanent Exhibition	25
Foreign Trade Zone Admission	26

… …

 The correct answer is "B".

✓ **JUST A SIDE NOTE:** "Re-warehousing" is the transfer of merchandise from one Customs bonded warehouse to another.

37. Cite the regulation that defines what the date of importation means?

A. 19 CFR 101.1
B. 19 CFR 24.1
C. 19 CFR 111.28
D. 19 CFR 159.1
E. None of the above

 As per 19 CFR 101.1:

§101.1 Definitions.

As used in this chapter, the following terms shall have the meanings indicated unless either the context in which they are used requires a different meaning or a different definition is prescribed for a particular part or portion thereof:

Business day. A "business day" means a weekday (Monday through Friday), excluding national holidays as specified in §101.6(a).

… …

Date of importation. **"Date of importation" means, in the case of merchandise imported otherwise than by vessel, the date on which the merchandise arrives within the Customs territory of the United States.** In the case of merchandise imported by vessel, "date of importation" means the date on which the vessel arrives within the limits of a port in the United States with intent then and there to unlade such merchandise.

… …

 The correct answer is "A".

✓ **NOTE:** As referenced in the above definition of "date of importation", and in the same 19 CFR 101.1, "Customs territory of the United States" is defined as:

"Customs territory of the United States" includes only the States, the District of Columbia, and Puerto Rico.

38. Which of the following cannot be entered on a carnet?

A. Mail importations
B. Merchandise transported by road vehicles
C. Commercial samples
D. Certain advertising films
E. Jewelry shown to solicit orders

 As per 19 CFR 114.31(a):

§114.31 Restrictions.

(a) *Mail importations.* Carnets shall not be accepted for importations by mail.

(b) *Temporary importations.* Merchandise not entitled to temporary importation under bond shall not be imported under cover of an A.T.A. or TECRO/AIT carnet.

(c) *Transportation in bond.* Except as provided in §18.43 of this chapter, merchandise not entitled to transportation in bond shall not be transported under cover of a TIR carnet.

 The correct answer is "A".

✓ **JUST A SIDE NOTE:** A carnet can be used instead of a Certificate of Registration (CBP Form 4455). A Certificate of Registration is used to register an item (with CBP) to be exported and returned, supporting the owner's claim for duty-free entry upon re-entry into the U.S.

39. What type of entry is required for goods brought into the customs territory of the United States by the National Aeronautics and Space Administration from space or from a foreign country as part of an international program of the National Aeronautics and Space Administration?

A. 01 - Formal Entry

B. 11 - Informal Entry

C. 51 - Defense Contract Management Command - International (DCMC-I) (formerly DCASR) is the importer of record and filer of the entry

D. 52 - Any U.S. Federal Government agency (other than DCMAO) is the importer of record

E. Entry is not required.

As per HTSUS Chapter 98 Subchapter VIII (IMPORTATIONS OF THE UNITED STATES GOVERNMENT), U.S. Note 1:

U.S. Note

1. **With respect to** subheading 9808.00.80, **goods brought into the customs territory of the United States by the National Aeronautics and Space Administration from space or from a foreign country as part of an international program of the National Aeronautics and Space Administration** shall not be considered an importation, and **an entry of such materials shall not be required.**

 The correct answer is "E".

✓ **JUST A SIDE NOTE:** Following the above-mentioned Chapter 98 Subchapter VIII, is Chapter 98 Subchapter IX (IMPORTATIONS OF FOREIGN GOVERNMENTS AND INTERNATIONAL ORGANIZATIONS), which, among other things, provides for duty-free treatment of gifts from foreign governments to U.S. governmental organizations.

40. Merchandise for which entry is required will be entered within _________________ after landing from a vessel, aircraft or vehicle, or after arrival at the port of destination in the case of merchandise transported in bond.

A. 5 calendar days
B. 10 calendar days
C. 15 calendar days
D. 20 calendar days
E. 25 calendar days

 As per 19 CFR 141.5:

§141.5 Time limit for entry.

Merchandise for which entry is required will be entered within 15 calendar days after landing from a vessel, aircraft or vehicle, or after arrival at the port of destination in the case of merchandise transported in bond. Merchandise for which timely entry is not made will be treated in accordance with §4.37 or §122.50 or §123.10 of this chapter.

 The correct answer is "C".

✓ **NOTE:** Sections §4.37, §122.50, and §123.10 all refer to General Order (GO), which is purgatory for potentially unclaimed or abandoned merchandise.

41. Any person outside the Customs Service who has reason to believe that any merchandise produced whether by mining, manufacture, or other means, in any foreign locality with the use of convict labor, forced labor, or indentured labor under penal sanctions, is likely to be, imported into the United States and that merchandise of the same class is being produced in the United States in such quantities as to meet the consumptive demands of the United States may communicate his belief to any port director or the Commissioner of Customs. Every such communication shall contain, or be accompanied by all of the below EXCEPT:

A. **A full statement of the reasons for the belief.**

B. **A detailed description or sample of the merchandise.**

C. **All pertinent facts obtainable as to the production of the merchandise abroad.**

D. **If the foreign merchandise is believed to be mined, produced or manufactured with forced labor or indentured labor under penal sanctions include detailed information as to the production and consumption of the particular class of merchandise in the United States and the names and addresses of domestic producers likely to be interested in the matter.**

E. **Location of foreign mining, production or manufacture at issue.**

As per 19 CFR 12.42 (a) & (d):

(b) Any person outside CBP who has reason to believe that merchandise produced in the circumstances mentioned in paragraph (a) of this section is being, or is likely to be, imported into the United States may communicate his belief to any port director or the Commissioner of CBP. **Every such communication shall contain, or be accompanied by:**

(1) A full statement of the reasons for the belief;

(2) A detailed description or sample of the merchandise; and

(3) All pertinent facts obtainable as to the production of the merchandise abroad.

(d) Upon receipt by the Commissioner of CBP of any communication submitted pursuant to paragraph (a) or (b) of this section and found to comply with the requirements of the pertinent paragraph, the Commissioner will cause such investigation to be made as appears to be warranted by the circumstances of the case and **the Commissioner or his designated representative will consider any representations offered by foreign interests, importers, domestic producers, or other interested persons.**

The CBP exam answer key states that "E" is the correct answer. However, the regulations here do not say that a person making this claim to Customs shall/must include "names and addresses of domestic producers", etc. The regulations say only that Customs will take these additional factors into consideration, but not necessarily as part of the three elements ("A", "B", and "C") required from the claimant.

✓ **JUST A SIDE NOTE:** Customs defines "forced labor" as "all work or service which is exacted from any person under the menace of any penalty for its nonperformance and for which the worker does not offer himself voluntarily."

42. Protest content shall contain all of the following information EXCEPT:

A. **The name and address of the protestant, i.e., the importer of record or consignee, and the name and address of his agent or attorney if signed by one of these.**

B. **The importer number of the protestant. If the protestant is represented by an agent having power of attorney, the importer number of the agent should also be shown.**

C. **The number and date of the entry**

D. **A copy of the bill of lading**

E. **The nature of, and justification for, the objection set forth distinctly and specifically with respect to each category, payment, claim, decision, or refusal.**

As per 19 CFR 174.13(a):

§174.13 Contents of protest.

(a) *Contents, in general.* A protest shall contain the following information:

(1) **The name and address of the protestant**, *i.e.*, the importer of record or consignee, and the name and address of his agent or attorney if signed by one of these;

(2) **The importer number of the protestant**. If the protestant is represented by an agent having power of attorney, the importer number of the agent shall also be shown;

(3) **The number and date of the entry**;

(4) The date of liquidation of the entry, or the date of a decision not involving a liquidation or reliquidation;

(5) A specific description of the merchandise affected by the decision as to which protest is made;

(6) **The nature of, and justification for** the objection set forth distinctly and specifically with respect to each category, payment, claim, decision, or refusal;

(7) The date of receipt and protest number of any protest previously filed that is the subject of a pending application for further review pursuant to subpart C of this part and that is alleged to involve the same merchandise and the same issues, if the protesting party requests disposition in accordance with the action taken on such previously filed protest;

(8) If another party has not filed a timely protest, the surety's protest shall certify that the protest is not being filed collusively to extend another authorized person's time to protest; and

(9) A declaration, to the best of the protestant's knowledge, as to whether the entry is the subject of drawback, or whether the entry has been referenced on a certificate of delivery or certificate of manufacture and delivery so as to enable a party to make such entry the subject of drawback (see §§181.50(b) and 191.81(b) of this chapter).

 A copy of the bill of lading is not required to file a protest. The correct answer is "D".

✓ **JUST A SIDE NOTE:** Protests may be submitted electronically via ACE (no longer available via ABI), or via hard copies with CBP Form 19.

43. Upon receipt of service of a summons in an action initiated in the Court of International Trade, all of the following items shall be immediately transmitted to the Court of International Trade as part of the official record by the Customs officer concerned, EXCEPT:

A. Consumption or other entry
B. Commercial Invoice
C. Special Customs Invoice
D. Official samples
E. Copy of a bill from CBP for duties owed

 As per 19 CFR 176.11:

§176.11 Transmission of records to Court of International Trade.

Upon receipt of service of a summons in an action initiated in the Court of International Trade the following items shall be immediately transmitted to the Court of International Trade as part of the official record by the Customs officer concerned:

(a) **Consumption or other entry**;

(b) **Commercial invoice**;

(c) **Special Customs invoice**;

(d) Copy of protest and any amendments thereto;

(e) Copy of denial or protest in whole or in part;

(f) Importer's exhibits;

(g) **Official samples**;

(h) Any official laboratory reports;

(i) The summary sheet;

(j) In any case in which one or more of the items listed in paragraphs (a) through (i) of this section do not exist, the Customs officer shall include a statement to that effect, identifying the items which do not exist.

 A copy of a bill from CBP for duties owed is not required in this instance. The correct answer is "E".

✓ **JUST A SIDE NOTE:** The United States Court of International Trade (USCIT), located in New York City, is a U.S. federal court that reviews and makes decisions on duty-related actions by CBP. The court was formerly known as The United States Customs Court.

44. In accordance with 19 C.F.R. 162.74, an oral prior-disclosure must be confirmed by a written record of the information conveyed to CBP, to the concerned Fines, Penalties, and Forfeitures Officer, within _______________.

A. Within 10 days of the date of the oral disclosure

B. Within 30 days of the date of the oral disclosure

C. Within 10 days of the date of identifying a potential violation

D. Within 30 days of the date of identifying a potential violation (or such longer period as CBP may provide)

E. Within 30 days of the date of receiving notice that CBP has commenced a formal investigation

As per 19 CFR 162.74(a):

§162.74 Prior disclosure.

(a) *In general*—(1) A prior disclosure is made if the person concerned discloses the circumstances of a violation (as defined in paragraph (b) of this section) of 19 U.S.C. 1592 or 19 U.S.C. 1593a, either orally or in writing to a Customs officer before, or without knowledge of, the commencement of a formal investigation of that violation, and makes a tender of any actual loss of duties, taxes and fees or actual loss of revenue in accordance with paragraph (c) of this section. A Customs officer who receives such a tender in connection with a prior disclosure shall ensure that the tender is deposited with the concerned local Customs entry officer.

(2) A person shall be accorded the full benefits of prior disclosure treatment if that person provides information orally or in writing to Customs with respect to a violation of 19 U.S.C. 1592 or 19 U.S.C. 1593a if the concerned Fines, Penalties, and Forfeitures Officer is satisfied the information was provided before, or without knowledge of, the commencement of a formal investigation, and the information provided includes substantially the information specified in paragraph (b) of this section. **In the case of an oral disclosure, the disclosing party shall confirm the oral disclosure by providing a written record of the information conveyed to Customs in the oral disclosure to the concerned Fines, Penalties, and Forfeitures Officer within 10 days of the date of the oral disclosure.** The concerned Fines, Penalties and Forfeiture Officer may, upon request of the disclosing party which establishes a showing of good cause, waive the oral disclosure written confirmation requirement. Failure to provide the written confirmation of the oral disclosure or obtain a waiver of the requirement may result in denial of the oral prior disclosure.

The correct answer is "A".

✓ **NOTE:** The sub-paragraph continues by further explaining that the CBP officer may waive the written follow-up requirement, if so requested by the disclosing party, and at the discretion of the officer.

45. Which of the following circumstances do NOT need to be disclosed when a party makes a valid prior disclosure of a violation of 19 USC 1592?

A. The importation identified by entry number, drawback claim number or by port of entry, and the approximate date of entry.

B. The class or kind of merchandise involved in the violation.

C. The material false statements, omissions or acts.

D. The name and contact information of the person responsible for the violation.

E. The true and accurate information or data that should have been provided.

As per 19 CFR 162.74(b):

(b) *Disclosure of the circumstances of a violation.* The term "discloses the circumstances of a violation" means the act of providing to Customs a statement orally or in writing that:

(1) Identifies the class or kind of merchandise involved in the violation;

(2) Identifies the importation or drawback claim included in the disclosure by entry number, drawback claim number, or by indicating each concerned Customs port of entry and the approximate dates of entry or dates of drawback claims;

(3) Specifies the material false statements, omissions or acts including an explanation as to how and when they occurred; and

(4) Sets forth, to the best of the disclosing party's knowledge, the true and accurate information or data that should have been provided in the entry or drawback claim documents, and states that the disclosing party will provide any information or data unknown at the time of disclosure within 30 days of the initial disclosure date. Extensions of the 30-day period may be requested by the disclosing party from the concerned Fines, Penalties, and Forfeitures Officer to enable the party to obtain the information or data.

A prior disclosure need not include the name and contact information of the person responsible for the violation. The correct answer is "D".

✓ **NOTE:** As made reference to in this exam question, "19 U.S.C. 1592" means United States Code, Title 19, Section 1592, which provides for "Penalties for fraud, gross negligence, and negligence".

46. A penalty or claim for liquidated damages is assessed and fewer than 180 days remain from the date of penalty or liquidated damages notice. Before the statute of limitations may be asserted as a defense, the Fines, Penalties, and Forfeitures Officer may specify in the notice a reasonable period of time, but not less than _______, for the filing of a petition for relief.

A. **5 working days**
B. **7 working days**
C. **10 working days**
D. **30 working days**
E. **60 workings days**

 As per 19 CFR 172.3(e):

(e) *Exception for certain cases.* **If a penalty or claim for liquidated damages is assessed and fewer than 180 days remain from the date of penalty or liquidated damages notice before the statute of limitations may be asserted as a defense, the Fines, Penalties, and Forfeitures Officer may specify in the notice a reasonable period of time, but not less than 7 working days, for the filing of a petition for relief**. If a petition is not filed within the time specified, the matter will be transmitted promptly to the appropriate Office of the Chief Counsel for referral to the Department of Justice.

 The correct answer is "B".

✓ **JUST A SIDE NOTE:** Generally speaking, the CBP statute of limitations is 5 years.

47. Which statement regarding Protest is FALSE?

A. **A protest shall not be filed against the decision of the port director on reliquidation upon any question not involved in the reliquidation.**

B. **If the protest relates to an administrative action involving exclusion of merchandise from entry or delivery under any provision of the Customs laws, the port director shall review and act on a protest filed in accordance with section 514(a)(4), Tariff Act of 1930, as amended (19 U.S.C. 1514(a)(4)), within 30 days from the date the protest was filed.**

C. **If the port director fails to allow or deny a protest which is the subject of a request for accelerated disposition within 30 days from the date of the mailing of such request, the protest shall be deemed to have been denied at the close of the 30th day following such date of mailing.**

D. **A written protest against a decision of CBP must be filed in quadruplicate on CBP Form 19 or a form of the same size clearly labeled "Protest" and setting forth the same content in its entirety, in the same order, addressed to CBP.**

E. **Within 60 calendar days after issuing a protest review decision, CBP will publish the decision in the Customs Bulletin or otherwise make it available for public inspection. Disclosure is governed by 6 CFR part 5 and 19 CFR part 103.**

 As per 19 CFR 174.32:

§174.32 Publication.

Within 90 calendar days after issuing a protest review decision, CBP will publish the decision in the Customs Bulletin or otherwise make it available for public inspection. Disclosure is governed by 6 CFR part 5 and 19 CFR part 103.

Multiple choice "E" states "60 calendar days" when in fact CBP has "90 calendar days" to publish their protest review decision. "E" is the false statement and correct answer.

✓ **JUST A SIDE NOTE:** The Customs Bulletin is a government publication made available for the trade community. As per CBP's website:

Customs Bulletin and Decisions provides a weekly compilation of decisions, rulings, regulations, notices, and abstracts concerning customs and related matters of the U.S. Customs and Border Protection, U.S. Court of Appeals for the Federal Circuit and U.S. Court of International Trade. As a service to the trade community, CBP maintains an electronic archive of Customs Bulletin and Decisions dating from January 2, 2002.

https://www.cbp.gov/trade/rulings/bulletin-decisions

Category VIII – Free Trade Agreements

48. Which of the following has a Merchandise Processing Fee (MPF) requirement?

A. Israel FTA
B. Oman FTA
C. Peru TPA
D. Jordan FTA
E. Insular Possessions

 As per 19 CFR 24.23(c):

(c) *Exemptions and limitations.* (1) **The ad valorem fee, surcharge, and specific fees provided for under paragraphs (b)(1) and (b)(2) of this section will not apply to**:

(i) Except as provided in paragraph (c)(2) of this section, articles provided for in chapter 98, Harmonized Tariff Schedule of the United States (HTSUS; 19 U.S.C. 1202);

(ii) Products of **insular possessions** of the U.S. (General Note 3(a)(iv), HTSUS);

… …

(5) The ad valorem fee, surcharge, and specific fees provided for under paragraphs (b)(1) and (b)(2) of this section will not apply to products of **Israel** that are entered, or withdrawn from warehouse for consumption, on or after September 16, 1998 (the effective date of a determination published in the FEDERAL REGISTER on September 1, 1998, under section 112 of the Customs and Trade Act of 1990).

… …

(11) The ad valorem fee, surcharge, and specific fees provided under paragraphs (b)(1) and (b)(2)(i) of this section will not apply to goods that qualify as originating goods under §202 of the United States—**Oman** Free Trade Agreement Implementation Act (see also General Note 31, HTSUS) that are entered, or withdrawn from warehouse for consumption, on or after January 1, 2009.

(12) The ad valorem fee, surcharge, and specific fees provided under paragraphs (b)(1) and (b)(2)(i) of this section will not apply to goods that qualify as originating goods under §203 of the United States-**Peru** Trade Promotion Agreement Implementation Act (*see also* General Note 32, HTSUS) that are entered, or withdrawn from warehouse for consumption, on or after February 1, 2009.

… …

The Jordan Free Trade Agreement does not exempt applicable entries from the MPF. The correct answer is "D".

✓ **JUST A SIDE NOTE:** The Morocco FTA is another rare case of a Free Trade Agreement not exempt from the MPF.

49. The _______ that completes and signs the NAFTA Certificate of Origin has _______ calendar days after the date of discovery of incorrect information in the Certificate to notify in writing all persons to whom the Certificate was originally given of the error.

A. **CBP Officer; 10**

B. **Freight Forwarder; 15**

C. **Importer of Record; 15**

D. **Exporter or producer; 30**

E. **Ship's captain; 5**

As per 19 CFR 181.11(d):

(d) *Notification of errors in Certificate.* **An exporter or producer** in the United States who has completed and signed a Certificate of Origin, and who has reason to believe that the Certificate contains information that is not correct, **shall within 30 calendar days** after the date of discovery of the error **notify in writing all persons to whom the Certificate was given** by the exporter or producer of any change that could affect the accuracy or validity of the Certificate.

✓ **JUST A SIDE NOTE:** A snapshot of CBP Form 434 (NAFTA Certificate of Origin) is provided on the following page.

DEPARTMENT OF HOMELAND SECURITY
U.S. Customs and Border Protection

OMB No. 1651-0098
Exp. 04-30-2020

NORTH AMERICAN FREE TRADE AGREEMENT CERTIFICATE OF ORIGIN

19 CFR 181.11, 181.22

1. EXPORTER NAME, ADDRESS AND EMAIL TAX IDENTIFICATION NUMBER:	2. BLANKET PERIOD FROM *(mm/dd/yyyy)* TO *(mm/dd/yyyy)*
3. PRODUCER NAME, ADDRESS AND EMAIL TAX IDENTIFICATION NUMBER:	4. IMPORTER NAME, ADDRESS AND EMAIL TAX IDENTIFICATION NUMBER:

5. DESCRIPTION OF GOOD(S)	6. HS TARIFF CLASSIFICATION NUMBER	7. PREFERENCE CRITERION	8. PRODUCER	9. NET COST	10. COUNTRY OF ORIGIN

I CERTIFY THAT:

- THE INFORMATION ON THIS DOCUMENT IS TRUE AND ACCURATE AND I ASSUME THE RESPONSIBILITY FOR PROVING SUCH REPRESENTATIONS. I UNDERSTAND THAT I AM LIABLE FOR ANY FALSE STATEMENTS OR MATERIAL OMISSIONS MADE ON OR IN CONNECTION WITH THIS DOCUMENT;
- I AGREE TO MAINTAIN AND PRESENT UPON REQUEST, DOCUMENTATION NECESSARY TO SUPPORT THIS CERTIFICATE, AND TO INFORM, IN WRITING, ALL PERSONS TO WHOM THE CERTIFICATE WAS GIVEN OF ANY CHANGES THAT COULD AFFECT THE ACCURACY OR VALIDITY OF THIS CERTIFICATE;
- THE GOODS ORIGINATED IN THE TERRITORY OF ONE OR MORE OF THE PARTIES, AND COMPLY WITH THE ORIGIN REQUIREMENTS SPECIFIED FOR THOSE GOODS IN THE NORTH AMERICAN FREE TRADE AGREEMENT AND UNLESS SPECIFICALLY EXEMPTED IN ARTICLE 411 OR ANNEX 401, THERE HAS BEEN NO FURTHER PRODUCTION OR ANY OTHER OPERATION OUTSIDE THE TERRITORIES OF THE PARTIES; AND
- THIS CERTIFICATE CONSISTS OF ______ PAGES, INCLUDING ALL ATTACHMENTS.

11.	11a. AUTHORIZED SIGNATURE		11b. COMPANY
	11c. NAME		11d. TITLE
	11e. DATE *(mm/dd/yyyy)*	11f. TELEPHONE NUMBERS *(Voice)* *(Facsimile)*	11g. EMAIL

CBP Form 434 (11/16)

Page 1 of 2

50. Which of the following statements regarding the North American Free Trade Agreement (NAFTA) Certificate of Origin is NOT true?

A. The Certificate of Origin may be applicable to a single or multiple importation(s) into the United States.

B. A Certificate of Origin is not required for non-commercial importations.

C. The Certificate of Origin shall be signed by the importer.

D. If the Certificate of Origin is illegible or defective, the importer shall be given a period of not less than 5 working days to submit a corrected Certificate.

E. The Certificate of Origin shall be completed in the English language or in the language of the country from which the good is exported.

 As per 19 CFR 181.22(b):

§181.22 Maintenance of records and submission of Certificate by importer.

… …

(b) *Submission of Certificate.* An importer who claims preferential tariff treatment on a good under §181.21 of this part shall provide, at the request of the Center director, a copy of each Certificate of Origin pertaining to the good which is in the possession of the importer. A Certificate of Origin submitted to CBP under this paragraph or under §181.32(b)(3) of this part:

(1) Shall be on CBP Form 434, or its electronic equivalent including privately-printed copies thereof, or on such other form as approved by the Canadian or Mexican customs administration, or, as an alternative to CBP Form 434 or such other approved form, in an approved computerized format or such other medium or format as is approved by the Office of International Trade, U.S. Customs and Border Protection, Washington, DC 20229. An alternative format must contain the same information and certification set forth on CBP Form 434;

(2) **Shall be signed by the exporter** or by the exporter's authorized agent having knowledge of the relevant facts;

(3) Shall be completed either in the English language or in the language of the country from which the good is exported. If the Certificate is completed in a language other than English, the importer shall also provide to the Center director, upon request, a written English translation thereof;

(4) Shall be accepted by CBP for four years after the date on which the Certificate was signed by the exporter or producer; and

(5) May be applicable to:

(i) A single importation of a good into the United States, including a single shipment that results in the filing of one or more entries and a series of shipments that results in the filing of one entry; or

(ii) Multiple importations of identical goods into the United States that occur within a specified period, not exceeding 12 months, set out therein by the exporter or producer.

 The NAFTA Certificate of Origin is signed by the exporter, not the importer. The correct answer is "C".

✓ **JUST A SIDE NOTE:** For NAFTA eligible shipments $2,500 or less, a short statement certifying NAFTA eligibility, specifying party type, name, title, address, signature, and date can take the place of the official NAFTA Certificate of Origin

51. An importer makes an entry of Phenobarbital Sodium originating from Mauritius that qualifies for a free rate of duty under the special tariff treatment programs. They use special preference indicator "K" on the CBP Form 7501. Pursuant to which General Note of the Harmonized Tariff Schedule are they making their claim under?

A. General Note 29
B. General Note 34
C. General Note 4
D. General Note 13
E. General Note 8

 As per HTSUS General Note 13:

13. Pharmaceutical products. Whenever a rate of duty of "Free" followed by **the symbol "K"** in parentheses appears in the "Special" subcolumn for a heading or subheading, any product (by whatever name known) classifiable in such provision which is the product of a country eligible for tariff treatment under column 1 shall be entered free of duty, provided that such product is included in the pharmaceutical appendix to the tariff schedule. Products in the pharmaceutical appendix include the salts, esters and hydrates of the International Non-proprietary Name (INN) products enumerated in table 1 of the appendix that contain in their names any of the prefixes or suffixes listed in table 2 of the appendix, provided that any such salt, ester or hydrate is classifiable in the same 6-digit tariff provision as the relevant product enumerated in table 1.

 The correct answer is "D".

✓ **JUST A SIDE NOTE:** The Pharmaceutical Appendix to the Tariff Schedule (see below snapshot) follows the Chemical Appendix to the Tariff Schedule, which follows Chapter 99.

Harmonized Tariff Schedule of the United States (2018)
Annotated for Statistical Reporting Purposes

PHARMACEUTICAL APPENDIX TO THE TARIFF SCHEDULE

2

Table 1.
This table enumerates products described by International Non-proprietary Names INN which shall be entered free of duty under general note 13 to the tariff schedule. The Chemical Abstracts Service CAS registry numbers also set forth in this table are included to assist in the identification of the products concerned. For purposes of the tariff schedule, any references to a product enumerated in this table includes such product by whatever name known.

ABACAVIR	136470-78-5	ACETORPHINE	25333-77-1
ABAFUNGIN	129639-79-8	ACETRYPTINE	3551-18-6
ABAGOVOMAB	792921-10-9	ACETYLCHOLINE CHLORIDE	60-31-1
ABAMECTIN	65195-55-3	ACETYLCYSTEINE	616-91-1
ABANOQUIL	90402-40-7	ACETYLDIGITOXIN	1111-39-3
ABAPERIDONE	183849-43-6	ACETYLLEUCINE	99-15-0
ABARELIX	183552-38-7	ACETYLMETHADOL	509-74-0
ABATACEPT	332348-12-6	ACEVALTRATE	25161-41-5
ABCIXIMAB	143653-53-6	ACEXAMIC ACID	57-08-9
ABECARNIL	111841-85-1	ACICLOVIR	59277-89-3
ABETIMUS	167362-48-3	ACIFRAN	72420-38-3

52. What regulation would you find the verification authority for the US-Korea Free Trade Agreement (UKFTA)?

A. 19CFR 10.616
B. 19CFR10.784
C. 19CFR 10.926
D. 19CFR10.1026
E. 19CFR 10.2026

 As per 19 CFR 10.1026:

§10.1026 Verification and justification of claim for preferential tariff treatment.

(a) *Verification.* A claim for preferential tariff treatment made under §10.1003(b) or §10.1011 of this subpart, including any statements or other information submitted to CBP in support of the claim, will be subject to such verification as the Center director deems necessary. In the event that the Center director is provided with insufficient information to verify or substantiate the claim, the Center director finds a pattern of conduct, indicating that an importer, exporter, or producer has provided false or unsupported declarations or certifications, or the exporter or producer fails to consent to a verification visit, the Center director may deny the claim for preferential treatment. A verification of a claim for preferential tariff treatment under UKFTA for goods imported into the United States may be conducted by means of one or more of the following:

(1) Written requests for information from the importer, exporter, or producer;

(2) Written questionnaires to the importer, exporter, or producer;

(3) Visits to the premises of the exporter or producer in the territory of Korea, to review the records of the type referred to in §10.1009(c)(1) of this subpart or to observe the facilities used in the production of the good, in accordance with the framework that the Parties develop for conducting verifications; and

(4) Such other procedures to which the Parties may agree.

(b) *Applicable accounting principles.* When conducting a verification of origin to which Generally Accepted Accounting Principles may be relevant, CBP will apply and accept the Generally Accepted Accounting Principles applicable in the country of production.

 The correct answer is "D".

✓ **JUST A SIDE NOTE:** The regulations on the UKFTA are located in Part 10, Subpart R, Sections 10.1001 thru. 10.1034.

53. An importer fails to produce a NAFTA Certificate of Origin for an entry claiming duty free treatment after CBP issued a Request for Information asking the importer to provide a valid NAFTA Certificate of Origin. Which of the following is true concerning a possible recordkeeping penalty action by CBP?

A. The importer is not subject to a recordkeeping penalty because only the exporter is required to retain the NAFTA Certificate of Origin.

B. The importer is not subject to a recordkeeping penalty because the NAFTA Certificate of Origin is not on the "(a)(1)(A) list".

C. If CBP liquidates the entry without NAFTA duty preference, CBP cannot also issue a recordkeeping penalty.

D. The importer may be subject to a recordkeeping penalty for failure to comply with the lawful demand.

E. CBP may issue a recordkeeping penalty only after serving a Customs summons in addition to the Request for Information.

As per 19 CFR 163.6(b):

163.6 Production and examination of entry and other records and witnesses; penalties.

… …

(b) *Failure to produce entry records*—(1) *Monetary penalties applicable.* The following penalties may be imposed if a person fails to comply with a lawful demand for the production of an entry record and is not excused from a penalty pursuant to paragraph (b)(3) of this section:

(i) If the failure to comply is a result of the willful failure of the person to maintain, store, or retrieve the demanded record, such person shall be subject to a penalty, for each release of merchandise, not to exceed $100,000, or an amount equal to 75 percent of the appraised value of the merchandise, whichever amount is less; or

(ii) If the failure to comply is a result of negligence of the person in maintaining, storing, or retrieving the demanded record, such person shall be subject to a penalty, for each release of merchandise, not to exceed $10,000, or an amount equal to 40 percent of the appraised value of the merchandise, whichever amount is less.

(2) *Additional actions*—(i) *General.* In addition to any penalty imposed under paragraph (b)(1) of this section, and except as otherwise provided in paragraph (b)(2)(ii) of this section, if the demanded entry record relates to the eligibility of merchandise for a column 1 special rate of duty in the Harmonized Tariff Schedule of the United States (HTSUS), the entry of such merchandise:

… …

correct answer is "D".

✔ **JUST A SIDE NOTE:** As evident in the above-mentioned excerpt from the regulations, penalties for refusing to provide documents to CBP are much stiffer than penalties for failing to produce documents due to negligence or lapses in recordkeeping.

Category IX – Foreign Trade Zones

54. A ______________ bonded warehouse is known as a general order warehouse, established for the storage and disposition exclusively of general order merchandise.

A. Class 3
B. Class 5
C. Class 8
D. Class 9
E. Class 11

 As per 19 CFR 19.1(a):

§19.1 Classes of customs warehouses.

(a) *Classifications.* Customs warehouses shall be designated according to the following classifications:

(1) *Class 1.* Premises that may be owned or leased by the Government, when the exigencies of the service as determined by the port director so require, and used for the storage of merchandise undergoing examination by Customs, under seizure, or pending final release from Customs custody. Merchandise will be stored in such premises only at Customs direction and will be held under "general order."

(2) *Class 2.* Importers' private bonded warehouses used exclusively for the storage of merchandise belonging or consigned to the proprietor thereof. A warehouse of class 4 or 5 may be bonded exclusively for the storage of goods imported by the proprietor thereof, in which case it shall be known as a private bonded warehouse.

(3) *Class 3.* Public bonded warehouses used exclusively for the storage of imported merchandise.

(4) *Class 4.* Bonded yards or sheds for the storage of heavy and bulky imported merchandise; stables, feeding pens, corrals, or other similar buildings or limited enclosures for the storage of imported animals; and tanks for the storage of imported liquid merchandise in bulk. If the port director deems it necessary, the yards shall be enclosed by substantial fences with entrances and exit gates capable of being secured by the proprietor's locks. The inlets and outlets to tanks shall be secured by means of seals or the proprietor's locks.

(5) *Class 5.* Bonded bins or parts of buildings or of elevators to be used for the storage of grain. The bonded portions shall be effectively separated from the rest of the building.

(6) *Class 6.* Warehouses for the manufacture in bond, solely for exportation, of articles made in whole or in part of imported materials or of materials subject to internal-revenue tax; and for the manufacture for home consumption or exportation of cigars in whole of tobacco imported from one country.

(7) *Class 7.* Warehouses bonded for smelting and refining imported metal-bearing materials for exportation or domestic consumption.

(8) *Class 8.* Bonded warehouses established for the purpose of cleaning, sorting, repacking, or otherwise changing in condition, but not manufacturing, imported merchandise, under Customs supervision and at the expense of the proprietor.

(9) *Class 9.* Bonded warehouse, known as "duty-free stores", used for selling, for use outside the Customs territory, conditionally duty-free merchandise owned or sold by the proprietor and delivered from the Class 9 warehouse to an airport or other exit point for exportation by, or on behalf of, individuals departing from the Customs territory for destinations other than foreign trade zones. Pursuant to 19 U.S.C. 1555(b)(8)(C), "Customs territory", for purposes of duty-free stores, means the Customs territory of the U.S. as defined in §101.1(e) of this chapter, and foreign trade zones (see part 146 of this chapter). All distribution warehouses used exclusively to provide individual duty-free sales locations and storage cribs with conditionally duty-free merchandise are also Class 9 warehouses.

(10) [Reserved]

(11) *Class 11.* Bonded warehouses, known as "general order warehouses," established for the storage and disposition exclusively of general order merchandise as described in §127.1 of this chapter.

 The correct answer is "E".

55. _________________ is the procedure for delivery of merchandise to a zone without prior application and approval on Customs Form 214.

A. Constructive Transfer
B. Activation
C. Transfer
D. Admit
E. Direct Delivery

 As per 19 CFR 146.39(a):

§146.39 Direct delivery procedures.

(a) *General.* This procedure is for delivery of merchandise to a zone without prior application and approval on Customs Form 214.

 Direct Delivery is the name of the procedure. The correct answer is "E".

✓ **NOTE:** CBP Form 214 is for the "Application for Foreign-Trade Zone Admission and/or Status Designation".

56. Warehouse withdrawals under blanket permit must be filed on which Form?

A. CBP Form 7512
B. CBP Form 7501
C. Customs Form 301
D. CBP Form 19
E. Customs Form 28

 As per 19 CFR 19.6(d):

§19.6 Deposits, withdrawals, blanket permits to withdraw and sealing requirements.

… …

(d) *Blanket permits to withdraw*—(1) *General.* (i) Blanket permits may be used to withdraw merchandise from bonded warehouses for:

… …

(2) ***Withdrawals under blanket permit***. Withdrawals may be made under blanket permit without any further CBP approval, and must be documented by placing a copy of the withdrawal document in the proprietor's permit file folder. **Each withdrawal must be filed on CBP Form 7501**, or its electronic equivalent, and must be consecutively numbered, prefixed with the letter "B". The withdrawal must specify the quantity and value of each type of merchandise to be withdrawn. Each copy must bear the summary statement described in §144.32(a) of this chapter, reflecting the balance of merchandise covered by the warehouse entry. Any joint discrepancy report of the proprietor and the bonded carrier, licensed cartman or lighterman, or weigher, gauger, or measurer for a supplementary withdrawal must be made on the copy and reported to the port director as provided in paragraph (b)(1) of this section. A copy of the withdrawal must be retained in the records of the proprietor as provided in §19.12(d)(4) of this part. Merchandise must not be removed from the warehouse prior to the preparation of the supplementary withdrawal. If merchandise is so removed, the proprietor will be subject to liquidated damages as if it were removed without a CBP permit.

 The correct answer is "B".

✓ **JUST A SIDE NOTE:** Warehouse withdrawals for exportation used to be able to be processed via CBP Form 7512. However, now only CBP Form 7501 may be used for such withdrawals.

57. What CBP Form is used for permission to manipulate, manufacture, exhibit, or destroy merchandise in a FTZ?

A. CBP Form 7501
B. CBP Form 216
C. CBP Form 214
D. CBP Form 3461
E. CBP Form 6043

 As per 19 CFR 146.52(a):

§146.52 Manipulation, manufacture, exhibition or destruction; Customs Form 216.

(a) *Application.* Prior to any action, the operator shall file with the port director an application (or blanket application) on **Customs Form 216 for permission to manipulate, manufacture, exhibit, or destroy merchandise in a zone**. After Customs approves the application (or blanket application), the operator will retain in his recordkeeping system the approved application.

 The correct answer is "B".

✓ **JUST A SIDE NOTE:** A blanket application to manipulate, etc. in a foreign trade zone may be approved for up to one year of manipulation, etc. activity.

58. Brown Bag, Inc. is looking to register their trademarks. They presently have 4 different classes of goods. How much will they be charged to register all their trademarks?

A. $.00. This is a free service.
B. $190.00
C. $380.00
D. $570.00
E. $760.00

 As per 19 CFR 133.3(b):

§133.3 Documents and fee to accompany application.

… …

(b) *Fee.* The application shall be accompanied by a fee of $190 for each trademark to be recorded. However**, if the trademark is registered for more than one class of goods (based on the class, or classes, first stated on the certificate of registration, without consideration of any class, or classes, also stated in parentheses) the fee for recordation shall be $190 for each class** for which the applicant desires to record the trademark with the United States Customs Service. For example, to secure recordation of a trademark registered for three classes of goods, a fee of $570 is payable. A check or money order shall be made payable to the United States Customs Service.

 $190 (fee) x 4 (classes) = $760. The correct answer is "E".

✓ **JUST A SIDE NOTE:** The above-mentioned trademark registration is for recordation of trademark with Customs purposes. A trademark application to the United States Patent and Trademark Office (USPTO) is a separate application and the fee starts at $225 per class. The United States Patent and Trademark Office is the federal agency for granting U.S. patents and registering trademarks.

59. Bob's Big Bargains Unlimited imported a shipment of designer branded t-shirts that were determined to bear counterfeit trademarks and seized by CBP. The relevant trademarks were recorded with CBP. The shipment contained 500 shirts with an invoice value of $5.00 each, a bargain compared to the manufacturer's suggested retail price of $50.00 for the genuine designer branded t-shirt. This was the second intellectual property rights seizure since the importer started his business a few months ago. The importer's previous seizure involved piratical plush toys that infringed numerous copyrights recorded with CBP. The civil penalty that CBP may assess for the importer's second seizure can be no more than:

A. $2,500
B. $25,000
C. $5,000
D. $50,000
E. None of the above.

As per 19 CFR 133.27(b):

133.27 Civil fines for those involved in the importation of merchandise bearing a counterfeit mark.

In addition to any other penalty or remedy authorized by law, CBP may impose a civil fine under 19 U.S.C. 1526(f) on any person who directs, assists financially or otherwise, or aids and abets the importation of merchandise for sale or public distribution that bears a counterfeit mark resulting in a seizure of the merchandise under 19 U.S.C. 1526(e) (see §133.21 of this subpart), as follows:

(a) *First violation.* For the first seizure of merchandise under this section, the fine imposed will not be more than the value the merchandise would have had if it were genuine, according to the manufacturer's suggested retail price in the United States at the time of seizure.

(b) *Subsequent violations:* **For the second and each subsequent seizure under this section, the fine imposed will not be more than twice the value the merchandise would have had if it were genuine, according to the manufacturer's suggested retail price in the United States at the time of seizure.**

 500 (shirts) x $50 (genuine value) x 2 (twice the value) = $50,000. The correct answer is "D".

✓ **NOTE:** The exam key incorrectly states that the answer is "B". However, this calculation does not include the "twice the value" consideration that can be charged for this second seizure.

60. A mail shipment of one counterfeit handbag valued at $500, bearing a spurious mark identical with, or substantially indistinguishable from, a mark registered on the Principal Register of the U.S. Patent and Trademark Office and recorded with CBP, is exempt from prohibition under section 526, Tariff Act of 1930, as amended (19 U.S.C.§ 1526), if:

A. **The item is intended for personal use, and the exemption for the same type of article has not been taken within the 30-day period.**

B. **The item is intended for personal use, and the quantity does not exceed the exemption of one article of the type bearing the protected trademark.**

C. **The circumstances allowing exemption from trademark or trade name restriction(s) set forth in §133.22(c) or §133.23(d) are established.**

D. **The addressee appears in person at the appropriate Customs office and, at that time, removes or obliterates the marks in a manner acceptable to the Customs officer.**

E. **None of the above.**

 As per 19 CFR 148.55:

§148.55 Exemption for articles bearing American trademark.

(a) *Application of exemption.* An exemption is provided for trademarked articles accompanying any person arriving in the United States which would be prohibited entry under section 526, Tariff Act of 1930, as amended (19 U.S.C. 1526), or section 42 of the Act of July 5, 1946 (60 Stat. 440; 15 U.S.C. 1124), because the trademark has been registered with the U.S. Patent and Trademark Office and recorded with Customs. **The exemption may be applied** to those trademarked articles of foreign manufacture bearing a trademark owned by a citizen of, or a corporation or association created or organized within, the United States **when imported for the arriving person's personal use in the quantities provided in paragraph (c) of this section**. Unregistered and unrecorded trademarked articles are not subject to quantity limitation.

(b) *Limitations*—(1) *30-day period.* **The exemption in paragraph (a) of this section shall not be granted to any person who has taken advantage of the exemption for the same type of article within the 30-day period** immediately prior to his arrival in the United States. The date of the person's last arrival on which he claimed this exemption shall be considered to be the date he last took advantage of the exemption.

(2) *Sale of exempted articles.* If an article which has been exempted is sold within one year of the date of importation, the article or its value (to be recovered from the importer), is subject to forfeiture. A sale subject to judicial order or in the liquidation of an estate is not subject to the provisions of this paragraph.

(c) *Quantities.* Generally, each person arriving in the United States may apply the **exemption to one article** of the type bearing a protected trademark. The Commissioner shall determine if a quantity of an article in excess of one may be entered and, with the approval of the Secretary of the Treasury, publish in the FEDERAL REGISTER a list of types of articles and the quantities of each entitled to the exemption. If the holder of a protected trademark allows importation of a quantity in excess of one of its particular trademarked article, the total of those trademarked articles authorized by the trademark holder may be entered without penalty.

a The conditions that must at least BOTH be met for the counterfeit to be exempt from importation prohibition for the described counterfeit are separately included in BOTH "A" AND "B". However, this complete combination of conditions is not singularly offered as a choice in any one of the choices. Accordingly, the correct answer is "E" (none of the above).

✓ **NOTE:** Multiple choice "C" makes reference to 133.22(c) and 133.23(d) which provide for relief from detention for counterfeit trademark and gray market items respectively, but not under section 526, Tariff Act of 1930.

61. Which statement is FALSE?

A. **Merchandise bearing a trademark that has been accorded Lever-rule protection under 19 C.F.R. part 133, may be imported into the United States if it bears a conspicuous and legible label designed to remain on the merchandise or its packaging stating that "the product is not a product authorized by the United States trademark owner for importation and is physically and materially different from the authorized product.**

B. **Protection for a recorded trade name shall remain in force as long as the trade name is used.**

C. **If there is a change in the name of the owner of a recorded trademark, but no change in ownership, written notice thereof shall be given to the IPR & Restricted Merchandise Branch, CBP Headquarters, accompanied by a fee of $190.00.**

D. **A "copying or simulating" trademark or trade name is one which may so resemble a recorded mark or name as to be likely to cause the public to associate the copying or simulating mark or name with the recorded mark or name.**

E. **The importation of infringing copies or phonorecords of works copyrighted in the U.S. is prohibited by Customs. The importation of lawfully made copies is not a Customs violation.**

 As per 19 CFR 133.6(b):

§133.6 Change in name of owner of recorded trademark.

If there is a change in the name of the owner of a recorded trademark, but no change in ownership, written notice thereof shall be given to the IPR & Restricted Merchandise Branch, CBP Headquarters, accompanied by:

(a) A status copy of the certificate of registration certified by the U.S. Patent and Trademark Office showing title to be presently in the name as changed; and

(b) A fee of $80, which covers all trademarks included in the application which have been previously recorded with the U.S. Customs and Border Protection. A check or money order shall be made payable to the U.S. Customs and Border Protection.

 The associated fee is $80, not $190. The correct answer is "C".

✓ **JUST A SIDE NOTE:** IPR, which stands for Intellectual Property Rights, is a "Priority Trade Issue" of Customs as they say counterfeit goods pose risks to "national security and the health and safety of consumers".

62. Which section of 19 CFR references the appropriate size for country of origin marking if a country other than the country of origin appears in close proximity?

A. 19 CFR 134.46
B. 19 CFR 134.21
C. 19 CFR 134.4
D. 19 CFR 134.45
E. 19 CFR 134.12

 As per 19 CFR 134.46:

§134.46 Marking when name of country or locality other than country of origin appears.

In any case in which the words "United States," or "American," the letters "U.S.A.," any variation of such words or letters, or the name of any city or location in the United States, or the name of any foreign country or locality other than the country or locality in which the article was manufactured or produced appear on an imported article or its container, and those words, letters or names may mislead or deceive the ultimate purchaser as to the actual country of origin of the article, **there shall appear legibly and permanently in close proximity to such words, letters or name, and in at least a comparable size, the name of the country of origin preceded by "Made in," "Product of," or other words of similar meaning.**

 The correct answer is "A".

✓ **INTERESTINGLY ENOUGH:** CBP reports that in 2015 the top seized commodities (by number of seizures, not necessarily by values) are…

1. Wearing Apparel/Accessories
2. Consumer Electronics
3. Footwear
4. Watches/Jewelry
5. Pharmaceuticals/Personal Care
6. Handbags/Wallets
7. Optical Media
8. Computers/Accessories
9. Labels/Tags
10. Toys

63. Which of the following is NOT an exception to marking requirements?

A. Steel Bands
B. Playing Cards
C. Cut Flowers
D. Barbed Wire
E. Sawed Lumber

As per 19 CFR 134.33:

§134.33 J-List exceptions.

Articles of a class or kind listed below are excepted from the requirements of country of origin marking in accordance with the provisions of section 304(a)(3)(J), Tariff Act of 1930, as amended (19 U.S.C. 1304(a)(3)(J)). However, in the case of any article described in this list which is imported in a container, the outermost container in which the article ordinarily reaches the ultimate purchaser is required to be marked to indicate the origin of its contents in accordance with the requirements of subpart C of this part. All articles are listed in Treasury Decisions 49690, 49835, and 49896. A reference different from the foregoing indicates an amendment.

Articles	References
… …	
Bands, steel.	
… …	
Cards, playing.	
… …	
Flowers, cut.	
… …	
Lumber, sawed	T.D.s 49750; 50366(6).
… …	
Wire, except barbed.	

Wire, "except barbed", is exempt from the country of origin marking requirement per the above excerpt of the J-List. "Barbed wire" is not on the list and therefore must adhere to the marking requirements. The correct answer is "D".

✓ **JUST A SIDE NOTE:** In addition to the above-mentioned J-List exemptions, there are additional "general exceptions" to marking requirements as outlined in 134.32, an excerpt of which is included below.

§134.32 General exceptions to marking requirements.

The articles described or meeting the specified conditions set forth below are excepted from marking requirements (see subpart C of this part for marking of the containers):

(a) Articles that are incapable of being marked;

(b) Articles that cannot be marked prior to shipment to the United States without injury;

(c) Articles that cannot be marked prior to shipment to the United States except at an expense economically prohibitive of its importation;

… …

64. Which statement is FALSE with regards to Marking?

A. **Any intentional removal, defacement, destruction, or alteration of a marking of the country of origin required by section 304, Tariff Act of 1930, as amended (19 U.S.C. 1304), and this part in order to conceal this information may result in criminal penalties of up to $5,000 and/or imprisonment for 1 year, as provided in 19 U.S.C. 1304(h).**

B. **If within 30 days from the date of the notice of redelivery, or such additional period as the port director may allow for good cause shown, the importer does not properly mark or redeliver all merchandise previously released to him, the port director shall demand payment of liquidated damages incurred under the bond in an amount equal to the entered value of the articles not properly marked or redelivered.**

C. **The adjectival form of the name of a country shall be accepted as a proper indication of the name of the country of origin of imported merchandise provided the adjectival form of the name does not appear with other words so as to refer to a kind or species of product. For example, such terms as "English walnuts" or "Brazil nuts" are unacceptable.**

D. **Articles of foreign origin imported into any possession of the United States outside its Customs territory and reshipped to the United States are not subject to all marking requirements applicable to like articles of foreign origin imported directly from a foreign country to the United States.**

E. **An article which is to be processed in the United States by the importer or for his account shall not be considered to be within the specifications of section 304(a)(3)(G), of the Tariff Act of 1930, as amended (19 U.S.C. 1304(a)(3)(G)), if there is a reasonable method of marking which will not be obliterated, destroyed, or permanently concealed by such processing.**

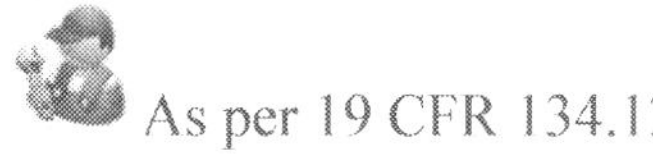
As per 19 CFR 134.12:

§134.12 Foreign articles reshipped from a U.S. possession.

Articles of foreign origin imported into any possession of the United States outside its Customs territory and reshipped to the United States **are subject to all marking requirements** applicable to like articles of foreign origin imported directly from a foreign country to the United States.

"D" states that foreign articles reshipped from a U.S. possession are "not" subject to the marking requirements. This is a false statement. The correct answer is "D".

JUST A SIDE NOTE: U.S. possessions include …

American Samoa
Guam
Northern Mariana Islands
Puerto Rico
U.S. Virgin Islands
The Minor Outlying Islands

65. Powers of attorney issued by a partnership shall be limited to a period not to exceed ___ years from the date of execution. All other powers of attorney may be granted for an unlimited period.

A. 2
B. 5
C. 6
D. 8
E. 10

As per 19 CFR 141.34:

§141.34 Duration of power of attorney.

Powers of attorney issued by a partnership shall be limited to a period not to exceed 2 years from the date of execution. All other powers of attorney may be granted for an unlimited period.

The correct answer is "A".

✓ **JUST A SIDE NOTE:** Below is an example of an Individual or Partnership Certification, which is an optional attachment to a Power of Attorney.

INDIVIDUAL OR PARTNERSHIP CERTIFICATION

CITY ______________________________
COUNTY ____________________________ } ss:
STATE _____________________________

On this ________ day of ______________ , 20____ , personally appeared before me ________________________________ residing at ________________________________ ________________________________ , personally known or sufficiently identified to me, who certifies that ________________________________ (is)(are) the individual(s) who executed the foregoing instrument and acknowledged it to be ________________________ free act and deed.

(Notary Public)

66. Which of the below is FALSE concerning a Power of Attorney?

A. A power of Attorney to a minor shall not be accepted.

B. Powers of attorney issued by a partnership shall be limited to a period not to exceed 2 years from the date of execution.

C. A power of attorney executed by a nonresident principal shall not be accepted if the agent designated thereby is a resident and is authorized to accept service of process against such nonresident.

D. A trustee may execute a power of attorney for the transaction of Customs business incident to the trusteeship.

E. Customs Form 5291 may be used for giving power of attorney to transact Customs business.

As per 19 CFR 141.36:

§141.36 Nonresident principals in general.

A power of attorney executed by a nonresident principal shall not be accepted **unless** the agent designated thereby is a resident and is authorized to accept service of process against such nonresident.

The regulations say "unless", which means "except if", and multiple choice "C" only states "if", which, although quite subtle, makes it a false. The correct answer is "C".

✓ **JUST A SIDE NOTE:** As referenced in multiple choice "E", 19 CFR 141.32 (see below) explains that Customs Form 5291 (POWER OF ATTORNEY) is just one of many variations of the form that may be used to give customs power of attorney.

§141.32 Form for power of attorney.

Customs Form 5291 may be used for giving power of attorney to transact Customs business. If a Customs power of attorney is not on a Customs Form 5291, it shall be either a general power of attorney with unlimited authority or a limited power of attorney as explicit in its terms and executed in the same manner as a Customs Form 5291. The following is an example of an acceptable general power of attorney with unlimited authority:

KNOW ALL MEN BY THESE PRESENTS, THAT

____

(Name of principal)

____________________,

____ (State legal designation, such as corporation, individual, etc.) residing at ______________ and doing business under the laws of th State of ______, hereby appoints

____

(Name, legal designation, and address)

as a true and lawful agent and attorney of the principal named above with full power and authority to do and perform every lawful act and thing the said agent and attorney may deem requisite and necessary to be done for and on behalf of the said principal without limitation of any kind as fully as said principal could do if present and acting, and hereby ratify and confirm all that said agent and attorney shall lawfully do or cause to be done by virtue of these presents until and including ______, (date) or until notice of revocation in writing is duly given before that date.

Date __________, 19__;.

___ ____

(Principal's signature)

67. A corporate surety power of attorney is executed on which CBP Form?

A. CBP FORM 3299
B. CBP FORM 3173
C. CBP FORM 5106
D. CBP FORM 5291
E. CBP FORM 5297

 As per 19 CFR 113.37(g):

(g) *Power of attorney for the agent or attorney of the surety.* Corporations may execute powers of attorney to act in their behalf in the following manner:

(1) *Execution and contents.* **Corporate surety powers of attorney may be submitted to CBP on the CBP Form 5297** and may be scanned and submitted as an email attachment, or submitted by facsimile (fax) or mail.

(i) Corporate surety name and number,

(ii) Name and address of agent or attorney, and social security number or other surety-generated 9-digit alphanumeric identification number for the agent or attorney.

(iii) Port(s) where the agent or attorney is authorized to act,

(iv) Date of execution of power of attorney,

(v) Seal of the corporate surety,

(vi) Signature of any two principal officers of corporation, and

(vii) Dollar amount of authorization.

… …

 The correct answer is "E".

✓ **<u>JUST A SIDE NOTE:</u>** A Corporate Surety Power of Attorney is used by a surety (insurance) company to expressly authorize the named employee to execute customs bonds on its behalf. It also stipulates for which (if not all) ports, and up to how much $. A snapshot of both pages of CBP Form 5297 (CORPORATE SURETY POWER OF ATTORNEY) is on the following page for your reference.

1. THIS FORM MUST BE TYPED.
2. DO NOT ALTER THIS FORM.
3. ORIGINAL TO BE SUBMITTED TO CBP. (See Option explained in Instruction No. 2.)

DEPARTMENT OF HOMELAND SECURITY
U.S. Customs and Border Protection

OMB NO. 1651-0050 EXP. 09/30/2020

CORPORATE SURETY POWER OF ATTORNEY

CBP USE ONLY
DATE RECEIVED
EFFECTIVE DATE

☐ **GRANT** (Instruction No. 3a.)
☐ **CHANGE** to Grant on file (Instruction No. 3b.)
☐ **REVOCATION.** The below-described powers previously granted are hereby revoked. (Instruction No. 3c.)

GRANTEE:	NAME ☐ This is a name change SOCIAL SECURITY NUMBER	ADDRESS ☐ This is an address change	
GRANTOR:	SURETY COMPANY'S CORPORATE NAME	SURETY NO.	STATE UNDER WHOSE LAWS ORGANIZED AS A SURETY

Port code(s) for CBP port(s) in which authorized to do business and limit on any single obligation -**OR**- port(s) being added to the original grant.

PORT	LIMIT	PORT	LIMIT	PORT	LIMIT	PORT	LIMIT	PORT	LIMIT	PORT	LIMIT

Grantor appoints the above-named person (Grantee) as its attorney in fact to sign its name as surety to, and to execute, seal, and acknowledge any bond so as to bind the surety corporation to the same extent as if done by a regularly elected officer, limited only to the extent shown above as to Customs and Border Protection port and amount on any single bond obligation. This grant, or change to a grant on file, or revocation, as specified, shall become active on the effective date shown provided the CBP Form 5297 is received at a port office 5 days before the effective date shown; otherwise the specified actions will be come active at the close of business 5 working days after the date of receipt at the port office.

In witness whereof, the said Grantor, by virtue of authority conferred by its Board of Directors, has caused these presents to be sealed with its corporate seal and attested by any two principal officers.	Date Attested Use a facsimile of corporate seal, and not impression seal.	Name and Title Signature (Sign in ink):	Name and Title Signature (Sign in ink):

CBP Form 5297 (06/08) Distribution: 3 copies **Page 1 of 2**

U.S.Ports and Codes	
Anchorage,AK	31
Baltimore,MD	13
Boston, MA	04
Buffalo, NY	09
Charleston, SC	16
Cleveland, OH	41
Chicago, IL	39
Dallas-Ft. Worth, TX	55
Detroit,MI	38
Duluth, MN	36
El Paso, TX	24
Great Falls, MT	33
Honolulu, HI	32
Houston-Galveston,TX	53
Laredo, TX	23
Los Angeles, CA	27
Miami, FL	52
Milwaukee, WI	37
Minneapolis, MN	35
Mobile, Al	19
New York,NY	10
New Orleans, LA	20
Nogales, AZ	26
Norfolk,VA	14
Ogdensburg, NY	07
Pembina, ND	34
Philadelphia, PA	11
Portland, ME	01
Portland, OR	29
Port Arthur, TX	21
Providence, RI	05
San Diego,CA	25
San Francisco,CA	28
San Juan, PR	49
Savannah,GA	17
St. Albans,VT	02
St. Louis, MO	45
Seattle, WA	30
Tampa, FL	18
Virgin Islands,U.S.	51
Washington,DC	54
Wilmington, NC	15

Explanations:

1. A Corporate Surety Power of Attorney, CBP Form 5297, must be executed for each of the following actions; grant an individual a power of attorney; change a name and/or address, and/or add districts to a power on file; revoke a power previous granted.

2. Form submission option: Each of the following conditions will require filing a copy of the CBP Form 5297: (a) if the port director permits the submission of the form to be made at any port within the district. (b) If the grantee desires to use the power of attorney at a location covered by the power, but other than the locations where the power was submitted, before CBP computer processing has been completed. For example: If both conditions are applicable, two copies of the CBP Form 5297 must be submitted with the original.

3. The box adjacent to the action executed on this CBP Form 5297 must be checked. The effective date for the action checked should be shown. (a) If grant is checked: The information required to grant a power of attorney are self-explanatory with the exception of the following: Port Information: Each port in which the power is granted must be shown except if the power both applies to all ports and the amount limit is the same in every one of those ports, enter the word "ALL" on the first line under "Port."
Limit Information: (1) If any amount limit differs between any of the ports in which the power is granted, individual amount limits must be shown for each of the ports listed. (2) If all the amount limits are the same for each district in which the power is granted and the amounts equal the surety company limit published in the Treasury Department Circular 570, enter the word ""Equal" on the first line under "Limit." (3) If all of the amount limits are the same for each port in which the power is granted and the amounts are not equal to the surety company limit published in the Treasury Department Circular 570, enter the amount limit on the first line under "Limit" and enter the word "SAME" on the second line.
Surety: The number required is the 3 digit identification code assigned by CBP Headquarters to a surety company, listed on Treasury Circular 570, at the time the surety company initially give notice to CBP that the company will be writing CBP bonds.
(b) To change a Corporate Surety Power of Attorney already on file, the previously field power granted must be revoked and a new power (CBP 5297) must be filed EXCEPT changes to the name and/or address and the addition of districts to a power on file. (1) To make a name and/or address change, the same information that was submitted to establish the existing power on file is required except the new name and/or address must be shown in the space provided and the port code(s) and related obligation limit(s) can be left blank. (2) To add ports, the same information that was submitted to establish the existing power on file is required except only the new districts and related obligation limits are necessary in the space provided.
(c) If revocation is checked: A revocation divests the designated agent's or attorney's power of attorney in all ports. Except for the following, the information required to revoke the power of attorney is self-explanatory: The ports in which authorized to do business and the associated single obligation limits do not have to be shown.

Privacy Act Statement: The following notice is given pursuant to section 7(b) of the Privacy Act of 1974 (5 U.S.C. 552a). Furnishing the information on this form, including the Social Security Number is mandatory. The primary use of the Social Security Number is to verify, in the CBP automated system, at the time an agent submits a CBP bond for approval that the individual was granted a Corporate Surety Power of Attorney by the Surety Company on the bond. Section 7 of Act of July 30, 1947, chapter 390, 61 Stat. 646, authorizes the collection of this information.

Paperwork Reduction Notice: The Paperwork Reduction Act says we must tell you why we are collecting this information, how we will use it, and whether you have to give it to us. We ask for this information to carry out U.S. Customs and Border Protection laws of the United States. We need it to ensure that persons transacting business with Customs have the proper bond coverage to secure their transactions as required by law and regulation. Your response is required to enter into any transaction in which a bond is a prerequisite under the Tariff Act of 1930, as amended.

Statement Required by 5 CFR 1320.21: The estimated average burden associated with this collection of information is 15 minutes per respondent or recordkeeper depending on individual circumstances. Comments concerning the accuracy of this burden estimate and suggestions for reducing this burden should be directed to U.S. Customs and Border Protection, Information Services Division, Washington, DC 20229, and to the Office of Management and Budget, Paperwork Reduction project (1651-0050).

CBP Form 5297 (06/08) **Page 2 of 2**

Category XIII – Practical Exercise

Practical Exercise 1: Please use the following CBP Form 7501 to answer questions 68 and 69.

Form Approved OMB No. 1651-0022
EXP. 10-31-2017

DEPARTMENT OF HOMELAND SECURITY
U.S. Customs and Border Protection
ENTRY SUMMARY

1. Filer Code/Entry No.	BMB-0404201-5
2. Entry Type	
3. Summary Date	10/22/2015
4. Surety No.	421
5. Bond Type	8
6. Port Code	0708
7. Entry Date	10/30/2015
8. Importing Carrier	GREEN BOY EXPRESS
9. Mode of Transport	30
10. Country of Origin	US
11. Import Date	10/30/2015
12. B/L or AWB No.	GBE125138
13. Manufacturer ID	USCARNEW3467AL
14. Exporting Country	CA
15. Export Date	10/30/2015
16. I.T. No.	
17. I.T. Date	
18. Missing Docs	
19. Foreign Port of Lading	
20. U.S. Port of Unlading	
21. Location of Goods/G.O. No.	
22. Consignee No.	22-357954000
23. Importer No.	22-357954000
24. Reference No.	
25. Ultimate Consignee Name and Address	City State SC Zip 29488
26. Importer of Record Name and Address	CAROLINA NEWBURG INC, City ALBANY State SC Zip 29488

27. Line No.	28. Description of Merchandise: 29. A. HTSUS No. B. ADA/CVD No.	30. A. Grossweight B. Manifest Qty.	31. Net Quantity in HTSUS Units	32. A. Entered Value B. CHGS C. Relationship	33. A. HTSUS Rate B. ADA/CVD Rate C. IRC Rate D. Visa No.	34. Duty and I.R. Tax (Dollars / Cents)
001	10/30/2015 INVOICE NUMBER 98017218 U.S GOODS RETURNED, WITHOUT HAVING BEEN ADVANCED IN VALUE IN COND. BY ANY PROCESS OR MANF. OR OTHER MEANS WHILE ABROAD, OTHR.			NOT RELATED		
	9801.00.1012	1425	1621 GWT	9832. C200	FREE	FREE
	MERCHANDISE PROCESSING FEE INV. VAL 9832.00 USF ENT. VAL 9832.00 USF					

Other Fee Summary for Block 39	35. Total Entered Value	CBP USE ONLY		TOTALS
499 MPF	$ 9,832.00	A. LIQ CODE	B. Ascertained Duty	37. Duty 0.00
	Total Other Fees $	REASON CODE	C. Ascertained Tax	38. Tax 0.00
			D. Ascertained Other	39. Other
			E. Ascertained Total	40. Total

36. DECLARATION OF IMPORTER OF RECORD (OWNER OR PURCHASER) OR AUTHORIZED AGENT

I declare that I am the ☐ importer of record and that the actual owner, purchaser, or consignee for CBP purposes is as shown above, OR ☐ owner or purchaser or agent thereof. I further declare that the merchandise ☐ was obtained pursuant to a purchase or agreement to purchase and that the prices set forth in the invoices are true, OR ☐ was not obtained pursuant to a purchase or agreement to purchase and the statements in the invoices as to value or price are true to the best of my knowledge and belief. I also declare that the statements in the documents herein filed fully disclose to the best of my knowledge and belief the true prices, values, quantities, rebates, drawbacks, fees, commissions, and royalties and are true and correct, and that all goods or services provided to the seller of the merchandise either free or at reduced cost are fully disclosed.
I will immediately furnish to the appropriate CBP officer any information showing a different statement of facts.

41. DECLARANT NAME	TITLE	SIGNATURE	DATE
BMB MANAGEMENT BROKERS,	ATTORNEY IN FACT		10/22/2015

42. Broker/Filer Information (Name, address, phone number)	43. Broker/Importer File No.
BMB MANAGEMENT BROKERS, NOWHERE, SC 29488	0708-98017218

Paperwork Reduction Act Notice CBP Form 7501 (06/09)

68. For the above entry summary, what would the proper entry type code be for Block 2?

A. 25
B. 03
C. 11
D. 06
E. None of the above

As per HTSUS Chapter 98 & 19 CFR 143.21(k):

Heading/ Subheading	Stat. Suf-fix	Article Description	Unit of Quantity	Rates of Duty 1 General	Rates of Duty 1 Special	2
9801.00.10		Products of the United States when returned after having been exported, or any other products when returned within 3 years after having been exported, without having been advanced in value or improved in condition by any process of manufacture or other means while abroad......	....	Free		
	10	Articles previously exported with intent to reimport after temporary use abroad......	X			
	12	Articles returned temporarily for repair, alteration, processing or the like, the foregoing to be reexported......	X			
		Other:				

---

§143.21 Merchandise eligible for informal entry.

The following types of merchandise are among those which may be entered under informal entry (see §§141.52 and 143.22 of this chapter):

(a) Shipments of merchandise not exceeding \$2,500 in value (except for articles valued in excess of \$250 classified in Chapter 99, Subchapters III and IV, HTSUS);

… …

(k) **Products of the United States, when the aggregate value of the shipment does not exceed \$10,000 and the products are imported—**

(1) **For the purposes of repair or alteration prior to reexportation, or**

(2) After having been either rejected or returned by the foreign purchaser to the United States for credit.

… …

Although the value is \$9832, which is a possible indicator of a formal entry, a quick lookup of the HTSUS shows that the item is a product of the U.S. being imported for the purpose of repair or alteration. There is no indication that the entry is subject to quota, and 143.21(k) shows that this merchandise is eligible for an informal entry, which the 7501 instructions will tell you is entry type code "11". The correct answer if "C".

✓ **JUST A SIDE NOTE:** For a Section 321 Entry (also known as a "Section Entry"), which is an easy and duty-free entry method for most items \$800 or less, there is no entry type code as the Entry Summary Form is not required for Section Entries. "Section 321" gets its name from the United States Code section it is located under, 19 U.S.C. 1321(a)(2).

69. What is the payable amount of Merchandise Processing Fees (MPF) on the above entry?

A) $2.00
B) $6.00
C) $25.00
D) $485.00
E) EXEMPT

 As per 19 24.23(c):

§24.23 Fees for processing merchandise.

… …

(c) *Exemptions and limitations.* (1) **The ad valorem fee, surcharge, and specific fees provided for under paragraphs (b)(1) and (b)(2) of this section will not apply to:**

(i) Except as provided in paragraph (c)(2) of this section, articles provided for in chapter 98, Harmonized Tariff Schedule of the United States (HTSUS; 19 U.S.C. 1202);

(ii) Products of insular possessions of the U.S. (General Note 3(a)(iv), HTSUS);

(iii) Products of beneficiary countries under the Caribbean Basin Economic Recovery Act (General Note 7, HTSUS);

(iv) Products of least-developed beneficiary developing countries (General Note 4(b)(i), HTSUS); and

(v) Merchandise described in General Note 19, HTSUS, merchandise released under 19 U.S.C. 1321, and merchandise imported by mail.

(2) In the case of any article provided for in subheading 9802.00.60 or 9802.00.80, HTSUS:

(i) The surcharge and specific fees provided for under paragraphs (b)(1)(ii) and (b)(2) of this section will remain applicable; and

(ii) The ad valorem fee provided for under paragraph (b)(1)(i) of this section will be assessed only on that portion of the cost or value of the article upon which duty is assessed under subheadings 9802.00.60 and 9802.00.80.

Items classified in Chapter 98, with the exception of 9802.00.60 and 9802.00.80, are all exempt from the Merchandise Processing Fee. The correct answer is "E".

✔ **JUST A SIDE NOTE:** As mentioned above, the MPF is charged for items classified under 9802.00.60 and 9802.00.80. The HTSUS descriptions for each are included below.

9802.00.60

Any article of metal (as defined in U.S. note 3(e) of this subchapter) manufactured in the United States or subjected to a process of manufacture in the United States, if exported for further processing, and if the exported article as processed outside the United States, or the article which results from the processing outside the United States, is returned to the United States for further processing

9802.00.80

Articles, except goods of heading 9802.00.90 and goods imported under provisions of subchapter XIX of this chapter and goods imported under provisions of subchapter XX, assembled abroad in whole or in part of fabricated components, the product of the United States, which (a) were exported in condition ready for assembly without further fabrication, (b) have not lost their physical identity in such articles by change in form, shape or otherwise, and (c) have not been advanced in value or improved in condition abroad except by being assembled and except by operations incidental to the assembly process such as cleaning, lubricating and painting.

Practical Exercise 2: Please use the following CBP Form 7501 to answer questions 70-75.

Form Approved OMB No. 1651-0022
EXP. 10-31-2017

DEPARTMENT OF HOMELAND SECURITY
U.S. Customs and Border Protection
ENTRY SUMMARY

1. Filer Code/Entry No.	2. Entry Type	3. Summary Date
4. Surety No. / 5. Bond Type	6. Port Code	7. Entry Date

8. Importing Carrier	9. Mode of Transport	10. Country of Origin	11. Import Date
12. B/L or AWB No.	13. Manufacturer ID	14. Exporting Country	15. Export Date

16. I.T. No.	17. I.T. Date	18. Missing Docs	19. Foreign Port of Lading	20. U.S. Port of Unlading

21. Location of Goods/G.O. No.	22. Consignee No.	23. Importer No.	24. Reference No.

25. Ultimate Consignee Name and Address	26. Importer of Record Name and Address
City State Zip	City State Zip

27. Line No.	28. Description of Merchandise — 29. A. HTSUS No. B. ADA/CVD No.	30. A. Grossweight B. Manifest Qty.	31. Net Quantity in HTSUS Units	32. A. Entered Value B. CHGS C. Relationship	33. A. HTSUS Rate B. ADA/CVD Rate C. IRC Rate D. Visa No.	34. Duty and I.R. Tax — Dollars Cents

Other Fee Summary for Block 39	35. Total Entered Value $	CBP USE ONLY		TOTALS
	Total Other Fees $	A. LIQ CODE	B. Ascertained Duty	37. Duty
		REASON CODE	C. Ascertained Tax	38. Tax
			D. Ascertained Other	39. Other
			E. Ascertained Total	40. Total

36. DECLARATION OF IMPORTER OF RECORD (OWNER OR PURCHASER) OR AUTHORIZED AGENT

I declare that I am the ☐ importer of record and that the actual owner, purchaser, or consignee for CBP purposes is as shown above, OR ☐ owner or purchaser or agent thereof. I further declare that the merchandise ☐ was obtained pursuant to a purchase or agreement to purchase and that the prices set forth in the invoices are true, OR ☐ was not obtained pursuant to a purchase or agreement to purchase and the statements in the invoices as to value or price are true to the best of my knowledge and belief. I also declare that the statements in the documents herein filed fully disclose to the best of my knowledge and belief the true prices, values, quantities, rebates, drawbacks, fees, commissions, and royalties and are true and correct, and that all goods or services provided to the seller of the merchandise either free or at reduced cost are fully disclosed.
I will immediately furnish to the appropriate CBP officer any information showing a different statement of facts.

41. DECLARANT NAME	TITLE	SIGNATURE	DATE

42. Broker/Filer Information (Name, address, phone number)	43. Broker/Importer File No.

Paperwork Reduction Act Notice CBP Form 7501 (06/09)

70. The shipment of quota merchandise is subject to antidumping. What entry type code would you use in Block 2 of the CBP Form 7501?

A. 01
B. 02
C. 03
D. 06
E. 07

 As per Form 7501 Instructions, Block 2:

Consumption Entries	
Free and Dutiable	01
Quota/Visa	02
Antidumping/Countervailing Duty (AD/CVD)	03
Appraisement	04
Vessel Repair	05
Foreign Trade Zone Consumption	06
Quota/Visa and AD/CVD combinations	**07**
Duty Deferral	08
Informal Entries	
Free and Dutiable	11
Quota Other than textiles	12
Warehouse Entries	
Warehouse	21
Re-Warehouse	22
Temporary Importation Bond	23

 The shipment in question is subject to BOTH "quota" AND "antidumping". The correct answer is "E".

✔ **INTERESTINGLY ENOUGH:** As of January 2018, there are no "absolute quotas" in effect. There are a few current universal "tariff-rate quotas" (see below), as well as many tariff-rate quotas on specific Free Trade Agreements.

Tariff-Rate Quota Item (HTSUS Heading/Classification)
Brooms (9603)
Whiskbrooms (9603.10.05)
Other Brooms (9603.10.40)
Ethyl Alcohol (9901.00.50)
Milk and Cream (0404.20.20)
Olives (Chapter 20)
Satsumas (Mandarins) (2008.30.42)
Tuna (1604.14.22)
Upland Cotton (9903.52)

71. In Block 2 on the Entry summary, what does ABI/N/L mean?

A. Statement paid by check or cash
B. Statement paid on a periodic monthly basis
C. Summary not paid on statement
D. "Live" entry/entry summary not paid on statement
E. Statement paid via ACH for a "live" entry/entry summary

 As per Form 7501 Instructions, Block 2:

BLOCK 2) ENTRY TYPE

… …

Automated Broker Interface (ABI) processing requires an ABI status indicator. This indicator must be recorded in the entry type code block. It is to be shown for those entry summaries with ABI status only, and must be shown in one of the following formats:

ABI/S = ABI statement paid by check or cash
ABI/A = ABI statement paid via Automated Clearinghouse (ACH)
ABI/P = ABI statement paid on a periodic monthly basis
ABI/N = ABI summary not paid on a statement

Note: Either a slash (/) or hyphen (-) may be used to separate ABI from the indicator
(i.e., ABI/S or ABI-S).

A "LIVE" entry is when the entry summary documentation is filed at the time of entry with estimated duties. Warehouse withdrawals are always considered "LIVE" entries. When a "LIVE" entry/entry summary is presented, an additional indicator is required to be shown in the following formats:

ABI/A/L = ABI statement paid via ACH for a "live" entry/entry summary
ABI/N/L = ABI "live" entry/entry summary not paid on a statement
"LIVE" or "L" = non-ABI "live" entry/entry summary

 The correct answer is "D".

✓ **JUST A SIDE NOTE:** For live entries, importers using Automated Clearing House (ACH) for payment to Customs may pay on the 10th day after entry date. Otherwise live entries must be submitted to Customs together with payment (e.g. cashier's check, etc.).

72. What would the mode of transportation be in Block 9 for Pedestrian?

A. 11
B. 20
C. 32
D. 33
E. 50

 As per Form 7501 Instructions, Block 9:

BLOCK 9) MODE OF TRANSPORT

Record the mode of transportation by which the imported merchandise entered the U.S. port of arrival from the last foreign country utilizing the following two digit numeric codes:

10 - Vessel, non-container (including all cargo at first U.S. port of unlading aboard a vessel regardless of later disposition; lightered, land bridge and LASH all included). If container status unknown, but goods did arrive by vessel, use this code.
11 - Vessel, container
12 - Border, Waterborne (used in cases where vessels are used exclusively to ferry automobiles, trucks, and/or rail cars, carrying passengers and baggage and/or cargo and merchandise, between the U.S. and a contiguous country).
20 - Rail, non-container
21 - Rail, container
30 - Truck, non-container
31 - Truck, container
32 - Auto
33 - Pedestrian
34 - Road, other
40 - Air, non-container
41 - Air, container
50 - Mail
60 - Passenger, hand-carried
70 - Fixed transport installation (includes pipelines, powerhouse, etc.)

For merchandise arriving in the customs territory from a U.S. FTZ, leave blank.

 The correct answer is "D".

✓ **INTERESTINGLY ENOUGH:** The U.S. port of San Ysidro (pronounced San Ee-Seed-Row) is the border crossing between San Diego & Tijuana. According to the U.S. General Services Administration (GSA), it is one of the busiest land border crossings in the world with approximately 25,000 pedestrians, alone, crossing the border from Mexico to the U.S. each day.

73. When an entry summary covers merchandise from more than one country of origin, MULTI must be recorded in which block?

A. 2
B. 5
C. 8
D. 10
E. 14

 As per Form 7501 Instructions, Block 10:

BLOCK 10) COUNTRY OF ORIGIN

Record the country of origin utilizing the International Organization for Standardization (ISO) country code located in Annex B of the HTS.

The country of origin is the country of manufacture, production, or growth of any article. If the article consists of material produced, derived from, or processed in more than one foreign territory or country, or insular possession of the U.S., it shall be considered a product of that foreign territory or country, or insular possession, where it last underwent a substantial transformation. For reporting purposes only on the CBP Form 7501, whenever merchandise has been returned to the U.S. after undergoing repair, alteration, or assembly under HTS heading 9802, the country of origin should be shown as the country in which the repair, alteration, or assembly was performed.

When merchandise is invoiced in or exported from a country other than that in which it originated, the actual country of origin shall be specified rather than the country of invoice or exportation.

When an entry summary covers merchandise from more than one country of origin, record the word "MULTI" in this block. In column 27, directly below the line number, prefixed with the letter "O," indicate the ISO code corresponding to each line item
… …

 The correct answer is "D", Block 10.

✓ **JUST A SIDE NOTE:** The reason that, for column 27, the above instructions say to place the letter "O" in front of the two-letter country of origin for each respective line item on the Entry Summary is in order to differentiate between a free trade agreement (FTA) claim and a non-FTA claim. For example, if one is claiming the Korea Free Trade Agreement on a line item, they would have "KR" typed in column 27 for that line item. If, on the other hand, a good originated from Korea, but the Korea Free Trade Agreement is NOT being claimed they would have "OKR" typed in column 27 for that line item.

74. The ISO country code "CA" for Canada for goods of Canadian Origin is no longer reported as a country of origin. As of May 15, 1997, the Canadian Province codes replaced the code "CA". The CA code, in addition to the province code, is acceptable in each case below EXCEPT?

A. **Withdrawals of goods from warehouses for consumption.**
B. **Entries of goods from Foreign Trade Zones into the Commerce of the U.S.**
C. **Informal entries.**
D. **Imports of Canadian origin arriving from countries other than Canada.**
E. **Cargo selectivity entries certified from entry summary, i.e. full cargo selectivity entries provided with entry data only or border cargo selectivity entries.**

 As per Form 7501 Instructions, Block 10:

BLOCK 10) COUNTRY OF ORIGIN

… …

• **Special Note for Goods of Canadian Origin**

The ISO country code "CA" for Canada for goods of Canadian Origin will no longer be reported as a country of origin. As of May 15, 1997, the Canadian Province codes will replace the code "CA". The following conditions in which the "CA" is acceptable, in addition to the Province Codes:

1. Withdrawals of goods from warehouses for consumption.

2. Entries of goods from Foreign Trade Zones into the Commerce of the U.S.

3. Informal entries.

4. Imports of Canadian origin arriving from countries other than Canada.

5. **Cargo selectivity entries not certified from entry summary**, i.e. full cargo selectivity entries provided with entry data only or border cargo selectivity entries.

6. Data elements intended specifically for other government agencies, e.g. FDA , DOT, and EPA which only allow "CA" to be used as the origin code.

Additional information related to reporting the correct ISO country code for goods of Canadian Origin can be found in CSMS#97-000267 and 02-000071 .

a "CA" as the country of origin indicator is acceptable for Canadian cargo selectivity entries NOT certified (ABI certified, etc.) from the entry summary. The key word here is "not". The false statement and correct answer is "E".

✓ **NOTE:** "Cargo Selectivity" is a system CBP uses that determines which entries are to be examined, and whether or not an examination is to be intensive (i.e. physical check of cargo).

75. On a warehouse withdrawal, the original warehouse entry number should be recorded at the bottom of block________.

A. 2
B. 25
C. 26
D. 29
E. 32

 As per Form 7501 Instructions:

BLOCK 25) ULTIMATE CONSIGNEE NAME AND ADDRESS

At the time of Entry Summary, record the name and address of the individual or firm purchasing the merchandise or, if a consigned shipment, to whom the merchandise is consigned. If those parties are not known, indicate to whose premises the merchandise is being shipped. If this information is the same as the importer of record, leave blank.

Note: For express consignment shipments and land border shipments, at the time of Entry Summary, record the name and address of the individual or firm for whose account the merchandise is shipped. The account of party is the actual owner, who is holder of title to the goods.

In the space provided for indicating the state, report the ultimate state of destination of the imported merchandise, as known at the time of entry summary filing. If the contents of the shipment are destined to more than one state or if the entry summary represents a consolidated shipment, report the state of destination with the greatest aggregate value. If in either case, this information is unknown, the state of the ultimate consignee, or the state where the entry is filed, in that order, should be reported. However, before either of these alternatives is used, a good faith effort should be made by the entry filer to ascertain the state where the imported merchandise will be delivered. In all cases, the state code reported should be derived from the standard postal two-letter state or territory abbreviation.

On a warehouse withdrawal, the original warehouse entry number should be recorded at the bottom of this block.

a The original warehouse entry number would be entered under the consignee details in block 25. The correct answer is "B".

✓ **JUST A SIDE NOTE:** Bonded warehouses are similar to Free Trade Zones (FTZ) in many aspects, but one difference is that only the Free Trade Zone offers an importer the benefit of an "inverted tariff". An inverted tariff occurs when a relatively lower duty rate applies to finished goods assembled in the FTZ from parts that would otherwise be subject to higher duty rates.

Category XIV – Value

76. Ace Auto Imports in Albany, NY purchases 3 Rolls Royce cars from Everything British Auto Dealers in London, England. The invoice, prepared for the sale and shipment of these goods, lists the total price paid or payable as 300,000 British Pounds. The cars were shipped by vessel from Liverpool, England on May 3, 2016 and arrived in Newark, New Jersey on May 10, 2016. The certified rate for the pound on May 3, 2016 was US$ 1.35. The certified rate for the pound on May 10, 2016 was US$ 1.40.

The value to be declared for entry purposes would be:

A $300,000
B. $222,222
C. $420,000
D. $405,000
E. $214,285

As per 19 CFR 159.32 & 19CFR 152.1(c):

(19 CFR 159.32)

Subpart C—Conversion of Foreign Currency

… …

§159.32 Date of exportation.

The date of exportation for currency conversion shall be fixed in accordance with §152.1(c) of this chapter.

(19 CFR 152.1)

… …

(c) *Date of exportation.* **"Date of exportation,"** or the "time of exportation" referred to in section 402, Tariff Act of 1930, as amended (19 U.S.C. 1401a), **means the actual date the merchandise finally leaves the country of exportation for the United States**. If no positive evidence is at hand as to the actual date of exportation, the Center director shall ascertain or estimate the date of exportation by all reasonable ways and means in his power, and in so doing may consider dates on bills of lading, invoices, and other information available to him.

a The currency conversion rate for customs entry is based on the date of export, not the date of import. The date of export is the date the shipment is exported (i.e. leaves first country in route to destination country). So, we'll multiply the exchange rate at the time of export by the foreign currency value. 1.35 (USD) x 300,000.00 (GBP) = 405,000.00 USD. The correct answer is "D".

✓ **JUST A SIDE NOTE:** Even if, for example, the goods transited Canada on May 7th in route to the United States, the country of export would still be the United Kingdom (GB), and the date of export would still be May 3rd.

77. All of the below are true, EXCEPT:

A. **"Selling commission" means any commission paid to the seller's agent, who is related to or controlled by, or works for or on the behalf of, the manufacturer or seller.**

B. **"Packing costs" means the cost of all containers (exclusive of instruments of international traffic) and coverings of whatever nature and of packing, whether for labor or materials, used in placing merchandise in condition, packed ready for shipment to the United States.**

C. **"Price actually paid or payable" means the total payment (whether direct or indirect, and exclusive of any charges, costs, or expenses incurred for transportation, insurance, and related services incident to the international shipment of the merchandise from the country of exportation to the place of importation in the United States) made, or to be made, for imported merchandise by the buyer to, or for the benefit of, the buyer.**

D. **"Related persons" means any person directly or indirectly owning, controlling, or holding with power to vote, five percent or more of the outstanding voting stock or shares of any organization, and that organization.**

E. **"Identical merchandise" means merchandise identical in all respects to, and produced in the same country and by the same person as, the merchandise being appraised.**

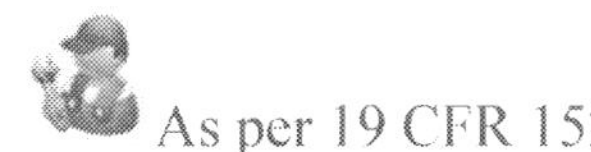
As per 19 CFR 152.102(f):

(f) *Price actually paid or payable*. **"Price actually paid or payable" means the total payment** (whether direct or indirect, and exclusive of any charges, costs, or expenses incurred for transportation, insurance, and related services incident to the international shipment of the merchandise from the country of exportation to the place of importation in the United States) made, or to be made, for imported merchandise **by the buyer to, or for the benefit of, the seller.**

Paraphrased, the regulations explain that the "price actually paid or payable" means "payment by the buyer to the SELLER", but multiple choice "C" incorrectly says "payment by the buyer to the BUYER". The incorrect statement, and thus correct answer is "C".

.

✓ **JUST A SIDE NOTE:** A selling commission (i.e. payment to the selling agent) is to be added to the "price actually paid or payable" and increases the entry value. A buying commission (i.e. payment to the buying agent) is not added to the price/value.

78. Generally accepted accounting principles refer to any generally recognized consensus or substantial authoritative support regarding any of the below EXCEPT:

A. Which financial statements should be prepared.

B. What information should be disclosed and how it should be disclosed.

C. Which changes in assets and liabilities should not be recorded.

D. Which economic resources and obligations should be recorded as assets and liabilities.

E. How the assets and liabilities and changes in them should be measured.

 As per 19 CFR 152.102(c):

(c) *Generally accepted accounting principles.* (1) "Generally accepted accounting principles" refers to any generally recognized consensus or substantial authoritative support regarding:

(i) Which economic resources and obligations should be recorded as assets and liabilities;

(ii) **Which changes in assets and liabilities should be recorded**;

(iii) How the assets and liabilities and changes in them should be measured;

(iv) What information should be disclosed and how it should be disclosed; and

(v) Which financial statements should be prepared.

(2) The applicability of a particular set of generally accepted accounting principles will depend upon the basis on which the value of the imported merchandise is sought to be established, and the relevant country for the point in contention.

(3) Information submitted by an importer, buyer, or producer in regard to the appraisement of merchandise may not be rejected by Customs because of the accounting method by which that information was prepared, if the preparation was in accordance with generally accepted accounting principles.

a "C" states "should NOT be recorded", versus the regulations that say "should be recorded". "C" is the exception and the correct answer.

✓ **JUST A SIDE NOTE:** Generally accepted accounting principles (GAAP) is defined by Investopedia as: a common set of accounting principles, standards and procedures that companies must follow when they compile their financial statements. GAAP is a combination of authoritative standards (set by policy boards) and the commonly accepted ways of recording and reporting accounting information. GAAP improves the clarity of the communication of financial information.

79. Which statement is FALSE?

A. **Fair market value is the price actually paid or payable for all imported merchandise.**

B. **If the production of an engineering or development assist occurred in the United States and one or more foreign countries, the value of the assist is the value added outside the United States.**

C. **Imported merchandise may be appraised on the basis of arbitrary or fictitious values.**

D. **Materials, components, parts, and similar items incorporated in the imported merchandise, would be considered an assist.**

E **"Related persons" are members of the same family, including brothers and sisters (whether by whole or half-blood), spouse, ancestors, and lineal descendants.**

 As per 19 CFR 152.108(g):

§152.108 Unacceptable bases of appraisement.

For the purposes of this subpart, imported merchandise may not be appraised on the basis of:

(a) The selling price in the United States of merchandise produced in the United States;

(b) A system that provides for the appraisement of imported merchandise at the higher of two alternative values;

(c) The price of merchandise in the domestic market of the country of exportation;

(d) A cost of production, other than a value determined under §152.106 for merchandise that is identical merchandise, or similar merchandise, to the merchandise being appraised;

(e) The price of merchandise for export to a country other than the United States;

(f) Minimum values for appraisement;

(g) Arbitrary or fictitious values.

 As per the above section of the regulations and as per common sense, the correct answer is "C".

✓ **JUST A SIDE NOTE:** As per 19 CFR 152.101(b): Imported merchandise will be appraised on the basis, and in the order, of the following:

(1) The transaction value provided for in §152.103;

(2) The transaction value of identical merchandise provided for in §152.104, if the transaction value cannot be determined, or can be determined but cannot be used because of the limitations provided for in §152.103(j);

(3) The transaction value of similar merchandise provided for in §152.104, if the transaction value of identical merchandise cannot be determined;

(4) The deductive value provided for in §152.105, if the transaction value of similar merchandise cannot be determined;

(5) The computed value provided for in §152.106, if the deductive value cannot be determined; or

(6) The value provided for in §152.107, if the computed value cannot be determined.

80. A used mold was provided free of charge to a Korean manufacturer by the U.S. importer. The used mold cost the importer $75,000. Because of its poor condition, the importer had it repaired for $2,500 before shipping the mold to Korea. The importer paid freight cost of $1,000 and the Korean manufacturer paid $500 import duty for the mold. What is the total value of the assist?

A. $75,000
B. $76,000
C. $77,500
D. $78,500
E. $79,000

 As per 19 CFR 152.103(d):

§152.103 Transaction value.

… …

(d) *Assist.* If the value of an assist is to be added to the price actually paid or payable, or to be used as a component of computed value, the Center director shall determine the value of the assist and apportion that value to the price of the imported merchandise in the following manner:

(1) If the assist consists of materials, components, parts, or similar items incorporated in the imported merchandise, or items consumed in the production of the imported merchandise, acquired by the buyer from an unrelated seller, **the value of the assist is the cost of its acquisition**. If the assist were produced by the buyer or a person related to the buyer, its value would be the cost of its production. In either case, **the value of the assist would include transportation costs to the place of production**.

(2) If the assist consists of tools, dies, molds, or similar items used in the production of the imported merchandise, acquired by the buyer from an unrelated seller, the value of the assist is the cost of its acquisition. If the assist were produced by the buyer or a person related to the buyer, its value would be cost of its production. If the assist has been used previously by the buyer, regardless of whether it had been acquired or produced by him, the original cost of acquisition or production would be adjusted downward to reflect its use before its value could be determined. If the assist were leased by the buyer from an unrelated seller, the value of the assist would be the cost of the lease. In either case, **the value of the assist would include transportation costs to the place of production. Repairs or modifications to an assist may increase its value.**

Example 1. A U.S. importer supplied detailed designs to the foreign producer. These designs were necessary to manufacture the merchandise. The U.S. importer bought the designs from an engineering company in the U.S. for submission to his foreign supplier.

Should the appraised value of the merchandise include the value of the assist?

No, design work undertaken in the U.S. may not be added to the price actually paid or payable.

Example 2. A U.S. importer supplied molds free of charge to the foreign shipper. The molds were necessary to manufacture merchandise for the U.S. importer. The U.S. importer had some of the molds manufactured by a U.S. company and others manufactured in a third country.

Should the appraised value of the merchandise include the value of the molds?

Yes. It is an addition required to be made to transaction value.

a The value of the assist will include the importer's cost of acquiring the equipment ($75,000) + the cost of repairs ($2,500) + freight costs ($1,000) = $78,500. Foreign duties are not added. The correct answer is "D".

✓ **JUST A SIDE NOTE:** As per CBP, assists means any of the following:
1) Materials, components, parts, and similar items incorporated in the imported merchandise.
2) Tools, dies, molds, and similar items used in the production of the imported merchandise.
3) Merchandise consumed in the production of the imported merchandise.
4) Engineering, development, artwork, design work, and plans and sketches that are undertaken elsewhere than in the United States and are necessary for the production of the imported merchandise.

Book 1 Part 11

Exam with Broker Commentary

October 2016 Customs Broker License Examination

This section of the study guide analyzes an actual customs broker exam. It presents the actual question and its multiple choices. For HTSUS classification questions, the author of this book has included abbreviated HTSUS Article Descriptions notated directly to the right of each multiple choice classification for the student's convenience and ease of reference purposes. As necessary, and in proportion to the complexity of each particular exam question, an analysis of the question and path to the correct answer has been provided. Direct excerpts from the HTSUS, 19 CFR, etc. are also included as supporting points of reference for each answer, as necessary. This exam (without commentary, etc.) and its answer key, as well as other previous customs exams can be downloaded directly from Customs' website at...

http://www.cbp.gov/document/publications/past-customs-broker-license-examinations-answer-keys

Exam Refs:

Harmonized Tariff Schedule of the United States
Title 19, Code of Federal Regulations
Customs and Trade Automated Interface Requirements (CATAIR)

- **Appendix B - Valid Codes**
- **Appendix D - Metric Conversion**
- **Appendix E - Valid Entry Numbers**
- **Appendix G - Common Errors**
- **Glossary of Terms**

Instructions for Preparation of CBP Form 7501
Right to Make Entry Directive, 3530-002A

Exam Breakdown by Subject:

Category I –	**Marking**	**Questions 1-3**
Category II –	**Power of Attorney**	**Questions 4-9**
Category III –	**Intellectual Property Rights**	**Questions 10-13**
Category IV –	**Practical Exercise**	**Questions 14-21**
Category V –	**Broker Compliance**	**Questions 22-27**
Category VI –	**Anti-Dumping/Countervailing**	**Questions 28-30**
Category VII –	**Bonds**	**Questions 31-34**
Category VIII –	**Classification**	**Questions 35-47**
Category IX –	**Drawback**	**Questions 48-51**
Category X –	**Free Trade Agreements**	**Questions 52-57**
Category XI –	**Value**	**Questions 58-61**
Category XII –	**Fines and Penalties**	**Questions 62-65**
Category XIII –	**Entry**	**Questions 66-76**
Category XIV –	**Foreign Trade Zones**	**Questions 77-80**

Category I: Marking

1. A CBP officer examines a shipment of widgets and determines that they are not legally marked. Which of the following statements is FALSE?

A. The importer may export the shipment

B. The importer may mark the shipment within 60 days

C. The importer may destroy the shipment

D. Failure to export, destroy or mark the shipment within the specified timeframe will result in additional duties of 10%

E. Failure to export, destroy or mark the shipment within the specified timeframe will result in liquidated damages equivalent to the value of the merchandise.

 As per 19 CFR 134.2 & 134.54(a):

134.2 Additional duties.
Articles not marked as required by this part shall be ***subject to additional duties of 10 percent of the final appraised value unless exported or destroyed under Customs supervision*** *prior to liquidation of the entry, as provided in 19 U.S.C. 1304(f). The 10 percent additional duty is assessable for failure either to mark the article (or container) to indicate the English name of the country of origin of the article or to include words or symbols required to prevent deception or mistake.*

134.54 Articles released from Customs custody.
(a) Demand for liquidated damages. If within 30 days from the date of the notice of redelivery, or such additional period as the port director may allow for good cause shown, the importer does not properly mark or redeliver all merchandise previously released to him, ***the port director shall demand payment of liquidated damages incurred under the bond in an amount equal to the entered value of the articles not properly marked or redelivered.***

 The answer is "B".

✓ **JUST A SIDE NOTE:** "Marking" refers to "Country of Origin Marking".

2. What is the amount of additional duties to which articles NOT marked as required under 19 CFR Part 134 may be subject?

A. $5,000 for each violation discovered.

B. 10 percent of the final appraised value of the merchandise.

C. The lesser of the domestic value of the merchandise or four times the loss of duties, taxes and fees; or if no loss of duties, taxes and fees, 40 percent of dutiable value of the merchandise.

D. A maximum of $10,000 for any one incident.

E. The entire bond amount in the case of an entry with single entry bond or in the case of continuous bond, the amount if the merchandise had been released under a single entry bond.

 As per 19 CFR 134.2:

134.2 Additional duties.
Articles not marked as required by this part shall be subject to additional duties of 10 percent of the final appraised value *unless exported or destroyed under Customs supervision prior to liquidation of the entry, as provided in 19 U.S.C. 1304(f). The 10 percent additional duty is assessable for failure either to mark the article (or container) to indicate the English name of the country of origin of the article or to include words or symbols required to prevent deception or mistake.*

 The correct answer is “B”.

✓ **JUST A SIDE NOTE:** Below is a good example of a deceptive (or at the very least, misleading) country of origin marking…

AN AMERICAN COMPANY
Package and Product Designed in the U.S.A.
MADE IN CHINA

3. What item is NOT a General Exception to the marking requirements?

A. Articles which are crude substances
B. Articles that are incapable of being marked
C. Products of possessions of the United States
D. Goods of a NAFTA country which are original works of art
E. Products of American fisheries which are not free of duty

As per 19 CFR 134.32:

134.32 General exceptions to marking requirements.

The articles described or meeting the specified conditions set forth below are excepted from marking requirements (see subpart C of this part for marking of the containers):

(a) Articles that are incapable of being marked;

(b) Articles that cannot be marked prior to shipment to the United States without injury;

(c) Articles that cannot be marked prior to shipment to the United States except at an expense economically prohibitive of its importation;

(d) Articles for which the marking of the containers will reasonably indicate the origin of the articles;

(e) Articles which are crude substances;

… …

(k) Products of American fisheries which are free of duty;

(l) Products of possessions of the United States;

(m) Products of the United States exported and returned;

(n) Articles exempt from duty under §§10.151 through 10.153, §145.31 or §145.32 of this chapter;

(o) Articles which cannot be marked after importation except at an expense that would be economically prohibitive unless the importer, producer, seller, or shipper failed to mark the articles before importation to avoid meeting the requirements of the law;

(p) Goods of a NAFTA country which are original works of art; and

(q) Goods of a NAFTA country which are provided for in subheading 6904.10 or heading 8541 or 8542 of the Harmonized Tariff Schedule of the United States (HTSUS) (19 U.S.C. 1202).

Products of American fisheries which are "NOT free of duty" are not exempt. The correct answer is "E".

✓ **INTERESTINGLY ENOUGH:** "American Fisheries" refers to the 200 miles wide belt that runs along the coasts of the United States. This zone is known as the Exclusive Economic Zone (EEZ).

Category II: Power of Attorney

4. Which of the following is NOT a true statement concerning Power of Attorney (POA)?

A. **Written notification to the client of the option to pay CBP directly is to be cited within the POA document or be attached to the POA.**
B. **Brokers are not required to file POA with the Port Director but must retain them and make them available to CBP upon demand.**
C. **The name of the Broker on the POA must match the name on the Broker's license. If the Broker has been approved to use a trade or fictitious name, the Broker's name must be included on the POA followed by "doing business as" the approved trade or fictitious name.**
D. **POA must be retained until revoked. Letters of Revocation must be retained for 3 years after the date of revocation or 2 years after the date the client ceases to be an active client.**
E. **POA issued by a partnership shall be limited to a period not to exceed 2 years from the date of execution.**

 As per 19 CFR, 111.29(b), 141.46, 111.30(c), 111.23(b), 141.34:

111.29 (b) Notice to client of method of payment—(1) ***All brokers must provide their clients with the following written notification:***

If you are the importer of record, payment to the broker will not relieve you of liability for customs charges (duties, taxes, or other debts owed CBP) in the event the charges are not paid by the broker. Therefore, if you pay by check, ***customs charges may be paid with a separate check payable to the "U.S. Customs and Border Protection"*** *which will be delivered to CBP by the broker.*

... ...

(i) ***On, or attached to, any power of attorney*** *provided by the broker to a client for execution on or after September 27, 1982; and*

141.46 Power of attorney retained by customhouse broker.
Before transacting Customs business in the name of his principal, a customhouse broker is required to obtain a valid power of attorney to do so. ***He is not required to file the power of attorney with a port director. Customhouse brokers shall retain powers of attorney with their books and papers, and make them available*** *to representatives of the Department of the Treasury as provided in subpart C of part 111 of this chapter.*

111.30(c) Change in name. ... ... The name must not be used until the approval of Headquarters has been received. In the case of a trade or fictitious name, ***the broker must affix his own name in conjunction with each signature of the trade or fictitious name when signing customs documents.***

111.23 (b) Period of retention. The records described in this section, other than powers of attorney, must be retained for at least 5 years after the date of entry. ***Powers of attorney must be retained until revoked, and revoked powers of attorney and letters of revocation must be retained for 5 years after the date of revocation or for 5 years after the date the client ceases to be an "active client"*** *as defined in §111.29(b)(2)(ii), ...*

141.34 Duration of power of attorney.
Powers of attorney issued by a partnership shall be limited to a period not to exceed 2 years *from the date of execution. All other powers of attorney may be granted for an unlimited period.*

 As with most all CBP record retention, 5 years is the requirement. The correct answer is "D".

Using the information provided below, please answer Questions 5 through 9.

Below are two Powers of Attorney (POA). The first was received by Daniel Evans, General Manager, East Coast Freight Forwarder & Logistics, Inc. (a freight forwarder), from General Merchants Corp., on December 31, 2008 (POA1). The second was issued by East Coast Freight Forwarder & Logistics, Inc. to Russell Morris, a customs broker doing business as Quick Brokers, on January 2, 2009 (POA 2). The importing history between the customs broker on behalf of the importer of record demonstrates that entries were made on February 1, 2009; March 1, 2009 and May 22, 2009.

POA 1: East Coast Freight Forwarder & Logistics, Inc. from General Merchants Corp.

CUSTOMS POWER OF ATTORNEY

I hereby authorize East Coast Freight Forwarders & Logistics, Inc. to act as General Merchants Corp. agent and customs broker and to file entry/entry summary for all commercial shipments from January 1, 2009 onwards. General Merchants Corp. authorizes other duly licensed customs brokers to act as Grantor's agent.

(Capacity): BUYER Date: DECEMBER 31, 2008 (Signature) (Signed)

POA 2: East Coast Freight Forwarder & Logistics, Inc. to Russell Morris dba Quick Brokers

CUSTOMS POWER OF ATTORNEY

KNOW ALL MEN BY THESE PRESENTS: That GENERAL MERCHANTS CORP doing business as a corporation under the laws of the State of Texas residing or having a place of business at 2960 EL ZAPATO LAREDO, TEXAS hereby constitutes and appoints RUSSELL MORRIS dba QUICK BROKERS, which may act through any of it's licensed officers or employees duly authorized to sign documents by power of attorney as a true and lawful agent and attorney of the grantor named above for and in the name, place, and stead of said grantor from this date and in ALL Customs Ports and in no other name, to make, endorse, sign, declare, or swear to any entry, withdrawal, declaration, certificate, bill of lading, carnet, or other document required by law or regulation in connection with the importation, transportation, or exportation of any merchandise shipped or consigned by or to said grantor; to perform any act or condition which may be required by law or regulation in connection with such merchandise; to receive any merchandise deliverable to said grantor.

To receive, endorse and collect checks issued for Customs duty refunds in grantor's name drawn on the Treasurer of the United States.

This power of attorney is to remain in full force and effect until revocation in writing is duly given to and received by grantee (if the donor of this power of attorney is a partnership, the said power shall in no case have any force or effect in the United States after the expiration 2 years from the dates of its execution);

IN WITNESS WHEREOF: the said GENERAL MERCHANTS CORP. has caused these presents to be sealed and signed:

(Signature) (Signed) (Print Name) DANIEL EVANS

(Capacity) ATTORNEY IN FACT Date: JANUARY 2, 2009

Witness: (if required) ______ (Signature) ______

If you are the importer of record, payment to the broker will not relieve you of liability for customs charges (duties, taxes, or other debts owed CBP) in the event the charges are not paid by the broker. Therefore, if you pay by check, customs charges may be paid with a separate check payable to U.S. Customs and Border Protection which shall be delivered to CBP by the broker. Importers who wish to utilize this procedure must contact our office in advance to arrange timely receipt of duty checks.

5. Which person or entity may act as the intended importer of record?

A. General Merchants Corp.

B. East Coast Logistics, Inc.

C. The nominal consignee

D. Quick Brokers

E. Daniel Evans A.I.F.

 As per RIGHT TO MAKE ENTRY DIRECTIVE 3530-002a, SECTION 5.1.2 & 5.3.1 & 5.3.2:

5.1.2 Section 484 provides that ***only the "importer of record" has the right to make entry. "Importer of Record" is defined as the owner or purchaser of the goods****, or when designated by the owner, purchaser, or consignee, a licensed Customs broker.*

5.3.1 The terms "owner" and "purchaser" include any party with a financial interest in a transaction, including, but not limited to, the actual owner of the goods, the actual purchaser of the goods, a buying or selling agent, a person or firm who imports on consignment, a person or firm who imports under loan or lease, a person or firm who imports for exhibition at a trade fair, a person or firm who imports goods for repair or alteration or further fabrication, etc. Any such owner or purchaser may make entry on his own behalf or may designate a licensed Customs broker to make entry on his behalf and may be shown as the importer of record on the CF 7501. ***The terms "owner" or "purchaser" would not include a "nominal consignee" who effectively possesses no other right, title, or interest in the goods except as he possessed under a bill of lading, air waybill, or other shipping document.***

5.3.2 Examples of nominal consignees not authorized to file Customs entries are express consignment operators (ECO), freight consolidators who handle consolidated shipments as described in 5.10 below, and Customs brokers who are not permitted to transact business in Customs ports where a shipment is being entered.

 The purchaser, General Merchants Corp., is the intended importer of record (IOR). They have not otherwise designated the customs broker to act as IOR on their behalf. The correct answer is "A".

✓ **JUST A SIDE NOTE:** "5.10" of the above-mentioned directive just refers to "Warehouse entries and withdrawals".

6. Based on the information provided for POA 1, which statement is TRUE?

A. **POA 1 allows the forwarder to create a subagency relationship (i.e., assign the POA to a broker)**

B. **POA 1 allows the East Coast Logistics, Inc. to classify and value the imported merchandise, and report the outcome to U.S. Customs and Border Protection**

C. **The Vice President of an incorporated business entity must sign the POA 1.**

D. **POA 1 is invalid since it does not allow for the service of process.**

E. **POA 1 must be on CBP Form 5291 "Power of Attorney"**

As per 19 CFR 141.31(a) & 141.32:

141.31 General requirements and definitions.
(a) Limited or general power of attorney. ***A power of attorney may be executed for the transaction by an agent or attorney of a specified part or all the Customs business of the principal.***

141.32 Form for power of attorney.
Customs Form 5291 may be used for giving power of attorney to transact Customs business. ***If a Customs power of attorney is not on a Customs Form 5291, it shall be either a general power of attorney with unlimited authority or a limited power of attorney*** *as explicit in its terms and executed in the same manner as a Customs Form 5291. The following is an example of an acceptable general power of attorney with unlimited authority:*

KNOW ALL MEN BY THESE PRESENTS, THAT

____

(Name of principal)

____________________,

____ (State legal designation, such as corporation, individual, etc.) residing at ______________ and doing business under the laws of the State of ______, hereby appoints

____

(Name, legal designation, and address)

as a true and lawful agent and attorney of the principal named above with full power and authority to do and perform every lawful act and thing the said agent and attorney may deem requisite and necessary to be done for and on behalf of the said principal without limitation of any kind as fully as said principal could do if present and acting, and hereby ratify and confirm all that said agent and attorney shall lawfully do or cause to be done by virtue of these presents until and including ______, (date) or until notice of revocation in writing is duly given before that date.

Date __________, 19__;.

___ ____

(Principal's signature)

The question's POA 1 is a general (i.e. not limited) POA from the importer that, explicitly in writing, "authorizes other duly licensed customs brokers to act as (their) agent". The correct answer is "A".

✓ **NOTE:** "Customs Form 5291" is no longer an official CBP form. Most companies just create their own by following the above guidelines, and adding a generous portion of their own terms and conditions.

7. Based on the information provided for POA 2, which statement is FALSE?

A. POA 2 identifies a resident principal.

B. POA 2 omits the "notice to client of method of payment".

C. Failure of the broker to retain a valid POA may result in a monetary penalty in an amount not to exceed an aggregate of $30,000.00 for one or more violations.

D. POA 2 may be granted for an unlimited period of time.

E. POA 2 authorizes the broker to sign documents in Puerto Rico.

 As per the question's reference POA 2:

If you are the importer of record, payment to the broker will not relieve you of liability for customs charges (duties, taxes, or other debts owed CBP) in the event the charges are not paid by the broker. Therefore, if you pay by check, ***customs charges may be paid with a separate check payable to U.S. Customs and Border Protection*** *which shall be delivered to CBP by the broker. Importers who wish to utilize this procedure must contact our office in advance to arrange timely receipt of duty checks.*

 The correct answer is "B".

✔ **JUST A SIDE NOTE:** In reference to the harsh tone of multiple choice "C"... Although a customs broker may be penalized up to a maximum of $30,000 for any violation or aggregate of violations, simply misplacing a single POA would only amount to a $1,000 penalty per POA. Furthermore, this amount could be mitigated down, depending on the circumstances. Appendix C to 19 CFR Part 171 spells this out...

... ...

E. Penalties for failure to retain powers of attorney from clients to act in their names.

1. The penalty notice should also cite 19 CFR 141.46 as the regulation violated.

2. ***Assessment amount—$1,000 for each power of attorney not on file.***

3. Mitigation—for a first offense, mitigate to an amount between $250 and $500 unless extraordinary mitigating factors are present, in which case full mitigation should be afforded. An extraordinary mitigating factor would be a fire, theft or other destruction of records beyond broker control. Subsequent offenses—no mitigation unless extraordinary mitigating factors are present.

4. Penalty should be mitigated in full if it can be established that a valid power of attorney had been issued to the broker, but it was misplaced or destroyed through clerical error or mistake.

... ...

8. Upon review of both POA's, which statement is FALSE?

A. The customs broker may prepare and present the entry summary to CBP

B. East Coast Freight Forwarder & Logistics, Inc. may authorize the customs broker to forward a completed CBP Form 3461

C. The customs broker shall exercise responsible supervision and control when transacting customs business.

D. The POA may be completed and signed after the merchandise has been released from CBP custody.

E. General Merchants Corp. is a resident corporate principal.

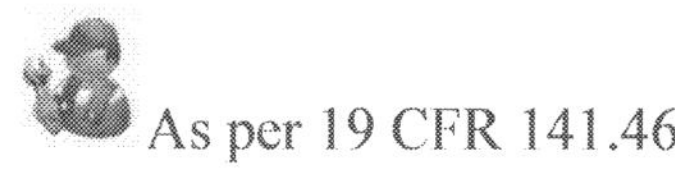

As per 19 CFR 141.46:

141.46 Power of attorney retained by customhouse broker.

***Before** transacting Customs business in the name of his principal, a customhouse broker is required to obtain a valid power of attorney to do so.* *He is not required to file the power of attorney with a port director. Customhouse brokers shall retain powers of attorney with their books and papers, and make them available to representatives of the Department of the Treasury as provided in subpart C of part 111 of this chapter.*

Common sense and Customs say the correct answer is "D".

✓ **JUST A SIDE NOTE:** For practical reasons, a Customs Power of Attorney is usually completed by the importer/client without specifying the length of POA validity. The client, however, can choose to specify that the POA is effective for a single shipment, or only for a defined period of time.

9. The Customs broker shall retain POA 2 for a period of 5 years starting on __________.

A. December 31, 2008

B. January 2, 2009

C. February 1, 2009

D. March 1, 2009

E. May 22, 2009

 As per 19 CFR 111.23(b):

(b) Period of retention. The records described in this section, other than powers of attorney, must be retained for at least 5 years after the date of entry. ***Powers of attorney must be retained until revoked, and revoked powers of attorney and letters of revocation must be retained for 5 years after the date of revocation or for 5 years after the date the client ceases to be an "active client"*** *as defined in §111.29(b)(2)(ii), whichever period is later. When merchandise is withdrawn from a bonded warehouse, records relating to the withdrawal must be retained for 5 years from the date of withdrawal of the last merchandise withdrawn under the entry.*

 The customs broker last transacted customs business for the client on May 22, 2009. The correct answer is "E".

✓ **JUST A SIDE NOTE:** The revocation of a Customs Power of Attorney must be in writing. Per 19 CFR 141.35:

141.35 Revocation of power of attorney.

Any power of attorney shall be subject to revocation at any time by written notice given to and received by the port director.

10. Which of the following is NOT required when submitting an application to record a trademark?

A. The name, address and citizenship of the trademark owner or owners

B. The name or trade style to be recorded

C. The name and principal business address of each foreign person or business entity authorized or licensed to use the trade name and statement as the use authorized

D. The name of the person submitting the application if different from the owner

E. A description of the merchandise with which the trade name is associated

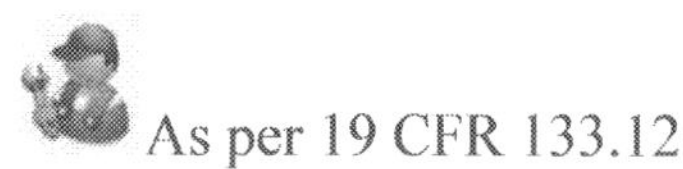

As per 19 CFR 133.12:

133.12 Application to record a trade name.

An application to record a trade name shall be in writing addressed to the IPR & Restricted Merchandise Branch, 1300 Pennsylvania Avenue, NW., Washington, DC 20229, and shall include the following information:

*(a) The **name, complete business address, and citizenship of the trade name owner or owners** (if a partnership, the citizenship of each partner; if an association or corporation, the State, country, or other political jurisdiction within which it was organized, incorporated or created);*

*(b) The **name or trade style to be recorded**;*

*(c) The **name and principal business address of each foreign person or business entity authorized or licensed to use the trade name and a statement as to the use authorized**;*

(d) The identity of any parent or subsidiary company, or other foreign company under common ownership or control which uses the trade name abroad (see §133.2(d)); and

*(e) A **description of the merchandise with which the trade name is associated**.*

The correct answer is "D".

✓ **JUST A SIDE NOTE:** A good example of a trademark is the "Swoosh" logo, a trademark of Nike, Inc.

11. A "counterfeit mark" is a (n)_______mark that is identical with, or substantially indistinguishable from, a mark registered on the Principal Register of the U.S. Patent and Trademark Office.

A. Authentic

B. Irregular

C. Unreadable

D. Unrecognizable

E. None of the above

 As per 19 CFR 133.21(a):

133.21 Articles suspected of bearing counterfeit marks.

(a) ***Counterfeit mark defined. A "counterfeit mark" is a spurious mark*** *that is identical with, or substantially indistinguishable from, a mark registered on the Principal Register of the U.S. Patent and Trademark Office.*

 The correct answer is "E" (None of the above).

✓ **JUST A SIDE NOTE:** According to Wikipedia's definition, "spurious can refer to: seeming to be genuine but false, based on false ideas or facts".

12. The following, if introduced or attempted to be introduced into the U.S. contrary to law, shall be seized:

A. Merchandise marked intentionally in violation of Title 19, United States Code, section 1304

B. Merchandise, the importation or entry of which is subject to any restriction or prohibition imposed by law relating to health, safety, or conservation and which is not in compliance with the applicable rule, regulation or statute

C. Merchandise whose importation or entry requires a license, permit or other authorization of a U.S. government agency, and which is not accompanied by such license, permit or authorization

D. Merchandise subject to quantitative restrictions, unless appropriate visa, permit license, or similar document, or stamp is presented to CBP

E. Merchandise that is stolen, smuggled, or clandestinely imported or introduced

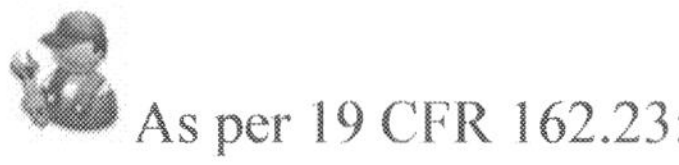
As per 19 CFR 162.23:

162.23 Seizure under section 596(c), Tariff Act of 1930, as amended (19 U.S.C. 1595a(c)).

(a) ***Mandatory seizures****. The following, if introduced or attempted to be introduced into the United States contrary to law, shall be seized pursuant to section 596(c), Tariff Act of 1930, as amended (19 U.S.C. 1595a(c)):*

(1) ***Merchandise that is stolen, smuggled, or clandestinely imported or introduced****;*

... ...

(b) ***Permissive seizures****. The following, if introduced or attempted to be introduced into the United States contrary to law, may be seized pursuant to section 596(c), Tariff Act of 1930, as amended (19 U.S.C. 1595a(c)):*

(1) ***Merchandise the importation or entry of which is subject to any restriction or prohibition imposed by law relating to health, safety, or conservation, and which is not in compliance with the applicable rule, regulation or statute;***

(2) ***Merchandise the importation or entry of which requires a license, permit or other authorization of a United States Government agency, and which is not accompanied by such license, permit or authorization;***

... ...

(5) ***Merchandise marked intentionally in violation of 19 U.S.C. 1304****;*

... ...

(7) ***Merchandise subject to quantitative restrictions****, found to bear a counterfeit visa, permit, license, or similar document, or stamp from the United States or from a foreign government or issuing authority pursuant to a multilateral or bilateral agreement (but see paragraph (e), of this section).*

All of the above multiple choice scenarios are subject to seizure. Exam credit was given to all examinees. It appears they misworded multiple choice "D".

13. CBP officers examine a commercial shipment of T-shirts and find that many of the t-shirts bear suspect versions of popular trademarks. Upon further investigation, the officers find that the suspect marks are recorded with CBP. Through the broker, the officers notify the importer in writing that the shipment has been detained and request information that would assist CBP in determining whether the detained merchandise bears counterfeit marks. The importer does not respond to the notice and the trademark owners, when contacted, advise that the suspect marks were not applied with authorization. CBP seizes the merchandise on the basis that it bears counterfeit marks. The importer wishes to challenge CBP's decision. What options does the importer have?

A. **Request a change of entry type from formal to informal**

B. **Re-export the commodity to the country of exportation**

C. **File an in-bond to another port for entry**

D. **File a petition for relief**

E. **Pay the counterfeit duty and enter the shipment anyway**

 As per 19 CFR 133.21(g):

(g) Consent of the mark owner; failure to make appropriate disposition. The owner of the mark, within thirty days from notification of seizure, may provide written consent to the importer allowing the importation of the seized merchandise in its condition as imported ***or its exportation****, entry after obliteration of the mark, or other appropriate disposition. Otherwise, the merchandise will be disposed of in accordance with §133.52 of this part,* ***subject to the importer's right to petition for relief*** *from forfeiture under the provisions of part 171 of this chapter.*

The exam key states that the correct answer is "D". However, we can clearly see from the above paragraph (g), that the owner of the mark may, at the owner's discretion, allow the importer to (among other options) re-export/export the shipment back (i.e. multiple choice "B").

✓ **JUST A SIDE NOTE:** Imported goods that are subsequently exported back to the country of export, or exported to a third country are called "re-exports" by Customs.

Category III: Intellectual Property Rights

Using the information provided below, answer questions **14 – 18**.

On April 12, 2015, an importer in the U.S. receives 500 single action economy stopwatches shipped by air from Munich, Germany. The shipment was entered and released through ABI by CBP on April 8, 2015. The stopwatches are packaged for retail sale and are invoiced at U.S. $ 24 F.O.B per stopwatch. The stopwatches are classified under HTSUS 9102.99.60 e/o nominee. The Watch Information Sheet indicates the following:

Manufacturer: Bern Watch Inc.
Model: A1020 Single Action Stopwatch
Features:
* Perfect for industrial use
* Start/stop by crown, reset by 10 o'clock button
* Preset push button
* Long hand 60 sec per turn, 1/100 min. increments
* 30 minute short hand
* Rugged steel case
* 1 year warranty
* Quality movement made in Switzerland

Type of Display:	Mechanical with hands	
Type of Movement:	Mechanical	Value US$ 18.50
Type of Case:	Base Metal, Chrome Plated	Value US$ 5.00
Type of Packaging:	Clear Plastic Blister Pack	Value US$ 0.50
Battery Powered:	No	
Automatic Winding:	No	
Number of jewels in movement:	13	
Country of Origin:	Switzerland	

---

14. What is the DUTY due on this entry?

A. $ 560.00

B. $ 535.00

C. $ 235.00

D. $ 730.00

E. $ 23.50

As per HTSUS 9102.99.60:

9102.99.60	1/	With movement valued over $15 each...........	1/	$1.16 each + 6% on the case

 The correct answer is "D".

580.00 (500 watches x $1.16 ea. duty)
+ 150.00 ($5.00 casing x 500 watches x 0.06 duty)
= 730.00

✓ **JUST A SIDE NOTE:** The above assessment is a good example of compound duty. Compound duty is where there are duties on an item based on its 1) value AND on its 2) quantity, or weight, or volume, etc.

15. What is the merchandise processing fee due on this entry?

A. $ 2.00

B. $ 25.00

C. $ 41.57

D. $ 485.00

E. Watches are exempt from MPF.

 As per 19 CFR 24.23(b):

(b) Fees—(1) Formal entry or release—(i) Ad valorem fee—(A) General. Except as provided in paragraph (c) of this section, ***merchandise that is formally entered or released is subject to the payment to CBP of an ad valorem fee of 0.3464 percent.*** *The 0.3464 ad valorem fee is due and payable to CBP by the importer of record of the merchandise at the time of presentation of the entry summary and is based on the value of the merchandise as determined under 19 U.S.C. 1401a. In the case of an express consignment carrier facility or centralized hub facility, each shipment covered by an individual air waybill or bill of lading that is formally entered and valued at $2,500 or less is subject to a $1.00 per individual air waybill or bill of lading fee and, if applicable, to the 0.3464 percent ad valorem fee in accordance with paragraph (b)(4) of this section.*

(B) Maximum and minimum fees. Subject to the provisions of paragraphs (b)(1)(ii) and (d) of this section relating to the surcharge and to aggregation of the ad valorem fee respectively, the ad valorem fee charged under paragraph (b)(1)(i)(A) of this section ***must not exceed $485 and must not be less than $25.***

 The correct answer is "C".

12,000.00 (Entered value of 500 watches x $24.00 ea.)
x .003464 (MPF)
= 41.57

✔ **NOTE:** As per the above 19 CFR excerpt, for formal entries, such as this one, the MPF minimum is $25 and maximum is $485.

16. What is the International Standard Country Code (ISO) for the country of origin?

A. CF

B. CH

C. CN

D. SZ

E. DE

 As per HTSUS, Annex B (International Standard Country Codes):

Sweden..	SE
Switzerland..	CH
Syrian Arab Republic.......................................	SY

 The correct answer is "B".

✓ **INTERESTINGLY ENOUGH:** According to Wikipedia:

A watch is considered Swiss, according to the Swiss law if:

- *its movement is Swiss and,*
- *its movement is cased up in Switzerland and;*
- *the manufacturer carries out the final inspection in Switzerland*

17. Which statement regarding the plastic blister packaging is TRUE?

A. The packaging is classified with the stopwatches.

B. The packaging is classified separately as articles of plastic.

C. The packaging costs are deducted from the entered value.

D. The packaging must include the importer's name.

E. The packaging must include the manufacturer's name.

 As per HTSUS, GRI 5 (b):

5. In addition to the foregoing provisions, the following rules shall apply in respect of the goods referred to therein:

   (a) Camera cases, musical instrument cases, gun cases, drawing instrument cases, necklace cases and similar containers,specially shaped or fitted to contain a specific article or set of articles, suitable for long-term use and entered with the articles for which they are intended, shall be classified with such articles when of a kind normally sold therewith. This rule does not,however, apply to containers which give the whole its essential character;

   (b) Subject to the provisions of rule 5(a) above, packing materials and packing containers entered with the goods therein shall be classified with the goods if they are of a kind normally used for packing such goods. However, this provision is not binding when such packing materials or packing containers are clearly suitable for repetitive use.

The type of packaging used to contain the stopwatches, "clear plastic blister pack", is clearly NOT suitable for repetitive use. Accordingly, the packaging is NOT classified separately and is instead entered with the stopwatches that they contain. The correct answer is "A".

✓ **INTERESTINGLY ENOUGH:** A "blister pack" is a pre-molded, bubble-like, and semi-rigid plastic packaging that in some forms resemble a skin blister. Ironically, "skin packaging" is different than blister packaging in that it is more of a film-like plastic closely molded onto the product.

18. Six months after the entry summary for the stopwatches was filed, the importer informs the broker he gave a die (purchased from a nonrelated U.S. firm at a cost of U.S. $500) to Bern Watch Inc., without charge, to be used only for the manufacturing of the 500 stopwatches. Transportation and duty costs to the importer to get the die to Bern were an additional U.S. $70. Based on this information, the broker should:

A. Take no action because the entry summary is already projected for liquidation.

B. Submit a SIL to CBP with a check for US $570 because this is a proceed to the seller, Bern Watch Inc.

C. Submit a SIL or a Prior Disclosure to CBP because this is an assist valued at US $500.

D. Submit a SIL or a Prior Disclosure to CBP because this is an assist valued at US $570.

E. Submit as a SIL requesting that the entered value be reduced by the amount of the assist and that the subsequent difference in duty and fees be refunded.

 As per 19 CFR 152.103(d):

(d) Assist. If the value of an assist is to be added to the price actually paid or payable, or to be used as a component of computed value, the port director shall determine the value of the assist and apportion that value to the price of the imported merchandise in the following manner:

(1) If the assist consist of materials, components, parts, or similar items incorporated in the imported merchandise, or items consumed in the production of the imported merchandise, acquired by the buyer from an unrelated seller, the value of the assist is the cost of its acquisition. If the assist were produced by the buyer or a person related to the buyer, its value would be the cost of its production. In either case, the value of the assist would include transportation costs to the place of production.

(2) ***If the assist consists of tools, dies, molds, or similar items used in the production of the imported merchandise, acquired by the buyer from an unrelated seller, the value of the assist is the cost of its acquisition.*** *If the assist were produced by the buyer or a person related to the buyer, its value would be cost of its production. If the assist has been used previously by the buyer, regardless of whether it had been acquired or produced by him, the original cost of acquisition or production would be adjusted downward to reflect its use before its value could be determined. If the assist were leased by the buyer from an unrelated seller, the value of the assist would be the cost of the lease.* ***In either case, the value of the assist would include transportation costs to the place of production.*** *Repairs or modifications to an assist may increase its value.*

 The correct answer is "D".

500.00 (value of die)
+ 70.00 (transportation and duty costs to place of production)
= 570.00

✓ **NOTE:** The Supplemental Information Letter (SIL) program is no longer used. Instead, a Post Entry Amendment (PEA) can be submitted up to 20 business days prior to the scheduled liquidation date of the entry. Usually the scheduled liquidation date is 314 calendar days after the customs entry date.

Using the invoice provided below, answer questions **19** through **21**.

COMMERCIAL INVOICE

EL GORDO de S.A.

Shipper/Exporter		**No. and Date of Invoice**
El Gordo's Fajita Shack de S.A. . 2568 Bagdad Matamoros, Tamaulipas Mexico		US001836 Lunes, Julio 14, 2007
For Account and Risk of Messers		**No. and Date of L/C**
Crocketts Cafe 301 Alamo Plaza San Antonio, TX 78205		**L/C Issuing Bank**
Notify Party R.Person, 956.729.3070		**Remarks** P/O No.: TPS001 Not subject to AD/CVD cases
Port of Lading Matamoros, Tamaulipas Mexico	**Final Destination** San Antonio	
Carrier	**Departure on or about** July 17, 2007	Marks and Numbers of Pkgs. Fernando's Fire Salsa 25/1. 16 Ounce Jar.

Description of Goods	Quantity	Unit Price	Amount
1. Country of Origin: Mexico Salsa: Ingredients - Tomato puree, peppers (jalapeno, ancho, cascabel), vinegar, onions, garlic, salt, cottonseed oil, bay leaves, and spices. PN: HOTSAUCEFI One pound jar	10000 pieces	0.35 USD	$3500
2. Country of Origin: Vietnam Shrimp: Peeled, headless weight 33 – 45 per kg., dusted w/flour, quick frozen	400 kgs.	0.90 USD	$360
(2%, Net 15 Days) **TOTAL**			**$3,860**

Master Bill: 001-63324833
House Bill: COSC56676406
Estimated Entry Date 07/18/07

19. What is the classification of the salsa?

A. 2002.90.8050 Tomatoes prepared or preserved otherwise than by vinegar or acetic acid>>Other>>Other>>Other

B. 2005.91.9700 Other vegetables prepared or preserved otherwise than by vinegar or acetic acid, not frozen, other than products of heading 2006>>Other vegetables and mixtures of vegetables>>Bamboo Shoots>>Other

C. 2103.20.4020 Sauces and preparations therefore; mixed condiments and mixed seasonings; mustard flour and meal and prepared mustard>>Tomato ketchup and other tomato sauces>>Other>>In containers holding less than 1.4kg

D. 2103.90.9051 Sauces and preparations therefore; mixed condiments and mixed seasonings; mustard flour and meal and prepared mustard>>Other>>Other>>Other>>Tomato-based preparations for sauces>>In containers holding less than 1.4kg

E. 2103.90.9091 Sauces and preparations therefore; mixed condiments and mixed seasonings; mustard flour and meal and prepared mustard>>Other>>Other>>Other>>Other

As per HTSUS Chapter 21:

Heading/ Subheading	Stat. Suf- fix	Article Description	Unit of Quantity	Rates of Duty 1 General	1 Special	2
2103		Sauces and preparations therefore; mixed condiments and mixed seasonings; mustard flour and meal and prepared mustard:				
2103.10.00	00	Soy sauce	kg	3%	Free (A, AU, BH, CA, CL, CO, D, E, IL, JO, KR, MA, MX, OM, P, PA, PE, SG)	35%
2103.20		Tomato ketchup and other tomato sauces:				
2103.20.20	00	Tomato ketchup	kg	6%	Free (A, AU, BH, CA, CL, CO, D, E, IL, JO, KR, MA, MX, OM, P, PA, PE, SG)	35%
2103.20.40		Other		11.6%	Free (A+, BH, CA, CL, CO, D, E, IL, JO, MX, OM, P, PA, PE, SG) 3.3% (KR) See 9912.21.05-9912.21.20 (MA) See 9913.96.57-9913.96.66 (AU)	50%
	20	In containers holding less than 1.4 kg	kg			
	40	Other	kg			

I'd just like to opine that the person who wrote the exam made a poor selection of an over-ambiguous example to test classification skills in this first classification-type question. Without getting into the Explanatory Notes (EN), let's just say that salsa is defined as a "spicy tomato sauce". As per GRI 3(a), the subheading 2103.20 provision for "tomato sauces" provides the most accurate and complete description of the article, salsa. The correct answer is "C".

✓ **INTERESTINGLY ENOUGH:** "Salsa" in Latin means "salty".

20. Column 31 of the CBP Form 7501 should indicate _____ for the salsa.

A. 4,536 kilograms

B. 10,000 pounds

C. 10,000 pieces

D. 16 ounces

E. 2,2046 kilograms

 As per FORM 7501 INSTRUCTIONS, Column 31:

COLUMN 31) NET QUANTITY IN HTS UNITS

When a unit of measure is specified in the HTS for an HTS number, report the net quantity in the specified unit of measure*, and show the unit of measure after the net quantity figure. Record quantities in whole numbers for statistical purposes unless fractions of units are required for other CBP purposes. Fractions must be expressed as decimals.*

 For the salsa classification 2103.20.4020, a unit of measure of "kg" is specified. The correct answer is "A".

Here's the math…

10,000 (number of jars of salsa per the commercial invoice)
x 0.453592 kg (each salsa jar = 1 pound = 0.453592 kg)
= 4,536 (rounded to nearest kilogram)

✓ **NOTE:** Best to bring a metric/standard conversion cheat sheet to the exam, just in case a question like this shows up.

21. The shrimp is identified as line item 002 of the Entry Summary. The correct information for identifying line number 002 from the abbreviated Entry Summary at Blocks 27 through 29 is:

A.

27.	28. Description of Merchandise		
Line No.	29. A. HTSUS No. B. ADA/CVD Case No.	30. A. Gross Weight B. Manifest Qty.	31. Net Quantity in HTSUS Units
002 O-VN	SHRIMP, Frozen dusted 1605.20.1030		

B.

27.	28. Description of Merchandise		
Line No.	29. A. HTSUS No. B. ADA/CVD Case No.	31. A. Gross Weight B. Manifest Qty.	31. Net Quantity in HTSUS Units
002 O-MX	SHRIMP, Frozen dusted 0306.23.0040		

C.

27.	28. Description of Merchandise		
Line No.	29. A. HTSUS No. B. ADA/CVD Case No.	32. A. Gross Weight B. Manifest Qty.	31. Net Quantity in HTSUS Units
002	SHRIMP, Frozen dusted 1605.90.6060		

D.

27.	28. Description of Merchandise		
Line No.	29. A. HTSUS No. B. ADA/CVD Case No.	33. A. Gross Weight B. Manifest Qty.	31. Net Quantity in HTSUS Units
002 VN	SHRIMP, Frozen dusted 0306.23.0040		

E.

27.	28. Description of Merchandise		
Line No.	29. A. HTSUS No. B. ADA/CVD Case No.	34. A. Gross Weight B. Manifest Qty.	31. Net Quantity in HTSUS Units
002	SHRIMP, Frozen dusted 1605.20.1030		

 As per FORM 7501 INSTRUCTIONS, Block 10:

When an entry summary covers merchandise from more than one country of origin**, record the word "MULTI" in this block. **In column 27, directly below the line number, prefixed with the letter "O," indicate the ISO code corresponding to each line item.

The salsa was made in Mexico and the shrimp in Vietnam (i.e. multi-origin). Accordingly, the country of origin for the shrimp, ISO code "VN", will be preceded by the letter "O". The correct answer is "A".

✔ **NOTE:** The HTS numbers in blocks 29 are fictitious, or at least from the sub-heading level. However, there is sufficient information presented in blocks 27 to select the correct answer.

22. If a Customs broker receives payment of duty, taxes and fees from a client after the due date to CBP, the broker must transmit the payment to the Government ___________________.

A. within 24-48 hours

B. within 5 calendar days

C. within 5 working days

D. within 10 calendar days

E. within 10 working days

As per 19 CFR 111.29(a):

111.29 Diligence in correspondence and paying monies.

(a) Due diligence by broker. Each broker must exercise due diligence in making financial settlements, in answering correspondence, and in preparing or assisting in the preparation and filing of records relating to any customs business matter handled by him as a broker. Payment of duty, tax, or other debt or obligation owing to the Government for which the broker is responsible, or for which the broker has received payment from a client, must be made to the Government on or before the date that payment is due. ***Payments received by a broker from a client after the due date must be transmitted to the Government within 5 working days from receipt by the broker.*** *Each broker must provide a written statement to a client accounting for funds received for the client from the Government, or received from a client where no payment to the Government has been made, or received from a client in excess of the Governmental or other charges properly payable as part of the client's customs business, within 60 calendar days of receipt. No written statement is required if there is actual payment of the funds by a broker.*

 The correct answer is "C".

✓ **JUST A SIDE NOTE:** Form of payment to CBP may be, among others described in 19 CFR 24.1, U.S. Currency (i.e. cash), cashier's check, certified check, and uncertified check (i.e. personal or business check) if certain conditions are met by the uncertified check writer.

23. How long does the Broker have to submit new employee information to Customs & Border protection?

A. 10 Business days after employment for 30 consecutive days.

B. 30 Calendar days after employment for 30 consecutive days

C. 15 Calendar days after employment initiated.

D. 30 Business days after employment initiated.

E. 10 Calendar days after employment for 30 consecutive days.

 As per 19 CFR 111.28(b):

(b) Employee information—(1) Current employees—(i) General. Each broker must submit, in writing, to the director of each port at which the broker intends to transact customs business, a list of the names of persons currently employed by the broker at that port. The list of employees must be submitted upon issuance of a permit for an additional district under §111.19, or upon the opening of an office at a port within a district for which the broker already has a permit, and before the broker begins to transact customs business as a broker at the port. For each employee, the broker also must provide the social security number, date and place of birth, current home address, last prior home address, and, if the employee has been employed by the broker for less than 3 years, the name and address of each former employer and dates of employment for the 3-year period preceding current employment with the broker. After the initial submission, an updated list, setting forth the name, social security number, date and place of birth, and current home address of each current employee, must be submitted with the status report required by §111.30(d).

(ii) ***New employees. In the case of a new employee, the broker must submit to the port director the written information required under paragraph (b)(1)(i) of this section within 10 calendar days after the new employee has been employed by the broker for 30 consecutive days.***

(2) Terminated employees. Within 30 calendar days after the termination of employment of any person employed longer than 30 consecutive days, the broker must submit the name of the terminated employee, in writing, to the director of the port at which the person was employed.

(3) Broker's responsibility. Notwithstanding a broker's responsibility for providing the information required in paragraph (b)(1) of this section, in the absence of culpability by the broker, Customs will not hold him responsible for the accuracy of any information that is provided to the broker by the employee.

 The correct answer is "E".

✔ **JUST A SIDE NOTE:** As per 19 CFR 111.1: (customs broker) "responsible supervision and control" is defined as:

that degree of supervision and control necessary to ensure the proper transaction of the customs business of a broker, including actions necessary to ensure that an employee of a broker provides substantially the same quality of service in handling customs transactions that the broker is required to provide.

24. Certain documents required for the entry of merchandise must be maintained by brokers for 5 years from the date of entry and must be made available upon reasonable notice for inspection by CBP. The following documents are examples of those that are subject to this requirement, EXCEPT:

A. Evidence of the right to make entry

B. Invoices

C. Packing lists

D. Bond information

E. Export certificates for beef or sugar-containing products subject to tariff-rate quota

As per 19 CFR 163.4(b)(2):

163.4 Record retention period.

(a) General. Except as otherwise provided in paragraph (b) of this section, any record required to be made, kept, and rendered for examination and inspection by Customs under §163.2 or any other provision of this chapter shall be kept for 5 years from the date of entry, if the record relates to an entry, or 5 years from the date of the activity which required creation of the record.

***(b) Exceptions**. (1) Any record relating to a drawback claim shall be kept until the third anniversary of the date of payment of the claim.*

(2) Packing lists shall be retained for a period of 60 calendar days from the end of the release or conditional release period, whichever is later, or, if a demand for return to Customs custody has been issued, for a period of 60 calendar days either from the date the goods are redelivered or from the date specified in the demand as the latest redelivery date if redelivery has not taken place.

(3) A consignee who is not the owner or purchaser and who appoints a customs broker shall keep a record pertaining to merchandise covered by an informal entry for 2 years from the date of the informal entry.

(4) Records pertaining to articles that are admitted free of duty and tax pursuant to 19 U.S.C. 1321(a)(2) and §§10.151 through 10.153 of this chapter, and carriers' records pertaining to manifested cargo that is exempt from entry under the provisions of this chapter, shall be kept for 2 years from the date of the entry or other activity which required creation of the record.

(5) If another provision of this chapter sets forth a retention period for a specific type of record that differs from the period that would apply under this section, that other provision controls.

The correct answer is "C".

✓ **JUST A SIDE NOTE:** A packing list, also sometimes referred to as a packing slip, is a shipping document that lists the contents, quantities, weights and dimensions of each package. In theory, it is a standard shipping document. In practice, however, it is not commonly used at present.

25. An ABI participant who has had his/her ABI privileges revoked, due to fraud or misstatement of material fact, has _______days to appeal to the Assistant Commissioner, Information and Technology from the date of the written notice of revocation.

A. 0 - appeals are not granted for fraud
B. 10
C. 20
D. 30
E. 60

 As per 19 CFR 143.8:

143.8 Appeal of suspension or revocation.

If the participant files a written appeal with the Assistant Commissioner, Information and Technology, within 10 days following the date of the written notice of action to suspend or revoke participation as provided in §§143.6 and 143.7, the suspension or revocation of participation shall not take effect until the appeal is decided, *except in those cases where the Executive Director, Trade Policy and Programs, Office of International Trade, or the Director, User Support Services Division, respectively, determines that participation was obtained through fraud or the misstatement of a material fact, or that continued participation would pose a potential risk of significant harm to the integrity and functioning of the system. The CBP officer who receives the appeal shall stamp the date of receipt of the appeal and the stamped date is the date of receipt for purposes of the appeal. The Assistant Commissioner shall inform the participant of the date of receipt and the date that a response is due under this paragraph. The Assistant Commissioner shall render his decision to the participant, in writing, stating his reasons therefor, by letter mailed within 30 working days following receipt of the appeal, unless this period is extended with due notification to the participant.*

 The correct answer is "B".

✓ **JUST A SIDE NOTE:** Sections 143.6 & 143.7 provide for "Failure to maintain performance standards" and "Revocation of ABI participation" respectively. They pertain to the quality and integrity of data transmissions to CBP via Automated Broker Interface (ABI).

26. When a complaint or charge against a broker is investigated, who determines if there is sufficient basis to recommend that charges be preferred against that broker?

A. Commissioner
B. Port director
C. Special agent
D. Import specialist
E. Hearing officer

 As per 19 CFR 111.56:

111.56 Review of report on investigation.

The port director will review the report of investigation to determine if there is sufficient basis to recommend that charges be preferred against the broker. *He will then submit his recommendation with supporting reasons to the Assistant Commissioner for final determination together with a proposed statement of charges when recommending that charges be preferred.*

 The correct answer is "B".

✓ **JUST A SIDE NOTE:** 19 CFR 111.53 lists the possible grounds for customs broker disciplinary action:

(a) The broker has made or caused to be made in any application for any license or permit under this part, or report filed with Customs, any statement which was, at the time and in light of the circumstances under which it was made, false or misleading with respect to any material fact, or has omitted to state in any application or report any material fact which was required;

(b) The broker has been convicted, at any time after the filing of an application for a license under §111.12, of any felony or misdemeanor which:

(1) Involved the importation or exportation of merchandise;

(2) Arose out of the conduct of customs business; or

(3) Involved larceny, theft, robbery, extortion, forgery, counterfeiting, fraudulent concealment, embezzlement, fraudulent conversion, or misappropriation of funds;

(c) The broker has violated any provision of any law enforced by Customs or the rules or regulations issued under any provision of any law enforced by Customs;

(d) The broker has counseled, commanded, induced, procured, or knowingly aided or abetted the violations by any other person of any provision of any law enforced by Customs or the rules or regulations issued under any provision of any law enforced by Customs;

(e) The broker has knowingly employed, or continues to employ, any person who has been convicted of a felony, without written approval of that employment from the Assistant Commissioner;

(f) The broker has, in the course of customs business, with intent to defraud, in any manner willfully and knowingly deceived, misled or threatened any client or prospective client; or ... ...

27. ABC Brokers, Inc. legally changed its name to Zumba Brokers, Inc. Before doing Customs business under the new name, the broker must submit evidence of his authority to use the new name to which of the following offices?

A. Office of the Chief Counsel
B. Office of International Trade
C. Regulatory Audit Division
D. Office of the Commissioner
E. National Finance Center in Indianapolis

 As per 19 CFR 111.30(c):

*(c) Change in name. **A broker who changes his name, or who proposes to operate under a trade or fictitious name** in one or more States within the district in which he has been granted a permit and is authorized by State law to do so, **must submit to the Office of International Trade**, U.S. Customs and Border Protection, Washington, DC 20229, evidence of his authority to use that name. The name must not be used until the approval of Headquarters has been received. In the case of a trade or fictitious name, the broker must affix his own name in conjunction with each signature of the trade or fictitious name when signing customs documents.*

 The correct answer is "B".

✓ **JUST A SIDE NOTE:** Not to be confused with the International Trade Association (or ITA, under Department of Commerce), the Office of International Trade (also referred to as Office of Trade, or OT, under Department of Homeland Security),

consolidates the trade policy, program development, and compliance measurement functions of CBP into one office.

Category VI: Antidumping/Countervailing Duties

28. What duty is levied when imported merchandise receives a bounty or grant when exported with material injury to an U. S. manufacturer?

A. Foreign Export Duties
B. Quota
C. Anti-Dumping Duties
D. Countervailing Duties
E. Marking

As per the CATAIR, Glossary of Terms:

Cotton Fee	An assessment collected on imported upland cotton and products containing upland cotton. The class code is 056.
Countervailing Duty	Countervailing duty is levied when imported merchandise receives a bounty or grant when exported with material injury to an U.S. manufacturer.
CSMS	Cargo Systems Messaging Service

The correct answer is "D".

✓ **JUST A SIDE NOTE:** Only about 6 pages in length, the CBP and Trade Automated Interface Requirements (CATAIR) Glossary *identifies document specific and ACS terminology and is provided for reference.* Here's another snapshot of the document that provides some more insight on the variety of terms described in the CATAIR Glossary.

FIRMS Code	Facilities Information and Resources Management System (FIRMS) code identifies the CBP facility where goods are located.
Foreign Trade Zone (FTZ)	Secured areas legally outside of a nation's CBP territory.
FROB	Foreign Remain On Board
GATT	General Agreement on Tariff and Trade
General Order (G.O.)	Premises owned or leased by the U.S. Government and used for the storage of merchandise undergoing CBP examination or under seizure, or pending final release from CBP custody. Unclaimed merchandise stored in such premises is held under "general order".

29. What is the correct collection code for antidumping duties?

A. 499
B. 012
C. 013
D. 501
E. 311

 As per FORM 7501 INSTRUCTIONS, Block 39:

… …

The applicable collection code must be indicated on the same line as the fee or other charge or exaction. Report the fees in the format below:

AD	012
CVD	013
Tea Fee	038
Misc. Interest	044
Beef Fee	053
Pork Fee	054
Honey Fee	055
Cotton Fee	056
Pecan Fee	057
Sugar Fee	079
Potato Fee	090
Mushroom Fee	103
Watermelon	104
Blueberry Fee	106
Avocado	107
Mango	108
Informal Entry MPF	311
Dutiable Mail Fee	496
Merchandise Processing Fee (MPF)	499
Manual Surcharge	500
Harbor Maintenance Fee (HMF)	501

… …

 The correct answer here is "B".

✔ **JUST A SIDE NOTE:** "Dumping" is when a party sells its product abroad at a price lower than it does in its domestic market. "Anti-dumping" is the imposition of additional duties on that party's imports in an effort to protect the domestic market parties.

30. An entry made on July 18, 2003, is under a statutory suspension of liquidation because it is subject to an antidumping order, and is later liquidated on December 20, 2004. A protest must be filed in order to be considered timely filed.

A. within 180 days of December 20, 2004, the date of liquidation

B. within 90 days of December 20, 2004, the date of liquidation

C. within one year of December 20, 2004, the date of liquidation

D. within one year of July 18, 2003, the date entry

E. 30 days before December 20, 2004, the date of liquidation

 As per 19 CFR 174.12(e):

(e) Time of filing. ***Protests must be filed****, in accordance with section 514, Tariff Act of 1930, as amended (19 U.S.C. 1514),* ***within 90 days of a decision relating to an entry made before December 18, 2004****, or within 180 days of a decision relating to an entry made on or after December 18, 2004,* ***after any of the following****:*

(1) ***The date of notice of liquidation*** *or reliquidation, or the date of liquidation or reliquidation, as determined under §§159.9 or 159.10 of this chapter;*

(2) The date of the decision, involving neither a liquidation nor reliquidation, as to which the protest is made (for example: The date of an exaction; the date of written notice excluding merchandise from entry, delivery or demanding redelivery to CBP custody under any provision of the customs laws; the date of written notice of a denial of a claim filed under section 520(d), Tariff Act of 1930, as amended (19 U.S.C. 1520(d)), or; within 90 days of the date of denial of a petition filed pursuant to section 520(c)(1), Tariff Act of 1930, as amended (19 U.S.C. 1520(c)(1)), relating to an entry made before December 18, 2004); or

(3) The date of mailing of notice of demand for payment against a bond in the case of a surety which has an unsatisfied legal claim under a bond written by the surety.

 The correct answer is "B".

✓ **JUST A SIDE NOTE:** Currently, protests can be filed within 180 days of liquidation. After 180 days, a prior disclosure is the only way to rectify an issue with Customs.

Category VII: Bonds

31. When a resident of France temporarily imports articles under subheading 9813.00.50, HTSUS, and formal entry is made, the importer of record shall be required to file a bond in what amount?

A. An amount equal to 110 percent of estimated duties and fees
B. An amount equal to 110 percent of estimated duties
C. An amount equal to three times the entered value
D. An amount equal to 200 percent of estimated duties and fees, if payable
E. An amount equal to the entered value plus duties, taxes and fees

 As per 19 CFR 10.31(f):

*(f) With the exceptions stated herein, a bond shall be given on CBP Form 301, containing the bond conditions set forth in §113.62 of this chapter, in an amount equal to double the duties, including fees, which it is estimated would accrue (or such larger amount as the port director shall state in writing or by the electronic equivalent to the entrant is necessary to protect the revenue) had all the articles covered by the entry been entered under an ordinary consumption entry. In the case of samples solely for use in taking orders entered under subheading 9813.00.20, HTSUS, motion-picture advertising films entered under subheading 9813.00.25, HTSUS, and **professional equipment, tools of trade and repair components for such equipment or tools entered under subheading 9813.00.50, HTSUS, the bond required to be given shall be in an amount equal to 110 percent of the estimated duties, including fees**, determined at the time of entry. If appropriate a carnet, under the provisions of part 114 of this chapter, may be filed in lieu of a bond on CBP Form 301 (containing the bond conditions set forth in §113.62 of this chapter). Cash deposits in the amount of the bond may be accepted in lieu of sureties. When the articles are entered under subheading 9813.00.05, 9813.00.20, or ... ...*

 The correct answer is "A".

✓ **JUST A SIDE NOTE:** This exam question is a good example of a Temporary Import under Bond (TIB). Here's a snapshot of 9813.00.50 from HTSUS Chapter 98, Subchapter 13/XIII (ARTICLES ADMITTED TEMPORARILY FREE OF DUTY UNDER BOND):

9813.00.50	1/	Professional equipment, tools of trade, repair components for equipment or tools admitted under this heading and camping equipment; all the foregoing imported by or for nonresidents sojourning temporarily in the United Statesand for the use of such nonresidents........	....	Free, under bond, as prescribed in U.S. note 1 to this subchapter	Free (AU, BH, CA, CL, IL, JO, KR, MA, MX, OM, P, PA, PE, SG)

32. For Government entries secured by stipulation, bond type ______ should be used in conjunction with surety code _______.

A. 8; 998

B. 9;999

C. 9; 998

D. 0; 999

E. 0; 998

As per 19 CFR 10.101(d) & FORM 7501 INSTRUCTIONS, Block 5:

19 CFR 10.101(d) Bond. ***No bond shall be required in support of an immediate delivery application provided for in this section if a stipulation in the form as set forth below is filed with the port director in connection with the application:***

____ I, ____, ____ (Title), a duly authorized representative of the____

____

(Name of United States Government department or agency) stipulate and agree on behalf of such department or agency that all applicable provisions of the Tariff Act of 1930, as amended, and the regulations thereunder, and all other laws and regulations, relating to the release and entry of merchandise will be observed and complied with in all respects.

____

(Signature)

FORM 7501 INSTRUCTIONS, BLOCK 5) BOND TYPE

Record the single digit numeric code as follows:

0 - U.S. Government or entry types not requiring a bond
8 - Continuous
9 - Single Transaction

Bond type "0" should be used in conjunction with surety code "999" for government entries secured by stipulation *as provided for in 19 C.F.R. § 10.101(d).*

Bond type "8" or "9," as appropriate, should be used in conjunction with surety code "998" when cash or government securities are deposited in lieu of surety.

Bond type "9" should be used in conjunction with surety code "999" when surety has been waived in accordance with 19 C.F.R. § 142.4 (c). A single entry bond should be attached to the entry summary package.

The correct answer is "D".

✓ **JUST A SIDE NOTE:** In this case, no customs bond is necessary because CBP does not deem the bond necessary in order to secure payment from another U.S. Government department or agency.

33. If the principal gets free release of any serially numbered shipping container classifiable under subheading 9801.00.10 or 9803.00.50, HTSUS, the principal agrees to all of the following, EXCEPT?

A. To advance the value or improve its condition abroad or claim (or make a previous claim) drawback on, any container released under subheading 9801.00.10, HTSUS
B. To pay the initial duty due and otherwise comply with every condition in subheading 9803.00.50, HTSUS, on any container released under that item
C. To mark that container in the manner required by CBP
D. To keep records which show the current status of that container in service and the disposition of that container if taken out of service
E. To remove or strike out the markings on that container when it is taken out of service or when the principal transfers ownership of it

 As per 19 CFR 113.66(b):

(b) Agreement to Comply With the Provisions of subheading 9801.00.10, or 9803.00.50 Harmonized Tariff Schedule of the United States (HTSUS). If the principal gets free release of any serially numbered shipping container classifiable under subheading 9801.00.10 or 9803.00.50, HTSUS, the principal agrees:

(1) ***Not to advance the value or improve its condition abroad or claim (or make a previous claim) drawback on, any container released under subheading 9801.00.10****, HTSUS;*

(2) To pay the initial duty due and otherwise comply with every condition in subheading 9803.00.50, HTSUS, on any container released under that item;

(3) To mark that container in the manner required by CBP;

(4) To keep records which show the current status of that container in service and the disposition of that container if taken out of service; and

(5) To remove or strike out the markings on that container when it is taken out of service or when the principal transfers ownership of it.

 The correct answer is "A".

✓ **JUST A SIDE NOTE:** The HTSUS subheadings 9801.00.10 & 9803.00.50 provide for free entry, respectively:

9801.00.10 Products of the United States when returned after having been exported, or any other products when returned within 3 years after having been exported, without having been advanced in value or improved in condition by any process of manufacture or other means while abroad

9803.00.50 Substantial containers and holders, if products of the United States (including shooks and staves of United States production when returned as boxes or barrels containing merchandise), or if of foreign production and previously imported and duty (if any) thereon paid, or if of a class specified by the Secretary of the Treasury as instruments of international traffic, repair components for containers of foreign production which are instruments of international traffic, and accessories and equipment for such containers, whether the accessories and equipment are imported with a container to be reexported separately or with another container, or imported separately to be reexported with a container

34. If a port director believes the acceptance of a transaction such as a "03" antidumping entry secured by a continuous bond would place the revenue in jeopardy, or otherwise hamper the enforcement of Customs and Border Protection laws or regulations, he/she shall require additional security according to:

A. 19 C.F.R. § 151.65

B. 19 C.F.R. § 113.13

C. 19 C.F.R. § 152.101

D. 19 C.F.R. § 152.107

E. 19 C.F.R. § 171.1

 As per 19 CFR 113.13(d):

(d) Additional security. Notwithstanding the provisions of this section or any other provision of this chapter, ***if CBP believes that acceptance of a transaction secured by a continuous bond would place the revenue in jeopardy or otherwise hamper the enforcement of all applicable laws or regulations, CBP may immediately require additional security.***

 The correct answer is "B".

✓ **JUST A SIDE NOTE:** If CBP deems the bond amount to be insufficient, the importer, or customs broker on behalf of the importer, will request the surety (i.e. the importer's customs bond insurance company) to increase the bond amount accordingly.

35. A driver bit is interchangeable and designed to be fitted into hand-operated power drills and impact drivers in order to drive a screw. What is the classification of the driver bit?

A. 8207.90.6000 Interchangeable tools for handtools, whether or not power operated, or for machine-tools (for example, for pressing, stamping, punching, tapping, threading, drilling, boring, broaching, milling, turning or screwdriving), including dies for drawing or extruding metal, and rock drilling or earth boring tools; base metal parts thereof>>Other interchangeable tools, and parts thereof>>Other>>Other>>Not suitable for cutting metal, and parts thereof>>For handtools, and parts thereof

B. 8207.90.7585 Interchangeable tools for handtools, whether or not power operated, or for machine-tools (for example, for pressing, stamping, punching, tapping, threading, drilling, boring, broaching, milling, turning or screwdriving), including dies for drawing or extruding metal, and rock drilling or earth boring tools; base metal parts thereof>>Other interchangeable tools, and parts thereof>>Other>>Other>>Not suitable for cutting metal, and parts thereof>>Other

C. 8204.20.0000 Hand-operated spanners and wrenches (including torque meter wrenches but not including tap wrenches); socket wrenches, with or without handles, drives or extensions; base metal parts thereof>>Socket wrenches, with or without handles, drives and extensions, and parts thereof

D. 8205.40.0000 Handtools (including glass cutters) not elsewhere specified or included; blow torches and similar self-contained torches; vises, clamps and the like, other than accessories for and parts of machine tools; anvils; portable forges; hand- or pedal-operated grinding wheels with frameworks; base metal parts thereof>>Screwdrivers, and parts thereof

E. 8466.10.0175 Parts and accessories suitable for use solely or principally with the machines of headings 8456 to 8465, including work or tool holders, self-opening dieheads, dividing heads and other special attachments for machine tools; tool holders for any type of tool for working in the hand>>Tool holders and self-opening dieheads>>Other

 As per HTSUS Section XVI (Machinery and Electronics Chapters 84 & 85), Note 1(o):

Notes

1. ***This section does not cover:***

... ...

(o) ***Interchangeable tools of heading 8207*** *or brushes of a kind used as parts of machines (heading 9603); similar interchangeable tools are to be classified according to the constituent material of their working part (for example, in chapter 40, 42, 43, 45 or 59 or heading 6804 or 6909);*

Multiple choices "C" (wrenches and wrench parts) and "E" (tool holders and self-opening dieheads) do not describe the product, so let's start by eliminating these two. Moreover, "E" is excluded per the Section XVI note. Now, notice that the item in question, a hand-operated power drill driver bit is "prima facie" (i.e. classifiable under more than one heading/classification). Accordingly, we try to classify using GRI 3(a), which says the most specific classification is preferred to less descriptive classifications. Thus heading 8207 ("A" and "B") is preferred over the "handtools not elsewhere specified" heading of 8205 ("D"). The driver bit is for "handtools", and so we select "A" as the correct answer.

Heading/ Subheading	Stat. Suf- fix	Article Description	Unit of Quantity	Rates of Duty 1 General	Rates of Duty 1 Special	2
8207 (con.)		Interchangeable tools for handtools, whether or not power operated, or for machine-tools (for example, for pressing, stamping, punching, tapping, threading, drilling, boring, broaching, milling, turning or screwdriving), including dies for drawing or extruding metal, and rock drilling or earth boring tools; base metal parts thereof: (con.)				
8207.90		Other interchangeable tools, and parts thereof:				
8207.90.15	00	Files and rasps, including rotary files and rasps, and parts thereof	doz	1.6%	Free (A, AU, BH, CA, CL, CO, D, E, IL, JO, KR, MA, MX, OM, P, PA, PE, SG)	15%
		Other:				
8207.90.30		Cutting tools with cutting part containing by weight over 0.2 percent of chromium, molybdenum, or tungsten or over 0.1 percent of vanadium		5%	Free (A, AU, BH, CA, CL, CO, D, E, IL, JO, KR, MA, MX, OM, P, PA, PE, SG)	60%
	30	Hobs and other gear cutting tools	X			
		For woodworking:				
	75	Cutterheads with interchangeable tools	X			
	80	Other	X			
	85	Other	X			
		Other:				
8207.90.45	00	Suitable for cutting metal, and parts thereof	X	4.8% 1/	Free (A, AU, BH, CA, CL, CO, D, E, IL, JO, KR, MA, MX, OM, P, PA, PE, SG)	50%
		Not suitable for cutting metal, and parts thereof:				
8207.90.60	00	For handtools, and parts thereof	X	4.3%	Free (A, AU, BH, CA, CL, CO, D, E, IL, JO, KR, MA, MX, OM, P, PA, PE, SG)	45%
8207.90.75		Other		3.7% 1/	Free (A, AU, BH, CA, CL, CO, D, E, IL, JO, KR, MA, MX, OM, P, PA, PE, SG)	35%
	45	Cutterheads with interchangeable tools	X			
	85	Other	X			

36. One 13oz. jar of 100% petroleum jelly labeled as skin protectant is put up for retail sale. How would you classify the petroleum jelly?

A. 3301.29.51 Essential oils (terpeneless or not), including concretes and absolutes; resinoids; extracted oleoresins; concentrates of essential oils in fats, in fixed oils, in waxes or the like, obtained by enfleurage or maceration; terpenic by products of the deterpenation of essential oils; aqueous distillates and aqueous solutions of essential oils>>Essential oils other than those of citrus fruit>>Other>>Other

B. 2712.10.00 Petroleum jelly; paraffin wax, microcrystalline petroleum wax, slack wax, ozokerite, lignite wax, peat wax, other mineral waxes and similar products obtained by synthesis or by other processes, whether or not colored>>Petroleum jelly

C. 3304.99.10 Beauty or make-up preparations and preparations for the care of the skin (other than medicaments), including sunscreen or sun tan preparations; manicure or pedicure preparations>>Other>>Other>>Petroleum jelly put up for retail sale

D. 3403.11.50 Lubricating preparations (including cutting-oil preparations, bolt or nut release preparations, antirust or anticorrosion preparations and mold release preparations, based on lubricants) and preparations of a kind used for the oil or grease treatment of textile materials, leather, furskins or other materials, but excluding preparations containing, as basic constituents, 70 percent or more by weight of petroleum oils or oils obtained from bituminous minerals>>Containing petroleum oils or oils obtained from bituminous minerals>>Preparations for the treatment of textile materials, leather, furskins or other materials>>Other

E. 2711.12.00 Petroleum gases and other gaseous hydrocarbons>>Liquefied>>Propane

As per HTSUS, Chapter 27, Additional U.S. Note 8:

*8. **Subheading 2712.10.00 does not include petroleum jelly, suitable for use for the care of the skin, put up in packings of a kind sold at retail for such use (subheading 3304.99.10).***

The item in question, 100% petroleum jelly put up for retail sale, is specifically provided for in HTSUS subheading 3304.99.10. Moreover, the above-mentioned Chapter 27 note precludes "B" from consideration. The correct answer is "C".

✓ **NOTE:** The actual HTSUS classifications are 10-digits in length, but have been truncated to 8-digits in this exam question, possibly in an attempt to simplify things.

Heading/ Subheading	Stat. Suf- fix	Article Description	Unit of Quantity	Rates of Duty 1 General	Rates of Duty 1 Special	Rates of Duty 2
3303.00		Perfumes and toilet waters:				
		Not containing alcohol:				
3303.00.10	00	Floral or flower waters	liters	Free		20%
3303.00.20	00	Other	kg	Free		75%
3303.00.30	00	Containing alcohol	kg	Free		88¢/kg + 75%
3304		Beauty or make-up preparations and preparations for the care of the skin (other than medicaments), including sunscreen or sun tan preparations; manicure or pedicure preparations:				
3304.10.00	00	Lip make-up preparations	X	Free		75%
3304.20.00	00	Eye make-up preparations	X	Free		75%
3304.30.00	00	Manicure or pedicure preparations	X	Free		75%
		Other:				
3304.91.00		Powders, whether or not compressed		Free		75%
	10	Rouges	X			
	50	Other	X			
		Other:				
3304.99.10	00	Petroleum jelly put up for retail sale	X	Free		75%
3304.99.50	00	Other	X	Free		75%
3305		Preparations for use on the hair:				
3305.10.00	00	Shampoos	X	Free		75%
3305.20.00	00	Preparations for permanent waving or straightening	X	Free		75%
3305.30.00	00	Hair lacquers	kg	Free		88¢/kg + 75%
3305.90.00	00	Other	kg	Free		88¢/kg + 75%
3306		Preparations for oral or dental hygiene, including denture fixative pastes and powders; yarn used to clean between the teeth (dental floss), in individual retail packages:				
3306.10.00	00	Dentifrices	X	Free		75%
3306.20.00	00	Yarn used to clean between the teeth (dental floss)	kg	Free		88¢/kg + 75%
3306.90.00	00	Other	kg	Free		88¢/kg + 75%

37. A two-piece box is constructed of rigid cardboard. Within the box is a paperboard sleeve and plastic "c" clip, upon which a watch will be mounted. Logos and graphics related to the style of watch being sold are printed on the exterior of the box. This packaging will be imported in the United States without watches. Upon importation the watch will be put into the boxes for retail sale. This container is not suitable for long term use. What is classification of the box?

A. 3923.10.0000 Articles for the conveyance or packing of goods, of plastics; stoppers, lids, caps and other closures, of plastics>>Boxes, cases, crates and similar articles

B. 3923.29.0000 Articles for the conveyance or packing of goods, of plastics; stoppers, lids, caps and other closures, of plastics>>Sacks and bags (including cones)>>Of other plastics

C. 4202.92.9015 Trunks, suitcases, vanity cases, attache cases, briefcases, school satchels, spectacle cases, binocular cases, camera cases, musical instrument cases, gun cases, holsters and similar containers; traveling bags, insulated food or beverage bags, toiletry bags, knapsacks and backpacks, handbags, shopping bags, wallets, purses, map cases, cigarette cases, tobacco pouches, tool bags, sports bags, bottle cases, jewelry boxes, powder cases, cutlery cases and similar containers, of leather or of composition leather, of sheeting of plastics, of textile materials, of vulcanized fiber or of paperboard, or wholly or mainly covered with such materials or with paper>>Other>>With outer surface of sheeting of plastic or of textile materials>>Other>>Other>>With outer surface of textile materials>>Other, jewelry boxes of a kind normally sold at retail with their contents

D. 4202.92.9036 Trunks, suitcases, vanity cases, attache cases, briefcases, school satchels, spectacle cases, binocular cases, camera cases, musical instrument cases, gun cases, holsters and similar containers; traveling bags, insulated food or beverage bags, toiletry bags, knapsacks and backpacks, handbags, shopping bags, wallets, purses, map cases, cigarette cases, tobacco pouches, tool bags, sports bags, bottle cases, jewelry boxes, powder cases, cutlery cases and similar containers, of leather or of composition leather, of sheeting of plastics, of textile materials, of vulcanized fiber or of paperboard, or wholly or mainly covered with such materials or with paper>>Other>>With outer surface of sheeting of plastic or of textile materials>>Other>>Other>>With outer surface of textile materials>>Other>>Other

E. 4819.50.4040 Cartons, boxes, cases, bags and other packing containers, of paper, paperboard, cellulose wadding or webs of cellulose fibers; box files, letter trays and similar articles, of paper or paperboard of a kind used in offices, shops or the like>>Other packing containers, including record sleeves>>Other>>Other>>Rigid boxes and cartons

a The item in question is a rigid cardboard (i.e. paperboard) box with a paperboard sleeve and plastic clip. Let's go about solving this one via the process of elimination. It is not a plastic "sack" or "bag", so we may disregard "B". It does not have an "outer surface of textile materials", so we may disregard "C" and "D". Now, at this point, we could (with an open mind) say that the item is potentially classifiable under "A" as a box of plastic, or under "E" as a box of cardboard/paperboard. In other words, the item is prima-facie (i.e. classifiable under more than 1 heading). So, we first try to classify by GRI 3(a), which says the most specific classification description is preferred to other classifications. This is not necessarily the case here, so next we try to classify via GRI 3(b), which says to classify the composite item based on its essential character. The cardboard/paperboard, from which the item is mostly constructed of, imparts the essential character of the item, more so than does the relatively insignificant "plastic 'c' clip". The correct answer is "E".

✓ **JUST A SIDE NOTE:** Cardboard is "heavy paper pulp–based (paper)board"

Heading/ Subheading	Stat. Suf- fix	Article Description	Unit of Quantity	Rates of Duty 1 General	Special	2
4819		Cartons, boxes, cases, bags and other packing containers, of paper, paperboard, cellulose wadding or webs of cellulose fibers; box files, letter trays and similar articles, of paper or paperboard of a kind used in offices, shops or the like:				
4819.10.00		Cartons, boxes and cases, of corrugated paper or paperboard		Free		35%
	20	Sanitary food and beverage containers	kg			
	40	Other	kg			
4819.20.00		Folding cartons, boxes and cases, of non-corrugated paper or paperboard		Free		35%
	20	Sanitary food and beverage containers	kg			
	40	Other	kg			
4819.30.00		Sacks and bags, having a base of a width of 40 cm or more		Free		35%
	20	Shipping sacks and multiwall bags, other than grocers' bags	kg			
	40	Other	kg			
4819.40.00		Other sacks and bags, including cones		Free		35%
	20	Shipping sacks and multiwall bags, other than grocers' bags	kg			
	40	Other	kg			
4819.50		Other packing containers, including record sleeves:				
4819.50.20	00	Sanitary food and beverage containers	kg	Free		35%
4819.50.30	00	Record sleeves	kg	Free		19.3c/kg
4819.50.40		Other		Free		35%
	20	Fiber drums, cans, tubes and similar containers	kg			
		Other:				
	40	Rigid boxes and cartons.	kg			
	60	Other	kg			
4819.60.00	00	Box files, letter trays, storage boxes and similar articles, of a kind used in offices, shops or the like	kg	Free		35%

38. What is the classification of women's cheerleading briefs made of 100% nylon knit fabric?

A. 6108.29.9000	Women's or girls' slips, petticoats, briefs, panties, night dresses, pajamas, negligees, bathrobes, dressing gowns and similar articles, knitted or crocheted>>Briefs and panties>>Of other textile materials>>Other
B. 6114.30.3070	Other garments, kitted or crocheted>>Of man-made fibers>>Other>>Other>>Women's or girls'
C. 6104.63.2060	Women's or girls' suits, ensembles, suit-type jackets, blazers, dresses, skirts, divided skirts, trousers, bib and brace overalls, breeches and shorts (other than swimwear), knitted or crocheted>>Trousers, big and brace overalls, breeches and shorts>>Of synthetic fibers>>Other>>Other>>Shorts>>Girls'>>Other
D. 6104.69.2060	Women's or girls' suits, ensembles, suit-type jackets, blazers, dresses, skirts, divided skirts, trousers, bib and brace overalls, breeches and shorts (other than swimwear), knitted or crocheted>>Trousers, big and brace overalls, breeches and shorts>>Of other textile materials>>Of artificial fibers>>Trousers, breeches and shorts>>Other>>Shorts
E. 6307.90.9889	Other made up articles, including dress patterns>>Other>>Other>>Other>>Other>>Other

a The item in question, "cheerleading briefs" (also known as bloomers), are considered prima facie. Meaning, in the HTSUS, they could potentially be classified as underwear-like "briefs" (heading 6108), "shorts" (heading 6104), or "other garments" (heading 6114)? Since neither GRI 3(a), nor GRI 3(b) are definitively applicable here, we try GRI 3(c), which says to classify based on the heading that occurs last in numerical order. The correct answer is "B".

✓ **NOTE:** The difference between "synthetic" fibers and "artificial" fibers is that "artificial" fibers are made from naturally-occurring substances, such plant cellulose. Both are "man-made". Nylon is a synthetic fiber.

Heading/ Subheading	Stat. Suf-fix	Article Description	Unit of Quantity	Rates of Duty 1 General	Rates of Duty 1 Special	2
6114 (con.)		Other garments, knitted or crocheted: (con.)				
6114.30 (con.)		Of man-made fibers: (con.)				
6114.30.30		Other		14.9%	Free (AU, BH, CA, CL, CO, IL, JO, KR, MA, MX, OM, P, PA, PE, SG)	90%
		Jumpers:				
	12	Containing 23 percent or more by weight of wool orfine animal hair (459)	doz. kg			
	14	Other (659)	doz. kg			
		Sunsuits, washsuits, one-piece playsuits and similar apparel:				
	20	Boys' (237)	doz. kg			
	30	Women's or girls' (237)	doz. kg			
		Coveralls, jumpsuits and similar apparel:				
		Men's or boys':				
	42	Containing 23 percent or more by weight of wool or fine animal hair (459)	doz. kg			
	44	Other (659)	doz. kg			
		Women's or girls':				
	52	Containing 23 percent or more by weight of wool or fine animal hair (459)	doz. kg			
	54	Other (659)	doz. kg			
		Other:				
	60	Men's or boys' (659)	doz. kg			
	70	Women's or girls' (659)	doz. kg			

39. What is the classification of a men's 100% knit cotton sleeveless muscle shirt?

A. 6105.10.0010 Men's or boy's shirts, knitted or crocheted>>Of cotton>>Men's
B. 6110.20.2069 Sweaters, pullovers, sweatshirts, waistcoats (vests) and similar articles, knitted or crocheted>>Of cotton>>Other>>Other>>Other>>Other
C. 6105.20.2010 Men's or boys' shirts, knitted or crocheted>>Of man-made fibers>>Other>>Boys'
D. 6106.10.0010 Women's or girls' blouses and shirts, knitted or crocheted>>Of cotton>>Women's
E. 6205.20.2066 Men's or boys' shirts>>Of cotton>>Other>>Other>>Other>>Men's

 As per HTSUS Chapter 61, Note 4:

4. Headings 6105 and 6106 do not cover garments with pockets below the waist, with a ribbed waistband or other means of tightening at the bottom of the garment, or garments having an average of less than 10 stitches per linear centimeter in each direction counted on an area measuring at least 10 centimeters by 10 centimeters. ***Heading 6105 does not cover sleeveless garments.***

 And, as per HTSUS Chapter 62, Note 1:

1. ***This chapter (62)*** *applies only to made up articles of any textile fabric other than wadding,* ***excluding knitted or crocheted articles*** *(other than those of heading 6212).*

An initial assessment of the exam question makes it appear that 6105.10.0010 ("A") is the correct classification. However, as per GRI 1, we must base our classification on heading descriptions AND Section and Chapter Notes. The above-mentioned Chapter 61, Note 4 precludes this heading and choices "A" and "C" from being used for "sleeveless" articles. "D" describes women's clothing, and is thus disregarded. And, as per the above-mentioned Chapter 61, Note 1, we may disregard chapter 62 ("E"). Finally, a reasonable argument could be made that a "muscle shirt" is an article similar to a sweatshirt (i.e. heading 6110), and that accordingly, the correct answer is "B".

✓ **NOTE:** It is our opinion that a more appropriate classification for the item question, a sleeveless muscle shirt, lies in HTSUS 6109.10.0018, which provides for T-Shirts, singlets, **tank tops** and similar garments, knitted or crocheted>>Of cotton>>Men's or boys'>>Tank topes and other singlets>>Men's

Heading/ Subheading	Stat. Suf-fix	Article Description	Unit of Quantity	Rates of Duty 1 General	Rates of Duty 1 Special	2
6110 (con.)		Sweaters, pullovers, sweatshirts, waistcoats (vests) and similar articles, knitted or crocheted: (con.)				
6110.20 (con.)		Of cotton: (con.)				
6110.20.20		Other		16.5%	Free (AU, BH, CA, CL, CO, IL, JO, MA, MX, OM, P, PA, PE, SG) 8.2% (KR)	50%
	05	Boys' or girls' garments imported as parts of playsuits (237)	doz. kg			
		Other:				
		Sweaters:				
	10	Men's (345)	doz. kg			
	15	Boys' (345)	doz. kg			
	20	Women's (345)	doz. kg			
	25	Girls' (345)	doz. kg			
		Vests, other than sweater vests:				
	30	Men's or boys' (359)	doz. kg			
	35	Women's or girls' (359)	doz. kg			
		Sweatshirts:				
	41	Men's (338)	doz. kg			
	44	Boys' (338)	doz. kg			
	46	Women's (339)	doz. kg			
	49	Girls' (339)	doz. kg			
		Other:				
		Men's or boys':				
	67	Knit to shape articles described in statistical note 6 to this chapter (338)	doz. kg			
	69	Other (338)	doz. kg			
		Women's or girls':				
	77	Knit to shape articles described in statistical note 6 to this chapter (339)	doz. kg			
	79	Other (339)	doz. kg			

40. What is the proper classification of a fluorine-based polyether polymer, in primary form? This is also chemically known as trifluoromethyl- poly[oxy-2-(trifluoromethyl)-trifluoroethylene]-poly(oxy- difluoromethylene)-trifluoromethyl ether.

A. 3403.99.0000 Lubricating preparations (including cutting-oil preparations, bolt or nut release preparations, antirust or anticorrosion preparations and mold release preparations, based on lubricants) and preparations of a kind used for the oil or grease treatment of textile materials, leather, furskins or other materials, but excluding preparations containing, as basic constituents, 70 percent or more by weight of petroleum oils or oils obtained from bituminous minerals>>Other>>Other

B. 3907.20.0000 Polyacetals, other polyethers and epoxide resins, in primary forms; polycarbonates, alkyd resins, polyallyl esters and other polyesters, in primary forms>> Other polyethers

C. 9902.23.11/3907.20.0000

9902.23.11: 1-Propene, 1,1,2,3,3,3-hexafluoro-, oxidized, polymerized (CAS No. 69991-67-9) (provided for in subheading 3904.69.50)

3907.20.0000: (see above "B")

D. 3907.30.0000 Polyacetals, other polyethers and epoxide resins, in primary forms; polycarbonates, alkyd resins, polyallyl esters and other polyesters, in primary forms>>Epoxide resins

E. 9902.01.85/3907.30.0000

9902.01.85: Epoxy molding compounds, of a kind used for encapsulating integrated circuits (provided for in subheading 3907.30.00)

3907.30.0000: (see above "D")

a We are not chemists. However, with a reasonable degree of certainty, we can say that "A" does not describe the item in question. Nor do 9902.23.11, 3907.30.0000, or 9902.01.85, which eliminates choices "C", "D", and "E". Through this process of elimination we can deduce that the correct answer is "B".

✓ **JUST A SIDE NOTE:** Although rarely used, Chapter 99 of the HTSUS imposes additional duties and/or restrictions on a handful of regular HTSUS classifications found throughout the HTSUS (i.e. Chapter 1 thru. Chapter 98). The regular HTSUS classification will be annotated with a note to refer to a Chapter 99 classification, which will further described, in detail, whether the additional classification in Chapter 99 will be necessary or not.

Heading/ Subheading	Stat. Suf-fix	Article Description	Unit of Quantity	Rates of Duty 1 General	Special	2
3906		Acrylic polymers in primary forms:				
3906.10.00	00	Poly(methyl methacrylate)	kg	6.3%	Free (A, AU, BH, CA, CL, CO, D, E, IL, JO, KR, MA, MX, OM, P, PA, PE, SG)	37%
3906.90		Other:				
3906.90.10	00	Elastomeric	kg	Free		20%
		Other:				
3906.90.20	00	Plastics	kg	6.3% 1/	Free (A, AU, BH, CA, CL, CO, D, E, IL, JO, KR, MA, MX, OM, P, PA, PE, SG)	37%
3906.90.50	00	Other	kg	4.2% 2/	Free (A, AU, BH, CA, CL, CO, D, E, IL, JO, K, KR, MA, MX, OM, P, PA, PE, SG)	25%
3907		Polyacetals, other polyethers and epoxide resins, in primary forms; polycarbonates, alkyd resins, polyallyl esters and other polyesters, in primary forms:				
3907.10.00	00	Polyacetals	kg	6.5%	Free (A, AU, BH, CA, CL, CO, D, E, IL, JO, K, KR, MA, MX, OM, P, PA, PE, SG)	2.2¢/kg + 33.5%
3907.20.00	00	Other polyethers	kg	6.5% 3/	Free (A, AU, BH, CA, CL, CO, D, E, IL, JO, K, KR, MA, MX, OM, P, PA, PE, SG)	2.2¢/kg + 33.5%
3907.30.00	00	Epoxide resins	kg	6.1% 4/	Free (A, AU, BH, CA, CL, CO, D, E, IL, JO, K, KR, MA, MX, OM, P, PA, PE, SG)	15.4¢/kg + 47%
3907.40.00	00	Polycarbonates	kg	5.8%	Free (A, AU, BH, CA, CL, CO, D, E, IL, JO, MA, MX, OM, P, PA, PE, SG) 2.9% (KR)	15.4¢/kg + 45%
3907.50.00	00	Alkyd resins	kg	6.5%	Free (A, AU, BH, CA, CL, CO, D, E, IL, JO, KR, MA, MX, OM, P, PA, PE, SG)	15.4¢/kg + 45%
3907.60.00		Poly(ethylene terephthalate)		6.5%	Free (A*, AU, BH, CA, CL, CO, D, E, IL, JO, K, MA, MX, OM, P, PA, PE, SG) 3.2% (KR)	15.4¢/kg + 45%
	30	Packaging grade (bottle grade and other, with an intrinsic viscosity of 0.70 or more but not more than 0.88 deciliters per gram)	kg			

1/ See heading 9902.24.15.
2/ See heading 9902.02.80.
3/ See headings 9902.02.98, 9902.23.10-9902.23.12, 9902.23.14, 9902.23.15, and 9902.23.17-9902.23.19.
4/ See heading 9902.01.85.

41. A package of trail mix is made up of a loose blend of nut kernels, seeds and candy. It contains raw almonds 26.4% C/O USA; raw cashews 22% C/O Vietnam, India or Brazil; raw pumpkin seeds 17.6% C/O China; raw walnut halves 10% C/O USA; candy coated milk chocolate pieces 15% C/O USA; and raw sunflower seeds 9% C/O USA. All of the ingredients will be imported into Canada, where they will be mixed together in the indicated proportion and packaged for export to the United States. No other processing will be done in Canada. What is the classification of the trail mix?

A. 0813.50.0020 Fruit, dried, other than that of headings 0801 to 0806; mixtures of nuts or dried fruits of this chapter>>Mixtures of nuts or dried fruits of this chapter>>Containing only fruit

B. 0813.50.0040 Fruit, dried, other than that of headings 0801 to 0806; mixtures of nuts or dried fruits of this chapter>>Mixtures of nuts or dried fruits of this chapter>>Containing only nuts

C. 0812.90.1000 Fruit and nuts, provisionally preserved (for example, by sulfur dioxide gas, in brine, in sulfur water or in other preservative solutions), but unsuitable in that state for immediate consumption>>Other>>Mixtures of two or more fruits

D. 0813.50.0060 Fruit, dried, other than that of headings 0801 to 0806; mixtures of nuts or dried fruits of this chapter>>Mixtures of nuts or dried fruits of this chapter>>Other

E. 2008.97.1040 Fruit, nuts and other edible parts of plants, otherwise prepared or preserved, whether or not containing added sugar or other sweetening matter or spirit, not elsewhere specified or included>>Other, including mixtures other than those of subheading 2008.19>>Mixtures>> In airtight containers and not containing apricots, citrus fruits, peaches or pears>>Other

 As per HTSUS Chapter 20, Note 1(a):

*1. **This chapter does not cover:***
*(a) **Vegetables, fruit or nuts, prepared or preserved by the processes specified in chapter** 7, **8** or 11;*

The item in question, essentially raw (i.e. unprepared) mixed nuts, are provided for in heading 0813. Accordingly, and, as per the above-mentioned Chapter 20 Note, we may disregard "E" (i.e. Chapter 20). We assume that the item is suitable for immediate consumption and not provisionally preserved, so we may disregard "C". In addition to nuts, the trail mix contains milk chocolate pieces, so the 0813.50.0060 classification of "other" (than containing only nuts) accurately describes the product. The correct answer is "D".

✔ **JUST A SIDE NOTE:** According to Wikipedia…

A **nut** is a fruit composed of a hard shell and a **seed**, which is generally edible. In a general context, however, a wide variety of dried seeds are called nuts, but in a botanical context, there is an additional requirement that the shell does not open to release the seed (indehiscent).

Heading/ Subheading	Stat. Suf-fix	Article Description	Unit of Quantity	Rates of Duty 1 General	Rates of Duty 1 Special	Rates of Duty 2
0813 (con.)		Fruit, dried, other than that of headings 0801 to 0806; mixtures of nuts or dried fruits of this chapter: (con.)				
0813.50.00		Mixtures of nuts or dried fruits of this chapter		14%	Free (A+, AU, BH, CA, CL, CO, D, E, IL, JO, KR, MA, MX, OM, P, PA, PE, SG)	35%
	20	Containing only fruit	kg			
	40	Containing only nuts	kg			
	60	Other	kg			
0814.00		Peel of citrus fruit or melons (including watermelons), fresh, frozen, dried or provisionally preserved in brine, in sulfur water or in other preservative solutions:				
0814.00.10	00	Orange or citron	kg	Free		4.4¢/kg
0814.00.40	00	Lime	kg	1.6¢/kg	Free (A, AU, BH, CA, CL, CO, D, E, IL, JO, KR, MA, MX, OM, P, PA, PE, SG)	4.4¢/kg
0814.00.80	00	Other	kg	1.6¢/kg	Free (A+, AU, BH, CA, CL, CO, D, E, IL, JO, KR, MA, MX, OM, P, PA, PE, SG)	4.4¢/kg

42. Stainless steel tattooing needles are designed for use in a hand-held tattooing machine which features a self-contained electric motor. The needles are dipped in ink and placed in the handheld machine which utilizes a vibratory action to drive the needle in an up-and-down fashion. This causes the needle tips to pierce the top layer of skin and deposit the ink into the second or dermal skin layer. What is the classification of the tattooing needles?

A. 8207.90.6000	Interchangeable tools for handtools, whether or not power operated, or for machine-tools (for example, for pressing, stamping, punching, tapping, threading, drilling, boring, broaching, milling, turning or screwdriving), including dies for drawing or extruding metal, and rock drilling or earth boring tools; base metal parts thereof>>Other interchangeable tools, and parts thereof>>Other>>Other>>Not suitable for cutting metal, and parts thereof>>For handtools, and parts thereof
B. 8453.90.5000	Machinery for preparing, tanning or working hides, skins or leather or for making or repairing footwear or other articles of hides, skins or leather, other than sewing machines; parts thereof>>Parts>>Other
C. 8467.99.0190	Tools for working in the hand, pneumatic, hydraulic or with self-contained electric or nonelectric motor, and parts thereof>>Parts>>Other>>Other
D. 8479.90.9496	Machines and mechanical appliances having individual functions, not specified or included elsewhere in this chapter; parts thereof>>Parts>>Other>>Other>>Other
E. 8487.90.0080	Machinery parts, not containing electrical connectors, insulators, coils, contacts or other electrical features, and not specified or included elsewhere in this chapter>>Other>>Other

 As per HTSUS Section XVI (contains Chapters 84 & 85), Notes 1:

*1. **This section does not cover:***

... ...

*(k) **Articles of chapter** 82 or 83;*

... ...

The item in question is a needle, a tool which is for use in a hand-held tattooing machine. The item can be classified using GRI 1, which says to classify based on Headings, Chapter Notes and Section Notes. Section XVI, Note 1 says that if an item can be classified in Chapter 82, then do not classify in Chapters 84. The correct answer is "A".

✓ **JUST A SIDE NOTE:** This exact same question appeared on the 2013 October exam. Recycled questions and answers are certainly not uncommon on the exam.

Heading/ Subheading	Stat. Suf-fix	Article Description	Unit of Quantity	Rates of Duty 1 General	Rates of Duty 1 Special	2
8207 (con.)		Interchangeable tools for handtools, whether or not power operated, or for machine-tools (for example, for pressing, stamping, punching, tapping, threading, drilling, boring, broaching, milling, turning or screwdriving), including dies for drawing or extruding metal, and rock drilling or earth boring tools; base metal parts thereof: (con.)				
8207.90		Other interchangeable tools, and parts thereof:				
8207.90.15	00	Files and rasps, including rotary files and rasps, and parts thereof	doz.	1.6%	Free (A, AU, BH, CA, CL, CO, D, E, IL, JO, KR, MA, MX, OM, P, PA, PE, SG)	15%
		Other:				
8207.90.30		Cutting tools with cutting part containing by weight over 0.2 percent of chromium, molybdenum, or tungsten or over 0.1 percent of vanadium		5%	Free (A, AU, BH, CA, CL, CO, D, E, IL, JO, KR, MA, MX, OM, P, PA, PE, SG)	60%
	30	Hobs and other gear cutting tools	X			
		For woodworking:				
	75	Cutterheads with interchangeable tools	X			
	80	Other	X			
	85	Other	X			
		Other:				
8207.90.45	00	Suitable for cutting metal, and parts thereof	X	4.8% 1/	Free (A, AU, BH, CA, CL, CO, D, E, IL, JO, KR, MA, MX, OM, P, PA, PE, SG)	50%
		Not suitable for cutting metal, and parts thereof:				
8207.90.60	00	For handtools, and parts thereof	X	4.3%	Free (A, AU, BH, CA, CL, CO, D, E, IL, JO, KR, MA, MX, OM, P, PA, PE, SG)	45%
8207.90.75		Other		3.7% 1/	Free (A, AU, BH, CA, CL, CO, D, E, IL, JO, KR, MA, MX, OM, P, PA, PE, SG)	35%
	45	Cutterheads with interchangeable tools	X			
	85	Other	X			

43. Certain women's bowling shoes, while imported as a pair, have separate identities. Both shoes have uppers of 100 percent rubber/plastics. The left shoe has an outer sole of rubber/plastics. The right shoe has an outer sole consisting of rubber/plastics and a large textile sliding pad. The textile pad comprises the majority of the surface area facing the ground. The shoes are below-the-ankle, do not have a foxing or foxing-like band, are not protective, and are secured to the foot with laces. What is the classification of this pair of bowling shoes?

A. 6402.19.1541	Other footwear with outer soles and uppers of rubber or plastics>>Sports footwear>>Other>>Having uppers of which over 90 percent of the external surface area … … is rubber or plastics … … >>Other>>For women
B. 6402.91.0500	Other footwear with outer soles and uppers of rubber or plastics>>Sports footwear>>Other footwear>>Covering the ankle>>Incorporating a protective metal toe-cap>> Having uppers of which over 90 percent of the external surface area … … is rubber or plastics … …
C. 6402.99.3165	Other footwear with outer soles and uppers of rubber or plastics>>Other footwear>>Other>>Other>> Having uppers of which over 90 percent of the external surface area … … is rubber or plastics … … >>Other>>Other>>Other>>For women>>Other
D. 6404.19.3960	Footwear with outer soles of rubber, plastics, leather or composition leather and uppers of textile materials>>Footwear with outer soles of rubber or plastics>>Other>> Footwear with open toes or open heels; footwear of the slip-on type, that is held to the foot without the use of laces or buckles or other fasteners, … …
E. 6405.90.9000	Other footwear>>Other>>Other

 As per HTSUS Chapter 64, Note 4(b), and Additional U.S. Note 5:

4. Subject to note 3 to this chapter:

*(b) **The constituent material of the outer sole** shall be taken to be the material having the greatest surface area in contact with the ground, **no account being taken of accessories or reinforcements such as spikes, bars, nails, protectors or similar attachments**.*

*5. **For the purposes of determining the constituent material of the outer sole pursuant to note 4(b) of this chapter, no account shall be taken of textile materials which do not possess the characteristics usually required for normal use of an outer sole, including durability and strength.***

The exam key lists "E" as the correct answer. We disagree, and believe "A" to be the correct classification. Based on the above Chapter 64 Note and Chapter 64 Additional U.S. Note, the right shoe's textile sliding pad should NOT be taken into account. Coincidentally, credit was given to all examinees for this question.

✓ **JUST A SIDE NOTE:** "Foxing", according to the Footwear Distributors and Retailers of America (FDRA),

is a strip of material, separate from the sole and upper, that secures the joint where the upper and sole meet.

Subheading	Suf-fix	Article Description	Unit of Quantity	1 General	1 Special	2
6402		Other footwear with outer soles and uppers of rubber or plastics:				
		Sports footwear:				
6402.12.00	00	Ski-boots, cross-country ski footwear and snowboard boots	prs.	Free		35%
6402.19		Other:				
		Having uppers of which over 90 percent of the external surface area (including any accessories or reinforcements such as those mentioned in note 4(a) to this chapter) is rubber or plastics (except footwear having foxing or a foxing-like band applied or molded at the sole and overlapping the upper and except footwear designed to be worn over, or in lieu of, other footwear as a protection against water, oil, grease or chemicals or cold or inclement weather):				
6402.19.05		Golf shoes		6%	Free (AU, BH, CA, CL, CO, D, E, IL, JO, KR, MA, MX, OM, P, PA, PE, R, SG)	35%
	30	For men	prs.			
	60	For women	prs.			
	90	Other	prs.			
6402.19.15		Other		5.1%	Free (AU, BH, CA, CL, CO, D, E, IL, JO, KR, MA, MX, OM, P, PA, PE, R, SG)	35%
	20	For men	prs.			
	41	For women	prs.			
	61	Other	prs.			
		Other:				
6402.19.30		Valued not over $3/pair		Free		84%
	31	For men	prs.			
	61	Other	prs.			
6402.19.50		Valued over $3 but not over $6.50/pair		76¢/pr. + 32%	Free (AU, BH, CA, CL, CO, D, E, IL, JO, KR, MA, MX, OM, P, PA, PE, R, SG)	$1.58/pr. + 66%
	31	For men	prs.			
	61	Other	prs.			
6402.19.70		Valued over $6.50 but not over $12/pair		76¢/pr. + 17%	Free (AU, BH, CA, CL, CO, D, E, IL, JO, KR, MA, MX, OM, P, PA, PE, R, SG)	$1.58/pr. + 35%
	31	For men	prs.			
	61	Other	prs.			
6402.19.90		Valued over $12/pair		9%	Free (AU, BH, CA, CL, CO, D, E, IL, JO, KR, MA, MX, OM, P, PA, PE, R, SG)	35%
	31	For men	prs.			
	61	Other	prs.			
6402.20.00	00	Footwear with upper straps or thongs assembled to the sole by means of plugs (zoris)	prs.	Free		35%

44. What is the classification of a woman's handbag with outer surface of textile materials and with a fiber content of 30% nylon, 30% cotton and 40% rayon?

A. 4202.22.4040 Trunks, suitcases, vanity cases, attache cases, … …, handbags, … … similar containers, of leather or of composition leather, of sheeting of plastics, of textile materials, of vulcanized fiber or … …>>Handbags, whether or not with a shoulder strap, including those without handle>>With outer surface of sheeting of plastic or of textile materials>>With outer surface of textile materials>>Wholly or in part of braid>>Other>>Other>>Other

B. 4202.22.6000 Trunks, suitcases, vanity cases, attache cases, … …, handbags, … … similar containers, of leather or of composition leather, of sheeting of plastics, of textile materials, of vulcanized fiber or … …>>Handbags, whether or not with a shoulder strap, including those without handle>>With outer surface of sheeting of plastic or of textile materials>>With outer surface of textile materials>>Other>> Of vegetable fibers and not of pile or tufted construction>>Other

C. 4202.22.8030 Trunks, suitcases, vanity cases, attache cases, … …, handbags, … … similar containers, of leather or of composition leather, of sheeting of plastics, of textile materials, of vulcanized fiber or … …>>Handbags, whether or not with a shoulder strap, including those without handle>>With outer surface of sheeting of plastic or of textile materials>>With outer surface of textile materials>>Other>> Other>>Other>>Of cotton

D. 4202.22.8050 Trunks, suitcases, vanity cases, attache cases, … …, handbags, … … similar containers, of leather or of composition leather, of sheeting of plastics, of textile materials, of vulcanized fiber or … …>>Handbags, whether or not with a shoulder strap, including those without handle>>With outer surface of sheeting of plastic or of textile materials>>With outer surface of textile materials>>Other>> Other>>Other>>Of man-made fibers

E. 4202.22.8080 Trunks, suitcases, vanity cases, attache cases, … …, handbags, … … similar containers, of leather or of composition leather, of sheeting of plastics, of textile materials, of vulcanized fiber or … …>>Handbags, whether or not with a shoulder strap, including those without handle>>With outer surface of sheeting of plastic or of textile materials>>With outer surface of textile materials>>Other>> Other>>Other>>Other

a The item in question is a textile handbag consisting of different materials in 30% nylon, 30% cotton and 40% rayon, and is considered "prima facie" (i.e. potentially classifiable under more than one heading) here. Simply put, once at GRI 3(b), we can mathematically say that the man-made fibers (i.e. nylon and rayon) impart the essential (textile) character of the handbag. The correct answer is "D".

✓ **JUST A SIDE NOTE:** "Vegetable fibers", according to Wikipedia,

are generally based on arrangements of cellulose, often with lignin: examples include cotton, hemp, jute, flax… …

Heading/ Subheading	Stat. Suf- fix	Article Description	Unit of Quantity	Rates of Duty 1 General	Rates of Duty 1 Special	2
4202 (con.)		Trunks, suitcases, vanity cases, attache cases, briefcases, school satchels, spectacle cases, binocular cases, camera cases, musical instrument cases, gun cases, holsters and similar containers; traveling bags, insulated food or beverage bags, toiletry bags, knapsacks and backpacks, handbags, shopping bags, wallets, purses, map cases, cigarette cases, tobacco pouches, tool bags, sports bags, bottle cases, jewelry boxes, powder cases, cutlery cases and similar containers, of leather or of composition leather, of sheeting of plastics, of textile materials, of vulcanized fiber or of paperboard, or wholly or mainly covered with such materials or with paper: (con.)				
		Handbags, whether or not with shoulder strap, including those without handle: (con.)				
4202.22 (con.)		With outer surface of sheeting of plastic or of textile materials: (con.)				
		With outer surface of textile materials: (con.)				
		Other:				
		Of vegetable fibers and not of pile or tufted construction:				
4202.22.45	00	Of cotton (369)	No. kg	6.3%	Free (AU, BH, CA, CL, CO, IL, JO, KR, MA, MX, OM, P, PA, PE, SG) 4.9% (E)	40%
4202.22.60	00	Other (871)	No. kg	5.7%	Free (AU, BH, CA, CL, CO, IL, JO, KR, MA, MX, OM, P, PA, PE, SG) 4.4% (E)	40%
		Other:				
4202.22.70	00	Containing 85 percent or more by weight of silk or silk waste	No. kg	7%	Free (AU, BH, CA, CL, CO, D, E, IL, JO, KR, MA, MX, OM, P, PA, PE, SG)	65%
4202.22.80		Other		17.6%	Free (AU, BH, CA, CL, CO, IL, JO, KR, MA, MX, OM, P, PA, PE, SG) 16.6% (E)	65%
	30	Of cotton (369)	No. kg			
	50	Of man-made fibers (670)	No. kg			
	70	Of paper yarn	No. kg			
	80	Other (871)	No. kg			

45. How would you classify a glass jar of spread that includes both peanut butter and grape jelly? The peanut butter and jelly each comprise 50% of the product.

A. The item would be classified as peanut butter. (2008.11)
B. The item would be classified as grape jelly. (2007.99.7500)
C. The item would be classified as a glass jar. (7010.90.50)
D. The item would be classified as a 'mixed condiment/seasoning'. (2103.90)
E. The item must be classified using the tariff numbers for both peanut butter and grape jelly.

 As per HTSUS GRI 2(b) and 3(a), 3(b), and 3(c):

2.
… …

(b) Any reference in a heading to a material or substance shall be taken to include a reference to mixtures or combinations of that material or substance with other materials or substances. Any reference to goods of a given material or substance shall be taken to include a reference to goods consisting wholly or partly of such material or substance. The classification of goods consisting of more than one material or substance shall be according to the principles of rule 3.

3. When, by application of rule 2(b) or for any other reason, goods are, prima facie, classifiable under two or more headings, classification shall be effected as follows:

(a) The heading which provides the most specific description shall be preferred to headings providing a more general description. However, when two or more headings each refer to part only of the materials or substances contained in mixed or composite goods or to part only of the items in a set put up for retail sale, those headings are to be regarded as equally specific in relation to those goods, even if one of them gives a more complete or precise description of the goods.

(b) Mixtures, composite goods consisting of different materials or made up of different components, and goods put up in sets for retail sale, which cannot be classified by reference to 3(a), shall be classified as if they consisted of the material or component which gives them their essential character, insofar as this criterion is applicable.

(c) When goods cannot be classified by reference to 3(a) or 3(b), they shall be classified under the heading which occurs last in numerical order among those which equally merit consideration.

The item in question, a spread consisting of 50% peanut butter and 50% grape jelly, is prima facie. As per GRI 2(b), mixtures are implied, meaning one classification can be used for an item containing a mixture of multiple items. So, we may disregard "E".

Next in order, we try to classify based on GRI 3(a), which says the heading with the most specific description is preferred to less descriptive headings. Heading 2103 provides for the relatively vague description of "mixed condiments", so we may disregard "D" here.

Next in order, we move on to GRI 3(b), which says to classify based on the material that gives the item its essential character. Well, neither the peanut butter nor the grape jelly clearly give the product its essential character over the other. The glass jar definitely does not give the product its essential character, so we may disregard "C" at this point.

Finally, we're forced to move on the GRI 3(c), which says to classify using the heading that numerically occurs last. 2008 (peanut butter heading) occurs after 2007 (grape jelly heading). The correct answer is "A".

✓ **NOTE:** GRI 5(b) also dictates that containers, such as the glass jars in this exam question, are to be classified with the goods they contain.

Heading/ Subheading	Stat. Suf- fix	Article Description	Unit of Quantity	Rates of Duty 1 General	1 Special	2
2008		Fruit, nuts and other edible parts of plants, otherwise prepared or preserved, whether or not containing added sugar or other sweetening matter or spirit, not elsewhere specified or included:				
		Nuts, peanuts (ground-nuts) and other seeds, whether or not mixed together:				
2008.11	00	Peanuts (ground-nuts):				
		Peanut butter and paste:				
2008.11.02	00	Described in general note 15 of the tariff schedule and entered pursuant to its provisions	kg	Free		15¢/kg
2008.11.05	00	Described in additional U.S. note 5 to this chapter and entered pursuant to its provisions	kg	Free		15¢/kg
2008.11.15	00	Other 1/	kg	131.8%	Free (BH, CL, JO, MX, SG) 35.10% (P) 61.5% (PE) 65.9% (KR) 87.8% (CO) 131.8% (PA)(s) See 9912.12.05, 9912.12.20 (MA) See 9913.12.05, 9913.12.20 (AU) See 9915.20.05- 9915.20.20 (P+) See 9916.12.05, 9916.12.20 (OM)	155%
		Blanched peanuts:				
2008.11.22	00	Described in general note 15 of the tariff schedule and entered pursuant to its provisions	kg	6.6¢/kg	Free (A+, AU, BH, CA, CL, CO, D, E, IL, JO, KR, MA, MX, OM, P, PA, PE, SG)	15¢/kg
2008.11.25	00	Described in additional U.S. note 2 to chapter 12 and entered pursuant to its provisions	kg	6.6¢/kg	Free (A, BH, CA, CL, CO, D, E, IL, JO, KR, MA, OM, P, PA, PE, SG)	15¢/kg
2008.11.35	00	Other 2/	kg	131.8%	Free (BH, CL, JO, MX, SG) 61.5% (PE) 65.9% (KR) 70.60% (P) 87.8% (CO) 131.8% (PA)(s) See 9908.12.01 (IL) See 9912.12.05, 9912.12.20 (MA) See 9913.12.05, 9913.12.20 (AU) See 9915.12.05, 9915.12.20, 9915.12.40 (P+) See 9916.12.05, 9916.12.20 (OM)	155%

46. Which statement is False?

A. For legal purposes, the classification of goods in the subheadings of a heading shall be determined according to the terms of those subheadings and any related subheading notes and, mutatis mutandis, to the above rules, on the understanding that only subheadings at the same level are comparable. For the purposes of this rule, the relative section, chapter and subchapter notes also apply, unless the context otherwise requires.

B. Subject to the provisions in section 213 of the Caribbean Basin Economic Recovery Act, goods which are imported from insular possessions of the United States shall receive duty treatment no less favorable than the treatment afforded such goods when they are imported from a beneficiary country under such Act.

C. Goods of Canada, when marked or eligible to be marked with their country of origin, that comply with the terms of the Automotive Products Trade Act are exempt from the Merchandise Processing Fee (MPF) when entered with the Special Program Indicator (SPI) "B#" prefacing the 10-digit HTS number.

D. Instruments of international traffic, such as containers, lift vans, rail cars and locomotives, truck cabs and trailers, etc. are exempt from formal entry procedures but are required to be accounted for when imported and exported into and out of the United States, respectively, through the manifesting procedures required for all international carriers by the United States Customs Service. Fees associated with the importation of such instruments of international traffic shall be reported and paid on a periodic basis as required by regulations issued by the Secretary of the Treasury and in accordance with 1956 Customs Convention on Containers (20 UST 30; TIAS 6634).

E. Schedule C provides a list of U.S. Customs districts, the ports included under each district, and the corresponding numeric codes used in compiling the U.S. foreign trade statistics. The Schedule contains a code for each official U.S. Customs district and port, with some additional codes provided to meet specific compiling requirements of the foreign trade statistics program.

 As per HTSUS Annex C:

ANNEX C
***Schedule D - Classification of U.S. Customs Districts and Ports** for U.S. Foreign Trade Statistics*
... ...

Schedule C (a.k.a. HTSUS Annex A) provides a list of numeric "classifications of country and territory designations for U.S. foreign trade statistics". For example, Canada's Schedule C code is 122.0.

Schedule D (a.k.a. HTSUS Annex C) provides a list of U.S. "customs district and port codes". For example, Baltimore, Maryland's port code is 1303. The false statement, and correct answer is "E".

✓ **JUST A SIDE NOTE:** The HTSUS contains 3 annexes. Annex A (Schedule C numeric country codes), Annex B (alpha country codes [e.g. "CA" for Canada]), and Annex C (Schedule D district & port codes).

STATISTICAL ANNEXES

47. What is the classification of a steel piston designed for a reciprocating positive displacement liquid pump that is used in the oil industry?

A. 8413.91.90	Pumps for liquids, whether or not fitted with a measuring device; liquid elevators; part thereof>>Parts>>Of pumps>>Other
B. 7326.90.85	Other articles of iron or steel>>Other>>Other>>Other>>Other
C. 9015.90.00	Surveying (including photogrammetrical surveying), hydrographic, oceanographic, hydrological, meteorological or geophysical instruments and appliances, excluding compasses; rangefinders; parts and accessories thereof>>Parts and accessories
D. 8413.50.00	Pumps for liquids, whether or not fitted with a measuring device; liquid elevators; part thereof>>Other reciprocating positive displacement pumps
E. 8414.90.90	Air or vacuum pumps, air or other gas compressors and fans; ventilating or recycling hoods incorporating a fan, whether or not fitted with filters; parts thereof>>Parts>>Other

 As per HTSUS Section XVI (contains Chapters 84 & 85), Note 2:

2. Subject to note 1 to this section, note 1 to chapter 84 and to note 1 to chapter 85, ***parts of machines*** *(not being parts of the articles of heading 8484, 8544, 8545, 8546 or 8547)* ***are to be classified according to the following rules:***

(a) Parts which are goods included in any of the headings of chapter 84 or 85 (other than headings 8409, 8431, 8448, 8466, 8473, 8487, 8503, 8522, 8529, 8538 and 8548) are in all cases to be classified in their respective headings;

(b) ***Other parts, if suitable for use solely or principally with a particular kind of machine, or with a number of machines of the same heading*** *(including a machine of heading 8479 or 8543)* ***are to be classified with the machines of that kind or in heading*** *8409, 8431, 8448, 8466, 8473, 8503, 8522, 8529 or 8538 as appropriate. However, parts which are equally suitable for use principally with the goods of headings 8517 and 8525 to 8528 are to be classified in heading 8517;*

(c) All other parts are to be classified in heading 8409, 8431, 8448, 8466, 8473, 8503, 8522, 8529 or 8538 as appropriate or, failing that, in heading 8487 or 8548.

This exam question is a good example of the classification of "parts", and especially relevant for Chapters 84 (mechanical items, generally speaking) and 85 (electrical items, generally speaking). THE BIG QUESTION ABOUT PARTS IS… do we classify the part as a stand-alone item (e.g. a steel piston), or as a "part of" another item (e.g. part of a pump). Well, the answer and procedure for doing so can be found in the applicable Section and/or Chapter Notes. As per the above Section XVI Note 2(a), (except for a small group of headings) parts are to be classified by as a stand-alone item if they are provided for in a heading. There is no such heading for these "steel pistons", so we move on to Section XVI, Note 2(b), which says if 2(a) does not apply, AND if the part is designed for a particular machine, then classify as a "part of" that machine. That is the case in this scenario. The correct answer is "A".

✓ **JUST A SIDE NOTE:** Here's another, yet different example of the classification of parts… As referenced in the above Section XVI, Note 2(a), (excluded) heading 8544 provides for cables and wires. As dictated in the note, essentially all cables and wires, even if parts of a greater product, are to remain classified in heading 8544.

Heading/ Subheading	Stat. Suf-fix	Article Description	Unit of Quantity	Rates of Duty 1 General	Rates of Duty 1 Special	2
8413 (con.)		Pumps for liquids, whether or not fitted with a measuring device; liquid elevators; part thereof: (con.)				
8413.70		Other centrifugal pumps:				
8413.70.10	00	Stock pumps imported for use with machines for making cellulosic pulp, paper or paperboard	No.	Free		35%
8413.70.20		Other		Free		35%
	04	Submersible pumps	No.			
		Other:				
		Single-stage, single-suction, close-coupled:				
	05	With discharge outlet under 5.08 cm in diameter	No.			
	15	With discharge outlet 5.08 cm or over in diameter	No.			
		Single-stage, single-suction, frame- mounted:				
	22	With discharge outlet under 7.6 cm in diameter	No.			
	25	With discharge outlet 7.6 cm or over in diameter	No.			
	30	Single-stage, double-suction	No.			
	40	Multi-stage, single- or double-suction	No.			
	90	Other	No.			
		Other pumps; liquid elevators:				
8413.81.00		Pumps		Free		35%
	20	Turbine pumps	No.			
	30	Household water systems, self-contained; and windmill pumps	No.			
	40	Other	No.			
8413.82.00	00	Liquid elevators	No.	Free		35%
		Parts:				
8413.91		Of pumps:				
8413.91.10	00	Of fuel-injection pumps for compression-ignition engines	X	2.5%	Free (A, AU, B, BH, C, CA, CL, CO, D, E, IL, JO, MA, MX, OM, P, PA, PE, SG) 1.2% (KR)	35%
8413.91.20	00	Of stock pumps imported for use with machines for making cellulosic pulp, paper or paperboard	X	Free		35%
8413.91.90		Other		Free		35%
	10	Of subheading 8413.30.90	X			
	50	Of hydraulic fluid power pumps	X			
	80	Other	X			
8413.92.00	00	Of liquid elevators	X	Free		35%

48. Merchandise or articles that for commercial purposes are identical and interchangeable in all situations are called:

A. Multiple products

B. Fungible merchandise or articles

C. Commercially interchangeable merchandise

D. Designated merchandise

E. Substituted merchandise or articles

 As per 19 CFR 191.2(o):

(o) Fungible merchandise or articles. ***Fungible merchandise or articles means merchandise or articles which for commercial purposes are identical and interchangeable in all situations.***

 The correct answer is "B".

✓ **JUST A SIDE NOTE:** The word "fungibility" comes from Latin "fungibilis" from "fungi", meaning "to perform", related to "function" and "defunct". Examples of fungible items are cash, salt, etc.

49. How long must records pertaining to the filing of a drawback claim be kept?

A. Five years from the date of entry

B. Ten years from the date the claim is filed

C. Indefinitely

D. At least until the third anniversary of the date of payment of the claim

E. At least until the fifth anniversary of the date of payment of the claim

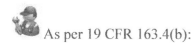

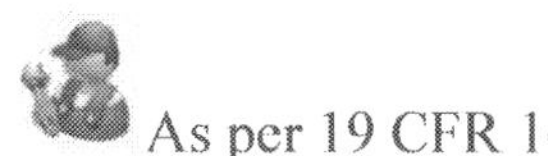 As per 19 CFR 163.4(b):

(b) Exceptions. ***(1) Any record relating to a drawback claim shall be kept until the third anniversary of the date of payment of the claim.***

(2) Packing lists shall be retained for a period of 60 calendar days from the end of the release or conditional release period, whichever is later, or, if a demand for return to Customs custody has been issued, for a period of 60 calendar days either from the date the goods are redelivered or from the date specified in the demand as the latest redelivery date if redelivery has not taken place.

(3) A consignee who is not the owner or purchaser and who appoints a customs broker shall keep a record pertaining to merchandise covered by an informal entry for 2 years from the date of the informal entry.

(4) Records pertaining to articles that are admitted free of duty and tax pursuant to 19 U.S.C. 1321(a)(2) and §§10.151 through 10.153 of this chapter, and carriers' records pertaining to manifested cargo that is exempt from entry under the provisions of this chapter, shall be kept for 2 years from the date of the entry or other activity which required creation of the record.

(5) If another provision of this chapter sets forth a retention period for a specific type of record that differs from the period that would apply under this section, that other provision controls.

 The correct answer is "D".

✓ **JUST A SIDE NOTE:** "Drawback", as per CBP's website, is described as

the refund of certain duties, internal revenue taxes and certain fees collected upon the importation of goods. Such refunds are only allowed upon the exportation or destruction of goods under U.S. Customs and Border Protection supervision.

50. To comply with manufacturing drawback (direct identification and substitution), the use of domestic merchandise taken in exchange for imported merchandise of the same kind and quality shall be treated as use of the imported merchandise if no certificate of delivery is issued covering the transfer of the imported merchandise. The provision is known as a/an_______?

A. Interchange

B. Fungibility

C. Trade Good

D. Exchange Merchandise

E. Tradeoff

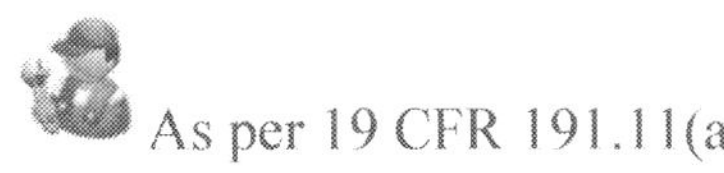
As per 19 CFR 191.11(a):

191.11 Tradeoff.

(a) Exchanged merchandise. To comply with §§191.21 and 191.22 of this part, ***the use of domestic merchandise taken in exchange for imported merchandise of the same kind and quality*** *(as defined in §191.2(x)(1) of this part for purposes of 19 U.S.C. 1313(b))* ***shall be treated as use of the imported merchandise if no certificate of delivery is issued covering the transfer of the imported merchandise. This provision shall be known as tradeoff*** *and is authorized by §313(k) of the Act, as amended (19 U.S.C. 1313(k)).*

The correct answer is "E".

✓ **JUST A SIDE NOTE:** As of October 2016, all drawback claims must be submitted electronically, via ACE (Automated Commercial Environment) instead of ACS/ABI. Manual drawback claims can still be submitted, but ACE claims will be given processing priority over manual claims.

51. A drawback claimant proposes to destroy unmerchantable distilled spirits, wine, or beer and must return the merchandise to CBP custody. The returned merchandise must be destroyed under the supervision of a CBP officer and the completed destruction shall be documented on________.

A. CBP Form 7551
B. CBP Form 7553
C. CBP Form 7501
D. CBP Form 3495
E. CBP Form 3461

 As per 19 CFR 191.166(b):

191.166 Destruction of merchandise.

(a) Action by the importer. A drawback claimant who proposes to destroy rather than export the distilled spirits, wine, or beer shall state that fact on Customs Form 7551.

(b) Action by Customs. ***Distilled spirits, wine, or beer returned to Customs custody at the place approved by the drawback office where the drawback entry was filed shall be destroyed under the supervision of the Customs officer who shall certify the destruction on Customs Form 7553.***

 The correct answer is "B".

✔ **JUST A SIDE NOTE:** CBP's Information Center has the following notice about drawback refunds:

If you have exported or intend to export goods previously imported with duty paid, there is a possibility you can get a refund of the duty. Drawback is a mechanism that Customs and Border Protection (CBP) has to enable importers to get a refund of duty paid on imported goods when they are exported or destroyed. **Be aware the process of filing for drawback can be involved and the time it takes to receive refunds can be lengthy.**

You must have proof of the export or destruction, as well as proof that duty was originally paid. A bill of sale or airway bill is valid proof of export and a CBP Officer must witness the destruction of the goods. Without proof of export or the destruction, the claim is not substantiated.

52. Which of the following is NOT true about the North American Free Trade Agreement (NAFTA) Certificate of Origin?

A. The Certificate must be signed by the exporter or the exporter's authorized agent having knowledge of the relevant facts.

B. The Certificate must be in the possession of the importer at the time preferential treatment is claimed, unless waived by the Port Director pursuant to 19 CFR 181.22(d)(1).

C. A Certificate which is photocopied, faxed, or scanned on a computer disc is acceptable.

D. A Certificate is required for each importation on which NAFTA is claimed, but does not need to accompany each shipment.

E. A producer who is not an exporter may prepare and sign a Certificate, relieving the exporter of his/her obligation to do so.

 As per 19 CFR 181.11(b):

(b) Preparation of Certificate in the United States. An exporter in the United States who completes and signs a Certificate of Origin for the purpose set forth in paragraph (a) of this section shall use Customs Form 434, or its electronic equivalent or such other medium or format as approved by the Canadian or Mexican customs administration for that purpose. ***Where the U.S. exporter is not the producer of the good, that exporter may complete and sign a Certificate on the basis of:***

(1) Its knowledge of whether the good qualifies as an originating good;

(2) Its reasonable reliance on the producer's written representation that the good qualifies as an originating good; or

(3) A completed and signed Certificate for the good voluntarily provided to the exporter by the producer.

a Although not explicitly stated in the regulations, it's common sense that a signed NAFTA certificate provided to the exporter by the producer does not relieve the exporter of his or her obligations of the certificate. The correct answer is "E".

✓ **JUST A SIDE NOTE:** If an item eligible for NAFTA is not originally claimed at the time of the importation, CBP will allow post-importation NAFTA claims for refunds within one year after the date of importation.

53. The phrase "goods wholly obtained or produced entirely in the territory of Canada, Mexico and/or the United States" refers to all of the following goods, EXCEPT:

A. mineral goods extracted in the territory of one or more of the NAFTA parties

B. live animals born and raised in the territory of one or more of the NAFTA parties

C. goods obtained from hunting, trapping or fishing in the territory of one or more of the NAFTA parties

D. goods produced on board factory ships from the goods referred to in subdivision (n)(v) provided such factory ships are registered or recorded with that NAFTA party and fly its flag;

E. vegetable goods, as such goods are defined in this schedule, imported in the territory of one or more of the NAFTA parties

As per HTSUS, General Note 12 (NAFTA) (n):

(n) As used in subdivision (b)(i) of this note, the phrase "goods wholly obtained or produced entirely in the territory of Canada, Mexico and/or the United States" means--

(i) mineral goods extracted in the territory of one or more of the NAFTA parties;

(ii) vegetable goods, as such goods are defined in this schedule, harvested in the territory of one or more of the NAFTA parties;

(iii) live animals born and raised in the territory of one or more of the NAFTA parties;

(iv) goods obtained from hunting, trapping or fishing in the territory of one or more of the NAFTA parties;

(v) goods (fish, shellfish and other marine life) taken from the sea by vessels registered or recorded with a NAFTA party and flying its flag;

(vi) goods produced on board factory ships from the goods referred to in subdivision (n)(v) provided such factory ships are registered or recorded with that NAFTA party and fly its flag;

(vii) goods taken by a NAFTA party or a person of a NAFTA party from the seabed or beneath the seabed outside territorial waters, provided that a NAFTA party has rights to exploit such seabed;

(viii) goods taken from outer space, provided such goods are obtained by a NAFTA party or a person of a NAFTA party and not processed outside the NAFTA parties;

(ix) waste and scrap derived from-- ... ...

"Imported" (i.e. not harvested) vegetable goods are not meant to qualify as "goods wholly obtained or produced entirely in the territory Canada, Mexico and/or the United States" (i.e. NAFTA). The correct answer is "E".

54. Which Country would qualify under the African Growth and Opportunity Act (AGOA)?

A. Barbados

B. Republic of Togo

C. Trinidad

D. Tobago

E. Jordon

 As per HTSUS, General Note 16 (AGOA) (a):

16 Products of Countries Designated as Beneficiary Countries under the African Growth and Opportunity Act (AGOA).

(a) The following sub-Saharan African countries, having been designated as beneficiary sub-Saharan African countries for purposes of the African Growth and Opportunity Act (AGOA), have met the requirements of the AGOA *and, therefore, are to be afforded the tariff treatment provided in this note, shall be treated as beneficiary sub-Saharan African countries for purposes of this note:*

Republic of Angola
Republic of Benin
Republic of Botswana
Burkina Faso

Republic of Cameroon
Republic of Cape Verde Federal
Republic of Chad
Union of the Comoros
Republic of Congo
Republic of Côte d'Ivoire
Republic of Djibouti
Ethiopia
Gabonese Republic
Republic of Ghana
Republic of Guinea
Republic of Kenya
Kingdom of Lesotho
Republic of Liberia
Republic of Madagascar (Madagascar)
Republic of Mali (Mali)
Republic of Malawi
Islamic Republic of Mauritania
Republic of Mauritius
Republic of Mozambique
Republic of Namibia
Republic of Niger
Republic of Nigeria
Republic of Rwanda
Democratic Republic of Sao Tome and Principe
Republic of Senegal
Republic of Seychelles
Republic of Sierra Leone
Republic of South Africa
Republic of Guinea-Bissau (Guinea-Bissau)
United Republic of Tanzania
Republic of Togo
Republic of Uganda
Republic of Zambia

 All AGOA qualifying countries are listed here. The correct answer is "B".

✓ **JUST A SIDE NOTE:** The AGOA, a U.S. government program, was enacted in the year 2000, and has been renewed until at least 2025.

55. With respect to Mexico, the term territory means all of the following except:

A. the states of the Federation and the Federal District

B. the islands, including the reefs and keys, in adjacent seas

C. the islands of Cayman and Revillagigedo situated in the Pacific Ocean

D. the continental shelf and the submarine shelf of such islands, keys and reefs

E. the waters of the territorial seas, in accordance with international law, and its interior maritime waters

 As per HTSUS, General Note 12 (NAFTA) (q):

*(q) For purposes of this note, the term **"territory" means**--*
... ...
*(ii) **with respect to Mexico,***

(A) the states of the Federation and the Federal District,
(B) the islands, including the reefs and keys, in adjacent seas,
*(C) **the islands of Guadalupe and Revillagigedo situated in the Pacific Ocean,***
(D) the continental shelf and the submarine shelf of such islands, keys and reefs,
(E) the waters of the territorial seas, in accordance with international law, and its interior maritime waters,
(F) the space located above the national territory, in accordance with international law, and
(G) any areas beyond the territorial seas of Mexico within which, in accordance with international law, including the United Nations Convention on the Law of the Sea, and its domestic law, Mexico may exercise rights with respect to the seabed and subsoil and their natural resources; and
... ...

NAFTA Mexican territory includes the islands of "Guadalupe" and "Revillagigedo", NOT the "Cayman" Islands. The correct answer is "C".

✓ **JUST A SIDE NOTE:** The Cayman Islands are located in the Caribbean Sea, and are considered a territory of Great Britain.

56. How long does the importer have to claim preferential tariff treatment on an originating good if preferential tariff treatment was not claimed at importation?

A. Within 5 days after the date of importation

B. Within 90 days after the date of importation

C. Within one year after the date of importation

D. Within 60 days after the date of importation

E. Within 30 days after the date of importation

 As per 19 CFR 181.31:

Notwithstanding any other available remedy, including the right to amend an entry so long as liquidation of the entry has not become final, ***where a good would have qualified as an originating good when it was imported into the United States but no claim for preferential tariff treatment on that originating good was made at that time under §181.21(a) of this part, the importer of that good may file a claim for a refund of any excess duties at any time within one year after the date of importation*** *of the good in accordance with the procedures set forth in §181.32 of this part. Subject to the provisions of §181.23 of this part, Customs may refund any excess duties by liquidation or reliquidation of the entry covering the good in accordance with §181.33(c) of this part.*

a The exam question does not specify for which free trade program the post-importation duty refund claim would be for. The above-mentioned CFR excerpt refers to NAFTA, however the one year post-importation claim window applies also to the free trade agreements for Chile, Dominican Republic, Oman, Peru, Korea, Panama, and Colombia. The correct answer is "C".

✔ **NOTE:** Generally speaking, the post-importation claim should include the four following elements.

(1) A written or electronic declaration or statement stating that the good was an originating good at the time of importation and setting forth the number and date of the entry or entries covering the good;

(2) A copy of a written or electronic certification demonstrating that the good qualifies for preferential tariff treatment;

(3) A written statement indicating whether the importer of the good provided a copy of the entry summary or equivalent documentation to any other person. If such documentation was so provided, the statement must identify each recipient by name, CBP identification number, and address and must specify the date on which the documentation was provided; and

(4) A written statement indicating whether or not any person has filed a protest relating to the good under any provision of law; and if any such protest has been filed, the statement must identify the protest by number and date.

57. The NAFTA de minimis provision allows for non-originating materials that do not satisfy the required tariff shift when incorporated into a finished textile product to be disregarded when determining NAFTA eligibility, IF:

A. **The value of the materials is not more than 7 percent of the value of the good.**

B. **The total weight of those components or materials is not more than 7 percent of the total weight of the good.**

C. **The value of the materials is more than 7 percent of the value of the good.**

D. **The total weight of those components or materials is more than 7 percent of the total weight of the good.**

E. **The value of the materials is more than 15 percent of the value of the goods**

As per 19 CFR 102.13(c):

102.13 De Minimis.

... ...

(c) Foreign components or materials that do not undergo the applicable change in tariff classification** set out in §102.21 or satisfy the other applicable requirements of that section **when incorporated into a textile or apparel product** covered by that section **shall be disregarded in determining the country of origin of the good if the total weight of those components or materials is not more than 7 percent of the total weight of the good.

Generally speaking, the De Minimis level (i.e. the allowable percentage of non-originating materials) for textile products is 7% of "weight", and for non-textile products 7% "value". The correct answer is "B".

✓ **JUST A SIDE NOTE:** "Textile or Apparel Products" means ANY item classified in Chapters 50 thru. 63 (i.e. HTSUS Section XI), AND other miscellaneous items, such as textile bags, textile footwear, etc., classified under the following headings and sub-headings:

3005.90
3921.12.15
3921.13.15
3921.90.2550
4202.12.40-80
4202.22.40-80
4202.32.40-95
4202.92.04-08
4202.92.15-30
4202.92.60-90
6405.20.60
6406.10.77
6406.10.90
6406.99.15

6501
6502
6504
6505.90
6601.10-99
7019.19.15
7019.19.28
7019.40-59
8708.21
8804
9113.90.40
9404.90
9612.10.9010

Category XI: Valuation

58. Which of the following is considered an assist and should be included in the entered value of headphones?

A. The cost of engineering plans produced in Las Vegas, Nevada for a headphone.

B. The cost of wiring purchased at full price by the foreign producer of headphones in Shenzhen, China.

C. The cost of copier paper supplied free of charge by the U.S. importer to the foreign producer of headphones in Shenzhen, China, for wedding invitations.

D. The cost of plastic earpiece components supplied free of charge by a U.S. importer to the foreign producer of headphones in Shenzhen, China.

E. The cost of computer training classes supplied free of charge by a U.S. importer to the foreign producer of headphones for use in training employees how to track time worked and leave.

 As per 19 CFR 152.102 (a):

(a) Assist. (1) ***"Assist" means any of the following if supplied directly or indirectly, and free of charge or at reduced cost, by the buyer of imported merchandise for use in connection with the production or the sale for export to the United States of the merchandise:***

(i) Materials, components, parts, and similar items incorporated in the imported merchandise.

(ii) Tools, dies, molds, and similar items used in the production of the imported merchandise.

(iii) Merchandise consumed in the production of the imported merchandise.

(iv) Engineering, development, artwork, design work, and plans and sketches that are undertaken elsewhere than in the United States and are necessary for the production of the imported merchandise.

Of the five options provided, the plastic earpiece components are the only free-of-charge/discounted, non-US design work items directly attributable to the production of the headphones. The correct answer is "D".

✓ **JUST A SIDE NOTE:** The purpose, in spirit, of adding any assist value to an import's invoice value is to help prevent the under-valuation of the import.

59. Which statement is true?

A. Interest on overdue bills will be assessed on the delinquent principal amount by 60-day periods. No interest charge will be assessed for the 60-day period in which the payment is actually received at the "Send Payment To" location designated on the bill.

B. Imported merchandise may not be appraised on the basis of, the price of merchandise in the domestic market of the country of exportation.

C. For the purpose of the entry of theatrical scenery, properties and apparel under subheading 9817.00.98, Harmonized Tariff Schedule of the United States, animals imported for use or exhibition in theaters or menageries may not be classified as theatrical properties.

D. A person transacting business in connection with entry or clearance of vessels or other regulation of vessels under the navigation laws is required to be licensed as a broker.

E. For purposes of administering quotas, "official office hours" shall mean 8:30 a.m. to 4:30 a.m. in all time zones.

 As per 19 CFR 152.108(c):

152.108 Unacceptable bases of appraisement.

For the purposes of this subpart, ***imported merchandise may not be appraised on the basis of:***

(a) The selling price in the United States of merchandise produced in the United States;

(b) A system that provides for the appraisement of imported merchandise at the higher of two alternative values;

(c) The price of merchandise in the domestic market of the country of exportation;

(d) A cost of production, other than a value determined under §152.106 for merchandise that is identical merchandise, or similar merchandise, to the merchandise being appraised;

(e) The price of merchandise for export to a country other than the United States;

(f) Minimum values for appraisement;

(g) Arbitrary or fictitious values.

a In regards to multiple choice "A", interest on overdue bills will be assessed on the delinquent principal amount by 30-day periods (Ref: 19 CFR 24.3a(c)). In regards to "C", neither the Chapter 98 Notes, nor the sub-heading 9817.00.98 state that animals may not be classified as theatrical properties (Ref: HTSUS Chapter 98). In regards to "D", a person transacting business in connection with entry or clearance of vessels or other regulation of vessels under the navigation laws is not required to be licensed as a broker (Ref: 19 CFR 111.2(a)). In regards to "E", CBP "hours of business" are 8:30 to 5:00 (Ref: 19 CFR 101.6). The correct answer is "B".

60. Which of the following is NOT an assist?

A. Materials, components, parts, and similar items incorporated in the imported merchandise that are supplied directly and free of charge by the buyer of the imported merchandise.

B. Tools, dies, molds, and similar items used in the production of the imported merchandise that are supplied indirectly and at a reduced cost by the buyer of the imported merchandise.

C. Engineering, development, artwork, design work, and plans and sketches that are undertaken elsewhere than in the United States and are necessary for the production of the imported merchandise that are supplied directly and free of charge by the buyer of the imported merchandise.

D. Merchandise consumed in the production of the imported merchandise that are supplied indirectly and at a reduced cost by the buyer of the imported merchandise.

E. Merchandise consumed in the production of the imported merchandise that are supplied directly and free of charge by the seller of the imported merchandise.

As per 19 CFR 152.102 (a):

(a) Assist. (1) "Assist" means any of the following if supplied directly or indirectly, and free of charge or at reduced cost, by the buyer of imported merchandise for use in connection with the production or the sale for export to the United States of the merchandise:

(i) Materials, components, parts, and similar items incorporated in the imported merchandise.

(ii) Tools, dies, molds, and similar items used in the production of the imported merchandise.

(iii) Merchandise consumed in the production of the imported merchandise.

(iv) Engineering, development, artwork, design work, and plans and sketches that are undertaken elsewhere than in the United States and are necessary for the production of the imported merchandise.

"Seller"-provided (as opposed to importer-provided) items used in production are NOT considered assists. Such costs are just regular seller/exporter cost of goods sold. The correct answer is "E".

✓ **JUST A SIDE NOTE:** Import "assists" are not at all illegal. However, they must be reported by being added to the transaction value (i.e. the price actually paid or payable) of the import.

61. "Generally accepted accounting principles" refers to any generally recognized consensus or substantial authoritative support regarding all of the following, EXCEPT:

A. Which economic resources and obligations should be recorded as assets and liabilities

B. Which changes in assets and liabilities should be recorded

C. How the assets and liabilities and changes in them should be measured

D. What information should not be disclosed and how it should be disclosed

E. Which financial statements should be prepared

 As per 19 CFR 152.102 (c):

(c) Generally accepted accounting principles. (1) ***"Generally accepted accounting principles" refers to any generally recognized consensus or substantial authoritative support regarding:***

(i) Which economic resources and obligations should be recorded as assets and liabilities;

(ii) Which changes in assets and liabilities should be recorded;

(iii) How the assets and liabilities and changes in them should be measured;

(iv) ***What information should be disclosed and how it should be disclosed****; and*

(v) Which financial statements should be prepared.

 The key word is the "not" in multiple choice and correct answer "D".

✓ **JUST A SIDE NOTE:** Generally Accepted Accounting Principles (GAAP) are the international standard guidelines for the practice of accounting.

Category XII: Fine and Penalties

62. Which is NOT a valid element to a prior disclosure per 19 CFR 162.74?

A. **Specifies the material false statements, omissions or acts including an explanation as to how and when they occurred.**

B. **Identification of the class or kind of merchandise involved in the violation.**

C. **Actual loss of duties, taxes, and fees must be tendered.**

D. **Provide any information or data unknown at the time of disclosure within 60 days of the initial disclosure date.**

E. **Identifies the importation or drawback claim included in the prior disclosure.**

 As per 19 CFR 162.74(b):

162.74 Prior disclosure.

... ...

(b) Disclosure of the circumstances of a violation. ***The term "discloses the circumstances of a violation" means the act of providing to Customs a statement orally or in writing that:***

(1) Identifies the class or kind of merchandise involved in the violation;

(2) Identifies the importation or drawback claim included in the disclosure by entry number, drawback claim number, or by indicating each concerned Customs port of entry and the approximate dates of entry or dates of drawback claims;

(3) Specifies the material false statements, omissions or acts including an explanation as to how and when they occurred; and

(4) Sets forth, to the best of the disclosing party's knowledge, the true and accurate information or data that should have been provided in the entry or drawback claim documents, ***and states that the disclosing party will provide any information or data unknown at the time of disclosure within 30 days of the initial disclosure date.*** *Extensions of the 30-day period may be requested by the disclosing party from the concerned Fines, Penalties, and Forfeitures Officer to enable the party to obtain the information or data.*

 The correct answer is "D".

✓ **JUST A SIDE NOTE:** The reason for the 30 day grace period is that timing is of the essence when it comes to the submittal of a prior disclosure. A prior disclosure affords the disclosing party favorable government treatment in the case of a violation, but the prior disclosure must be presented to CBP before the importer's knowledge of an investigation. A fully detailed report to CBP can be drafted after the initial prior disclosure communication.

63. Section 592(d) demands for actual losses of duty ordinarily are issued in connection with a ____________ action.

A. Liquidated damages

B. Seizure remission decision

C. Liquidation Notice

D. Penalty

E. Bill

 As per 19 CFR 171 Appendix B, (J) Section 592(d) Demands:

***Section 592(d) demands for actual losses of duty ordinarily are issued in connection with a penalty action**, or as a separate demand without an associated penalty action. In either case, information must be present establishing a violation of section 592(a). In those cases where the appropriate Customs field officer determines that issuance of a penalty under section 592 is not warranted (notwithstanding the presence of information establishing a violation of section 592(a)), but that circumstances do warrant issuance of a demand for payment of an actual loss of duty pursuant to section 592(d), the Customs field officer shall follow the procedures set forth in section 162.79b of the Customs Regulations (19 CFR 162.79b). Except in cases where less than one year remains before the statute of limitations may be raised as a defense, information copies of all section 592(d) demands should be sent to all concerned sureties and the importer of record if such party is not an alleged violator. Also, except in cases where less than one year remains before the statute of limitations may be raised as a defense, Customs will endeavor to issue all section 592(d) demands to concerned sureties and non-violator importers of record only after default by principals.*

 The correct answer is "D".

✓ **JUST A SIDE NOTE:** "Section 592" refers to "Section 592 of the Tariff Act of 1930", the act which "prohibits persons, by fraud, gross negligence or negligence, from entering or introducing, attempting to enter or introduce, or aiding and abetting the entry or introduction of merchandise into the commerce of the United States ."

Appendix B to Part 171 is titled "Customs Regulations, Guidelines for the Imposition and Mitigation of Penalties for Violations of 19 U.S.C. 1592". This "19 U.S.C. 1592" provides for laws for penalties for fraud, gross negligence, and negligence

"U.S.C. stands for United States Code". New laws are assigned a number and recorded in the U.S.C. The CFR, on the other hand, is subsequently created or amended to explain in detail these laws and how they will be implemented and enforced.

64. A broker counsels a client that certain gemstones are absolutely free of duty and need not be declared upon entry into the United States. The client arrives in the United States and fails to declare a quantity of gemstones worth $45,000. A penalty of $30,000 may be imposed against the broker for such counseling, yet not to exceed $30,000. What personal penalty would the client incur, under the provision of title 19, United States Code, section 1497?

A. None

B. $10,000

C. $15,000

D. $30,000

E. $45,000

As per 19 CFR 171, Appendix C, VI. Section 1641(d)(1)(D)—Counseling, Commanding, Inducing, Procuring or Knowingly Aiding and Abetting Violations by Any Other Person of Any Law Enforced by the Customs Service:

A. If the law violated by another moves only against property, a monetary penalty equal to the domestic value of such property or $30,000 whichever is less, may be imposed against the broker who counsels, commands or knowingly aids and abets such violation.

B. If the law violated provides for only a personal penalty against the actual violator, a penalty may be imposed against the broker in an amount equal to that assessed against the violator, but in no case can the penalty exceed $30,000.

C. If the broker is assessed a penalty under the statute violated by the other person, he may be assessed a penalty under this section in addition to any other penalties.

D. Examples of violations of this subsection:

***1. A broker counsels a client that certain gemstones are absolutely free of duty and need not be declared upon entry into the United States. The client arrives in the United States and fails to declare a quantity of gemstones worth $45,000. A penalty of $30,000 may be imposed against the broker for such counseling. The client would incur a personal penalty of $45,000** under the provisions of title 19, United States Code, section 1497, but the penalty against the broker cannot exceed $30,000.*

... ...

The exam question is taken from the regulations example verbatim. The correct answer is "E".

✓ **JUST A SIDE NOTE:** Appendix C to Part 171is titled "Customs Regulations Guidelines for the Imposition and Mitigation of Penalties for Violations of 19 U.S.C. 1641". This "19 U.S.C. 1641" provides for laws governing customs brokers.

65. The port director may review transactions for correctness and take action under his general authority to correct errors, including those in appraisement where appropriate, at the time of all the below except.

A. Liquidation of an entry

B. Voluntary reliquidation completed within 90 days after liquidation

C. Voluntary correction of an exaction within 180 days after the exaction was made

D. Reliquidation made pursuant to a valid protest covering the particular merchandise as to which a change is in order

E. Modification, pursuant to a valid protest, of a transaction or decision which is neither a liquidation nor reliquidation.

 As per 19 CFR 173.2:

The port director may review transactions for correctness, and take appropriate action under his general authority to correct errors, including those in appraisement where appropriate, at the time of:

(a) Liquidation of an entry;

(b) Voluntary reliquidation completed within 90 days after liquidation;

(c) Voluntary correction of an exaction within 90 days after the exaction was made;

(d) Reliquidation made pursuant to a valid protest covering the particular merchandise as to which a change is in order; or

(e) Modification, pursuant to a valid protest, of a transaction or decision which is neither a liquidation or reliquidation.

 An exaction by CBP may be corrected within "90 days" (i.e. NOT 180 days). The correct answer is "C".

✓ **JUST A SIDE NOTE:** Charges and exactions are "specific sums of money (other than ordinary customs duties) on imported merchandise".

66. The following motor vehicles may be imported by any person and do not have to be shown to be in compliance with emission requirements or modified before entitled to admissibility, except for which of the following:

A. Gasoline-fueled light-duty trucks and light-duty motor vehicles manufactured before January 1, 1968

B. Diesel-fueled light-duty motor vehicles manufactured before January 1, 1979

C. Diesel-fueled light-duty trucks manufactured before January 1, 1976

D. Motorcycles manufactured before January 1, 1978

E. Gasoline-fueled and diesel-fueled heavy-duty engines manufactured before January 1, 1970

 As per 19 CFR 12.73(e):

(e) Exemptions and exclusions from emission requirements based on age of vehicle. ***The following motor vehicles, except as shown, may be imported by any person and do not have to be shown to be in compliance with emission requirements or modified before entitled to admissibility:***

(1) Gasoline-fueled light-duty trucks and light-duty motor vehicles manufactured before January 1, 1968;

(2) Diesel-fueled light-duty motor vehicles manufactured before January 1, 1975;

(3) Diesel-fueled light-duty trucks manufactured before January 1, 1976;

(4) Motorcycles manufactured before January 1, 1978;

(5) Gasoline-fueled and diesel-fueled heavy-duty engines manufactured before January 1, 1970; and

(6) Motor vehicles not otherwise exempt from EPA emission requirements and more than 20 years old. Age is determined by subtracting the year of production (as opposed to model year) from the year of importation. The exemption under this subparagraph is available only if the vehicle is imported by an ICI.

 The exemption cut-off year for diesel-fueled light-duty vehicles is 1975, not 1979. The correct answer is "B".

✔ **JUST A SIDE NOTE:** This Section 73 of 19 CFR Part 12 works in the U.S. Environmental Protection Agency (EPA) emission requirements. The EPA's complete regulations are separately found in Title 40 CFR.

67. Where in 19 CFR would you find information relation to importations prohibited by Section 307, Tariff Act of 1930?

A. 19 CFR 10.107

B. 19 CFR 12.42

C. 19 CFR 127.32

D. 19 CFR 141.112

E. 19 CFR 192.12

As per 19 CFR 12.42:

Merchandise Produced By Convict, Forced, or Indentured Labor

§12.42 Findings of Commissioner of Customs.

(a) ***If any port director or other principal Customs officer has reason to believe that any class of merchandise that is being, or is likely to be, imported*** *into the United States is being produced, whether by mining, manufacture, or other means, in any foreign locality with the use of convict labor, forced labor, or indentured labor under penal sanctions, including forced child labor or indentured child labor under penal sanctions,* ***so as to come within the purview of section 307, Tariff Act of 1930****, he shall communicate his belief to the Commissioner of Customs. Every such communication shall contain or be accompanied by a statement of substantially the same information as is required in paragraph (b) of this section, if in the possession of the port director or other officer or readily available to him.*

… …

 The correct answer is "B".

✓ **JUST A SIDE NOTE:** "Section 307 of the Tariff Act of 1930" (19 U.S.C. 1307) is for the purpose of reducing child labor and forced labor.

68. All of the following articles are articles that may NOT be designated as an eligible article for purposes of the GSP, EXCEPT:

A. Watches, except as determined by the President pursuant to section 503(c)(1)(8) of the Trade Act of 1974, as amended

B. Import-sensitive steel articles

C. Import-sensitive electronic articles

D. Any agricultural product of chapters 2 through 52, inclusive, that is subject to a tariff-rate quota, if entered in a quantity in excess of the in-quota quantity for such product;

E. Textile and apparel articles which were eligible articles for purposes of this note on January 1, 1994

 As per HTSUS General Note 4(c) (Generalized System of Preferences):

(c) Articles provided for in a provision for which a rate of duty of "Free" appears in the "Special" subcolumn followed by the symbols "A" or "A" in parentheses are those designated by the President to be eligible articles for purposes of the GSP pursuant to section 503 of the Trade Act of 1974.* ***The following articles may not be designated as an eligible article for purposes of the GSP****:*

(i) textile and apparel articles which were NOT eligible articles for purposes of this note on January 1, 1994;

(ii) watches, except as determined by the President pursuant to section 503(c)(1)(B) of the Trade Act of 1974, as amended;

(iii) import-sensitive electronic articles;

(iv) import-sensitive steel articles;

(v) footwear, handbags, luggage, flat goods, work gloves and leather wearing apparel, the foregoing which were not eligible articles for purposes of the GSP on April 1, 1984;

(vi) import-sensitive semimanufactured and manufactured glass products;

(vii) any agricultural product of chapters 2 through 52, inclusive, that is subject to a tariff-rate quota, if entered in a quantity in excess of the in-quota quantity for such product; and

(viii) any other articles which the President determines to be import-sensitive in the context of the GSP.

 "NOT" is the key word that determines that the correct answer is "E".

✓ **INTERESTINGLY ENOUGH:** On this date, January 1, 1994, GSP eligibility for Mexico was replaced by NAFTA eligibility.

69. Which statement is TRUE?

A. "Guaranteeing association" means an association approved by the Office of Trade to guarantee the payment of obligations under carnets covering merchandise entering the Customs territory of the United States under a Customs Convention or multilateral Agreement to which the United States has acceded.

B. The importation into the United States of plants and plant products is subject to regulations and orders of the Food and Drug Administration. Customs officers and employees shall perform such functions as are necessary or proper to carry out such regulations and orders.

C. Any packages containing merchandise subject to an absolute quota, which is filled shall be returned to the postmaster for return to the sender immediately as undeliverable mail.

D. Unless a formal entry or entry by appraisement is required, a mail entry on Customs Form 7501 shall be issued and forwarded with the package to the postmaster for delivery to the addressee.

E. Under the Trade Facilitation and Trade Enforcement Act of 2015, the port director shall pass free of duty and tax any shipment of merchandise, as defined in § 101.1, imported by one person per week and having a fair retail value, in the country of shipment not exceeding $200, unless he has reason to believe that the shipment is one of several lots covered by a single order or contract and that it was sent separately for the express purpose of securing free entry therefore or of avoiding compliance with any pertinent law or regulation.

As per 19 CFR 114.1(c), 19 CFR 12.10, 19 CFR 132.22, 19 CFR 132.24, & 19 CFR 10.151:

114.1 Definitions.
... ...
(c) Guaranteeing association. "Guaranteeing association" means an association ***approved by the Commissioner*** *to guarantee the payment of obligations under carnets covering merchandise entering the Customs territory of the United States under a Customs Convention* ***or bilateral Agreement*** *to which the United States has acceded.*

12.10 Regulations and orders of the Department of Agriculture.
The importation into the United States of plants and plant products is subject to regulations and orders of the ***Department of Agriculture*** *restricting or prohibiting the importation of such plants and plant products. ... ...*

132.22 When quota is filled.
Any packages containing merchandise subject to an absolute quota which is filled shall be returned to the postmaster for return to the sender immediately as undeliverable mail. The addressee will be notified on Customs Form 3509 or in any other appropriate manner that entry has been denied because the quota is filled.

132.24 Entry.
Unless a formal entry or entry by appraisement is required, a mail entry on ***Customs Form 3419*** *shall be issued and forwarded with the package to the postmaster for delivery to the addressee and collection of any duties in the same manner as for any other mail package subject to Customs treatment.*

10.151 Importations not over $800.
Subject to the conditions in §10.153 of this part, the port director shall pass free of duty and tax any shipment of merchandise, as defined in §101.1 of this chapter, imported by one person ***on one day*** *having a fair retail value, as evidenced by an oral declaration or the bill of lading (or other document filed as the entry) or manifest listing each bill of lading, in the country of shipment* ***not exceeding $800****, ...*

The only correct statement and answer is multiple choice "C".

70. If merchandise is withheld from release by CBP due to an active withhold release order, an importer has up to __________ after the article was imported to provide information to CBP to contend that its goods were not mined, produced, or manufactured with any form of labor specified in section 307, Tariff Act of 1930.

A. **1 month**
B. **6 months**
C. **3 months**
D. **2 months**
E. **12 months**

As per 19 CFR 12.43(a):

2.43 Proof of admissibility.

(a) If an importer of any article detained under §12.42(e) or (g) desires to contend that the article was not mined, produced, or manufactured in any part with the use of a class of labor specified in section 307, Tariff Act of 1930, ***he shall submit to the Commissioner of Customs within 3 months after the date the article was imported a certificate of origin****, or its electronic equivalent, in the form set forth below, signed by the foreign seller or owner of the article. If the article was mined, produced, or manufactured wholly or in part in a country other than that from which it was exported to the United States, an additional certificate, or its electronic equivalent, in such form and signed by the last owner or seller in such other country, substituting the facts of transportation from such other country for the statements with respect to shipment from the country of exportation, shall be so submitted.*

Certificate of Origin
I, ________, foreign seller or owner of the merchandise hereinafter described, certify that such merchandise, consisting of ________ (Quantity) of ________ (Description) in __________ (Number and kind of packages) bearing the following marks and numbers ______ was mined, produced, or manufactured by ________ (Name) at or near ________, and was laden on board ___________ (Carrier to the United States) at ________ (Place of lading) (Place of final departure from country of exportation) which departed from on ______; (Date); and that __________ (Class of labor specified in finding) was not employed in any stage of the mining, production, or manufacture of the merchandise or of any component thereof.

Dated ______

(Signature)

The importer has 3 months to certify that the goods were not obtained through child or forced labor. The correct answer is "C".

✔ **JUST A SIDE NOTE:** As per 19 CFR 12.42(h):

(h) The following findings made under the authority of section 307, Tariff Act of 1930 are currently in effect with respect to the merchandise listed below:

Merchandise	Country	T.D.
Furniture, clothes hampers, and palm leaf bags	Ciudad Victoria, Tamaulipas, Mexico	53408 54725

71. Importation is prohibited, except as authorized by the issuance of a permit by the Director, U.S. Fish and Wildlife Service, for all the below, EXCEPT:

A. Any species of European rabbit the genus Oryctolagus
B. Any species of Indian wild dog, red dog, or dhole of the genus Cuon
C. Any live specimens or egg of the species of so-called "pink starling" or "rosy pastor" Sturnus roseus
D. Any live fish or viable eggs of the family Clariidae
E. Any species of the so-called Bumblebee bat

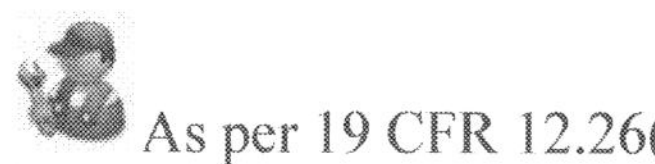
As per 19 CFR 12.26(a):

12.26 Importations of wild animals, fish, amphibians, reptiles, mollusks, and crustaceans; prohibited and endangered and threatened species; designated ports of entry; permits required.

(a)(1) The importation into the United States, the Commonwealth of Puerto Rico, and the territories and possessions of the United States of live specimens of:

(i) Any species of the so-called "flying fox" or fruit bat of the genus Pteropus;

(ii) Any species of mongoose or meerkat of the genera Atilax, Cynictis, Helogale, Herpestes, Ichneumia, Mungos, and Suricata;

(iii) ***Any species of European rabbit the genus Oryctolagus;***

(iv) ***Any species of Indian wild dog, red dog, or dhole of the genus Cuon;***

(v) Any species of multimammate rat or mouse of the genus Mastomys;

(vi) ***Any live specimens or egg of the species of so-called "pink starling" or "rosy pastor" Sturnus roseus;***

(vii) The species of dioch (including the subspecies black-fronted, red-billed, or Sudan dioch) Quelea quelea;

(viii) Any species of Java sparrow, Padda oryzivora;

(ix) The species of red-whiskered bulbul, Pycnonotus jocosus;

(x) ***Any live fish or viable eggs of the family Clariidae;***

(xi) Any other species of wild mammals, wild birds, fish (including mollusks and crustacea), amphibians, reptiles, or the offspring or eggs of any of the foregoing which the Secretary of the Interior may prescribe by regulations to be injurious to human beings, to the interest of agriculture, horticulture, forestry, or to wildlife or the wildlife resources of the United States, is prohibited, except as may be authorized by the issuance of a permit by the Director, U.S. Fish and Wildlife Service, U.S. Department of the Interior, Washington, DC ... ...

The importation of the bumblebee bat is not prohibited. However, unless otherwise authorized, the U.S. Fish and Wildlife Service Form 3-177 will be required at the port of entry. The correct answer is "E".

✓ **JUST A SIDE NOTE:** The Fish and Wildlife Service regulations are contained in Title 50 of the CFR.

72. In the case of nonconsumable vessel stores and equipment returned to the United States under subheading 9801.00.10, HTSUS, the entry summary may be made on CBP Form 3311, or its electronic equivalent. The entry summary on CBP Form 3311, or its electronic equivalent, must be executed in duplicate by the entrant and supported by the entry documentation required by §142.3 of this chapter. Before an entry summary on CBP Form 3311, or its electronic equivalent, may be accepted for nonconsumable vessel stores and equipment, the CBP officer must be satisfied with all of the following, EXCEPT:

A. The articles are products of the United States.

B. The articles have not been improved in condition or advanced in value while abroad

C. No drawback has been or will be paid

D. No duty equal to an internal revenue tax is payable under subheading 9801.00.80, HTSUS.

E. Duty equal to an internal revenue tax is payable under subheading 9801.00.80, HTSUS

 As per 19 CFR 10.1(h):

(h) Nonconsumable vessel stores and equipment. (1) In the case of nonconsumable vessel stores and equipment returned to the United States under subheading 9801.00.10, HTSUS, the entry summary may be made on CBP Form 3311, or its electronic equivalent. The entry summary on CBP Form 3311, or its electronic equivalent, must be executed in duplicate by the entrant and supported by the entry documentation required by §142.3 of this chapter. Before an entry summary on CBP Form 3311, or its electronic equivalent, may be accepted for nonconsumable vessel stores and equipment, the CBP officer must be satisfied that:

(i) The articles are products of the United States.

(ii) The articles have not been improved in condition or advanced in value while abroad.

(iii) No drawback has been or will be paid, and

(iv) ***No duty equal to an internal revenue tax is payable under subheading 9801.00.80, HTSUS.***

... ...

 The correct answer is "E".

✓ **JUST A SIDE NOTE:** CBP Form 3311 is the "Declaration for Free Entry of Returned American Products" statement.

73. A radiation generator unit is sent to Japan for repair under warranty and returned. The value of the equipment prior to repair is $45000. The value of the repairs is $4000. The equipment is properly classified under subheading 9022.90.0050, HTSUS, and subheading 9802.00.4040, HTSUS, is properly claimed. What is the merchandise processing fee?

A. **$0.00**

B. **$169.74**

C. **$25.00**

D. **$155.88**

E. **$13.86**

 As per 19 CFR 24.23(c):

(c) Exemptions and limitations. (1) ***The ad valorem fee, surcharge****, and specific fees provided for under paragraphs (b)(1) and (b)(2)* ***of this section will not apply to:***

(i) Except as provided in paragraph (c)(2) of this section, ***articles provided for in chapter 98****, Harmonized Tariff Schedule of the United States (HTSUS; 19 U.S.C. 1202);*

(ii) Products of insular possessions of the U.S. (General Note 3(a)(iv), HTSUS);

(iii) Products of beneficiary countries under the Caribbean Basin Economic Recovery Act (General Note 7, HTSUS);

(iv) Products of least-developed beneficiary developing countries (General Note 4(b)(i), HTSUS); and

(v) Merchandise described in General Note 19, HTSUS, merchandise released under 19 U.S.C. 1321, and merchandise imported by mail.

... ...

Although "duty" will be assessed for the $4000 in repairs at the duty rate applicable to the classification 9022.90.0050, the "Merchandise Processing Fee" for this Chapter 98 customs entry will not be assessed due to the above-mentioned exemption. The correct answer is "A".

✓ **JUST A SIDE NOTE:** The chapter 98 classifications that are not exempt from the Merchandise Processing Fee (MPF) rate of .003464 are HTSUS 9802.00.60 and 9802.00.80, which provide for articles of metal exported for further processing, and certain articles exported for simple assembly abroad respectively.

74. The person claiming a certification of exemption from entry for undeliverable articles under General Note 3(e), HTSUS, is subject to the following conditions, EXCEPT:

A. The merchandise was intended to be exported to a foreign country
B. The merchandise is being returned within 45 days of departure from the United States
C. The merchandise did not leave the custody of the carrier or foreign customs
D. The merchandise is being returned to the United States because it was undeliverable to the foreign consignee.
E. The merchandise was sent abroad to receive benefit from, or fulfill obligations to, the United States as a result of exportation.

 As per 19 CFR 141.4(c):

(c) Undeliverable articles. The exemption from entry for undeliverable articles under General Note 3(e), HTSUS, is subject to the following conditions:

(1) The person claiming the exemption must submit a certification (documentary or electronic) that:

(i) The merchandise was intended to be exported to a foreign country;

(ii) The merchandise is being returned within 45 days of departure from the United States;

(iii) The merchandise did not leave the custody of the carrier or foreign customs;

(iv) The merchandise is being returned to the United States because it was undeliverable to the foreign consignee; and

(v) ***The merchandise was not sent abroad to receive benefit from, or fulfill obligations to, the United States as a result of exportation.***

(2) Upon request by CBP, the person claiming the exemption shall provide evidence required to support the claim for exemption.

 Yet another "NOT" gotcha attempt by exam writer. The correct answer is "E".

✓ **JUST A SIDE NOTE:** Below is an excerpt from the above-referenced HTSUS General Note 3(e):

(e) Exemptions. For the purposes of general note 1--

(i) corpses, together with their coffins and accompanying flowers,

(ii) telecommunications transmissions,

(iii) records, diagrams and other data with regard to any business, engineering or exploration operation whether on paper, cards, photographs, blueprints, tapes or other media,

(iv) articles returned from space within the purview of section 484a of the Tariff Act of 1930,

(v) articles exported from the United States which are returned within 45 days after such exportation from the United States as undeliverable and which have not left the custody of the carrier or foreign customs service, ...

75. Which of the following operations performed abroad would not be regarded as an assembly operation?

A. Laminating
B. Sewing
C. Mixing or Combining of liquids
D. Gluing
E. Welding

 As per 19 CFR 10.16(a):

10.16 Assembly abroad.

(a) Assembly operations. The assembly operations performed abroad may consist of any method used to join or fit together solid components, such as welding, soldering, riveting, force fitting, gluing, laminating, sewing, or the use of fasteners, and may be preceded, accompanied, or followed by operations incidental to the assembly as illustrated in paragraph (b) of this section. ***The mixing or combining of liquids, gases, chemicals, food ingredients, and amorphous solids with each other or with solid components is not regarded as an assembly.***

Example 1. A television yoke is assembled abroad from American-made magnet wire. In the foreign assembly plant the wire is despooled and wound into a coil, the wire cut from the spool, and the coil united with other components, including a terminal panel and housing which are also American-made. The completed article upon importation would be subject to the ad valorem rate of duty applicable to television parts upon the value of the yoke less the cost or value of the American-made wire, terminal panel and housing, assembled therein. The winding and cutting of the wire are either assembly steps or steps incidental to assembly.

Example 2. An aluminum electrolytic capacitor is assembled abroad from American-made aluminum foil, paper, tape, and Mylar film. In the foreign assembly plant the aluminum foil is trimmed to the desired width, cut to the desired length, interleaved with paper, which may or may not be cut to length or despooled from a continuous length, and rolled into a cylinder wherein the foil and paper are cut and a section of sealing tape fastened to the surface to prevent these components from unwinding. Wire or other electric connectors are bonded at appropriate intervals to the aluminum foil of the cylinder which is then inserted into a metal can, and the ends closed with a protective washer. As imported, the capacitor is subject to the ad valorem rate of duty applicable to capacitors upon the value less the cost or value of the American-made foil, paper, tape, and Mylar film. The operations performed on these components are all either assembly steps or steps incidental to assembly.

Example 3. The manufacture abroad of cloth on a loom using thread or yarn exported from the United States on spools, cops, or pirns is not considered an assembly but a weaving operation, and the thread or yarn does not qualify for the exemption. However, American-made thread used to sew buttons or garment components is qualified for the exemption because it is used in an operation involving the assembly of solid components.

 The simple mixing or combining of materials is not regarded as "assembly" abroad. The correct answer is "C".

✔ **JUST A SIDE NOTE:** Articles assembled abroad from U.S. components are eligible for partial exemption from duties by utilization of HTSUS 9802.00.80 (i.e. "a duty upon the full value of the imported article, less the cost or value of such products of the United States").

76. Any person outside the Customs Service who has reason to believe that any merchandise produced whether by mining, manufacture, or other means, in any foreign locality with the use of convict labor, forced labor, or indentured labor under penal sanctions, is likely to be, imported into the United States and that merchandise of the same class is being produced in the United States in such quantities as to meet the consumptive demands of the United States may communicate his belief to any port director or the Commissioner of Customs. Every such communication shall contain, or be accompanied by all of the below, EXCEPT:

A. a full statement of the reasons for the belief

B. a detailed description or sample of the merchandise

C. all pertinent facts obtainable as to the production of the merchandise abroad

D. if the foreign merchandise is believed to be mined, produced or manufactured with forced labor or indentured labor under penal sanctions include detailed information as to the production and consumption of the particular class of merchandise in the United States and the names and addresses of domestic producers likely to be interested in the matter

E. location of foreign mining, production or manufacture at issue

 As per 19 CFR 12.42(b):

(b) Any person outside the Customs Service who has reason to believe that merchandise produced in the circumstances mentioned in paragraph (a) of this section is being, or is likely to be, imported into the United States and, if the production is with the use of forced labor or indentured labor under penal sanctions, that merchandise of the same class is being produced in the United States in such quantities as to meet the consumptive demands of the United States may communicate his belief to any port director or the Commissioner of Customs. ***Every such communication shall contain, or be accompanied by, (1) a full statement of the reasons for the belief, (2) a detailed description or sample of the merchandise, and (3) all pertinent facts obtainable as to the production of the merchandise abroad. If the foreign merchandise is believed to be mined, produced, or manufactured with the use of forced labor or indentured labor under penal sanctions, such communication shall also contain (4) detailed information as to the production and consumption of the particular class of merchandise in the United States and the names and addresses of domestic producers likely to be interested in the matter.***

Reporting to CBP of the location of foreign mining, production or manufacture at issue is not required. The correct answer is "E".

✓ **JUST A SIDE NOTE:** Uncommon to all previous exams, this year's exam makes regular reference to the regulations pertaining to merchandise produced by convict, forced, or indentured labor (i.e. 19 CFR 12.42 & 12.43).

CATERGORY XIV: Foreign Trade Zones

77. After merchandise is warehoused, the importer has 5 years from what DATE to remove the merchandise, provided an extension was not granted by the port director?

A. **Release Date**

B. **Entry Summary Date**

C. **Exportation Date**

D. **Importation Date**

E. **Liquidation Date**

As per 19 CFR 146.64(d):

(d) Time limit. ***Merchandise may neither be placed nor remain in a Customs bonded warehouse after 5 years from the date of importation*** *of the merchandise.*

 The correct answer is "D".

.

✓ **JUST A SIDE NOTE:** Merchandise in a Foreign Trade Zone (FTZ) may be transferred from an FTZ for 1) exportation, 2) transport to a different port, 3) consumption (entry), or 4) (bonded) warehouse.

78. What is the time limit for physical removal from a foreign trade zone of merchandise that has been permitted for transfer to Customs territory?

A. Within 30 business days of issuance of a Customs permit.

B. Within 5 calendar days of issuance of a Customs permit.

C. Within 90 business days of issuance of a Customs permit.

D. Within 5 business days of issuance of a Customs permit.

E. None of the above.

 As per 19 CFR 146.71(c):

(c) Time limit. Except in the case of articles for use in a zone, merchandise for which a Customs permit for transfer to Customs territory has been issued must be physically removed from the zone ***within 5 working days of issuance of that permit.*** *The port director, upon request of the operator, may extend that period for good cause. Merchandise awaiting removal within the required time limit will not be further manipulated or manufactured in the zone, but will be segregated or otherwise identified by the operator as merchandise that has been constructively transferred to Customs territory.*

 The correct answer is "D".

✓ **JUST A SIDE NOTE:** CBP's website describes, in general, what products and activities are allowed in FTZ's:

The Foreign-Trade Zones Board may exclude from a zone any merchandise that is in its judgment detrimental to the public interest, health, or safety. The Board may place restrictions on certain types of merchandise, which would limit the zone status allowed, the kind of operation on the merchandise in a zone, the entry of the merchandise into the commerce, or similar transactions or activities.

Many products subject to an internal revenue tax may not be manufactured in a zone. These products include alcoholic beverages, products containing alcoholic beverages except domestic denatures distilled spirits, perfumes containing alcohol, tobacco products, firearms, and sugar. In addition, the manufacture of clock and watch movements is not permitted in a zone.

No retail trade of foreign merchandise may be conducted in a FTZ. However, foreign and domestic merchandise may be stored, examined, sampled, and exhibited in a zone.

79. The person with the right to make entry shall file a Customs entry or file an application for admission of the merchandise to the foreign trade zone on Customs Form 214 within ______ days after identifying an OVERAGE.

A. **5**

B. **7**

C. **10**

D. **15**

E. **30**

As per 19 CFR 146.53(d):

(d) Overage. The person with the right to make entry shall file, ***within 5 days after identification of an overage****, an application for admission of the merchandise to the zone on Customs Form 214 or file a Customs entry for the merchandise. If a Customs Form 214 or a Customs entry is not timely filed, and the port director has not granted an extension of the time provided, the merchandise shall be sent to general order.*

The correct answer is "A".

✓ **JUST A SIDE NOTE:** For regular, non-FTZ merchandise, if an import shipment has been sitting at the port for more than 15 days without a customs entry or in-bond transfer assigned to it, the import will enter into General Order (GO) status. If still unclaimed after 6 months in General Order, the shipment will legally be made available for public auction.

80. A CBP Form 7512 must be presented to CBP for .

A. merchandise to be withdrawn from a bonded warehouse for consumption

B. admission into a foreign trade zone

C. presentation of quota class merchandise withdrawn from continuous customs custody

D. a drawback claimant to claim manufacturing drawback on merchandise transferred from continuous customs custody

E. merchandise to be withdrawn from a bonded warehouse for immediate transportation, immediate exportation, or transportation and exportation

 As per 19 CFR 18.10:

18.10 Kinds of entry.

(a) The following entries and withdrawals may be made for merchandise to be transported in bond:

(1) Entry for immediate transportation without appraisement.

(2) Warehouse or rewarehouse ***withdrawal for transportation****.*

(3) Warehouse or rewarehouse ***withdrawal for exportation or for transportation and exportation.***

(4) Entry for transportation and exportation.

(5) Entry for exportation.

(b) The copy of each entry or withdrawal made in any of the classes named in paragraph (a) of this section which is retained in the office of the forwarding port director shall be signed by the party making the entry or withdrawal. In the case of shipments to the Virgin Islands (U.S.) under paragraph (a), (3), (4), or (5) of this section, one additional copy of the entry or withdrawal on ***Customs Form 7512 shall be filed*** *and shall be mailed by the receiving port director to the port director, Charlotte Amalie, St. Thomas, Virgin Island (U.S.). Before shipping merchandise in bond to another port for the purpose of warehousing or rewarehousing, the shipper should ascertain whether warehouse facilities are available at the intended port of destination.*

 The correct answer is "E".

✓ **JUST A SIDE NOTE:** Essentially, CBP Form 7512 is a carrier's request to CBP to move in-bond items to another port or to export.

Book 1 Part 12

Exam with Broker Commentary

April 2016 Customs Broker License Examination

This section of the study guide analyzes an actual customs broker exam. It presents the actual question and its multiple choices. For HTSUS classification questions, the author of this book has included abbreviated HTSUS Article Descriptions notated directly to the right of each multiple choice classification for the student's convenience and ease of reference purposes. As necessary, and in proportion to the complexity of each particular exam question, an analysis of the question and path to the correct answer has been provided. Direct excerpts from the HTSUS, 19 CFR, etc. are also included as supporting points of reference for each answer as necessary. This exam (without commentary, etc.) and its answer key, as well as other previous customs exams can be downloaded directly from Customs' website at…

http://www.cbp.gov/document/publications/past-customs-broker-license-examinations-answer-keys

Exam Refs:

Harmonized Tariff Schedule of the United States
Title 19, Code of Federal Regulations
Customs and Trade Automated Interface Requirements (CATAIR)

- **Appendix B - Valid Codes**
- **Appendix D - Metric Conversion**
- **Appendix E - Valid Entry Numbers**
- **Appendix G - Common Errors**
- **Glossary of Terms**

Instructions for Preparation of CBP Form 7501
Right to Make Entry Directive, 3530-002A

Exam Breakdown by Subject:

Category I –	**Practical Exercises**	**Questions 1-3**
Category II –	**Powers of Attorney**	**Questions 4-6**
Category III –	**Entry**	**Questions 7-16**
Category IV –	**Foreign Trade Zones**	**Questions 17-20**
Category V –	**Classification**	**Questions 21-32**
Category VI –	**Valuation**	**Questions 33-38**
Category VII –	**Free Trade Agreements**	**Questions 39-44**
Category VIII –	**Drawback**	**Questions 45-49**
Category IX –	**Antidumping/Countervailing**	**Questions 50-52**
Category X –	**Marking**	**Questions 53-57**
Category XI –	**Broker Compliance**	**Questions 58-65**
Category XII –	**Fines and Penalties**	**Questions 66-71**
Category XIII –	**Bonds**	**Questions 72-76**
Category XIV –	**Intellectual Property Rights**	**Questions 77-80**

Please use the table below to answer questions 1-3.

Form Approved OMB No. 1651-0022
EXP. 10-31-2017

DEPARTMENT OF HOMELAND SECURITY
U.S. Customs and Border Protection
ENTRY SUMMARY

1. Filer Code/Entry No.	BMB-1007201-5
2. Entry Type	03 ABI/P
3. Summary Date	06/17/2015
4. Surety No.	201
5. Bond Type	8
6. Port Code	5301
7. Entry Date	06/17/2015
8. Importing Carrier	OOCL CANADA
9. Mode of Transport	11
10. Country of Origin	TW
11. Import Date	06/10/2015
12. B/L or AWB No.	OOLU 2534567390
13. Manufacturer ID	TWCHACHU301TAI
14. Exporting Country	TW
15. Export Date	05/28/2015
16. I.T. No.	V1622934183
17. I.T. Date	
18. Missing Docs	
19. Foreign Port of Lading	52809
20. U.S. Port of Unlading	2709
21. Location of Goods/G.O. No.	S639 BNSF HOUSTON
22. Consignee No.	99-887766500
23. Importer No.	99-887766500
24. Reference No.	23-456789100
25. Ultimate Consignee Name and Address	City / State DE / Zip
26. Importer of Record Name and Address	PLASTIC CORPORATION OF NOWHERE, 7804 MARKET ST, City OCEANBREEZE, State FL, Zip 45678

27. Line No.	28. Description of Merchandise / 29. A. HTSUS No. B. ADA/CVD No.	30. A. Grossweight B. Manifest Qty.	31. Net Quantity in HTSUS Units	32. A. Entered Value B. CHGS C. Relationship	33. A. HTSUS Rate B. ADA/CVD Rate C. IRC Rate D. Visa No.	34. Duty and I.R. Tax (Dollars / Cents)
	2000 PCS					
001	POLY(VINYL ALCOHOLS)					
TW	3905.30.0000	41600	40000 KG	92976	3.2%	2975.23
	TSCA:P			C5784		
	A-583-841-001				0.0308	2863.66
	MERCHANDISE PROCESSING FEE				0.3464%	322.07
	I.V. 98760.00					
	-NDC 5783.85	BLOCK 39 SUMMARY				
	E.V. 92976.15	MERCHANDISE PROCESSING FEE		499 322.07		
		HARBOR MAINT. FEE		501 116.22		

Other Fee Summary for Block 39: 2863.66 _____ ANTIDUMPING DUTY

35. Total Entered Value $ 92976.00

Total Other Fees $ 3301.95

CBP USE ONLY		TOTALS
A. LIQ CODE	B. Ascertained Duty	37. Duty 2975.23
REASON CODE	C. Ascertained Tax	38. Tax
	D. Ascertained Other	39. Other 3301.95
	E. Ascertained Total	40. Total 6277.18

36. DECLARATION OF IMPORTER OF RECORD (OWNER OR PURCHASER) OR AUTHORIZED AGENT

I declare that I am the ☐ importer of record and that the actual owner, purchaser, or consignee for CBP purposes is as shown above, OR ☐ owner or purchaser or agent thereof. I further declare that the merchandise ☐ was obtained pursuant to a purchase or agreement to purchase and that the prices set forth in the invoices are true, OR ☐ was not obtained pursuant to a purchase or agreement to purchase and the statements in the invoices as to value or price are true to the best of my knowledge and belief. I also declare that the statements in the documents herein filed fully disclose to the best of my knowledge and belief the true prices, values, quantities, rebates, drawbacks, fees, commissions, and royalties and are true and correct, and that all goods or services provided to the seller of the merchandise either free or at reduced cost are fully disclosed.
I will immediately furnish to the appropriate CBP officer any information showing a different statement of facts.

41. DECLARANT NAME | TITLE | SIGNATURE | DATE

42. Broker/Filer Information (Name, address, phone number)

43. Broker/Importer File No.

CBP Form 7501 (06/09)

1) In Block 2, "Entry Type", what does ABI/P represent?

a) ABI statement paid by check or cash
b) ABI statement paid via Automated Clearinghouse (ACH)
c) ABI statement paid on a periodic monthly basis
d) ABI summary not paid on statement
e) ABI statement paid via ACH for a "live" entry/entry summary

 As per CBP Form 7501 Instructions, BLOCK 2) ENTRY TYPE:

... ...

Automated Broker Interface (ABI) processing requires an ABI status indicator. This indicator must be recorded in the entry type code block. It is to be shown for those entry summaries with ABI status only, and must be shown in one of the following formats:

ABI/S = ABI statement paid by check or cash
ABI/A = ABI statement paid via Automated Clearinghouse (ACH)
ABI/P = ABI statement paid on a periodic monthly basis
ABI/N = ABI summary not paid on a statement

"ABI" stands for Automated Broker Interface. The "P" stands for Periodic (Monthly Statement). The correct answer is "c".

✓ **JUST A SIDE NOTE:** Periodic Monthly Statement (PMS) is a feature in Automated Commercial Environment (ACE) that allows importers and brokers flexibility to pay for all entries released in a month as a single payment, and as late as the 15th working day of the following month, interest free.

2) In "Other Fee Summary for Block 39", what is the collection code for Antidumping Duties?

a) 012
b) 013
c) 044
d) 055
e) 103

 As per CBP Form 7501 Instructions, OTHER FEE SUMMARY FOR BLOCK 39:

The applicable collection code must be indicated on the same line as the fee or other charge or exaction. Report the fees in the format below:

AD 012
CVD 013
Tea Fee 038
Misc. Interest 044
Beef Fee 053
Pork Fee 054
Honey Fee 055
Cotton Fee 056
Pecan Fee 057
Sugar Fee 079
Potato Fee 090
Mushroom Fee 103
Watermelon 104
Blueberry Fee 106
Avocado 107
Mango 108
Informal Entry MPF 311
Dutiable Mail Fee 496
Merchandise Processing Fee (MPF) 499
Manual Surcharge 500
Harbor Maintenance Fee (HMF) 501

a The "Other Fee Summary for Block 39" line should read "2863.66 012 ANTIDUMPING DUTY". The correct answer is "a".

✓ **JUST A SIDE NOTE:** The Merchandise Processing Fee (MPF) and Harbor Maintenance Fee (HMF) are also usually included in the same "Other Fee Summary for Block 39", though they are not for this exam entry summary.

3) If refunds, bills, or notices of extension or suspension of liquidation are sent to an individual or firm other than the importer of record, which block would be used to record the IRS, EIN, SSN, or CBP assigned number?

a) Block 13
b) Block 15
c) Block 22
d) Block 23
e) Block 24

 As per CBP Form 7501 Instructions, BLOCK 24) REFERENCE NUMBER:

BLOCK 24) REFERENCE NUMBER

***Record the IRS EIN, SSN, or CBP assigned number of the individual or firm to whom refunds, bills, or notices of extension or suspension of liquidation are to be sent (if other than the importer of record** and only when a CBP Form 4811 is on file). Proper format is listed under the instructions for Consignee Number. Do not use this block to record any other information.*

 The answer is "e".

✔ **JUST A SIDE NOTE:** The above-referenced CBP Form 4811 is simply a "Special Address Notification" form. Snapshot of which is below for your reference.

DEPARTMENT OF HOMELAND SECURITY

U.S. Customs and Border Protection

SPECIAL ADDRESS NOTIFICATION

I request that: (Mark only one code)

10 ☐ Bills, Refunds and Notices of Liquidation

40 ☐ Bills and Notices

34 ☐ Checks and Notices

20 ☐ Checks for Refunds or Drawback only

23 ☐ Bills and Checks

30 ☐ Bills Only

24 ☐ Notices of Liquidation only

be addressed to the undersigned in care of the agent whose Importer Number is shown below whenever it appears as Reference Number on an Entry Summary (CBP 7501) for which I am (my organization is) the Importer of Record.

Agent's Name ____________________ Agent's Number ____________ (Show hyphens)

My (organization's) Importer No. (Show hyphens)

☐ Principal
☐ Member of Firm
☐ __________ of the Corp.

(Signature) (Date) (Title)

Note: A Report of Importer Number (CBP 5106) must be on file for each Importer Number appearing on this form.

CBP Form 4811 (10/01)

4) What form is used for giving power of attorney to transact Customs business?

a) CBP Form 5291
b) CBP Form 3347
c) CBP Form 4647
d) CBP Form 368
e) CBP Form 7501

As per 19 CFR 141.32:

141.32 Form for power of attorney.

Customs Form 5291 may be used for giving power of attorney to transact Customs business. *If a Customs power of attorney is not on a Customs Form 5291, it shall be either a general power of attorney with unlimited authority or a limited power of attorney as explicit in its terms and executed in the same manner as a Customs Form 5291. The following is an example of an acceptable general power of attorney with unlimited authority:*

KNOW ALL MEN BY THESE PRESENTS, THAT

____

(Name of principal)

_____________________,

(State legal designation, such as corporation, individual, etc.) residing at ______________ and doing business under the laws of the State of ______, hereby appoints

(Name, legal designation, and address)

as a true and lawful agent and attorney of the principal named above with full power and authority to do and perform every lawful act and thing the said agent and attorney may deem requisite and necessary to be done for and on behalf of the said principal without limitation of any kind as fully as said principal could do if present and acting, and hereby ratify and confirm all that said agent and attorney shall lawfully do or cause to be done by virtue of these presents until and including ______, (date) or until notice of revocation in writing is duly given before that date.

Date __________, 20__;.

(Principal's signature)

The answer is "a".

✔ **JUST A SIDE NOTE:** Although the above-mentioned form may be used to assign a customs power of attorney for an importer, most customs brokerage operations create their own unique form and include their terms and conditions with the form.

5) Where a limited partnership is the Grantor of a power of attorney, ____________ must accompany the power of attorney.

a) a copy of the partnership agreement
b) CBP Form 7501
c) a nonnegotiable check for duties due to U.S. Customs and Border Protection
d) a copy of the articles of incorporation
e) fingerprint cards and proof of citizenship of the partners

 As per 19 CFR 141.39(a)(2):

141.39 Partnerships.

(a)(1) General. A power of attorney granted by a partnership shall state the names of all members of the partnership. One member of the partnership may execute a power of attorney in the name of the partnership for the transaction of all its Customs business.

(2) Limited partnership. A power of attorney granted by a limited partnership need only state the names of the general partners who have authority to bind the firm unless the partnership agreement provides otherwise. ***A copy of the partnership agreement must accompany the power of attorney.*** *For this purpose, a partnership or limited partnership means any business association recognized as such under the laws of the state where the association is organized.*

 The correct answer is "a".

✓ **JUST A SIDE NOTE:** Simply put, a "partnership agreement" (a.k.a. articles of partnership) is a legal contract between two or more parties that spells out the rights and obligations of the parties entering into the agreement.

6) A Customs Power of Attorney issued by a partnership shall be limited to _____ year(s).

a) 1
b) 5
c) 2
d) 10
e) unlimited

 As per 19 CFR 141.34:

141.34 Duration of power of attorney.

Powers of attorney issued by a partnership shall be limited to a period not to exceed 2 years from the date of execution. *All other powers of attorney may be granted for an unlimited period.*

 The correct answer is "c".

✓ **JUST A SIDE NOTE:** Although a Power of Attorney (POA) for a non-partnership organization may be granted for a limited time period, for a defined time period, or for a specific shipment referenced within the POA.

7) Absolute quota merchandise imported in excess of the admissible quantity may NOT be____________________.

a) held in a Foreign Trade Zone (FTZ) for the opening of the next quota period
b) held in a warehouse for the opening of the next quota period
c) exported
d) destroyed under CBP supervision
e) entered at a higher rate of duty

 As per 19 CFR 132.5(c):

(c) Disposition of excess merchandise. ***Merchandise imported in excess of either an absolute or a tariff-rate quota may be held for the opening of the next quota period by placing it in a foreign-trade zone or by entering it for warehouse, or it may be exported or destroyed under Customs supervision.***

There are several options for handling an import in excess of an "absolute quota", though entering it in at a higher duty rate is not one of those options. Entering a quota shipment in at a higher duty rate is only an option for a "tariff rate quota." The correct answer is "e".

✓ **JUST A SIDE NOTE:** An "absolute quota" is also referred to, and is the same thing as a "quantitative quota."

8) A work of fine art arrived at the Port of Miami and was admitted temporarily into the United States under chapter 98, subchapter XIII of the Harmonized Tariff Schedule of the United States. Eleven months later, the importer wants the work of art to remain in the United States under Chapter 98, Subchapter XIII for eight additional months and to be exported from the Port of Boston. What course of action should the importer take?

- **a) File a consumption entry**
- **b) File a written application for extension on CBPF 3173 to the Commissioner of CBP**
- **c) File a written application for extension on CBPF 3173 to the Port Director of Miami before the initial twelve months has lapsed**
- **d) File a written application for extension on CBPF 3173 after the twelve months has lapsed to the Director of Field Operations for the Port of Miami**
- **e) File a written application for extension on CBPF 3173 to the Port Director of Boston**

 As per 19 CFR 10.37:

10.37 Extension of time for exportation.

The period of time during which merchandise entered under bond under chapter 98, subchapter XIII, Harmonized Tariff Schedule of the United States (19 U.S.C. 1202), may remain in the customs territory of the United States, may be extended for not more than two further periods of 1 year each, or such shorter period as may be appropriate. Extensions may be granted by the director of the port where the entry was filed upon written application on CBP Form 3173*, provided the articles have not been exported or destroyed before the receipt of the application, and liquidated damages have not been assessed under the bond before receipt of the application. Any untimely request for an extension of time for exportation shall be referred to the Director, Commercial and Trade Facilitation Division, Office of International Trade, CBP Headquarters, for disposition. Any request for relief from a liquidated damage assessment in excess of a Fines, Penalties, and Forfeitures Officer's delegated authority shall be referred to the Director, Border Security and Trade Compliance Division, Office of International Trade, CBP Headquarters, for disposition. No extension of the period for which a carnet is valid shall be granted.*

 The correct answer is "c".

✓ **JUST A SIDE NOTE:** HTSUS 9813.00.70 is the classification for:

Works of the free fine arts, engravings, photographic pictures and philosophical and scientific apparatus brought into the United States by professional artists, lecturers or scientists arriving from abroad for use by them for exhibition and in illustration, promotion and encouragement of art, science or industry in the United States.

9) For merchandise entered under any temporary monthly entry program established by CBP before July 1, 1989, for the purpose of testing entry processing improvements, provided that those importations involve the same importer and exporter, the fee for processing merchandise for each day's importations at an individual port will be the lesser of the 0.3464 percent ad valorem merchandise processing fee and:

a) $25.00
b) $400.00
c) $425.00
d) $485.00
e) $500.00

 As per 19 CFR 24.23(d)(1):

(d) Aggregation of ad valorem fee. (1) ***Notwithstanding any other provision of this section, in the case of entries of merchandise made under any temporary monthly entry program established by CBP before July 1, 1989, for the purpose of testing entry processing improvements, the ad valorem fee charged under paragraph (b)(1)(i) of this section for each day's importations at an individual port will be the lesser of the following,*** *provided that those importations involve the same importer and exporter:*

(i) $400; or

(ii) The amount determined by applying the ad valorem rate under paragraph (b)(1)(i)(A) of this section to the total value of such daily importations.

 The correct answer is "b".

✔ **NOTE:** The above-referenced "paragraph (b)(1)(i)(A)" refers to the MPF rate of 0.3464 percent.

✔ **JUST A SIDE NOTE:** "Ad Valorem" means the duties or fees percentage rate is multiplied against the entered value of the item (as opposed to duty based on weight or surface area).

10) Bills resulting from dishonored checks or dishonored Automated Clearinghouse (ACH) transactions are due ______________.

a) within 2 days of the date of issuance of the bill
b) within 10 days of the date of issuance of the bill
c) within 15 days of the date of issuance of the bill
d) within 20 days of the date of issuance of the bill
e) within 30 days of the date of issuance of the bill

 As per 19 CFR 24.3(e):

(e) Except for bills resulting from dishonored checks or dishonored Automated Clearinghouse (ACH) transactions, all other bills for duties, taxes, fees, interest, or other charges are due and payable within 30 days of the date of issuance of the bill. ***Bills resulting from dishonored checks or dishonored ACH transactions are due within 15 days of the date of issuance of the bill.***

 The correct answer is "c".

✓ **JUST A SIDE NOTE:** Automated Clearinghouse (ACH) is simply a electronic method of payment between two parties. An ACH payment is relatively cheap and multiple payments can be batched together, as opposed to a wire transfer. If an entry is processed as an Automated Broker Interface (ABI) entry, then duties and fees may be paid by the customs broker or importer by ACH.

11) A prospective participant interested in transmitting data electronically through the Automated Broker Interface (ABI) must submit which of the following documents to CBP?

a) Power of attorney
b) Letter of intent
c) Custom's bond
d) Hold harmless agreement
e) Broker's license number

 As per 19 CFR 143.2:

143.2 Application.

A prospective participant in ABI shall submit a letter of intent *to the port director closest to his principal office, with a copy to the Assistant Commissioner, Information and Technology, or designee. The letter of intent shall set forth a commitment to develop, maintain and adhere to the performance requirements and operational standards of the ABI system in order to ensure the validity, integrity and confidentiality of the data transmitted. The letter of intent must also contain the following, as applicable:*

 The correct answer is "b".

✓ **JUST A SIDE NOTE:** The Letter of Intent must include the following items, as listed in section 143.2:

(a) A description of the computer hardware, communications and entry processing systems to be used and the estimated completion date of the programming;

(b) If the participant has offices in more than one location, the location of each office and the estimated start-up date for each office listed;

(c) The name(s) of the participant's principal management and contact person(s) regarding the system;

(d) If the system is being developed or supported by a data processing company, the data processing company's name and the contact person;

(e) The software vendor's name and the contact person; and

(f) The participant's entry filer code and average monthly volume.

12) Any person, whose protest has been denied, in whole or in part, may contest the denial by _____________.

a) filing a request for accelerated disposition with U.S. Customs and Border Protection
b) filing a request for further review of the protest
c) submitting an amended protest with the Port Director of New York within 180 days of the protest denial
d) filing a civil action in the United States Court of International Trade
e) filing a protest with U.S. Customs and Border Protection after 180 days of the protest denial

 As per 19 CFR 174.31:

Any person whose protest has been denied, in whole or in part, may contest the denial by filing a civil action in the United States Court of International Trade *in accordance with 28 U.S.C. 2632 within 180 days after*—

 The correct answer is "d".

✓ **JUST A SIDE NOTE:** Protests may be filed within 180 days after the entry liquidation date, or within 180 days after the Customs action that is being protested.

13) What is the timeframe to submit the adjusted summary along with payment of duties, taxes and fees once the quota has gone on hold and Headquarters has authorized release of merchandise?

a) within 5 working days after presentation
b) within 10 working days after presentation
c) within 5 working days after authorized release
d) within 10 working days after authorized release
e) any time after the authorization from Headquarters

 As per 19 CFR 132.13(a):

132.13 Quotas after opening.
(a) Procedure when nearing fulfillment. To secure for each importer the rightful quota priority and status for his quota-class merchandise, and to close the quota simultaneously at all ports of entry:

... ...

(iii) Quota Proration. When it is determined that entry summaries for consumption or withdrawals for consumption must be amended to permit only the quantity of tariff-rate and absolute quota merchandise determined to be within the quota, the entry summaries for consumption or withdrawals for consumption must be returned to the importer for adjustment. The time of presentation for quota purposes in that event shall be the same as the time of the initial presentation of the entry summaries for consumption or withdrawals for consumption or their electronic equivalents, provided:

(A) ***An adjusted entry summary for consumption, or withdrawals for consumption, or their electronic equivalents, with estimated duties attached, is deposited within 5 working days after Headquarters authorizes release of the merchandise****, and*

 The correct answer is “c”.

✔ **JUST A SIDE NOTE:** In general, when a quota reaches the threshold of 95% of its limit, Customs puts a hold on the quota. This is done to provide more of an equal opportunity for affected importers to make entry prior to the closing of the quota.

14) Which of the following circumstances requires a separate entry for any portion of a split shipment?

a) The importer pre-filed an entry with U.S. Customs and Border Protection
b) The portion of the shipment that arrived six calendar days after the first portion
c) The portion of the shipment that arrived at a different port and was transported in-bond to the port of destination where entry was made for the other portions of the shipment
d) The portion of merchandise that arrives twelve calendar days after the first portion
e) The portion arriving after the importer of record filed and was granted a special permit for immediate delivery when the first portion arrived

 As per 19 CFR 141.57(b):

141.57 Single entry for split shipments.

(a) At election of importer of record. At the election of the importer of record, ***Customs may process a split shipment****, pursuant to section 484(j)(2), Tariff Act of 1930 (19 U.S.C. 1484(j)(2)),* ***under a single entry, as prescribed under the procedures set forth in this section.***

(b) Split shipment defined. A "split shipment", for purposes of this section, means a shipment:

(1) Which may be accommodated on a single conveyance, and which is delivered to and accepted by a carrier in the exporting country under one bill of lading or waybill, and is thus intended by the importer of record to arrive in the United States as a single shipment;

(2) Which is thereafter divided by the carrier, acting on its own, into different portions which are transported and consigned to the same party in the United States; and

(3) Of which the first portion and all succeeding portions arrive at the same port of entry in the United States, as listed in the original bill of lading or waybill; and all the succeeding portions arrive at the port of entry within 10 calendar days of the date of the first portion. *If any portion of the shipment arrives at a different port, such portion must be transported in-bond to the port of destination where entry of the shipment is made.*

a The later portion of a split shipment must arrive within 10 days of the first portion in order for Customs to process both portions under a single entry. The multiple choice "d" scenario has the later portion arriving 12 days after the first portion, thus requiring a separate entry. The correct answer is "d".

✓ **JUST A SIDE NOTE:** A "split shipment" most often occurs when an airline does not have sufficient space to carry the entire shipment on one flight.

15) Dutiable merchandise imported and afterwards exported, even though duty thereon may have been paid on the first importation, is liable to duty on every subsequent importation into the Customs territory of the United States for:

a) Personal and household effects taken abroad by a resident of the United States and brought back on his or her return to this country
b) Automobiles and other vehicles taken abroad for noncommercial use
c) Articles exported for exhibition under certain conditions
d) Domestic animals taken abroad for temporary pasturage purposes and returned within 11 months
e) Articles exported under lease to a foreign manufacturer

As per 19 CFR 141.2:

141.2 Liability for duties on reimportation.

Dutiable merchandise imported and afterwards exported, even though duty thereon may have been paid on the first importation, is liable to duty on every subsequent importation into the Customs territory of the United States, but this does not apply to the following:

(a) Personal and household effects taken abroad by a resident of the United States and brought back on his return to this country (see §148.31 of this chapter);

(b) Professional books, implements, instruments, and tools of trade, occupation, or employment taken abroad by an individual and brought back on his return to this country (see §148.53 of this chapter);

(c) Automobiles and other vehicles taken abroad for noncommercial use (see §148.32 of this chapter);

... ...

(f) Articles exported for exhibition under certain conditions (see §§10.66 and 10.67 of this chapter);

(g) ***Domestic animals taken abroad for temporary pasturage purposes and returned within 8 months*** *(see §10.74 of this chapter);*

(h) Articles exported under lease to a foreign manufacturer (see §10.108 of this chapter); or

(i) Any other reimported articles for which free entry is specifically provided.

a Domestic animals taken abroad (e.g. Canada) for temporary pasturage for 8 months or less are not liable for duty on subsequent importations. If they are taken abroad for more than 8 months, as in the scenario for multiple choice "d", then they are dutiable. The correct answer is "d".

✓ **NOTE:** The actual exam copy was incorrectly written with the word "EXCEPT" at the end of this question, rendering the problem invalid. Thus, we have removed the word from this rendition of the exam problem.

16) What is the Shipping/Packaging Unit Code for Bulk Liquid?

a) BL
b) BJ
c) BU
d) LG
e) VL

 As per CATAIR – Appendix B, Shipping/Packaging Unit Codes:

TZ	*Tubes, In Bundle/Bunch/Truss*
VA	*Vat*
VG	*Bulk Gas (At 1031 MBAR and 15 degrees Celsius)*
VI	*Vial*
VL	***Bulk Liquid***
VO	*Bulk, Solid, Large Particles ("Nodules")*
VP	*Vacuum-packed*
VQ	*Bulk, Liquified Gas (At Normal Temperature)*
VR	*Bulk, Solid, Granular Particles ("Grains")*
VY	*Bulk, Solid, Fine Particles ("Powders")*
WB	*Wicker bottle*

 The correct answer is "e".

✓ **JUST A SIDE NOTE:** "CATAIR" stands for Customs (or CBP) and Trade Automated Interface Requirements. Basically speaking, it spells out how a customs broker can communicate electronically with CBP. It is technical in nature and mainly for persons working with customs brokerage-type software development.

Category IV: Foreign Trade Zones

17) What is the correct entry type code to be entered on an entry summary filed for Foreign Trade Zone (FTZ) consumption merchandise?

a) 03
b) 06
c) 21
d) 23
e) 61

As per Form 7501 Instructions, BLOCK 2) ENTRY TYPE:

BLOCK 2) ENTRY TYPE

Record the appropriate entry type code by selecting the two-digit code for the type of entry summary being filed. The first digit of the code identifies the general category of the entry (i.e., consumption = 0, informal = 1, warehouse = 2). The second digit further defines the specific processing type within the entry category. The following codes shall be used:

Consumption Entries	
Free and Dutiable	*01*
Quota/Visa	*02*
Antidumping/Countervailing Duty (AD/CVD)	*03*
Appraisement	*04*
Vessel Repair	*05*
Foreign Trade Zone Consumption	***06***
Quota/Visa and AD/CVD combinations	*07*
Duty Deferral	*08*
Informal Entries	
Free and Dutiable	*11*
Quota Other than textiles	*12*
Warehouse Entries	
Warehouse	*21*
Re-Warehouse	*22*
Temporary Importation Bond	*23*
… …	

The correct answer is "b".

✓**JUST A SIDE NOTE:** A "Foreign Trade Zone", though directly supervised by Customs, is considered to be outside U.S. Customs territory. It is also commonly referred to as a "Free Trade Zone".

18) Prior to any action within a Foreign Trade Zone (FTZ), the operator shall file with the port director an application for permission to manipulate, manufacture, exhibit, or destroy merchandise. Which Customs Form is used for that purpose?

a) Customs Form 214
b) Customs Form 216
c) Customs Form 300
d) Customs Form 4607
e) Customs Form 7512

 As per 19 CFR 146.52(a):

146.52 Manipulation, manufacture, exhibition or destruction; Customs Form 216.

(a) Application. ***Prior to any action, the operator shall file with the port director an application (or blanket application) on Customs Form 216 for permission to manipulate, manufacture, exhibit, or destroy merchandise in a zone.*** *After Customs approves the application (or blanket application), the operator will retain in his recordkeeping system the approved application.*

 The correct answer is "b".

✓ **JUST A SIDE NOTE:** Here's a snapshot of the above-mentioned CBP Form 216.

OMB Control Number: 1651-0029; Expiration Date: 06/30/2015

DEPARTMENT OF HOMELAND SECURITY
U.S.Customs and Border Protection

APPLICATION FOR FOREIGN-TRADE ZONE ACTIVITY PERMIT

19 CFR 146.52, 146.66

1. ZONE NO. AND LOCATION *(Address)*

2. ZONE ADMISSION NO

3. APPLICATION DATE

4. TYPE OF ACTIVITY FOR WHICH PERMIT REQUESTED
☐ Manipulate ☐ Manufacture ☐ Exhibit ☐ Destroy ☐ Temporary Removal

5. FULL DESCRIPTION OF THE ACTIVITY *(Include designation of the exact place in zone where the operation is to be performed and, in the case of a proposed manipulation or manufacture, a statement as to whether merchandise with one zone status is to be packed, commingled, or combined with merchandise having different zone status. If additional space required, attach separate sheet. If first application for manufacturing of this kind, state whether Foreign-Trade Zones board has occurred in proposed operation.)*

6. ZONE LOT NO. OR UNIQUE IDENTIFIER	7. MARKS AND NUMBERS	8. DESCRIPTION OF MERCHANDISE	9. QUANTITY	10. WEIGHTS MEASURES	11. ZONE STATUS

If any merchandise is to be manipulated in any way or manufactured, I agree to maintain the records provided for in sections 146.21(a), 146.23, and 146.52(d) of the Customs Regulations and to make them available to CBP officers for inspection.

12. APPLICANT FIRM NAME	13. BY *(Signature)*	14. TITLE
APPROVED BY FOREIGN-TRADE ZONE OPERATOR ➧	15. BY *(Signature)*	16. TITLE

PERMIT

The application made above is hereby approved and permission is granted to manipulate, manufacture, exhibit, destroy, or temporarily removed, as requested, on condition that the applicable regulations are complied with and the records required to be maintained will be available for inspection.

17. PORT DIRECTOR OF CBP. By *(Signature)*	18. TITLE	19. DATE

FTZ OPERATOR'S

20. TO THE PORT DIRECTOR OF CBP:
I certify that the goods described herein have been disposed of as directed except as noted below.

21. FOR THE FTZ OPERATOR. *(Signature)*	22. TITLE	23. DATE

CBP Form 216 (05/10)

19) XYZ Corp. operates a manufacturing facility within a Foreign Trade Zone (FTZ). XYZ Corp. manufactures bottles using raw materials imported from Asia and admitted into the FTZ as non-privileged foreign merchandise on a Form 214. The finished bottles are then sold and delivered daily to U.S. beverage companies. Which of the following is true?

a) XYZ Corp. does not need to file entry, as the bottles are considered products of the United States.
b) XYZ Corp. may enter all of its merchandise on their reconciliation report.
c) XYZ Corp. is not allowed to file pro forma invoices for this merchandise.
d) XYZ Corp. may file weekly entries.
e) XYZ Corp. does not need to file entry, as the entry was made when the raw materials were admitted into the FTZ.

As per 19 CFR 146.63(c):

146.63 Entry for consumption.

... ...

(c) Estimated production—(1) Weekly entry. ***When merchandise is manufactured or otherwise changed in a zone (exclusive of packing) to its physical condition as entered within 24 hours before physical transfer from the zone for consumption, the port director may allow the person making entry to file an entry on Customs Form 3461, or its electronic equivalent, for the estimated removals of merchandise during the calendar week.*** *The Customs Form 3461, or its electronic equivalent, must be accompanied by a pro forma invoice or schedule showing the number of units of each type of merchandise to be removed during the week and their zone and dutiable values. Merchandise covered by an entry made under the provisions of this section will be considered to be entered and may be removed only when the port director has accepted the entry on Customs Form 3461, or its electronic equivalent. If the actual removals will exceed the estimate for the week, the person making entry shall file an additional Customs Form 3461, or its electronic equivalent, to cover the additional units before their removal from the zone. Notwithstanding that a weekly entry may be allowed, all merchandise will be dutiable as provided in §146.65. When estimated removals exceed actual removals, that excess merchandise will not be considered to have been entered or constructively transferred to the Customs territory.*

 The correct answer is "d".

✔ **JUST A SIDE NOTE:** "Privileged Foreign Status" means that the merchandise will be classified and assessed duty based on its condition when admitted into the FTZ (front end). "Non-privileged Foreign Status" means the merchandise will be classified and assessed duty based on its condition when it formally leaves the FTZ (back end). The difference here is significant because often items are manufactured within the FTZ, transforming them into merchandise with different classifications and duty rates.

20) On November 15, 2015, a shipment of t-shirts enters an FTZ, and does not undergo any manipulation or manufacturing while in the FTZ. On April 20, 2016, the owner of the t-shirts decides to enter 5,000 of them for sale at the local swap meet. Which form is required to enter the t-shirts?

a) Form 3495
b) Form 214
c) Form 301
d) Form 7523
e) Form 7501

 As per 19 CFR 146.62(b):

146.62 Entry.

... ...

(b) Documentation. (1) ***Customs Form 7501, or its electronic equivalent, or the entry summary will be accompanied by the entry documentation****, including invoices as provided in parts 141 and 142 of this chapter. The person with the right to make entry shall submit any other supporting documents required by law or regulations that relate to the transferred merchandise and provide the information necessary to support the admissibility, the declared values, quantity, and classification of the merchandise. If the declared values are predicated on estimates or estimated costs, that information must be clearly stated in writing at the time an entry or entry summary is filed.*

 The correct answer is "e".

✓ **JUST A SIDE NOTE:** Another commonly used FTZ-related term is "zone-restricted merchandise". Zone-restricted merchandise means that the designated merchandise in the FTZ cannot be entered for consumption, and is considered exported. Essentially, it cannot be touched except to export or to destroy.

21) Which of the following products is NOT covered in Chapter 26: Ores, Slag & Ash?

a) Iron ores and concentrates, including roasted iron pyrites
b) Copper Ores and Concentrates
c) Slag wool, rock wool or similar mineral wools
d) Nickel Ores and Concentrates
e) Cobalt ores and concentrates

 As per HTSUS Chapter 26, Note 1:

Notes

1. This chapter does not cover:

(a) Slag or similar industrial waste prepared as macadam (heading 2517);
(b) Natural magnesium carbonate (magnesite), whether or not calcined (heading 2519);
(c) Sludges from the storage tanks of petroleum oils, consisting mainly of such oils (heading 2710);
(d) Basic slag of chapter 31;
(e) Slag wool, rock wool or similar mineral wools (heading 6806);
(f) Waste or scrap of precious metal or of metal clad with precious metal; other waste or scrap containing precious metal or precious metal compounds, of a kind used principally for the recovery of precious metal (heading 7112); or
(g) Copper, nickel or cobalt mattes produced by any process of smelting (section XV).

Here's a relatively easy classification question. If there are items that a particular HTSUS Section or Chapter DO NOT cover, then those items will be listed in that Section's Note 1 or Chapter's Note 1.

 The correct answer is "c".

✓ **JUST A SIDE NOTE:** "Slag" is the by-product of smelting a metal from that metal's raw ore.

22) Which of the following rules does NOT apply if merchandise is entered duty free into the U.S. under Harmonized Tariff Schedule of the United States (HTSUS) number 9802.00.5010 or 9802.00.8040?

a) The country of origin must be the U.S. or a CBI country.
b) The country of export must be a CBI country.
c) The additional tariff number must be reported with the 9802 number and the number cannot begin with 2709 or 2710.
d) The additional HTS number cannot be associated with a textile category number unless the number is from chapter 62.
e) None of the above

 As per CATAIR, Appendix B, CBTPA NOTES:

The following must apply if merchandise is entered duty free into the U.S. under HTS number 9802.00.5010 or 9802.00.8040.

- *The country of origin must be the U.S. or a CBI country.*
- *The country of export must be a CBI country.*
- *An additional tariff number must be reported with the 9802 number and the number cannot begin with 2709 or 2710.*
- *The additional HTS number* ***cannot be associated with a textile category number unless the number is from chapter 64****.*

In our humble opinion, this is not at all a practical exam question. This is a classification question, so the examinee would naturally be searching in HTSUS Chapter 98 for the answer. Instead, the answer is found in the CATAIR on page 31 (of 43 pages).

Nevertheless, the correct answer here is "d".

✓ **JUST A SIDE NOTE:** The Caribbean Basin Trade Partnership Act (CBTPA) is a trade preference program that includes beneficiary countries such as Costa Rica, Guatemala, and Panama. The Caribbean Basin Initiative (CBI) program preceded the CBTPA and essentially includes the same list of countries.

23) Textile or apparel product is any good classifiable in Chapters 50 through 63 of the Harmonized Tariff Schedule of the United States (HTSUS), and any good classifiable under which one of the following HTSUS headings or subheadings?

a) 9113.90.40
b) 1213.00
c) 2833
d) 4407.10
e) None of the above

 As per 19 CFR 102.21(b):

102.21 Textile and apparel products.

… …

(b) Definitions*. The following terms will have the meanings indicated when used in this section:*
… …

(5) Textile or apparel product. A textile or apparel product is any good classifiable in Chapters 50 through 63, Harmonized Tariff Schedule of the United States (HTSUS), and any good classifiable under one of the following HTSUS headings or subheadings:

3005.90	*6501*
3921.12.15	*6502*
3921.13.15	*6504*
3921.90.2550	*6505.90*
4202.12.40-80	*6601.10-99*
4202.22.40-80	*7019.19.15*
4202.32.40-95	*7019.19.28*
4202.92.04-08	*7019.40-59*
4202.92.15-30	*8708.21*
4202.92.60-90	*8804*
6405.20.60	***9113.90.40***
6406.10.77	*9404.90*

… …

Here's another obscure exam classification question. Who would think to look in Part 102 (Rules of origin) of 19 CFR to look this up?

Nonetheless, the correct answer is "a". Hang in there—they're not all this complicated.

✔ **JUST A SIDE NOTE:** HTSUS 9113.90.40 is the classification for watch straps of textile material.

24) What is the classification for the 10th copy of a bronze statue cast from an original mold created twenty (20) years after the original artist has died?

a) 7419.91.0050 Other articles of copper>>Other>>Cast, molded, stamped or forged, but not further worked>>Other

b) 7419.99.5050 Other articles of copper>>Other>>Other>>Other>>Other>>Other

c) 8306.21.0000 Bells, gongs and the like, nonelectric, of base metal; statuettes and other ornaments, of base metal; photograph, picture or similar frames, of base metal; mirrors of base metal; and base metal parts thereof>>Statuettes and other ornaments, and parts thereof>>Plated with precious metal, and parts thereof

d) 9703.00.0000 Original sculptures and statuary, in any material.

e) None of the above

As per HTSUS Chapter 97, Additional U.S. Note 1:

Additional U.S. Notes

*1. **Heading 9703 covers not only original sculpture made by the sculptor, but also the first 12 castings, replicas or reproductions made from a sculptor's original work or model, by the sculptor himself or by another artist, with or without a change in scale and whether or not the sculptor is alive at the time the castings, replicas or reproductions are completed.***

The item in question, a bronze cast statue, is a prima facie item (i.e. classifiable under more than one heading). As far as we know, no single heading differentiates itself from the others as being more specific, so the item cannot be classified by application of GRI 3(a). The item is not a composite or set item, so GRI 3(b) (essential character) cannot be applied. Hence, as the last option for classifying a prima facie item, GRI 3(c), we choose the classification that occurs numerically last in the HTSUS, which is 9703.00.0000. The correct answer is "d".

✓ **NOTE:** GRI 1(notes and headings) is also applied here as the Chapter 97 Additional U.S. Note 1 specifies that the bronze statue in question is considered by the HTSUS to be an "original" statue.

Heading/ Subheading	Stat. Suf-fix	Article Description	Unit of Quantity	Rates of Duty 1 General	Rates of Duty 1 Special	Rates of Duty 2
9701		Paintings, drawings and pastels, executed entirely by hand, other than drawings of heading 4906 and other than hand-painted or hand-decorated manufactured articles; collages and similar decorative plaques; all the foregoing framed or not framed:				
9701.10.00	00	Paintings, drawings and pastels	X	Free		Free
9701.90.00	00	Other	X	Free		Free
9702.00.00	00	Original engravings, prints and lithographs, framed or not framed	X	Free		Free
9703.00.00	00	Original sculptures and statuary, in any material	X	Free		Free
9704.00.00	00	Postage or revenue stamps, stamp-postmarks, first-day covers, postal stationery (stamped paper) and the like, used or unused, other than those of heading 4907	X	Free		Free
9705.00.00		Collections and collectors' pieces of zoological, botanical, mineralogical, anatomical, historical, archeological, paleontological, ethnographic or numismatic interest		Free		Free
		Numismatic (collector's) coins:				
	30	Gold	Au g			
	60	Other	X			
	70	Archaeological, historical, or ethnographic pieces	X			
	91	Other	X			
9706.00.00		Antiques of an age exceeding one hundred years		Free		Free
	20	Silverware	X			
	40	Furniture	X			
	60	Other	X			

25) The Miami Sound Machine music store is importing cellos from a manufacturer in Spain for a client in Orlando, FL. Included in the shipment are forty of each of the following: cellos, black and red cello cases, and bows. The store will sell each cello, case, and bow as a unit to the Florida client. Which of the following statements describes how these items will be classified?

a) The cellos, cases, and bows all must be separately classified.
b) The cases and bows shall be classified with the cellos.
c) The bows shall be classified with the cellos, but the cases must be separately classified.
d) The bows shall be classified with the cases, but the cellos must be separately classified.
e) The cases shall be classified with the cellos, but the bows must be separately classified.

 As per HTSUS, General Rules of Interpretation (GRI) 3(b) & GRI 5(a):

*GRI 3(b) Mixtures, **composite goods** consisting of different materials or made up of different components, and goods put up in sets for retail sale, which cannot be classified by reference to 3(a), **shall be classified as if they consisted of the material or component which gives them their essential character**, insofar as this criterion is applicable.*

*GRI 5(a) Camera cases, **musical instrument cases**, gun cases, drawing instrument cases, necklace cases and similar containers, specially shaped or fitted to contain a specific article or set of articles, suitable for long-term use and **entered with the articles for which they are intended, shall be classified with such articles when of a kind normally sold therewith. This rule does not, however, apply to containers which give the whole its essential character.***

The item in question, a cello with bow and case, should be entered as a single HTS classification. Using GRI 3(b) we can say that the cello, not the bow, gives the shipment its essential character. Using GRI 5(a) we can say that the case should be classified with the cello as well. The correct answer is "b".

✓ **NOTE:** The question states that the store is "importing cellos", so from that we may safely assume here that the cello cases do not impart the essential character.

Heading/ Subheading	Stat. Suf-fix	Article Description	Unit of Quantity	Rates of Duty 1 General	Rates of Duty 1 Special	Rates of Duty 2
9202		Other string musical instruments (for example, guitars, violins, harps):				
9202.10.00	00	Played with a bow	No.	3.2%	Free (A, AU, BH, CA, CL, CO, E, IL, JO, KR, MA, MX, OM, P, PA, PE, SG)	37.5%
9202.90		Other:				
		Guitars:				
9202.90.20	00	Valued not over $100 each, excluding the value of the case	No.	4.5%	Free (A, AU, BH, CA, CL, CO, E, IL, JO, KR, MA, MX, OM, P, PA, PE, SG)	40%
9202.90.40	00	Other	No.	8.7%	Free (A, AU, BH, CA, CL, CO, E, IL, JO, KR, MA, MX, OM, P, PA, PE, SG)	40%
9202.90.60	00	Other	No.	4.6%	Free (A, AU, BH, CA, CL, CO, E, IL, JO, KR, MA, MX, OM, P, PA, PE, SG)	40%

26) A clothing set for a child measures 85 centimeters, consists of a 100 percent cotton woven dress, and coordinates 100 percent cotton knit diaper cover. The items are imported together, presented as a set, and intended to be worn together by the same person. What is (are) the classification(s) for this clothing set?

a) 6111.20.6030/6209.20.1000

6111.20.6030 Babies' garments and clothing accessories, knitted or crocheted>>Of cotton>>Other>>Other>>Other>>Imported as parts of sets
6209.20.1000 Babies' garments and clothing accessories>>Of cotton>>Dresses

b) 6111.20.6070/6209.20.1000

6111.20.6070 Babies' garments and clothing accessories, knitted or crocheted>>Of cotton>>Other>>Other>>Other>>Other
6209.20.1000 Babies' garments and clothing accessories>>Of cotton>>Dresses

c) 6111.20.6030/6209.20.5045

6111.20.6030 Babies' garments and clothing accessories, knitted or crocheted>>Of cotton>>Other>>Other>>Other>>Imported as parts of sets
6209.20.5045 Babies' garments and clothing accessories>>Of cotton>>Other>>Other>>Other>>Imported as parts of sets

d) 6111.20.6020 Babies' garments and clothing accessories, knitted or crocheted>>Of cotton>>Other>>Other>>Sets

e) 6209.20.5035 Babies' garments and clothing accessories>>Of cotton>>Other>>Other>>Sets

As per HTSUS Section XI (includes Textile Chapters 50 thru. 63), Note 14:

14. Unless the context otherwise requires, textile garments of different headings are to be classified in their own headings even if put up in sets for retail sale. For the purposes of this note, the expression "textile garments" means garments of headings 6101 to 6114 and headings 6201 to 6211.

The item in question is a child's outfit set consisting of a diaper cover (heading 6111) and a dress (heading 6209). As per the above-mentioned Section Note, the two items in the set are to be classified separately since they each belong to different headings. Accordingly, we may disregard multiple choice options "d" and "e".

Multiple choice "c" classification 6209.20.5045 is for Other (than dresses), so we may disregard it. Multiple choice "b" classification 6111.20.6070 is for Other (than Imported as parts of sets), so we may disregard it. Multiple choice "a" is the only option that, without any contradictions, correctly describes the clothing set. The correct answer is "a".

✔ **NOTE:** Here's a good example of just applying GRI 1 to classify. We classified based on the Section Note (GRI 1), and based on the heading terms (also GRI 1).

Heading/ Subheading	Stat. Suf- fix	Article Description	Unit of Quantity	Rates of Duty 1 General	Special	2
6111		Babies' garments and clothing accessories, knitted or crocheted:				
6111.20		Of cotton:				
6111.20.10	00	Blouses and shirts, except those imported as parts of sets (239)	doz. kg	19.7%	Free (AU, BH, CA, CL, CO, IL, JO, KR, MA, MX, OM, P, PA, PE, SG)	90%
6111.20.20	00	T-shirts, singlets and similar garments, except those imported as parts of sets (239)	doz. kg	14.9%	Free (AU, BH, CA, CL, CO, IL, JO, KR, MA, MX, OM, P, PA, PE, SG)	90%
6111.20.30	00	Sweaters, pullovers, sweatshirts, waistcoats (vests) and similar articles, except those imported as parts of sets (239)	doz. kg	14.9%	Free (AU, BH, CA, CL, CO, IL, JO, KR, MA, MX, OM, P, PA, PE, SG)	90%
6111.20.40	00	Dresses (239)	doz. kg	11.5%	Free (AU, BH, CA, CL, CO, IL, JO, KR, MA, MX, OM, P, PA, PE, SG)	45%
		Other:				
6111.20.50	00	Trousers, breeches and shorts, except those imported as parts of sets (239)	doz. kg	14.9%	Free (AU, BH, CA, CL, CO, IL, JO, KR, MA, MX, OM, P, PA, PE, SG)	90%
6111.20.60		Other		8.1%	Free (AU, BH, CA, CL, CO, IL, JO, KR, MA, MX, OM, P, PE, SG) See 9822.09.65, 9919.61.01-9919.61.02 (PA)	90%
	10	Sunsuits, washsuits and similar apparel (239)	doz. kg			
	20	Sets (239)	doz. kg			
		Other:				
	30	Imported as parts of sets (239)	doz. kg			
	50	Babies' socks and booties (239)	doz.pr. kg			
	70	Other (239)	doz. kg			

Heading/ Subheading	Stat. Suf-fix	Article Description	Unit of Quantity	Rates of Duty 1 General	Special	2
6209		Babies' garments and clothing accessories:				
6209.20		Of cotton:				
6209.20.10	00	Dresses (239)	doz. kg	11.8%	Free (AU, BH, CA, CL, CO, IL, JO, KR, MA, MX, OM, P, PA, PE, SG)	90%
6209.20.20	00	Blouses and shirts, except those imported as parts of sets (239)	doz. kg	14.9%	Free (AU, BH, CA, CL, CO, IL, JO, KR, MA, MX, OM, P, PA, PE, SG)	37.5%
		Other:				
6209.20.30	00	Trousers, breeches and shorts, except those imported as parts of sets (239)	doz. kg	14.9%	Free (AU, BH, CA, CL, CO, IL, JO, KR, MA, MX, OM, P, PA, PE, SG)	90%
6209.20.50		Other		9.3%	Free (AU, BH, CA, CL, CO, IL, JO, KR, MA, MX, OM, P, PA, PE, SG)	90%
	30	Sunsuits, washsuits and similar apparel (239)	doz. kg			
	35	Sets (239)	doz. kg			
		Other:				
	45	Imported as parts of sets (239)	doz. kg			
	50	Other (239)	doz. kg			

(This Page Intentionally Left Blank)

27) For the purposes of subheading 2601.11.0060, the term "coarse" refers to iron ores with a majority of individual particles having a diameter ______________.

a) less than 3.50 mm
b) between 1 to 2 mm
c) exceeding 4.75mm
d) between 2 to 3 mm
e) less than 4.50 mm

 As per HTSUS Chapter 26, Statistical Note 2:

Statistical Notes

1. The quantity of metal content to be reported shall be the assay quantity without deductions.

2. For the purposes of subheading 2601.11.0060, the term "coarse" refers to iron ores with a majority of individual particles having a diameter exceeding 4.75 mm.

 As per the above-mentioned Chapter 26 note, "c" is clearly the correct answer.

✔ **NOTE:** The HTSUS Section and Chapter Notes may include four separately named "notes". They are the "Notes", "Subheading Notes", "Additional U.S. Notes", and "Statistical Notes". As their names suggest, they somewhat differ in their breadth of applicability. The main things to remember is that they are all potentially helpful in the classification process, and that they are all also fair game on the exam.

Heading/ Subheading	Stat. Suf- fix	Article Description	Unit of Quantity	Rates of Duty 1 General	Special	2
2601		Iron ores and concentrates, including roasted iron pyrites:				
		Iron ores and concentrates, other than roasted iron pyrites:				
2601.11.00		Non-agglomerated		Free		Free
	30	Concentrates	t			
		Ores:				
	60	Coarse	t			
	90	Other	t			
2601.12.00		Agglomerated		Free		Free
	30	Pellets	t			
	60	Briquettes	t			
	90	Other	t			
2601.20.00	00	Roasted iron pyrites	t	Free		Free
2602.00.00		Manganese ores and concentrates, including ferruginous manganese ores and concentrates with a manganese content of 20 percent or more, calculated on the dry weight		Free		2.2¢/kg on manganese content
	40	Containing less than 47 percent by weight of manganese	kg Mn kg			
	60	Containing 47 percent or more by weight of manganese	kg Mn kg			
2603.00.00		Copper ores and concentrates		1.7¢/kg on lead content	Free (A, AU, BH, CA, CL, CO, E, IL, JO, KR, MA, MX, OM, P, PA, PE, SG)	8.8¢/kg on copper content + 3.3¢/kg on lead content + 3.7¢/kg on zinc content
	10	Copper content	Cu kg 1/			
	20	Lead content	Pb kg 1/			
	30	Zinc content	Zn kg 1/			
	40	Silver content	Ag g 1/			
	50	Gold content	Au g 1/			
2604.00.00		Nickel ores and concentrates		Free		Free
	40	Nickel content	Ni kg 1/			
	80	Other metal content	kg 1/			
2605.00.00	00	Cobalt ores and concentrates	kg Co kg	Free		Free
2606.00.00		Aluminum ores and concentrates		Free		$1/t
		Bauxite, calcined:				
	30	Refractory grade	t			
	60	Other	t			
	90	Other	t			

28) Bitrex, also known as Denatonium Benzoate, is an aromatic, cyclic amide indicated for use as a denaturant and bittering agent. It is imported from Singapore and classified in HTS 2924.29.7100. The importer has provided the Chemical Abstract Service (CAS) number, 3734-33-6, and certified that it is not listed in the Chemical Appendix to the Tariff Schedule. What is the rate of duty for Bitrex?

a) 0%
b) 3.7%
c) 5.9%
d) 6.5%
e) 15.4%/kg + 58%

 As per HTSUS General Note (GN) 13 (Pharmaceutical products):

13. Pharmaceutical products. Whenever a rate of duty of "Free" followed by the symbol "K" in parentheses appears in the "Special" subcolumn for a heading or subheading, any product (by whatever name known) classifiable in such provision which is the product of a country eligible for tariff treatment under column 1 shall be entered free of duty, provided that such product is included in the pharmaceutical appendix to the tariff schedule. *Products in the pharmaceutical appendix include the salts, esters and hydrates of the ... ...*

 AND as per the HTSUS Pharmaceutical Appendix:

... ...

DENAGLIPTIN	*483369-58-0*
DENATONIUM BENZOATE	***3734-33-6***
DENAVERINE	*3579-62-2*

... ...

The HTSUS number 2924.29.7100 includes Special Program Indicator (SPI) "K". Accordingly, the item in question, Denatonium Benzoate, may potentially be eligible for duty free treatment under the Agreement on Trade in Pharmaceutical Products program. In searching the HTSUS Pharmaceutical Appendix, Denatonium Benzoate is found to be listed. Thus, as per General Note 13, the shipment may be entered duty free. The correct answer is "a".

✔ **NOTE:** The above GN 13 Note includes the condition "which is the product of a country eligible for tariff treatment under column 1". Singapore is an eligible country. Only the countries Cuba and North Korea are column 2 countries (i.e. not column 1).

✔ **NOTE:** As referenced in the classification article description, Additional U.S. Note 3: to Section VI says:
3. The term "products described in additional U.S. note 3 to section VI" refers to any product not listed in the Chemical Appendix to the Tariff Schedule and--

(a) For which the importer furnishes the Chemical Abstracts Service (C.A.S.) registry number and certifies that such registry number is not listed in the Chemical Appendix to the Tariff Schedule; or ... ...

✔ **JUST A SIDE NOTE:** A "denaturant" is added to alcohol to render it undrinkable, particularly for the purpose of discouraging recreational drinking.

Heading/ Subheading	Stat. Suf- fix	Article Description	Unit of Quantity	Rates of Duty 1 General	Rates of Duty 1 Special	Rates of Duty 2
2924 (con.)		Carboxyamide-function compounds; amide-function compounds of carbonic acid: (con.)				
		Cyclic amides (including cyclic carbamates) and their derivatives; salts thereof: (con.)				
2924.29 (con.)		Other: (con.)				
		Aromatic: (con.)				
		Other: (con.)				
		Other:				
2924.29.65	00	5-Bromoacetyl-2-salicylamide	kg	6.5%	Free (A, AU, BH, CA, CL, CO, E, IL, JO, KR, MA, MX, OM, P, PA, PE, SG)	15.4¢/kg + 58%
		Other:				
2924.29.71	00	Products described in additional U.S. note 3 to section VI	kg	6.5% 114/	Free (A+, AU, BH, CA, CL, CO, D, E, IL, JO, K, KR, L, MA, MX, OM, P, PA, PE, SG)	15.4¢/kg + 58%
2924.29.76		Other		6.5% 115/	Free (A+, AU, BH, CA, CL, CO, D, E, IL, JO, K, KR, L, MA, MX, OM, P, PA, PE, SG)	15.4¢/kg + 58%
	10	Acetoacetanilide	kg			
	20	Acetoacet-2,5-dimethoxy-4-chloroanilide	kg			
	30	*p*-Aminobenzamide	kg			
	90	Other	kg			
		Other:				
2924.29.80	00	2,2-Dimethylcyclopropylcarboxamide	kg	Free		30.5%
2924.29.95	00	Other	kg	6.5%	Free (A, AU, BH, CA, CL, CO, E, IL, JO, K, KR, MA, MX, OM, P, PA, PE, SG)	30.5%

29) What is the classification for 48 hair combs, worn in the hair, made of silver (a precious metal), valued at $22 per dozen pieces?

a) 9615.19.2000 Combs, hair-slides and the like; hairpins, curling pins, curling grips, hair-curlers and the like, other than those of heading 8516, and parts thereof>>Combs, hair-slides and the like>>Other>>Combs>>Valued not over $4.50 per gross

b) 7113.11.2080 Articles of jewelry and parts thereof, of precious metal or of metal clad with precious metal>>Of precious metal whether or not plated or clad with precious metal>>Of silver, whether or not plated or clad with other precious metal>>Other>>Valued not over $18 per dozen pieces or parts

c) 9615.11.1000 Combs, hair-slides and the like; hairpins, curling pins, curling grips, hair-curlers and the like, other than those of heading 8516, and parts thereof>>Combs, hair-slides and the like>>Of hard rubber or plastics>>Combs>>Valued not over $4.50 per gross

d) 7113.11.5080 Articles of jewelry and parts thereof, of precious metal or of metal clad with precious metal>>Of precious metal whether or not plated or clad with precious metal>>Of silver, whether or not plated or clad with other precious metal>>Other>>Other>>Other

e) 9615.19.4000 Combs, hair-slides and the like; hairpins, curling pins, curling grips, hair-curlers and the like, other than those of heading 8516, and parts thereof>>Combs, hair-slides and the like>>Other>>Combs>>Valued over $4.50 per gross

 As per HTSUS Chapter 96, Note 4:

*4. **Articles of this chapter, other than those of headings** 9601 to 9606 or **9615, remain classified in the chapter** whether or not composed wholly or partly of precious metal or metal clad with precious metal, of natural or cultured pearls, or precious or semiprecious stones (natural, synthetic or reconstructed). However, headings 9601 to 9606 and **9615 include articles in which** natural or cultured pearls, precious or semiprecious stones (natural, synthetic or reconstructed), **precious metal** or metal clad with precious metal **constitute only minor constituents.***

 And As per HTSUS Chapter 71, Note 9:

9. For the purposes of heading 7113, the expression "articles of jewelry" means:

(a) Any small objects of personal adornment (for example, rings, bracelets, necklaces, brooches, earrings, watch chains, fobs, pendants, tie pins, cuff links, dress studs, religious or other medals and insignia); and
... ...

Per the Chapter 96, Note 4, items of precious metal that DON"T constitute only minor constituents should be classified elsewhere than in heading 9615. The item is made of silver, so we may disregard heading 9615 options "a", "c", and "e".

The item is valued at over $18 per dozen, so we eliminate option "b". The correct answer is "d".

✔ **JUST A SIDE NOTE:** The unit of measure "gross" means 12 dozen (i.e. 144). So, in using the exam question as an example, $22 per dozen ÷ 12 = 1.833 grosses.

Heading/ Subheading	Stat. Suf-fix	Article Description	Unit of Quantity	Rates of Duty 1 General	Rates of Duty 1 Special	Rates of Duty 2
		III. JEWELRY, GOLDSMITHS' AND SILVERSMITHS' WARES AND OTHER ARTICLES				
7113		Articles of jewelry and parts thereof, of precious metal or of metal clad with precious metal:				
		Of precious metal whether or not plated or clad with precious metal:				
7113.11		Of silver, whether or not plated or clad with other precious metal:				
7113.11.10	00	Rope, curb, cable, chain and similar articles produced in continuous lengths, all the foregoing, whether or not cut to specific lengths and whether or not set with imitation pearls or imitation gemstones, suitable for use in the manufacture of articles provided for in this heading	X	6.3%	Free (A, AU, BH, CA, CL, CO, E, IL, JO, KR, MA, MX, OM, P, PA, PE, SG)	80%
		Other:				
7113.11.20		Valued not over $18 per dozen pieces or parts		13.5%	Free (A, AU, BH, CA, CL, CO, E, IL, JO, KR, MA, MX, OM, P, PA, PE, SG)	110%
	15	Containing jadeite or rubies	X			
	80	Other	X			
7113.11.50		Other		5%	Free (A*, AU, BH, CA, CL, CO, E, IL, JO, KR, MA, MX, OM, P, PA, PE, SG)	80%
	15	Containing jadeite or rubies	X			
	80	Other	X			

30) What is the classification of a woman's 70% rayon (artificial) / 30% wool knit suit comprised of a divided skirt and a suit coat? The skirt and suit coat are of the same fabric construction, color, composition, style and size.

a) 6204.19.2000 Women's or girls' suits, ensembles, suit-type jackets, blazers, dresses, skirts, divided skirts, trousers, bib and brace overalls, breeches and shorts (other than swimwear)>>Suits>>Of other textile materials>>Of artificial fibers>>Other

b) 6104.13.1000 Women's or girls' suits, ensembles, suit-type jackets, blazers, dresses, skirts, divided skirts, trousers, bib and brace overalls, breeches and shorts (other than swimwear), knitted or crocheted>>Suits>>Of synthetic fibers>>Containing 23% or more by weight of wool or fine animal hair

c) 6104.19.1000 Women's or girls' suits, ensembles, suit-type jackets, blazers, dresses, skirts, divided skirts, trousers, bib and brace overalls, breeches and shorts (other than swimwear), knitted or crocheted>>Suits>>Of other textile materials>>Of artificial fibers>>Containing 23% or more by weight of wool or fine animal hair

d) 6204.39.3010 Women's or girls' suits, ensembles, suit-type jackets, blazers, dresses, skirts, divided skirts, trousers, bib and brace overalls, breeches and shorts (other than swimwear)>>Suit-type jackets and blazers>>Of other textile materials>>Of artificial fibers>>Other>>Women's

e) 6104.19.1500 Women's or girls' suits, ensembles, suit-type jackets, blazers, dresses, skirts, divided skirts, trousers, bib and brace overalls, breeches and shorts (other than swimwear), knitted or crocheted>>Suits>>Of other textile materials>>Of artificial fibers>>Other

 As per HTSUS Chapter 61, Note 3(a):

3. For the purposes of headings 6103 and 6104:

(a) The term "suit" means a set of garments composed of two or three pieces made up, in respect of their outer surface, in identical fabric and comprising:
- one suit coat ... ... and
***- one garment designed to cover the lower part of the body** and consisting of trousers, breeches or shorts (other than swim- wear), a skirt **or a divided skirt**, having neither braces nor bibs.*
***All of the components of a "suit" must be of the same fabric construction, color and composition; they must also be of the same style and of corresponding or compatible size.** ... ...*

First off, the item in question is a "knit" suit, so we'll disregard heading 6204 (i.e. the non-knitted heading) choices "a" and "d". The suit is made of "artificial" fibers, not "synthetic", so we disregard "b". The suit is 30% wool, so we choose "c" and not "e". The correct answer is "c".

✔ **JUST A SIDE NOTE:** Chapter 54 (man-made filaments) defines "synthetic fibers" and "artificial fibers" as:

Synthetic Fibers: *By polymerization of organic monomers to produce polymers such as polyamides, polyesters, polyolefins or polyurethanes, or by chemical modification of polymers produced by this process (for example, poly(vinyl alcohol) prepared by the hydrolysis of poly(vinyl acetate)).*

Artificial Fibers: *By dissolution or chemical treatment of natural organic polymers (for example, cellulose) to produce polymers such as cuprammonium rayon (cupro) or viscose rayon, or by chemical modification of natural organic polymers (for example, cellulose, casein and other proteins, or alginic acid), to produce polymers such as cellulose acetate or alginates.*

Heading/ Subheading	Stat. Suf-fix	Article Description	Unit of Quantity	Rates of Duty 1 General	Rates of Duty 1 Special	Rates of Duty 2
6104		Women's or girls' suits, ensembles, suit-type jackets, blazers, dresses, skirts, divided skirts, trousers, bib and brace overalls, breeches and shorts (other than swimwear), knitted or crocheted:				
		Suits:				
6104.13		Of synthetic fibers:				
6104.13.10	00	Containing 23 percent or more by weight of wool or fine animal hair (444)........	No. kg	Free		54.5%
6104.13.20	00	Other (644)........	No. kg	14.9%	Free (AU, BH, CA, CL, CO, IL, JO, KR, MA, MX, OM, P, PA, PE, SG)	72%
6104.19		Of other textile materials:				
		Of artificial fibers:				
6104.19.10	00	Containing 23 percent or more by weight of wool or fine animal hair (444)........	No. kg	8.5%	Free (AU, BH, CA, CL, CO, IL, JO, KR, MA, MX, OM, P, PA, PE, SG)	54.5%
6104.19.15	00	Other (644)........	No. kg	Free		72%
6104.19.40	00	Containing 70 percent or more by weight of silk or silk waste (744)........	No. kg	0.9%	Free (AU, BH, CA, CL, CO, E, IL, JO, KR, MA, MX, OM, P, PA, PE, SG)	60%
6104.19.50	00	Of wool or fine animal hair (444)........	No. kg	13.6%	Free (AU, BH, CA, CL, CO, IL, JO, KR, MA, MX, P, PA, PE, SG) 2.7% (OM)	54.5%
6104.19.60		Of cotton........	....	9.4%	Free (AU, BH, CA, CL, CO, IL, JO, KR, MA, MX, OM, P, PA, PE, SG)	90%
	10	Jackets imported as parts of suits (335)........	doz. kg			
	20	Skirts and divided skirts imported as parts of suits (342)........	doz. kg			
	30	Trousers, breeches and shorts imported as parts of suits (348)........	doz. kg			
	40	Waistcoats imported as parts of suits (359)........	doz. kg			

31) What is the classification for leather golf bags?

a) 4202.92.4500 Trunks, suitcases, vanity cases, attache cases, briefcases, school satchels, spectacle cases, … …, sports bags, bottle cases, jewelry boxes, powder cases, cutlery cases and similar containers, of leather or of composition leather, … …>>Other>>With outer surface of sheeting of plastic or of textile materials>>Travel, sports and similar bags>>Other

b) 6305.90.0000 Sacks and bags, of a king used for the packing of goods>>Of other textile materials

c) 9506.39.0080 Articles and equipment for general physical exercise, gymnastics, athletics, other sports (including table-tennis) or outdoor games, not specified or included elsewhere in this chapter; swimming pools and wading pools; parts and accessories thereof>>Golf clubs and other golf equipment; parts and accessories thereof>>Other

d) 4202.91.0010 Trunks, suitcases, vanity cases, attache cases, briefcases, school satchels, spectacle cases, … …, sports bags, bottle cases, jewelry boxes, powder cases, cutlery cases and similar containers, of leather or of composition leather, … …>>Other>>With outer surface of leather or of composition leather>>Golf bags

e) 9506.99.6080 Articles and equipment for general physical exercise, gymnastics, athletics, other sports (including table-tennis) or outdoor games, not specified or included elsewhere in this chapter; swimming pools and wading pools; parts and accessories thereof>>Other>>Other>>Other>>Other

 As per HTSUS Chapter 95, Note 1(d):

Notes

1. This chapter does not cover:

… …

***(d) Sports bags or other containers of heading 4202**, 4303 or 4304;*

To begin with, as per the above-mentioned Chapter 95 note, the sports bag in question is to be classified in heading 4202 here, so we eliminate multiple choice options "b", "c", and "e".

Next, since "a" is for golf bags made of plastic or textile material, we eliminate it. The correct classification for the leather golf bags and the answer is in multiple choice "d".

✔ **JUST A SIDE NOTE:** The Chapter 95 note makes reference to headings 4303 and 4304, which are for articles of (real) fur and artificial fur respectively.

Heading/ Subheading	Stat. Suf- fix	Article Description	Unit of Quantity	Rates of Duty 1 General	Rates of Duty 1 Special	Rates of Duty 2
4202 (con.)		Trunks, suitcases, vanity cases, attache cases, briefcases, school satchels, spectacle cases, binocular cases, camera cases, musical instrument cases, gun cases, holsters and similar containers; traveling bags, insulated food or beverage bags, toiletry bags, knapsacks and backpacks, handbags, shopping bags, wallets, purses, map cases, cigarette cases, tobacco pouches, tool bags, sports bags, bottle cases, jewelry boxes, powder cases, cutlery cases and similar containers, of leather or of composition leather, of sheeting of plastics, of textile materials, of vulcanized fiber or of paperboard, or wholly or mainly covered with such materials or with paper: (con.)				
		Other:				
4202.91.00		With outer surface of leather or of composition leather	....	4.5%	Free (AU, BH, CA, CL, CO, D, IL, JO, KR, MA, MX, OM, P, PA, PE, R, SG) 3.5% (E)	35%
	10	Golf bags	No.			
	30	Travel, sports and similar bags	No.			
	90	Other	No.			
4202.92		With outer surface of sheeting of plastic or of textile materials:				
		Insulated food or beverage bags:				
		With outer surface of textile materials:				
4202.92.04	00	Beverage bags whose interior incorporates only a flexible plastic container of a kind for storing and dispensing potable beverages through attached flexible tubing	No. kg	7%	Free (A, AU, BH, CA, CL, CO, E, IL, JO, KR, MA, MX, OM, P, PA, PE, SG)	40%
4202.92.08		Other	....	7%	Free (AU, BH, CA, CL, CO, E, IL, JO, KR, MA, MX, OM, P, PA, PE, SG)	40%
	05	Of cotton (369)	No. kg			
	07	Of man-made fibers (670)	No. kg			
	09	Other (870)	No. kg			
4202.92.10	00	Other	No. kg	3.4%	Free (A, AU, BH, CA, CL, CO, E, IL, JO, KR, MA, MX, OM, P, PA, PE, SG)	80%

32) A pneumatic handheld impact riveter is imported by a civil aircraft manufacturer in Philadelphia. The riveter is specially designed and is used for attaching metal sheeting on aircraft. What is the classification of the riveter?

a) 8705.10.0010	Special purpose motor vehicles, other than those principally designed for the transport of persons or goods (for example, wreckers, mobile cranes, fire fighting vehicles, concrete mixers, road sweepers, spraying vehicles, mobile workshops, mobile radiological units)>>Mobile cranes>>Cable operated
b) 8803.20.0030	Parts of goods of heading 8801 or 8802>>Undercarriages and parts thereof>>For use in civil aircraft>>Other
c) 8467.21.0010	Tools for working in the hand, pneumatic, hydraulic or with self-contained electric or nonelectric motor, and parts thereof>>With self-contained electric motor>>Drills of all kinds>>Rotary>>Battery powered
d) 8467.19.1000	Tools for working in the hand, pneumatic, hydraulic or with self-contained electric or nonelectric motor, and parts thereof>>Pneumatic>>Other>>Suitable for metal working
e) 8203.30.0000	Metal cutting shears and similar tools, and parts thereof

 As per HTSUS Section XVII (Chapters 86 thru. 89), Note 2(e):

*2. **The expressions "parts" and "parts and accessories" do not apply to the following articles, whether or not they are identifiable as for the goods of this section:***

... ...

*(e) **Machines or apparatus of headings 8401 to 8479**, or parts thereof; articles of heading 8481 or 8482 or, provided they constitute integral parts of engines or motors, articles of heading 8483;*

 AND as per HTSUS Section XV (Chapters 72 thru. 83), Note 1(f):

*1. **This section does not cover:***

... ...

*(f) **Articles of section XVI (Chapters 84 & 85)**;*

Just based on the heading / classification descriptions of each multiple choice option, the examinee could possibly arrive at the correct answer. However, for the sake of practice, we'll acknowledge the related section notes and address each classification here.

The item in question, a pneumatic handheld impact riveter, is definitely not a mobile crane, so we disregard multiple choice "a". We may disregard "b" as per the Section XVII, machines for (use on) the goods of Chapters 86 thru. 89 are to be classified in Chapter 84. We may disregard "c" as the item in question is pneumatic (i.e. air powered), not battery powered. We may also disregard "e" as the Section XV note precludes it from consideration. Therefore, by application of GRI 1 (notes and heading descriptions) and by the process of elimination, we deduce that the correct answer is "d".

✔ **JUST A SIDE NOTE:** Headings 8801 and 8802 are for non-powered aircraft (e.g. hot air balloons) and powered aircraft (e.g. airplanes) respectively.

Heading/ Subheading	Stat. Suf-fix	Article Description	Unit of Quantity	Rates of Duty 1 General	Rates of Duty 1 Special	Rates of Duty 2
8467		Tools for working in the hand, pneumatic, hydraulic or with self-contained electric or nonelectric motor, and parts thereof:				
		Pneumatic:				
8467.11		Rotary type (including combined rotary-percussion):				
8467.11.10		Suitable for metal working		4.5%	Free (A, AU, BH, CA, CL, CO, E, IL, JO, KR, MA, MX, OM, P, PA, PE, SG)	30%
	40	Grinders, polishers and sanders	No.			
	80	Other	No.			
8467.11.50		Other		Free		27.5%
	10	Rock drills	No.			
	20	Drills, other than rock drills; screwdrivers and nut runners	No.			
	40	Wrenches, other than nut runners	No.			
	90	Other	No.			
8467.19		Other:				
8467.19.10	00	Suitable for metal working	No.	4.5%	Free (A, AU, BH, CA, CL, CO, E, IL, JO, KR, MA, MX, OM, P, PA, PE, SG)	30%
8467.19.50		Other		Free		27.5%
	30	Pneumatic, hand-held force feed lubricating equipment	No.			
	60	Designed for use in construction or mining	No.			
	90	Other	No.			

33) ABC Steel purchased carbon steel bars from a manufacturer in Ontario, Canada. ABC Steel paid $19,000, ex-factory, in Canadian dollars. The steel bars arrived at the Detroit Port of Entry via semi-tractor trailer on 5/6/2015, and the shipment was released the same day. The applicable currency exchange rate is .793021. The invoice price does not include duty at 2.9%, merchandising processing fee at .3464%, or freight charges of $1,628. What is the entered value of this shipment?

a) $17,372
b) $19,000
c) $15,067
d) $13,017
e) $18,403

 As per 19 CFR 152.103(a):

152.103 ***Transaction value.***

(a) Price actually paid or payable—(1) General. In determining transaction value, the price actually paid or payable will be considered without regard to its method of derivation. *It may be the result of discounts, increases, or negotiations, or may be arrived at by the application of a formula, such as the price in effect on the date of export in the London Commodity Market. The word "payable" refers to a situation in which the price has been agreed upon, but actual payment has not been made at the time of importation. ... ...*

Here's a fairly straightforward and practical exam question. The Transaction Value, which excludes duties, fees, freight, insurance, etc., for this shipment is the ex-factory/ex-works value of 19,000.00 in Canadian Dollars. To calculate the Entered Value (EV), which must be in U.S. Dollars (USD), we can simply take this value (in foreign currency) and multiply it by the applicable exchange rate.

19,000.00 CAD x 0.793021 (exchange rate) = $15,067.40 USD

The entered value is rounded to $15,067.00. The correct answer is "c".

✓ **JUST A SIDE NOTE:** In many cases, the "Certified Quarterly Rate" is used to convert commercial invoices in foreign currencies to U.S. Dollars. 19 CFR 159.34 explains:

159.34 Certified quarterly rate.

(a) Countries for which quarterly rate is certified. For the currency of each of the following foreign countries, there will be published in the Customs Bulletin, for the quarter beginning January 1, and for each quarter thereafter, the rate or rates first certified by the Federal Reserve Bank of New York for such foreign currency for a day in that quarter:

Australia, Austria, Belgium, Brazil, Canada, Denmark, Finland, France, Germany, Hong Kong, India, Iran, Ireland, Italy, Japan, Malaysia, Mexico, Netherlands, New Zealand, Norway, People's Republic of China, Philippines, Portugal, Republic of South Africa, Singapore, Spain, Sri Lanka (Ceylon), Sweden, Switzerland, Thailand, United Kingdom, Venezuela.

(b) When certified quarterly rate is used. The certified quarterly rate established under paragraph (a) of this section shall be used for Customs purposes for any date of exportation within the quarter, ...

34) What is the amount of duties and fees for goods entered in the U.S. for a shipment with the following characteristics?

- **Contains seven (7) 31mm ball bearings with integral shafts**
- **Is manufactured by XYZ Company from Germany with a value of $7,598.00.**
- **Has an applicable anti-dumping duty deposit rate is 68.89%, HTS 8482.10.1080 @2.4% duty rate and MPF.3464%**

a) $5260.57
b) $5234.26
c) $5416.61
d) $5442.93
e) $208.66

Here we just take the value of the shipment and multiply it against each of the listed duties and fees rates, and then add the resulting totals.

5234.26 (7598 x .6889)
+ 182.35 (7598 x 0.024)
+ 26.32 (7598 x 0.003464)
= 5442.93

The correct answer is "d".

✔ **NOTE:** The exam states that the total is $5442.92. This is incorrect, so we revised "d" to $5442.93.

35) Which of the following individuals is NOT considered when determining a related party transaction, as defined in the Tariff Act of 1930?

a) Employer and Employee

b) Members of the same family, including brothers and sisters (whether by whole or half-blood), spouse, ancestors, and lineal descendants

c) Any officer or director of an organization and such organization

d) Any person, directly or indirectly, owning, controlling or holding with power to vote, less-than four percent of the outstanding voting stock or shares of any organization and such organization.

e) An officer or director of an organization and an officer or director of another organization, who is also an officer or director in the other organization.

 As per 19 CFR 152.102(g):

(g) Related persons. ***"Related persons" means:*** *(1) Members of the same family, including brothers and sisters (whether by whole or half-blood), spouse, ancestors, and lineal descendants.*

(2) Any officer or director of an organization, and that organization.

(3) An officer or director of an organization and an officer or director of another organization, if each individual also is an officer or director in the other organization.

(4) Partners.

(5) Employer and employee.

(6) ***Any person directly or indirectly owning, controlling, or holding with power to vote, five percent or more of the outstanding voting stock or shares of any organization, and that organization.***

(7) Two or more persons directly or indirectly controlling, controlled by, or under common control with, any person.

The correct answer is "d". Owning "five percent or more" of the outstanding shares is the related persons threshold.

✔ **JUST A SIDE NOTE:** Customs may somewhat scrutinize "related persons" transactions to ensure that the relationship does not influence customs values.

36) Which of the following is an exclusion from transaction value?

a) The packing costs incurred by the buyer with respect to the imported merchandise
b) The transportation cost of the merchandise after its importation, when identified separately from the price actually paid or payable
c) A mold used in the production of the imported goods, supplied free of charge by the buyer to the manufacturer
d) The price actually paid or payable for the imported merchandise
e) A selling commission incurred by the buyer with respect to the imported merchandise

 As per 19 CFR 152.103(b):

(b) Additions to price actually paid or payable. (1) ***The transaction value of imported merchandise is the price actually paid or payable for the merchandise when sold for exportation to the United States, plus amounts equal to:***

(i) The packing costs incurred by the buyer with respect to the imported merchandise;

(ii) Any selling commission incurred by the buyer with respect to the imported merchandise;

(iii) The value, apportioned as appropriate, of any assist;

(iv) Any royalty or license fee related to the imported merchandise that the buyer is required to pay, directly or indirectly, as a condition of the sale of the imported merchandise for exportation to the United States; and

(v) The proceeds of any subsequent resale, disposal, or use of the imported merchandise that accrue, directly or indirectly, to the seller.

 Freight is not included as part of the price actually paid or payable. The correct answer is "b".

✓ **NOTE:** An easy-to-remember and worth-repeating tool on what to add to the price actually paid or payable is to remember the acronym **"C.R.A.P.P." (Commissions, Royalties, Assists, Packaging, Proceeds)**.

37) The foreign commercial invoice before you shows a value of $7200 with an addition of $800 for "distributor fee", for a total invoice value of $8000. The nature of the fee charged by the seller was to compensate the exclusive U. S. distributor who, by agreement with the foreign seller, receives 10% of all sales in the U. S. as a commission. They receive this regardless of whether or not they actually make the sale. What is the $800?

a) Not part of Transaction Value
b) A buying commission to be added to the price actually paid or payable
c) A buying commission; part of the price actually paid or payable
d) A selling commission to be added to the price actually paid or payable
e) A selling commission; part of the price actually paid or payable

 As per 19 CFR 152.103(b):

(b) Additions to price actually paid or payable. (1) ***The transaction value of imported merchandise is the price actually paid or payable for the merchandise when sold for exportation to the United States, plus amounts equal to:***

(i) The packing costs incurred by the buyer with respect to the imported merchandise;

(ii) ***Any selling commission incurred by the buyer with respect to the imported merchandise;***

(iii) The value, apportioned as appropriate, of any assist;

(iv) Any royalty or license fee related to the imported merchandise that the buyer is required to pay, directly or indirectly, as a condition of the sale of the imported merchandise for exportation to the United States; and

(v) The proceeds of any subsequent resale, disposal, or use of the imported merchandise that accrue, directly or indirectly, to the seller.

 The correct answer is "d".

✓ **JUST A SIDE NOTE:** Generally speaking, a buying commission is a payment made by the importer to their agent. On the other hand, a selling commission is a payment made by the exporter to their agent.

38) A U.S. television manufacturer contracts with a manufacturer in China to produce 500 bare printed circuit boards at a cost of $50 per board. The U.S. television manufacturer also contracts with a design company in New York to prepare the schematics for use in the production of the bare printed circuit boards at a cost of $20,000. Upon completion, the bare printed circuit boards are exported from China to Malaysia for further processing into printed circuit board assemblies for televisions at a cost of $200 per assembly. The completed printed circuit board assemblies are shipped to the U.S. television manufacturer and an invoice from the Malaysia manufacturer in the amount of $100,000 is included in the shipment at the time of importation. What is the transaction value of this shipment?

a) $20,000
b) $100,000
c) $120,000
d) $125,000
e) $145,000

 As per 19 CFR 152.102(a):

(a) Assist. (1) ***"Assist" means any of the following if supplied directly or indirectly, and free of charge or at reduced cost, by the buyer of imported merchandise for use in connection with the production or the sale for export to the United States of the merchandise:***
... ...

(iv) Engineering, development, artwork, design work, and plans and sketches that are undertaken elsewhere than in the United States and are necessary for the production of the imported merchandise.

(2) No service or work to which paragraph (a)(1)(iv) of this section applies will be treated as an assist if the service or work:

(i) Is performed by an individual domiciled within the United States;

a The Malaysian invoice value is $100,000 (500 boards x $200 ea.) for the imported printed circuit board assemblies. However, the assist for the initial Chinese manufacturing of $25,000 (500 boards x $50 ea.) must be added to this to make market value. $100,000 + $25,000 = $125,000.

We do not add the cost of $20,000 for the NY company's preparation of the schematics. Costs for engineering work and design work, etc. are only added as an assist to the transaction value if such work was done outside of the United States. The correct answer is "d".

✓ **JUST A SIDE NOTE:** "Make Market Value" (MMV) is the term used for adding dutiable values to the Invoice Value (IV) to calculate the Entered Value (EV) on the annotated commercial invoice. Using the above-scenario as an example:

Invoice Value $100,000
MMV $25,000

Entered Value $125,000

VII: Free Trade Agreements

39) Which of the following elements determine whether a particular good qualifies under the Generalized System of Preferences (GSP) value content requirement?

a) Cost or value of originating materials
b) Direct cost of processing
c) Cost or value of originating materials plus direct costs of processing that are greater than or equal to 35% of the appraised value of the good
d) Cost or value of originating materials plus direct costs of processing that are less than 35% of the appraised value of the goods.
e) Cost or value of originating materials plus direct costs of processing that are greater than or equal to 45% of the appraised value of the good.

 As per GN 4:

The symbol "A" indicates that all beneficiary developing countries are eligible for preferential treatment with respect to all articles provided for in the designated provision. The symbol "A" indicates that certain beneficiary developing countries, specifically enumerated in subdivision (d) of this note, are not eligible for such preferential treatment with regard to any article provided for in the designated provision.* ***Whenever an eligible article which is the growth, product, or manufacture of a designated beneficiary developing country listed in subdivision (a) of this note is imported into the customs territory of the United States directly from such country or territory, such article shall be eligible for duty-free treatment*** *as set forth in the "Special" subcolumn, unless excluded from such treatment by subdivision (d) of this note;* ***provided that, in accordance with regulations promulgated by the Secretary of the Treasury the sum of (1) the cost or value of the materials produced in the beneficiary developing country or any 2 or more countries which are members of the same association of countries which is treated as one country under section 507(2) of the Trade Act of 1974, plus (2) the direct costs of processing operations performed in such beneficiary developing country or such member countries is not less than 35 percent of the appraised value*** *of such article at the time of its entry into the customs territory of the United States. No article or material of a beneficiary developing country shall be eligible for such treatment by virtue of having merely undergone simple combining or packing operations, or mere dilution with water or mere dilution with another substance that does not materially alter the characteristics of the article.*

Basically, if qualifying Materials + Processing ≥ 35% then the item probably qualifies for GSP. The correct answer is "c".

✔ **NOTE:** Here's a snapshot of just a few of the GSP beneficiary developing countries as listed in HTSUS General Note 4(a):

Independent Countries

Afghanistan
Albania
Algeria
Angola
Armenia
Azerbaijan
Belize
Benin
Bhutan
Bolivia
… …

Grenada
Guinea
Guinea-Bissau
Guyana
Haiti
India
Indonesia
Iraq
Jamaica
Jordan

Republic of Yemen
Rwanda
Saint Lucia
Saint Vincent and the Grenadines
Samoa
Sao Tomé and Principe
Senegal
Serbia

40) A Merchandise Processing Fee (MPF) is exempt for originating goods from which Free Trade Agreement listed below?

a) Jordan JOFTA
b) Australia AUFTA
c) Morocco MAFTA
d) China CHFTA
e) Egypt QIZ

 As per 19 CFR 24.23(c):

24.23 ***Fees for processing merchandise.***

... ...

(c) Exemptions and limitations. (1) ***The ad valorem fee, surcharge, and specific fees provided for under*** *paragraphs (b)(1) and (b)(2) of* ***this section will not apply to:***

... ...

(8) The ad valorem fee, surcharge, and specific fees provided under paragraphs (b)(1) and (b)(2)(i) of this section will not apply to goods that qualify as originating goods under §203 of ***the United States-Australia Free Trade Agreement*** *Implementation Act (see also General Note 28, HTSUS) that are entered, or withdrawn from warehouse for consumption, on or after January 1, 2005.*

 The correct answer is "b".

✔ **JUST A SIDE NOTE:** Many other Free Trade Agreements (FTA) are also exempt from the Merchandise Processing Fee (MPF), such as NAFTA, Singapore FTA, Chile FTA, Korea FTA, Panama TPA (Trade Promotion Agreement).

✔ **JUST A SIDE NOTE:** Currently there is no such thing as a China FTA, as referenced in the above exam question.

41) Where no claim for preferential treatment under the North American Free Trade Agreement was made at the time of importation, an importer may file a claim for preferential treatment under NAFTA within ________.

a) 1 year from the date of exportation of the goods
b) 1 year from the date of the importation of the goods
c) 1 year from the date of liquidation of the entry
d) 80 days from the date of liquidation of the entry
e) 314 days from the date of exportation of the goods

 As per 19 CFR 181.31 (NAFTA Post-importation):

181.31 Right to make post-importation claim and refund duties.

Notwithstanding any other available remedy, including the right to amend an entry so long as liquidation of the entry has not become final, ***where a good would have qualified as an originating good when it was imported into the United States but no claim for preferential tariff treatment on that originating good was made at that time*** *under §181.21(a) of this part,* ***the importer of that good may file a claim for a refund of any excess duties at any time within one year after the date of importation*** *of the good in accordance with the procedures set forth in §181.32 of this part. Subject to the provisions of §181.23 of this part, Customs may refund any excess duties by liquidation or reliquidation of the entry covering the good in accordance with §181.33(c) of this part.*

 The correct answer is "b".

✔ **JUST A SIDE NOTE:** A NAFTA Certificate of Origin (CBP Form 434) is required to support a NAFTA preferential tariff treatment claim. A snapshot of what the form looks like included below:

DEPARTMENT OF HOMELAND SECURITY
U.S. Customs and Border Protection

NORTH AMERICAN FREE TRADE AGREEMENT
CERTIFICATE OF ORIGIN

19 CFR 181.11, 181.22

1. EXPORTER NAME, ADDRESS AND EMAIL TAX IDENTIFICATION NUMBER:	2. BLANKET PERIOD FROM (mm/dd/yyyy) TO (mm/dd/yyyy)
3. PRODUCER NAME, ADDRESS AND EMAIL TAX IDENTIFICATION NUMBER:	4. IMPORTER NAME, ADDRESS AND EMAIL TAX IDENTIFICATION NUMBER:

5. DESCRIPTION OF GOOD(S)	6. HS TARIFF CLASSIFICATION NUMBER	7. PREFERENCE CRITERION	8. PRODUCER	9. NET COST	10. COUNTRY OF ORIGIN

I CERTIFY THAT:

- THE INFORMATION ON THIS DOCUMENT IS TRUE AND ACCURATE AND I ASSUME THE RESPONSIBILITY FOR PROVING SUCH REPRESENTATIONS. I UNDERSTAND THAT I AM LIABLE FOR ANY FALSE STATEMENTS OR MATERIAL OMISSIONS MADE ON OR IN CONNECTION WITH THIS DOCUMENT;
- I AGREE TO MAINTAIN AND PRESENT UPON REQUEST, DOCUMENTATION NECESSARY TO SUPPORT THIS CERTIFICATE, AND TO INFORM, IN WRITING, ALL PERSONS TO WHOM THE CERTIFICATE WAS GIVEN OF ANY CHANGES THAT COULD AFFECT THE ACCURACY OR VALIDITY OF THIS CERTIFICATE;
- THE GOODS ORIGINATED IN THE TERRITORY OF ONE OR MORE OF THE PARTIES, AND COMPLY WITH THE ORIGIN REQUIREMENTS SPECIFIED FOR THOSE GOODS IN THE NORTH AMERICAN FREE TRADE AGREEMENT AND UNLESS SPECIFICALLY EXEMPTED IN ARTICLE 411 OR ANNEX 401, THERE HAS BEEN NO FURTHER PRODUCTION OR ANY OTHER OPERATION OUTSIDE THE TERRITORIES OF THE PARTIES; AND
- THIS CERTIFICATE CONSISTS OF [ ] PAGES, INCLUDING ALL ATTACHMENTS.

11.	11a. AUTHORIZED SIGNATURE		11b. COMPANY
	11c. NAME		11d. TITLE
	11e. DATE (mm/dd/yyyy)	11f. TELEPHONE NUMBERS (Voice) (Facsimile)	11g. EMAIL

CBP Form 434 (11/14)

42) The NAFTA Certificate of Origin must be retained in the _____.

a) U.S. by the importer until notification of liquidation is received from CBP
b) NAFTA country of origin by the producer for one year after liquidation
c) NAFTA country of origin by the producer for five years after liquidation
d) U.S. for five years after entry of the good with all relevant documentation
e) NAFTA country of origin for five years after date of liquidation

 As per 19 CFR 181.22(a):

181.22 Maintenance of records and submission of Certificate by importer.

(a) Maintenance of records. ***Each importer claiming preferential tariff treatment for a good imported into the United States shall maintain in the United States, for five years after the date of entry of the good, all documentation relating to the importation of the good. Such documentation shall include a copy of the Certificate of Origin and any other relevant records*** *as specified in §163.1(a) of this chapter.*

 The correct answer is "d".

✓ **JUST A SIDE NOTE:** A NAFTA Certificate of Origin may be made for a single shipment, or it may be made to cover multiple shipments on what's commonly referred to as a "blanket certificate", valid up to 1 year.

43) When an importer is making a claim of preferential tariff treatment under the United States-Australia Free Trade Agreement, the importer indicates their claim on the CBP Form 7501. Which of the following special program indicator should be used?

a) A+
b) MX
c) AU
d) CL
e) K

 As per HTSUS GN 3(c):

(c) Products Eligible for Special Tariff Treatment.

*(i) Programs **under which special tariff treatment may be provided, and the corresponding symbols for such programs as they are indicated in the "Special" subcolumn, are as follows:***

Generalized System of Preferences....................A, A or A+*
United States-Australia Free Trade Agreement....................AU
Automotive Products Trade Act....................B
United States-Bahrain Free Trade Agreement Implementation Act....................BH
Agreement on Trade in Civil Aircraft....................C
North American Free Trade Agreement:
Goods of Canada, under the terms of general note 12 to this schedule....................CA
Goods of Mexico, under the terms of general note 12 to this schedule....................MX
United States-Chile Free Trade Agreement....................CL
African Growth and Opportunity Act....................D
*Caribbean Basin Economic Recovery Act....................E or E**
United States-Israel Free Trade Area....................IL
United States-Jordan Free Trade Area Implementation Act....................JO
Agreement on Trade in Pharmaceutical Products....................K
Dominican Republic-Central America-United States Free Trade Agreement.................... P or P+
Uruguay Round Concessions on Intermediate Chemicals for Dyes....................L
United States-Caribbean Basin Trade Partnership Act....................R
United States-Morocco Free Trade Agreement Implementation Act....................MA
United States-Singapore Free Trade Agreement....................SG
United States-Oman Free Trade Agreement Implementation Act....................OM
United States-Peru Trade Promotion Agreement Implementation Act....................PE
United States-Korea Free Trade Agreement Implementation Act....................KR
United States-Colombia Trade Promotion Agreement Implementation Act....................CO
United States-Panama Trade Promotion Agreement Implementation Act....................PA

 The correct answer is "c".

✓ **JUST A SIDE NOTE:** If "AU" precedes the HTS number on the Entry Summary (CBP Form 7501), that means the Australia FTA is being claimed for that Entry Summary line. If, instead, "0AU" (zero-A-U) precedes the HTS number on the Entry Summary, that means the country of origin is Australia for that Entry Summary line, and no Australia FTA is being claimed.

44) Which of the following is NOT a direct cost of processing operations performed in the beneficiary developing country?

a) **All actual labor costs involved in the growth, production, manufacture, or assembly of the specific merchandise, including fringe benefits, on-the-job-training, and the cost of engineering, supervisory, quality control, and similar personnel**

b) **General expenses of doing business which are either not allocable to the specific merchandise or are not related to the growth, production, manufacture, or assembly of merchandise, such as administrative salaries, casualty and liability insurance, advertising, and salaries, commissions, or expenses**

c) **Dies, molds, tooling, and depreciation on machinery and equipment which are allocable to the specific merchandise**

d) **Costs of inspecting and testing the specific merchandise**

e) **Research, development, design, engineering, and blueprint costs insofar as they are allocable to the specific merchandise**

As per 19 CFR 10.178:

10.178 Direct costs of processing operations performed in the beneficiary developing country.

(a) Items included in the direct costs of processing operations. As used in §10.176, the words ***"direct costs of processing operations" means those costs either directly incurred in, or which can be reasonably allocated to, the growth, production, manufacture, or assembly of the specific merchandise under consideration. Such costs include, but are not limited to:***

(1) ***All actual labor costs*** *involved in the growth, production, manufacture, or assembly of the specific merchandise, including fringe benefits, on-the-job training, and the cost of engineering, supervisory, ...*

(2) ***Dies, molds, tooling, and depreciation*** *on machinery and equipment which are allocable to the specific merchandise;*

(3) ***Research, development,*** *design, engineering, and blueprint costs insofar as they are allocable to the specific merchandise; and*

(4) ***Costs of inspecting and testing*** *the specific merchandise.*

(b) Items not included in the direct costs of processing operations. ***Those items which are not included within the meaning of the words "direct costs of processing operations" are those which are not directly attributable to the merchandise under consideration or are not "costs" of manufacturing the product. These include, but are not limited to:***

(1) ***Profit****; and*

(2) ***General expenses of doing business*** *which are either not allocable to the specific merchandise or are not related to the growth, production, manufacture, or assembly of the merchandise, such as administrative salaries, casualty and liability insurance, advertising, and salesmen's salaries, commissions, or expenses.*

 The correct answer is "b".

✓ **JUST A SIDE NOTE:** Direct costs, such as manufacturing labor, are traceable to the finished product. On the other hand, other expenses that are naturally fixed, such as telephone bills, are not considered direct costs.

45) Which form must be presented to CBP to request exportation of merchandise that is intended for a rejected merchandise drawback claim?

a) CBP Form 7512
b) CBP Form 7551
c) CBP Form 7553
d) CBP Form 7523
e) CBP Form 7533

 As per 19 CFR 191.42 (c):

(c) Notice. ***A notice of intent to export or destroy merchandise which may be the subject of a rejected merchandise drawback claim*** *(19 U.S.C. 1313(c)) must be provided to the Customs Service to give Customs the opportunity to examine the merchandise.* ***The claimant, or the exporter (for destruction, see §191.44), must file at the port of intended redelivery to Customs custody a Notice of Intent to Export, Destroy, or Return Merchandise for Purposes of Drawback on Customs Form 7553*** *at least 5 working days prior to the date of intended return to Customs custody. Waiver of prior notice for exportations under 19 U.S.C. 1313(j) (see §191.91 of this part) is inapplicable to exportations under 19 U.S.C. 1313(c).*

 The correct answer is "c".

✔ **JUST A SIDE NOTE:** See below snapshot of what the relatively rarely used CBP Form 7553 looks like:

OMB No. 1651-0075 Exp. 12/31/2014

DEPARTMENT OF HOMELAND SECURITY
U.S. Customs and Border Protection

NOTICE OF INTENT TO EXPORT, DESTROY OR RETURN MERCHANDISE FOR PURPOSES OF DRAWBACK
19 CFR 191

PAPERWORK REDUCTION ACT NOTICE: This request is in accordance with the Paperwork Reduction Act. We ask for the information in order to enforce the laws of the United States, to fulfill the U.S. Customs Regulations, to ensure that the claimant is entitled to drawback, and to have the necessary information which permits CBP to calculate and refund (or increase) the correct amount of duty and/or tax. Your response is required to obtain a benefit. The estimated average burden associated with this collection of information is 33 minutes per respondent depending on individual circumstances. Comments concerning the accuracy of this burden estimate and suggestions for reducing this burden should be directed to U.S. Customs and Border Protection, Asset Management, Washington, DC 20229, and to the Office of Management and Budget, Paperwork Reduction Project (1651-0075) Washington, DC 20503.

1. Exporter or Destroyer
Name
Address
I.D. Number

2. Drawback Entry No.
3. Intended Action ☐ Export ☐ Destroy
4. Intended Date of Action (MM/DD/YYYY)
5. Drawback Center

6. Contact Name
Address
Phone Ext.
FAX

DATE RECEIVED

7. Location of Merchandise
8. Method of Destruction
9. Location of Destruction
10. Exporting Carrier Name (if known)
11. Intended Port of Export
12. Unique Identifier No.
13. T & E No.
14. Country of Ultimate Destination
15. Import Entry No.
16. Description of Merchandise (Include Part/Style/Serial Numbers)
17. Drawback Amount
18. Quantity & Unit of Measure
19. HTSUS No./Schedule B

20. Drawback to be filed as:
☐ Unused Merchandise Drawback ☐ J1 ☐ J2
☐ Manufacturing Drawback
☐ Same Condition Drawback under NAFTA
☐ Distilled Spirits, Wine or Beer under 26 U.S.C. 5062 (c)
☐ Rejected Merchandise
☐ Shipped without Consent
☐ Defective at Time of Importation
☐ Not Conforming to Sample or Specifications

21. Preparer
Printed Name X Signature Title Date

THIS FORM MUST BE SUBMITTED WITH THE DRAWBACK CLAIM

CBP USE ONLY

22. Examination ☐ Required or ☐ Waived (Additional information may be required if exam requested, T & E may be required)
23. Present Merchandise to CBP at:
24. Destruction to be Witnessed by Customs ☐ Yes ☐ No
25. Printed Name
Phone Number
26. Signature & Badge No.
X
27. Date
28. Port
29. Comments/Results of Examination or Witnessing of Destruction. (Merchandise matches invoice description)
30. Date Destroyed or Exam Conducted
31. Printed Name of Examining Officer
Phone Number Ext.
32. Signature & Badge No.
X
Date

CBP Form 7553 (07/08)

46) A person may be certified in the drawback compliance program after meeting the core requirements established under this program. In order to be certified as a participant in the drawback compliance program or negotiated alternative drawback compliance program, the party must be able to demonstrate all of the following EXCEPT:

a) Understanding of the legal requirements for filing claims, including the nature of the records that are required to be maintained and produced and the time period involved
b) Having established procedures explain the Customs requirements to those employees involved in the preparation of claims, and the maintenance and production of required records.
c) Having a dependable individual(s) who will be responsible for compliance under the program, and maintenance and production of required records.
d) Having an established a record maintenance program approved by Customs regarding original records or, if approved by Customs, alternative records or recordkeeping formats for other than the original records.
e) Having procedures for notifying the importer of variances in, or violations of, the drawback compliance or other alternative negotiated drawback compliance program, and for taking corrective action when notified by the importer of violations and problems regarding such program.

As per 19 CFR 191.192(b):

(b) Core requirements of program. ***In order to be certified as a participant in the drawback compliance program or negotiated alternative drawback compliance program, the party must be able to demonstrate that it:***

(1) ***Understands the legal requirements for filing claims****, including the nature of the records that are required to be maintained and produced and the time periods involved;*

(2) ***Has in place procedures that explain the Customs requirements*** *to those employees involved in the preparation of claims, and the maintenance and production of required records;*

(3) Has in place procedures regarding the preparation of claims and maintenance of required records, and the production of such records to Customs;

(4) ***Has designated a dependable individual*** *or individuals who will be responsible for compliance under the program, and maintenance and production of required records;*

(5) ***Has in place a record maintenance program approved by Customs*** *regarding original records, or if approved by Customs, alternative records or recordkeeping formats for other than the original records; and*

(6) ***Has procedures for notifying Customs of variances*** *in, or violations of, the drawback compliance or other alternative negotiated drawback compliance program, and for taking corrective action when notified by Customs of violations and problems regarding such program.*

Multiple choice "e" says "procedures for notifying 'the importer' of variances." Whereas, 19 CFR 191.192(b)(6) states "procedures for notifying 'Customs' of variances." The correct answer is "e".

✓ **JUST A SIDE NOTE:** The Drawback Compliance Program is a voluntary certification program open to importers and customs brokers. Its benefits include, but may not be limited to, reduced penalties and reduced warnings from Customs.

47) The method by which fungible merchandise or articles are identified on the basis of calculation by recordkeeping of the amount of drawback that may be attributed to each unit of merchandise or articles in the inventory. Which of the following approved accounting method is utilized by Customs and Border Protection?

a) Average
b) Inventory turn-over for limited purposes
c) Low-to-High
d) Last-in, first out
e) First-in, first out

 As per 19 CFR 191.14(c):

... ...

(4) Average—(i) General. ***The average method is the method by which fungible merchandise or articles are identified on the basis of the calculation by recordkeeping of the amount of drawback that may be attributed to each unit of merchandise or articles in the inventory.*** *In this method, the ratio of:*

(A) The total units of a particular receipt of the fungible merchandise in the inventory at the time of a withdrawal to;

(B) The total units of all receipts of the fungible merchandise (including each receipt into inventory) at the time of the withdrawal;

(C) Is applied to the withdrawal, so that the withdrawal consists of a proportionate quantity of units from each particular receipt and each receipt is correspondingly decreased. Withdrawals and corresponding decreases to receipts are rounded to the nearest whole number.

Actually, all five multiple choice options are actual accounting methods approved and utilized by CBP, depending on the company and situation. In this scenario, the "average method" is utilized. The correct answer is "a".

✓ **JUST A SIDE NOTE:** "Fungibility" means the interchangeability of identical items. It is a Latin-based word and related to the word "function". A good example of fungible merchandise is salt, and is defined by Customs as:

Fungible merchandise or articles means merchandise or articles which for commercial purposes are identical and interchangeable in all situations.

48) Upon review of a drawback claim, if the claim is determined to be incomplete, the claim will be rejected and Customs will notify the filer in writing. The filer shall then have the opportunity to complete the claim subject to the requirement for filing a complete claim within _______________.

a) 2 days
b) 30 days
c) 1 years
d) 2 years
e) 3 years

 As per 19 CFR 191.52(a):

191.52 Rejecting, perfecting or amending claims.

(a) Rejecting the claim. ***Upon review of a drawback claim, if the claim is determined to be incomplete (see §191.51(a)(1)), the claim will be rejected and Customs will notify the filer in writing. The filer shall then have the opportunity to complete the claim subject to the requirement for filing a complete claim within 3 years.***

 The correct answer is "e".

✔ **JUST A SIDE NOTE:** A (duty) drawback is the (partial or in full) refund of import duties on an item subsequently exported or destroyed.

49) Which of the following parties does NOT have authority to sign drawback documents?

a) Owner of a sole proprietorship
b) An individual acting on his/her behalf
c) Licensed Customs broker without a power of attorney
d) A full partner of a partnership
e) President, Vice President, Secretary, Treasurer, or any employee legally authorized to bind the corporation

 As per 19 CFR 191.6(a):

191.6 Authority to sign drawback documents.

(a) ***Documents listed in paragraph (b) of this section shall be signed only by one of the following:***

(1) The president, a vice-president, secretary, treasurer, or any other employee legally authorized to bind the corporation;

(2) A full partner of a partnership;

(3) The owner of a sole proprietorship;

(4) Any employee of the business entity with a power of attorney;

(5) An individual acting on his or her own behalf; or

(6) ***A licensed Customs broker with a power of attorney.***

 A licensed customs broker WITHOUT a power of attorney does not have such authority. The correct answer is "c".

✓ **JUST A SIDE NOTE:** A licensed customs broker CAN, without a power of attorney, file a "Section 321" entry for an importer. Basically, a Section 321 entry is a simplified entry with very little document requirements, and can be done on most imports valued at $800 or less (previously $200 or less). This is also known as a Low Value Shipment (LVS).

50) Qualifying expenditures which may be offset by a distribution of assessed antidumping and countervailing duties must fall within the categories described below with the exception of?

"These expenditures must be incurred after the issuance, and prior to the termination, of the antidumping duty order or finding or countervailing duty order under which the distribution is sought. Further, these expenditures must be related to the production of the same product that is the subject of the related order or finding, with the exception of expenses incurred by associations which must relate to a specific case."

a) Manufacturing facilities
b) Housing
c) Personnel training
d) Health Care Benefits for employees paid for by the employer
e) Equipment

 As per 19 CFR 159.61(c):

(c) Qualifying expenditures. Qualifying expenditures which may be offset by a distribution of assessed antidumping and countervailing duties must fall within the categories described in paragraphs (c)(1) through (c)(10) of this section. ... ...

(1) ***Manufacturing facilities;***

(2) ***Equipment;***

(3) Research and development;

(4) ***Personnel training;***

(5) Acquisition of technology;

(6) ***Health care benefits for employees paid for by the employer;***

(7) Pension benefits for employees paid for by the employer;

(8) Environmental equipment, training, or technology;

(9) Acquisition of raw materials and other inputs; and

(10) Working capital or other funds needed to maintain production.

 Employee housing expenses are not eligible for antidumping payments. The correct answer is "b".

✓ **JUST A SIDE NOTE:** "Affected domestic producers" are eligible to receive subsidy payments pulled from Customs collected antidumping and countervailing duty receipts.

51) Which entry types(s) may be used for merchandise subject to antidumping/countervailing duties (AD/CVD)?

a) 03
b) 07
c) 34
d) 38
e) All of the above

 As per CBP Form 7501 Instructions, BLOCK 2) ENTRY TYPE:

BLOCK 2) ENTRY TYPE

Record the appropriate entry type code by selecting the two-digit code for the type of entry summary being filed. The first digit of the code identifies the general category of the entry (i.e., consumption = 0, informal = 1, warehouse = 2). The second digit further defines the specific processing type within the entry category. The following codes shall be used:

Consumption Entries	
Free and Dutiable	*01*
Quota/Visa	*02*
Antidumping/Countervailing Duty (AD/CVD)	***03***
Appraisement	*04*
Vessel Repair	*05*
Foreign Trade Zone Consumption	*06*
Quota/Visa and AD/CVD combinations	***07***
Duty Deferral	*08*
Informal Entries	
Free and Dutiable	*11*
Quota Other than textiles	*12*
Warehouse Entries	
Warehouse	*21*
Re-Warehouse	*22*
Temporary Importation Bond	*23*
Trade Fair	*24*
Permanent Exhibition	*25*
Foreign Trade Zone Admission	*26*
Warehouse Withdrawal	
For Consumption	*31*
Quota/Visa	*32*
AD/CVD	***34***
Quota/Visa and AD/CVD combinations	***38***

... ...

 The correct answer is "e".

✓ **JUST A SIDE NOTE:** Antidumping/Countervailing Duty entry type "03" is by far the most common of all AD/CVD entry types filed.

52) ___________ is required prior to liquidation of an entry subject to an antidumping/countervailing duty order or those duties will be doubled upon liquidation.

a) A Certificate of manufacturing
b) A sales receipt
c) A reimbursement certificate
d) Meeting with Import Specialists
e) An Invoice

 As per 19 CFR 351.402 (f):

... ...

(2) Certificate. ***The importer must file prior to liquidation a certificate in the following form*** *with the appropriate District Director of Customs:*

> *I hereby certify that I (have) (have not) entered into any agreement or understanding for the payment or for the refunding to me, by the manufacturer, producer, seller, or exporter, of all or any part of the antidumping duties or countervailing duties assessed upon the following importations of (commodity) from (country): (List entry numbers) which have been purchased on or after (date of publication of antidumping notice suspending liquidation in the Federal Register) or purchased before (same date) but exported on or after (date of final determination of sales at less than fair value).*

... ...

 The correct answer is "c".

✓ **JUST A SIDE NOTE:** The above-mentioned certificate and statement is also known as an Antidumping/Countervailing Duty Non-Reimbursement Certificate. It can be completed for a single shipment or as a one year-blanket certificate. Basically, it makes the importer certify that they will not receive compensation from the foreign supplier to help off-set the antidumping duties that CBP levies on the import.

53) Which of the following parties CANNOT request a county-of-origin advisory ruling or final determination?

a) A foreign Manufacturer, producer, or exporter, or a United States importer of the merchandise

b) A manufacturer, producer, or wholesaler in the United States of a like product

c) United States members of a labor organization or other association of workers whose members are employed in the manufacture, production, or wholesale in the United States of a like product

d) A trade or business association a majority of whose members manufacture, produce, or wholesale a like product in the United States

e) The Port Director to where the merchandise has arrived

 As per 19 CFR 177.23:

177.23 Who may request a country-of-origin advisory ruling or final determination.

A country-of-origin advisory ruling or final determination may be requested by:

(a) ***A foreign manufacturer, producer, or exporter, or a United States importer of merchandise,***

(b) ***A manufacturer, producer, or wholesaler in the United States of a like product,***

(c) ***United States members of a labor organization*** *or other association of workers whose members are employed in the manufacture, production, or wholesale in the United States of a like product, or*

(d) ***A trade or business association*** *a majority of whose members manufacture, produce, or wholesale a like product in the United States.*

 The correct answer is "e".

✓ **JUST A SIDE NOTE:** Such country of origin rulings and classification rulings are recorded and indexed at CBP's Customs Rulings Online Search System (CROSS). This CBP website is an excellent free resource for importers and customs brokers. Currently there are over 190,000 searchable Customs rulings here.

www.rulings.cbp.gov

54) How many days does CBP have before it is required to notify the importer that it is detaining goods to determine admissibility relative to possible counterfeit trademarks?

a) 5 business days
b) 5 calendar days
c) 7 calendar days
d) 10 business days
e) 10 calendar days

 As per 19 CFR 133.21(b):

(b) Detention, notice, and disclosure of information—(1) Detention period. CBP may detain any article of domestic or foreign manufacture imported into the United States that bears a mark suspected by CBP of being a counterfeit version of a mark that is registered with the U.S. Patent and Trademark Office and is recorded with CBP pursuant to subpart A of this part. The detention will be for a period of up to 30 days from the date on which the merchandise is presented for examination. In accordance with 19 U.S.C. 1499(c), if, after the detention period, the article is not released, the article will be deemed excluded for the purposes of 19 U.S.C. 1514(a)(4).

(2) Notice of detention to importer and disclosure to owner of the mark—(i) Notice and seven business day response period. ***Within five business days from the date of a decision to detain suspect merchandise, CBP will notify the importer in writing of the detention*** *as set forth in §151.16(c) of this chapter and 19 U.S.C. 1499. CBP will also inform the importer that for purposes of assisting CBP in determining whether the detained merchandise bears counterfeit marks:*
... ...

 The correct answer is "a".

✓ **JUST A SIDE NOTE:** 19 CFR 133.21(a) defines a "counterfeit mark" as "a spurious mark that is identical with, or substantially indistinguishable from, a mark registered on the Principal Register of the U.S. Patent and Trademark Office."

55) What is the fee for recording a trademark with CBP for a United States Patent and Trademark Office (USPTO) registration that includes four classes of goods?

a) $190
b) $0
c) $300
d) $760
e) $380

 As per 19 CFR 133.3(b):

(b) Fee. The application shall be accompanied by a fee of $190 for each trademark to be recorded. However, ***if the trademark is registered for more than one class of goods*** *(based on the class, or classes, first stated on the certificate of registration, without consideration of any class, or classes, also stated in parentheses)* ***the fee for recordation shall be $190 for each class*** *for which the applicant desires to record the trademark with the United States Customs Service. For example, to secure recordation of a trademark registered for three classes of goods, a fee of $570 is payable. A check or money order shall be made payable to the United States Customs Service.*

 $190 x 4 classes = $760. The correct answer is "d".

✓ **JUST A SIDE NOTE:** There are currently 45 trademark classes, as organized by the World Intellectual Property Organization. Trade mark classes include goods such as paints, pharmaceuticals, vehicles, etc., as well as services such as advertising, transportation, education, etc.

56) Which article is NOT exempt from country of origin marking requirements when imported into the United States?

a) A unicycle that was manufactured in 1953
b) A clothes dryer machine made in Wisconsin
c) An original oil painting produced in France
d) A printed poster produced in Italy
e) A set of glasses to be used by the importer

 As per 19 CFR 134.32:

134.32 General exceptions to marking requirements.

The articles described or meeting the specified conditions set forth below are excepted from marking requirements *(see subpart C of this part for marking of the containers):*

(a) Articles that are incapable of being marked;

(b) ***Articles that cannot be marked prior to shipment to the United States without injury****;*

(c) Articles that cannot be marked prior to shipment to the United States except at an expense economically prohibitive of its importation;

(d) Articles for which the marking of the containers will reasonably indicate the origin of the articles;

(e) Articles which are crude substances;

(f) ***Articles imported for use by the importer*** *and not intended for sale in their imported or any other form;*
... ...

(i) ***Articles which were produced more than 20 years prior*** *to their importation into the United States;*
... ...

(m) ***Products of the United States*** *exported and returned;*
... ...

 The correct answer is "d".

✔ **NOTE:** The following section, 19 CFR 134.33 contains the "J-List", which is a more specific list of items exempt from country of origin requirements. Excerpt below:

Articles
Art, works of.
Articles classified under subheadings 9810.00.15, 9810.00.25, 9810.00.40 and 9810.00.45, Harmonized Tariff Schedule of the United States
Articles entered in good faith as antiques and rejected as unauthentic.

57) Additional duties will be assessed at ___________ for failure to mark the article (or container) to indicate the English name of the country of origin of the article or to include words or symbols required to prevent deception or mistake.

a) 5%
b) 10%
c) 15%
d) 20%
e) 100%

 As per 19 CFR 134.2:

134.2 Additional duties.

Articles not marked as required by this part shall be subject to additional duties of 10 percent of the final appraised value *unless exported or destroyed under Customs supervision prior to liquidation of the entry, as provided in 19 U.S.C. 1304(f). The 10 percent additional duty is assessable for failure either to mark the article (or container) to indicate the English name of the country of origin of the article or to include words or symbols required to prevent deception or mistake.*

 The correct answer is "b".

✓ **NOTE:** Country of origin markings must be reasonably legible, durable, and noticeable enough for the ultimate purchaser.

58) The license of a broker that is a corporation or association can be revoked by operation of law if it fails for _____ continuous days to have at least one officer of the corporation or association who holds a valid individual broker license.

a) 30
b) 60
c) 120
d) 160
e) 180

 As per 19 CFR 111.45(a):

111.45 Revocation by operation of law.

(a) License. ***If a broker that is a partnership, association, or corporation fails to have, during any continuous period of 120 days, at least one member of the partnership or at least one officer of the association or corporation who holds a valid individual broker's license, that failure will, in addition to any other sanction that may be imposed under this part, result in the revocation by operation of law of the license*** *and any permits issued to the partnership, association, or corporation. The Assistant Commissioner or his designee will notify the broker in writing of an impending revocation by operation of law under this section 30 calendar days before the revocation is due to occur.*

 The correct answer is "c".

✓ **JUST A SIDE NOTE:** "120 days" means 120 calendar days. If Customs explicitly specifies "working days", that means weekends and federal holidays are not included in the counting of days.

59) The negligent failure to produce entry documents required by law or regulation for the entry of merchandise after a lawful demand by CBP, will subject the person who is required to maintain the documents to a penalty, per release of merchandise. What is the maximum penalty?

- **a) $100,000 or an amount equal to 75% of the appraised value of the merchandise, whichever is less**
- **b) $25,000 and 50% of the appraised value of the merchandise**
- **c) $10,000 or an amount equal to 40% of the appraised value of the merchandise, whichever amount is less**
- **d) $1,000,000 or an amount equal to 75% of the appraised value of the merchandise, whichever amount is less**
- **e) No penalty applicable**

 As per 19 CFR 163.6(b):

(b) Failure to produce entry records—(1) Monetary penalties applicable. The following penalties may be imposed if a person fails to comply with a lawful demand for the production of an entry record and is not excused from a penalty pursuant to paragraph (b)(3) of this section:

(i) If the failure to comply is a result of the willful failure of the person to maintain, store, or retrieve the demanded record, such person shall be subject to a penalty, for each release of merchandise, not to exceed $100,000, or an amount equal to 75 percent of the appraised value of the merchandise, whichever amount is less; or

(ii) ***If the failure to comply is a result of negligence of the person in maintaining, storing, or retrieving the demanded record, such person shall be subject to a penalty, for each release of merchandise, not to exceed $10,000, or an amount equal to 40 percent of the appraised value*** *of the merchandise, whichever amount is less.*

... ...

The correct answer is "c".

✓ **JUST A SIDE NOTE:** "Entry Records" usually include the CBP Form 7501 (entry summary), CBP Form 3461 (release), Commercial Invoice, Bill of Lading (or Air Waybill), and any applicable certificates.

60) Requests for alternative methods of storage for records, other than those that are required to be maintained as original records under laws and regulations administered by other Federal government agencies, must be made from which of the following offices?

a) Port Director, in the port where the records will be stored
b) Broker Management Office, Washington, DC
c) Regulatory Audit, Charlotte, NC
d) Director of Field Operations, in the District where the records will be stored
e) National Finance Office, Indianapolis, IN

 As per 19 CFR 163.5(b):

(b) Alternative method of storage—(1) General. ***Any of the persons listed in §163.2 may maintain any records, other than records required to be maintained as original records under laws and regulations administered by other Federal government agencies, in an alternative format, provided that the person gives advance written notification of such alternative storage method to the Regulatory Audit****, U.S. Customs and Border Protection, 2001 Cross Beam Dr., Charlotte, North Carolina 28217, and provided further that the Director of Regulatory Audit, Charlotte office does not instruct the person in writing as provided herein that certain described records may not be maintained in an alternative format. The written notice to the Director of Regulatory Audit, Charlotte office must be provided at least 30 calendar days before implementation of the alternative storage method, must identify the type of alternative storage method to be used, and must state that the alternative storage method complies with the standards set forth in paragraph (b)(2) of this section. If an alternative storage method covers records that pertain to goods under CBP seizure or detention or that relate to a matter that is currently the subject of an inquiry or investigation or administrative or court proceeding, the appropriate CBP office may instruct the person in writing that those records must be maintained as original records and therefore may not be converted to an alternative format until specific written authorization is received from that CBP office. A written instruction to a person under this paragraph may be issued during the 30-day advance notice period prescribed in this section or at any time thereafter, must describe the records in question with reasonable specificity but need not identify the underlying basis for the instruction, and shall not preclude application of the planned alternative storage method to other records not described therein.*

(2) Standards for alternative storage methods. Methods commonly used in standard business practice for storage of records include, but are not limited to, machine readable data, CD ROM, and microfiche. Methods that are in compliance with generally accepted business standards will generally satisfy CBP requirements, provided that the method used allows for retrieval of records requested within a reasonable time after the request and provided that adequate provisions exist to prevent alteration, destruction, or deterioration of the records. The following standards must be applied by recordkeepers when using alternative storage methods:
... ...

 The correct answer is "c".

✓ **JUST A SIDE NOTE:** Entry documents are required to be kept for 5 years after the customs entry date.

61) Which of the following is NOT "Customs Business" as defined in the Code of Federal Regulations?

a) The payment of duties, taxes and fees
b) Corporate compliance activity
c) Determining the admissibility of merchandise
d) Determining the classification and valuation of merchandise
e) The preparation and filing of CBP Form 7501

 As per 19 CFR 111.1:

Customs business. "Customs business" means those activities involving transactions with CBP concerning the entry and admissibility of merchandise, its classification and valuation, the payment of duties, taxes, or other charges assessed or collected by CBP on merchandise by reason of its importation, and the refund, rebate, or drawback of those duties, taxes, or other charges. "Customs business" also includes the preparation, and activities relating to the preparation, of documents in any format and the electronic transmission of documents and parts of documents intended to be filed with CBP in furtherance of any other customs business activity, whether or not signed or filed by the preparer. However, ***"customs business" does not include the mere electronic transmission of data received for transmission to CBP and does not include a corporate compliance activity.***

 The correct answer is "b".

✓ **JUST A SIDE NOTE:** The regulations' definition of "customs broker" means a licensed customs broker. However, outside of the regulations, the term "customs broker" does not necessarily mean the individual is licensed by CBP.

62) When a broker is employed for the transaction of customs business by an unlicensed person, who is not the actual importer, the broker must transmit ________________.

a) the entry in ACS immediately, as this type of transaction is new and only accepted in ACS

b) the entry in ACE immediately, as this type of transaction is new and only accepted in ACE

c) a copy of the importer's bill for services rendered or a copy of the entry

d) Customs Form 5106 for the unlicensed person

e) a Power of Attorney to Customs and Border Protection on behalf of the unlicensed person

As per 19 CFR 111.36(a):

111.36 Relations with unlicensed persons.

(a) Employment by unlicensed person other than importer. ***When a broker is employed for the transaction of customs business by an unlicensed person who is not the actual importer, the broker must transmit to the actual importer either a copy of his bill for services rendered or a copy of the entry****, unless the merchandise was purchased on a delivered duty-paid basis or unless the importer has in writing waived transmittal of the copy of the entry or bill for services rendered.*

The correct answer is "c".

✓ **JUST A SIDE NOTE:** Many freight forwarding companies do not possess their own customs brokerage departments. So, when such a freight forwarder imports a shipment into the U.S., they will often contract out the customs clearance to a 3rd party customs broker, and include that customs broker's invoice and the customs entry packet with their own freight forwarding services invoice to the importer.

63) XYC Brokerage is located in New York. It is permitted to conduct Customs business in the ports of New York, Florida, California, and Alabama. The individual qualifying the permit in New York leaves the brokerage. Which statement is correct?

a) **The broker has only 120 days to replace the individual qualifying the permit in New York.**

b) **The broker may demonstrate to the Port Director in New York that the licensed individual qualifying the Alabama permit can exercise responsible supervision and control over the business conducted in New York.**

c) **A waiver from the requirements of CR 111.11 can be granted because that is where the corporate license was issued.**

d) **There is no requirement to replace the licensed individual in New York as long as it is shown that the quality of work rendered by the employees in New York is the same as that rendered by the licensed individual.**

e) **XYC Brokerage has only 180 days to replace the individual qualifying the permit in New York.**

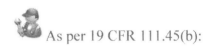

 As per 19 CFR 111.45(b):

(b) Permit. ***If a broker who has been granted a permit for an additional district fails, for any continuous period of 180 days, to employ within that district*** *(or region, as defined in §111.1, if an exception has been granted pursuant to §111.19(d))* ***at least one person who holds a valid individual broker's license, that failure will****, in addition to any other sanction that may be imposed under this part,* ***result in the revocation of the permit by operation of law.***

 The correct answer is "e".

✓ **JUST A SIDE NOTE:** When a customs broker receives their license from their port director, they are also eligible to receive a permit for the district in which that port is located. Essentially, this is their primary permit. After receipt of which, they may apply for additional district permits or for a national permit.

64) If a broker that is a partnership, association, or corporation fails to have at least one member or officer who holds a valid individual broker's license during any continuous period of _____________, the license and any permits will be revoked by operation of law.

a) 30 days
b) 60 days
c) 120 days
d) 180 days
e) 360 days

 As per 19 CFR 111.45(a):

(a) License. ***If a broker that is a partnership, association, or corporation fails to have, during any continuous period of 120 days, at least one member of the partnership or at least one officer of the association or corporation who holds a valid individual broker's license, that failure will,*** *in addition to any other sanction that may be imposed under this part,* ***result in the revocation by operation of law of the license and any permits issued to the partnership, association, or corporation.*** *The Assistant Commissioner or his designee will notify the broker in writing of an impending revocation by operation of law under this section 30 calendar days before the revocation is due to occur.*

 The correct answer is "c".

✔ **JUST A SIDE NOTE:** This type of exam question that asks how long a business may operate without a licensed customs broker is frequently asked on the exams. Just try to remember the answer is "120" days for the license question, and "180" days for additional permit question.

65) What is the deadline for a Licensed Customs Broker to file a status report?

a) March 31st of the reporting year
b) January 1st of each year
c) February 1st of each third year
d) December 31st of each third year
e) April 30th of each second year

 As per 19 CFR 111.30(d):

(d) Status report—(1) General. ***Each broker must file a written status report with Customs on February 1, 1985, and on February 1 of each third year after that date.*** *The report must be accompanied by the fee prescribed in §111.96(d) and must be addressed to the director of the port through which the license was delivered to the licensee (see §111.15). A report received during the month of February will be considered filed timely. No form or particular format is required.*

 The correct answer is "c".

✔ **JUST A SIDE NOTE:** Currently, the above-mentioned (triennial) status report fee is $100, which can be paid in the form of a company or personal check, and enclosed in envelope with the status report.

66) From June 2015 to September 2015, an importer entered five shipments of widgets as consumption entries despite his Customs attorney having advised him the widgets are subject to an antidumping case. In October 2015, CBP determined that the widgets should have been entered as antidumping entries and that the appropriate cash deposit rate for the widgets at the time of entry was 0.00%. Which of the following best describes the culpability of the importer for a penalty under 19 U.S.C. § 1592?

a) The importer is not culpable because there was no loss of revenue.
b) The importer is not culpable because, as the cash deposit rate is 0.00%, he is not liable for antidumping duties.
c) The importer is not culpable because CBP had previously released five shipments of the same merchandise, which is a contributory Customs error.
d) The importer may be culpable because the error affects CBP's determination of whether an unfair trade practice has been committed.
e) The importer is culpable, but he will not receive a penalty if his customs attorney can show that his advice was given prior to the commencement of any CBP investigation.

As per 19 CFR 171, APPENDIX B:

(B) Definition of Materiality Under Section 592

A document, statement, act, or ***omission is material if it has the natural tendency to influence or is capable of influencing agency action including, but not limited to a Customs action regarding****: (1) Determination of the classification, appraisement, or admissibility of merchandise (e.g., whether merchandise is prohibited or restricted); (2) determination of an importer's liability for duty (including marking, antidumping, and/or countervailing duty); (3) collection and reporting of accurate trade statistics; (4) determination as to the source, origin, or quality of merchandise; (5)* ***determination of whether an unfair trade practice has been committed under the anti-dumping or countervailing duty laws or a similar statute****; (6) determination of whether an unfair act has been committed involving patent, trademark, or copyright infringement; or (7) the determination of whether any other unfair trade practice has been committed in violation of federal law. The "but for" test of materiality is inapplicable under section 592.*

The correct answer is "d".

✓ **JUST A SIDE NOTE:** "Culpable" means a person being held responsible for something the person did or did not do.

67) A prior disclosure must ______.

a) disclose the circumstances of the exportation violation

b) include the disclosing party's calculation of the loss of revenue

c) specify the material false statements, omissions or acts and explain how and when they occurred

d) be submitted in response to a government issued notice of formal investigation

e) not involve entries subject to a drawback claim

 As per 19 CFR 162.74(b):

(b) Disclosure of the circumstances of a violation. ***The term "discloses the circumstances of a violation" means the act of providing to Customs a statement orally or in writing that****:*

(1) Identifies the class or kind of merchandise involved in the violation;

(2) Identifies the importation or drawback claim included in the disclosure by entry number, drawback claim number, or by indicating each concerned Customs port of entry and the approximate dates of entry or dates of drawback claims;

(3) ***Specifies the material false statements, omissions or acts including an explanation as to how and when they occurred****; and*

(4) Sets forth, to the best of the disclosing party's knowledge, the true and accurate information or data that should have been provided in the entry or drawback claim documents, and states that the disclosing party will provide any information or data unknown at the time of disclosure within 30 days of the initial disclosure date. Extensions of the 30-day period may be requested by the disclosing party from the concerned Fines, Penalties, and Forfeitures Officer to enable the party to obtain the information or data.

 The correct answer is "c".

✔ **JUST A SIDE NOTE:** A prior disclosure may be initiated either orally or in writing. If a conversation took place, however, it should be documented and sent to the appropriate CBP office within 10 days of the oral disclosure. As a wise man once said, if it isn't in writing, it didn't happen.

68) When filing a prior disclosure, the disclosing party may choose to make the tender of actual loss of duties, taxes, and fees, or actual loss of revenue. When must the disclosing party make the tender of actual loss of duties, taxes, and fees, or actual loss of revenue?

a) Within 1 year of filing the prior disclosure

b) At the time of the claimed prior disclosure or within 30 days after Customs notifies the person in writing of Customs calculation of the actual loss of duties, taxes and fees or actual loss of revenue

c) At the time of the claimed prior disclosure or within 90 days after Customs notifies the person in writing of Customs calculation of the actual loss of duties, taxes and fees or actual loss of revenue

d) Within 1 year of filing the prior disclosure or within 30 days after Customs notifies the person in writing of Customs calculation of the actual loss of duties, taxes and fees or actual loss of revenue

e) Within 90 days after Customs notifies the person in writing of Customs calculation of the actual loss of duties, taxes and fees or actual loss of revenue

 As per 19 CFR 162.74(c):

(c) Tender of actual loss of duties, taxes and fees or actual loss of revenue. A person who discloses the circumstances of the violation shall tender any actual loss of duties, taxes and fees or actual loss of revenue. ***The disclosing party may choose to make the tender either at the time of the claimed prior disclosure, or within 30 days after CBP notifies the person in writing of CBP calculation of the actual loss of duties, taxes and fees or actual loss of revenue.*** *The Fines, Penalties, and Forfeitures Officer may extend the 30-day period if there is good cause to do so.*

... ...

Failure to tender the actual loss of duties, taxes and fees or actual loss of revenue finally calculated by CBP shall result in denial of the prior disclosure.

 The correct answer is "b".

✓ **JUST A SIDE NOTE:** One reason a company might decide to submit a prior disclosure without accompanying duties is to secure prior disclosure status prior to the initiation of a CBP investigation.

69) Petition for relief must be filed within _________from the date of mailing to the bond principal the notice of claim for liquidated damages or penalty secured by a bond.

a) 2 days
b) 10 days
c) 30 days
d) 60 days
e) 90 days

 As per 19 CFR 172.3(b):

(b) When filed. ***Petitions for relief must be filed within 60 days from the date of mailing to the bond principal*** *the notice of claim for liquidated damages or penalty secured by a bond.*

 The correct answer is "d".

✓ **JUST A SIDE NOTE:** "Liquidated damages" are demands for payment by CBP to a principal's (e.g. importer's) surety (i.e. customs bond company). Petitions and supplemental petitions for relief are requests to have the penalties mitigated (i.e. reduced).

70) An error in the liquidation of an entry covering household or personal effects may be corrected by the port director even though a timely protest was not filed if entry was made before December 18, 2004 and an application for refund is filed with the port director ________________and no waiver of compliance with applicable regulations is involved other than a waiver which the port director has authority to grant. Where the port director has no authority to grant the waiver, the application will be referred to the Commissioner of CBP.

a) Within 10 days after the date of entry
b) Within 30 days after the date of entry
c) Within 60 days after the date of entry
d) Within 90 days after the date of entry
e) Within 1 year after the date of entry

 As per 19 CFR 173.5:

173.5 Review of entry covering household or personal effects.

An error in the liquidation of an entry covering household or personal effects may be corrected by the port director even though a timely protest was not filed if entry was made before December 18, 2004 and an application for refund is filed with the port director within 1 year after the date of the entry *and no waiver of compliance with applicable regulations is involved other than a waiver which the port director has authority to grant. Where the port director has no authority to grant the waiver, the application will be referred to the Commissioner of CBP.*

 The correct answer is "e".

✓ **JUST A SIDE NOTE:** Part 173 of these customs regulations is titled "ADMINISTRATIVE REVIEW IN GENERAL". It provides procedures and authority for CBP to review and relatively casually amend errors associated with old entries.

71) If the Fines, Penalties, and Forfeitures Officer has reasonable cause to believe that a violation of section 592, Tariff Act of 1930, as amended (19 U.S.C. 1592), has occurred, and determines that further proceedings are warranted, he shall issue to the person concerned a notice of his intent to issue a claim for a monetary penalty. The prepenalty notice shall be issued whether or not a seizure has been made. The prepenalty notice shall contain all of the below EXCEPT:

a) Description of merchandise
b) State the actual loss of duties, if any and demand payment immediately
c) Specify all laws and regulations allegedly violated
d) Disclose all material facts which established the alleged violation
e) State whether the alleged violations occurred as the result of fraud, gross negligence or negligence

 As per 19 CFR 162.77(b):

(b) Contents—(1) Facts of violation. ***The prepenalty notice shall:***

(i) Describe the merchandise,

(ii) Set forth the details of the entry or introduction, the attempted entry or introduction, or the aiding or abetting of the entry, introduction, or attempt,

(iii) Specify all laws and regulations allegedly violated,

(iv) Disclose all material facts which establish the alleged violation,

(v) State whether the alleged violation occurred as the result of fraud, gross negligence, or negligence, and

(vi) ***State the estimated loss of duties, if any, and, taking into account all circumstances, the amount of the proposed monetary penalty.***

 The prepenalty notice will state the "estimated" (i.e. not "actual") loss of duties, etc. The correct answer is "b".

✓ **JUST A SIDE NOTE:** "Section 592 of Tariff Act of 1930" provides for penalties for errors in statements to CBP.

72) If the principal gets free release of any serially numbered shipping container classifiable under subheading 9801.00.10 or 9803.00.50, Harmonized Tariff Schedule of the United States (HTSUS), the principal agrees to all of the following EXCEPT:

a) **To advance the value and improve its condition abroad or claim (or make a previous claim) drawback on any container released under subheading 9801.00.10, HTSUS.**
b) **To pay the initial duty due and otherwise comply with every condition in subheading 9803.00.50, HTSUS, on any container released under that item**
c) **To mark that container in the manner required by Customs**
d) **To keep records which show the current status of that container in service and the disposition of that container if taken out of service**
e) **To remove or strike out the markings on that container when it is taken out of service or when the principal transfers ownership of it**

 As per 19 CFR 113.66(b):

(b) Agreement to Comply With the Provisions of subheading 9801.00.10, or 9803.00.50 Harmonized Tariff Schedule of the United States (HTSUS). ***If the principal gets free release of any serially numbered shipping container classifiable under subheading 9801.00.10 or 9803.00.50, HTSUS, the principal agrees:***

(1) ***Not to advance the value or improve its condition abroad or claim (or make a previous claim) drawback on, any container released under subheading 9801.00.10, HTSUS;***

(2) To pay the initial duty due and otherwise comply with every condition in subheading 9803.00.50, HTSUS, on any container released under that item;

(3) To mark that container in the manner required by CBP;

(4) To keep records which show the current status of that container in service and the disposition of that container if taken out of service; and

(5) To remove or strike out the markings on that container when it is taken out of service or when the principal transfers ownership of it.

 With the release, the importer agrees "NOT to advance the value" of the container. The correct answer is "a".

✓ **JUST A SIDE NOTE:** The above-referenced subheadings 9801.00.10 and 9803.00.50 provide for:

9801.00.10 *Products of the United States when returned after having been exported, without having been advanced in value or improved in condition by any process of manufacture or other means while abroad.*

9803.00.50 *Substantial containers and holders, if products of the United States (including shooks and staves of United States production when returned as boxes or barrels containing merchandise), or if of foreign production and previously imported and duty (if any) thereon paid ... ...*

73) With regards to the disposition of merchandise on a basic custodial bond, the principal agrees to all of the following EXCEPT:

a) If a bonded carrier, to report promptly the arrival of merchandise at the destination port by delivering to CBP the manifest or other approved notice.

b) If a cartage or lighterage business, to deliver promptly and safely to CBP any merchandise placed in the principal's custody together with any related cartage and lighterage ticket and manifest.

c) To dispose of merchandise in a manner authorized by CBP Regulations.

d) To file timely with CBP any report required by CBP Regulations.

e) In the case of Class 9 warehouses, to provide reasonable assurance of exportation of only merchandise subject to excise taxes that is withdrawn under the sales ticket procedure of §144.37(h) of this chapter.

 As per 19 CFR 113.63(c):

(c) Disposition of Merchandise. The principal agrees:

(1) If a bonded carrier, to report promptly the arrival of merchandise at the destination port by delivering to CBP the manifest or other approved notice;

(2) If a cartage or lighterage business, to deliver promptly and safely to CBP any merchandise placed in the principal's custody together with any related cartage and lighterage ticket and manifest;

(3) To dispose of merchandise in a manner authorized by CBP regulations; and

(4) To file timely with CBP any report required by CBP regulations.

(5) ***In the case of Class 9 warehouses, to provide reasonable assurance of exportation of merchandise withdrawn under the sales ticket*** *procedure of §144.37(h) of this chapter.*

a Assurance of exportation for all (i.e. not just excise tax-type) merchandise withdrawn under the referenced procedure. The correct answer is "e".

✓ **JUST A SIDE NOTE:** A "Class 9 warehouse" is a duty-free store. A "sales ticket" is the duty-free store's sales receipt to their customer that provides Customs' required details of the transaction such as description and quantity of goods sold, etc.

74) The principal agrees to comply with all Importer Security Filing requirements set forth in part 149 of this chapter, including but not limited to, providing security filing information to Customs and Border Protection in the manner and in the time period prescribed by regulation. If the principal defaults with regard to any obligation, the principal and surety (jointly and severally) must pay liquidated damages of _______ for each violation.

a) $1,000
b) $2,000
c) $5,000
d) $10,000
e) $15,000

 As per 19 CFR 113.62(j):

(j) The principal agrees to comply with all Importer Security Filing requirements set forth in part 149 of this chapter including but not limited to providing security filing information to CBP in the manner and in the time period prescribed by regulation. ***If the principal defaults with regard to any obligation, the principal and surety (jointly and severally) agree to pay liquidated damages of $5,000 for each violation.***

 The correct answer is "c".

✓ **JUST A SIDE NOTE:** "Severally" means separately, as the examinee can possibly deduce from the context of the paragraph.

75) A bond is not required on an importation of a vehicle when:

a) A vehicle that conforms to the EPA & DOT standards is purchased by a U.S. Citizen for resale in the United States within one year of importation.

b) The vehicle is imported by a U.S. military employee on commission for another person.

c) The vehicle conforms to the EPA & DOT standards and was recently purchased abroad by a nonresident already living in the United States who had the vehicle shipped directly from the foreign factory to his U.S address for his personal use while employed in the United States.

d) An EPA & DOT conforming vehicle is imported in connection with the arrival of a nonresident, to be used in the United States only for his or her personal transportation, and will not be resold within 1 year after the date of importation.

e) A bond is required on all types of vehicle importations.

As per 19 CFR 142.4(a):

142.4 Bond requirements.

(a) At the time of entry. ***Except as provided in §10.101(d) of this chapter, or paragraph (c) of this section, merchandise shall not be released from Customs custody at the time Customs receives the entry documentation or the entry summary documentation which serves as both the entry and the entry summary, as required by §142.3 unless a single entry or continuous bond*** *on Customs Form 301, containing the bond conditions set forth in §113.62 of this chapter, executed by an approved corporate surety, or secured by cash deposits or obligations of the United States, as provided for in §113.40 of this chapter,* ***has been filed****. When any of the imported merchandise is subject to a tariff-rate quota and is to be released at a time when the applicable quota is filled, the full rates shall be used in computing the estimated duties to determine the amount of the bond.*

The correct answer is "e".

✓ **NOTE:** The CBP states that the correct answer is "d", however we respectfully disagree on this one.

✓ **NOTE:** 19 CFR 10.101(d) is for U.S. Government entries. 19 CFR 142.4(c) is for informal entries.

76) Too Loud Audio imported three speakers as samples for use in taking orders under a Temporary Importation Bond (TIB) on June 1, 2012, subheading classification 9813.00.20. They have extended the expiration period by two one-year time periods. In May, 2015 the broker notifies the importer that the TIB is about to reach its expiration date. The importer has indicated that it will not be able to export or destroy the speakers by the TIB's expiration date. What is the importer's best option?

a) **Extend the TIB for an additional one-year time period**

b) **File an anticipatory breach and pay liquidated damages of 110% of all duties and the merchandise processing fee**

c) **Export similar speakers of the same value**

d) **File an anticipatory breach and pay liquidated damages for double the duties and the merchandise processing fee**

e) **Sell the speakers**

 As per 19 CFR 10.39(e) & (f):

... ...

(4) Upon the payment of an amount equal to double the duty which would have accrued on the articles had they been entered under an ordinary consumption entry, or ***equal to 110 percent of such duties where that percentage is prescribed in §10.31(f)****, if such amount is determined to be less than the full amount of the bond.*

(f) ***Anticipatory breach. If an importer anticipates that the merchandise entered under a Temporary Importation Bond will not be exported or destroyed in accordance with the terms of the bond, the importer may indicate to Customs in writing before the bond period has expired of the anticipatory breach.*** *At the time of written notification of the breach, the importer shall pay to Customs the full amount of liquidated damages that would be assessed at the time of breach of the bond, and the entry will be closed. The importer shall notify the surety in writing of the breach and payment. By this payment, the importer waives his right to receive a notice of claim for liquidated damages as required by §172.1(a) of this chapter.*

 The correct answer is "b".

✓ **JUST A SIDE NOTE:** Temporary imports under bond are to be exported within 1 year of their importation. However, if approved, the TIB may be extended twice, 1 year each for each extension. This means the total time allowed for a TIB may not exceed 3 years.

77) Which of the following is NOT provided for in 19 CFR 133 to dispose of merchandise seized for infringement of a trademark recorded with U.S. Customs and Border Protection?

a) Forfeiture followed by destruction of the infringing merchandise
b) Release of the infringing merchandise by way of a gift to a charitable institution having a need for the same when there is consent of the trademark owner, obliteration of the offending mark, and a determination by CBP that the merchandise is not unsafe or hazardous
c) Exportation of the infringing merchandise without obliteration of the offending mark when it is one other than a counterfeit
d) Release of the infringing merchandise after obliteration when the offending mark is counterfeit
e) None of the above

 As per 19 CFR 133.51(b) & 133.52(c):

133.51 Relief from forfeiture or liquidated damages.
... ...
(b) Conditioned relief. In appropriate cases, **except for articles bearing a counterfeit trademark, relief** ***from a forfeiture may be granted pursuant to a petition for relief upon the following conditions*** *and such other conditions as may be specified by the appropriate Customs authority:*

(1) ***The unlawfully imported or prohibited articles are exported or destroyed under Customs supervision and at no expense to the Government;***

(2) ***All offending trademarks or trade names are removed or obliterated prior to release of the articles:***
... ...

133.52 Disposition of forfeited merchandise.
... ...
(c) ***Articles bearing a counterfeit trademark****. Merchandise forfeited for violation of the trademark laws shall be destroyed, unless it is determined that the merchandise is not unsafe or a hazard to health and the Commissioner of Customs or his designee has the written consent of the U.S. trademark owner, in which case the Commissioner of Customs or his designee may dispose of the merchandise,* ***after obliteration of the trademark, where feasible, by:***

(1) Delivery to any Federal, State, or local government agency that, in the opinion of the Commissioner or his designee, has established a need for the merchandise; or

(2) ***Gift to any charitable institution that, in the opinion of the Commissioner or his designee, has established a need for the merchandise****; or*

19 CFR 133.51 explains that articles may be released if trademarks are removed "except for articles bearing a 'counterfeit' trademark". The correct answer is "d".

✓ **NOTE:** The exam questions mentions an "infringement" of a trademark, which is not necessarily a "counterfeit" of a trademark. All counterfeits are infringements, though not all infringements are counterfeit (i.e. fraudulent) cases.

78) If a violation of the trademark or copyright laws is not discovered until after entry and deposit of estimated duty, the entry shall be endorsed with an appropriate notation and the duty refunded as an erroneous collection upon exportation or destruction of the prohibited articles in accordance with ________________of this chapter.

a) 19CFR 10.581 or 10.709
b) 19CFR 24.3 or 24.3a
c) 19CFR 158.41 or 158.45
d) 19CFR 174.2 or 174.12
e) 19CFR 191.176 or 191.183

 As per 19 CFR 133.53:

133.53 Refund of duty.

If a violation of the trademark or copyright laws is not discovered until after entry and deposit of estimated duty, the entry shall be endorsed with an appropriate notation and the duty refunded as an erroneous collection upon exportation or destruction of the prohibited articles ***in accordance with §158.41 or §158.45 of this chapter.***

 The correct answer is "c".

✓ **JUST A SIDE NOTE:** 19 CFR Sections 158.41 and 158.45 cover the destruction of prohibited merchandise and the exportation of the merchandise, respectively.

79) Which of the following is appropriate to challenge the seizure of merchandise for a violation of 19 USC 1526(e), as implemented by 19 CFR 133.21(d)?

a) Filing a protest under 19 CFR 174
b) Filing a petition under 19 CFR 172
c) Filing a ruling request under 19 CFR 177
d) All of the above
e) None of the above

 As per 19 CFR 133.21(g):

(g) Consent of the mark owner; failure to make appropriate disposition. The owner of the mark, within thirty days from notification of seizure, may provide written consent to the importer allowing the importation of the seized merchandise in its condition as imported or its exportation, entry after obliteration of the mark, or other appropriate disposition. Otherwise, the merchandise will be disposed of in accordance with §133.52 of this part, ***subject to the importer's right to petition for relief from forfeiture under the provisions of part 171 of this chapter.***

a Petition for relief from forfeiture is located in part 171 (FINES, PENALTIES, AND FORFEITURES). The correct answer is "e" (none of the above).

✓ **NOTE:** The exam question says "as implemented by 19 CFR 133.21**(d)**", though we believe this must be a typo, and was meant to read "as implemented by 19 CFR 133.21**(g)**".

✓ **JUST A SIDE NOTE:** "19 USC 1526(e)" is, in a way, the United States Code (USC) equivalent of Title 19 Code of Federal Regulations (CFR) 133.52 (Disposition of forfeited merchandise). New laws are assigned a number and recorded in the USC. The CFR is subsequently created or amended to explain in detail these laws and how they will be implemented.

80) Which of the following is TRUE with respect to imported merchandise after the U.S. International Trade Commission (ITC) finds a violation of section 337 of the Tariff Act (19 USC 1337) and issues an exclusion order, as implemented by CBP under 19 CFR 12.39?

a) **The exclusion order is not effective until 60 days after issuance, at which point merchandise subject to the exclusion order no longer may be entered.**

b) **Merchandise subject to the exclusion order may be entered under a single entry bond, in an amount set by the ITC, from the time the exclusion order issues until the time it expires.**

c) **Merchandise subject to the exclusion order may be entered under bond, in an amount set by the ITC that is secured by the importer's basic importation bond.**

d) **Merchandise subject to the exclusion order may be entered under bond as provided for in 19 CFR 113, until the determination of a violation becomes final.**

e) **Merchandise subject to the exclusion order may not be entered after the exclusion order has issued.**

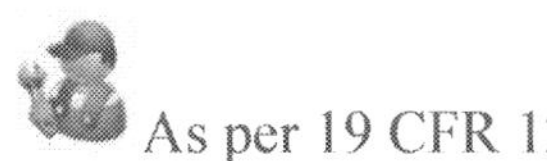 As per 19 CFR 12.39(b):

(b) Exclusion from entry; entry under bond; notice of exclusion order. (1) If the Commission finds a violation of section 337, or reason to believe that a violation exists, it may direct the Secretary of the Treasury to exclude from entry into the United States the articles concerned which are imported by the person violating or suspected of violating section 337. The Commission's exclusion order remains in effect until the Commission determines, and notifies the Secretary of the Treasury, that the conditions which led to the exclusion no longer exist, or until the determination of the Commission on which the order is based is disapproved by the President.

*(2) **During the period the Commission's exclusion order remains in effect, excluded articles may be entered under a single entry bond** in an amount determined by the International Trade Commission to be sufficient to protect the complainant from any injury. **On or after the date that the Commission's determination of a violation of section 337 becomes final**, as set forth in paragraph (a) of this section, **articles covered by the determination will be refused entry**. If a violation of section 337 is found, the bond may be forfeited to the complainant under terms and conditions prescribed by the Commission. To enter merchandise that is the subject of a Commission exclusion order, importers must:*

(i) File with the port director prior to entry a bond in the amount determined by the Commission that contains the conditions identified in the special importation and entry bond set forth in appendix B to part 113 of this chapter; and

(ii) Comply with the terms set forth in 19 CFR 210.50(d) in the event of a forfeiture of this bond.
... ...

 The correct answer is "d".

✓ **JUST A SIDE NOTE:** "19 USC 1337" covers "Unfair Practices in Import Trade".

Book 2 Part 1

Book 2 Introduction

How to Start Your Own CHB Business

Most customs brokers have thought to themselves, "what would it be like to run my own customs brokerage business?" Well, once you have a little experience under your belt and have acquired some resources and potential clients, then utilizing this book will end up saving you much wasted time and frustration.

What caused me to write this book is that when I first decided to start my own customs brokerage business, instructions on doing so from US Customs or the customs brokerage community were nowhere to be found. I resolved to methodically log and document all the steps that I actually took in setting up my own customs brokerage business from start to finish. I knew that doing so would prove to be an invaluable service for others following the same path.

$ Money Saving Tip $

Some regional banks offer free checking accounts with relatively high interest that might suit your new small business. ACH services may be extra, so shop around. See also kasasa.com

So, with this book, the reader is able to bypass the trial and error method that I used when setting up my own customs brokerage business. This guide systematically outlines, step-by-step, how to most efficiently open your own customs brokerage business—and how to do it on a budget.

You may have a long list of prospective customers or few such contacts. Either way, your ambition to offer a service, superior to any other in your market, will, by itself, eventually grow your business. Refer to this book for direction, be pro-active, yet patient, and GROW YOUR BUSINESS.

Book 2 Part 2

Necessary Links

Customs website:
cbp.gov

Code of Federal Regulations (CFR) Online:
www.eCFR.gov

Harmonized Tariff Schedule (HTS) Online:
hts.usitc.gov/current

Customs Forms:
cbp.gov/xp/cgov/toolbox/forms/

IRS Small Business:
irs.gov/businesses/small/index.html

$ Money Saving Tip $
Have not yet been able to purchase your own 19 CFR or HTSUS? The online versions of these texts are convenient, easily searchable (e.g., use your computer's "find" function [Ctrl + F] to quickly locate item descriptions and HTS numbers within these PDF files), and they're always up-to-date.

Book 2 Part 3

Start with Customs

Start Here

Customs Broker License

First, let's assume that you do have your customs broker license. If you don't, then let's get that first. Read part one of this book on how to become a licensed customs broker. If you're already studying for the exam, then keep it up and good luck—the international trade community needs more licensed brokers and you're nearly there.

To Operate Under a Trade Name

Some individual customs brokers operate under their own personal names (e.g. John Doe). Others choose to give their small business a name (e.g. John Doe, DBA Perfect Customs Brokerage). Either way will work, but if you choose to operate under an assumed business name or Doing Business As (DBA) trade name, then Customs requires that the individual customs broker first submit a proposal to operate under a trade name in the form of a letter (see sample letter on the following page, and also refer to 19 CFR 111.30(c) to verify all information is up-to-date) to the Customs Broker Compliance Branch before proceeding with district permit application, filer code application, etc.

In your letter to Broker Compliance, refer to and attach evidence of your authority to use the trade name (usually in the form of your State's department of licensing confirmation letter or license). Also be sure to include your customs broker license number with this and all other such correspondence to Customs.

Customs will review your letter and will send back written approval to you within a couple weeks. They may be kind enough to email or fax confirmation back to you if politely asked to do so in your letter.

$ Money Saving Tip $

Need to courier docs overseas? Although no current US domestic service still exists, DHL, or an authorized reseller of DHL, can sometimes offer small businesses international rates at nearly half that of standard UPS and FedEx rates.

Sample: Proposal to operate under a trade name

John Doe
Perfect Customs Brokerage
3000 NE 309th Ave
Port City, WA 98682
Tel: 360-123-4567
(email address)

(Date)

U.S. Customs and Border Protection
1300 Pennsylvania Ave., NW
Attn: 1400 L St., Broker Compliance Branch
Washington, DC 20229

Re: Proposal to operate under a trade name

Dear Sir or Madam,

Per 19 CFR 111.30 (c) I am submitting evidence of my authority to use the trade name (John Doe, DBA) **"Perfect Customs Brokerage"** per attached acknowledgement letter from the Washington State Department of Licensing (unified business identifier number 600000000).

Best Regards,

John Doe
License#12345

District Permit Request

A customs broker can only conduct customs business in the ports that he or she has permits for. The first permit that you will want to apply for is for the district in which you will initially be making customs entries.

Afterwards a national permit can be applied for, yet only subsequently to receipt of the district permit. An individual customs broker may utilize remote location filing (RLF) if he or she has a national permit. RLF will allow you to make entry on regular informal or formal entry at any port even if you don't have an office at that port. At this point, however, RLF is just something to keep in mind and consider down the road. Just go to cbp.gov and search "remote location filing" for more information on the subject, if you would like.

Include the following information in your **district** permit application (see sample letter on following page)...

1) Broker license number, date of issuance, and delivered through port (attach copy of license)

2) Your office address (attach copy of lease agreement or title)

3) Evidence of right to use assumed business name if applicable (attach approval from state)

4) Name of individual broker to exercise responsible supervision and control (usually your name)

5) List of other districts for which you have a permit (write "none" if none)

6) "Records retained at" address, and recordkeeping contact name

7) All other persons employed by applicant (write "none" if none)

8) Note $100.00 permit fee (attach check, and see 19 CFR 111.96 to verify amount is up-to-date).

9) Note $138.00 annual user fee (attach check, and see 19 CFR 111.96 to verify amount is up-to-date).

Be sure to make your checks out to "Customs and Border Protection". As of 2017, the 19 CFR still oddly instructs payments to be made out to the "United States Customs Service". Also be sure to keep a copies of all such correspondence with Customs for your records.

Sample: District Permit Request

John Doe
DBA Perfect Customs Brokerage
3000 NE 309th Ave
Port City, WA 98682
Tel: 360-123-4567
(email address)

(Date)

Ms. Jane Smith, Port Director, CBP

Re: Application for District Permit for Port of Port City

Dear Ms. Smith,

Please accept this letter as application for a district permit to perform customs business in the port of Port City. Required information per CFR19, 111.19 (b) is as follows:
1) Broker License Number 12345, Date of issuance 4/22/05 (delivered through port of New Orleans, copy of license attached)
2) Office address: 3000 NE 309th Ave, Port City, WA 98682 Tel: 360-123-4567 (copy of lease attached)
3) Copy of document which reserves applicant's business name with the state of Washington (attached)
4) Individual broker to exercise responsible supervision and control: John Doe
5) Other districts for which I have a permit: None
6) Records retained at: 3000 NE 309th Ave, Port City, WA 98682. Recordkeeping contact: John Doe
7) All other persons employed by applicant: None
8) $100.00 permit fee (attached)
9) $138.00 annual user fee (attached)

Best Regards,

John Doe, License#12345

Filer Code Request

Each broker conducting business with Customs will be issued a three-character (alpha, numeric, or alpha-numeric) code that will be included with entry numbers for all customs entries. This three-character code is called the "filer code". To obtain a filer code, submit a filer code request letter (separate from the district permit request), and include the following information (see sample letter on following page)...

1) Full legal name of requestor (you)
2) Business contact (probably you)
3) Business address and telephone number
4) Broker license number, date of issuance, and "delivered through" port.

$ Money Saving Tip $

Need inexpensive or free accounting software such as "BS1 Free Accounting Software"? Check out CNET's website for downloads and reviews. Search for business software>>accounting and billing software. download.com

NOTE: The requests for district permit and filer code can be submitted together (verify with the port director or equivalent just in case). They will provide you with a receipt for your checks, and will notify you of approval within about two to three weeks.

Sample: Filer Code Request

John Doe
DBA PERFECT Customs Brokerage
3000 NE 309th Ave
Port City, WA 98682
Tel: 360-123-4567
(Email address)

(Date)

Ms. Jane Smith
Port Director
Customs and Border Protection (Port of Port City)

Re: Filer Code Request

Dear Ms. Smith,

Please accept this letter as application for a filer code. Information required to process this application is as follows:

1) Full legal name of requestor: John Doe
2) Business contact (Individual broker to exercise responsible supervision and control): John Doe
3) Business address: 3000 NE 309th Ave, Port City, WA 98682 Tel: 360-123-4567
4) Broker License Number 12345, Date of issuance 4/22/05 (delivered through port of New Orleans)

Thank you very much for your consideration. Please feel free to contact me should you require further information.

Best Regards,

John Doe
License#12345

Book 2 Part 4

Type of Organization

Keep it simple

Legal Designation

While you're patiently waiting for Customs to get back to you on your district permit and filer code applications, it may be a good time to focus on the structure of the business. Many large freight forwarder and customs brokerage operations are incorporated. For your start-up business, however, it may be best to keep it simple. By that I mean that I mean consider initially registering your new business with your state as a sole proprietorship rather than an LLC or corporation.

I would not suggest a partnership for any type of business. The saying goes "the 'partnership' is the one ship that won't sail"? Hours worked and perceptions of contributions to the partnership will vary, eventually leading to discontent and resentment between the parties involved.

As your business grows you can later decide to expand on your sole proprietorship by easily converting to an S-Corporation. You can also purchase liability and/or errors and omissions insurance from an insurance or surety bond company to help protect your company and your personal interests.

$ Money Saving Tip $

Some companies charge a substantial monthly fee to list your business in their publications. Note, however, that there are many free print directories, online directories, and search engines for you to register with.

Taxes

Taxes on your business will depend on several different factors, including legal designation, estimated income, and local tax code. It will be worth your time to consult with a recommended CPA in your area to try to gain a better understanding of your specific tax considerations. A consultation may cost you some money upfront (maybe about $100.00 for a short visit?), but will, without a doubt, give you peace of mind that is hard to put a price on.

One thing that every business owner must do, however, is to separate personal finances from business finances. This means setting up a separate bank account for your business. All business-related expenses come out of your business' account, and all business-related income goes into this account—no exceptions. Doing so will allow you to accurately compute your taxes, as well as let you know if your business is making a profit.

As a general rule of thumb, set aside about 1/4 of all withdrawn profits into yet another separate bank account (most may prefer a savings type account) for your business so that you will have these funds available for taxes. So, for example, if taking out $1,000.00 from your business' checking account, only $750.00 will go into your personal bank account, and the other $250.00 will go into and remain in your business' savings account in preparation for your quarterly tax payments and annual tax time. Again, consult with a good CPA for details that will be relevant to you own unique situation.

An EIN (employee identification number) is not absolutely necessary to run your sole-proprietor business (as opposed of other forms of business), but some of your vendors may require this ID number when applying for credit with them. You may obtain an EIN from the IRS if you wish by applying online at the following...

irs.gov/smallbiz

The IRS's small business website also provides very informative online tutorials, among other useful tools. You can even sign up for a free newsletter to help keep you up-to-date on IRS-related regulations and tips.

<u>$ Money Saving Tip $</u>
Use the EFTPS (Electronic Federal Tax Payment System) method of paying your IRS taxes. It is the quickest, most accurate, and the cheapest method of all for a small business. Go to irs.gov/smallbiz to learn more regarding EFTPS.

Book 2 Part 5

Marketing Your CHB Business

Get the Word Out

Still waiting for your district permit and filer code? Now is a perfect time to start working on your marketing plan.

You do not have to spend a lot of money to advertise your business. Here are just a few of the best methods of getting your business' name out there. And, they're all free.

Customs Website

Ask your port director (or equivalent) if they can list your new business on CBP's list of brokers as soon as your filer code is created. All active brokers are listed by the port within they operate on the Customs website (cbp.gov), and importers often search and are shepherded here (by Customs, etc.) when looking for someone to clear their shipment. Getting listed may take a little patience and persistence, but the amount of exposure your company gets from this is well worth the wait.

Port Website

Most ports (e.g. The Port of Tacoma, The Port of Norfolk, etc.) have very business-friendly websites. Among the various port-related resources they often provide for the benefit of local commerce, is a directory of local warehouses, trucking companies, freight forwarders, and customs brokers. Contact your port (air, ocean, or both) and ask to be added to the list. This service should also be free, and is another great way to receive a reference from a credible source.

Other Marketing Advice

I also recommend the book *Guerilla Marketing* by Jay Conrad Levinson. This book is just full of creative, yet proven ideas to advertise your on-a-budget business. It is extensive in its description of all different types of effective marketing techniques.

$ Money Saving Tip $

Making multiple trips to Customs, etc.? Deduct about 50¢ per mile as an expense. See irs.gov/smallbiz for the current rate.

Book 2 Part 6

ABI Vendor

Test Drive it for the Right Fit

Selecting an ABI Vendor

Finding "any" ABI provider is easy. However, choosing the "right-fit-for-your-company" ABI provider takes some shopping around.

An initial one-time licensing fee will run anywhere from $10,000.00 to $2,000.00. After that, monthly maintenance fees for ABI providers can be as expensive as $1,000.00 per month or as low as about $200.00 per month. Most offer a full array of ABI capabilities, but some may offer more accounting and other optional features than others. Some require you to buy an on-site server to run their software off of, while others allow you to do everything online thru the use of their server—as if you were creating and sending an email from your Hotmail or Gmail email account.

Feel free to compare the actual functionality of a couple different vendors with actual one-on-one demo's, either in-person or remotely online. Also, get a good feel for a company's culture. Your instincts should tell you whether they will offer excellent or below-average customer service for when you have a question or problem with their system. My best advice to you on the subject is to not only choose your ABI vendor based on their pricing, but also based on their technical and customer support expertise. We chose SmartBorder smartborder.com, after trying two other ABI vendors. They absolutely made ABI Certification a relatively pain-free process. It is easy for me to endorse them because I know their product is one of the best in the industry (note: this is a non-paid endorsement). Their system is accessible from anywhere with an internet connection, and handles necessary Customs transactions such as: Entries (7501,3461), RLF, ISF, truck manifest, ocean manifest, electronic invoice, In-bond 7512, Exports, Reconciliation, Protests, OGA filing, 5106, Statement processing, and PMS.

A current listing of all ABI vendors, certified by US Customs, can be found at cbp.gov/document/guidance/abi-software-vendors-list

Reproducing Customs Forms

The Customs Forms Management Office (located in Washington, DC) requires all ABI providers to submit their versions of US Customs forms (3461, 7501, etc.) to their office for approval before the forms are printed and used by individual brokers (via their laser or inkjet printers). Customs is concerned that their forms be kept uniform, and Customs may request this letter of approval at anytime.

Interestingly enough, not all ABI providers seem to have this important letter of proof, so it is important to request that your prospective ABI provider provide a copy of this letter for your file before you commit to buying their product.

Letter of Intent

Once you have received your district permit and filer code from Customs, you will ask the ABI provider to provide a letter of intent template (see sample letter on following page, and see 19 CFR 143.2 to verify information is up-to-date) that you or your ABI provider can send to the Customs Office of Information and Technology (OIT). The only thing that you will need to add to the template should be your new filer code and a signature. Have the letter of intent mailed to the OIT or call them at (703) 650-3500 to ask if you can fax the letter in order to expedite the process. Make sure that your ABI provider also gets a copy of the submitted letter. Go to www.cbp.gov and type "getting started with ABI" for current instructions in detail or go to the following URL: cbp.gov/document/guidance/letter-intent-instructions

$ Money Saving Tip $

Thinking of printing your own business cards or promotional material? Instead, why not consider outsourcing the task to a local printing company? It's the most convenient and cost effective way.

Sample: ABI Letter of Intent

John Doe
Perfect Customs Brokerage
3000 NE 309th Ave
Port City, WA 98682
Tel: 360-123-4567
(Email address)

(Date)

Office of Information and Technology
Director of Client Representatives Branch
7501 Boston Blvd. 2nd Floor, Room 211
Springfield, VA 22153

RE: Letter of intent to participation in ACS/ABI.

Per 19 CFR 143.2, this letter of intent sets forth our commitment to develop, maintain and adhere to the performance requirements and operational standards of the ABI system in order to ensure the validity, integrity and confidentiality of the data transmitted.

1) The following is a description of the computer hardware, communications and entry processing systems to be used and the estimated completion date of the programming: (***ABI provider will advise these details***).
2) Our offices are located at: 3000 NE 309th Ave
Port City, WA 98682. Contact: John Doe.
Estimated Start Date: Feb. 1st 2017.
3) The name of the participant's principal management and contact person regarding the system: John Doe
4) The system is being developed by the following data processing company: PDQ Systems.
Contact: Denise Richards
5) Entry filer code: XYZ

Please feel free to contact us should you have any questions.

Best regards,

John Doe, LCB, License#12345

The letter of intent will be processed in about a week. Customs will assign an "ABI representative" (not to be confused with your "ABI vendor") to you. He or she will contact you to introduce themselves, and you can advise your ISA confirmation number (see next paragraph) at that time as well. Once an ABI rep is assigned, you will work closely with him or her and with your ABI provider to test your ABI transmissions. Ask your ABI provider to help you prepare for and walk you through this ABI testing period, which can be completed within a couple days (depending on your provider).

VPN Interconnection Security Agreement

The Trade Virtual Private Network (VPN) Interconnection Security Agreement (ISA) is how Customs informs the ABI applicant of the importance of keeping the connection between your computer and Customs' servers secure. Go to the following online form, read the agreement, and complete and submit the security agreement acceptance form.

apps.cbp.gov/tvpn/tvpn.asp

Once the VPN ISA has submitted you will receive a confirmation number via email. Simply reply to the confirmation email from Customs to complete the ISA acceptance process. Keep this confirmation number and provide it to your ABI representative when they contact you.

Book 2 Part 7

Selecting a Surety Company

That was Easy

The surety company that you choose will be able to issue single transaction bonds and continuous bonds to accompany your customs entries.

Before deciding on a surety company, check with your ABI provider to see if they integrate a specific company's bonds in their system. If they do, and if the surety's rates are reasonable, then use them.

Otherwise, selecting a surety company can still be much easier than selecting an ABI provider as prices seem to be relatively competitive between competing surety companies. Ask for a few quotes to get a better idea of what's out there.

$ Money Saving Tip $

Want shipping industry news for free? Sign up for the Journal of Commerce's free newsletter at joc.com

We recommend choosing a surety company that does not charge a minimum for your single transaction bonds, and one that has an easy-to-use bond application system. Some may let you get your single transaction bonds directly online (web-based), while others will have you download (stand-alone) software that will allow you to issue bonds directly from your desktop.

To get a current listing of Customs approved surety companies that can provide you with a quote go to www.cbp.gov and search for "surety names/codes". Or try typing the following URL https://www.cbp.gov/document/forms/surety-names-and-codes-0

Book 2 Part 8

Running Your CHB Business

Do it Differently

The day-to-day operations of your new customs brokerage business is entirely up to you. You can get as creative as you want. That's to your advantage. Most of the customs brokerage businesses out there appear to be doing the same thing. And some may have (just as any corporation is susceptible to) lost their soul.

Power of Attorney

A signed customs power of attorney (POA) from the importer is required in order for a customs broker to conduct customs business on behalf of that importer.

In regards to the POA, an individual customs broker can do one of two things. One option is to purchase a boilerplate-type POA form in bulk from another company. The National Customs Brokers & Forwarders Association of America (NCBFAA), for example, has published several different versions of the power of attorney for the transportation industry. The NCBFAA Power of Attorney can be located and purchased at the NCBFAA website under "Publications and Resources" and then under "Commercial Docs".
ncbfaa.org

One of your other options is to refer to Customs' example of the power of attorney (as written in 19 CFR 141.32) as a benchmark, and customize it to fit your company (see sample POA on following page). For starters, we recommend this method as it is FREE and could be made more user-friendly for customers than the long form published by the NCBFFAA.

As a side note, as you have your customer fill out the power of attorney, ask them to also complete and return what I call the "customers instructions to broker" (see sample following POA). The importer can use this form to describe their imported product, and clarify delivery and billing details. This supplemental form also serves the purpose of letting your new client know that you care about their input, and provides up-front information in writing.

Sample: Customs Power of Attorney

Customs Power of Attorney

KNOW ALL MEN BY THESE PRESENTS, THAT

____
(Full name of company or individual)

____
(Legal designation, such as corp., individual, sole prop., LLC, or partnership)

located at

____
(Business Address)

and doing business under the laws of the State of

______________, using EIN or SSN__________________
hereby appoints the grantee, **John Doe, DBA Perfect Customs Brokerage** as a true and lawful agent and attorney of the principal named above with full power and authority to do and perform every lawful act and thing the said agent and attorney may deem requisite and necessary to be done for and on behalf of the said principal without limitation of any kind as fully as said principal could do if present and acting, and hereby ratify and confirm all that said agent and attorney shall lawfully do or cause to be done by virtue of these presents until written notice of revocation is delivered to the grantee. In the case of a partnership, this power of attorney will only be effective two years from the date below.

_____________________________ __________________
(Principal's signature) *(Date)*

Sample: Customer Instructions to Broker

Customer Instructions to Broker

1) The product that I am importing can best be described as…

____

(What is it? What is it made of?)

____

(What is it used for? What is it used in conjunction with?)

2) Please deliver to…

____

(delivery address)

____

(delivery location contact name and telephone#)

*This location **does / doesn't** have a loading dock. (Please circle one)*

3) Please bill to…

____

(billing address)

____

(billing contact name and telephone#)

ACH Payment

Complete Customs Form 401 (ACH Credit Enrollment Application) and fax, email, or mail the completed application to the Customs Revenue Division. Upon receipt, they will send instructions to you on ACH payer procedures as well as show you how to send an ACH pre-note test (necessary test for ACH user approval) through your bank to Customs. Once approved, you can work with your ABI provider and bank to get everything else set up. Until then, Customs will accept checks submitted with the entry or entry summary. Go to cbp.gov and search "signing up for ach" for details and current instructions. Or try going direct via the following URL: https://www.cbp.gov/trade/trade-community/automated/automated-systems/gs-automated-systems/ach/signing

Accounting Software

If you're not a seasoned CPA (like the rest of us), then keeping track of your company's finances may require the acquisition of a bare-bones, easy-to-use accounting software solution. If your ABI provider offers accounting software that is integrated within their ABI software product, then feel free to use that as it may help simplify things.

If they do not offer such integrated accounting software, then stand-along accounting software such as QuickBooks® will work as well. Because of its widespread use, many ABI providers include functions in the ABI software that allow you to easily transfer data to and from QuickBooks.

Pricing

Be aware of your competitors' pricing. You may want to beat their pricing and/or offer importers a much more simplified version of the typical customs brokerage invoice. If you can boast about your great rates then feel free to compare yours to the "typical" customs broker on your website or via other methods of advertising.

Creativity can also enter into your method of pricing of your customs brokerage services. You might not have the cash on hand that a larger business has, so you could offer a substantial discount to an importer if he or she submits payment to you at the time of or before delivery of her shipment. This will help you to cash flow your business, as well as give you a chance to go out and meet your customers.

Truckers

Contact several different truckers and get an account setup with them before your first shipment. Most will require you to complete a credit check application, while others will ask for payment to be made on a COD basis for the first couple of shipments. Either way, it is nice to have a friend in your trucking company.

Necessary Office Equipment

In regards to necessary office equipment, a minimalist would only really need a computer, printer, telephone, and shredder (Customs requires all information-sensitive material to be shredded rather than put in the dumpster). Some ABI vendors may require you to purchase a stand-alone server in order to operate their software.

$ Money Saving Tip $
Cleared a small shipment and have some free time? Deliver using your own car or rent a truck (your car insurance co. may have weight restrictions). This is also a good chance to see your customer.

Recordkeeping

Customs requires brokers to keep records (either in paper or electronic form) of transaction for five years from the entry date. The IRS requires an individual or business to keep tax-related records for three years (though some recommend keeping longer).

However, there is no need to invest in a row of file cabinets if you're on a budget. Just go to Wal-Mart or Target and buy manila file folders, some hanging files to organize them in, and a few banker boxes to hang the hanging files in. Not only is this method more economical, but the banker boxes are easier to move around and store.

Working with Customs

Customs doesn't care whether the customs broker that is submitting an entry to them works for the largest freight forwarder in America, or whether he or she is working off a card table in the corner of their apartment. Just do your best to build a reputation as an honest and straight-forward broker, and Customs will treat you fairly.

Also, be aware that Customs is a government institution and things take time (including their role in processing your fore mentioned applications and request submittals).

In closing, I would simply like to wish you a sincere "keep your head up" on your customs brokerage business.

! Final Tips !
Finally, I recommend that you try to avoid the use debt to finance your business. Instead of "jumping from" your current job/situation, time it right and "jump to" your own business opportunity. Have a "long-term game plan" and grow the business with a patient heart.

References

United States Customs and Border Protection Home Page.
http://www.cbp.gov/
Web 2018.

United States Government Printing Office Home Page.
Title 19 Electronic Code of Federal Regulations "Customs Duties"
http://www.ecfr.gov/
Web 2018.

Wikipedia
http://www.wikipedia.org/
Web 2018.

United States International Trade Commission Home Page
"Harmonized Tariff Schedule of the United States"
http://www.usitc.gov/
Web 2018.

Made in the USA
Middletown, DE
02 February 2019